S0-BYC-570

War and Social Change in Modern Europe
The Great Transformation Revisited

This book revisits the historical terrain of Karl Polanyi's *The Great Transformation* (1944). Recent years have seen a remarkable resurgence of interest in Polanyi's powerful account of the rise and demise of Europe's nineteenth-century market system. However, this book argues that Polanyi's analysis is, in important ways, inaccurate and misleading. Sandra Halperin traces the persistence of traditional class structures during the development of industrial capitalism in Europe and the way in which these structures shaped states and state behavior and generated conflict. She documents European conflicts between 1789 and 1914, including small- and medium-scale conflicts often ignored by researchers, and links these conflicts to structures characteristic of industrial capitalist development in Europe before 1945. Ultimately, the book shows how and why these conflicts both culminated in the world wars and brought about a "great transformation" in Europe. Its account of this period challenges not only Polanyi's analysis but a variety of influential perspectives on nationalism, development, conflict, international systems change, and globalization.

Sandra Halperin is a Reader in International Relations and Politics at the University of Sussex. Her written work includes two books, *In the Mirror of the Third World: Capitalist Development in Modern Europe* and *Global Civil Society and Its Limits* (co-edited with Gordon Laxer), as well as contributions to numerous edited volumes and major journals. Dr. Halperin received her degree from the University of California, Los Angeles.

for D.O.W.

War and Social Change in Modern Europe

The Great Transformation Revisited

SANDRA HALPERIN

University of Sussex

CAMBRIDGE
UNIVERSITY PRESS

PUBLISHED BY THE PRESS SYNDICATE OF THE UNIVERSITY OF CAMBRIDGE
The Pitt Building, Trumpington Street, Cambridge, United Kingdom

CAMBRIDGE UNIVERSITY PRESS
The Edinburgh Building, Cambridge CB2 2RU, UK
40 West 20th Street, New York, NY 10011-4211, USA
477 Williamstown Road, Port Melbourne, VIC 3207, Australia
Ruiz de Alarcón 13, 28014 Madrid, Spain
Dock House, The Waterfront, Cape Town 8001, South Africa

http://www.cambridge.org

© Sandra Halperin 2004

This book is in copyright. Subject to statutory exception
and to the provisions of relevant collective licensing agreements,
no reproduction of any part may take place without
the written permission of Cambridge University Press.

First published 2004

Printed in the United States of America

Typeface Sabon 10/12 pt.   *System* LATEX 2$_\varepsilon$ [TB]

A catalog record for this book is available from the British Library.

Library of Congress Cataloging in Publication Data

Halperin, Sandra.
War and social change in modern Europe : The great transformation revisited /
Sandra Halperin.
    p.   cm.
Includes bibliographical references and index.
ISBN 0-521-81806-0 – ISBN 0-521-54015-1
1. Europe – Economic conditions.   2. Europe – Social conditions.   I. Title.
HC240.H31353 2003
330.94′028–dc21   2003053226

ISBN 0 521 81806 0 hardback
ISBN 0 521 54015 1 paperback

Contents

Tables   *page* viii

Preface   ix

INTRODUCTION

1   Conflict and Change in World Politics   3
    Industrial Expansion in Nineteenth-Century Europe: A Critique
       of the Polanyian View   5
    Conflict and Change: A Class Approach   15
    The Great Transformation, Revisited   38

I. SOCIAL FORCES, INDUSTRIAL EXPANSION, AND CONFLICT IN
EUROPE'S NINETEENTH-CENTURY MARKET SYSTEM

2   The First Transformation: Social Forces in the Rise of Europe's
    Nineteenth-Century Market System   51
    The Aristocratic-"Absolutist" Conflict   51
    National Political Revolutions and the Struggle for the State   55
    The New Balance of Social Power and the New European Order   64
    Class Conflict, Revolution, and War   72

3   Europe's Nineteenth-Century Industrial Expansion:
    A "Bottom Up" Perspective   78
    Introduction   78
    The Dual Economy   79
    Domestic Markets   82
    The Circuit of Capital   108
    Conclusions: Dualism and "Dependent Development" in Europe's
       Nineteenth-Century Industrial Expansion   117

4 Europe's Century of War, 1815–1914   119
   Conflict and Dualistic Industrial Expansion   120
   Labor Conflicts   125
   Enfranchisement Conflicts   131
   Ethnic Conflicts   134
   Imperialist Conflicts   136
   Conclusions   144

5 World War I and the Postwar Retrenchment   145
   Imperialism and War in Europe   146
   The Post–World War I Retrenchment   150
   The Decline of the Aristocracy   151
   Labor   153
   Democracy Between the Wars   158
   Minorities   162
   Imperialism in the Interwar Years   165
   Conclusions   170

II. THE INTERREGNUM

6 The Polarization of European Society, 1918–1939   175
   Liberal Challenge, Conservative Response: The Class Compromise
      of 1848   176
   The Socialist Threat   180
   World War I and Mass Mobilization   183
   Postwar Revolutionary Currents and the Fascist Reaction   187
   The Polarization of European Society   196
   Conclusions   199

7 The Politics of Appeasement and Counterrevolution:
   International Relations in Europe, 1918–1939   200
   British Appeasement Policies   201
   The "Appeasers"   217
   Alternative Interpretations   222
   Conclusions   229

III. THE GREAT TRANSFORMATION

8 The Post–World War II Order   235
   Europe's Post–World War II Social Peace and Prosperity   236
   Social Structure and Development in Postwar Europe   251
   Peace in Europe   262
   Conclusions   267

Contents

9   The Great Transformation and the Eternal Return:
    "Globalization" Reconsidered   269
    *Nineteenth-Century Industrial Expansion: The "Great
       Transformation" Revisited*   272
    Globalization: The "Great Transformation" Reversed?   281
    Globalization Redux? The Incommensurability Thesis Examined   287
    Conclusions: Lessons from History   294

Appendix 1. Europe Defined   297
*Appendix 2. A Sample of Europe's Class, Ethnic, and Imperialist
    Conflicts, 1789–1945*   299
*Appendix 3. European (Regional and Extraregional) Wars,
    Insurrections, Rebellions, Revolutions, Uprisings, Violent Strikes,
    Riots, and Demonstrations, 1789–1945*   312
Works Cited   445
Index   499

Tables

1.1. Wars Fought Outside Europe by European States   *page* 7

3.1. The Nature of Britain's "Bourgeois Revolution":
Two Models Compared   83

3.2. The Nature of Britain's Nineteenth-Century Industrial
Expansion: Two Models Compared   84

3.3. Mean Coefficient of Growth of Selected U.K. Industries,
1781–1913   86

3.4. Cartels and Combinations   90

3.5. Changes in the Average Real Wages in Industry, 1850–1914   96

3.6. Change in Average Real Wages or Income of the Employed
Agricultural Poor, 1850–1914   97

3.7. Average Annually Cumulated Percentage Change, 1895–1913,
in Real Wages, Industrial Productivity, Wage/Income Ratio in
Industry, and Barter Terms for Industry   97

3.8. Percent of Population in Towns of 20,000+ in Europe (1910)   99

4.1. Comparison of European Wars, Eighteenth and
Nineteenth Centuries   120

4.2. Number and Intensity of European Wars, 1815–1914   121

4.3. Intervention by European States in Class (Labor and
Enfranchisement) and Ethnic Conflicts in Other
Regional States   125

4.4. Strikes in Britain in the 1870s   129

4.5. Percent of European Population Enfranchised, 1910   131

6.1. Social Polarization in Europe during the Interwar Years   197

8.1. Minorities in Europe, 1910–1930   265

8.2. Europe's Magnitude 3+ Wars, 1945–1990   266

9.1. Advantages for Capitalists of Capitalism That Is Nationally
Embedded and Disembedded, 1950–1975 and 1975–2000   292

Preface

In recent years, the perception of large-scale change has fueled a resurgence of interest in history and a renewed appreciation of its importance for analyzing processes of change. This interest is founded, in large part, on hope that a better understanding of the past can offer insights into current trends of change.[1] History is, indeed, a source of insight; but because it is also the arena within which we debate questions about the future, the writing and reading of it is a partisan affair. Finding insights in the past depends, therefore, on our ability to evaluate critically the historical accounts on which we rely: how they emerged and why they gained the status of authority; how they were shaped by and how, in turn, they helped to shape the central conflicts of our time and of the recent past.

COLD WAR SOCIAL SCIENCE

Social theory and historiography, both in Europe and in the United States, was importantly influenced by the "social question" – by concerns with counteracting disorder and revolution and maintaining social order and stability.[2] By the end of the nineteenth century, however, the elements that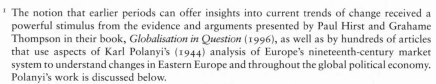

---

[1] The notion that earlier periods can offer insights into current trends of change received a powerful stimulus from the evidence and arguments presented by Paul Hirst and Grahame Thompson in their book, *Globalisation in Question* (1996), as well as by hundreds of articles that use aspects of Karl Polanyi's (1944) analysis of Europe's nineteenth-century market system to understand changes in Eastern Europe and throughout the global political economy. Polanyi's work is discussed below.

[2] Eric Wolf explains the "social question" as follows:

> With the accelerating of capitalist enterprise in the eighteenth century, [the] structure of state and classes came under increasing pressure from new and "rising" social groups and categories that clamored for the enactment of their rights against those groups defended and represented by the state. Intellectually, this challenge took the form of asserting the validity of new social, economic, political, and ideological ties,

were central to this investigation in Europe had become increasingly peripheral to American social science. The "social question" continued to be the focus of social theory in the United States, but increasingly it was investigated in ways that severed it from issues relating to historical agency and social change, class and power, and the character of fundamental social relations.

Political developments in the twentieth century – revolutionary currents between the wars and the spread of socialism and of socialist reforms throughout Europe in the 1940s – appeared to further encourage this tendency. Probably the most important factor in shaping the direction of American social theory, however, was America's post–World War II "development project." This project had a decisive impact, not only on American social science but, through its influence, on post–World War II social theory generally.

The central concern of America's "development project" was to shape the future of the "developing world" in ways that would ensure that it would not be drawn into the Soviet communist bloc.[3] The United States and other capitalist countries had contained the spread of socialism between 1917 and 1939; but following the interruption of World War II and within a period of a few years, socialism had made huge gains: social democratic reforms were institutionalized in varying degrees throughout Europe, and the Communist pattern of organization had spread to much of Eastern Europe and to China. To prevent it from spreading still further and wider – to the colonial areas in Africa and Asia that had become independent from European powers – the United States enlisted its social scientists to study and devise ways of promoting capitalist economic development and political stability.

By the early 1950s, this "development project" was well under way and it continued, through generous funding and institutional inducements, to attract a steady and ever-expanding flow of research and writing from across the social sciences.[4] Within a couple of decades, contributions from political

now conceptualized as "society," against the state. The rising tide of discontent pitting "society" against the political and ideological order erupted in disorder, rebellion, and revolution. The specter of disorder and revolution raised the question of how social order could be restored and maintained, indeed, how social order was possible at all. (Wolf 1982: 8)

On the emergence of the social question, see Fischer 1966; a good discussion of the impact of the "social question" on the development of contemporary social science is in Wolf 1982: 7–19, and Katznelson 1997.

[3] On the "development project," see, e.g., McMichael 1996a: 13–76; McMichael 1996b; and So 1990: chap. 1. See also the essays in Chomsky et al. 1997 and Simpson 1999.

[4] Government funding was made available for the establishment of centers for "area studies" linked to American strategic interests, for training in "defense" languages, and to support overseas research. See, e.g., Simpson 1994; Diamond 1992; Nader 1997; and Wallerstein 1997. In addition, nongovernmental organizations, such as the Social Science Research Council, which was especially instrumental in the establishment of "area studies" and which funded workshops and conferences, fellowships and grants, summer training institutes,

scientists, economists, sociologists, psychologists, anthropologists, and de-mographers had markedly converged around a common set of analytic conventions and general themes. Eventually, these produced a common grounding for research and writing in all areas of social scientific inquiry. The "development project" may have amplified already existing trends, but it ultimately succeeded in thoroughly recasting social science in line with its own political aims. A key factor in this achievement was the production and widespread use of analytic and conceptual innovations that fused the aims of social science with those of the development project.

The decisive impact of the "development project" can be seen not only in social science research but in the writing of history. In fact, in what has surely been one of its greatest accomplishments, the "development project" helped to produce and gain wide acceptance of what this book argues was a radically revisionist account of European industrial capitalist development. Previously, research and writing on European industrial development had focused on what, throughout the nineteenth century, had been seen as its most characteristic aspects: domination, exploitation, uneven development, inequality, political instability, and authoritarianism. These had been the principal foci of the narratives and analyses of countless social scientists and reformers; the speeches, official documents and reports, and other writings of European statesmen; and the work of the century's greatest literary figures.

 But in the accounts of modern European history produced in America after World War II, all these aspects of industrial capitalist development, all the elements that for nineteenth-century social scientists had revealed its intrinsic costs and engendered pessimism and doubt about it,[5] recede into the background. Instead, the emergence of industrial capitalism and democracy in Europe is depicted as resulting from a gradual, evolutionary change. Slowly but steadily wealth diffuses; gradually, but inevitably, equality and liberty spread into increasingly wider domains. It is a reassuring and inspiring tale of progress, a story devoid of bloody conflict, power, and privilege, of suffering, division, and struggle. Thus, while the ideological fervor and politics of the Cold War were suppressing not only communism but socialist and other reformist and progressive elements in the "developing world," it was

---

scholarly exchanges, and publications, forged links between government and universities, and among researchers, practitioners, and policy makers. For collaboration between universities, nongovernmental organizations, and intelligence services, see, e.g., Cumings 2002.

[5] Pessimism and doubt about whether the ever-expanding productive capacity of society leads to human happiness was expressed by the classical theoreticians of liberalism as, for instance, David Ricardo, in this reflection:

> Happiness is the object to be desired, and we cannot be quite sure that, provided he is equally well-fed, a man may not be happier in the enjoyment of the luxury of idleness than in the enjoyment of a neat cottage and good clothes. And after all we do not know if these would fall to his share. His labour might only increase the enjoyment of his employer. (1887: 138)

working, also, through the "development project" to suppress, in history, the role of these elements in achieving welfare states and the democratization of national politics in Europe.

A number of features of contemporary social scientific and historical research and writing in the United States are the focus of particular concern in this book. The first is the absence of class and class analysis.[6] For ideological reasons and, specifically because of its association with Marxism, class analysis was rejected in the United States as doctrinaire (and thus irrelevant to the purposes and aims of social scientific research and good historical practice). Marxism is an exploration of the role of class processes (processes of the production, appropriation, and distribution of surplus value) and class struggles in human history. Thus, the rejection of classical Marxism by liberal (and also "post-Marxist"[7]) historiography entailed, first and foremost, a rejection of the notion of class and of class conflict.

The rejection of class is the basis of a number of other analytic orientations characteristic of American social science and historiography. Among these are two conceptualizations that together have worked effectively to foreclose investigation into how societal processes and relationships shape state action and the state system. The first of these is the conception of the state as wholly, "relatively," or "potentially" autonomous from social forces. Despite the variety of conceptual refinements that, in recent years, have been produced by scholars in a variety of disciplines, most social science research and writing is based, either explicitly or implicitly, on a notion of the state as autonomous from dominant class interests.[8] The second conceptualization

---

[6] Notable exceptions abound: the work of Maurice Zeitlin, Perry Anderson, Gospa Esping-Anderson, Ira Katznelson, and Aristide Zolberg immediately comes to mind.

[7] A variety of political and intellectual stances on the left dissociate the socialist project from class and class struggle and reject the primacy of class politics in favor of "democratic struggles" and "new social movements." On this, see Ellen Meiksins Wood (1998b).

[8] In most of the dominant approaches to theorizing about the state, the state is conceived of as autonomous from dominant classes and as an independent institution acting in its own right. In Weberian/institutional and liberal modernization approaches, the differentiation of an autonomous governing subsystem is seen as resulting from or connected to a process of rationalization compelled by the imperatives of modernization (e.g., Huntington 1968; Weber 1978: 1006–69); of the division of labor, either within society (see, e.g., and following Durkheim 1975, Parsons 1951, 1966; Eisenstadt 1966; Bendix 1977) or within the world capitalist system (e.g., Wallerstein 1974); or of advances in military technology (e.g., Hintze 1962, 1975; Finer 1975; Tilly 1990). The autonomous state is also a feature of neoclassical economic and rational choice approaches (e.g., North and Thomas 1973; North 1981, 1990), newer statist or state-centric approaches (e.g., Krasner 1977; Skocpol 1979; Evans, Rueschemeyer, and Skocpol 1985), and neo-Marxist theories of the state. During the 1970s, Marxist-oriented analysts were concerned with exploring and explaining "the relative autonomy of the state" from direct control by the dominant class. In this conception of the state, the state is thought of as above class struggle by reason of its monopoly of force, and therefore autonomous relative to social dynamics. It rules and controls society by virtue of capabilities that differentiate it from social groups. Its most threatening enemies are other states,

is of the interstate environment as a sociologically neutral "anarchy." Main-stream theories contend that because states operate in an "anarchical" and, therefore, militarily dangerous and threatening environment, they can have or pursue no interest or purpose in their relations with other states other than that of maximizing their own security.[9] These two assumptions are, however, quite problematic. In addition to providing a distorted view of the history of state formation and interstate relations, they have confounded attempts to theorize the interrelations among global, state, and local social structures, and to develop theoretically coherent analyses of change. More-over, by providing a rationale for defining a distinction between interna-tional and domestic processes and structures, they have helped to obfuscate relations of connection, interaction, and interdependence that are causally related to many of the outcomes that social science is concerned with ex-plaining. Conflict and war research provides a particularly unfortunate ex-ample. The analytical distinction commonly drawn between international and domestic conflict obscures critical linkages and continuities not only among different conflicts and among different sorts of conflicts but among the structures and processes that help to produce and resolve them, as well. In particular, it forecloses investigation into patterns of conflict throughout transnational social formations and how these conflicts and formations are related to large-scale change.

KARL POLANYI'S *THE GREAT TRANSFORMATION*

The resurgence of interest in history has produced in recent years a remark-able revival of interest in Karl Polanyi's *The Great Transformation*. Written in 1944, this powerful account of the rise and demise of Europe's nineteenth-century market system remains one of the most influential analyses of insti-tutional transformation and the emergence of new structures. It has figured prominently in debates about transitions under way in Eastern Europe and the post-Soviet area, as well as in debates about "globalization" and the rise of a global market. One of the great charismatic books of the twentieth century, it continues to be a source of inspiration for political economists, international relations theorists, sociologists, and historians endeavoring to understand the multiple challenges and transformations facing national, re-gional, and global structures in the twenty-first century. It may be, as has been

and successful protection against these enemies serves to justify and legitimate state control over social groups or classes. This is the liberal state, a neutral mechanism for aggregating preferences or integrating society – except that relations of domination prevail between the state and civil society, rather than consensually based authority, as in liberal theories. For a discussion of neo-Marxist theories of the state, see Poulantzas and Miliband 1973; Holloway and Picciotto 1978; Jessop 1982, 1990; and Carnoy 1984.

[9] See, e.g., Masters 1964; the articles in Art and Jervis 1973; Waltz 1979, 1990; Grieco 1988; Milner 1991; Shimko 1992; Mearsheimer 1994–95; and Powell 1994.

said, that "no work of economic history except *Capital* and *The Protestant Ethic and the Spirit of Capitalism* has had more influence."[10]

Interest in Polanyi's *The Great Transformation* has focused on features of its analysis that appear to depart from and significantly improve upon more conventional studies of change produced after World War II.[11] However, its analysis as a whole is based on many of the same exclusions and biases found both in other studies of change and in American social science generally. Because of these, Polanyi misses key dimensions of the historical transformations he discusses, and he develops conceptualizations and conclusions that, in important ways, are inaccurate and misleading.

Consider, for instance, Polanyi's conception of agency. According to Polanyi, the basic dynamic shaping both the development of industrial capitalism in Europe and its transformation in the course of the world wars is the antagonism that emerged in the nineteenth century between "society as a whole" and the "soulless institutions" of the self-regulating market system (Polanyi 1944: 219). Despite the record of industrial and political struggles that recurred throughout the nineteenth century, and the language of class that emerged to express and shape them, this history largely fades from view. Polanyi assigns no role to class in shaping the rise and spread of the market system; and in the demise of the system, its role, according to Polanyi, does not begin until the 1920s.[12]

By ignoring the class structures that were emerging from the introduction of capitalist forms of ownership and production, Polanyi misses the political dynamics of what is perhaps the most crucial chapter in modern history for understanding current trends of change: the dismantling of Europe's eighteenth-century national welfare systems (see Chapter 2) and regulated markets, and the social conflicts that emerged as a result. He misconceives the character of Europe's industrial expansion and the translocal institutional complex that underpinned it. He also overlooks the key role of social conflicts and imperialist wars both in Europe's industrial expansion and in bringing about and shaping the outcome of the great transformation that occurred in the course of the world wars. Polanyi conceives of society as organic and sociologically undifferentiated, and of state and global structures as sociologically neutral. Thus, like many other influential studies of large-scale change (e.g., Skocpol 1979; Gilpin 1981), Polanyi is unsuccessful

---

[10] Hejeebu and McCloskey 1999: 286. A review of online citation indices several years ago yielded 1,688 references to Polanyi in articles published during the 1990s. While this does not definitively support claims about his popularity, it might serve as an indication of what a more thorough and careful search might produce.

[11] See Chapter 1 for a discussion of other influential accounts of large-scale change.

[12] For Polanyi's most extended discussion of classes, see Polanyi 1944: chap. 13. According to Polanyi, it was only after World War I and with the "final phase of the fall of market economy" that "the conflict of class forces entered decisively" (1944: 219).

in his attempt to theorize the interrelationship of global structures, states, and social forces, and how it produces change.

The arguments in this book are presented in relation to Polanyi's *The Great Transformation* for a number of reasons. The spirit and central concerns so vividly expressed in Polanyi's book inspired the research and writing of this one, and this one focuses on the same terrain, and for the same purpose: to clarify the mechanisms and possibilities of progressive change. In a sense, then, this book is ultimately less a critique of Polanyi's masterpiece than it is a testament to its enduring power. Polanyi's analysis provides a compelling and provocative example of the analytic orientations that this book is challenging, and his analysis of large-scale change not only is one of the most influential ever produced, it is also being used extensively to analyze current trends of change (i.e., "globalization"). Thus, Polanyi's analysis is not itself the target of the critique so much as an eminent representative of the sort of analyses and interpretations that, as this book hopes to show, cloud important issues; consequently, there will not be a sustained textual engagement with it.

Since this book focuses on class divisions and struggle, it might be assumed that it castigates Polanyi in order to elevate Marx. If that were its purpose, the book would be structured very differently. It would set out Marx's analysis of Europe's industrial capitalist development, endeavor to show the unerring accuracy and completeness of it, and then on that basis argue that accounts like Polanyi's that deviate from it in any way must be in that way inferior to it. But that is not what this book does. More often than not, and even where Marxist categories are used, the account of European industrial development developed in this book challenges Marx's analysis as well as Polanyi's.[13]

The errors in Polanyi's analysis that are the concern of this book are linked in further discussions of them (Chapter 1) to his failure to consider the role of social structures and conflict in shaping the overall pattern of European economic and social development after the Industrial Revolution. This might be seen as a reflection of the time and place in which it was produced. The writing of *The Great Transformation* took place in the United States in 1944, and was supported by a two-year fellowship from the Rockefeller Foundation.[14] Polanyi's occasionally awkward attempts to avoid agreement

---

[13] Thus, for instance, while subsequent chapters distinguish between the methods of absolute and relative surplus value production, they use the distinction to show that the general pattern of industrial expansion in Europe differed from that described by most Marxist, as well as non-Marxist, scholars.

[14] His later writings, when he was at Columbia University, were supported by funds from the Ford Foundation (on this, see Hejeebu and McCloskey 1999). He later went to Canada when his wife was forced because of her Communist background to leave the United States. It is impossible to say whether or how his circumstances influenced the work he produced in the United States at that time, but the analytic orientation of *The Great Transformation* is, nonetheless, fully compatible with Cold War ideological positions.

with Marx might be seen in this light, as well as his view of the state and other nineteenth-century European institutions as "liberal." He had a tendency to treat as historical fact what remained but a hope of early nineteenth-century liberals: that politics and economics could be separated so that no one class would monopolize political power for its own purposes.

Thus, while he recognizes the transformative force of the Industrial Revolution, inconsistent with this, and perhaps for the purpose of distancing himself from Marx, he rejects the notion that the development of productive forces is the major element in historical change. Polanyi rightly points out that "the road to the free market was opened and kept open by an enormous increase in continuous, centrally organized and controlled interventionism" (1944: 140), but, consistent with liberal conceptions of the state, he then goes on to treat the state as largely autonomous from social forces. Though he wants to "de-naturalize" the *rise* of the unregulated market, he then treats its operation and, in many respects, its demise, as analogous to a force of nature. Thus, while he is unsparing in his depiction of the horrors of industrialization, he is careful to avoid the exploitation, monopoly, and political repression that created and sustained them for more than a century. Instead, these horrors appear in his account as the outcome of a sociologically neutral plague-like visitation on "society as a whole"; for Polanyi's market system is not only "unregulated" – once in operation, it appears to be largely self-sustaining. States, embodying the contradictory impulses that governed the time, put in place "pro-market" laws but also helped to undermine the market through the introduction of protectionist legislation. As we would expect in a society afflicted by plague, the overall character and purpose of government action and social activity was focused on securing protection (through, e.g., tariffs and social legislation). Moreover, as with plague, the actions of states and groups to secure protection, for whomever and by whatever means, contributed to the protection, and was therefore in the interest, of "society as a whole."

Absent from Polanyi's analysis is a detailed exploration of the "first transformation" that, at the end of the eighteenth century, brought about the rise of the unregulated market system. A consideration of the class structure and the class-specific interests that shaped the rise of the unregulated market might have focused his attention on the varying capacities of different groups to gain protection, and the recurring social conflicts and imperialist wars throughout the period.

RETHINKING THE GREAT TRANSFORMATION

In contrast to Polanyi, I argue that the dismantling of market regulations and systems of national welfare prevailing at that time in Britain, France, and elsewhere in Europe represented the victory not of new liberal commercial interests but of rural, pre-industrial, and autocratic structures of power and

authority. The assumption that a "new" industrial capitalist class rose to power in the first transformation causes him to characterize as "liberal" key structures and features of nineteenth-century Europe, including the state, the Concert of Europe, and Europe's "peace." States were not liberal, but exclusionary and nobilitarian (Chapter 2). The central dynamic of Europe's industrial expansion was not a double movement of protection by and for "society as a whole" against the expanding market system, but a dualism *within* society itself (Chapter 3).

Polanyi and those who follow him are gravely mistaken about the reality of the so-called long peace of the nineteenth century. Far from being a period of peace gradually overtaken by the contradictions of the unregulated market, this period was born in violence and remained violent throughout (Chapter 4). European states fought *in Europe* fourteen interstate wars and twelve wars against the populations of other states; outside Europe, they fought some fifty-eight wars. The appendix records 540 conflicts between the first and second transformations, and these must be treated as not a complete record but as a sample only.

The differences of conceptualization and analytic perspective between Polanyi's analysis and the one presented in this book have important implications. Consider, for instance, how the terrain of Polanyi's analysis would appear if it focused not on the relative absence of multilateral great power conflict in Europe but on the recurring social conflicts and the continual imperialist wars both within and outside Europe that, in Polanyi's account, are absent. What if the change in the form of the state that occurred as part of the "first transformation" represented not the rise to power of a "new" and liberal industrial capitalist class but the means by which landed wealth consolidated its power over the state and, as a result, over the economy? What if it were shown that key groups within society sought protection not from the market but from pressures for redistribution and reform that threatened their monopoly and privilege? What if it were shown that, at least in nineteenth-century Europe, there was no such thing as an "unregulated market" – that markets were always and everywhere regulated by states in order to effect the outcome of their transactions? This book endeavors to show all of this, and to draw the implications for contemporary trends of change.

Polanyi begins his analysis with the international system because, in his view, the system was crucial to the emergence and consolidation of liberal states and the unregulated market. He therefore offers what might be termed a "top down" analysis: he starts with the nature of the overarching international system and then shows how that system shaped the emergence and development of local social institutions. But the terrain appears very different if it is traversed, as is done in this book, in reverse – that is, from a "bottom up" exploration of social relations, conflicts, and interests, and how these shaped the emergence and development of state and international structures. This book focuses not on the international system but on the system of social relations and how they are reproduced both in sites of production and throughout social formations, not on the balance of state power in Europe but on the balance of social power.

What if Polanyi had lived to see the beginning of the rise, once again, of the "unregulated" market? Polanyi believed that the great transformation from free unregulated markets to welfare states represented a permanent change. If the "unregulated" market was assumed to be not an unprecedented phenomenon but a recurring one, how might his analysis of it have changed? The assumption that something is unprecedented and that its emergence simultaneously triggers a mechanism that leads inevitably to its demise (e.g., Polanyi's "double movement") might encourage an overly general and benign view of it. The Czech writer Milan Kundera aptly renders this idea:

> If the French Revolution were to recur eternally, French historians would be less proud of Robespierre. But because they deal with something that will not return, the bloody years of the Revolution have turned into mere words, theories and discussions, have become lighter than feathers, frightening no one. There is an infinite difference between a Robespierre who occurs only once in history and a Robespierre who eternally returns, chopping off French heads.[15]

The purpose of revisiting the history of Europe's nineteenth-century market system is to explore the relevance of the relationships it reveals for current trends of change, but since current events revise our views of past ones, the aim is also to consider how current trends of change help to illuminate the past.

CLASS AND CLASS AGENCY

The present study revisits the terrain of Karl Polanyi's "Great Transformation," focusing on the class nature of the institutional complex underlying Europe's nineteenth-century market economy and the class interests that shaped and were served by the expansion of industrial capitalism. Its overall argument focuses on the importance of the balance of class power for understanding change (as do, among others, Rueschemeyer et al. 1992).

Its analysis of class differs from those used in various Marxist approaches in two ways. First, it focuses on the class relation as it extends beyond the production process to the sphere of circulation and consumption[16] and politics. Second, it focuses on the class nature of both the state and the interstate system. States are rooted in a common social structure[17] that predated their

---

[15] *The Unbearable Lightness of Being*, trans. Michael Henry Heim (New York: Harper and Row, 1984), p. 2.
[16] In Marx, these spheres are not really separable. See, e.g., the Introduction to Marx's *Grundrisse*.
[17] Social structure is conceived in terms of a collection of institutions, rules of behavior, norms, and roles "that are relatively invariant in the face of turnover of individuals and relatively

formation and that overlapped and intersected with local class structures (see Chapter 2). Elites continued to operate within this system of social institutions, relationships, and norms, and within institutional arrangements that linked local interests and institutions to international mechanisms of control.

Recognizing this, the book argues that the development of prosperous, stable democratic societies was achieved much later than is commonly thought, and not gradually or smoothly, as is often assumed, but as a result of a shift in the balance of class power in Europe in the course of two world wars. The relative peace and stability that characterized much of Europe after 1945 was a consequence of this shift and of the redistribution of political power, wealth, and income that it helped to bring about (Chapter 8).

The nearly simultaneous Industrial and French Revolutions have, for generations of students of Western history, represented the critical turning point in the development of industrial capitalism and democracy in Europe. However, these events represented not a revolutionary break with the past, but only the beginning of a process that was slow, bloody, had many setbacks, and finally culminated in two world wars. A vast frontier lay between the Industrial Revolution and the achievement of industrial capitalism in Europe. Nearly a century and a half after the French Revolution, lower classes and ethnic minorities in Europe were still effectively excluded from political life and from opportunities for economic advancement. Various forms of economic protection and monopoly, as well as restrictions on labor organization and on political participation, enabled a small elite of landowners and wealthy industrialists to monopolize land as well as the entire field of industry and trade. This produced a dual pattern of development that, in all aspects, resembles the dual economies described by theories of contemporary third world development and erroneously restricted in their application to that world.[18]

Dualistic industrial expansion in Europe was characterized by the use of methods that deskilled labor and kept it fragmented and impoverished, together with the development of exogenous demand and consumption through the export of capital and goods. A generally low level of industrialization and the production of high-cost goods for export avoided

resilient to the idiosyncratic preferences and expectations of individuals" (March and Olsen 1984: 740). This structure reproduces a given balance of class forces. They vary along a number of dimensions: social mobility, relations of power, distribution of resources, and the balance of power among different classes.

[18] The evidence that this book presents suggests that models of development devised to explain the dynamics of contemporary third world development apply equally as well to Europe's industrial expansion. This extends arguments developed in a previous book, *In the Mirror of the Third World: Industrial Capitalist Development in Modern Europe* (1997). There, as here, I argue that the features that collectively comprise "dependent development" were as characteristic of European development up until the world wars as they are of the contemporary third world.

(1) redistribution of the national income – the need to provide workers with the purchasing power to consume the goods that they produced – and (2) the creation of a significant factory proletariat. This ensured that the benefits of expanding production would be retained solely by the property-owning classes.

The struggle between labor and capital, while carried on in different societies and in different ways, brought about broadly similar outcomes. Dualistic structures emerged not through the common or concerted action of Europe's ruling class but as a result of the structural relations of connection that constituted Europe's transnational elite, and the similarities and interdependencies that it created among states. The ruling classes of European states were not separate-but-similar classes. They were part of a single transregional elite whose broadly similar characteristics, interests, capabilities, and policies were constituted and reproduced through relations of interaction, connection, and interdependence (Chapter 1). These relations of connection had for centuries created similarities and interdependencies among states (Chapter 2). As the various economies of Europe began to expand in the nineteenth century, their advanced sectors were tied more closely to those within the economies of other European countries than to the more backward sectors within their own (Chapter 3). As a result, and as time went on, economic development in Europe took place within, and was crucially shaped by, an increasingly interdependent industrial system. This system, and the structural relations of connection and interaction that produced it, ensured that problems relating to the establishment of capitalist labor markets and new labor processes were resolved in broadly similar ways.

On the eve of World War I, the dominant social, economic, and political systems of Europe paralleled those that existed at the time in other regions and that exist still in many areas in the contemporary third world. Its most effective elites were traditional and aristocratic and not bourgeois; landowning and rent receiving, not capitalist or entrepreneurial; religious, not secular; oligarchic, not democratic. Industry was penetrated by feudal forms of organization and characterized by monopolism, protectionism, cartellization, and corporatism; forming small islands within impoverished, backward agrarian economies. Political institutions had not significantly affected the character of popular representation; the great majority of adults were excluded from political participation. In Europe, as in areas of the third world today, elites were interested not in development but in power. Economic expansion was external, rather than internal, and based on the enlargement of foreign markets rather than of domestic ones. States sought to increase their distributive share, rather than to increase the total social output. This pattern of economic expansion produced recurring social conflicts in Europe as well as imperialist rivalries and tensions, both within and outside the region.

EUROPEAN CONFLICTS

Karl Polanyi begins his analysis in *The Great Transformation* with the assertion that Europe experienced a hundred years of relative peace between 1815 and 1914. But throughout the nineteenth century, European states were continually at war with populations and states both within Europe and elsewhere in the world. Attempts to maintain or eradicate restrictions on political rights and economic opportunities generated minority and class conflicts at home. Attempts to secure protected external markets in lieu of developing internal markets generated imperialist conflicts.

This book records *all* conflicts waged by, within, and among European states between 1815 and 1914, both within Europe and without, including small- and medium-scale domestic conflicts usually not considered, together with large-scale interstate ones. It may appear peculiar to "lump together" conflicts of vastly different magnitude, motive, and apparent importance. However, small- and medium-scale events are connected to big ones, and familiar types of international conflict are interwoven and causally connected with internal class conflict.[19] Recording the whole range of conflict activity over time reveals the essentially transnational and regional dynamics underlying conflict. It shows that the same actors repeatedly became engaged in the same sort of conflicts over a long period of time, that no conflict was purely an internal affair, and that conflicts of various types and sizes and in a variety of settings were, in significant ways, interconnected.

The importance of investigating the entire range of conflict activity throughout an interconnected area over time was made clear to me by the Iranian Revolution in 1979. The revolution came as a complete surprise to political observers, Western and Israeli intelligence services, Middle East scholars, war researchers, and journalists. Recall U.S. President Jimmy Carter's famous toast at a dinner for the Shah of Iran. In a manner reminiscent of Chamberlain's declaration of "peace in our time" following the Munich Pact, Carter raised his wine glass and toasted Iran as "a pillar of stability in the region." Years later, when I began to study the pattern of conflict throughout the region, I discovered that there had been almost continual outbreaks of violent conflict in Iran starting in 1963: demonstrations and riots – sometimes a million strong – were almost routine in the years leading up to the revolution. But war researchers, analysts, and scholars had simply failed to perceive, in terms of both its nature and its magnitude, the significance of this pattern of violent activity. In studying the causes, conditions,

---

[19] A number of influential studies have explored the international ramifications of domestic class conflict and the ways in which international conflict is interwoven with and caused by internal class conflict. The historian Eckart Kehr (1975, 1977) is only the most notable example. Kehr's arguments about the domestic roots of German foreign policy in 1914 were rediscovered and elaborated in the 1970s by, e.g., Berghahn 1971 and Wehler 1985. For a discussion of the Kehrite view, see Berghahn 1994: ix–xvii, and Mommsen 1973: 3–16.

and consequences of European conflict, I resolved, therefore, to undertake a detailed and systematic investigation of all violent conflict throughout the region.

THE ORGANIZATION OF THE STUDY

This book, like Polanyi's, is about two transformations: first, the eradication of communal control over economic life, and second, its reinstatement. Its overall argument is that "great transformations" such as occurred in the course of the world wars are made possible by shifts in the balance of social power. Chapter 1 elaborates this argument, while the subsequent chapters are structured to examine various chronological aspects of the overall argument. In Part I, the class-analytic perspective developed in Chapter 1 is used to reread the history of the Industrial Revolution (Chapter 2), the dynamic of expansion abroad and restriction at home that defines ruling class responses to it (Chapter 3), the social and imperialist conflicts that it engenders (Chapter 4), and how these conflicts produced the first Great War of the twentieth century (World War I) and its social revolutionary aftermath (Chapter 5). Part II describes "the interregnum": the polarization of European society between the wars (Chapter 6) and, associated with this, the politics of appeasement and World War II (Chapter 7). Then, Part III explores the causes and conditions of the class compromise that brought about a return to systems of nationally regulated capitalism after World War II (Chapter 8); it then extends the argument forward in time to a consideration of globalization (Chapter 9).

THE PLAN OF THE BOOK

The study is designed, in part, to challenge ideological orientations within contemporary social scientific inquiry and, specifically, those that foreclose an investigation into class divisions and the interests and politics that arise from them. After examining some influential examples of these analyses, Chapter 1 shows how Polanyi's analysis is undermined by analytic elements common to them and in similar ways. A class analytic perspective is then used to highlight the theoretical weaknesses and empirical flaws of Polanyi's analysis and to sketch the contours of an alternative interpretation of Europe's industrial development and of how and why European society was transformed during the world wars.[20]

[20] This is a work of synthesis that presents a mix of historical insights, comparative contrasts, and statistical data (though not statistical testing). It is based not on new research but on a reading of the available works of modern historians and on scholarly evidence that is widely accessible and in other contexts widely used to reinterpret the past. It draws together and fleshes out themes that emerge repeatedly in the works of modern scholars, but are

At the center of the argument is the contention that European industrial expansion was characterized not by the double movement of expansion and protection that Polanyi described but by a dualism grounded in internal repression and external expansion. Societies industrialized on the basis of the expansion and integration not of internal markets, as standard accounts assume, but of external ones. This enabled European economies to expand with the least amount of disruption and leveling of the social structure.

The onset of the Industrial Revolution brought to an end an unprecedented period of social peace in Europe and began a century of social conflict. Deregulation of markets, dismantling of national welfare systems (in Britain, France, and elsewhere), and the imposition of capitalist forms of ownership and factory production set in motion recurring social conflicts that, during the nineteenth century, spread throughout Europe (Chapter 2).

Dominant classes expanded industrial production in ways that enabled them to consolidate their position within the class struggles that emerged at the end of the eighteenth century, to monopolize gains from the new forms of production, and to leave intact to the greatest extent possible the traditional bases of their social and political power (Chapter 3). Throughout the century, externally oriented expansion generated social conflicts at home and imperialist conflicts abroad (Chapter 4).

By the beginning of the twentieth century, external expansion as an engine of growth had begun to approach its limit and, as it did, imperialist rivalries came to focus once again on Europe itself. The mobilization of Europe's masses in 1914 to fight in Europe the first of a two-phased culminating war of European imperialism set in motion what a century of externally oriented expansion had succeeded in preventing: social revolution and a vastly accelerated process of social change (Chapter 5). As a result, during the interwar years the domestic and international relations of European states became increasingly polarized under the impact of a more or less continuous round of violent strikes, riots, demonstrations and street fighting, rebellions, coups, and revolutions (Chapter 6). As Europe's ruling classes became increasingly preoccupied with the threats of socialism at home and Bolshevism abroad, the concern with stopping the spread of Communism became inextricably bound up with the preservation and defense of the traditional structures of European society. British and French appeasement policies were a reflection of this preoccupation and led to World War II (Chapter 7).

The Second World War completed what the first had begun: a shift in the balance of class power throughout Europe. This made possible the many

given insufficient emphasis there. It draws on available statistical data, but reads them with a different set of lenses. Thus, it shows how these same data may be suggestive of new conclusions. At times the sources cited in the text do not reflect the most recent research and writing on the subjects at hand, but are older sources that have been overlooked or given insufficient attention.

important other changes generally attributed to the war and its impact. By bringing about a redistribution of political power, wealth, and income, the war enabled states in Europe to put their economies on an entirely new footing. This was the "great transformation" that occurred in Europe as a result of the world wars and that marked the beginning of an era of unprecedented growth and of relative peace and political stability in Europe (Chapter 8). After 1945, development was internally oriented and relatively more balanced, making possible, for a time, greater prosperity and political stability. However, by the 1970s, a reappearance of flux, uncertainty, and more intense conflict in political life had become apparent in Europe, in both the East and the West. In both parts of Europe, it was possible to discern the formation of new class structures, with features reminiscent of nineteenth-century European society and, as a result, a resurgence of nationalism and class conflict. At the same time, and in both East and West, increasing deregulation of industry and markets, privatization of state assets, and the curtailment of state welfare functions suggest parallels to aspects of the pre–world war international political economy. The implications of the historical analysis of previous chapters are drawn for these trends that, collectively, many refer to as "globalization" (Chapter 9). In light of the analysis of previous chapters, "globalization" appears as the continuation of social and political conflicts that began with Europe's industrial expansion two centuries ago. The lesson for social scientists and historians that might be drawn from that is one that sociologist Barrington Moore endeavored to communicate in an essay written in 1958. In "Strategy in Social Science," Moore argued that the major issue confronting contemporary social theorists is the same as that which confronted Tocqueville, Mosca, Marx, Weber, and Durkheim: the feasibility of creating rational societies under the conditions of industrialism.

Inasmuch as "globalization" is a continuation of struggles that began with the Industrial Revolution and, in particular, with the deregulation and changes in production that gave rise to unregulated markets in the nineteenth century, the dilemmas, dangers, and opportunities that "globalization" presents are ones that social thinkers have grappled with since the dawn of the industrial age. Our ability to address them effectively depends on our willingness to take up the themes and aspects of industrial capitalism that were the primary focus of their work.

This book began as a Ph.D. dissertation at the University of California, Los Angeles, where I was inspired by a supremely talented group of scholars. In the intervening years, and as I worked on other, related projects, colleagues at the University of Pittsburgh and at the University of Sussex provided me with encouragement and intellectual sustenance: at Pittsburgh, Charles Gochman and Jonathan Harris; at Sussex, Ronen Palan, Kees van der Pijl, and Julian Saurin. Comments by David Gibbs and Henk Overbeek on earlier drafts of the book manuscript and, especially, Mark Blythe's detailed and incisive comments on the penultimate and final drafts helped make this a better book than it would otherwise have been. None of them, of course, is to be held responsible for its shortcomings.

David Wilkinson has been a beacon illuminating my way down many roads I may never have explored but for him. This book would not exist but for his support and example. It is with gratitude for his wisdom and generosity of spirit that I dedicate this book to him.

INTRODUCTION

I

Conflict and Change in World Politics

In *The Great Transformation* (1944), Karl Polanyi chronicled the rise of a self-regulating market system in Europe in the early nineteenth century and the "great transformation" that occurred when the system collapsed in the course of the world wars.[1] Two features of this chronicle, in particular, have made the book a focus of interest for scholars over the more than half a century since it was written. First, its account of the social implications of the new system presented an eloquent and powerful testimonial to the ravages generated by the commodification of land and labor and the operation of unregulated markets. Second, in explaining how and why the system collapsed through a contradictory "double movement" of expansion and protection, Polanyi offered a key and enduring insight into a universal dynamic of growth and change.

Polanyi's analysis was concerned to demolish two notions that pervade liberal thought. First, in arguing that the market emerged as a result of deliberate state action, Polanyi rejected completely the notion that the self-regulating market was in any way "natural" or that it "evolved" or arose spontaneously as a result of the expansion of trade. His keen insights into how the international institutional context shaped the development of national markets strengthened the argument. Polanyi's most insistent claim was that the unregulated market constitutes a threat to human society, and he argued that, irrespective of whatever indices are marshaled to show an improvement in living standards in the nineteenth century, the fact remains that the unregulated market wrought a social catastrophe in Europe.

Much of Polanyi's book, and the interest it has generated, focuses on the elaboration of this "double movement" and its consequences: the emergence simultaneously of the market system and of a protective countermove to

[1] The "great transformation" about which Polanyi wrote has been interpreted wrongly to mean "the commodification of money, land, and labor" (see, e.g., Katznelson 1986: 14; Zolberg 1986: 413).

check its action with regard to labor, land, and money,[2] and the pattern of stresses and strains that it generated and that ultimately led to two world wars and to the collapse of the system.

Despite the phenomenal resurgence of interest in Polanyi's work in recent years, the insight that a "double movement" shaped industrial development in Europe has not been sufficiently incorporated into our understanding of modern European history, nor have its implications for comparative-historical studies been recognized. Europe's industrial development was shaped by protectionism to a far greater extent than is generally recognized. I argue that before World War II, protectionism had enabled a small elite of landowners and wealthy industrialists to monopolize land and the entire field of industry and trade. As a result, the pattern of development in Europe before World War II was far more similar to contemporary third world development than is commonly thought.

Polanyi's focus on the interrelationship of global structures, states, and social forces offered important insights into how to study these subjects as well. Increasingly, contemporary analysts of social change are recognizing the need to conceptualize and theorize the interaction and fundamental interdependencies between domestic and international structures and processes (e.g., Skocpol 1979; Gilpin 1981; Spruyt 1996; Katznelson and Shefter 2002).

Polanyi's analysis of the institutional complex underpinning Europe's "nineteenth-century civilization" (Polanyi 1944: 3) assumed that changes in the organization of the international economy provide particular kinds of opportunities for states to act that, in turn, shape the extent to which social forces will be able to influence state policy.[3] Thus, working from the top down, Polanyi focused first on the international balance of power system (and the "Hundred Years' Peace" that it made possible) and the gold standard. These and the "liberal state" were the creation of the self-regulating market system (a series of connected markets). He argued that with the collapse of the market system in the course of the world wars, a new global opportunity structure would emerge and lay the basis for a new political and economic order in Europe. However, soon after the publication of *The Great Transformation*, it became clear that this expectation would not be fulfilled.[4] In fact, following World War II, the United States was determined to restore a world economy based on the principles

---

[2] Polanyi argued that "While on the one hand markets spread all over the face of the globe and the amount of goods grew to unbelievable proportions, on the other hand a network of measures and policies was integrated into powerful institutions designed to check the action of the market relative to labor, land and money" (1944: 76).

[3] A good discussion of Polanyi's analytic schema, on which I depend for this brief consideration, is Block and Somers 1984: 72–75.

[4] See Polanyi's article, "Our Obsolete Market Mentality" (1947), reprinted in Polanyi 1971: 59–77.

of a self-regulating market, and this worked to effectively block moves toward the establishment of socialist markets locally and new economic arrangements internationally.[5] The market system *had* been transformed in important ways, but not, as Polanyi had assumed, because of changes at the top.[6]

The fact that the expected outcome of the great transformation failed to materialize in just the way Polanyi said it would does not depreciate his rich and insightful analysis, but it does invite closer scrutiny of his analytic schema and, in particular, his assumptions about how the world economy, states, and social forces are interrelated.

The next section focuses on these assumptions. It revisits the institutional complex underlying Europe's nineteenth-century market economy, starting, where Polanyi's analysis begins, with the international system. It finds that contradictions and problems stemming from his assumptions about the character and relations among the world economy, states, and social forces lead him logically to a flawed and misleading interpretation of nineteenth-century European institutions and of how and why they were transformed in the course of the world wars.

INDUSTRIAL EXPANSION IN NINETEENTH-CENTURY EUROPE: A CRITIQUE OF THE POLANYIAN VIEW

The Balance of Power System – and the "Hundred Years' Peace"?

Europe's nineteenth-century balance of power system was maintained by a "Concert of Europe" that, according to Polanyi, was dominated by haute finance and by its concern for the preservation of liberal, free-market institutions. Motivated by this concern, the Concert acted as an "international peace interest."[7] For Polanyi, one of the most striking features of

---

[5] For insightful analyses, see, e.g., Block 1977; van der Pijl 1984: 50–137.

[6] As Polanyi himself recognized; see Polanyi 1947. A year after the publication of *The Great Transformation*, Polanyi wrote an article on the transformation of liberal capitalism that reiterated the analytical position he had elaborated in his book.

He argued that to understand the transformation of liberal capitalism, we must look first to the international environment, "since it is in the international field that the methods of private enterprise have broken down – as shown by the failure of the gold standard; and it is in that field that adherence to such methods constitutes a direct obstacle to practical solutions" (Polanyi 1945: 89).

[7] Though "business and finance were responsible for many wars," they were also responsible for "the fact that a general conflagration was avoided" (1944: 16). Business and finance maintained peace by providing the balance of power system with "concrete organized interests" (1944: 17):

Haute finance functioned as a permanent agency of the most elastic kind. Independent of single governments, even of the most powerful, it was in touch with all; independent

nineteenth-century Europe was what he called the "Hundred Years' Peace." The Concert lost its ability to keep the peace when the growth of protectionism and imperialist rivalries began to destroy the self-regulating market and the liberal state. The collapse of these institutions undermined the gold standard that, in turn, destroyed the balance-of-power system and in 1914 led to war.[8]

This characterization of the nature of the Concert of Europe and its role in European affairs is misleading. While the Concert may have been dominated by haute finance, it was also the tool of Europe's monarchs and aristocracies who, after twenty-five years of war in Europe, feared that another major European war would trigger revolution and destruction of the social order.[9] It was committed not to free markets and liberal states but to protection and autocracy. It was this commitment that motivated the series of Concert-sponsored antirevolutionary military actions in Europe.

In describing Europe's nineteenth century as a "century of peace," Polanyi is referring only to the relative absence, between 1815 and 1914, of multilateral great power wars in Europe. But while that may be the case, it is also true that during this period, European states were continually engaged in conflict with their own populations, with other European states and populations, and with territories and states outside Europe. Fourteen wars were fought in Europe between and among Britain, France, Germany, Spain, Russia, Denmark, Austria, Italy, Greece, and Serbia.[10] Twelve wars were fought by Britain, France, Russia, and Austria against foreign populations in

---

of the central banks, even of the Bank of England, it was closely connected with them. . . . the secret of the successful maintenance of general peace lay undoubtedly in the position, organization, and techniques of international finance. (1944: 10)

[8] The Concert of Europe ceased to operate in 1904 when Britain formed the Entente Cordiale with France. Then, in 1907, an Anglo-Russian agreement completed a triple alliance in opposition to Germany, Italy, and Austria-Hungary. With the split of Europe into two hostile power groupings, the balance of power system collapsed. There was an attempt to restore the system after World War I using the League of Nations in place of the Concert of Europe. But the League failed, according to Polanyi, because the defeated countries were not genuine power units.

[9] While in some respects the Concert of Europe sought to serve as a counterweight to the absolutist states of the Holy Alliance, it also guaranteed to them membership in the club of European great powers and that they would be consulted about any major change in the European status quo.

[10]
1821	France, Spain	1870–71	Prussia, France
1828–29	Russia, Turkey	1876	Russia, Turkey
1848–50	Denmark, Prussia	1877–78	Russia, Turkey
1853–56	Russia, Turkey	1897	Greece, Turkey, U.K., France, Austria
1864	Denmark, Prussia	1912–13	Serbia, Turkey
1866	Prussia, Austria	1913	the Balkans
1866	Italy, Austria	1911–12	Italy, Turkey

TABLE 1.1. *Wars Fought Outside Europe by European States*

1807–37	Netherlands in Central Sumatra	1871–72	France in Algeria
1823–26	Britain in Burma	1873–1908	Netherlands in Achin
1825–30	Britain in Tasmania	1878–80	Britain in Afghanistan
1836–52	France in Argentina	1878–81	Russia in Geok Tepe
1836–52	Britain in Argentina	1881	France in Tunisia
1838–42	Britain in Afghanistan	1881–85	Britain in Sudan
1839–42	Britain in China	1882	Britain in Egypt
1839–47	France in Algeria	1882–85	France in China
1843	Britain in India	1885–86	Britain in Burma
1833–36	Portugal in Zambesi in Delagoa Bay	1891–94	Netherlands in the Malay Archipelago
1845–46	Britain in India	1892–94	Belgium in East Congo
1846–49	Netherlands in Bali	1894–96	Italy in Abyssinia
1848–49	Britain in India	1894–1901	France in Madagascar
1850–52	Britain in South-East Africa	1896–1900	Britain in Sudan
1853	Britain in Burma	1897–98	Britain in India
1856–57	Britain in Persia	1897–1901	Britain in Uganda
1856–60	Britain in China	1898	Britain in Sierra Leone
1856–60	France in China	1898	Spain vs. the U.S.
1857	France in Senegal	1899–1900	Britain in China
1857–59	Britain in India	1899–1900	France in China
1859–60	Netherlands in South Celebes	1899–1900	Russia in China
1859–60	Spain vs. Morocco	1899–1900	Italy in China
1859–63	Netherlands in South Borneo	1899–1900	Germany in China
1859–64	Russia in Circassia	1899–1902	Britain in S. Africa
1861–67	Britain in Mexico	1903–8	Germany in S.W. Africa
1865–68	Russia in Bokhara	1904–5	Russia in Japan
1867–68	Britain in Abyssinia	1911–17	Italy in Libya
		1912	France in Morocco

Europe.[11] During that period, European states also fought some fifty-eight wars outside Europe, as shown in Table 1.1.

According to Polanyi, Europe enjoyed one hundred years of peace after 1815 because haute finance acted, through the agency of the Concert of Europe, as an "international peace interest" in the nineteenth century. In this, Polanyi advances a popular current of liberal thought that associates

[11]
1821	Austria in Piedmont	1849	France in Italy
1826–33	Britain in Portugal	1849	Russia in Hungary
1826–33	France in Portugal	1859	France in Italy
1833–40	Britain in Spain	1859	Austria in Piedmont
1848–49	Austria in Piedmont	1860–61	France in Italy
1848	France in Italy	1866–69	Britain in Crete

high finance with peace. But he can do so only by restricting his focus to the occurrence, or nonoccurrence, of interstate wars in Europe. In fact, European states were continually at war during the nineteenth century, and in the very areas of the world where finance capital had migrated. That is why Lenin, Hobson, and others associated finance capital not with peace but with war. Polanyi's association of finance with peace is problematic, not only because of the imperialist wars fought by European powers throughout the century, but because European states were also continually at war with their own populations, as well as those of other territories and states both within Europe and around the world.

However, Polanyi also ignores the recurring and increasingly violent class conflicts that characterized European domestic relations throughout the nineteenth century. This critical dimension of European industrial development is almost entirely missing from Polanyi's account. According to Polanyi, it was only in the 1920s and 1930s, during the "final phase of the fall of market economy," that class conflicts emerged in Europe (1944: 219).

Yet the Concert of Europe was primarily and centrally concerned with class conflicts. The "peace interest" that it promoted was linked to this concern and with defending the existing sociopolitical order against revolutionary threats. Europe's monarchs and aristocracies realized that "if they weakened each other by a war comparable in size to the Napoleonic wars they would open the gates to their own internal destruction" (Holborn 1951: 36). As Viscount Castlereagh, Britain's foreign secretary from 1812 to 1822, recognized, with "revolutionary embers more or less existing in every state of Europe...true wisdom is to keep down the petty contentions of ordinary times, and to stand together in support of the established principles of social order."[12] As Eric Hobsbawm notes: "it was evident to all intelligent statesmen that no major European war was henceforth tolerable, for such a war would almost certainly mean a new revolution, and consequently the destruction of the old regimes" (1962: 126).

Polanyi's analysis is consistent with that of the many scholars who have drawn a contrast between the recurring violence that has accompanied industrialization in many parts of the contemporary third world and the supposedly peaceful domestic relations and relatively smooth development of industrial capitalism and democracy in Europe. But recurring violent conflict was a fundamental dimension of European industrial development. Ethnic and nationalist, religious and ideological conflicts; riots, insurrections, rebellions, revolutions, uprisings, violent strikes, and demonstrations; and coups, assassinations, political repression, and terrorism were characteristic of European societies up until 1945.

Polanyi begins his analysis with Europe's supposed century of peace because it is essential to his conception of Europe's nineteenth-century market

---

[12] *Correspondence*, Third Series, vol. 11, p. 105; in Hobsbawm 1962: 126.

system. For Polanyi, Europe's "unprecedented" one hundred years' peace is powerful evidence of the dominance in Europe of a 'new' liberal bourgeoisie, and the establishment of free markets, free trade, and the liberal state. The fact of war and social conflict involving European states throughout the nineteenth century not only challenges Polanyi's notion of Europe's hundred years' peace; it also casts doubt on institutional features of Europe's nineteenth-century market system that, in Polanyi's analysis, are logically connected to it.

The "Liberal" State?

As Polanyi rightly pointed out, "the road to the free market was opened and kept open by an enormous increase in continuous, centrally organized and controlled interventionism" (1944: 140). However, according to his account, the state subsequently assumed a predominantly liberal character and, consistent with conceptions of the state in liberal theory, functioned as an autonomous actor. Polanyi's characterization of nineteenth-century European states as both "liberal" and autonomous falls far from the mark: throughout the century, states in Europe were not liberal but exclusionary, not autonomous but nobilitarian.[13]

The "self-regulating" market was, as Polanyi acknowledged, an ideal, but it was farther from being a reality than he recognized. Throughout the nineteenth century, states in Europe adopted interventionist economic policies with regard to labor, industry, markets, and trade. In a free market, economic transactions are governed by the free play of all people's unrestricted and competitive pursuit of their economic advantage. However, throughout most of the nineteenth century this freedom was not seen as applicable to workers. Polanyi argued that the self-regulating market began to operate fully in 1834, when workers in England became "free," that is, gained sufficient mobility to sell their labor power in the market. But after 1834 labor was only theoretically free.[14] In practice, its mobility was impeded by a variety of state-enforced legal and extralegal devices,[15] as was its ability

---

[13] The nobilitarian state: a state administered by notables as, for instance, Britain throughout the nineteenth century (Weber 1978: 974). More on the nobilitarian character of the state below.

[14] Some scholars argue that the New Poor Law of 1834 that, Polanyi claims, introduced the market system, was designed to preserve the power of the traditional landed classes (e.g., Brundage 1974, 1979).

[15] In Prussia, for instance, Junkers demanded certificates of morality from anyone who moved to a new estate. Thus, a Junker had only to deny a laborer such a certificate to prevent him from leaving his own estate (Reddy 1987: 172). Until 1890, workers in France had to produce an identification booklet (*livret*) attesting that they had met all debts and other obligations to past employers or be barred from further employment and subject to arrest for vagrancy. A provision barring workers from changing employment during most of the year and requiring that they show they had a source of income for "protection" was in use until

to engage in collective resistance and bargaining.[16] State legislation, as well as wealth, power, and the active collaboration of parish officers and justices of the peace, enabled employers to deny workers the right to bargain, to bind workers by long and inflexible contracts (e.g., the coalminers' "yearly bond" in parts of Britain), and to make them liable to imprisonment for breach of employment (by a law of contract codified in 1823, not applicable to employers). Wage levels were determined not by market forces or through collective bargaining but by employers. Employers supplemented their profits by requiring workers to make payments in kind and forced purchases in company shops and by imposing fines for any infraction of whatever measure they chose to devise (Hobsbawm 1968: 122).

If European states were not liberal in domestic economic affairs, neither were they with respect to foreign trade. The period 1860–75 represents the only free trade interlude in an otherwise protectionist century. It was not until the 1860s that Britain repealed the Navigation Laws and Usury Laws and abolished restrictions on exports and all but a few duties on imports. Starting in the late 1870s and continuing until the end of the Second World War, there was a steady closure and constriction of markets everywhere in Europe.[17]

1883 in Finland and 1885 in Sweden. In Hungary, a law passed in 1907 forbade agricultural workers from leaving their place of employment or receiving outside visitors without the permission of their landlords (Goldstein 1983: 59).

[16] Though in Britain trade unions ceased to be formally illegal in 1824, efforts to destroy them continued. The courts did everything in their power to curb unions and prohibit strikes. *Temperton v. Russell* (1893) ruled against boycotts; *Trollope v. London Building Trades Federation* (1895) declared union officers who published blacklists of nonunion firms and free laborers to be guilty of conspiracy; *Lyons v. Wilkins* (1899) outlawed "picketing to persuade"; the Taff Vale decision of 1901 held unions liable for damages incurred by individual members during a strike; the Osborne judgment of 1909 declared that unions could not levy dues for political purposes (Meacham 1972: 1352–53).

Many European countries supplemented their basic restrictions on unions and strikes with additional regulations that severely curtailed workers' freedoms. Strikes were legalized in England in 1834, but Master and Servant Acts remained in use by judges to threaten striking workers with jail. Peaceful picketing was not clearly recognized as legal in the United Kingdom until 1906 (Goldstein 1983: 60–61). Unions and strikes were technically legalized in Hungary in 1872 and 1884, but until 1904, provisions of the Hungarian penal code outlawed "gatherings for the purpose of extracting wages" and "violent arguments for the furtherance of wage claims" (Goldstein 1983: 59). Even after labor unions were legalized in France in 1884, police and troops were routinely dispatched to major and some minor strikes, and clashes with workers were frequent (Goldstein 1983: 68). Vaguely worded legislation in Sweden, Germany, and Belgium was used to harass labor officials and jail workers who engaged in picketing or wage disputes.

[17] The Great Depression and the agrarian distress of 1873–86 was the impetus for the raising of tariff walls throughout Europe. France developed a comprehensive system of agricultural protection in the 1880s (Meredith 1904: chaps. 4 and 5). Bismarck popularized all-around protectionism in 1879. By the end of the Depression, Germany had surrounded itself with protective tariffs, established a general cartel organization, set up an all-around social

The state, in Polanyi's view, was acting in the interests of society as a whole because, embodying the contradictory impulses of nineteenth-century development, it passed protectionist legislation as well as "pro-market" laws.[18] But nineteenth-century European states were not class-neutral. Before the world wars these states were aligned with the dominant landed and industrial class in Europe. In Britain, France, Germany, Sweden, Russia, and elsewhere in Europe this alignment was encouraged by the social integration of top state personnel with the upper classes, especially the landed upper class.[19]

From about the 1870s onward liberals such as Vilfredo Pareto, Herbert Spencer, and Max Weber wrote with dismay about the "persistence" of traditional landed, bureaucratic, and military elites.[20] The British state, as Max Weber pointed out, remained an "administration of notables" throughout the nineteenth century (Weber 1978: 974). Until 1905, every British cabinet, whether Conservative or Liberal, was dominated by the traditional landed elite.[21] The French bureaucracy fell completely into the hands of the traditional notability during the Second Empire (1852–70). In 1871, over two-thirds of the deputies elected to the Chamber of Deputies were local notables from old aristocratic families. At the beginning of the Fourth Republic in 1945, the state bureaucracy still recruited from the privileged social strata (Badie and Birnbaum 1982: 113–14; Cole and Campbell 1989: 48–49). The German bureaucracy also remained under the control of the aristocracy throughout the nineteenth century. In 1910, nobles occupied nine out of eleven cabinet positions, all of the upper legislative house, 25 percent of lower legislative seats, 55 percent of all army ranks of colonel and above, 80 percent of ambassadorships, 11 out of 12 administrative headships, 23 out of 27 regional administrative headships, and 60 percent of all prefectures (Goldstein 1983: 252). Sweden's "highly status-conscious nobility" still dominated the

insurance system, and was practicing high-pressure colonial policies (Polanyi 1944: 216). Austria also turned to protectionism in the 1870s, as did Italy in the 1880s, and Britain after World War I. It was in the crisis of 1873 and during the subsequent depression years that the foundation of the modern cartel movement was laid (Rosenberg 1934) and that a second great wave of European imperialism was launched that, increasingly, focused European imperialist ambitions on Europe itself.

[18] Polanyi's argument that workers were afforded protection, too, recalls G. E. M. de Ste. Croix's description of the Roman Empire: "The rulers of the empire rarely if ever had any real concern for the poor and unprivileged as such; but they sometimes realised the necessity to give some of them some protection . . . either to prevent them from being utterly ruined and thus become useless as taxpayers, or to preserve them as potential recruits for the army" (1981: 502).

[19] Craig 1956; Dangerfield 1961; Shapiro 1962; Thompson 1963; Clark 1966: 206–74; Rosenberg 1966; Gillis 1968; Kitchen 1968; Guttsman 1969; Ridley and Blondel 1969; Cecil 1970; Struve 1973; Peiter 1976; Röhl 1976; Sheehan 1976; Weber 1976; Spring 1977; Zeldin 1979; Weiner 1981; Checkland 1985: 163–258; Greenleaf 1985.

[20] See, Weber 1978: 974; and, e.g., Spencer 1898: chaps. 22, 23, 24; 1902: 122–41; 1981 [1884]; Mosca 1939 [1896]; Michels 1949; Pareto 1968.

[21] Thomas 1939: 4. Brief exceptions are the Liberal ministries of 1892–95.

upper ranks of the bureaucracy in the mid-1920s (Rueschemeyer et al. 1992: 92; Samuelsson 1968: 214). Right up to the eve of the Revolution of 1917, the Russian governmental apparatus was dominated exclusively by the nobility (Beetham 1974: 199).

If the nineteenth-century European state was not class-neutral, neither were its policies. State policies were generally consistent with the immediate interests of the landowners. As a result, landowners did not experience significant political setbacks with respect to tariffs, labor legislation, land reform, state allocations, tax policy, or internal terms of trade until after World War II.[22]

Though tariff policy varied throughout Europe and fluctuated throughout the nineteenth century, at no time anywhere was agriculture left without substantial protection. Landowners were also able to block efforts at agrarian reform, to maintain the social and political isolation of agrarian labor, and to secure favorable state tax and pricing policies.[23] Moreover, by ensuring the survival of various forms of corporatism and creating new ones, states provided landowners and wealthy industrialists with privileged access to the state and to all the resources at its command. At the same time, state policies ensured the exclusion of workers from political life and from opportunities for economic advancement by maintaining a vast restrictive system of legal, social, and land institutions. States brutally repressed labor organization and ensured that the mass of the population would be barred from any possibility of gaining significant institutionalized economic, social, or political power.

The interventionist policies of states redounded principally to the benefit of dominant classes. State policies maintained a vast restrictive system of legal, social, and land institutions that effectively excluded workers from political life and from opportunities for economic advancement (on suffrage and other restrictions, see Chapter 3). Most important of all, states supported an expansion of production based on imperialist exploitation of other states and territories, both within and outside Europe. By limiting the geographic and sectoral spread of industrial capitalism, this process of expansion enabled elites to increase production and profits while retaining their monopoly of land and capital. As a result, industrial expansion in Europe was essentially dualistic: repression and restriction at home and imperialist expansion abroad. It was this "double movement," rather than the Polanyian one of protection and expansion, that characterized Europe's nineteenth-century industrial capitalism.

---

[22] It is often assumed that the repeal of the Corn Laws marked the end of the power of the landlords in Britain. But it did not. More on this below in the chapter.

[23] When states found it necessary to introduce price control on grain and other food staples and in order to reduce the "wage bill" for industrialists, they took measures to prevent prices from dropping too low and cutting into the profits of large landowners. Price controls, as well as taxes on agricultural exports, were also offset by low agricultural land taxes.

The "Double Movement" of Industrial Capitalist Development

For Polanyi, nineteenth-century protectionism in Europe was a movement neither of states nor particular groups within states but of society as a whole. For him, the protectionist countermovement was primarily a social and cultural phenomenon. It represented the reassertion of the dominance of society over markets. In his view, land, labor, and money are social substances, rather than bases of class formation and class interests. Thus, different sectors differ only in the type of "social substance" that they seek to protect. Since land, labor, and money are "social substances," protection of them is a general, social interest. The working class was effective in gaining passage of various sorts of social legislation, he contends (and he vastly overstates the extent to which they succeeded in this), because when it sought protection it represented the general needs of society against the market. A "too narrow conception of interests," Polanyi maintains, leads "to a warped vision of social and political history" (154–55).

Thus, Polanyi describes a "spontaneous social protective reaction against the perils inherent in a self-regulating market system" (1944: 76) that came from all sectors of society.[24] Though it was groups, sections, and classes that acted, their interests cannot be understood apart from "the situation of society as a whole"; for the "challenge" was to society as a whole (1944: 152). All groups, sectors, and classes sought to gain protection, and all succeeded; and they did so because it was in the interest of society as a whole.[25]

This conception is the basis of the "double movement" of expansion and protectionism that, for Polanyi, explains the demise of Europe's nineteenth-century market economy. Because Polanyi fails to recognize the existence of exploiters and producers and their differential capacities, limitations, and potentialities, it is conceived and elaborated largely without reference to specific social relations or interests. The self-regulating market threatened society as a whole; it met with resistance from society as a whole; and when different classes within society endeavored to secure protection for themselves (the "protectionist countermove"), their efforts redounded to the benefit of society as a whole. The most important way in which groups, sectors, and classes

---

[24] Agrarians, manufacturers, and trade unionists all "wished to increase their incomes through protectionist action" (1944: 153). However, Polanyi characterizes the search for protection as primarily noneconomic. For "even where monetary values were involved," he asserts, they were secondary to other interests: "almost invariably professional status, safety and security, the form of a man's life, the breadth of his existence, the stability of his environment were in question" (1944: 154).

[25] Nations and peoples shielded themselves "from unemployment and instability with the help of central banks and customs tariffs, supplemented by migration laws.... Although each single restriction had its beneficiaries whose super-profits or -wages were a tax on all other citizens, it was often only the *amount* of the tax that was unjustified, not also protection itself. In the long run there was an all-round drop in prices which benefited all" (1944: 217).

act and are acted on and, in particular, the way in which they interrelate with state and global structures, is as an organic whole.

It is probably true that all groups within all societies act always to protect themselves. However, not everyone is equally victimized or disadvantaged by any particular process of change or by the expansion of markets. Some gained or had sufficient power to secure protection from or receive compensation for losses, or sufficient mobility to reposition themselves; others lost and lacked sufficient power or mobility to gain protection. In fact, as previously discussed, the type and extent of protection gained by different classes differed significantly, and it did so because throughout the nineteenth and early twentieth centuries, state legislation worked to protect the interests of dominant classes. Polanyi took no account of this, or of the class-specific interests that shaped the central institutions of Europe's market economy.[26] Classes are endowed with different power resources, and this influences the way social institutions develop, operate, and are transformed.

By ignoring the class structure that was emerging from the introduction of capitalist forms of ownership and production, and the class-specific nature of protectionism, Polanyi also failed to grasp the essential dualism that characterized Europe's industrial capitalist development.

The institutional complex underpinning Europe's nineteenth-century market economy set in motion and maintained a process of economic growth that was based on external expansion rather than on the development of domestic markets. This externally oriented expansion had the effect of limiting the geographic and sectoral spread of industrialization and the growth of organized labor. As a result, industrial expansion in Europe was characterized by dualism and monopoly, a lack of internal structural integration, and dependency on outside capital, labor, and markets. It was shaped not by a liberal, competitive ethos but by monopoly and by rural, pre-industrial, feudal, and autocratic structures of power and authority. These structures enabled dominant classes to preserve the traditional bases of their political and economic power, monopolize gains from industrial expansion, and exclude other classes and groups from political and economic life.

---

[26] His discussion of the Speenhamland Act of 1795 and the anti-Combination Laws of 1799 and 1801 illustrates the analytical position. Polanyi sees these measures as part of a spontaneous countermovement from all sectors of society set in motion by the commodification of labor. Their aim, he argues, was to protect workers from the market by providing them with the means to live outside the wage system and thus preventing them from gaining their status as workers within the market system (see Polanyi 1944: chap. 7). But these measures were not designed to protect workers. They drove wages down below subsistence and barred workers from seeking redress through collective resistance and bargaining. Landowners objected to Speenhamland because it set an external standard for subsistence income; thus, in 1834, the Poor Law Amendment Act swept away entirely the eighteenth-century social security system, and placed the administration of "relief" almost entirely in the hands of aristocratic Justices of the Peace (Ashford 1992: 154–55).

CONFLICT AND CHANGE: A CLASS APPROACH

The basic antagonism generated by industrial capitalist development, according to Polanyi, was that which developed between whole societies, on the one hand, and the institutions of the self-regulating market system, on the other. European societies in the nineteenth century were, in fact, being destroyed, Polanyi wrote, by "the blind action of soulless institutions the only purpose of which was the automatic increase of material welfare" (1944: 219). But this increase of material wealth was not automatic or class-neutral, and the actions of the institutions created to produce it were not "blind" but designed specifically for the purpose.

Because Polanyi ignores the industrial and political class struggles that characterized nineteenth- and early twentieth-century Europe, he assigns them no role in shaping the development and operation of the market system and its central institutions. Even after acknowledging the European class conflicts of the interwar years, he treats them as a symptom only, rather than a cause of the dissolution of the free market system, and declines to consider whether and in what ways classes or class conflict shaped the way in which nineteenth-century European institutions were transformed in the course of the world wars. His analysis, throughout, eschews the language of class that emerged to express and shape the struggles of Europe's industrial development and that provided the principal categories of social analysis employed by Europeans themselves to describe their own society during the nineteenth century.[27] As G. E. M. de Ste. Croix argues, "it is a healthy instinct on the part of historians in the empirical tradition to feel the need at least to *begin from* the categories and the terminology in use within the society they are studying – provided, of course, they do not remain imprisoned, therein" (1981: 35).

Before considering the utility of specific class categories for understanding the two transformations with which Polanyi was concerned, we first consider the utility of class more generally for the analysis of change. To

---

[27] "The idea of class," as William Reddy points out, "has been a central one in European politics ever since Sieyès wrote his pamphlet 'What Is the Third Estate?'" (1987: 22). It was recognized not just by revolutionaries but by Popes, as well. Pope Pius XI's 1931 encyclical, *Quadragesimo anno*, speaks of the serious threat that class struggle had posed at the end of the nineteenth century and asserts that it had been dispelled by Leo XIII's *Rerum novarum*. With the onset of the Industrial Revolution, the language of class supplanted the language of "ranks," "orders," "estates" (Morris 1979: 9; see also 18–20 for a comparison of the eighteenth-century language of status groups and the nineteenth-century discussion of conflict groups or classes), and the language of trade. "Working people, for the first time, altered their vocabularies and world views to speak and think of themselves as workers, rather than just as members of this or that trade. They generalized the sense of solidarity of trade beyond specific and segmented crafts" (Katznelson 1986: 23). The language of class reflected the changing nature and intensity of inequality and exploitation. It conveyed "what Europeans perceived as the fundamental social antagonisms arising from the unequal distribution of power and authority" (Dahrendorf 1959: 201–5).

enable us to do this, we turn to a consideration of two influential studies that endeavor to explain change: Theda Skocpol's *States and Social Revolutions* (1979) and Robert Gilpin's *War and Change in World Politics* (1981). Like Polanyi's study, both of these attempt to understand change in terms of the interrelationship of global structures, states, and social forces; both are top-down analyses; and in both, the failure to take into account social interests and purposes leads to empirical and theoretical weaknesses that undermine their conclusions.

The Transformation of International Systems, States, and Societies: Two Perspectives

Theda Skocpol's **States and Social Revolutions.** In her influential study, *States and Social Revolutions*, Theda Skocpol endeavors to explain how the inter-action of social forces, states, and the international system work to produce the conditions for social revolution. At the center of Skocpol's analysis are autonomous states operating in an anarchical international environment. Skocpol argues that the state can be seen as autonomous because it tends to give priority to securing national defense over the protection of any partic-ular interests of the ruling class or section thereof.

According to Skocpol, the absolutist state, especially as it developed in France, was a quasibureaucratic apparatus that opposed the dominant feu-dal class and realized goals fundamentally opposed to the interests of the feudal class by directly attacking its material base. Yet her *own* analysis sug-gests that state institutions played a clearly partisan role in the class struggles that triggered social revolutions. She argues that absolutist states were con-strained by "agrarian class structures and political institutions"; that, in fact, as a result of these constraints, anciens regimes were unable to respond to external military threats, and as a consequence broke down (1979: 85). She states that "the property and privileges of dominant classes" became vulner-able to attack when this occurred. Thus, according to her own analysis, it would appear that regimes, prior to their breakdown, protected the property and privileges of dominant classes, and that it was only the regimes' protec-tion that prevented "revolts from below" from threatening the property and privileges of the dominant class (1979: 285).

Skocpol argues that social revolution is brought about by external factors (usually military defeat) that change the relationship of state organizations to domestic political and social groups. Anciens regimes cannot respond to external events ("international military threats arising in the modern era"), and as a result states experience "revolutionary crises." When this occurs, "revolts from below" accomplish "changes in class relations that otherwise would not have occurred" (Skocpol 1979: 285).

However, it seems reasonable to assume that the breakdown of a regime will bring about system change only if internal groups come to power having interests fundamentally different from the interests of those previously in power. While external forces have the potential to change the balance of power among contending classes within the state, we would need to know the class interests of such forces to determine whether or not they would wish to do so. Usually, outside powers act to militarily strengthen anciens regimes; often, they act competitively to strengthen both sides. Or they may seek only to change the balance of power among the contending elites within a state. Thus, whether or not the breakdown of an ancien regime allows new classes to rise to power would depend not only on the relative strength of these new classes but also on the class interests of the intervening powers.

Skocpol's account of the French Revolution ends with the breakdown of state institutions and the flight of the scions of the ancien regime. But this leaves a crucial part of the story untold: the successful international effort to *restore* the ancien regime to power in France following the Revolution. Because she assumes that states exist within an international anarchy, she fails to consider when and why external forces have an interest in changing the balance of power among contending elites within the state and allowing new classes to rise to power. Since there is no relationship between the external and the internal challenge, the external challenge that brings about "a change in class relations" is a purely conjunctural element: it results from the purely coincidental confluence of external and internal challenges. In contrast, defining the class nature of the interests represented and served by a linkage between external and internal forces can tell us when or whether domestic forces in conjunction with external forces will bring about a fundamental change in the system.

Robert Gilpin's **War and Change in World Politics.** In *War and Change in World Politics* (1981), Robert Gilpin begins by stressing the need to take social interests and purposes into account in analyzing international systems change. He argues that any social or political system is created to advance a particular set of political, economic, or other types of interests, and that the interests most favored will reflect the relative power of the actors involved, that is, those of the most powerful members of the social system. But after emphasizing this central premise of sociological investigation, Gilpin then goes on to develop an analysis that, like Skocpol's, takes no account of social interests or purposes at the international level.

Gilpin advances a theory of international systems change that focuses on the rise and demise of successive hegemonic states. The mechanism of change in Gilpin's argument is "uneven development." When rival powers grow faster than the existing hegemon, the underlying distribution of power shifts, and a new hegemon rises to power. Wars occur during the transitional periods when one hegemon declines and a new one rises.

To return to Gilpin's initial assumption, an explanation of system change requires an explanation of how groups with fundamentally different interests come to power. But his explanation of how and why one hegemon is replaced by another tells us nothing about the interests of the two hegemons. Thus, it does not provide an explanation for system change.

If a social system reflects the interests of its dominant groups, then the system changes only when the interests of the dominant group change. The replacement of one dominant group with another brings about system change only if it has fundamentally different interests. Therefore, to explain system change it is not enough to know how or why the United States replaced Great Britain as the hegemonic power in the international system. To determine whether or not the system has changed, we need to know, as well, the interests of both powers. If the United States and Great Britain share a common interest in the same kind of system, then U.S. hegemony is not likely to change the system that existed under British hegemony; leadership changes, but the system will probably remain the same because the interests of the dominant groups are the same.

As noted, a basic assumption of sociological theory is that a social system is created to advance the interests of its dominant group. The system changes when the dominant class is replaced by a class having fundamentally different interests.[28] Change occurs when there is a change in the relationship of class forces. Thus, class analysis is essential to an understanding of social change. It allows us to distinguish fundamental, "organic" changes in social structure from relatively short-term, "conjunctural" changes or alterations, and to define their character and scope. It focuses attention on the way class structures determine the course of development and, consequently, how economic and social change differentially impacts various groups in society. In focusing on how society as a whole experienced the rise of the self-regulating market and the commodification of land, labor, and capital, Polanyi ignored the fact that, while we have abundant evidence of lower class misery, we have little evidence that the privileged classes suffered. Instead, he treated these political changes as if their impact was like that of a plague, visited on rich and poor alike and in equal measure. The story of the rise and expansion of industrial capitalism can be truly told only through an account of the experiences of classes, not of nations or whole societies.[29]

---

[28] The classical elite theorists Gaetano Mosca and Robert Michels do not seem to allow for a change in the fundamental character of the elite (see Mosca 1939: 404–9, 425, and 427; and Michels 1949: 74–77, 164–84, 377–92); Vilfredo Pareto does allow for it (see Pareto 1935: paras. 2057–59, 2178, 2183, 2187–93, 2202, 2252).

In most so-called revolutions, nothing like the complete breakdown of the old elite and its replacement by a new one happens. The phenomenon I am describing here – the replacement of a dominant elite by another with fundamentally different beliefs – would seem, at least from the evidence of the period I will be considering in this study, to be either an extreme abnormality or one that occurs only every century or so.

[29] As numerous writers have pointed out, elites in the third world enjoy the same level of income and standard of living as elites in the developed countries. The distortions that characterize

Classes and Class Conflict in Social Change

The absence of class as an analytic category in much of post–World War II theorizing about social change is often attributed to problems of conceptualization, as well as to difficulties in defining the class structure of capitalist society. Classes may be defined in a diversity of ways: in terms of property, factors of production, relations of authority, or professional and marketplace advantages. A class analysis can employ any one of these. But regardless of the definition chosen, an analyst must show that the basic distinction and relationship defined is one that is significant in explaining political forms and conflicts and can be expressed in general theoretical terms and examined in a specific historical context. G. E. M. de Ste. Croix, whose class analysis of ancient Greece and Rome (1981) illuminates neglected aspects of that well-trodden terrain, advises that the definition of class we adopt should be clear and consistent and correspond to historical realities and to the best sociological thought of the time and place to which it is to be applied.

With these criteria in mind, "class," for purposes of this study, is defined as "a group of persons in a community identified by their position in the whole system of social production, defined above all according to their relationship ... to the conditions of production and to other classes."[30] Class conflict becomes intrinsic to this definition when it is applied to the conditions of production that characterized the capitalist society of nineteenth-century Europe. While in all civilized societies the producers of necessities produce a surplus beyond what they actually consume themselves, in capitalist society, the fruits of that "surplus labor" are appropriated by a small minority who, by virtue of property rights, control the process of production. Class "is the collective social expression of the fact of [this] exploitation," of the appropriation of part of the product of the labor of others, "and of the way in which exploitation is embodied in a social structure" (Ste. Croix 1981: 43). It is a relationship of inequality and exploitation that gives rise to conflicts over the distribution of wealth, income, and power.

Many difficulties with class analysis stem from a tendency to conflate different dimensions of class.[31] In particular, class tends to be conflated with class consciousness and action, thus making the existence of the former dependent on the latter. But a class may exist irrespective of whether all its

---

"dependent development" are an effect of class structures and state policies that act to privilege and disadvantage different sectors within third world societies. Dependency is class dependency, not state dependency; it is a dependency internal to states, not between states. See Halperin 1997a for a review of the relevant arguments and evidence.

[30] Ste. Croix 1981: 43. Legal or constitutional privileges can enter into the determination of class because they affect the kind and scale of exploitation employed and suffered.

[31] For a discussion of the difficulties that arise from the tendency to conflate or confuse different analytic dimensions of class, see Katznelson 1986.

members are conscious of themselves as members of a class or choose to (or have the capacity to) engage in class-based movements and activities.[32]

In this, it is instructive to compare how we treat "nations" and questions of national consciousness and collective action with how we treat class and class consciousness and action. We accept that a nation may exist irrespective of whether all its members are conscious of themselves as belonging to that nation or actively participate in its national movement.[33] We recognize that nations are internally divided by a whole set of differences, and into a small active group of leaders and a mass of followers. Thus, even when we include national consciousness and collective action in definitions of "nation," we don't require that these be universal or continuous for a nation to exist. We accept formal, legal definitions of nations, and because we do, we also accept that nations are "real" and a relevant unit of analysis in social life. "Class" is not defined legally today (though it was in the past), and attempts to apply formal definitions are rejected as deterministic. In consequence, class is considered by many to be an ideological construct and, therefore, irrelevant to the aims of social scientific inquiry. As a result, our master narratives of social development and change are stories about the rise and exploits of nations, rather than of classes.

The intention here is *not* to deny that individuals are conscious of themselves as members of a nation, but rather to point out that we give far greater latitude to the analysis of nationalism than we do to that of class with respect to the question of consciousness. Analysts are generally able to refer to a group as a nation without being required to prove that all members of that group are actually conscious of themselves as being part of the nation in question. However, it is often argued that "working class" is not a relevant or useful social category unless we can show that all workers see themselves as belonging to it. While it is not necessary to demonstrate consciousness in order to treat collectivities as nations, it *is* deemed necessary for the analysis of classes. It is not the use of class in social analysis but its rejection that is ideological.

The question of consciousness should be treated as no more problematic in the analysis of class than it is in the analysis of nation. Not all members of a nation or of a class are conscious of themselves as bound to other members by a common identity and a common set of interests, understandings, and values. All nations and classes have a small core of leaders, thinkers, visionaries, and political activists who define, for the whole nation or class, the advantages and disadvantages of their circumstances within the wider social environment. We should not on this basis reject class analysis. Nor, on this basis, should we reject E. P. Thompson's conclusion that "when every caution

---

[32] For an excellent elaboration of this, see the discussion in Wood 1998b: chaps. 5 and 6.

[33] Here it is useful, though perhaps not necessary, to distinguish between a "nation-state" and a "nation" that is stateless and that constitutes a national minority within a state.

has been made, the outstanding fact of the period between 1790 and 1830" in Britain "is the formation of 'the working class,'" and that by 1832 "there were strongly based and self-conscious working-class institutions – trade unions, friendly societies, educational and religious movements, political organizations, periodicals – working-class intellectual traditions, working-class community-patterns, and a working class structure of feeling" (Thompson 1965: 129–30).

The relation of classes to their political agencies should be treated as no more problematic than that of a national group to its political agencies. Not all members of a nation or of a class share a disposition to behave in certain ways. This occurs, if at all, only when special circumstances, usually conflict and threats to core interests, create unity and cooperation among the different elements of a nation or of a class. Consider the similarities that suggest themselves in this description of class:

Class is a summary of countless day-to-day experiences, not all of which involve the expression of aggressive sentiments of identity and conflict. The people of Nottinghamshire did not all go around smashing machines, but they saw to it that the boys who did were not caught. Trades-union leaders were not averse to joining in a petition with the small manufacturer or sitting on a platform with a helpful Anglican parson, but this did not necessarily stop them from stoning blacklegs in a strike or sharpening pikes when all else failed. (Morris 1979: 45–46)

Class-based action can be defined as "organized antagonism with a nation-wide appeal to all members of a broad social level," as was evident, for instance, in Britain in the Parliamentary Reform Movement of 1816–19 (Perkin 1969: 209) and in the interconnected industrial conflicts of the 1820s and early 1830s (Randall and Charlesworth 1996: 5). With these elements of a general definition of class, and issues of class consciousness and agency identified and provisionally clarified (more on this below), it is possible to define the specific class structure that characterized the time and place with which this study is concerned.

Class Structure

"Class" can be analyzed by means of a highly differentiated class concept or a more simplified and abstract one. As Eric Wright points out, it depends on the context. Distinctions within classes on the basis of sector, status, gender, and race are important for exploring some kinds of problems (Wright's own work on the middle class is an example), but for others "it is appropriate to use a much more abstract, simplified class concept, revolving around the central polarized class relation of capitalism: capitalists and workers" (Wright 1999: 2). While the capitalist class or bourgeoisie is a heterogeneous class, with many different elements or "fractions," the circumstances of nineteenth-century Europe and, specifically, the revolutionary currents unleashed first by the French Revolution and the Napoleonic Wars and later by the revolutions of 1848, increasingly polarized European society along class lines and thus brought about the fusion and unity of various fractions of the capitalist class. As a result, the economic divisions of the class and other divisions of various kinds that might have given rise to intraclass conflict were of far less importance than the issues over which that class as a whole was more or less united. For example, while landed and industrial capital in Britain clashed over the Corn Laws, they were united in a struggle to prevent labor from achieving any significant political and economic power, and it was this struggle that dominated the nineteenth and early twentieth centuries in Europe. In times of acute class conflict, society becomes polarized, as did European society in the nineteenth and early twentieth centuries. Landowners, industrialists, and bankers, which, in other circumstances, analysts might treat as separate classes, united, and their unity assumed a definite political expression. Similarly, conflicts between large and small landowners, between monopolistic and competitive business, between liberal bourgeois and reactionary feudal overlords, and between domestic and foreign interests, became subsumed within the larger conflict situation.[34]

Landlords and industrial capitalists became fractions of a single class as a result of the revolutions that swept through Europe in 1848. During the revolutions, the willingness of the industrial bourgeoisie to press their demands through mobilizing the masses and the emergence of socialism as a mass movement brought about the unity and fusion of landed and industrial elites through class compromise. As a result of the compromise, between 1850 and 1870, the upper middle class was accepted into ruling coalitions and, in exchange, supported a system of imperialist expansion and restricted domestic development that preserved the basic contours of the traditional order.

As subsequent chapters show, after 1850, the social conflicts endemic throughout Europe during the nineteenth century increasingly worked to polarize European society until it effectively produced a two-class structure: an aggregate of people who produced surplus value from a subordinate position in terms of production functions, income, and status, and an aggregate of those who occupied the upper rungs of the economic ladder. Irrespective of whether they are "owning" classes or not, this latter class controlled the

---

[34] In Britain, as elsewhere, the dominant class consisted of a landowning aristocracy; the large manufacturing, financial, and commercial interests of capitalist enterprise; and those who fulfilled specific professional and other functions on behalf of them or who, by virtue of income, status, occupation, or kinship, were associated with them. Thus, those elements performing the functions of a middle class in the professions were also linked to the dominant class. As R. J. Morris rightly observes, "the bulk of the professions were a specialized sector of the ruling class which dealt with key aspects of economic and political domination: the lawyers with property, the church with ideology, the military officers with main force, and the medical men with the health of the producers of wealth as well as the health of the dominant class" (1979: 23).

operations of capitalist enterprise (as well as some of those whose status and position in society was directly dependent on them, e.g., household servants).

Working class formation and politics, when examined on a country-to-country basis, appear to have varied considerably in nineteenth-century Europe. The differences most frequently cited concern the degree of working-class integration into society, patterns of collective action, the relationship between economic and political demands, organizational capacities and strategies of unions and political parties, and the degree of militancy and commitment to a doctrine of class struggle or to revolution.[35] However, much of the discussion about these variations in working-class formation and politics exaggerates the range and importance of it. The effects of the institutions of capitalist forms of ownership, the situation of proletarianization, processes whereby labor is recruited, and the economic, social, and psychological effects of the conversion of peasants and artisans into workers were more or less the same everywhere,[36] and everywhere they provoked a more or less similar set of responses.[37] The individual worker, as Marx notes, "has no economic resources on which he can fall back"; he therefore "cannot 'wait' till his market price (the offered wage) goes up before selling his labour power." This situation "makes collective organisation of such sales by workers – i.e. unionisation and collective bargaining – a powerful inbuilt tendency under capitalism, reproducing itself universally wherever wage-labour appears" (Marx 1991: 73). Thus, despite the variations that existed in Europe during the nineteenth century, by the turn of the twentieth century, there was a convergence of outlook among workers;[38] as a result, the struggle between labor and capital, while carried on in different societies and in different ways, brought into being trade unions everywhere.

Whatever variations existed with respect to working-class activism, there was far less variation in the response that it evoked from the ruling class,

[35] Thus, in France, working-class formation was shaped by artisan traditions, a low degree of organizational mobilization, and a high degree of militancy; while in Germany, the working class had considerable organizational strength and a high degree of mobilization (see, e.g., Zolberg 1986).

[36] And this was regardless of whether industrialization came from within or from without. See, e.g., Hodgkin 1956: 63–83, which compares the motives and effects of rural migration to the new towns of Africa with that of rural migration to the new towns of early nineteenth-century England.

[37] "The forms of collective action industrial workers engaged in to improve their position in the labor market bore a strong family resemblance to one another across national boundaries." Unions and strikes became "common features of all industrial and industrializing societies," though there was variation in the frequency and character of strikes and in the outlook of unions (Zolberg 1986: 398).

[38] "The activities of the Second International provide some support for the proposition that at the turn of the twentieth century workers of the capitalist world came closer than ever before or since to sharing a common political doctrine, social democracy, and to collaborating in a common cause" (Zolberg 1986: 398–99).

and it was that response that was most determinative of important political outcomes. Whether the demand was for an eight-hour day, a living wage, universal and equal suffrage, or the overthrow of capitalist property relations, the response was swift, absolute, uncompromising, and supported by the state. Anything that challenged the ability of elites to hold on to their wealth filled them with dread in the same way that peasant uprisings had in the past. As is shown throughout this study, political and industrial demands for redistribution of power and wealth were opposed as ferociously as those calling for revolution. For, however it is defined, and however varied the circumstances of its formation and the characteristics of its organization, the working class constituted the only significant challenge to the power of capital. Defining distinct boundaries between classes during the nineteenth century is consequently not as difficult as it is in, say, post–World War II advanced industrial countries; for while conflict between labor and capital was not the only conflict within nineteenth-century European society, it was the most far-reaching and important.

The capitalist class in Europe was formed from a fusion of Europe's industrial and landowning classes. This class, overall, was dominated not by a new industrial capitalist bourgeoisie, but by Europe's traditional landowning and aristocratic elite. Almost all research and writing on European industrial capitalist development is conscious of the fact that European society was not revolutionized wholly and all at once by capital.[39] "Classes bear the mark of previous centuries," as Marx noted. As van der Pijl argues, "all class formation and social differentiation in general is premised on prior patterns of structuration" (1998: 32). But, in fact, most analyses do not take seriously the persistence and determinative impact of prior structures in class formation and political outcomes. Most tend to treat "old" structures as "residues" rather than as determinative of socioeconomic and political outcomes.

In Britain (as elsewhere in Europe), the Industrial Revolution advantaged the older and more conservative sectors of the British wealth structure (the great landowners and the bankers and merchants of the City of London) rather than the manufacturers and industrialists (Rubinstein 1983: 17; in Cain and Hopkins 1993: 37). This had a profound effect on the nature of Europe's industrial capitalist development. Throughout the nineteenth century, Europe's most effective elites were traditional and aristocratic, landowning and rent receiving, and oligarchic.

According to both liberal and Marxist theory, a new capitalist class emerged together with the new capitalist mode of production. This class is supposed to have played a highly revolutionary part in social and economic development by demolishing outworn institutions so as to replace them by a new system of production and new institutions to meet the needs

---

[39] Marx seems to recognize this in his *Grundrisse*; Lenin is preoccupied with the issue in his study of capitalism in Russia.

of capital. The nation-state arose as the political form of this new class. It came to power through nationalist revolutions and consolidated its power by means of the institutions of the nation-state. But the Industrial Revolution and the regime changes following it did not displace one ruling class by another. Instead, they were the means by which a ruling class successfully adapted to changing circumstances and gradually co-opted a new stratum. While in most European countries an industrial bourgeoisie emerged that demanded a bigger share of power, they did not, nor did they want to, overthrow and replace the old ruling class. Thus, the landowning class was the dominant element in this fusion.[40]

During the interwar period, the class compromise of 1848 began to unravel and intraclass conflicts began to emerge. This began a growing commitment by part of the European bourgeoisie to the "American Model" and, specifically, to methods of relative, as opposed to absolute, surplus value production. The dual economies that characterized Europe's economic expansion (elaborated in Chapter 3) eventually led to rivalry and conflict among European ruling groups and in 1914 to a major multilateral interstate war. Confronted with more powerful and militant working classes as a result of the war, industrial capitalist interests began to recognize the limits of the system, and an intraclass division opened up.

In Britain, these conflicts were associated with the reinstatement of the Gold Standard and the tensions that surrounded British commitments to it after World War I, as well as the growing competitive threat from Germany and America. A sharp division began to open up between the City of London and its interest in a worldwide system of freely moving goods and capital, and British heavy industry, represented by Chamberlain and a vision of imperial preferences and federation to compete with America and Germany. Business rivalries within the capitalist class contributed to the basic pressures of interclass rivalries in generating appeasement (Kurth 1979).

Though intraclass conflicts become more articulated during the interwar period, the polarization of classes during that time worked to allay them. Though things began to change as a result of World War I (see Chapter 5) and differences were most likely increasing, the revolutionary ferment of the interwar period and the polarization of classes that it produced worked effectively to keep the capitalist class unified. Thus, while some scholars have argued that intraclass struggles over different methods of production were determinative of the transformation that took place in the course of the wars (e.g., Sohn-Rethel, van der Pijl), Chapter 8 argues against this view. The contradictions of absolute surplus value production and imperialism that had led to World War I continued to dominate during the interwar period and produced fascism, imperialism in Europe, and the Second World War.

[40] See, e.g., Veblen 1915; Guttsman 1954: 22; Rosenberg 1966: 44; Dahrendorf 1967; Stern 1977; Thompson, 1977: 37; Mayer 1981: 123; Halperin 1997a: chap. 4.

Distinctions are conventionally drawn between class structures in different European societies and, particularly, between those in Western Europe that supposedly were dominated by an indigenous, independent capitalist bourgeoisie, and those European and non-European societies that were not. Often scholars will endeavor to capture these distinctions by defining two roads of industrial capitalist development. Broadly, these can be described as follows. The first road is characterized by a relatively open political space that developed, as supposedly it did in Britain, because a bourgeois revolution displaced the old landed aristocracy and the absolutist state (allied with one another, it is assumed). As a result, the aristocracy subsequently became "bourgeoisified" and offered no resistance to industrialization. The second road is characterized by a relatively closed political space maintained by well-entrenched agrarian elites. Here the aristocracy and the industrial bourgeoisie remained separate, with the aristocracy able to resist and block industrialization.

A recent example of the two-road schema is the distinction between "first wave" and "second wave" capitalisms and patterns of capitalist development that David Coates defines in his excellent examination of models of capitalism (2000). In first-wave capitalisms, the move from feudalism to capitalism and from agriculture to industry was historically distinct (or in the U.S. case with feudalism, nonexistent). As a result,

indigenous middle classes set the pace of economic change, presiding over an industrialization process . . . whose reach and penetration into the economy as a whole was relatively thorough and dense from very early on. . . . (227)

In second-wave capitalisms, the move from feudalism to capitalism was fused, and as a result, industrial bourgeoisies were weaker and modernizing aristocracies were stronger (Coates 2000: 227).

The two-road schema developed by Kees van der Pijl is based on a similar set of distinctions. Thus, in his "Lockean" states, represented in Europe by Britain, "the bourgeoisie came on the heels of its vanguard, ready to take its place"; while in "Hobbesian" states, "the vanguard is not likely dislodged as soon as the ascendant class is 'in place' socially" (1998: 78–79).

Lenin used the same set of characteristics on which these schemas are based to define the "American" and "Prussian" roads that he contrasted as historical alternatives. In Lenin's Prussian road, the continuing dominance of an agrarian class poses a major obstacle to capitalist development. Thus, in this road, while capitalist penetration undermines the old labor repressive system of agricultural production, it does not succeed in completely destroying it. Note, however, that only *one* of these roads is based on Europe: the second one is found not in Europe but in America.

In fact, Lenin's Prussian road provides a good description of Britain's road to capitalist development. In most two-road schemas, Britain's road is characterized as distinctly different from that of other European countries.

However, throughout the nineteenth and early twentieth centuries, Britain's industrial expansion, like that of other European countries, was dominated by its traditional landowning elite (see Chapter 3).

It is often assumed that the repeal of the Corn Laws marked the end of the power of the landlords in Britain. But the Corn Laws had been designed not to shore up a declining sector but to retain the high profits generated during the Napoleonic war years. Wheat prices did not fall until the onset of the Great Depression in the 1870s (see Hobsbawm 1968: 197). For most of the nineteenth century, British agriculture remained the biggest branch of the economy by far in terms of employment. In 1891 it still employed more than any other industrial group. Only in 1901, with the growth of the transport industry and metal industries complex, did it cease to be the largest branch of the economy in employment terms (Hobsbawm 1968: 195). And until 1914, nonindustrial Britain could easily outvote industrial Britain (Hobsbawm 1968: 196). Despite all that had been written about industrialists replacing landowners as the dominant element in the ruling elite, as late as 1914 industrialists "were not sufficiently organized to formulate broad policies or exert more than occasional influence over the direction of national affairs" (Boyce 1987: 8).

As a result Britain's Industrial Revolution was sectorally, as well as geographically, limited. Land in Britain, as elsewhere in Europe, was highly concentrated and became increasingly concentrated throughout the nineteenth century. Its farming system was among the least mechanized among advanced countries. These were not peripheral aspects of British industrialization. Nor were they attributable to the "survival" of a dying "feudal" substance, to pre-capitalist and ever-diminishing "forces of resistance" to industrial expansion. It was the traditional landowning elite who led capitalist development in Britain and elsewhere in Europe and who formed the basis of its "capitalist class," and it was this class that actively blocked land reform and the rationalization of agriculture in Britain.

Thus, in Europe, there was only one road. Everywhere in Europe, capitalist development was characterized not by a clear division between industrial and landed capital but by their fusion. While it is often said that in Britain, a new capitalist class fueled the expansion of industrial development, the nature of industrial capitalist development there, as elsewhere, was shaped by the political convergence of a landed aristocracy and large capitalist manufacturers.[41] Rosa Luxemburg got it precisely right: in England, there was

---

[41] In Britain, this had been achieved by the end of the eighteenth century (see, e.g., Hobsbawm 1962; Thompson 1965): "In Britain, an open land market meant that new wealth did not challenge old, but simply bought a landed estate.... At the same time the younger sons of landowners were joining the sons of urban tradesmen and master manufacturers among the merchants and professional men, thus strengthening the social bonds between landed and other forms of economic and social power" (Morris 1979: 15).

no revolutionary changeover from medieval to modern society, but "an early compromise which has preserved [into the twentieth century] the old remnants of feudalism." The old forms of medieval England "were not shattered or swept away, but filled with new content" (Luxemburg 1976: 232).

All European countries, including Britain, had relatively closed political spaces maintained by well-entrenched agrarian elites throughout the nineteenth century. There were differing degrees of closure and restriction, but while it is possible to quibble about the extent that closure and restriction varied, it was not substantial enough to constitute a different road. Either the aristocracy absorbed the industrial bourgeoisie and dominated it, protecting land and income structures, or the aristocracy resisted the industrial bourgeoisie and dominated it, protecting land and income structures. The road that emerges, either way, is the one of dualism and monopoly.

A critical distinction drawn in two-road schemas is the one that, in most of these, is held to be responsible for the emergence of different patterns of capitalist development: that is, whether a society developed on the basis of fusion or conflict with absolutism. The first-wave capitalisms, Lockean states, and American road were born of conflict, while their alternatives emerged as a result of fusion with absolutism. It is necessary, therefore, to clarify the nature of the conflict with absolutism that gave rise to modern nation-states and new industrial capitalist classes in Europe. In general, the conflict was over selective aspects of absolutism – those that scholars have identified with "enlightened" and "liberal" absolutism (see, e.g., Gagliardo 1967). Many of the revolutionary and progressive changes associated with the emergence of nation-states and a new capitalist class in fact originated not with a revolt against the mercantilist systems of absolutist states but with reforms of land, tax, educational, and legal systems that absolutist monarchs introduced as a means of abolishing serfdom and the guilds and establishing the conditions for the freer circulation of property and goods (see Chapter 2).

In fact, national revolutions and revolts had as their aim the eradication of many of these liberal reforms. Thus, the struggle was not with absolutism but with the price and wage controls, labor protections, and national welfare systems (in Britain, France, and elsewhere) that had been introduced by European monarchs beginning in the sixteenth century. The aristocracies that led and won those revolutions sought to seize control of the state in order to preserve their privileges and prerogatives and to privatize sources and means of producing wealth. They put an end to much of what was socially enlightened about liberal absolutism, retaining much of what was not in a new guise. What did survive and is often seen as the result of new revolutionary and progressive forces was, in fact, the work of absolutist monarchs. So, for instance, the features of France thought to resemble a bourgeois state in 1815 were the work not of the revolution, but of the ancien regime. It was the ancien regime that established the centralized administrative apparatus of the French state.

Absolute monarchies introduced standing armies, a permanent bureaucracy, national taxation, a codified law, and the beginnings of a unified market – all of which, as Perry Anderson rightly observes, seem "pre-eminently capitalist" (1979: 18–19). Moreover, it was France's ancien regime that had, long before 1789, begun the breakup of large estates into a multiplicity of small proprietorships. In fact, some students of the subject maintain that the number of landed proprietorships in France was scarcely smaller before 1789 than it is today (Johnson 1979: 155). Nor were the ideas and values supposedly born in the Revolution the product of a new and revolutionary class. After examining more closely the ancien regime, Tocqueville concluded, "Men had, it seemed, already many of the sentiments and opinions which I had always regarded as products of the Revolution, and in the same way many of the customs commonly thought to stem from it exclusively had already entered into our mores" (Tocqueville 1955: ix).

Yet the various ways of depicting two roads of industrial capitalist development obscure more than they reveal. In particular, the distinction commonly defined between societies that had or did not have "bourgeois revolutions" is overdrawn and misleading. No European country experienced a radical transformation of its social structure in the nineteenth century. Even where there was a large, independent capitalist bourgeoisie, it did not play the decisive role in the achievement of industrialization and democracy. Barrington Moore's (1966) "no bourgeoisie, no democracy" thesis could not be more wrong. Democracy was brought about by working-class power, which was a function of mobilization for war. As Rueschemeyer et al. argued, "Where labor is most suppressed, there we find the least progress towards democracy" (1992: 47). As is clearly shown below, it was the vast increase in the organizational strength, unity, and political power of labor in Europe, as a result of its mobilization not for industry but for war, that made possible the achievement of industrialization and democracy in Europe.

Europe's Pan-Regional Class Structure

The dominant class in Europe was a transnational class. States in Europe were built up within a pre-existing social formation, a region-wide system of social institutions, relationships, and norms. As a result, class structures throughout the region were similar, as were administrative and political structures.[42] Administration derived from the same principles; political assemblies were composed of the same elements and invested with the same powers. For centuries, and with the Church acting as an international

---

[42] The administration of medieval France, England, and Germany derived from the same general principles. The political assemblies were composed of the same elements and invested with the same powers. The same institutions could be found from the Polish frontier to the Irish Sea: the manor (*signeurie*), the seigneurial court presided over by the lord, the fief, the quitrent, feudal services, and trade and craft guilds. Sometimes the names were identical in

unifying agent, regulating economic life and political and class struggles across the region, political development, class struggles, social change, ideology, and culture remained essentially trans-European.[43] As many scholars have noted, Europe's elite was more closely tied by culture and concrete interests to an international class than to the classes below them.[44] The

all countries. And "behind all these institutions, and sponsoring them, was the same ideology" (Tocqueville 1955: 15–16; see also the essays in Crump and Jacob 1926; Hume 1975).

The church was the international arbiter of Western Europe's internal and external affairs, Christendom's court of last resort. It controlled education, social welfare, and the whole of intellectual life. It created a normative order across state, ethnic, class, and gender boundaries. Norms regarding property rights and free exchange "were guaranteed by a mixture of local customs and privileges, some judicial regulation by weak states, but above all by the common social identity provided by Christendom" (Mann 1988: 13–14). Princes were expected to enforce not merely the municipal law of their own realms but the common law of the whole community. The units viewed themselves as municipal embodiments of a universal community (see Mattingly 1955). The great revolt against papal authority at the end of the thirteenth century did not destroy the international order. It was still seen as a single community of some kind (Hinsley 1967: 242–52). In the thirteenth and fourteenth centuries, most states were constituted in accordance with legal principles that were essentially analogous wherever they were applied. St. Louis, Simon Montfort, Edward I, and Philip August "all approached their administrative tasks in much the same way." The cortes, states-general, diets, and parliaments that arose between the twelfth and fourteenth centuries, while reflecting different local customs, "were all representative assemblies, devised to comply with patterns of constitutionalism that antedated their existence and had always distinguished the political system of Europe from that of other societies" (Bozeman 1960: 452).

During the sixteenth and seventeenth centuries, Europe underwent a process of division into separate sovereignties. However, Westphalia made the reciprocal recognition of states of the sovereignty of other states represented at Westphalia the basis of a system of international law. An international society thus was established that consisted of an association of European states to which other states could be admitted only with their acquiesence. Western Europe retained a consciousness of essential unity. In the eighteenth century, legal theorists (Vattel, Grotius) and nonlegal writers (Montesquieu, Voltaire, Rousseau) emphasized that Europe's states were politically sovereign organizations that had, however, been drawn together by contiguity and historical development into an international system that was a unity (see, e.g., Voltaire 1935: chap. 2, p. 5). A cosmopolitan elite culture of court and salon spread across Europe in the eighteenth century. French became an international idiom of diplomatic and intellectual discourse.

[43] See, among others, Hill 1905; Meynial 1926; Voltaire 1935; Mattingly 1955; Tocqueville 1955; Pirenne 1958, 1969; Stubbs 1967; Granshof 1970; Strayer 1970; Balch 1978; Mann 1988.

[44] C. A. Macartney has described the three-fold national and social class structure that emerged in areas of Europe as a result of various waves of conquest: the original conquering races (Magyars, Germans, Swedes, Turks, Poles) who formed an upper class of landowners and administrators, the conquered serfs (Czechs, Slovaks, Slovenes, Vlachs, Ruthenes, White Russians, Finns, Lithuanians, and the non-Turkish races of the Balkans) who tilled the land, and midway between the two in legal status, the middle class of German, Polish, or Jewish colonists (Macartney 1934: 82–83).

Describing Europe in the 1780s, Eric Hobsbawm writes that throughout Europe "townsmen were often physically different from peasants.... Even townsmen of the same religion and nationality as the surrounding peasantry looked different: they wore different dress,

pan-regional elite, while bearing something like a family resemblance to one another, was often physically distinct from peasants within their own countries; often they were of a different nationality or religion or spoke a different language. Even where they had the same nationality and religion, their mode of life had in all respects more in common with elites elsewhere in Europe than with the lower classes within their own countries.[45]

The late eighteenth-century Industrial Revolution in Europe did not involve any fundamental change in this trans-European social system. The political convergence of large capitalist manufacturers with a dominant pan-European aristocracy shaped economic expansion in Europe during the nineteenth century in ways that worked to ensure the continuity of trans-European structures throughout the nineteenth and early twentieth centuries. In fact, the reorganization of social relations of production in Europe as a result of the Industrial Revolution brought different groups across states into closer relations of interdependence.

Often noted features of modern European history have helped to make this structure observable. The interdependent changes in the political structures of Poland, Denmark, Spain, and the Netherlands during the sixteenth and seventeenth centuries and the effects of the Napoleonic Wars are two

and indeed in most cases (except for the exploited indoor laboring and manufacturing population) were taller, though perhaps also slenderer" (Hobsbawm 1962: 27–28). On the eve of World War I, upper and lower classes were as sharply divided as ever. Roderick Floud describes the impoverished masses crowding the slums of London and other cities as so "stunted and wizened by illness and poverty" as to appear "as another race to upper class observers" (Floud 1997: 14). Others have written at length, for instance, about Britain's "two nations" (Disraeli 1950) and the difficulties of turning "peasants into Frenchmen" (Weber 1976).

[45] The French nobility, for instance, considered themselves to be a separate nation, one more closely tied to an international aristocracy than to the French classes below them. The Comte de Boulainvilliers, a French nobleman who wrote at the beginning of the eighteenth century, regarded the nobility as a constituting nation having more in common with a foreign people of the "same society and condition" than with their compatriots. Boulainvilliers argued that France is divided into two races that have at bottom nothing in common. They speak a common language, but they have neither common rights nor a common origin (*Histoire de l'ancien gouvernement de la France* (1727), vol. 1, p. 33; quoted in Arendt 1958: 162). Albert Thierry wrote, "The true French, incarnated in our day in the nobility and its partisans, are the sons of free men; the former slaves and all races alike employed primarily in labor by their masters are the fathers of the Third Estate" (*Considèrations sur l'histoire de France*, 5th ed. (Paris, 1868), chap. 2; cited in Cassirer 1946: 229). On the eve of the Revolution, the Comte Dubuat-Nançay proposed "the creation of a kind of *Internationale* of aristocracy of barbarian origin." The Comte argued that the true origin of the French nation was supposed to be identical with that of the Germans; the French lower classes, though no longer slaves, were not free by birth but by the grace of the nobility (*Les Origines de l'ancien gouvernement de la France, de l'Allemagne, et de Italie*, 1789). The outbreak of the Revolution forced great numbers of the French nobility to seek refuge in Germany and England, and a few years later the French exiles actually tried to form an *internationale* of aristocrats in order to stave off the revolt of those they considered foreign enslaved people.

examples.[46] In the nineteenth century, as in previous centuries, debates and conflicts over succession in Europe continued, as well as contention over who to support from among locally powerful groups in territories outside Europe (potential leaders with whom the imperial powers could work). Throughout the nineteenth century, the pan-regional social structure was particularly evident in the interventions and involvement of European states in ongoing interstate and domestic disputes (see Chapter 4). Since, as in previous centuries, the structure of rights throughout the region tended to advantage and disadvantage the same groups (everywhere in Europe the upper classes generally had the same privileges, and lower classes and ethnic minorities were, in general, subject to the same restrictions), conflicts in Europe throughout the nineteenth century were inherently transnational in nature and regional in scope (see Chapter 4). Since the belligerents in nineteenth- and early twentieth-century labor, enfranchisement, and ethnic conflicts belonged to transnational reference groups, the outcome of a conflict in one state bore on the relations of power between members of the same groups living in other states.

Though classes may take different forms in different societies, since they are constituent elements of any capitalist structure, they are ultimately a transnational phenomenon rooted in the structure of capitalist relations. However, the account of Europe's nineteenth-century industrial capitalist expansion developed in subsequent chapters treats Europe's capitalist class as essentially trans-European, rather than, as in Kees van der Pijl's influential theorization, part of a trans-Atlantic capitalist class.

Van der Pijl elaborates a process of trans-Atlantic class formation that coincided with the successive stages of the internationalization of capital. The comprehensive capital relation became global between 1688 and the present through these stages and their attendant social forms (diasporas, multinational corporations, planning groups). The period between 1840 and 1914 saw a process of combining the U.S. and British economies through the circuit of money capital and migration. The end of the U.S. Civil War began the process through which the United States "partly enlarged and partly replaced Britain's pre-eminence in the heartland and beyond" (1998: 70). A more or less united transnational capitalist class emerged, according to van der Pijl, as a result of World War I. The war, he argues, turned New York into the world's banking center.[47]

---

[46] See, e.g., Gourevitch 1978; Poggi 1978; Gilpin 1981: chap. 6; Parker 1988; Tilly 1990; Spruyt 1996. On the pan-European impact of the Napoleonic Wars, see, e.g., Tocqueville 1955; Hobsbawm 1962.

[47] 1998: 72. In fact, and as van der Pijl himself points out, London recovered as a banking center after the war, although, he contends, "increasingly as an 'offshore' center divorced from the actual British economy" (1998: 72). But London's banking center was always "offshore" (see Chapter 3). As Boyce has argued, the City of London, while making more fortunes than in the whole of British industry, depended "only slightly" on Britain's economic

But if classes bear the mark of past centuries, then, clearly, the European capitalist bourgeoisie in the nineteenth century was shaped by a different legacy than that of the U.S. capitalist class. As Gramsci argued, the lack of a feudal past and of parasitic classes and strata from the past allowed the United States to rationalize production and labor. In Europe, however, the decaying classes resisted the spread of "Americanism" to Europe because the new methods of production threatened to undermine them. Thus, the transnational networks of power that van der Pijl elaborates, and that are constructed by coalitions among fractions of the capitalist class, began to shape the socioeconomic and political character of industrial capitalist development in Europe only during the period of the world wars. Until then, different fractions of the capitalist bourgeoisie dominated in the United States. Thus, in Europe, and despite the migrations and monetary circuits that van der Pijl traces, capitalist development was shaped, until then, by predominantly trans-European rather than trans-Atlantic forces and structures.

Class Agency

Because of the essentially transnational nature of European society and the similarities and interdependencies that it created among states, as the various economies of Europe began to expand in the nineteenth century, their advanced sectors were tied more closely to those within the economies of other European countries than to the more backward sectors within their own (see Chapter 3). As a result, Europe's economic expansion took place within, and was crucially shaped by, an increasingly interdependent industrial system. Since interdependent parts must grow in some sort of balance if profitability is to be maintained,[48] the advanced sector in one country had an interest in supporting and maintaining the growth of advanced sectors in other countries, thus reinforcing and maintaining the uneven and dual pattern of economic expansion characteristic of industrial capitalist development everywhere in Europe. In the nineteenth century, as a result of the structural relations of connection and interaction that constituted the trans-European

---

performance (Boyce 1987: 18–19). In any case, in van der Pijl's account a trans-Atlantic capitalist class doesn't seem really to emerge until after World War II. He writes that it is only after World War II that Britain was "locked into a 'special relationship'" with the United States, a relationship that "constituted the core to which other states could accede . . . " (1998: 72); it was in the New Deal that the "American productive and class structure was recast around the progressive mode of accumulation (Fordism)," and the New Deal was not "extrapolated" to Western Europe until the Marshall Plan (1998: 119).

[48] As Chapter 3 shows, for much of the nineteenth century, the "advanced sectors" of European and other economies developed less through direct competition with each than by means of a mutually reinforcing circuit of investment and exchange.

class, similar relations were established in sites of production, and they were reproduced, in similar ways, by their maintenance throughout the social formation.

To clarify how these similar outcomes emerged in different states, it is useful to focus more specifically on the nature of the relationship among ruling groups throughout Europe. These groups were not "taxonomic groups," that is, groups "whose members show similar (formal) attributes but which need not actually connect or interact with one another." Relations among taxonomic groups are relations of similarity, but not necessarily of connection. Their similarity, therefore, does not explain why and how – through what connections – these groups might act similarly. However, if members of groups – whatever their similarities or differences – "relate to each other structurally or causally" (Sayer 1992: 244) and similarly, it is because the relations *themselves* are relations of connection. The ruling classes of European states were *not* separate but similar classes. Rather, they formed a single transregional elite, and their broadly similar characteristics, interests, capabilities, and policies were constituted and reproduced through interaction, connection, and interdependence. While the properties of dominant groups in different parts of Europe may have varied, the connections and interactions among them were rich and concrete and, in themselves, and within the constraints and opportunities present in different contexts, produced a set of common solutions to the problems of organizing production along new lines. It is generally the case that elites are interested in adopting the most up-to-date methods of multiplying their revenue, wealth, and power. The obvious success of the British elite in this regard would have been expected to inspire elites elsewhere in Europe to emulate British economic, social, administrative, and intellectual trends. That is why nationalist policies and rhetoric emerged across different European societies. As Liah Greenfeld shows (1992), groups in different countries were facing problems similar to those that, in England, had given rise to nationalism, and with modifications, copied the model developed in England.[49] Solutions developed in one country were, thus, observed and copied, with modifications relevant to the specific context. States and groups followed the leaders, emulated their goals, envied their triumphs, and adopted their policies.

Common problems arising from the establishment of a capitalist labor market and new labor processes were generally resolved throughout Europe

---

[49] As Charles Tilly observes with respect to nationalism more generally, "state-led processes created visible, prestigious, transferable models for exploitation and opportunity hoarding." As a result, "Throughout the world, administrative structures, constitutions, and declared commitments of regimes to development, stability, and democracy came to resemble each other far more than did the diversity of their material conditions and actual accomplishments"(1998: 180).

in broadly similar ways (see Chapters 2 and 3). The most acute problem that arose as industrial capitalist production began to expand in the nineteenth century was how to mobilize a mass of workers for the expansion of production while at the same time maintaining their subordination to capital.

The dominant solution to this problem was to very slowly and selectively introduce mechanization while predominantly using methods of production that kept workers unskilled and kept labor, as a whole, fragmented and poorly paid. However, this solution raised an additional problem. If the standard of consumption of the mass of the national population remained the same or was reduced, where would consumers be found for the products of expanded production? The overall solution, therefore, was to expand production principally for export to ruling groups in other countries. In this way, they could limit the development of mass purchasing power at home, while developing it among foreign groups and ruling bodies through the creation of public debt and investment in infrastructure, railroads, and armaments (see Chapter 3). Thus, there developed an exchange of raw materials and manufactured goods through an elite circuit of exchange, in which elites of different countries were integrated with the help of British financiers and firms.

Dominant classes have a common interest in exploiting labor (for profit). The ability to exploit labor by paying workers less than the value they produce is a necessary condition of creating surplus value and, thus, of realizing profit. All capitalists sought to realize the value of the rising mountain of goods that resulted from enlarged industrial production without a corresponding democratization of consumption. To exploit labor by paying less than the value produced, capitalists must maintain an advantageous balance of power. The numerical inferiority of capitalists makes this a critical task. At the beginning of Europe's industrial expansion it would have been one that was difficult to accomplish and, once accomplished, difficult to maintain. Since it is a necessary condition for realizing profit, it was a task faced by every dominant group seeking to increase profits by expanding production. How it was met, as Chapter 3 shows below, varied across different societies, according to its place in the circuit, the type of goods it produced for sale, and the relative power of capital and labor. However, similar capabilities, as well as a common Europe-wide context, tended to shape their interaction with labor in similar ways. In Britain, dominant classes ensured that the conditions for realizing profit were met by using methods of absolute surplus value production to maintain the subordination of labor in the sites of production and by maintaining these relations throughout the larger social formation (national and international). This became the model for industrial expansion throughout Europe.

Europe emerged into its first century of industrial capitalism from the crucible of the Great War. A quarter-century of war and revolutionary turmoil had made clear the central dilemma for dominant groups tempted by the possibilities of great profits to reorganize production along the lines of industrial capitalism: how to mobilize – train, educate, and, in other ways, empower – labor while, at the same time, maintaining the basic relation of capitalism, that is, the subordination of labor to capital. The Great War had revealed the dangers of a trained and compact mass army: many analogies, in fact, were drawn between the mass army of soldiers created in the Great War and the mass industrial army of workers needed for industrial capitalist production (see Chapter 2). At the same time, socialism had been born in the French Revolution, and its focus, in particular, on eradicating private property – something that dominant classes had achieved through a century or more of struggle – seemed, in combination with the revolutionary ferment unleashed by the war, to threaten an anticapitalist revolt of the masses. This was the context within which elites throughout Europe undertook to mobilize labor for industrial production.

Subsequent chapters show what occurred, the situation in which it occurred, who acted, and the instruments they used. They show that, in Europe, production was expanded largely for export and largely through the intensification of labor; that this was done at a time when strong revolutionary currents were flowing through Europe; that those who shaped and directed this development were landed elites and the industrial classes allied with them; and that they used the apparatus of the state and, in particular, the military and police. That the purpose of producing largely for other elites and ruling groups was to subordinate labor and monopolize the gains from industrial expansion can be inferred from all of the above.

Elites were cohesive and had much to gain. They controlled immense resources and were free to deploy them in a sustained pursuit of their aims. They either controlled the apparatus of the state directly or had access to political leaders and could trade their political support, or the withdrawal of political opposition, for concessions from them. They were therefore able to carry on a class struggle throughout the nineteenth century by means of a purposive, determined, and essentially coherent legislative, legal, military, and political assault on artisans, laborers, and peasants.

We are permitted to say that policies are "designed" – that is, that they are intended, calculated, planned, premeditated, and deliberate. However, as is often the case, there were unintended consequences of these policies, and in this case, there were important ones. By generating imperialist rivalries and conflicts that eventually led to multilateral great power war in Europe, external expansion had the unintended consequence of forcing governments and ruling elites to mobilize (and, thus, empower) the masses. This is precisely what it seemed a century of external expansion had enabled them to avoid. As a number of scholars have shown, war often produces social leveling, revolution, and shifts in the balance of social forces, and in the course of the world wars, this is, in fact, what happened in Europe.

Classes and States

A final consideration relevant to the issues of class agency is the relation of dominant classes to the state. Among theoreticians of the state, both liberal and neo-Marxist, the focus of concern in recent years has been to explain and analyze the autonomy of the state. From this perspective, the state is understood as a set of administrative and coercive structures or institutions that are wholly, relatively, or potentially autonomous from social forces. According to liberal theory, the growth of state autonomy is the outcome of a process of rationalization in which authority structures become differentiated from other structures and specialized. This differentiation, which frees the state from the control of particularistic subgroups,[50] historically is supposed to have occurred as a result of the divorce between the monarchy and the aristocracy and the consequent emergence of the modern and more "rational" nation-state (see, e.g., Parsons 1966). However, as previously discussed (and as Chapter 2 argues), nation-states were established in a rearguard movement by privileged classes to reverse the efforts of absolute monarchs to rationalize tax structures and introduce liberal reforms, to restore the union of state and aristocracy, and to limit the growing autonomy of the state.

Neo-Marxist theories of state autonomy emerged to explain a key problem in Marxist theory: if a new capitalist class came to power with the development of capitalism, why, in Kautsky's famous phrase, is it "a ruling class that doesn't rule"? The answer, according to neo-Marxist theories of state autonomy, is that the state exists and is structured in particular ways because of the requirements of capitalism. In other words, structural and impersonal constraints and pressures cause the state to serve the needs of capital, rather than the people who occupy positions of state power.

If we recognize that the owners of capital were *not* a fundamentally new class,[51] that the "traditional" elite formed the basis of the "capitalist class," that it was not replaced by some previously dominated class and, instead, remained the dominant class under new relations of production, the problem of explaining the disjuncture between political and economic power

---

[50] An early formulation of the thesis is Durkheim's: once the steadily increasing division of labor has made the state a "distinct organ of society," it can then "stand above all other interests," above "castes, classes, corporations, coteries of every sort, and every kind of economic person" (Durkheim 1975: 177).

[51] Because the emergence of the capitalist state coincided with the disappearance of serfdom, Marx and Engels assumed that feudal relations had also disappeared. This assumption was consistent with Marx's famous formula: "The mode of production of material life conditions the general character of the social, political and spiritual processes of life.... In broad outline the Asiatic, ancient, feudal and modern bourgeois modes of production can be designated as epochs marking progress in the economic development of society" (Marx 1970: 21–22).

disappears.[52] It then becomes clear that the national state that emerged with industrial capitalism *was* created by and for the capitalist bourgeoisie, and *was* the institution whereby that class imposed and defended its power and privileges against subordinate classes.

The fraction of the bourgeoisie that dominates, that is, wins political hegemony and enforces it through state power, is the fraction that actually makes the laws and rules and determines the pattern of capitalist development (see, e.g., Marx 1964). As subsequent chapters show, what the state is and what it can do shifts in response to changes in the balance of forces, not only between classes, but also within them. Before World War II, the top state personnel in Britain, France, Germany, Sweden, Russia, and elsewhere in Europe were drawn from or socially integrated with the "traditional" upper classes, especially the landed upper class (until 1905, it dominated every British cabinet). Because it dominated, state policies were generally consistent with its immediate interests, and as a result, landowners did not experience significant political setbacks with respect to tariffs, labor legislation, land reform, state allocations, tax policy, or internal terms of trade until after World War II.

In the next section, the terrain of Karl Polanyi's "Great Transformation" is revisited, focusing on the class nature of the institutional complex underlying Europe's nineteenth-century market economy and the class interests that shaped and were served by the expansion of industrial capitalism, the "Liberal State," and the "hundred years' peace." Working from the bottom up, it begins with a consideration of social forces and conflicts, and then traces their impact on the nature of states and state action and, via states, on the nature of the overarching interstate system. It recasts the protectionist countermove in terms of sectoral, rather than societal, interests; reconceives the nature of the state and its role in nineteenth-century European industrial expansion in terms of class interests; and explains how the European conflicts that recurred throughout the nineteenth and early twentieth centuries and culminated in the world wars were intrinsically related to the character of European industrialization before the world wars.

THE GREAT TRANSFORMATION, REVISITED

Social and historical change is best described neither as linear nor cyclical but as a spiral combining both linear developments and cyclical processes. Within a generally unilinear and progressive development of productive forces, we find, in social and political life, recurring problems and, historically, some

---

[52] Engels's oft-cited description of the supposedly relatively autonomous state really asserts the state's autonomy only from capitalists and workers, not from the ancien regime. In the new German Empire, under Bismarck, "capitalists and workers are balanced against each other and equally cheated for the benefit of the impoverished Prussian cabbage junkers" (Engels 1968: 290–91).

common set of responses to them. Social processes recur, but in a world that is ever changing as a result of technological developments. However, since things that have occurred in the past tend to recur,[53] the world is never entirely transformed.[54] Technological advances combine with repeated processes in social life to create growth as well as stagnation, social progress, and retrogression.

Among the many processes in social life that tend to recur is the process of accumulation set in motion by the discovery of new sources of wealth or means of creating it. All accumulation is based on exclusion. Where there are new opportunities of gaining wealth and power, those in positions of privilege will endeavor to control and monopolize them in order to preserve the structures and institutions of society on which their privileges depend and to prevent new groups or classes from gaining power. Thus, while they seek to profit from technological change and changes in productive forces, elites may also endeavor to limit their application and block the distribution of resources needed to spread their advantages more widely. The resulting rigidities are likely to generate stagnation, crisis, and conflict.

With the dawning of the industrial age, elites in Europe used the wealth and privileges that they had acquired in the past to ensure that processes of industrial development would not adversely affect their interests. Concerned with consolidating and maintaining their control of labor while, at the same time, mobilizing it for the expansion of production, as elaborated below, elites sought to increase profits by increasing absolute surplus value production at home and pursuing imperialist expansion abroad. This dualistic system of internal restriction and external expansion constituted the central feature of Europe's industrial expansion. The "double movement" of expansion and protection that Polanyi so compellingly argued was its central dynamic was but an element of it, and was generated not by the resistance of "society as a whole" to the self-regulating market but as part of a system of production fundamentally shaped by social class conflict.

This externally oriented system produced the essential dualism that has characterized industrial capitalist expansion both in Europe and in the contemporary third world. This dualism was characterized by a lack of internal structural integration and dependency on outside capital, labor, and/or markets. Great Britain, France, Italy, Germany, Spain, Portugal, the Austro-Hungarian Empire, Russia, Belgium, and much of the Balkans had a dynamic, foreign-oriented economic sector that failed to transform the rest of society (Halperin 1997a: chap. 5; and Chapter 3). Some countries experienced widely spread growth, though less widespread and much later

---

53 Capitalism comes and goes; so do democracy and prosperity, but in forms that vary in conjunction with the progressive development of productive forces.

54 The world is not capable of infinite transformation, as Friedrich Nietzsche observed ("The Eternal Return," in *The Will to Power* (New York: Vintage Books, 1967), 544–50).

than is usually supposed. In most, modern industrial sectors oriented to and dependent on international markets formed enclaves within nonindustrial, mainly agricultural, and backward hinterlands and were linked not to other sectors of the domestic economy but to similar industrial enclaves in other countries (see Chapter 3 and Halperin 1997a: chap. 5). Production was largely for external markets; trade was external; capital was invested abroad.[55]

Thus, on the eve of World War I, most of Europe was still rural and "preeminently pre-industrial," as Arno Mayer has argued (1981: 187, 301). Agriculture was still the single largest and weightiest sector in all the continental countries. Even after World War I, France drew her wealth principally from agriculture, and approximately half of her population was engaged in agricultural pursuits (Ogg 1930: 185). In 1914 almost half of Western Europe's working population was still employed in agriculture (including fishing and forestry), and rural dwellers still made up the largest part of the population in all the countries of continental Europe, except Germany. In many Western European industrial countries, the absolute numbers of those employed in agriculture did not decline dramatically until after 1945 when mechanization of production increased significantly.

Absolute Surplus Value Production and Imperialist Expansion

As bases of growth, increasing production principally for export or for mass, local consumption are genuine alternatives (as Chapter 3 argues). As the history of the post–World War II period makes clear, the expansion of domestic markets is a problem not of production but of distribution and consumption, and as subsequent chapters argue, in nineteenth-century Europe it was a matter of choice, of deliberate organization and collective effort, on the part of elites concerned with maintaining a specific distribution of resources that subordinated labor and preserved elite privileges.[56] Government-induced demand creation was not a twentieth-century invention: it was a key feature in Europe's nineteenth-century industrial expansion. Almost universally, government demand (in addition to foreign inputs) substituted for missing

---

[55] Capital flowed between London and the far reaches of the Empire, but not between London and the industrial north (Kindleberger 1964: 62). French industrial banks were mainly interested in underwriting foreign bonds rather than in lending to domestic industry (Collas 1908; Baldy 1922; Bouvier 1961: chap. 6).

[56] In Germany, the doctrine was preached that "the State should retard the march of technical innovation for fear of the economic damage caused to those who had invested in older methods" (Dobb 1963: 383–84). German landowners, fearing that the expansion of employment in factories would increase both the danger of socialism (as evidenced by the opinions expressed in the *Kreuzzeitung*, the most influential organ of German conservatism; Richter 1938: 48–52, in Tipton 1976: 115) and the power of the Polish population, were able through their opposition to hamper industrial development plans in the 1890s and to prevent their revival after 1902 (Tipton 1976: 115–16).

developmental "prerequisites" such as capital, skills, and a home market for industrial goods (Morris and Adelman 1988: 123–24). Everywhere in Europe, national governments were involved in building railways and ports, and in the expansion and control of credit institutions. Moreover, a significant aspect of Europe's industrial development throughout the nineteenth century was the demand stimulus of government weapons purchases for imperialist expansion.

Subordinating labor required that the mass of workers be kept poor, unskilled, uneducated, unorganized, and in excess of demand. Workers had to remain relatively poor because political power in nineteenth-century Europe was based on wealth (not citizenship). Workers had to remain unskilled, since skilled workers were more independent, scarce, and valuable, and could therefore command higher wages and regulate their own time. Thus, gradually but persistently, industrialists worked to make irrelevant the skilled laborers of previous centuries and restricted mechanization and skilled labor to those sectors of the economy producing for export (see Chapter 3).

Technological improvements were introduced in sectors producing for export, but even here, mechanization was introduced far later and less completely than is generally thought. In the rest of the economy, production continued to be carried out by methods of increasing absolute surplus production, that is, extending the length of the working day, intensifying work, and decreasing the standard of living of the labor force. These methods predominated in Europe far longer than is generally recognized. In most sectors of European economies, technological improvement came late, and only under pressure of military competition and war. In general, workers were unskilled and wages remained low. As a result, masses of unskilled workers remained "in reserve," keeping the overall market position of labor weak.[57]

The various legislative acts extending educational opportunities in Europe were designed not to find, advance, and instruct the talented children of the working class but to maintain a rigid division among the classes. Thus, while Britain's Education Act of 1870 granted the children of the working class the right to universal primary education, it was intended, as H. G. Wells wrote, "to educate the lower classes for employment on lower class

---

[57] Automatism is a feature not of technology but of capitalist production relations and is inherent in capitalist control over production. During the seventeenth, eighteenth, and early nineteenth centuries, handicrafts acted as an obstacle to consolidating the control of capital over production. As long as handicraft production played an essential role in the capitalist labor process, automatism did not take full command (Sohn-Rethel 1978a: 121). Sohn-Rethel (1978a) argues that the division of intellectual and manual labor is ruled by a logic of appropriation. The direct producers are no longer required or permitted to think for themselves. Thus, there is a division between head and hand. Taylorism in effect converts the machine operator into a part of the machinery.

lines, and with specially trained, inferior teachers who had no university qualifications."[58]

The one source of power left to workers was their sheer numbers. But since this mass is strong only when it is organized and united,[59] each advance in labor organization in Europe produced additional legal obstacles and setbacks. Thus, workers were barred from effective trade union organization and strike activity until well into the twentieth century.[60] Backed by the power of the state, elites were able to maintain political and economic restrictions on workers that kept wages low and labor weak, dependent, and controlled.

Subordinating labor in this way entailed securing markets abroad and expanding production for foreign rather than for local consumption. This ensured that since workers were not the principal buyers of what they produced, they would not need to be paid more than was necessary for bare subsistence. It meant, too, that the masses would no longer be able to exercise power through consumer choice or boycott as they had done in previous centuries when the production of goods in Europe had been largely for local markets. Had Europe developed a capitalist economy based on expanding the mass production of goods for local consumption, not only would wealth have had to be redistributed in favor of workers to enable them to buy what they produced, but their demands would have dominated commercially. External expansion, however, offered a means both to secure markets for increased production and to avoid increasing the power of labor.

Imperialism and Class

Polanyi argued that imperialist rivalries began to destroy the central institutions of nineteenth-century European society after 1879. However,

---

[58] Wells 1934, in Landes 1969: 341. Its essential function was "to discipline a growing mass of disaffected proletarians and integrate them into British society" (Landes 1969: 341). In 1897, fewer than 7 percent of grammar-school pupils in Britain came from the working class. The Education Act of 1902 set up a new system of secondary education designed to exclude the children of the working class from higher education. In 1936, a recommendation by the Consultative Committee of the Board of Education that all children should be given schooling to the age of fifteen was rejected by the government. Tawney recalls one argument against the proposal: "'The small fingers' of children of fourteen, we were told by a speaker in the House of Commons" on the proposed bill, "are indispensable to the survival of the Yorkshire textile industry." He goes on to observe that "the children of the rich, in addition to their other advantages, are apparently blessed by Providence with fingers plumper and more elongated" than those bestowed on children "whose parents happen to be poor" (Tawney 1952: 144).

[59] The one factor of success that the workers have at their command, as Marx pointed out, is mass. But this mass is strong only when it is compact and united. "Without compactness, without solidarity the workers would be doomed to failure" ("Inaugural Address and Provisional Rules of the International Workingmen's Association," London, 1864).

[60] See note 16.

imperialism was intrinsic to Europe's industrial expansion. If imperialism began to destroy Europe's nineteenth-century market system after 1879, it was because, after that time, imperialist ambitions began to focus increasingly on Europe itself. Imperialism in Europe during and immediately after the Napoleonic Wars had subordinated many areas of Europe to the Great Powers, either through direct rule or through administration, occupation, or annexation. Imperialist expansion in other regions of the world began in the 1820s. Subsequent chapters argue that imperialism was neither, as Polanyi argued, part of a protective countermovement that emerged simultaneously with the unregulated market nor, as Lenin and others argued, necessary to the development of capitalism.[61] Instead, it is argued here that expansionist policies were proposed and advocated by European elites as a means of increasing revenue and resources and as an alternative to alleviating land hunger and expanding opportunities for participation at home through redistribution and reform. The main capital exporters did not have capital-saturated domestic economies, as Lenin and others argued. In Britain and France, the two largest foreign investors during the nineteenth century, domestic industry clearly suffered because investors failed to exploit opportunities at home.[62] However, in Britain, increasing land concentration and the resulting inequalities in the distribution of wealth impeded the efficient use of disposable resources, making it more desirable for investors to export capital than to invest in the domestic economy.[63] It was therefore not the case that imperialism was necessary because capital could not expand in any other way. It was, rather, a means by which elites could increase their wealth without revolutionizing their societies through the expansion and integration of the domestic market.[64]

[61] Marxist thinkers such as Rosa Luxemburg and Lenin argued that imperialism was an inevitable result of capitalist development. Since capitalism is expansionist and competitive, if it is first developed in one or two countries, then it will expand in one way or another into other countries – the original capitalist countries will try to penetrate the others *economically* in a variety of ways. But the specific form of imperialism in the late nineteenth and early twentieth centuries – direct rule by the metropolitan nations – was a *noneconomic* means of expansion. Just as capitalism entails extraction of surplus value through economic means, capitalist expansion must also entail economic means. The foreign capital investments of Britain, France, and Belgium were concentrated in foreign railway construction, but also in docks, tramways, telegraphs and telephones, and gas and electric works. These are the sorts of investments by means of which imperial countries could develop and extend their domination over other internal markets. While this effectively capitalized the world, it did so through essentially noneconomic means.
[62] Sée 1942: 360; Lévy 1951–52: 228; Cairncross 1953: 225; Cameron 1961: 123, 152; Lewis 1972: 27–58; Trebilcock 1981.
[63] However, it has been argued that imperial investments were not more profitable than domestic investments. For the two largest investors, see Braunschwig 1960, for France; Davis and Huttenback 1988, for Britain.
[64] This is the Schumpeterian view, that imperialism was the product of the surviving "feudal substance" of a pre-capitalist Europe that had fused with bourgeois-capitalism (1955: 98, 119, 128). A more recent view, consistent with this one, is Cain and Hopkins 1993. In Weber's

Imperialist expansion had the effect of restricting the geographic and sectoral spread of industrial capitalism to within the constraints posed by the concentration of land ownership.

In the classical theory of economic development, the extension of the market depends on the extent of the division of labor, and this, in turn, depends on a more equitable distribution of land and other resources, of income, and of opportunity (Smith 1976b: 7–16). Thus, the redistribution of land was among the most critical issues affecting the growth of the internal market.[65] But at the beginning of the nineteenth century, most land was in the hands of a tiny fraction of the population, and land became increasingly concentrated in the course of the century. Imperialist expansion offered a means of securing cheaper food without transforming agriculture. However, land concentration eventually slowed the growth of industrial production.[66] When British industry fell behind international competitors, there were insufficient employment opportunities outside the export trade areas to absorb the export unemployment because no special effort had been made to stimulate production for home consumption.

Imperialism and War

Between the Napoleonic Wars (1815) and the beginning of World War I (1914), Europe did not enjoy a century of peace. Conflict emerged continually within and among the states of Europe and between those states

---

view, imperial expansion was usually associated with the economic interests of groups that sought monopoly profits instead of being content to manufacture and exchange goods in a formally free market. This form of monopoly capitalism was a parasitic form of genuine capitalism (1978: 920, 922; see also Gerth and Mills 1946: 162–71).

It might be argued that the history of the United States shows that the development of the home market is perfectly consistent with aggressive expansionism. The United States developed an internal market in the 1870s and yet, it might be argued, pursued imperialist expansion as well. However, while the United States gained a formal empire in the Caribbean and the Pacific following an American policy shift in 1898–99, that country "showed almost no interest in possession of territory as a protected sphere of trade or investment. It was necessary only to secure commercial entrepôts, naval bases, the site for a strategic canal and to solve existing social and economic problems in areas of established American influence, as in Samoa and Hawaii" (Fieldhouse 1973: 474). A comparison of U.S. and British expansionism reveals additional contrasts. In 1913 Britain was exporting 25 percent of its output, while the United States, the largest economy in the world at that time, was exporting only 7 percent. When U.S. foreign investment peaked in the 1920s, it was still exceeded by that of British investors. At the height of the Marshall Plan, in 1947, the level of foreign investment as a share of national income was around 3 percent; in the 1950s, it was 0.5 percent of national income (McCloskey 1981: 144; Floud 1997: 90).

[65] Morris and Adelman have found that "sustained and widespread economic growth is likely only with above-average equity in land distribution and with success in wresting political power from powerful resource-owning elites" (1989: 1425).

[66] See Morris and Adelman 1988: chap. 5 for a discussion.

and extraregional populations and states. During that period, attempts to maintain or eradicate restrictions on political rights and economic opportunities generated minority and class conflicts at home, and efforts to secure protected foreign markets in lieu of developing internal markets generated imperialist conflicts abroad and, increasingly, in Europe itself, as France, Great Britain, Russia, Austria-Hungary, Germany, Sweden, Belgium, the Netherlands, Italy, Spain, Portugal, Greece, Serbia, Bulgaria, Romania, and Poland embarked on imperial expansion, both within and outside Europe. These conflicts culminated in a massively destructive, two-phased final war of European imperialism.

The great wave of European imperialism launched by the Depression and agrarian distress of 1873–86, a "stupendous movement, without parallel in history" (Barraclough 1967: 63–64), sharply diminished the possibilities of overseas outlets within two decades.[67] By the turn of the century, as overseas expansionism began to approach its limit as an engine of growth, the imperialist ambitions of European states had come to focus with renewed urgency on Europe itself.[68]

Externally oriented expansion had led to a process of growth so distorted from a welfare point of view that, by the first decades of the twentieth century, it had produced stagnation and crisis. Thus, at the same time that interstate tensions in Europe were intensifying, European societies were becoming increasingly polarized by pressures for redistribution and reform. These tensions combined to produce, by 1914, the first of two massively destructive regional wars.

The First World War brought into conflict the two central features of European development: internal restriction and external expansion. For the

---

[67] Between 1876 and 1900, European control of Africa expanded from about one-tenth to nine-tenths of the continent. In the 1890s, France claimed a quarter of the total area and nearly a fifth of the population of China, Britain asserted exclusive interests in the whole basin of the Yangtse, with well over half the population of the empire, and Russia set its sights on Manchuria (Barraclough 1967: 61–62). Though there were still gains to be made in Africa and especially in Asia, given the poverty of these countries and their low rates of growth, their demand for manufactures was limited.

[68] As the world was increasingly being carved up by naval powers, the essentially landlocked Russian, Austro-Hungarian, and German Empires began to fight over Europe. Russia was obsessed with retaining its Serbian foothold in the Balkans. Austria was obsessed with the threat of Serbian nationalism – both within the Empire and in the Balkans generally. Germany was obsessed with keeping control of Alsace-Lorraine. The treaties concluded among the Central Powers during World War I provided for the acquisition by Austria-Hungary of Serbia, Montenegro, Albania, and Venice; and the acquisition by Germany of substantial territories in Eastern Europe, effective control of Belgium, and annexation of French coal regions. Treaties concluded among the Allies provided for the acquisition by Russia of Turkish provinces in Europe and those parts of Poland that in 1914 were controlled by Prussia and Austria. France sought a number of German territories: Alsace-Lorraine, the Saar Valley, and other territories on the left bank of the Rhine. Italy wanted, among other territories, the Trentino, Southern Tyrol, Trieste, and Istria.

threat of imperialism in Europe itself forced governments and ruling elites
to do precisely what a century of imperialist expansion had enabled them to
avoid: mobilize the masses. In the eighteenth century, governments had relied
on the social elite to pay for mercenary troops and to provide military leaders
to fight professional wars, and as a result, these wars had tended to heighten
existing social inequalities. But when mass armies were mobilized to fight
Napoleon's mass "citizen" armies, the participation of the lower classes,
both in the war effort and in areas of work and social life usually barred to
them, worked to enhance the power of labor and to strengthen its market
position.[69] Moreover, their loyalty had to be ensured by extending to them
various rights. Thus, serfdom was abolished and peasants were granted the
ownership of the land they cultivated concurrent with the military reforms
that Stein introduced in Prussia. Later, Alexander II in Russia introduced
reforms that both transformed the army from a professional into a conscript
force and abolished serfdom. In Austria, the adoption of universal military
service coincided with reforms that established a constitutional monarchy
(Andreski 1968: 69).

Thus, after the end of the Napoleonic Wars, and despite the difficulty of
raising and maintaining large numbers of mercenaries, experimentation with
citizen armies largely ended, and there was a return to old-style armies of
paid professionals, mercenaries, and "gentlemen" (Silver and Slater 1999:
190). The new weapon that had been introduced by Napoleon was used in
1870 by France and Germany, also with frightening consequences (the rising
of the Paris commune), and then not again until 1914.[70]

In 1914, aggressive imperialist threats on their frontiers forced states,
once again, to use what was then still the most powerful weapon of mass
destruction: the *lévee en masse*. Mass mobilization for World War I set in
motion a social revolution that, between 1917 and 1939, swept through all
of Europe. The efforts of Western governments and ruling elites to prevent its
further spread and escalation led directly to the Second World War. At its end,

---

[69] A number of scholars have argued that the alteration of class structures is an important effect
of war (Sorokin 1927, 1969; Titmuss 1958: 86; Andreski 1968: 33–38; Marwick 1974: 10;
1980: chap. 11). According to Pitirim Sorokin, war brings about "an extensive redistribution
of wealth" among groups and individuals within society (1927: 338) and "sudden changes
in the relative strength and position of various political parties, social estates and classes"
(1969: 501). In time of war, "the social rise of the poor and the disenfranchised and the social
sinking of wealthy and privileged groups, is more intensive than in time of peace" (1927:
348–49). Schumpeter, in a similar observation, noted that the transformation of social orders
is often accelerated by major wars (1976: 419).

[70] The new weapon involved "masses raised by universal conscription, armed and equipped by
large-scale state-intervention in industry" (Howard 1961: 9). For an overview of this issue,
see Howard 1961: 8–39. For the changes in France in 1870 and their connection to the rising
of the Paris Commune, see Taithe 2001: esp. 6–13, 22–28, 38–47. Russia conscripted large
numbers of men for the Crimean War, but contrast a description of the forces raised in Russia
for that war (Royle 1999: 91–92) with the account of France in 1870–71 (Taithe 2001).

the region was wholly transformed. While previous regional conflagrations had been followed by restorations (e.g., the Napoleonic Wars, the revolutions of 1830 and 1848, and World War I), the decisive shift in the balance of class power in Europe that had occurred as a result of World War II made restoration impossible. Instead, the vastly increased organizational strength and power of working classes and peasant masses and the decline of the aristocracy created the conditions for a historic class compromise and for the achievement in Western Europe of universal suffrage and the welfare state. Class compromise placed economies on an entirely different footing, leading to more balanced and internally oriented development and, for a time, to unprecedented growth and relative peace and stability.[71]

[71] Most of the wars involving European states after 1945 resulted from the attempts on the part of some West European states to hold on to colonial possessions. See Table 8.2, "Europe's Magnitude 3+ Wars, 1945–1990."

I

SOCIAL FORCES, INDUSTRIAL EXPANSION, AND CONFLICT IN EUROPE'S NINETEENTH-CENTURY MARKET SYSTEM

2

The First Transformation

Social Forces in the Rise of Europe's Nineteenth-Century Market System

Industrial capitalism in Europe grew up during the closing battles of a centuries-long aristocratic-"absolutist" conflict. Centralized bureaucratic state structures (absolutist states) were formed and originally functioned to protect the power of the traditional nobility. However, over time, rulers sought increasingly to gain autonomy from dominant groups within their domains. One way to do this was to secure an independent source of revenue through the creation of new classes. To achieve this, monarchs increasingly attempted to introduce liberal reforms that would attract foreign and minority elements to their lands and enable them to achieve sufficient freedom and mobility to generate a taxable revenue stream.[1] As the threat of new classes and state autonomy increased, the nobility sought to gain control of state institutions.

THE ARISTOCRATIC-ABSOLUTIST CONFLICT

The absolutist state[2] emerged when, between the thirteenth and fifteenth centuries, a crisis of feudalism threatened to destroy serfdom and thus to

---

[1] In France, Louis XIV (1643–1715), Louis XV (1715–74), and Louis XVI (1774–92); in England, Charles II (1660–68), who, having been educated at the court of Louis XIV, struggled to impose tax and judicial reforms against the opposition of the English bourgeoisie; in the Hapsburg lands, Frederick II (1740–86) and Joseph II (1765–90); in Prussia, Frederick William I (1688–1740) and Frederick II (1740–86).

[2] In historical writing, the term "absolutism" is used to refer to the government centralization that replaced the anarchical structures left over from the late medieval period. However, absolutism referred more to an ideal than to actual realities of government. Absolutist states were those that supposedly had a centralized administration applying laws uniformly over all the inhabitants of a territory. France, Spain, and Austria are considered to have been the only states to have actually achieved this ideal. But even these states continued to be conglomerates where rulers had to operate a different system within each of the constituent territories of their domains. Many states had foreign enclaves embedded in their territory, like the papal city of Avignon in France. Territories within a state often were dependent on a lord in another

undermine the feudal mode of production.[3] At the behest of the landed aristocracy, the feudal seigneuries were combined in the hands of a single seigneur as a means of protecting aristocratic property and privileges. As Perry Anderson describes it, the absolutist state was essentially "a redeployed apparatus of feudal domination, the new political carapace of a threatened nobility" (1974: 18). Although the state assumed some of the political powers previously exercised by the aristocracy, it did not seek to bring about any far-reaching changes in the social and economic domination of the rural aristocracy. Under feudalism, the authority to wage war, to tax, and to administer and to enforce the law had been privately owned as legal, hereditary rights by members of a military landed aristocracy. Under absolutism, the king's great vassals continued to own important elements of public power as hereditary and legally recognized property rights. Absolute monarchs belonged to the hierarchy of landed nobles and depended largely on their support. Thus, the central bureaucracy of the absolutist state operated to perpetuate the existence of the old feudal class and to make that class the main beneficiary of changes in the economy. The landed nobility was exempted almost entirely from taxes (absolute monarchies lived largely on the taxes of peasants), and it continued to own the bulk of the fundamental means of production in the economy and to occupy the great majority of positions within the total apparatus of political power.

In the sixteenth century, absolutist rulers attempted to end internal customs dues, to break up entailed estates, and to eliminate complex feudal regulations and customs that hampered economic expansion. Faced with resistance from the nobility, rulers sought increasingly to gain autonomy from them. They endeavored to induct foreign and minority elements into the state bureaucracy,[4] and they created professional armies dominated by

---

state, and customs barriers ran between different provinces of the same state. The term "absolutism" was used by those who became opposed to centralized administration when, after the sixteenth century, monarchs attempted to introduce policies and reforms that, today, are similar to those we associate with the welfare state and with progressive liberalism. Attempts to capture this contradiction in terms are seen in such phrases as "enlightened despotism" and "liberal absolutism." However, the word survives as a key analytic term in the study of early modern Europe, together with its negative connotations and the hostility that it was originally meant to express.

[3] This was a result of widespread peasant riots in Western Europe. See Hilton 1951. On various interpretations of the "crisis of feudalism," see Hilton 1951; Pirenne 1969; Perroy 1970; Sweezy et al. 1976; and Harvey 1991.

[4] Throughout history, rulers have sought to gain autonomy from their internal adversaries by developing an apparatus that operates independently of their subjects. This required a class of officials who were completely independent of society. In various times and places, rulers have staffed their central administration with eunuchs or celibate priests, estate-owned slaves, and members of otherwise disfranchised or excluded groups. Whenever possible, the ruler recruited his officials from foreigners, whose kin links are distant and who are completely dependent on him (Weber 1978: 1027).

mercenaries and controlled by civilian intendants chosen, generally, from outside the great aristocratic families.

But monarchs could not gain autonomy from the local nobility unless they could pay for their bureaucracies and armies from their own treasuries, that is, without having to make concessions to locally powerful groups. One way of doing this was to extend market privileges to foreigners and to found cities with foreign and minority industrialists and commercial classes in order to obtain high ground rents and subjects capable of paying high taxes.[5]

In the seventeenth and eighteenth centuries, this became an increasingly popular policy, not only in Britain[6] and France but elsewhere in Europe, as well. German colonists were invited by rulers in Poland, Bohemia, and Hungary and granted royal charters permitting them to acquire property and

---

[5] Eventually, these policies created a middle class nationally different from the surrounding population. Successive waves of conquest had originally left two distinct classes: one formed by the conquerors – Magyars, Germans, Swedes, Turks, Poles – and the other by the conquered – Czechs, Slovaks, Slovenes, Vlachs, Ruthenes, and White Russians, the Finnish and Lithuanian nations of the Baltic, and the non-Turkish races of the Balkans. The upper classes of the conquered population tended to assimilate culturally to the conquerors. For instance, when the Poles became the ruling class north of the Carpathians, the Ruthene aristocracy of East Galicia became completely Polonized in language, religion, and sentiment. As a result, there were Polish serfs, but there were no Ruthene nobles. The Austrian colonizers of the Ostmark admitted a certain number of Slav nobles to their number; Bosnian and Bulgarian nobles converted to Islam in order to preserve their estates and their position (Macartney 1934: 59). Elsewhere, for example, in France, the state made the productive apparatus dependent on the state and subject to its control. Later, states obtained outside sources or revenue by allowing a high degree of foreign ownership of industry and a variety of credit, ownership, technological, and marketing dependency relationships with international capital. By providing monarchs with alternative sources of revenue, these foreign and minority classes enabled monarchs to secure a degree of autonomy from traditional elites and, thus, to introduce reforms aimed at eliminating their fiscal privileges and seigneurial rights. In defense, traditional elites fomented nationalist revolutions and movements to defend local and corporate privilege (the "liberties" of the "nation") from the threat of redistributive and liberal reforms.

[6] Many historians assume that England never had a form of state that corresponded to the absolute monarchies of the continent because English monarchs could not take the property of their subjects without their consent in parliament. But continental absolutisms were also based on the rights of property. In England, the landowners used parliament to ensure that the main burden of supporting the state fell on the lower classes. In France, this was accomplished through the formal exemption of the ruling class from taxation. Parliament (in England) and formal privilege (in France) were two means of institutionalizing harmony between the needs of the state and the interests of the ruling class (Manning 1965: 256). Others have argued that England did not have an absolute monarchy because it was constrained by parliament. But, as Manning has pointed out, England's parliament was not set up over and against the state: it played an essential part in the establishment of the absolute state under Henry VIII and Elizabeth and was an integral part of the absolutist state (Manning 1965: 250–51). It survived from the medieval period and into the seventeenth century because, as a court, it was part of the legal system through which English monarchs governed. Perry Anderson appears to support this view in arguing that the centralization of royal power in England and noble representation were complementary, not opposing processes (Anderson 1974: 114; and, more generally, 113–42).

to pursue trades under their own German law.[7] The kings of Poland invited masses of Jews from Western Europe, as well as Germans, into Polish territories. Catherine the Great patronized German immigrants and encouraged substantial colonization on the Volga and the Black Sea to offset the power of local Tartar communities. The Hapsburgs recolonized lands reacquired from the Ottomans with Germans and other minorities to inhibit and contain the Magyars (Pearson 1983: 11). They lured German colonists with free land, free houses, and tax exemptions to the north of the Banat (in the Vojvodina) in 1718. The German immigration totaled 43,000 by 1770; this number had nearly doubled by 1787. By 1790, the German immigrants owned more land in the Banat than any other group (Lampe and Jackson 1982: 64–67).

As French monarchs increasingly pursued a policy of attracting foreign ethnic or religious groups to fill state offices and perform functions in commerce, trade, and the professions, these new groups threatened to undermine the position of resident groups. Louis XIII (1610–43) replaced aristocratic governors by civilian officials (intendants), and attempted (unsuccessfully) to eliminate the purchase of offices and of courts based on class. Louis XIV (1643–1715) granted the Huguenots an important role in creating the financial basis for the development of absolutism in mercantilism (Colbertism). In 1649, a year after Charles I of England was executed, the French nobility launched a revolt against these developments (the Fronde, 1649–53). Though the failure of this revolt resulted in the circumscription of their political power, they retained their ownership of land, exemption from taxation, and special judicial status.

In the eighteenth century, absolutist rulers, faced with growing fiscal crises, increasingly attempted to expand agricultural productivity and urban commerce. Especially after the Seven Years' War in 1763, which left all the major European countries with large new debts, European monarchs were concerned with undertaking a wide-ranging series of economic, fiscal, political, and social reforms: to improve agriculture, to encourage freer trade within their realms, to eliminate the privileges of religion and religious orders, to set up independent judiciaries, to substitute salaried officials for hereditary officeholders, and to improve the status of peasants. The landed and wealthy elite resisted every measure of reform and, throughout the century, were at constant odds with royal administrations.[8]

Frederick William I of Prussia (1688–1740) instituted educational, fiscal, and military reforms. His son, Frederick II (1740–86), introduced legal

---

[7] The German colonists, the new class of burghers, were "an immediate necessity in the political balancing act" (Tihany 1976: 48).

[8] The Fronde in France, the Catalonian Republic in Spain, the Neapolitan Revolution in Italy, the Estates Revolt in Bohemia, and the great Rebellion in England all involved a revolt of nobilities against the consolidation of absolutism. In France, Spain, Italy, and Austria, insurrections dominated or infected by noble disaffection were crushed.

reforms. Hapsburg rulers also introduced reforms. Joseph II (1765–90) attempted to institute far-reaching land and tax reforms, to abolish serfdom (1780) and the guilds, and to establish toleration for the denominations. The nobles were able to block many of these reforms, and after Joseph's death measures intended to improve the peasants' lot were rescinded completely. In France, Louis XV (1715–74) created a standing army (in 1726) in order to smash the autonomy of the towns and to prevent rebellions against economic reforms. He "nationalized" all army regiments, establishing a monopoly of the use of force and doing away with personal armies under the command of various local authorities (Badie and Birnbaum 1982: 108). Despite these inroads, under Louis XVI (1774–92), the aristocracy was able to retain its power and, gradually, to win a large share in administration (Lefebvre 1974: 19). Eventually, they sought control both of the central power and of local administration.

NATIONAL POLITICAL REVOLUTIONS AND THE STRUGGLE FOR THE STATE

Research and writing on nationalism tends to overlook the aristocratic origins and conservative nature of nationalism in Europe. Nationalism, in large part, is related to the struggle over religious tolerance and the status of foreign and minority elements, concerns that, in turn, were related to efforts by locally privileged groups to control capitalist development and to restrict it in ways that would preserve the traditional bases of their political and economic power. It is often claimed that the establishment of nation-states in Europe represented the emergence of rationalized, autonomous state institutions that operated to advance state or national interests.[9] But the central concern of nationalism was to eradicate the growing autonomy of the state, its institutions, and its personnel.[10]

Historically, the first European nationalisms were conceived in opposition to centralized bureaucratic reform. The English Revolutions of the seventeenth century, usually considered to be the first full manifestation of modern nationalism, were a reaction, largely by aristocrats, to the attempts of Charles II (1660–68) to impose tax and judicial reforms. The threat of liberal reform in France triggered the French Revolution. In the nineteenth century, the Prussian Junkers launched a movement for a new German state in which they could control the machinery of government and retain almost all their medieval supremacy over the peasantry of their demesnes, as well as their exemption from taxes. The liberal policies of Hapsburg monarchs gave rise to Magyar and Czech nationalism; reform-minded royalty of

---

[9] See, e.g., Wallerstein 1974: 51, 93–95, 237, 269, 349; Skocpol 1979: 203; Gellner 1983: 20, 46, 94; Tilly 1990: 14–15.

[10] On this, see Halperin 1993, 1997a: chap. 3.

the Austro-Hungarian Empire fueled German nationalism in the Empire; Ottoman reforms in the nineteenth century precipitated Balkan nationalisms (see Halperin 1997a: chap. 3).

In France, as elsewhere, the monarchy increasingly had preferred to fill official posts with technically competent and politically harmless middle-class men. However, there, as in many other countries, the nobility encroached steadily on these posts during the eighteenth century. With footholds established in the local and central administrations, they gained fiscal and tax exemptions that helped push France to the verge of bankruptcy and into crisis. As Georges Lefebvre points out, "technically the crisis was easy to meet: all that was necessary was to make everybody pay" (1974: 23). By the late 1780s, falling real wages, rising inflation, increasing feudal burdens, and bad harvests made it impossible to squeeze more from the common people. Faced with financial crisis, Louis's finance minister, Jacques Turgot (and his successors, Jacques Necker and Charles Alexandre de Calonne), insisted that it would be necessary to tax aristocratic incomes, abolish some guild restrictions, and lighten the feudal burdens of the peasantry.

But proposals to stimulate economic activity and increase the taxable wealth represented more than a threat to noble tax privileges. At stake was the growth of state autonomy; for, as Lefebvre notes, "if a budgetary balance could be restored, and maintained through the growth of national wealth, there would be no more need of erratic fiscal expedients and the king would escape from the control of the *parlements*" (1974: 24–25). Thus, the members of the aristocracy refused to pay without an extension of their privileges. They forced the king to recall that relic of feudalism, the Estates-General. They demanded that the king recognize that the aristocracy alone had the necessary rank to advise him and to command in his name; and that he grant them a monopoly of employments compatible with that rank (Lefebvre 1974: 15).

Until the French Revolution, the term "nation" had referred to the nobility and the clerical elite;[11] separate words existed to describe the whole population: *populus, peuple,* people, *popolo,* and *pueblo* (Seton-Watson 1977: 8). In the eighteenth century, the term "nation" referred to those classes

---

[11] See Zernatto 1944. From the fifteenth century, the term "nation" is used in this way in Europe. The Hungarian *natio* referred not to the generality of the people inhabiting the territory of Hungary or those of Hungarian speech, but only to persons of noble status. In the Peace of Satzmar of 1711, which ended the fighting between Hapsburg and Hungarian forces, the parties to the settlement were the Hapsburg dynasty and "the Hungarian nation," meaning "the barons, prelates, and nobles of Hungary" (Kedourie 1960: 14). The Polish "nation" under the old commonwealth consisted, in law as well as in fact, of the nobility (*szlachta*), a class that comprised about a tenth of the population (Snyder 1964: 123). Eventually, a "nation" was understood as that body of persons who could claim to represent, or to elect representatives for, a particular territory at councils, diets, or estates. By the eighteenth century, "nation" referred to those wealthy and educated classes who considered themselves alone capable of government, prestige, and power.

possessing wealth and education who considered themselves alone capable of government, prestige, and power. Thus, before the Revolution, the French nobility conceived of themselves as a separate "nation" from the French classes below them (Cassirer 1946: 229; Arendt 1958: 16). In the 1760s, the French *parlements* (bodies of magistrates drawn from the privileged classes) announced that they constituted a single united magistracy representing the whole country. Thereafter, those who ascribed to the view that the *parlements* should rule in place of the king called themselves "nationalists" (Palmer 1944: 105). Thereafter, in France and elsewhere, the terms "nationalist" and "nationalism" were put to a variety of other uses. But they continued to be used and to prove useful as a means of establishing laws and institutions that preserved the privileges and prerogatives of local elites.

When nationalism first penetrated Eastern Europe, it was used to bolster the conservative stand of the provincial nobility against imperial plans for reform and to intimidate the imperial power into concessions that were promptly monopolized by the upper classes. The classic example was Magyar nationalism, which, by raising the specter of popular nationalism, acquired for the Magyar nobility the *Ausgleich* and thereby a free hand in Hungary. They, like nobles elsewhere in Eastern Europe (e.g., Polish and Croat nobles), reserved for themselves alone the rights, responsibilities, and privileges of the "nation." In fact, "Magyar," "Pole," and "Croat" were as much labels denoting class privilege as ethnic affiliation (Pearson 1983: 32). Many of the "nationalist" uprisings in the Balkans during the nineteenth century were really revolts of the Islamicized nobility against reforms (e.g., in 1839 and 1856) that were intended to improve the position of the Christian masses, but that also infringed on noble prerogatives. The origins of the Russian Slavophil movement reach back to the reactions of the conservative element against the efforts of the seventeenth-century Muscovite rulers to modernize and westernize Russia.

The aristocratic character of nationalism was most apparent in cases where, after "national" independence was won, a foreign aristocrat was asked to become the head of the newly independent "nation"-state. Legitimacy and fitness to rule were determined not by ethnic or cultural criteria or by means of plebiscites but on the basis of noble blood. Thus, after the Walloons and Flemish peoples of Belgium successfully freed themselves from the rule of the Dutch, Belgian nationalist leaders offered the Belgian crown first to a royal heir of France and, when refused, to a German prince. Following the Greek national war of independence, a Bavarian prince was appointed to rule the new state of Greece. He was overthrown in 1862. But then the Greeks appointed a Danish prince to replace him. After Romania gained independence in 1877, Prince Charles of Hohenzollern-Sigmaringen continued to rule until 1914.[12] Bulgarian nationalists rose in opposition to foreign

---

[12] He had ruled as prince since 1866. He reigned as King Carol I from 1881 to 1914.

control of the Bulgarian administration, but then offered the throne to the German Prince Alexander of Battenberg. Battenberg was deposed in 1886 when he tried to reform the military. The throne was then offered to Prince Ferdinand of Saxe-Coburg-Gotha, who reigned until 1918. In 1905, Norwegians were successful in winning independence from Sweden, but then voted to have a Danish prince as king of their new state. During World War II, when the fortunes of war led to the establishment of an independent state of Croatia, nationalist leaders invited, among others, a member of the Italian Savoy dynasty to become king of Croatia.

Liberal and Marxist theories of nationalism associate the emergence of nation-states with the rise of a new capitalist bourgeoisie. Nationalism, according to these theories, emerged as an expression of this new class and its desire to establish the political and legal framework necessary to ensure the development of capitalism. However, scholars of both political persuasions have increasingly recognized that the role attributed to the bourgeoisie in the rise of nationalism and of nation-states (and its strength, unanimity, and omnipotence, generally) has been vastly overdrawn.[13] The urban bourgeoisie in most European states were often either foreign classes or were weak and regionally confined, and consequently dependent on the monarchy, the Church, or the landholding aristocracy.

In much of Central and Eastern Europe, the bourgeoisie was distinguished nationally, as well as socially, from the rest of the population. In fact, in the nineteenth century, the bourgeoisie (particularly in the East) consisted of foreign colonists – usually German, Jewish, or Greek, but also Polish and Italian – that were nationally, as well as socially, different from the surrounding population. Jews constituted the main urban class in Lithuania and Romania. For many centuries, Germans formed the urban class in Poland, Bohemia, and the Slavonic districts of southeastern Austria. All the larger towns of Hungary, including Pest, were essentially German well into the nineteenth century.

Obviously, where the bourgeoisie were foreign colonists, they could hardly claim to represent the nation. They were, in fact, an international class, having at their disposal an international network that was the basis of their prosperity. Their primary interest was in maintaining the autonomy of the cities and the links among them, rather than in establishing national markets. Polish industrialists, with all of Russia at their feet, took no part in the national movements of the nineteenth century. Industrialists and traders in the Hapsburg Empire preferred the great markets then open to them rather than the little markets of future national independence (Hobsbawm 1962: 166). The commercial classes in Italy did not take part in the revolutions of 1830

---

[13] See, e.g., Veblen 1915, 1959; Weber 1921; Gramsci 1949; Hexter 1961; Dahrendorf 1967; Engels 1969: 12; Luxemburg 1976: 175–82; Stern 1977; Hill 1981; Mayer 1981; Stone 1981; Clark 1985, 1986; Cannadine 1990.

and 1848, preferring the prosperity of trading all over the Mediterranean rather than the possibilities of a national Italian market.

The character of nationalist movements reflected the exclusiveness of their aristocratic leadership and aims. Though the notion that nation-states were established and maintained by popular will or consent was a central feature of the national mythologies that were developed in the nineteenth century,[14] movements to form states excluded large segments – usually the vast majority – of the population. Throughout the Age of Nationalism, most peasants were either ignorant of the nationalist cause or indifferent to it.[15] Nationalist leaders generally depended for their support on wealthy, elite elements, and made little effort to appeal to the masses. In fact, wars of "national liberation" or "national unification" were sometimes fought while, at the same time, bloody civil wars were dividing the "nation." In the Balkan "nationalist" struggles of the 1830s and 1850s, nobles fought to block Ottoman efforts to abolish their feudal privileges, while peasants fought the nobles. The Greek revolution was almost jeopardized by internecine quarrels (but finally salvaged by the intervention of the Great Powers). During the Italian wars of national unification in the 1850s and 1860s (the Risorgimento), the peasants fought their landlords, while their landlords fought the Austrians. The series of civil wars fought in the south during the 1860s probably produced as many casualties as those of all the wars against Austria fought for national independence.[16] At every moment of crisis in Italy's subsequent history – 1898, 1915, 1922, and 1943 – the battles of the Risorgimento resurfaced. In Germany, the wars of 1864, 1866, and 1870–71 were followed by a kind of civil war in the government's anti-Catholic Kulturkampf and in the divisions of aristocratic conservatives and bourgeois liberals along ideological and economic lines.

The nation-states that emerged in the nineteenth century reflected the conservative objectives of the nationalist movements that brought them into being. When state independence was won, rights were not extended to other

[14] For example, Fichte maintained that Germany came into being through a free contract of all people among themselves (*Staatsbürgervertrag*; 1834–35: vol. 3, p. 195). But, as Ernst Cassirer has argued, these notions have nothing to do with the actual historical origins of the state. They are principles of political order devised by theoreticians (1946: 172–75).

[15] On this, see Seton-Watson 1934: 221; Reddaway 1950: 378, 383; Kohn 1961: 33, 60; Hobsbawm 1962: 156; Macartney 1968: 387; Pech 1969: 153–4; Gramsci 1971: 100–103; Smith 1971: 219–20; Tihany 1976: 163; Djordjevic and Fischer-Galati 1981: 111–12, 162–63.

[16] See Smith 1971: 36, 273, and the works cited there, and also chapter 12. In his appeal to the Sicilians on May 5, 1860, Garibaldi proclaimed: "The misfortunes of Italy arise from the indifference of one province to the fate of the others" (*The Annual Register* 1861: 281). Paul Kennedy notes that recruitment for the armed services was difficult; placement of army units was calculated according to regional political considerations, rather than strategic principles; and civil-military relationships at the top were characterized by a mutual miscomprehension and distrust (1987: 205).

classes or nationalities.[17] In nearly all states, the franchise remained highly restricted until well into the twentieth century. In many states, minorities were dominated by a different nationality that exploited this domination in order either to enforce integration or to arrogate to itself special privileges, or both. Among those so dominated were the Irish, the Norwegians, the Flemish in Belgium; the Danes, Poles, Alsatians, and Lotharingians in post-1871 Germany; non-German minorities in Austria; all non-Magyar nationalities in Hungary; non-Russian minorities in Russia; the Finns, and later the Swedes in Finland; and the Welsh, Scots, Lapps, Frisians, Savoyards, Bretons, Basques, and Corsicans. Part of the nationalist crusade were the internal colonial policy of purging foreigners and various schemes for subjugating other portions of the population through language, religion, or other social identities. European states generally engaged in deliberate homogenization: adoption of state religions, expulsion of minorities, and institution of national languages.

There is no sense in which it can be said that the creation of nation-states represented an extension of liberty or an advance in human welfare. In many respects, nation-states were less liberal, less tolerant, and more oppressive than the absolutist states and empires that they replaced.[18] In fact, the linguistic, religious, and educational standardization instituted in the nation-states

---

[17] Where middle-class and lower-class elements joined nationalist movements, they did so in order to acquire rights of citizenship, as Eric Hobsbawm (1990) and others have argued. However, after enlisting the aid of the masses to win "national liberation" or nationalist crusades, elites showed themselves unwilling to extend liberties to other classes or groups.

[18] National minorities within nation-states suffered more under the tyranny of national majorities than in dynastic empires. Imperial civil services traditionally recruited on the basis of talent, a policy that could be turned to advantage by members of national minorities. In Europe, as this chapter has noted, monarchs had attempted to institute religious tolerance and freedom for minority and foreign elements to engage in trade, commerce, and the professions.

It might be argued that this discussion leaves out of account cases where nationalism has had as its aim delivering some group (defined as the "nation") from oppression by some other group (defined as "foreign"). But while this is decidedly a part of nationalism in some instances, and while benefits may be gained for some portion of the population by acquiring freedom from foreign rule, more often than not nationalism frees the mass of a population from one oppression only to deliver them to another. Immediately following the independence of Ecuador, the people found the perfect phrase to describe the period initiated with emancipation from Spain: "Last day of despotism and first of the same." As Agustin Cuerva notes, "popular wit was right on target, inasmuch as independence was going to mean for the exploited classes, no more than a substitution of the metropolitan officer with the native agent on various levels of national life" (1982: 3). Most studies of nationalism tend to disregard post-independence oppression by conationals as irrelevant to their inquiry. But persecution by conationals tends to be a concomitant of successful nationalist movements and of nation building and differs little, if at all, in its character and consequences from persecution by foreigners.

of Northwestern Europe during the nineteenth century contrasted sharply with the far greater tolerance for linguistic, cultural, and religious diversity that existed in the Ottoman Empire at that time. The Ottoman state did not impose Islamic law on its Christian and Jewish subjects. It neither compelled unbelievers to conform to the Muslim faith nor directed their lives. Out of this principle developed the millet system,[19] whereby the Ottoman state acknowledged the existence within itself of communities to whom a different type of law must apply. The Hapsburg Empire was also, at its end, more tolerant than the nation-states that replaced it.[20] The heir to the imperial throne, the Archduke Franz Ferdinand, whose assassination in 1914 was the first of a series of events leading to World War I, was instrumental in extending improved political representation to non-German minorities in the Empire and increasing their power relative to that of the Germans – the dominant nationality in the Empire. With the Moravian Compromise of 1905, the Bukovina Compromise of 1910, and the Polish-Ruthenian Compromise of early 1914, it appeared that the Empire was liberalizing as far and as rapidly as politically feasible until the very outbreak of World War I. In the new state of Czecho-Slovakia, tensions arose almost immediately between Czechs and Slovaks, and, in the new Kingdom of the Serbs-Croats-Slovenes (later renamed Yugoslavia), between Serbs and Croats. In Slovakia, Hungarian peasants were considered to be part of the "enemy nation" and were victims of political and economic exploitation (Seton-Watson 1945: 79, 297; Janics 1975). In the new states of Hungary and Austria, pressure increased on Jewish communities.

Nationalism and Imperialism

The age of nationalism and of the creation of nation-states in Europe was, from its start, an age of imperialism. Faced by fiscal crises, absolutist monarchs in the eighteenth century had attempted to increase agricultural productivity and urban commerce. The "national" governments and states that emerged beginning at the end of the eighteenth century sought to resolve these crises by expropriating properties owned by foreigners and minorities,

---

[19] There were seventeen millets recognized by the Ottoman government in 1914.

[20] While the Hapsburg Empire was not an ideal state, "before the First World War, summary trials, witch hunts, torture, public executions, secret death-sentences, concentration camps, deportations and dispossessions were unknown there; so were slave labor and child labor" (Kokoschka 1974, in Vansittart 1984: xii–xx). In describing a distant relative's relationship to his grandfather (a Pole in Lithuania), Czeslow Milosz writes that he can appreciate "how ironic nationalistic Europe seems to those who . . . had been exposed to an old-fashioned way of thinking that was far more humane than the new way, with its fanatical discrimination" (1968: 30).

and through imperialism.[21] Thus, nationalist movements called not for "nation-states" but for the resurrection or creation of empires (e.g., Napoleon's Empire, the Great Germany Crusade, the Italian fascist crusade to recreate a Roman empire, the Russian pan-Slav movement, the Polish nationalist crusade to resurrect the supranational Polish Commonwealth, and the Lithuanian national dream to resurrect the Kingdom of Lithuania). They called not for the political independence of national communities within national frontiers but for the widest possible extension of national boundaries, regardless of ethnic considerations and in fundamental opposition to the national idea. Nationalist ideologies expressed the hope of nations to extend their domination over other nations, through the political, economic, and cultural subordination of national minorities living within the territory under their control, through annexation of portions of other countries, or by acquisition of colonial possessions.

At the end of the eighteenth century, Napoleon fused French nationalism with the Roman imperial idea and, as the alleged heir of Charlemagne, united France, Western Germany, Italy, and the Low Countries in a new empire. German nationalism stressed the need to unify the German nation scattered across large parts of other states in Central and Eastern Europe. German nationalists also sought territories with wholly non-German populations. Italian nationalism became bound up with a mission to "complete the Risorgimento" (unification movement) through expansion into contiguous and overseas territories. This was a theme of Mazzini no less than it was of Mussolini.[22] Russian nationalism emerged in the nineteenth century in the

---

[21] Schumpeter attributed modern imperialism to the survival of residual political structures dating from the time of the absolute monarchy. Imperialism, in his view, like nationalism, is the expression of the tendency and outlook of the feudal aristocracy. The argument developed below appears in some respects to be consistent with this interpretation of imperialism. However, other than with respect to these points, it has little in common with the Schumpeterian view. Schumpeter argued that this imperialism was motivated by "objectless" tendencies toward forcible expansion. In his view, it resulted from irrational, purely instinctual tendencies, from warlike passions and inclinations that the aristocracy had developed throughout history (1955: 7, 83, 119, 125). This interpretation is not supported by the arguments developed below, both in this chapter and in the next.

[22] Writing in his newspaper *La Roma del Popolo* in 1871, Mazzini set out an imperialist international policy "to lay open to Italy every pathway leading to the Asiatic world, and to fulfill at the same time the mission of civilization pointed out by the times, through the systematic augmentation of Italian influence at Suez and Alexandria, and by seizing the earliest opportunities of sending a colonizing expedition to Tunis." He argued that

> in the inevitable movement of European civilization upon Africa, as Morocco belongs to Spain and Algeria to France, so does Tunis, key of the central Mediterranean, belong to Italy. Tunis, Tripoli, and Cyrenaica form a part – extremely important from its contiguity with Egypt, and through Egypt and Syria, with Asia – of that zone of Africa which truly belongs to the European system. And the Roman standard did float upon those heights in the days when, after the fall of Carthage, the Mediterranean was named our sea. We were masters of the whole of that region up to the fifth century.

form of pan-Slavism that, in Russia, was a doctrine justifying the imperial expansion of the Russian state.[23]

Hungarian nationalism did not simply call for the establishment of a Magyar nation-state, that is, independence for the "Kingdom of St. Stephen." Kossuth's program of March 3, 1848, envisaged the incorporation of Croatia-Slavonia, Transylvania, and the co-called Military Frontier in the Kingdom of Hungary, as well.[24] The Finnish cultural nationalism of the mid-nineteenth century produced a Greater Finland campaign for the acquisition of Karelia and Ingria, and a racially based movement for the greater solidarity of the Finns, Estonians, Mordvins, and other Finno-Ugrian groups. The Poles revolted in 1863, claiming independence not only for the Polish-speaking districts but for all land within their historic frontiers, including Lithuania and White Russia. In 1936, the Falangists in Spain revived the dream of resurrecting the glories of the Golden Century, of the great Catholic empire of the Hispanidad that had ruled in the Americas and in the South Seas. A pan-Celtic movement, formed in the late nineteenth century, sought to unite the Gaels, Welsh, and Bretons.

Expansionist ideas lay similarly at the core of Balkan nationalism. Balkan nationalists were interested not in dividing the Ottoman Empire according to the principles of nationality but in the creation of a Greater Serbia and a Greater Croatia, a Greater Bulgaria, a Greater Greece, a Greater Romania, and a Greater Macedonia. Croatian nationalism was expressed by the Illyrian movement, a national idea aiming at the cultural unification of the Croatians and the rest of the Southern Slavs.[25] Bulgarian nationalists envisioned

France has her eye upon it at the present, and will have it if we do not. (published in English translation in *Fortnightly Review*, April 1877, p. 579)

Mussolini shared Mazzini's hope for a "Third Rome," a Rome of the Italian people that would exercise world leadership as the Rome of the Caesars and the Rome of the Popes had done in antiquity and in the Middle Ages. On October 25, 1932, Mussolini told an audience in Milan: "the Twentieth Century will be the century of fascism, the century of Italian power, the century during which Italy will become for the third time the leader of mankind" (in Kohn 1955: 81).

[23] Not all of Russia's territorial ambitions were directed at Slavic lands. Other, Asian territories were claimed on strategic or economic grounds.

[24] Hungary, "whose struggle for national independence was so much admired in its time ... was nothing more than an attempt to assure class rule of the Magyar minority over a country of nine nationalities. The national "independence" of the Hungarians was bought by severing the Carpathian Slovaks from their brothers, the Sudeten Czechs; separating the Germans of Bratislava, Temesvar, and Transylvania from the Austrian Germans; and the Croats and Dalmatian Serbs from Croatia and the Slovenians" (Luxemburg 1976: 163). According to Luxemburg, the numerical relationship of nationalities in Hungary at that time was more or less as follows: Hungarians, 5,000,000; Romanians, 2,300,000; Slovaks, 1,670,000; Germans, 1,500,000; Croats, 900,000; Serbs, 830,000; and Ruthenians, 443,000.

[25] In 1860, a Serbo-Croatian agreement was drafted whereby Yugoslavia would be a common federative state consisting of the Serbs, the Croats, and the Bulgarians. In September 1866, the scope of this collaboration was expanded to include efforts toward the achievement

the resurrection of the medieval empire of Tsar Simeon, and fought three wars to regain it.[26] The Romanian unification movement, organized politically in 1856–57, called for unification of Moldavia and Wallachia,[27] and in the Romanian war of independence (1877–78), the ultimate national goal was the annexation of Transylvania and Bessarabia, as well. Romania emerged from World War I with frontiers very nearly attaining those of the province of Dacia to which the Roman Emperor Trajan sent colonists in the early second century A.D. and from which Romanians trace their lineage. Greek nationalism aimed at a general revolution that would result in the establishment of a Greek Balkan Empire, ruled by a descendant of the Russian imperial family (Botzaris 1962: 102–9). The Megali Idea (Great Idea) based on the notion of the resurrection of the glory and power of the Byzantine Empire was the ideological cornerstone of Greek national politics in the nineteenth century, culminating in the twentieth, when in 1936 the establishment of General Johannes Metaxas's fascist regime inaugurated the "Third Hellenic Civilization," with the Spartan salute as its symbol (Daphnas 1955).

THE NEW BALANCE OF SOCIAL POWER AND THE NEW EUROPEAN ORDER

The economies and societies of eighteenth-century Europe were very different from those developed by national states and governments in Europe in the nineteenth century. Governments in the eighteenth century had regulated local markets with the aim, among other things, of provisioning the local community and ensuring the well-being of the general population. In France, the government required that grain or other necessities be made available for sale to the poor before it was offered up for sale to outsiders. In Britain, marketing, licensing, and forestalling legislation set maximum prices on staple

---

of liberation of all Slavs from Ottoman and Austrian domination and the creation of a Yugoslav state. The "liberation movement" was to be started in Bosnia, in the summer of 1867, by means of an insurrection. The insurgents were to establish a government, convoke an Assembly, and proclaim union with Serbia. The Southern Slav state was to include Serbia, Bosnia, Herzegovina, Montenegro, northern Albania, Macedonia, Bulgaria, a large part of Thrace, Croatia, Srem, Dalmatia, Istria, Carniola, and the northern parts of Styria and of Karst (Djordjevic and Fischer-Galati 1981: 124; citing the "Circular of the Belgrade Central Committee for the Unification of the Southern Slavs Addressed to Committees Abroad," issued in March 1867).

[26] After 1878, Bulgaria's external activities were directed primarily toward the incorporation of Eastern Rumelia and toward the annexation of Macedonia. In September 1885, a secret Central Bulgarian Committee organized and launched an insurrection and coup, followed by the proclamation by a provisional government of the union of Eastern Rumelia and Bulgaria, a union eventually recognized by the Great Powers (Black 1943; Jelavich 1958).

[27] The union of the Principalities under Ottoman suzerainty was proclaimed at the end of 1857. In 1859, the representatives of Moldavia and Wallachia declared the de facto unification of the Principalities. This union became official in December 1861.

foods such as meat and grain. Magistrates (with the aid of local juries) were charged with surveying corn stocks in barns and granaries, ordering quantities to be sent to market, and attending the market to ensure that the poor were provided with corn at a favorable price. The government also controlled employment and settlement.

Governments in Europe were also active in the provision of welfare. Traditionally, assistance to the poor had been provided by monasteries and fraternities, town "stocks," almshouses, and church collections. But beginning in the sixteenth century, and all over Western Europe, states increasingly coordinated or provided poor relief. The government of England in the sixteenth century began a campaign to eliminate poverty. In step with a Europe-wide movement, it pushed for legislation to set up new institutions for poor relief and established a system of hospitals to provide medical care for paupers. In 1517, Cardinal Wolsey set out to eliminate vagrants and beggars. He instigated measures to control the spread of plague and organized commissions "to survey stocks of grain and arrange the regular provision of markets" (Slack 1990: 15). In 1536, the government pushed for legislation to set up new institutions for poor relief. In line with developments in other cities of Europe, a system of hospitals was established in London in the 1540s and 1550s to provide medical care for paupers. Legislation in 1572, 1598, and 1601 required churchwardens and overseers of the poor throughout England to raise parish rates and doles and local taxes and cash payments for those incapable of working, to set the able-bodied to work, and to apprentice poor children (Slack 1990). In the late seventeenth century, the right of the poor to relief in cases of extreme necessity ("indigency") became a legal entitlement. By 1700, England had a national welfare system.[28] France also

---

[28] Slack 1990: 22. Poor rates were universal in England, and every year remarkable sums were raised there and in Wales for pensions to the old, widowed, and disabled; relief for the ill and unemployed; casual payments to the able-bodied poor; and shoes, shirts, bread, fuel, lodging, medical aid, stocks of flax or wool to spin, spinning wheels or other work tools, and apprenticeships for children. Between 1696 and 1750, "expenditure on the poor doubled in real terms" and continued to rise until the 1780s (Slack 1990: 32–33). This was due to a number of factors. Pensions rose to meet most, rather than a small part, of living expenses, and economic crises between the 1690s and 1720s worked to "ratchet up" the rates from crisis to crisis; and there was a change in perceptions and expectations of what an adequate standard of living was and of the needs that the country could afford to meet (Slack 1990: 32–33). In addition, large, well-funded subscription charities, charity schools and hospitals, and hundreds of "friendly societies" flourished after 1660. By the end of the eighteenth century, these "associated charities" were transferring very large sums to the poor on top of the rates (Slack 1990: 52).

Pat Thane recently pointed out that "there is a real question as to whether the vastly richer Britain of the twentieth century is relatively more or less generous to its poor than the England of the seventeenth and eighteenth centuries. At present we do not have adequate techniques capable of making this comparison usefully in either a cultural or quantitative dimension" (1998: 55).

established a nation-wide welfare system in the eighteenth century (Lis and Soly 1979: 200–209). By 1770, Prussia had introduced measures establishing a cradle-to-grave welfare system that guaranteed every Prussian subject adequate food, sanitation, and police protection.[29]

In the eighteenth century, the masses were often able to exercise economic power as consumers. In England, capitalists depended on the sale of cereals and meat to millions of consumers. The economies of Europe at that time were still based on local markets and face-to-face relations between seller and consumer. In England, there was a "highly sensitive consumer-consciousness" among working people (Thompson 1993: 189) and a tradition of popular action to gain fair prices. Workers also acted to gain fair wages and to regulate their work time. During the eighteenth century, as entrepreneurs, seeking to escape government regulations through long-distance trade, expanded production for export,[30] competition for labor increased, and as it did, wages rose and laborers were able "to take on less work and spend more time at leisure without endangering their traditional standard of living."[31]

Thus, on the eve of the Industrial Revolution, governments in Europe were regulating markets on behalf of the local population. They controlled prices and wages, instituted protections for labor, and, in some places, had put in place national welfare systems. The masses were able to exercise power both as laborers and as consumers to gain fair wages and prices. For much of the eighteenth century, prices and population were relatively stable and living standards were rising. All this encouraged people to view the status quo as just, and this helped to preserve political stability.[32] In fact, from 1700 to the

---

[29] The legal measures were never fully implemented, however, because of the resistance to them of the aristocratic officeholders whose job it was to apply them. See Dorwart 1971 for a discussion of Prussia's "welfare state." This state, according to Dorwart, was created by the legislative and regulative acts of the Hohenzollern princes of Brandenburg-Prussia. Dorwart notes that, in the era before 1740, there was in every area of state intervention an "almost complete identity...with practically every area of regulation by the state in contemporary society" (Dorwart 1971: vii).

[30] British exports increased 67 percent; production for the home market increased only 7 percent.

[31] Gillis 1983: 41. "[S]tarting with a relatively cheap food supply and a shortage of labor before 1750" there existed

> a margin between income and expenditure on basic necessities which, between 1759 and 1780, was not reduced, and in many cases, must have become larger: food prices did not rise sufficiently to cancel out the original benefit; and relative labor shortages continued in many areas and in respect of many skills; and employers made no concerted or conscious attempts to reduce real wages to subsistence levels. (Eversley 1967: 220)

[32] Politics and political realms were relatively stable, ruled, as with the kings of France and England – Louis XV, George I, II, and III (pre-madness) – by men who, having no real problems or crises facing them, are recorded in history as men of little renown and character.

1770s, Europe had enjoyed one of the longest periods of domestic peace in its history.[33] However, in the latter part of the eighteenth century, locally powerful groups, seeking to enlarge profits by expanding production for export, pressed increasingly for a reorganization of economic relations and freedom of market relationships from legal control.[34] Governments ultimately bowed to their pressure and, having previously allowed changes in the institutions of property and the relationships of production, enclosures of land, and the concentration of capital and landownership, ended their limitations on exploitation for personal profit, protections for labor, including apprenticeship and wage regulations, and the provision of welfare. Europe began to industrialize with no commitment to social welfare and justice, and as it did, its long period of social peace came to an end.

The "Industrial Revolution"[35] and the End of the Peace

The system devised in Europe to expand production for export was based on the creation of a property-less class of people dependent on wages for making a living.[36] The process of creating this class began with the efforts

The century saw many changes, but relative peacefulness and stability was maintained in the course of them, as is reflected in the keywords of the age: enlightenment, mercantilism, science, and progress.

33 Between 1700 and the 1770s, no significant social upheaval disturbed Western Europe (Gillis 1983: 47; for England, see also Charlesworth 1983: 44, 48). This period was not wholly devoid of domestic conflict. For instance, sharp rises in the cost of living in Britain in 1740–41, 1757, and 1767 were accompanied by rioting over large parts of the country; and there were, of course, interstate wars (1740–48, 1756–63, 1776–83) and colonial movements for autonomy and secession (in the United States, 1776–83; Ireland, 1782–84; Belgium and Liège, 1787–90; Holland, 1783–87).

34 Textile manufacturers were opposed to regulations, taxes, and the welfare system; commercial banks wanted an end to restrictions on the free movement of capital.

35 Most experts pick the 1780s as the decisive decade of the Industrial Revolution. That sudden turn upward that marks the take-off period of the Industrial Revolution "can probably be dated with as much precision as possible . . . to some time within the twenty years from 1780 to 1800: contemporary with, but slightly prior to, the French Revolution" (Hobsbawm 1962: 46).

36 The changes that led to the emergence of this system were made possible by a shift in the balance of social power that, in Britain, France, and elsewhere in Europe, marked a decisive turning point in the centuries-long struggle of Europe's aristocracy against the policies and reforms of "absolutist" monarchs. To a great extent, this shift was a trans-European phenomenon rooted in events and trends of change that were region-wide. Throughout the region, income differentials widened as a result of enclosure movements of various kinds, the crisis of the seventeenth century, and inflation.

   Probably the most important of the factors in shifting the balance of class power in Europe was the economic contraction of the seventeenth century and the wars and social upheavals that followed. To fight the wars of the seventeenth century, European states had raised the largest armies since the Roman era (Fischer 1996: 97). The upkeep of massive and expensive mercenary armies, in addition to famine, war, depression, and inflation, drained

of larger landowners to enlarge and consolidate their holdings by abolishing open fields and common lands. The "enclosures" in England, "clearances" in Scotland, and "regulation" in eastern Germany were all part of this process, as was the consequent depopulation of the countryside, consolidation of estates, and development of laws relating to private property in land.[37]

In the middle of the eighteenth century, a wave of enclosures took place that, in England, involved a total amount of land eight or nine times as large as that involved in the enclosures undertaken there previously (Dobb 1963: 227). By the middle of the century, and in line with developments elsewhere, a fifth of the population of England and Wales was landless.[38]

With a tiny minority of the population owning, as private property, the means of production, the rest of the population was forced to work for hire in order to survive. To increase their profits while maintaining control over the masses of landless people working to produce it, property owners developed a system of production that increased the subordination of labor. Thus, production was expanded not by introducing technological improvements on a massive scale or by training and educating large numbers of workers but primarily by intensifying labor and depressing the standard of living of the masses to bare subsistence.[39] This was not a logical outcome

state revenues. In Britain, the decline of all international trade, and of the overseas merchants and mercantile interests on whom the Crown had depended, forced the Crown to rely on London merchants. This helped to shift power to their commercialized gentry allies and, eventually, to the middlemen merchants who had formed a network of domestic traders in alliance with rural elites. As a result, the struggle between aristocratic landowners and the overseas merchants and earlier mercantile interests (mobile wealth) allied with absolutism took a decisive turn. Landed wealth gained power over the economy in England in 1688; it succeeded in gaining power in France a century later (1789). In the century that began and ended with political revolution in England and in France, the dominance of absolutism and mercantilism was increasingly undermined by political changes that eventually gave rise to national states and industrial capitalism.

37 Collectively, these incidents constituted that "whole series of thefts, outrages, and popular miseries that accompanied the forcible expropriation of the people, from the last third of the fifteenth to the end of the eighteenth century." The effect of the appropriation of land by a small minority was to create conditions favorable to the release of labor from agriculture and the creation of a wage labor force "at liberty for the uses of industry" (Marx 1990: 889).

38 By that time, a fifth of the population of Sweden and Norway and two-fifths of the Finnish population were landless (Langer 1969: 11–12).

39 Relative and absolute surplus value production both yield more products in a given workday. With relative surplus value, the articles produced cost less labor than before. That is, labor is neither longer nor more intensive; rather, the productivity of labor increases. This shortens the portion of the working day needed to produce the workers' means of subsistence and costs less labor to produce each product than before. The expansion of production in Europe was based, predominantly, on an increase in absolute surplus value production. This yields more products in a given working day by increasing the normal intensity of labor: extending the length of the working day and/or intensifying work. As shown in Chapter 3, the methods

of the transition to a system of industrial production[40] nor did it represent an initial and brief stage in its development.[41] Production processes were devised not just to mobilize labor for the expansion of production but to enable property owners to control and discipline a compact and potentially powerful mass of workers by transforming them into mere instruments of production: "hands."[42] This was a radical and often brutal process that was effected through political and military, as well as economic, means. In France and Germany, the first factories were state prisons, "whose purpose was both to make money and to discipline the inmate population" (Gillis 1983: 162). Employers called into use the language and protocols of military operations. They saw themselves as "captains" of industry and their task as one of "conscripting, training, and commanding" an industrial "army" that they housed in large-scale, multifamily tenements or rental "barracks." In Prussia, miners wore uniforms and saluted their supervisors (Gillis 1983: 154).

Polanyi's description of the Industrial Revolution in *The Great Transformation* was consistent with that of the many "writers of all views and parties, conservatives and liberals, capitalists and socialists" who "invariably referred to social conditions under the Industrial Revolution as a

---

of this latter form predominated in Europe and, in particular, in the home of the Industrial Revolution far longer than is generally thought.

[40] Writers of all persuasions have observed the brutality of this transformation. But they tend to characterize it as logically connected to industrial production, rather than the outcome of deliberate choice. Andrew Ure, an early apologist of the factory system, set the tone of such discussions:

> The main difficulty in industrial production was above all, in training human beings to renounce their desultory habits of work, to identify themselves with the unvarying regularity of work of the complex automaton. It requires in fact a man of Napoleonic nerve and ambition to subdue the refractory tempers of work people accustomed to irregular spasms of diligence, and to urge on his multifarious and intricate constructions in the face of prejudice, passion, envy. (Andrew Ure, *The Philosophy of Manufacture* (1835); in Gillis 1983: 155)

But then note how John Gillis characterizes the process as one involving "the mastery and transformation of *human nature* by the revolutionary seizure of control over the human being's time, over his emotional as well as physical energy" (1983: 153–54).

[41] This Chapter 3 endeavors to show. It is generally thought that in the 1840s and 1850s, employers in Britain began to abandon extensive methods – extending the duration of labor and decreasing wages – and began to develop intensive methods of surplus value production. Doubtless, this is founded on a misapprehension concerning the consequences of the Acts of 1844 and 1850, which shortened the working day. However, with the shorter workday came an intensification of labor. As Marx noted, "capital's tendency, as soon as a prolongation of the hours of labor is once for all forbidden, is to compensate for this by systematically raising the intensity of labor, and converting every improvement in machinery into a more perfect means for soaking up labor-power" (Marx 1990: 542).

[42] Production processes, as Alfred Sohn-Rethel has pointed out, are structured in ways that enable capital to retain its control over the class struggle (Sohn-Rethel 1978a: 163).

veritable abyss of human degradation" (1944: 39). But in contrast to many of them, Polanyi failed to see or find significant the human effort, motives, and choices that created and maintained throughout more than a century the "soulless institutions" of Europe's nineteenth-century "self-regulating" market system. This was a century of greed.[43] Its institutions enabled a vast expansion of the economic surplus while, at the same time, leaving the majority of workers in Europe to face a struggle for elementary daily necessities and fear of unemployment. Between the 1760s and the end of the Napoleonic Wars, real wages declined in Britain (Dobb 1963: 239). From the mid-1790s until the late 1840s, while living standards rose on average for the whole population, severe maldistribution left large sections of the industrial population unaffected by these trends. Between 1815 and 1850, approximately one-third of the population of Europe lived below the level of subsistence and "at the brink of starvation"; another one-third lived at subsistence level but with no reserves for periods of unemployment or high food prices.[44]

Meanwhile, with enclosures, the loss of agricultural employment, and inflation from the Napoleonic Wars rapidly exceeding the capacity of Britain's system of poor relief, attacks on it continued and, eventually, succeeded in dismantling it and increasing the number and misery of those struggling to survive.[45] In 1795, the Speenhamland decision set a minimum income for subsistence and required that poor relief be limited to the local parish. But though it effectively restricted the mobility of labor and enabled employers

---

[43] Greed and its corruption of society is the great theme of nineteenth-century writers, such as Balzac (monarchist) and Dickens (democrat), as well as scores of lesser-known literary lights. There is a tendency to attribute the great emphasis on misery and greed in nineteenth-century discourse to the supposed greater measure of social consciousness at the time. But this is not so. The concern with poverty and greed in the nineteenth century was due to its unprecedented scope and magnitude.

[44] Goldstein 1983: 91. The question of whether poverty increased during this time is, of course, debated among historians. But, as Eric Hobsbawm pointed out, "the very fact that the question can be put already supplies a gloomy answer: nobody seriously argues that conditions are deteriorating in periods when they plainly do not, such as the 1950s....Indeed, during such periods the large areas of existing poverty tend to be forgotten, and have to be periodically rediscovered (at least by those who are not poor)" (1968: 91). Chapter 3 argues that figures that show rising real wages and standards of living in Britain during the first half of the nineteenth century are based on the export sector, where the methods of relative surplus value production predominated; in the rest of the economy, technological improvement came late and only under pressure of military competition and war, and workers were unskilled and wages were lower until the world wars.

[45] Critics of the welfare system demanded that the state define limits to entitlement to relief, restrict relief to the truly needy, and limit the generosity of those charged with overseeing the doles and pensions. These demands seem eminently reasonable. However, their real concerns are perhaps better represented by their arguments that charitable activities made poor rates unnecessary, and that poor relief destroyed incentives to work and encouraged pauperization (Slack 1990: 52–53).

to suppress wages below subsistence, the landowning class objected to it because it set an external standard for subsistence income. Thus, in 1834, the Poor Law Amendment Act swept away entirely the eighteenth-century social security system and placed the organization of local "Poor Law Guardians," the collection of poor law duties, and the administration of poor houses almost entirely under the administration of the aristocratic Justices of the Peace (Ashford 1992: 154–55).

With the end of governmental limitations on exploitation for personal profit and provisions for welfare, the frequency and intensity of conflict in Britain increased.[46] A series of social disturbances began in the 1770s. There were bread riots in 1766–67, 1773, 1782, 1795, and 1800.[47] The year 1776 marked the beginning of anti-machinery riots in Wiltshire and Somerset, which continued until the 1820s. As conflict was increasing in frequency and intensity, its nature was changing, as well. In the earlier years of the century, protest typically had been directed at remedying grievances, not overthrowing the system. "Risings of the poor" had been directed at "setting the price," not sacking or pilfering, and while they had "carried the resentment and suspicion of the poor against the rich," they were "disciplined and limited to specific targets" and "never acted to overturn existing social arrangements, only to adjust them in favor of the poor."[48]

There were uprisings elsewhere, as well. In 1782 (the same year as the Dutch Revolt), shopkeepers and artisans in Geneva rose up against the wealthy oligarchs of the city. There were riots in Utrecht in 1785 and in Amsterdam in 1786. In France, falling real wages, rising inflation, increasing feudal burdens, and bad harvests produced a series of bread riots that, throughout the 1770s and 1780s, became increasingly frequent and violent.[49] Insurrections and bread riots occurred at Rheims in 1770, at Poitiers in 1772, at Dijon, Versailles, St. Germain, Pontoise, and Paris in 1775, and at Aix-en-Provence in 1785. In the late 1780s, there were bread riots in Paris and throughout France. And then, in 1789, a governmental crisis

---

[46] There was not just an increase in the number of conflicts but an increase in their intensity, as well (see tables in Chapter 4).

[47] Perhaps the most well known of these were the Gordon Riots in 1780 – a week of insurrection during which the monarchy lost control of London.

[48] Morris 1979: 16. Adrian Randall and Andrew Charlesworth, comparing the Weaver's Strike in Gloucestershire in 1756, which was lauded at the time for its orderliness (1996: 8, citing the "Gloucester Journal," 1757), and the extensive food riots in the same county ten years later, describe the latter uprising in this way: "Spreading out from the markets in the towns where they seized food stocks and sold them at the 'just price,' the crowds, highly organized and surprisingly disciplined, marched around the district, visiting neighboring markets, mills, shops and warehouses to uncover hoarded food stocks and to set the price. The rioters had a strong sense of community participation. All were pressed, willing or not, into service in the work of 'regulating'" (1996: 10).

[49] Probably the most famous of these was the "flour war" in 1775 – a popular reaction to the high price of grain.

over attempts by the monarchy to equalize taxation ended with an aristocratic attempt to take over the French state. This, and a recurring round of bread riots, peasant revolts, and urban strike activity, triggered the French Revolution.

Thus, interclass conflict was intensifying at the same time as intraclass conflict, and together these moved Europe toward revolution and war.

CLASS CONFLICT, REVOLUTION, AND WAR

Workers figured prominently in the revolution. They made up 75 to 80 percent of those who stormed the Bastille (Rudé 1959: 246–48) and formed the greater part of the *sans-culottes* – a mostly urban movement of the laboring poor, small craftsmen, shopkeepers, artisans, and tiny entrepreneurs – who supplied the demonstrators, rioters, and constructors of barricades who, together, constituted the main striking-force of the revolution.[50] The *sans-culottes* emphasized the dignity of labor and just reward for individual effort, supported radical democracy in place of the legalistic revolution of 1789–91, brought down the monarchy in 1792 with their revolutionary activities, and expelled moderates from the Legislative Convention in 1793.

Aristocrats who attempted to take over the French state had miscalculated the independent intentions of the "Third Estate," which was dominated by the middle class,[51] but the Third Estate miscalculated the revolutionary power and intentions of the masses. With governments in Europe threatening to join French emigres to restore the monarchy and, in February 1792, with the conclusion of a protective alliance between Austria and Prussia, the liberal bourgeois Girondin faction of the French government pressed for a declaration of war (in April 1792, against Austria and Prussia); then, in August 1793, and in the midst of increasing social division and turmoil, they called on all "citizens" to unite against the foreign danger. Despite their fears of the political consequences of a popular mobilization for the war effort, they instituted a *levée en masse* (general call-up for the army) and inaugurated the world"s first experiment with a mass citizen army. The *levée en masse* had consequences that, if not entirely unforeseen, proved more dangerous than anticipated.

---

[50] Soboul 1958: 439–51. The traditional prestige and functions of nobles and clerics enabled them, in some rural areas, to win peasants, day laborers, and the unemployed, as well as craftsmen and artisans, to the cause of counterrevolution.

[51] The elected representatives of the Third Estate came from the ranks of lawyers, lesser magistrates, civil servants, men in commerce and trade, nontitled property owners, and other professional classes who often found their careers blocked because of their nonnoble origins. When the aristocracy and upper clergy, following legal precedent, tried to assert their ancient right to outvote the Third Estate two to one, the Third Estate retaliated: it declared itself the National Assembly and as such the sole representative of the nation in June 1789.

During the eighteenth century, wars had been the result of dynastic strug-gles for power, a kind of family quarrel within a ruling aristocracy.[52] They had been fought with "well-defined protocol by professional and armed forces recruited from all over Europe and officered by an equally interna-tional aristocratic cousinage" (Blainey 1973: 75). They brought about no alteration in social structures and thus had minimal impact on society. The *levée en masse*, however, worked to enhance the power of the lower and middle classes and, by doing so, accelerated the growth of radicalism that, during the Napoleonic Wars and in their aftermath, presented acute dangers to governments throughout Europe.

In the immediate postwar years, a revolutionary wave swept through Europe. England experienced one of the most violent periods of its history and by 1819 appeared to be on the verge of revolution.[53] In France, the thousands of men released from army service into civilian life contributed to the renewal of *sans-culotte* as well as trade union activity.[54] There, and also in Germany, Russia, and Spain, new, nonaristocratic republican, liberal, or reformist army officers sought to intervene in politics and, when they found their way blocked, joined the ranks of secret societies and radical movements (e.g., the Italian carbonieri, German Conditionals, and Russian Decembrist conspiracy). Foot soldiers and officers alike figured prominently in revolts and putsches in 1819, 1822, 1825, 1834, 1839, and 1844, and in the Europe-wide revolutions in 1820, 1830, and 1848. The army itself was seen as a tool of the left after the war: the *sans-culotte* and other foot soldiers saw it as the vanguard of democracy. The new military officers who owed their ascent to professional ability rather than wealth saw in its new forms of organization and knowledge the basis of a new social order. Thus, the new mass citizen armies of the French Revolutionary and Napoleonic Wars that had proved so effective were dismantled, and after 1815, there was a return to professional armies.

The Outcome of the Revolutionary Wars

Mass armies of volunteers and conscripts, because they were larger, cheaper, and, therefore, more expendable than mercenary or draft troops, had inau-gurated a new form of warfare. With professional armies, officers had been concerned to save valuable troops and, thus, to outmaneuver the enemy and avoid battle. But mass armies did not inspire the same concern for human

---

[52] Louis XVI was the brother-in-law of both the emperor and the king of Naples, and the cousin of Charles IV of Spain. His two brothers were sons-in-law of the king of Sardinia. The Hapsburgs ruled Austria, the Netherlands, and Spain.

[53] Beginning in 1815, England experienced one of the most violent periods in its history. On this, see Chapter 4.

[54] Labor organization had played an important role in radical movements in France and England during the 1790s.

costs, and as a consequence, their leaders pursued a strategy of all-out assault on the enemy. Thus, it has been said that the mass armies of this period inaugurated an era of "total war."[55] However, though the superiority of the new French weapon (the mass "citizen" army) was demonstrated when Prussia's army of aristocratic officers and conscripted peasants was resoundingly defeated, and though it was adopted by other states and used effectively in German and Spanish wars of liberation against the French, the new weapon, after having been used only once and with great and frightening effect, was not used again for nearly a century.[56]

Perhaps the most important outcome of this revolutionary and bloody period was the decisive end that it put to the aristocratic-"absolutist" feud. Fearful of the masses and their destructive power, monarchs and aristocracies forged a compromise based on common interests (in preserving the social order) and fears (of revolution) that would remain in place throughout the nineteenth century.[57] Monarchs abdicated their regulatory and welfare functions, and the aristocracy, revived under a new name, was given effective control of the state bureaucracy. States would now be ruled by legislative assemblies elected by indigenous adult males who owned significant amounts of property (the medieval *natio*s). Whatever reforms that would henceforth be undertaken would involve no threat to the power of aristocrats, only a reformulation of the terms under which it was exercised. States would expropriate the property of foreigners and minorities within their territories and restrict their political and economic participation. To discourage further revolutionary demands for social equality, state governments would help to create and to maintain systems of production and distribution that increased social distance between classes and that, staffed by a largely unskilled, uneducated, impoverished, and disenfranchised work force, would produce commodities, in ever-increasing quantities, for consumption abroad.

To maintain this system, states would back up existing forms of law enforcement with regular troops. Thus, in England, a force consisting of gentry and employers (the "Volunteers"), first raised in 1794 to restore social peace, operated to keep the peace throughout the first postwar decade. Beginning

---

55 "Total war" refers to warfare involving a high level of social mobilization and massive engagements. However, as I argue below, though the introduction of citizen armies during the French Revolutionary and Napoleonic wars made total war possible, except for the years 1793–1815, 1914–18, and 1939–45, it was not actually waged.

56 It was used to some extent again in France and Germany in 1870, with similarly frightening results (i.e., the Paris Commune). After that, it would not be used again until 1914.

57 Previously, in Britain, in the Glorious Revolution of 1688, "an early compromise" was concluded that had preserved "the old remnants of feudalism. The old forms of medieval England were not shattered or swept away, but filled with new content" (Luxemburg 1976: 232). After the French Revolution, monarchs and aristocracies no longer sought to activate the masses, but merchant and professional elements were willing to resort to their use. In 1848, the weapon was unleashed again. "New" money was admitted to the ranks of the privileged, and they all closed ranks against the poor once again.

in 1829, a bureaucratically organized police force backed by concentrations of regular troops was introduced into the working-class areas of industrial towns. By the late 1830s, over 30,000 troops were on permanent garrison duty in England. Beginning in the 1840s, local barracks and a state-controlled system of paramilitary and police forces were established as part of an organization headed by the Home Office, the local military command, and the local Home Office intelligence network (see Foster 1974: chaps. 3 and 4).

CONCLUSIONS

Class antagonism in Europe's industrial expansion began not in the 1920s, as Polanyi maintains, but in the last decades of the eighteenth century. Beginning in the 1770s, a movement to dismantle market regulations and systems of national welfare prevailing at that time in Britain, France, and elsewhere in Europe gained momentum. This movement, which had expressed itself previously in the aristocratic struggle against "absolutism," was carried on in its final stages under the banner of "nationalism." Thereafter, and throughout the nineteenth century, Europe experienced more or less continual conflict over the distribution of resources and the terms and conditions under which market forces operated.

Starting in England at the end of the eighteenth century, and in western continental countries around 1840, the lower classes in rural areas began to demand a larger share of the land and reduced obligations to the landlords. In the cities, they demanded higher wages and public works to provide employment, along with restrictions on the introduction of machinery.[58] As the power of organized labor grew and the strike replaced the food riot, conflicts involving labor became a continuous source of tension, leading to recurring outbreaks of violence nearly everywhere in Europe. Conflict between classes erupted for or against changes in property relations, higher wages, extension of the suffrage, redistribution of the national product, shorter hours of employment, and the right to secure bread at an affordable price, to organize, and to work in safe conditions. Enfranchisement, nationalist, and imperialist conflicts were connected with these struggles (see Chapter 4).

As labor solidarity developed, action to defend and improve living standards developed in a way that was "radically new, specifically illegal and in its practical application a direct challenge to state power" (Foster 1974: 43). Thus, as the century progressed, labor struggles increasingly overlapped with enfranchisement struggles. Nationalism, originally an outgrowth of class and social conflict, and despite the new uses that it found in the nineteenth century, remained integrally related to class conflict. Nationalism targeted foreign and minority elements. It transferred economic power to a dominant "national" group through restrictions on land ownership and confiscation

---

[58] Machinery that intensified labor and deprived skilled labor of employment.

of properties owned by groups it defined as foreigners or minorities. In this and other ways, nationalism was bound up with the struggle for control of industrial capitalist development locally, as well as of markets and sources of cheap food abroad. Thus, nationalist, as well as imperialist conflicts, were related to and interconnected with the class struggles that characterized the expansion of industrial capitalism during the century of greed.

The imposition of capitalist forms of ownership and factory production was the result not of some disembodied macroeconomic change but of a political change: a decisive shift in the balance of power between "absolutist" monarchs and aristocracies, in favor of the latter. Threatened by the extension of the market system and the growth of new commercial classes, aristocrats sought to make more secure their social and economic domination over lower classes and ethnic minorities, and thus shape industrial capitalist development in ways that would preserve their privileges and prerogatives. They initiated and led nationalist movements to block the growth of state autonomy and the power of new classes. The success of these movements ensured that civil servants would be drawn from local, indigenous privileged groups. They also eliminated extrasocietal sources of military power by eliminating mercenary armies. For example, in some newly established nation-states (e.g., Italy), the personal armies of the noble landowners became the foundation for the new national army. Thus, nationalism ensured that the coercive apparatus of the state would not have purposes and goals different from those of the dominant classes. Nationalism also deprived foreigners and minorities of their economic power and position and reduced their role in finance, commerce, and trade.

In some places aristocrats performed the role of governing and administering (e.g., in Germany); in other places a separate bureaucratic elite filled this role (e.g., in France, at times); in many cases, the role was filled by some combination of the two. In all cases, however, the governing elite of national states proved either unwilling or unable to successfully challenge the power of traditional elites and to effect meaningful reforms over their opposition. In fact, they typically developed or strengthened a variety of corporate structures that operated to give dominant classes privileged access to the state and to restrict access to the state by the popular sector. Thus, the "national" states and governments created in Europe did not bring a new class to power. Rather, they provided a new mechanism of control for traditional elites, one that enabled them to gain control of capitalist development and to channel it into noncompetitive, ascriptive, and monopolistic forms.

The "unregulated" market system that arose with the deregulation and the reorganization of economic relationships at the end of the eighteenth century was a product not of some disembodied force of progress but of concerted political action and the abandonment by the state of social commitments and responsibilities. It was not a prerequisite for industrialization, as developments in other parts of the world have since shown us. Those who demanded deregulation and an end to protections for labor and social security were concerned not with development and progress but with profit. Their aim was to preserve or create institutions that would enable them to exploit the human and material resources of their own and other societies for personal profit unhindered by commitments to social welfare and justice.

With the shift in the balance of social power, the abdication of governments from previously held responsibilities and commitments and the end of governmental limitations on exploitation for personal profit changed the nature and scope of exploitation and led to a protracted period of class conflict in Europe. To consolidate their position in this conflict and maintain their control over labor, dominant classes sought to keep labor poor (political power was based on wealth, not citizenship) and in excess of demand (in "reserve"). Gradually but persistently, they worked to destroy the market position of the skilled laborers of previous centuries who were more independent and valuable and could therefore command higher wages and regulate their own time.[59] By pursuing a strategy of expanding production largely for export, they obviated the need to furnish laborers with sufficient means to buy what they produced and deprived them of the ability to exercise power through consumer choice or boycott, as they had in the eighteenth century. They kept peasants and rural workers poor and weak by blocking land reform; monopolized domestic industry and international trade through the creation of cartels, syndicates, tariffs, and various other controls; instituted corporatist arrangements of a discriminatory and "asymmetrical" nature to place further limits on competition; and obstructed rising entrepreneurs and foreign competitors. As the next chapter shows, industrial expansion in Europe was shaped, therefore, not by a liberal, competitive ethos, as is emphasized in most accounts of European industrial development, but by feudal forms of organization; by monopolism, protectionism, cartellization, and corporatism; and by rural, pre-industrial, and autocratic structures of power and authority.

---

[59] See Sohn-Rethel (1978a) on the division of intellectual and manual labor that, Sohn-Rethel argues, is ruled by a logic of appropriation. The direct producers are no longer required or permitted to think for themselves. Thus, there is a division between head and hand. Taylorism in effect converts the machine operator into a part of the machinery.

3

Europe's Nineteenth-Century Industrial Expansion

A "Bottom Up" Perspective

INTRODUCTION

Karl Polanyi's analysis of industrial expansion in Europe focuses on what he considered to be the central institutions of Europe's nineteenth-century market system: at the international level, the balance of power system and the gold standard, and, locally, the liberal state and the unregulated market (which connects with others to form the larger unregulated "market system"). As noted earlier, Polanyi offers a top-down analysis: he starts with the nature of the overarching international system and shows how that system shaped the emergence and development of local social institutions. In contrast to Polanyi's analysis, this chapter develops a bottom-up analysis of Europe's nineteenth-century industrial expansion and market system. The previous chapter laid the essential groundwork by bringing into focus the genesis and nature of the configuration of class and state power that existed in Europe at the end of the Napoleonic Wars. The analysis continues in this chapter by showing how this social power was reproduced in and through the social relations of surplus extraction and production that predominated in nineteenth-century Europe. Specifically, it shows how local relations of production (political, social, and economic) restricted the home market for producer goods and articles of mass consumption while, at the same time, expanding markets for capital and goods among a network of wealth owners, ruling groups, and governments within and outside Europe. Thus, domestic economies remained limited and weakly integrated, while strong linkages were forged between their expanding sectors and those of foreign economies. The development of this dualistic system was an outcome not of more or less natural processes of uneven growth but of state-created and supported local and international institutions. Through local and interstate institutions (i.e., the Concert of Europe and its balance of power and imperialist "regimes"), states worked to strengthen and defend the dualistic and monopolistic structures that limited economic growth at home while at the same time facilitating and defending an aggressive expansion of markets abroad. Dualism preserved the political and economic bases of traditional groups by restricting growth to within the constraints posed by the concentration of capital and land ownership. In so doing, it also generated the structural distortions that, collectively, are erroneously associated exclusively with third-world "dependent" development.

THE DUAL ECONOMY

Dual economy models were developed to explain the economies of colonial countries. Their most characteristic feature is the existence of an island of Western economic institutions and organizations surrounded by traditional communities and institutions and an underdeveloped economy. According to liberal models, this dualism is characteristic of the initial stages of industrial development and arises as a result of more or less automatic processes of unbalanced growth between rural and urban or between successful and less successful sectors of the economy. A dynamic sector emerges within the larger traditional economy. Eventually, it disseminates its growth-stimulating effects throughout the traditional sector. In this way, it acts as the "leading sector" or "engine of growth" for the entire economy: as industrial life diffuses outward from the dynamic sector, the "traditional" sector declines and, eventually, disappears.[1]

But, neo-Marxist, dependency, and world systems analyses reject the application of this conception of dualism to the colonial economy (note: but *not* its application to the earlier development of Western economies!). In colonial economies, they point out, the modern economic sector fails to transform the rest of society and slave and feudal relations combine and coexist with capitalist and state-owned enterprises.[2] They argue that, while industrializing countries in the West had leading sectors that were essentially indigenous and closely interwoven with the other sectors of the economy (e.g., cotton textiles in the British "take-off" from 1783 to 1803, railroads in France from 1830 to 1860), the leading sectors found in contemporary developing countries are imposed by external agents[3] acting on behalf of the reproductive

[1] See, e.g., Rostow 1971 for the development and employment of the model and, specifically, of the concept of "leading sector." In the 1950s and 1960s, the notion of dualism had come into use in analyses that focused on the survival and persistence of traditional low-wage sectors both in developing and in developed states (Boeke 1953; Schatz 1956: 419–32; Amuzegar 1966: 651–61; Jorgenson 1966). It also later appeared in discussions of "corporatism" in Europe, as well as in Latin America, and discussions of "state capitalist" and "state socialist" systems in both Europe and the third world. For an introduction and bibliography on these perspectives, see Meier 1970: 125–88.

[2] See, e.g., Dos Santos 1970; Frank 1970; Amin 1974, 1976; Cardoso and Falleto 1979; Sunkel 1993.

[3] Imposed originally through colonialism and imperialism and, after decolonization, maintained and reproduced through various forms of neocolonialism.

requirements of advanced capitalist economies. These sectors remain largely alien to the other sectors, and the sectorally uneven capitalist development that results restricts the growth of the domestic economy. The foreign-oriented "corporate" sector encompasses all capital-intensive enterprise, whether in industry or in agriculture, utilities, transport, and the civil service. There, reproducible capital, financial profit, and wage relations exist on an appreciable scale. But there is no investment beyond the enclave – profits are either reinvested there or exported; improvements in technology do not diffuse outward to agriculture or to cottage industry. What income distribution takes place is confined to the corporate sector and does not occur between it and the noncorporate sector. Thus, the economy as a whole is characterized by a lack of internal structural integration and dependency on outside capital, labor, and markets.

Some theorists conceptualize this pattern of contemporary third-world development as emerging from the "internationalization of the domestic market." This happens because within third-world countries, there forms an "internationalized bourgeoisie" dominated by its "transnational kernel" (Sunkel 1973: 146) – "a complex of activities, social groups and regions in different countries...closely linked transnationally through many concrete interests as well as by similar styles, ways and levels of living and cultural affinities" (Cardoso and Faletto 1979: 135). This provides a good description of Europe's nineteenth- and early twentieth-century industrial expansion. In fact, dual economies and all the structures we associate with "dependent" development were as common to Europe before the world wars as they are to the contemporary third world.[4] Dualism and dependent development in both places was actively and dynamically perpetuated by local and transnational class relations and processes of class formation common both to Europe and to the developing world today. Elites in both places sought to preserve their wealth and privileges by avoiding the development of the domestic market

---

[4] As Phyllis Deane and many others have pointed out, a "distinctive and significant dimension" of British industrial growth was "the extent to which it was dependent on the international economy both for material inputs and for final demand" (Deane 1979: 294). The crucial input in Britain's cotton industry (its "leading sector"), cotton, was imported, so linkages were with foreign rather than domestic industries. Deane elaborates on this:

> It was a long time before cotton manufacture became a major consumer of coal. The industry was highly localized so that it did not create a spreading demand for new transport and building facilities. It was not until the second quarter of the nineteenth century that a textile-machinery industry developed on any scale. In short, the industry's links with other major producing sectors were quite limited and its repercussions on the rest of the economy were largely indirect.

The significance of these repercussions, Deane notes, "must remain a matter of judgment rather than measurement" (1979: 102). One of the aims of this chapter is to assess the significance of Britain's textile and other staple export industries for the rest of the British economy.

(and the social externalities associated with it) and depending, instead, on exogenous inputs and consumption as a means of expanding production and accumulating capital.

Many scholars claim that while, in the third world, dependent development prevented the indigenous bourgeoisie from acquiring either political or economic hegemony, in Britain, industrial development was "promoted and led by an independent capitalist middle class which fought against the old aristocracy as well as against the restrictive power of the state" (Chirot 1977: 223). Both Britain and France had had eighteenth-century "bourgeois revolutions" when middle-class elements (the Independents in the English Revolution and the Montagnards in the French Revolution) fought and won a struggle for state power against merchant and financial monopolists that had originated in the feudal land aristocracy (the Royalists and Monarchists of the English and French revolutions).[5] Barrington Moore argued that, as a result, Britain had a "fully capitalist bourgeoisie" in the nineteenth century that, with minimum help from the state, was able to "convert a large part of the globe into [its] trading area" (1966: 32). But, as Chapter 2 argued, it was the aristocracy that led and won the revolt against absolutism, both in Britain and elsewhere in Europe, and though concessions were granted to wealthy nonaristocratic industrialists after the 1848 revolutions, the aristocracy remained the dominant faction of the bourgeoisie throughout the nineteenth and early twentieth centuries. In consequence, it was the traditional elites that led capitalist development in Europe and formed the basis of its "capitalist class."[6]

Many have argued that this elite had become bourgeoisified by the eighteenth or nineteenth century. However, throughout the nineteenth century, the most effective elites were traditional and aristocratic, land owning and rent receiving, and oligarchic. This elite dominated the state apparatus and used it to channel industrial expansion into noncompetitive, ascriptive, monopolistic forms that ensured the continuity of rural, pre-industrial, feudal, and autocratic structures of power and authority. Thus, despite the claim that the establishment of nation-states in Europe represented the emergence of rationalized, "autonomous" state institutions that operated to advance "state" or "national" interests, and the large and influential body of writing concerning the "new" liberal age, the end of absolutism and the creation of the bourgeois state and bourgeois law did not bring about the separation of economic (class) power from political (state) power but, rather, a structure

---

[5] In England, the upper class closed ranks during the Napoleonic Wars against the menace of radicalism and revolution. Moore argues, however, that this reactionary phase was relatively brief, and "movement towards a freer society commenced anew during the nineteenth century" (1966: 31).

[6] The position remains true, however, for the United States, New Zealand, Canada, Australia, and perhaps for South Africa, as well.

of power that fused both for extraction of surplus, locally and abroad, by extra-economic compulsion.[7]

Table 3.1 lists (1) indices of a landowning elite that is (a) "commercialized and bourgeoisified" and (b) "pre-bourgeois." Listed also are (2) indices of modes of surplus-value extraction that reflect the character of (a) bourgeois and (b) pre-bourgeois classes. The following sections of this chapter argue that the characteristics shown in boldface in Table 3.1 were those that predominated in Britain throughout the nineteenth century.

The predominant characteristics of Britain's nineteenth-century industrial development are those listed under 2a and 2b. If 1a and 2a were substantial and increasing, these would suggest a bourgeoisified landowning class; their absence suggests an incomplete "bourgeois revolution" and social transformation.

Table 3.2 lists features that depict structures of class and state power and patterns of industrial development that overlap and are associated with a complete and an incomplete "bourgeois revolution." The features related to a successful revolution are those associated with conventional accounts of European industrial development (referred to here as the "European" model); those related to an incomplete bourgeois revolution are associated with the "dependency" model. The following sections of this chapter argue that the characteristics that are in boldface in Table 3.2 are those that predominated in Britain throughout the nineteenth century.

To further investigate these aspects of development and the character of Britain's nineteenth-century industrial expansion, we turn, next, to a consideration of the domestic market.

DOMESTIC MARKETS

It is generally assumed that foreign trade was the primary engine of economic growth in England in the eighteenth century and the major cause of its Industrial Revolution. The verdict of more recent scholarship, however, is that, while this trade was significant, it was the home market that gave the impetus to industrial growth in England between 1750 and 1780.[8] The proportion of Britain's industrial output consumed at home – four-fifths at the beginning of the century – was still about two-thirds at the end of it (Cole 1981: 39). The ratio of exports to gross national product for the

[7] This compulsion was in the form, locally, of the state-controlled system of paramilitary and police forces and concentrations of regular troops on permanent garrison duty, in the working-class areas of industrial towns; elsewhere, in the form of the opening up and control of territories for exploitation by armed aggression.

[8] "Between 1750 and 1780, the overseas market did not play a major role in providing the justification of the expansion for the country as a whole. If for some sectors, and some areas, exports were already vitally important, this certainly was not known to those responsible for the conduct of other sectors" (Eversley 1967: 221; see also Mathias 1983: 16, 94).

TABLE 3.1. *The Nature of Britain's "Bourgeois Revolution": Two Models Compared (**boldface** indicates characteristics that predominated throughout the nineteenth century)*

1. The landowning class	
a. Commercialized, bourgeoisified	*b. Pre-bourgeois*
• Willingness to sell land for money	• **Concentration of land ownership**
• Peasants transformed into a rural proletariat based on wage labor	• **Incomplete proletarianization of peasants; wages in kind; highly repressive labor conditions**
• Use of mechanized harvesting	• **Limited mechanization of agriculture**
• **Diversification of assets: speculation in nonlanded assets (stocks and bonds)**	• Landowner assets remain in landed property
• Commercialized distribution of crops	• **High-cost, single-crop, staple agriculture; a lack of flexibility in switching crops**[a]
• Commodification of agriculture: large-scale marketing of crops on a regional and global scale	• **Production for local consumption**

2. The mode of production	
a. Capitalist	*b. Pre-capitalist*[b]
• Labor is (1) free of feudal obligations, (2) **dispossessed (separated from the means of production)**	• Labor is (1) **bound by feudal obligations**, (2) in possession of means of production
• Surplus extracted from the dispossessed producer by economic "coercion"	• **Surplus extracted from the dispossessed producer by extra-economic compulsion**
• Generalized commodity production (production primarily for sale; labor power itself a commodity)[c]	• **Self-sufficient localized economy supplemented by simple circulation of commodities**
• Extended reproduction of capital and rise of organic composition of capital[c]	• **Simple reproduction where surplus is largely consumed**

[a] This was true of wheat production, for example, which comprised half of Britain's grain output in 1870 (Mathias 1983: 316).
[b] Based on the feudal mode of production, in which heavy extraction of surplus from small producers is applied through extra-economic coercion, and economic growth is primarily extensive – through the expansion of the area under cultivation.
[c] Found only in industrial sectors producing for export, as discussed below.

TABLE 3.2. *The Nature of Britain's Nineteenth-Century Industrial Expansion: Two Models Compared (**boldface** indicates characteristics that predominated throughout the nineteenth century)*

The "European" model	The "dependency" model[a]
Structure of class and state power	
• Strong, independent, industrial capitalist bourgeoisie	• **Alliance of capitalist bourgeoisie, the state, and the landholding aristocracy (and multinational corporations)**
• Separation of economic (class) power from political (state) power; creation of bourgeois state and bourgeois law	• **Fusion of economic power and political (state) power for extraction of surplus**
The industrial sphere	
• Liberal, competitive "bourgeois" ethos	• **Aristocratic values**
• Industrial competition	• **Monopolization of industry**
• Development of a domestic market for the products of national industry	• **Limited, weakly integrated domestic economy; strong linkages between sectors of it and foreign economies (dualism)**
• Diversified industrial structure with numerous linkages, including economically strategic capital goods industries	• **Dependence on a narrow range of export goods and a few trading partners**
• Diversification of the export structure, trade partners, and sources of capital and technology	• **Dependence on foreign supply of important factors of production (technology, capital)**
• Diffusion and more egalitarian distribution of purchasing power and assets	• **Inequality of income and land structures; growing gap between elites and masses**
• **"National" control over the investment of capital and the accumulation process**	• Limited developmental choices

[a] The following is a more complete list of elements that comprise "dependent development": 1. a history of colonialism; 2. the condition of being less developed and not yet well-integrated nation-states in an international environment dominated by more developed and homogeneous states; 3. dualism (i.e., the lack of integration of various parts of the domestic economy due to strong linkages between portions of the economy and foreign economies); 4. dependence on a narrow range of export goods and a few trading partners; 5. dependence on the foreign supply of important factors of production (technology, capital); 6. specialization in the production of raw materials and primary crops; more generally, limited developmental choices – the magnitude of a country's capacity for setting its own developmental course; 7. inequality (of both income and land tenure structures) and a growing gap between elites and masses; 8. absence of an independent indigenous capitalist bourgeoisie and a dominant role for the state in development; and 9. "formal" but inauthentic, partial, and unstable democracy.

An extended discussion of each of these is in Halperin 1997a, along with a refutation of the "incommensurability thesis" and arguments why colonialism and the nature and structure of international relations before and after World War II do *not* represent a bar to the application of the dependency model to European development before 1945.

British economy over the eighteenth century was about 8.4 percent in 1700, growing to 14.6 percent in 1760 (falling to 9.4 percent in 1780) and then increasing to about 15.7 percent in 1801 (Engerman 1994; see also Cole 1981: 38). Thus, the value of Britain's home trade was also far greater than its foreign trade in the eighteenth century (Ashton 1955: 63).

In fact, during the eighteenth century, England's breakthrough in production was equaled by one of home consumption. Britain's industrial output quadrupled during the century, and the bulk of this output was mass consumption goods. As McKendrick, Brewer, and Plumb have argued, it is "extremely improbable that all this extra consumption could be absorbed by the top layers of income" (1982: 29). In the course of the century, there was a marked improvement in the variety and quality of household furnishings, decorations, and "luxury" items among artisans and farmers. In fact, in Britain, "a greater proportion of the population than in any previous society in human history" was able "to enjoy the pleasures of buying consumer goods" and "not only necessities, but decencies, and even luxuries."[9]

Despite the growth of the domestic market in the eighteenth century, and the fact that at the end of the Napoleonic Wars abundant opportunities remained for investment and the expansion of production for home consumption, in the nineteenth century, the home market ceased to play a major role in Britain's industrialization.

Production for Export

Though the export of manufactured goods had accounted for only a small proportion of Britain's industrial output in the eighteenth century, foreign trade had expanded more rapidly than did the economy as a whole. Deane and Cole calculated that, if we start at the year 1700 with a base of 100 for all industries, by 1800 the export industries grew to 544, whereas the home industries grew to 152 and agriculture to 143 (1967: 78; Mathias 1983: 94). In other words, those industries oriented to foreign trade rose by 444 percent during the eighteenth century, while those industries oriented to domestic industry rose by 52 percent.

Export industries continued to expand faster than the economy as a whole throughout the nineteenth century. This is shown by comparing British industries that remained overwhelmingly dependent on home consumption (flour milling, bread, biscuits and pastry, the home meat trade, sugar

---

[9] By 1801, the home market accounted for about £90 million per annum or about £40 per household. Even allowing for inflation, this suggests a significant increase in per capita consumption of home products, and although obviously all householders did not reach this average, it is extremely improbable that all this extra consumption could be absorbed by the top layers of income (McKendrick, Brewer, and Plumb 1982: 29; see also Thirsk 1978).

TABLE 3.3. *Mean Coefficient of Growth of Selected U.K.*
Industries, 1781–1913

Industries producing largely for export		Industries producing largely for the home market	
Iron and steel products	4.2	Sugar	2.1
Pig iron	4.2	Bread and pastry	1.1
Coal	3.1	Flour	0.8
Cotton fabrics	3.0	Meat products[a]	0.8
Cotton yarn	2.8	Leather	0.1
Woolen fabrics	1.8		
TOTAL	3.2		1.0

[a] Figure is for 1855–1913.
Source: Hoffmann 1955: 83, 85.

production, and leather manufacture)[10] with those that relied mainly on export markets: cotton and woolen industries, iron and steel, shipbuilding, heavy engineering, coal mining, glass and earthenware, and jute industries.

Table 3.3 shows a breakdown of the two types of industries between 1781 and 1913. As these figures show, before World War I the output of Britain's export industries grew at a relatively quicker rate than that of industries producing for home consumption. As Chapter 8 shows, after World War I, this changed, and after World War II and until the 1960s, the proportion of resources devoted to exports declined. All of this begs the following question. After providing the means for the take-off of British industrial production, and long before it had been exhausted as a market for goods and capital, why did Britain's domestic economy cease to expand so that in 1914, it was undermechanized and poorly integrated relative to other advanced countries?

Aspects of the domestic economy relevant to an answer are considered below. The first issue to be considered is the structure of landholding and the increasing concentration of both land and the industrial sphere. Second is a discussion of the predominant methods of surplus extraction in industries producing goods for domestic household consumption and, specifically, their dependence on (1) wage levels and standards of employment that prevented workers from improving their standard of consumption and (2) traditional manufacturing. Finally, the question of underinvestment in the domestic economy and the export of capital is considered. While this is perhaps the issue that *first* comes to mind in contemplating the stagnation of Britain's domestic market, the debates about Britain's nineteenth-century foreign investment are best considered in light of the other issues, and so they are discussed first.

---

[10] This excludes goods produced both for the home market and for export: e.g., high-quality furniture, tools and utensils, glass, and building materials.

The Structure of Landholding

In nineteenth-century Britain, as is typical throughout the contemporary third world today, the structure of landholding and the low productivity of the labor force engaged in growing food for home consumption limited industrial production for the home market (see, e.g., Lewis 1978a: 224). Throughout the nineteenth century, the larger landowners continued to enlarge and consolidate their holdings. In 1897, some 175,000 people owned ten-elevenths of the land of England, and forty million people the remaining one-eleventh.[11] The landless rural population subsisted on low wages. The rest subsisted on small plots of land; these produced few crops for export or sale to industry, as most farmers had no access to loan capital for the purchase of tractors, metal plows, or chemical fertilizers. The majority of farms in England and Wales possessed neither a tractor nor a milking machine until World War II, despite their having been available for some thirty years or more. They remained relatively small and investment in them relatively low. As late as 1935, some 18 percent of all agricultural holdings comprised less than five acres, and a further 45 percent less than fifty acres.[12] On the eve of World War I, more than 60 percent of the adult agricultural laborers of the kingdom received less than the amount necessary for the maintenance of a laborer and his family on workhouse fare.[13]

A series of official inquiries undertaken in Britain during the 1870s and 1880s had revealed for the first time the extent of the territorial monopoly and collective wealth of landowners and had led to widespread demands for changes in the distribution and control of property and for much heavier taxation of unearned incomes.[14] There was an unprecedented upsurge in agrarian agitation and protest in many parts of the country. Tenants turned against their landlords, frequently refused to pay their rents, and stridently demanded an end to the system of great estates (Cannadine 1990: 36).

---

[11] Romein 1978: 195. In 1900, less than 1 percent of the population owned more than 40 percent of the land of Austria, Hungary, Romania, Germany, and Poland; less than 4 percent of the population owned 25 percent of the land of Denmark and France. Ten percent of landowners held 85 percent of Italy; less than 1 percent of the landowners controlled over 40 percent of the land of southern and central Spain (Goldstein 1983: 240).

[12] Benson 1989: 19. In France, the small peasant plots were inadequate to the needs of their owners and their size made it impossible to introduce the kinds of improvements needed to make them more productive. Production continued to be for local rather than national consumption.

[13] According to a semi-official Land Enquiry Committee report in 1912; cited in Ogg 1930: 174.

[14] An inquiry begun in 1871 resulted in a report published in 1876 entitled *Return of the Owners of Land*. Two further government inquiries followed during the 1880s, conducted by the Royal Commission on the Housing of the Working Classes and the Select Committee on Town Holdings. For a discussion of these inquiries and the responses to them, see Cannadine 1990: 54–87.

The culmination of these events came when Lloyd George, in his "Land Campaign" of 1912–14, launched an attack on the rural and the urban landowners. However, consideration of agrarian reform was postponed by the outbreak of war in 1914. In Britain, as in nearly all of Europe, serious agrarian reform did not take place until after World War II. When blockade and the shortage of shipping during World War II made it necessary to expand domestic food production, within five years British agriculture changed from one of the least to one of the most mechanized of farming systems in advanced countries. Arable acreage increased by 50 percent and the number of tractors and combine harvesters on British farms multiplied almost fourfold. Food imports decreased by half, and home output almost doubled with only about a 10 percent increase in the workforce (Hobsbawm 1968: 204–5).

Until World War II, increasing land concentration and the resulting inequalities in the distribution of wealth prevented the development of an internal market and a wider spread of economic growth. As in most of Europe, Britain's land tenure system left most peasants too poor to buy consumer goods. As Weber observed, landlords in Europe "confiscate[d] much of the purchasing power of the agricultural masses that could contribute toward the creation of a market for industrial products" (Weber 1978: 1101). Between 1870 and 1914, rural poverty was a significant factor in fueling a massive emigration of some 35 million Europeans from the region. On the eve of World War I, agrarian reform remained the most important problem confronting Britain (as well as France, Germany, Russia, and Eastern and Southern Europe).[15]

The Concentration of the Industrial Sphere

Like its agriculture, Britain's financial and industrial sectors were bound by monopoly and restriction. The regulative, protective system of mercantilism was only selectively dismantled, and by the end of the nineteenth century, there was a full-blown return to monopoly and regulation. The City of London, in which greater fortunes were made than in the whole of industry, remained "enmeshed in a pseudo baronial network of gentlemanly noncompetition."[16] Friedrich Engels made these observations of the City as it

---

[15] Morris and Adelman have found that "sustained and widespread economic growth is likely only with above-average equity in land distribution" (1989: 1425). In France, peasants had title to land, but the land tenure system was characterized by small parcels of land, and the peasants who worked them had limited access to credit.

[16] Hobsbawm 1968: 169. One of the key concerns of the national states that emerged with the defeat of absolutism was to deprive foreigners and minorities of their economic power and position and reduce their role in finance, commerce, and trade. Thus, despite its reputation for cosmopolitanism and the fact that, in the last decades before 1914, "the rare dynamic entrepreneurs of Edwardian Britain were, more often than not, foreigners or minority

entered the last decade of the nineteenth century:

Everything connected with the old government of the City of London – the constitution and the administration of the city proper – is still downright medieval. And this includes also the port of London [which has] in the past seventy years ... been delivered up to a small number of privileged corporations for ruthless exploitation. And this whole privileged monstrosity is being perpetuated and, as it were, made inviolable through an endless series of intricate and contradictory Acts of Parliament.... But while these corporations presume upon their medieval privileges ... their members have become regular bourgeois, who besides fleecing their customers, exploit their workers in the vilest manner and thus profit simultaneously from the advantages of medieval guild and modern capitalist society. (Engels 1971 [1889]: 396)

In the industrial sphere, traditional corporatist structures – guilds and patronage and clientelist networks – survived in some places and grew stronger. Elsewhere, new corporatist structures were created. As the nineteenth century progressed, industry became increasingly penetrated by monopoly and protection. The modern cartel movement began to develop in the crisis of 1873 and during the subsequent depression years. In Britain and France, industry maintained tacit limits on competition that were about as effective as formal contracts. However, despite the strong tendency in Britain to the kind of gentleman's agreement that makes cartels unnecessary, cartels did appear there in metallurgy, milling, chemicals, and glass making (see Table 3.4). In what David Landes aptly calls "a commercial version of the enclosure movement" (Landes 1969: 247), Britain answered the cartel movement with the "combine," which grouped sizable fractions of the productive units in a given trade in various degrees of amalgamation. Combines, like cartels, were designed to control the market by eliminating competition, fixing prices, sharing out supplies, buying raw materials en bloc, and cutting out middlemen. By 1900, there were no German enterprises of any consequence, except shipbuilding, that were unaffected profoundly by the cartel movement.[17] But by 1914, cartelization pervaded industry everywhere in Europe.[18] The complex of privileged corporations and vested interests in Western Europe, William McNeil observes, had become by 1914 "quite as formidable as those of the Old Regime" (McNeill 1974: 164–65).

---

groups" – Jews, Quakers, Germans, and Americans – (Hobsbawm 1968: 169), the City of London was operated by men of English or Scottish stock and members of the established church ("anti-semitism was as widespread in the City as elsewhere in the country"; Boyce 1987: 20).

[17] Thus, in the weaving industry, while in 1882 there were no fewer than 255,000 separate undertakings, of which 157,000 were carried on by single individuals, in 1907 the number of separate undertakings had fallen to 67,000 and the number carried on by separate individuals to 31,000. This was the general trend throughout German industry. Shipbuilding was probably the only major exception to it (Ogg 1930: 222).

[18] In the interest of space, the table leaves out Romania, Poland, Bulgaria, and other countries with cartelized industry. For a fuller discussion, see Halperin 1997a: chap. 7.

TABLE 3.4. *Cartels and Combinations*

Great Britain	Cement, iron, coal, steel, industrial spirits, whiskey, wallpaper, electrical industry, cable, salt, cotton, sewing thread, bleaching and dying, calico printing, artificial silk, chemicals, railways, tobacco, rubber, munitions, alcohol, yeast, matches, copper mining, insurance, bookselling, textiles, cement, porcelain, carpets
France	Sugar, petroleum refining, plate glass, iron, steel, heavy chemicals, pig iron, coal, chemicals, aluminum, porcelain, salt, soap, petroleum, buttons, paper, textiles
Germany	Iron, steel, chemicals, electrical industry, potash, cement, coal, dye, synthetic nitrates, rayon, salt, explosives, textiles, paints and lacquers, fertilizer, pharmaceuticals, shipbuilding, weaving, wire cable, zinc, copper, brass, nickel, lead, brick and tile, aluminum, foodstuffs, sugar, distilling, paper, toilet paper, bicycles, merry-go-rounds, railway carriages and wagons, ceramic industries, shipping and transport agencies
Belgium	Coal, coke, iron, steel, glass, plate glass, zinc, cement
Switzerland	Silk, cotton, lace, dying, lime, velvet, beer, brick, granite, tannery, milling, milk, chocolate, films, vinegar, paper, wood pulp, chemicals, brewery, cement, electricity, watches, cables, rubber, aluminum, matches
Scandinavia	Timber products, iron ore, electrical goods, glass, machines, molybdenum, copper, carbide, bricks, soda, cement, limestone, granite, flour, cellulose, paper, soap, peat, spirits, artificial manures, meat, cotton, chocolate, margarine, carbonic acid, tar, jute, canned goods, tin plate, textiles, superphosphate, shipping
Italy	Cotton textiles, iron, sugar, marble, paper, sulphur, steel screws, pumice stone, artificial fertilizer, silk, spirits, citric acid, milling, glass
Spain	Iron, wire, wire nails, screws, rolling stock, pyrites, coal, copper, lead, timber, resin, cement, mirror glass, table glass, paper, rubber goods, cotton weaving, jute weaving, rice, beer, artificial fertilizer, soap, nitrate, sugar, flour, meat, canned goods
Hungary	Iron, metal, stone, clay, coal mining, steel screws, spirits, mineral water, carbonic acid, petroleum, carbide, soda, beer, sugar, glue, dyes, borax, tartaric acid, tanning materials, magnesite, artificial fertilizer, matches, bricks, cement, candles, coffee substitutes, incandescent lamps, cables, cotton, cloth, woven goods, leather
Czechoslavakia	Lignite, railway materials, iron, string, spirits, steel, chains, cables, insulating materials, jute, cloth, screws, tubes, copper, brass, aluminum goods, mineral oils, carbide cement, asbestos, bottles, table glass, bricks, glue, cellulose, paper, sugar, chemicals, mining, ceramics, rubber, textiles, wood
Russia	Coal, iron, copper, cement, sugar, matches, tobacco, salt, spirits, mirror glass, paper, chemicals, cellulose, buttons, petroleum, glue, rubber, asbestos, glass, cotton, calico printing, book printing, agricultural machinery

Sources: Levy 1927: chap. 9; Curtis 1931: 411; Liefmann 1933: 25–30, 40–41; Clough 1952: 642; Teichova 1974: 60; Berend and Ranki 1976: 311–13; Lampe and Jackson 1982: 492; Tipton and Aldrich 1987a: 29. Reprinted from Halperin 1997a: chap. 7.

Absolute and Relative Surplus Value Production

The development of mass purchasing power was foreclosed by the nature of surplus extraction in industries producing for Britain's home market and, specifically, the predominance of methods of increasing absolute surplus value production. These methods ensured that workers would operate and be reproduced as a factor of production only, and not of consumption.

Profit is increased by producing goods with fewer or cheaper workers (i.e., by reducing the cost of labor). There are two ways to do this. The first way (increasing relative surplus production) is to use machines to increase productivity, so that fewer workers are needed to produce the same amount of articles. This means that each article costs less labor to produce. In other words, it reduces the cost of labor by using machines. However, these machines require skilled and relatively valuable (higher cost) workers.

Profit increases by increasing the magnitude of surplus value, and this is accomplished by decreasing necessary labor – the cost of physically reproducing labor (the *value* of labor). Theoretically, the value of labor (the cost of goods needed to physically reproduce it) is decreased by increasing the productivity of wage goods industries. Increased productivity in food and other wage goods sectors reduces the price of those goods, and thus the cost of labor (the cost of reproducing labor physically). However, this entails the reform of land tenure and agricultural systems and also increases the value of agricultural workers.

The second means of increasing profits (increasing absolute surplus value production) reduces the cost of labor not by increasing its productivity in wage goods industries but by a variety of alternative methods. It applies large quantities of unskilled or semi-skilled labor to production as is typical of primary export production in the contemporary third world. In Britain, whole families (women and children) were put to work to earn, together, the same wage once paid to a single "head of household." When the whole family contributes to its reproduction rather than a single head of household, the employer gets more workers for no additional cost. Absolute surplus value production also produces more articles by increasing the duration or the normal intensity of labor – by getting workers to work longer or faster or by reducing the periods of the working day when they are not actually working. In Britain, the value of labor was reduced by importing cheap food from abroad (or forcing workers to consume poorer quality food, as, for instance, in Ireland, where the cost of feeding workers was forced down by making them dependent on the potato crop for sustenance[19]).

British overseas investment and, in particular, British railway, harbor, and shipbuilding for Baltic and later North American grain produced a backflow

---

[19] The use of the potato allowed workers to survive on the lowest possible wage. Thus, "for nearly fifty years a regular dietary class-war took place, with potatoes encroaching on bread in the south, and with oatmeal and potatoes encroaching in the north" (Thompson 1975: 145).

of cheaply produced and regulated raw materials and foodstuffs that did not compete with domestic English agriculture and drove domestic working-class wages down. Britain imported a third of its food after 1870, including nearly half of its bread grains (Brown 1968: 166; Brown 1970: 66). Securing cheaper food and other wage goods from abroad in exchange for exported manufactured goods cheapened labor and decreased pressure on landlords to lower agricultural prices through the rationalization of agriculture. But the mass of the labor force gained nothing; food costs decreased but so, too, did wages.

The methods of absolute surplus value production predominated in Europe far longer than is generally recognized. It is probable that they did so because landowners preferred them. Certainly, there were good reasons for them to do so. In agriculture, increasing absolute surplus value production is preferable because investment in new technology involves new expenditure on fixed capital and skilled labor. Why pay for harvesters or tractors when you can increase the number of workers at no extra cost by spreading the same amount paid for wages over a longer workday[20] or a larger number of workers (whole families working to provision the household rather than just a single breadwinner)? Theoretically, employers wish to reduce the number of laborers employed, since the cost of wages is the main item in the cost of production, and because hiring more workers decreases the reserve army. But if a worker's wife and children are pulled into the work force, and the wage paid to him alone is reduced so that the employer gains a larger work force for the same amount of wages, and the wages paid out still enable the work force to reproduce itself physically, then these theoretical incentives for increasing relative surplus value disappear.[21] Moreover, in what must surely have been the most attractive advantage of increasing absolute surplus value production for Britain's landowning class, it does not require a rationalization or reorganization of land and farming systems.

In an economy dominated by a traditional landowning elite, as in Britain, the methods of increasing absolute value production will also be preferred in industry. Here, as in agriculture, increasing absolute surplus value production expands production and increased profits without additional cost – in either labor or machinery. New machinery requires not only an outlay of capital but an investment in workers' training that, in turn, converts workers into a "quasi-fixed factor" of production (Becker 1969). As in agriculture, in industry, the cost of new machinery and relatively skilled workers could

---

[20] "The lengthening of the workday ... permits an expansion of the scale of production without any change in the amount of capital invested in machinery and buildings" (Marx 1990: 529).

[21] See, for a discussion, Marx 1990: 517–18 and, as cited there, annual *Reports of the Inspectors of Factories, Reports of the Children's Employment Commission,* and *Reports on Public Health,* published in London.

be avoided by securing cheaper food and wage goods from abroad and applying the methods of absolute surplus value production. A change in the productivity of labor does not decrease the value of labor power (nor increase the magnitude of surplus value) unless the products of the industries affected are articles habitually consumed by the workers, but a change in the intensity or extensivity of labor causes a change in the magnitude of surplus value irrespective of the nature of the articles produced.[22]

Is there evidence that the methods of absolute surplus value production predominated in Britain throughout the nineteenth century? Yes. In fact, Britain was slow to mechanize its industry, and even where new machinery was introduced, there was a tendency to increase absolute surplus value production in order to keep new machinery working and, thus, to pay back its cost (Marx 1990: 526, 530–31). Only in the export sector did the methods of relative surplus value production predominate;[23] in the rest of the economy, technological improvement came late and only under pressure of military competition and war, and workers were unskilled and wages lower until the world wars.

Mechanization. Britain's Industrial Revolution was limited sectorally, as well as geographically.[24] Its industrial breakthrough in the 1780s and 1790s involved the mechanization of only one branch (spinning) of one industry (cotton). The other branch, weaving, remained unmechanized for forty years. The introduction of the factory system in spinning, in fact, actually *increased* the number of domestic weavers (to handle the expanded production in yarn). Thus, between 1806 and 1830, while the number of factory workers in textiles rose from 90,000 to 185,000, the number of domestic weavers increased to almost 240,000 (Gillis 1983: 41). Traditional manufacturing organized around the putting-out system continued to make profits of as much as 1000 percent (Gillis 1983: 159), and as long as it did, there was

---

[22]   In order to effect a fall in the value of labour-power, the increase in the productivity of labour must seize upon those branches of industry whose products determine the value of labour-power, and consequently either belong to the class of customary means of subsistence or are capable of supplying the place of those means.... But an increase in the productiveness of the labour in those branches of industry which supply neither the necessaries of life, nor the means of production for such necessaries, leaves the value of labour-power undisturbed. (Marx 1990: 432)

[23] Productivity increased in Britain in export sectors: mining, iron, steel, shipbuilding, and cotton textiles. Between 1850 and 1870, output in mining doubled, although the number of miners increased by less than half. Output in iron and steel and in machine making and shipbuilding tripled, although the numbers of workers only doubled. Cotton textile output doubled between 1850 and 1860, while the size of the work force remained the same (Barratt Brown 1970: 62).

[24] Geographically, the Industrial Revolution was limited to the great centers of the export industry in the North and "Celtic Fringe" (Manchester was the capital of the basic export industries).

little incentive to introduce new techniques having the capacity to produce social externalities.[25] There was no mechanization outside the cotton industry. By 1850, the total number of factory workers amounted to not much more than 5 percent in England (Lis and Soly 1979: 159). "There was no mechanized transport for fifty years, no mass-produced machinery for sixty and no large steel production for seventy" (Foster 1974: 20).

There was little attempt to mechanize industries producing goods for domestic household consumption.

The building industries grew by expanding employment, rather than by introducing innovations in either organization or technology. New techniques were introduced "slowly and with considerable reluctance." In the 1930s, half the industry's work force still practiced "their traditional handicrafts, especially in house-building, largely untouched by mechanization" (Benson 1989: 20).

Though Britain had pioneered electrotechnics, by 1913 the output of the British electrical industry was little more than a third of Germany's (Hobsbawm 1968: 180). Before World War II, less than a third of those employed in the transport sector were employed by the railways (28 percent in 1931). A majority of those engaged in transport worked for a small employer or were self-employed (Benson 1989: 22–23).

Despite the British origins of the machines and machine tools industry, it was not until the 1890s that automatic machine-tools production was introduced in Britain. The impetus came from the United States, and the desire on the part of employers "to break down the hold of the skilled craftsmen in the industry" (Hobsbwam 1968: 181). Gas manufacture was mechanized late, and as a result of pressure from trade unions.

Even Britain's export industries were slow to adopt new techniques or improvements, not only in textiles but in coal, iron, steel, railways, and shipbuilding. The supply of coal increased[26] not through the introduction of labor-saving techniques but by increasing the number of coal miners.[27] In the 1930s, "more than 40% of British coal was cut, and practically 50% conveyed, without the aid of machinery" (Benson 1989: 16).

Britain was preeminent in steel production and had pioneered major innovations in its manufacture. But with the exception of the Bessemer converter (1856), Britain was slow to apply the new methods and failed to keep up with subsequent improvements. By the early 1890s, Britain had fallen

---

[25] Antimachinery riots in Wiltshire and Somerset between 1776 and 1823 "very considerably delayed the introduction there of the spinning jenny, scribbling engine, and flying shuttle" (Charlesworth et al. 1996: 24).

[26] From 49 million tons in 1850 to 147 million in 1880.

[27] There were 200,000 coal miners in Britain in 1850, half a million in 1880, and 1.2 million in 1914 (Hobsbawm 1968: 116).

behind Germany and the United States.[28] American shipbuilding expanded at a faster rate than that of the British, and by 1860, it had almost caught up. Though British industrialization was based on the expansion of capital goods production for railway building, even here, rapid technical progress, as with engineering, came, finally, only when compelled by military competition and the modernizing armaments industry.[29]

Wages and Productivity. The predominance of methods of absolute surplus value production can be further explored by considering wages and productivity and, specifically, where and to what extent these increased with the expansion of production and how they were related. There is considerable contention regarding the progress of real wages in Britain in the first half of the nineteenth century. National aggregates of real wages are no more reliable as an indicator than is national income. They often conceal important differences within overall movements and trends. In the nineteenth century, gains in real wages were often offset by the lower volume of employment that tended to accompany a fall in prices of wage goods (Mathias 1983: 198–99). A host of other relations among changes in money wages, the volume of employment, and prices bearing on the cost and standard of living for the British working class have prevented any consensus from emerging with regard to these decades (see Mathias 1983: 196–98).

There is greater degree of consensus for their having risen, on the whole, between 1870 and 1914. Table 3.5 shows Cynthia Morris's and Irma Adelman's conclusions about the general trends from their widely cited study of patterns of economic development in Europe. For British industry as a whole, there was, according to Morris, a strong upward movement in real wages between 1870 and 1890 and an "upward movement but not strong" between 1890 and 1914.

Reflecting the character of British industry as a whole, Britain's labor market exhibited a sharp dualism. In the export sectors, workers earned higher wages and worked in relatively more skilled and more secure jobs, particularly in the cotton mills and in shipbuilding, transport, and mining. In these industries there developed a "labor aristocracy" consisting of "a maximum of 15%, and probably less," of its work force (Hobsbawm 1968: 161).

---

[28] For example, the Siemens-Martin open-hearth furnace (1867), which made it possible to increase productivity, and the Gilchrist-Thomas process (1877–78), which made it possible to use phosphoric ores for steel manufacture. With respect to the latter, Britain continued to import nonphosphoric ores and failed to exploit her own phosphoric ore deposits until the 1930s.

[29] See also the discussion in Mathias 1983: 373–93. Peter Mathias concludes, after surveying arguments that center on differences between earlier and later industrializing countries, that these do not explain the "failure in innovation and development, widespread in the British economy" (1983: 375).

TABLE 3.5. *Changes in the Average Real Wages in Industry, 1850–1914*

	Strong upward movement	Upward movement but not strong	Reasonably stable – no clear trend	Downward movement
Denmark	1870–1914	1850–70		
Sweden	1870–1914	1850–70		
Norway	1870–90 1890–1914	1850–70		
Britain	1870–90	1850–70 1890–1914		
Switzerland	1850–70	1890–1914	1870–90	
Belgium		1850–1914		
France		1850–1914		
Germany		1870–1914		1850–70
Italy		1870–1914		1850–70
Netherlands		1870–1914	1850–70	
Russia		1870–90	1890–1914	1850–70
Spain			1870–90?	1890–1914

Source: Morris and Adelman 1988: 353–66.

Outside this sector, the other 85 percent of the work force, including women, children, rural labor, and migrants, worked in low-wage unskilled jobs with little security, and in poor working conditions. Throughout the century, earnings for this mass of workers remained insecure and insufficient (see Table 3.6).

If we allow for differences among sectors, it is reasonable to conclude that real wages rose higher and faster in the sectors that were more mechanized. These required a more highly skilled work force and consequently offered higher wages; they also enjoyed higher productivity.

The real wages of industrial workers are made up of (1) the productivity of labor (output per worker in each industry expressed in units of that industry's product), (2) the share of that industry's product that goes to the wage-earner (e.g., the boot maker's wage in boots), and (3) the barter terms on which these units of the worker's own product can be exchanged for objects of his own consumption.

$$\text{Real Wage} = \text{Productivity} + \begin{array}{c}\text{Share of}\\\text{wage earner}\\\text{in product}\end{array} + \begin{array}{c}\text{Number of units of}\\\text{consumables obtained}\\\text{per unit of product}\end{array}$$

Increases in the rise of real wages were linked to rises in productivity, and it was in the export industries that both productivity and real wages rose highest and fastest. The outstanding contribution to the rise in real wages came from the rise in productivity, as can be seen in Table 3.7. In Britain, the real

TABLE 3.6. *Change in Average^a Real Wages or Income of the Employed Agricultural Poor, 1850–1914*

	Strong upward movement	Upward movement but not strong	Reasonably stable – no clear trend	Downward movement
Denmark	1870–90	1850–70		
		1890–1914		
Sweden	1870–1914	1850–70		
Norway	1870–1914	1850–70		
Belgium		1890–1914		1850–90
Britain		1850–1914		
Switzerland	1850–70	1890–1914	1870–90?	
France		1850–70	1870–90	
		1890–1914		
Germany		1870–1914		1850–70
Italy		1890–1914		1850–90
Netherlands		1870–1914	1850–70	
Russia		1870–90		1850–1914
Spain				1850–1914

^{a} "Average" means that where, for instance, wage earners and small peasants experienced differing trends, these were weighted according to their rough relative importance in the population.
Source: Morris and Adelman 1988: 353–66.

TABLE 3.7. *Average Annually Cumulated Percentage Change, 1895–1913, in Real Wages, Industrial Productivity, Wage/Income Ratio in Industry, and Barter Terms for Industry*

	Real wages	Industrial productivity	Wage/income ratio in industry	Barter terms for industry
Germany	1.27	1.93	−0.45	−0.20
Sweden	1.48	2.13	−0.24	−0.40
United Kingdom	−0.11	0.03	−0.32	0.16

Source: Brown 1968: 263.

wage per head was raised, as the product per worker was, for the most part, progressively raised. However, *"the share of this product handed over to the worker himself as his wage, did not rise or fall much"* (Brown 1968: 31; emphasis added). If the product increases while wages as a share of the product decline, then workers are worse off not in absolute terms but in relation to the value of what they produce. The *standard of consumption* of labor (the mass of the population) bears no relation to its productivity, to its increased power of production. Wage earners cannot buy back what, as workers, they produce. A rise in real wages does not necessarily mean that there is an increase in purchasing power or the standard of consumption. Even where the real wage increased, "improvement in working-class purchasing power could be, and frequently was, checked by a wide range of social and economic factors" (Benson 1989: 56). While wages rose with increases in productivity, there was, as Marx predicted in his *Inaugural Address to the International Working Men's Association* in 1864, *a growing disparity between productivity and real wages.* Marx argued that, as a result of this, the felt poverty of workers would increase despite whatever might happen to the absolute level of consumption, since wages would decline in relation to the wealth of society and the ruling class.

Labor and Consumption. The insufficiency and insecurity of wages for a considerable portion of both the rural and urban work force is, of course, directly relevant to the question of why the domestic economy ceased to expand in the nineteenth century. According to the conventional view, the separation of the direct producer from the means of production creates a home market for means of production and articles of consumption by converting the means of both production and subsistence into commodities (Lenin 1967: 68–69). It creates a home market, too, by transforming the great mass of the rural population into freely mobile wage earners who then migrate to the towns and factories where their labor is increasingly needed. Urban populations depend on the market to procure their needs. A rise in urbanization, therefore, leads to an expansion of the market for mass-produced goods for local consumption: food, buildings, clothing, shoes, furniture, tools, and utensils of all sorts. In England, the growth of capitalism swelled the urban population during the eighteenth century, and this encouraged the development of large-scale shoemaking and clothing industries and led to a great boom in the building industries. The growth of building led to a corresponding boom in the furniture, paperhanging, and artistic trades. The development of factories required stonemasons, carpenters, joiners, and furniture makers. The workers had to be provisioned by butchers, bakers, and metalworkers with food, cooking pots, cutlery, and other products.

But where labor "can command only a subsistence or near-subsistence wage from its buyers," laborers are "too poor to provide an intensive market for anything but the absolute essentials of subsistence: food, housing and a few elementary pieces of clothing and household goods" (Hobsbawm 1968: 135; see also Benson 1989: 41). Thus, during the nineteenth century, the growth of the urban population slowed, as millions of workers fled Europe in search of employment and the means of subsistence.[30] On the eve of

---

[30] B. R. Mitchell (1975: 12–15) gives figures showing the population growth in "major cities" of nineteenth-century Europe. These figures show that while population growth in "Greater London" remained roughly the same for the two periods, at 58 and 59 percent, respectively, growth in Britain's other major cities was greater between 1800 and 1850 than between 1850 and 1900: Birmingham, 68 and 55 percent; Liverpool, 79 and 47 percent; Manchester,

TABLE 3.8. *Percent of Population in Towns of 20,000 +
in Europe (1910)*

United Kingdom	62	Spain	17
Germany	35	Sweden	15
Netherlands	34	Austria	14
Italy	28	Greece	13
France	26	Hungary	13
Belgium	25	Portugal	12
Denmark	21	Romania	11
Switzerland	20	Russia (Europe only)	10
Norway	18		

Source: Goldstein 1983: 241.

World War I, nowhere in Europe did the urban population represent much more than a third of the total population of the country, except in Britain, where London (in 1914) was as large as the next twelve cities combined (Boyce 1987: 18; see Table 3.8).

Technological improvements and an increase in real wages were confined to the export sectors. The vast mass of workers remained solely a factor of production rather than of consumption. The nature of power and surplus extraction enabled elites to monopolize the gains of expanded production. Thus, regardless of whether or not workers earned more or consumed more, the mass of labor worked longer and harder and their increased productivity did not provide them with the purchasing power needed for a *higher standard of consumption*. There is no question that, relatively, the poor grew poorer as European societies grew richer.

Home Investment

The final issue to address in considering the underdevelopment and weak integration of Britain's home economy is the dearth of home investment throughout the nineteenth and early twentieth centuries. In the nineteenth century, Britain devoted a substantially smaller proportion of its national output and savings to home investment than did any of its major competitors.[31] In some respects London's institutions were more highly organized to provide capital to foreign investors than to British industry.[32] Capital flowed

---

70 and 53 percent; Bradford, 87 and 63 percent; Sheffield, 76 and 67 percent; Edinburgh, 59 and 48 percent; and Glasgow, 88 and 54 percent. Bristol is the sole exception: 53 and 60 percent.

[31] Floud 1981: 12–17. There was a brief home investment boom in the last years of the nineteenth century. One of the proximate causes of the Great Depression of the 1870s–90s was an abrupt paralysis of the market for foreign loans. The result was to increase investment at home.

[32] Committee on Finance and Industry, *Macmillan Report* (1931), p. 171.

between London and the far reaches of the Empire, but not between London and the industrial north. "A limited number of firms in a limited number of industries could get access to the London new-issues market – railroads, shipping, steel, cotton (after 1868), along with banks and insurance companies. And some attention was devoted to refinancing existing private companies. For the most part, however, the flow of savings was aimed abroad and not to domestic industries" (Kindleberger 1964: 62).

The French on the whole did not invest domestically in large-scale industrial enterprises during the nineteenth and early twentieth centuries. Foreign lending built up rapidly in the 1850s. It flourished in 1879–81, from 1896 to 1913, and from 1919 to 1930. The industrial banks were mainly interested in underwriting foreign bonds rather than in lending to domestic industry (Collas 1908; Baldy 1922). Industrial banks, such as the Crédit Mobilier, founded in 1852, quickly turned from loans to industry to securities promotion abroad. After the demise of the Crédit Mobilier in 1868, the next generation of banks, notably the Banque de Paris et des Pays-Bas and the Union Parisienne, followed the same pattern. Crédit Lyonnais quickly changed from an industrial bank to a deposit bank, and soon turned from industrial lending to *rentes* and foreign loans (Bouvier 1961: chap. 6). Three years after its founding in 1863, it started to restrict its loans to industry and to lend abroad. The merchant banks also concentrated mainly on the sale of foreign securities, rather than on securities for domestic industry (Bigo 1947: 124). Like industry, agriculture was hampered by a shortage of capital (Augé-Laribé 1955: 152). The savings of peasants were drained off by the Crédit Agricole and invested in *rentes* and foreign bonds (Kindleberger 1964: 44–45).

The usual explanation for the nineteenth-century trend, in Britain, France, and elsewhere in Europe, is that the domestic market was *not yet* developed enough to absorb the output of expanded production and to provide profitable investment opportunities for surplus capital. As a result, capitalists were *forced* to seek for larger markets and more profitable fields of investment abroad. This was the view of Lenin and of John Hobson, who contended, like many have since, that Britain's foreign investment and that of other advanced countries was a result of the superabundance of capital that had accumulated in them and the consequent pressure of capital for new fields of investment. This view, and particularly the notion that advanced countries had capital-saturated economies, was current at the time when Lenin and Hobson wrote and since has been embraced by a wide variety of theorists and historians.[33] While both Lenin and Hobson were, to varying

---

[33] Jules Ferry, the founder of the modern French colonial empire, expressed the general view in this speech, delivered in 1883:

> Is it not clear that the great states of modern Europe, the moment their industrial power is founded, are confronted with an immense and difficult problem, which is

degrees, concerned with the blockages that tended to produce the appearance of "saturation," the language of "saturation" and "pressure of surplus capital," both in the conventional historiography of nineteenth- and early twentieth-century Europe and in analyses of the contemporary international economy, tends to obscure the fact that capital exporters did not have then, and tend not to have now, capital-saturated domestic economies.[34]

Lenin recognized that economies were, in fact, *not* saturated and that profitable investment opportunities could be provided with an adequate and sustained rise in the consumption of the masses. But as John Strachey notes, this was, for Lenin, only "a theoretical possibility to be dismissed as utterly incompatible with the real balance of power in any capitalist society." And this view of things, Strachey rightfully points out, "was by no means unrealistic for the Britain of 1900–1914" (i.e., the Britain in which Lenin lived for a time "and which he studied intensively"; Strachey 1959: 117). The view of economies as suffering from "overproduction," "saturation," the "pressure of surplus capital," and the need for new markets is nonetheless misleading. As Hobson makes clear, the market that was "saturated" in Britain, in 1902 and before, was the one constituted solely by the wealthy classes. His observation might be extended to argue a broader point: that the discourse of "saturation" generally and implicitly assumes that the domestic market consists solely of owners of capital and that the mass of the population is irrelevant to demand and consumption of any goods other than those necessary for their own physical reproduction.

Certainly, the two largest foreign investors during the nineteenth century, Britain and France, suffered from inadequate investment at home. Numerous scholars have argued that funds used for British foreign investment could have found productive uses at home and that, had they remained at home, they could have "helped to augment the stock of domestic housing and other urban social overhead projects that would have expanded the domestic market for the expanded output of the British economy."[35] Arthur Lewis

the basis of industrial life, the very condition of existence – the question of markets? Have you not seen the great industrial nations one by one arrive at a colonial policy? And can we say that this colonial policy is a luxury for modern nations? Not at all, messieurs, this policy is, for all of us, a necessity, like the market itself. (Speech of October 11, 1883; quoted in Langer 1931: 286–87)

[34] See, e.g., Sée 1942: 360; Lévy 1951–52: 228; Cairncross 1953: 225; Cameron 1961: 123, 152; Lewis 1972: 27–58; Trebilcock 1981. More on this below.

[35] Brown 1970: x. See also Davis and Huttenback 1988. Recent scholarship supports the view of classical liberals such as Richard Cobden and John Bright, who argued that imperialism was against the interests of the taxpaying and productive sectors of British society. For a discussion of these views, see Cain 1979. It might appear that removing the export trade in 1801 would have resulted in a lowering of Britain's national income by 15.7 percent (see the discussion of the value of British exports, above). But, as Engerman points out, the resources used in the foreign trade sector could have found employment elsewhere. If Britain had not exported cotton, it could have used the resources to pave new roads, construct

insisted that if foreign lending had been on a smaller scale and investors
had exploited opportunities at home, the technical performance of British
industry would have been improved (Lewis 1972: 27–58, 1978a: 176–77;
see also Trebilcock 1981).

In the same vein, many studies have shown that France, the second largest
investor, was technologically backward and clearly in need of much larger
home investment.[36] French investments helped to industrialize considerable
parts of Europe, but by 1914, France's total industrial potential was only
about 40 percent of Germany's, and what coal, steel, and iron were produced were usually more expensive, coming from smaller plants and poorer
mines (Kennedy 1987: 222). However, French deposit banks, while furnish-
ing capital to German producers through loans to financial intermediaries,
were reluctant to provide capital for French industry.

Not only was investment needed at home, but according to Lance Davis
and Robert Huttenback (1988), after 1880 the rates of profits on Britain's
colonial investments fell below comparable returns from Britain itself.
During the next thirty-four years, returns from overseas investment were
"far below what presumably could have been earned by devoting the same
resources to the expansion of domestic industry." In general, these investments were also exposed to more risk than domestic investments.

Noting that "every advanced industrial nation has been tending to place a
larger share of its capital outside the limits of its own political area, in foreign
countries, or in colonies, and to draw a growing income from this source,"
Hobson argued that there was a strong tendency for Britain to generate too
little consumption and too much savings. Too little of the national income
was allocated to wage earners who did most of the nation's consumption,
and too much income was allocated to property owners who did most of the
nation's saving (1902: 51). He wrote that if the mass public

> raised its *standard of consumption* to keep pace with every rise of productive powers,
> there could be no excess of goods or capital.... Foreign trade would indeed exist,
> but there would be no difficulty in exchanging a small surplus of our manufactures
> for the food and raw material we annually absorbed, and all the savings that we
> made could find employment, if we chose, in home industries. (Hobson 1902: 81;
> emphasis added).

---

new buildings, or make beer. "As McCloskey reminds us, 'exports are not the same thing as
new income. They are new markets, not new income'" (Engerman 1994). For Germany, see
Wehler 1969; for France, see Langer 1931 and Wesseling 1997.

[36] A. K. Cairncross asserts that French industry was "starved for capital" (1953: 225). The
issue was a matter of debate from at least the 1830s. See Cameron 1961: 123, 152; and, for
citations, Landes 1954: 260n9. Henri Sée believes that foreign lending was a handicap to
French development after 1896, especially to agriculture (1942: 360). Maurice Lévy blamed
foreign lending for capital shortage, especially in the chemical industry and in urban transport
(1951–52: 228). Agriculture was also hampered by a shortage of capital (Augé-Laribé 1955:
152) as the savings of peasants were drained off by the Crédit Agricole and invested in *rentes*
and foreign bonds (Kindleberger 1964: 44–45).

Thus, "It is not industrial progress that demands the opening up of new markets and areas of investment, but mal-distribution of consuming power which prevents the absorption of commodities and capital within the country" (Hobson 1902: 85).

While Hobson saw this as a typical consequence of capitalism, he argued it was not a *necessary* one. "Home markets," he argued, "are capable of indefinite expansion" given "a constantly rising standard of national comfort. . . . Whatever is produced in England can be consumed in England, provided that the 'income' or power to demand commodities, is properly distributed" (1902: 88). If the Industrial Revolution had taken place "in an England founded upon equal access by all classes to land, education and legislation," then

foreign trade would have been less important . . . the standard of life for all portions of the population would have been high, and the present rate of national consumption would probably have given full, constant, remunerative employment to a far larger quantity of private and public capital than is now employed.

Instead, more than a quarter of the population of British towns "is living at a standard that is below bare physical efficiency" (1902: 86).

World systems and dependency theorists would agree with Hobson that the colonial trade was not necessary as a means of securing markets for surplus goods and capital. However, they contend that colonialism was necessary nonetheless. It provided a means of acquiring essential raw materials at favorable terms of trade and, thus, was crucial to the industrialization of Europe as a means both of acquiring raw materials and of accumulating capital (see, e.g., Wallerstein 1974: 38, 51, 93–95, 237, 269, 349).

This contention has become the focus of considerable dispute. According to P. K. O'Brien (1982), England's trade with the periphery, and the profits from it, made up still too small a percentage of its total economy to explain its expansion through the eighteenth century. Paul Bairoch has argued that the "core" countries had an abundance of the minerals of the Industrial Revolution (iron ore and coal); they were almost totally self-sufficient in raw materials and, in fact, exported energy to the third world.[37] Colonialism, Bairoch

---

[37] Bairoch 1993: 172. The minerals prominent in tropical trade today did not come to the fore until the end of the nineteenth century. Minerals amounted to only 13 percent of tropical exports in 1913, compared with 29 percent in 1965. In 1913, minerals were prominent in the exports only of Peru and Mexico (Lewis 1978a: 201). Moreover, Britain's terms of trade were unfavorable throughout the nineteenth and early twentieth centuries, until around 1920 (see figures in Strachey 1959: 149–51). Terms of trade improved for the less developed countries during the nineteenth century and the first decades of the twentieth. It was only after World War II (in the 1950s, and again in the 1980s) that terms of trade in primary goods deteriorated (Bairoch 1993: 113–14). The exception – and, as Arthur Lewis points out, it is an important one for Latin America (and for arguments developed in this chapter concerning cheap food imports) – is the terms of trade for sugar that, relative to manufactured goods, deteriorated by 25 to 35 percent between 1830 and 1910.

argues, was, therefore, not a necessity for industrial growth in Europe; in fact, it may have hampered national economic growth and development there:

If one compares the rate of growth during the nineteenth century it appears that non-colonial countries had, as a rule, a more rapid economic development than colonial ones. There is an almost perfect correlation. Thus colonial countries like Britain, France, the Netherlands, Portugal, and Spain have been characterized by a slower rate of economic growth and industrialization than Belgium, Germany, Sweden, Switzerland and the United States. The "rule" is, to a certain extent, also valid for the twentieth century. Thus Belgium, by joining the colonial "club" in the first years of the twentieth century, also became a member of the group characterized by slow growth. The loss of the Netherlands' colonial Empire after World War II coincided with a rapid acceleration in its economic development. (Bairoch 1993: 77)

Britain's decline, when it came, was heralded by its relative absence in the "new" industries that emerged at the end of the nineteenth century, and this may have been due, in part, Bairoch suggests, because its "ability to sell easily non-sophisticated manufactured goods to its colonies forestalled the need for modernization" (1993: 167).

Why, then, did investors not take advantage of unexploited fields of investment at home? Why did they neglect opportunities for profitable home investment, leaving British industry, throughout the nineteenth century and relative to that of its nearest competitors, slow to mechanize and to introduce new technologies? Why, instead, did they pursue investments overseas that were riskier, more difficult and costly to acquire, and, in some cases, not as lucrative? The next section attempts to answer these questions.

Britain's Nineteenth-Century Economy

Putting together the aspects of Britain's nineteenth-century industrial expansion discussed thus far, a composite picture emerges of Britain's nineteenth-century economy. Its most effective elites, those that shaped and directed the expansion of production, were aristocratic landowners and financiers, and its agricultural, financial, and industrial spheres reflected aristocratic interests and values. Land and industry became concentrated in fewer and fewer hands in the course of the century; methods of increasing absolute surplus value production and traditional manufacturing persisted; and an unprecedented degradation and intensification of labor, both within and outside

---

King Leopold of Belgium compared Africa to a "magnificent cake," suggesting, as Wesseling points out, that it was a luxury rather than a necessity (Wesseling 1997: 92). Bismarck, in a speech to the Reichstag on January 26, 1899, said of the German colonists in Africa: "They cannot prove that it is useful for the Reich. I, however, cannot prove that it is harmful to it, either" (Von Bismarck 1924–32: XIII, 386; quoted in Wesseling 1997: 90).

Europe, produced an increasing volume of goods and capital for circulation among a transnational network of property owners. Nowhere was there found the liberal, competitive, bourgeois ethos featured in conventional historiographical and social science lore.

Decisions about whether and how to increase or restructure production are based on calculations about the conditions necessary for the realization of profit. Certainly, disadvantageous social externalities produced by the introduction of new production methods and by an expansion of output would be part of those calculations. Had the "democratization of consumption" of the eighteenth century continued, and had a broad-based industrial growth developed, along with the mass purchasing power and internal market needed to support it, the class, land, and income structures on which the existing structure of social power in Britain rested would have been destroyed.

The consumer revolution and the expansion of production in the eighteenth century had important implications for the structure of British society. Mass consumption is associated with democracy, and elites were certainly aware of its corrosive effects. That these were widely recognized is evident in the laws regulating consumption that were everywhere evident throughout history, in Europe and elsewhere, and persist in many places throughout the world today.[38] Sumptuary laws restricted the personal consumption of goods based on class and income and were enacted in Europe between the fifteenth and eighteenth centuries, as in other places and times, to preserve and reinforce lines of distinction between classes. They were aimed largely at the masses and "uppity" middle-class elements. Laws forbidding the common people from clothing themselves like their betters were retained by many states well into the nineteenth century (see Dorwart 1971: 45–50; also Greenfield 1918; Baldwin 1926; Vincent 1969; and Hunt 1996). The consumer revolution of the eighteenth century and the emergence of a domestic market for mass-produced consumer goods, because they worked to undermine class distinctions and increase social mobility, were politically threatening and, thus, were not encouraged.

The commitment to limiting the expansion of industry and consumption at home was reflected in the continued allegiance of influential elites to mercantilist notions. Specifically, these included the notion that domestic trade does not make people rich, that low wages and restricted consumption were necessary to economic prosperity,[39] that foreign trade was the sole source of

---

[38] Dress restrictions based on income were common outside Europe as, for instance, in Japan. Today these laws persist, for instance, in northern Africa, where neither Tuareg women nor slaves are permitted to veil (El Guindi 1999: 124).

[39] As, for instance, the following sentiment: "There is a very great consumption of luxuries among the labouring poor of this kingdom: particularly among the manufacturing populace, by which they consume their time, the most fatal of consumptions" (anonymous, *An Essay on Trade and Commerce* (London, 1770), pp. 47, 153; in Marx 1990: 342n57).

surplus and, thus, accumulation, and that domestic trade was a means only of transferring wealth among individuals (rather than increasing the surplus).[40] Mercantilist policies promoting overseas trade had provided governments with a source of tax revenues and loan capital that had *fewer negative domestic consequences* than other available sources and enabled them to gain a certain degree of "autonomy" from the local nobility. Those mercantilist policies that had offered states a means of gaining autonomy from local elites had become a target of aristocratic wrath. But after aristocratic landholding and financial interests succeeded in gaining control of the state, these very same policies became useful to them, and probably for the very same purpose: as a means of acquiring autonomy from local social forces. Thus, while a mass of government rules and restrictions on economic activity "were swept out of the statute books" between 1760 and 1850 (Deane 1979: 220), many mercantilist policies and doctrines were retained. Promoting overseas, rather than domestic, commerce as a means of generating income was among these. And it is reasonable to assume that it was for the same reasons – that is, that it had fewer negative domestic consequences for those who were promoting it. By the twentieth century, mercantilist thought resonated strongly in the policies and doctrines associated with the various forms of fascism that emerged following World War I.

Mass production also had serious implications for the existing structure of social power in Britain. A fully industrialized economy requires mass mobilization. Mass mobilization for industry (as for war) creates, out of the relatively disadvantaged majority of the population, a compact and potentially dangerous force; thus, elites showed little interest in the expansion of industry at home. Marx, as in much of his writing, was here perhaps only reflecting a general perception of his times when he wrote:

The advance of industry...replaces the isolation of the labourers...by their revolutionary combination, due to association. The development of Modern Industry, therefore, cuts from under its feet the very foundation on which the bourgeoisie produces and appropriates products. (Marx 1967: 93–94)

It might be argued that owners of wealth were not conscious of the social externalities associated with the application of large masses of labor to production. This seems hardly plausible. The problems of setting to work and controlling masses of labor are not so substantially different in capitalist production as to have made all prior problems and their solutions irrelevant. For centuries, landlords had been confronted with the "great fear" of mass peasant uprisings and had organized production in ways that reinforced the existing relations of power and authority. The difference in capitalist production – and this is crucial – is not the strategic power that workers

---

[40] Mercantilism is a set of policies, regulations, and laws developed over the sixteenth through the eighteenth centuries.

have (peasants had that, too), but that for industry to grow and remain competitive, a sizable portion of the labor force must be educated, skilled, and mobile. If property owners were not conscious of the dangers of mass mobilization for industry, would they not have been after Marx spelled it out for them in the widely read and cited *Communist Manifesto*?

What is supportable, at any rate, is the following.

1. *Britain's "patrician hegemony" opposed any "aggressive development of industrialism" and the social transformation necessary to it* (Weiner 1981: 7, 10).

2. *The way in which Britain's production was reorganized and expanded did not envision or anticipate a corresponding expansion of consumption and markets at home.* Decisions about what to produce and how to produce it were based on the expectation not that the purchasing power for articles of mass consumption could be created at home, but that it could be created for capital goods, and for goods and services outside the normal budget of the wage earners among an ever-widening circle of elites and ruling groups throughout Europe and beyond.[41]

3. *Britain's economy developed chiefly through the expansion of absolute surplus value production and international trade.*

4. *The industrial production of high-cost goods for export avoided (1) redistribution of the national income – the need to provide workers with the purchasing power to consume the goods that they produced, and (2) the creation, for much of the nineteenth century, of a significant factory proletariat.*

5. *Elites succeeded in massively mobilizing resources for the development of investment opportunities abroad but failed to create additional productive capacity at home.*

The development of exogenous demand and consumption through the export of capital and goods, together with the continued use of methods of increasing absolute surplus value at home, ensured that the benefits of expanding production would be retained solely by the property-owning classes. In 1914, British industrialization was still sectorally and geographically limited in the way that dualistic colonial and post-colonial economies have been described. Landed and industrial property had become increasingly concentrated. Only in sectors producing for export was there mechanization, skilled labor, rising productivity, and real wages. These sectors did not have a profound impact on the rest of the economy. Revenues from these sectors were not invested in the expansion of production for the home market. There was

---

[41] Phyllis Deane observes, in the nineteenth century, "The evidence available certainly indicates that there was a shift in the distribution of incomes in favor of profits and rent and a change in the composition of output in favor of capital goods, exports and goods and services for upper-class consumption" (1979: 270).

little attempt to expand or mechanize industries producing goods for domestic household consumption. Instead, production expanded through the development of a circuit of capital that operated among a transnational aggregate of elites and governments. We now turn to a consideration of this circuit.

THE CIRCUIT OF CAPITAL

Europe's economy before World War II was based on the development of external markets for heavy industry and high-cost consumption goods, and through cooperation with or imperialist exploitation of other states and territories, both within and outside Europe.

In dual economies, intersectoral flows are limited. Instead, the dynamic sectors of European economies grew by means of an international circuit of investment and exchange. The major features of the circuit were as follows. Britain increased its industrial production by expanding its shipbuilding, boiler making, gun, and ammunition industries. This enabled it to penetrate and defend markets overseas, and then to build foreign railways, canals, and other public works; to build banks, telegraphs, and other public services owned by or dependent on governments; to establish foreign factories; and to develop foreign mines. British exports of capital provided purchasing power among foreign governments and elites for British goods, and this funded the development and transport of food and raw materials exports to Europe, thus creating additional foreign purchasing power and demand for British goods and also decreasing the price of food, and thereby the value of labor, in Britain.[42]

The City of London was at the center of this circuit of capital. London's capital markets expanded during the Napoleonic Wars through loans to the British government and to Britain's allies needed to meet the requirements of almost a quarter-century of warfare. After the war, City loans helped to reestablish reactionary governments in various continental countries. By the 1820s, net long-term lending had made its first significant and sustained appearance with loans raised for newly independent Latin American and Balkan governments. By the 1830s, loans were going to U.S. states. The flow of net foreign investment continued to rise throughout the 1840s and 1850s. In the mid-1850s, the stock of net overseas assets was around 8 percent of the stock of wealth owned by Britons at home and abroad. By 1870, it had risen to around 17 percent. Then there was a spectacular rise in overseas investment. In 1913, one-third of Britain's net wealth was invested overseas, as a result of annual flows of foreign investment; one-third of everything owned by Britons was in a foreign country (Floud 1997: 164). "Never before

---

[42] Britain's industrial wage-earners realized 55 to 60 percent of their wages in the form of food; the steady fall in prices of staple food imports after 1874 (grain, tea, sugar, lard, cheese, ham, and bacon; Mathias 1983: 345) allowed real wages in Britain to rise until World War I.

or since has one nation committed so much of its national income and savings to capital formation abroad."[43] As a result, the City of London, where more fortunes were made than in the whole of industry, depended "only slightly" on Britain's economic performance (Boyce 1987: 18–19).

The bulk of this outflow between 1880 and 1913 was to the Dominions, Europe, and the United States (over 55 percent; Barratt Brown 1970: xiv). Between 1865 and 1914, almost 70 percent of British new portfolio investment went into social overhead capital (railways, docks, tramways, telegraphs and telephones, gas and electric works, etc.) and, in particular, the enormously capital-absorbing railways (as did the bulk of French and Belgian foreign investment).[44] Only the production of modern armaments is more capital-absorbing (the mass production of armaments in the United States, and their export to Europe's great and small powers, began in the 1860s).[45] Increasing blocs of territory throughout the world became covered with networks of British-built and -financed railroads, provisioned by British steamships and defended by British warships.

The circuit developed originally through colonialism and imperialism. Britain established colonies in the Americas and the tropics that later became sources of raw materials and markets for British exports. By 1797, Britain's North American colonies and the West Indies accounted for 32 percent of British imports and 57 percent of exports (Thomas and McCloskey 1981). But markets abroad could be created either by bringing more countries

---

[43] McCloskey 1981: 143. The United States, which at the same time was the largest economy in the world, exported only 7 percent (Floud 1997: 90). At the height of the Marshall Plan, in 1947, the level of foreign investment as a share of national income was around 3 percent (McCloskey 1981: 144).

[44] Some 12 percent went into extractive industries (agriculture and mining); only 4 percent went into manufacturing (Edelstein 1981: 73).

[45] Dobb 1963: 296. Hobsbawm casts doubt on the notion that Britain's domestic railway building reflected efforts to expand and integrate the home market. At least in the short run, he argues, railway building in Britain did not reflect the transport needs of an industrial economy. All industrial areas were within easy access of water transport by sea, river, or canal, and water transport was and is by far the cheapest for bulk goods (coal mined in the north had been shipped inexpensively by sea to London for centuries). Moreover, regularity of flow, and not speed, was the important factor in transporting nonperishable goods; and this was supplied by water transport.

Hobsbawm argues that, in fact, "many of the railways constructed were and remained quite irrational by any transport criterion, and consequently never paid more than the most modest profits, if they paid any at all. This was perfectly evident at the time...." What was also evident is that investors were looking for "any investment likely to yield more than the 3.4 percent of public stocks." Railway returns eventually settled down at an average of about 4 percent (Hobsbawm 1968: 111; see also 113–15).

Mathias argues a different view of the importance of railways for Britain: "The importance of the coming of the railways as a service for the economy as a whole lies in the fact that they enabled economic activity in all other sectors of the economy to expand" (1983: 256; see also the rest of chap. 10).

into the world market or by squeezing other countries out of their markets. Britain and France both launched military crusades aimed at usurping exist-ing markets for textiles. British military operations forced open the Indian subcontinent and usurped India's international market for British cotton tex-tiles. During the Napoleonic Wars, France, through its "Continental System" and colonial expansion in Europe, attempted to turn Italy into a source of raw materials for French textiles and to usurp Italy's domination of inter-national markets for high-quality textiles. Ottoman vulnerability, revealed after Britain thwarted a French attack on Egypt during the Napoleonic Wars, provided a new field for exploitation. Britain developed Egypt and the Sudan as sources of cotton for its textile industry; while a French claim to Lebanon (by virtue of its Catholic Maronite community) ensured a nearby (relative to China) source of raw silk for the French silk industry.[46] Britain added territories to its colonial empire for strategic and commercial purposes (e.g., Singapore, Aden, the Falkland Islands, Hong Kong, and Lagos) and as a result of the movement and activities of land-hungry British emigrants (e.g., in South Africa, Canada, and Australia). Colonies also provided labor that was even cheaper than that which was available at home and, in any case, was an alternative to mobilizing labor at home.

European countries enslaved and forced 11 to 12 million Africans to go to work in their colonies in North and South America between 1600 and 1900. More than half (over 6 million) of these were forcibly exported from Africa during the eighteenth century, principally to British- and French-owned centers of production in the Caribbean (Jamaica and St. Domingue, or what later became Haiti). This trans-Atlantic slave trade did not come to a total end until the 1870s. Though Britain declared the slave trade illegal in 1807 (but actually abolished slavery in 1832), the slave trade continued illegally: almost 2 million more slaves were transported from Africa between 1810 and 1870, most to the major Caribbean sugar producer in the nine-teenth century, Cuba.

Though the slave trade came to an end in the 1870s (though, of course, slavery never did, or has, completely), labor could still be had more cheaply abroad. For in addition to the stream of slave labor from Africa to the Americas that was developed and set in motion by the colonial powers, another stream of migration developed consisting of contract laborers fed, in particular, by large numbers of Indian and Chinese contract laborers who went to the tropics and to Africa to work in the mines and on the plantations. Thus, while British legislators promoted the notion that Britain's prosecution of the Boer War was to secure jobs for British labor in South Africa, the

---

[46] France had a keen interest in securing supplies of raw silk from the mulberry plantations of Lebanon. Toward this end, France secured from the Ottoman Sultan in 1860 the right to act as protector of the Roman Catholic Maronite community of Lebanon.

jobs actually went to cheaper Chinese labor.[47] Thus, however piecemeal and
slow the progress of labor legislation was in European countries during the
nineteenth century, labor could be had more cheaply, and the methods of
absolute surplus value production applied with greater ease and freedom,
outside Europe. Conditions overseas generally facilitated a lower level of
wages, a longer working day, a greater exploitation of the labor of women
and children, the absence or nonapplication of social legislation, and the use
of forced labor or labor paid in kind.

Throughout the circuit, in Europe and among the extraregional states
and territories brought within its ambit, the same overall pattern of dualistic
growth was repeated, though with variations according to each country's
place in the circuit and the type of goods it produced for sale.

France, whose empire, export earnings, and foreign investment were second only to Britain's, exported high-cost textiles and luxury goods (e.g., silks,
laces, wines, and delicacies) and built and financed railroads in Russia with
French equipment and capital. Germany's dualistic industrial expansion took
off with its marriage not of "iron and finance," as in Britain, but of "iron
and rye," celebrated, in 1879, along with the enactment of an Anti-Socialist
Law and state legal enforcement of cartel agreements to limit production.
In Italy and Austria-Hungary, industrial development focused on expanding
heavy industry and gaining railway concessions in the Balkans.

Other states – Russia, the United States, Canada, and Australia – were
incorporated into the circuit as raw material producers. These increased
their production of agricultural and other raw materials exports to pay for
railways, iron and steel, armaments, and other foreign manufactures. Russia
paid for these imports and its interest on its enormous foreign debt by steadily
increasing agricultural exports even during famines (e.g., in 1891). In 1913,
some 74 percent of Russian exports consisted of agricultural produce and
timber (Munting 1982: 31). Colonial territories that became independent
states – as, for instance, states in the Balkans and in Latin America – remained
within the circuit. Local elites, whether in colonies, former colonies, or states
that had never been colonies, imported British capital and goods, developed
mines and raw materials exports, and built railways and ports in order to
extend, consolidate, and maintain their power and become wealthy.

---

47 "After having given people in Britain the idea that the main purpose of the war was to open
up the whole of South Africa to British immigration, it was very difficult to explain the need
for Chinese labor instead" (Pelling 1968: 97). Charles Fenwick, the Northumberland miners'
M.P., summed up the situation in his comments before the House of Commons. Recalling
that the government had pointed out to the working classes in Britain "what a happy hunting
ground" South Africa would be for the British laborer, and what a splendid outlet it would
be for the surplus population of this country, he noted, "Now it turned out that this country
had shed the blood of tens of thousands of its subjects not in the interests of British labour
but in the interests of Chinese labour." House of Commons, Series 4, 130, 71 (February 17,
1904); in Pelling 1968: 98.

But some former colonies did not develop the sharp dualism that characterized industrial expansion in Europe. In Australia, Canada, and New Zealand there was no pre-existing landed elite, and the colonists displaced, overwhelmed, or destroyed prior inhabitants. In these countries, revenues were not used solely to enrich a traditional landowning class and their allies, as they were in Europe and in Latin America. In the United States, where a strong landowning class developed in the south, a struggle between landowners and industrialists culminated in civil war and the victory of the industrial capitalist bourgeoisie.

Imperialism was, first and foremost, a means of securing markets for expanded production without the redistribution and reform necessary for the further development of the home market. Imperialist expansion was proposed and advocated by the aristocracies and nobilities of almost all European countries in the nineteenth century. Here, it is important to underline the distinction between support for the expansion that comes about through inherent, virtually automatic impulses (population growth, trade, geopolitical opportunity), and imperialism – expansion facilitated by military power and the conscious cultivation of myths of imperial mission. Aristocracies and nobilities promoted the British and French empires, the Great Germany crusade, the Russian pan-Slav movement, the Greek Megali Idea and the fascist crusade to recreate a Roman empire; the movements for a Greater Serbia, a Greater Croatia, a Greater Bulgaria, a Greater Romania, and a Greater Macedonia; and crusades to resurrect the supranational Polish Commonwealth and the supranational Kingdom of Lithuania.[48]

British, German, Italian, and Russian landowning elites were the most active champions of imperialist expansion. Britain's imperialists were the aristocracy and later the Tories (Barratt Brown 1970: 53–54). Italian imperialism was promoted by the Church and the landowning nobility. In Germany, the most persistent and zealous champions of imperial expansion were the landowners organized in the powerful Bund der Landwirte and other agrarian groups in Germany, as well as the Pan-German League, representing both the great landowners and the large industrialists (see, e.g., Wertheimer 1924; Meyer 1955). The Russian nobility and large landowners represented in the pan-Slav movement championed the cause of Russian imperial expansion (Mazour 1951). In addition to landowners, large industrialists pressed for imperialist expansion. Among the most influential imperialists were representatives of iron and steel and heavy industry (railroads and shipping), such as Joseph Chamberlain in Britain and Jules Ferry in France and the large

---

[48] A pan-Celtic movement to unite Gaels, Welsh, and Bretons was formed in the late nineteenth century. There was also a pan-Scandinavian movement in the nineteenth century, but its aims were limited, apparently, to closer economic integration among the Nordic nations (Denmark, Iceland, Norway, Sweden, and Finland).

industrialists in Germany who, after the 1870s, joined with landowners in the Pan-German League (see, e.g., Langer 1931: chap. 9).

A number of scholars have drawn attention to the social structural basis of imperialism. Joseph Schumpeter (1955) argued that imperialism was the product of the surviving "feudal substance" of precapitalist Europe and a manifestation of the aggressive mercantilist ethos of the ancien regime. This "feudal substance," which Schumpeter recognized had "fused with bourgeois-capitalism," had actually shaped not only its imperialist policies but its essential character. Cain and Hopkins (1993) have argued that overseas expansion, which "played a vital role in maintaining property and privilege at home," was fueled by "gentlemanly capitalism," a form of capitalism centered on an alliance among aristocrats, city financiers, and the professional classes who, in alliance with political decision makers, promoted their common interest in creating an international regime based on antidemocratic values. "It is no coincidence," Cain and Hopkins point out, "that the most pervasive images of imperialism and empire were those which projected gentility rather than industry" (1993: 45).

In general, imperialism operated through a set of practices that, in its overall character, resembled the intraelite interactions characteristic of medieval Europe's transterritorial commonwealth. Puchala and Hopkins (1983) suggest this in their description of imperialism between 1870 and 1914. First, they note the distinctive pattern of activity that characterized imperialism:

extracted raw materials flowed from colonies to European imperial centers, light manufactures flowed back; investment capital flowed outward from European centers, profits and returns flowed back; administrators, soldiers, entrepreneurs, and missionaries went abroad to rule new lands, make new fortunes, and win new converts to their political, economic or religious causes. (1983: 68)

Then, they point to the regulation of this activity by a regime that "prescribed certain modes of behavior for imperial powers vis-à-vis each other and toward their respective colonial subjects." The managers of the regime were the ministries and ministers of major states. These "made the rules of the colonial game," and "diplomats, soldiers, businessmen, and settlers played accordingly." Other subnational actors were involved, as well: "church societies, militarist lobbies, and bankers," and in some countries, these "exercised substantial influence over the formulation of colonial policy" (1983: 67). While "there were conflicts, frictions, and collisions at points where empires came geographically together and occasional armed skirmishes outside of Europe," there were also "periodic conferences called to settle colonial issues, and countless bilateral treaties and agreements between colonial powers that defined borders on distant continents, transferred territories or populations, and codified the privileges and obligations of each colonial power with respect to the domains of others" (Puchala and Hopkins 1983: 68).

Two additional questions remain about the social groups and interests associated with imperialism. First, if landowning and other elites championed imperialism, did not other sectors of society do so, as well? Hobson noted that financial interests had a "policy of owning newspapers for the sake of manufacturing public opinion" in favor of imperialism. In European cities such as Berlin, Vienna, and Paris, many of the influential newspapers were held by financial houses, which used them not primarily to make direct profits out of them but in order to put into the public mind beliefs and sentiments that would influence public policy. As a result, "the Press worked to popularise the notion of the need for and glory of acquiring access to or ownership of overseas territories" (Hobson 1902: 60).

However, despite these efforts, in Germany, colonialism was "a late and marginal concern." Colonial politics existed "in the margins of major politics and as far as the government and parliament were concerned, it remained a question of secondary importance." The public regarded it with indifference, though sometimes after a spectacular victory, the public flared "into a collective but brief enthusiasm which was quickly doused by irritation over expenses and losses in these far-off places." In France, "[t]here existed no genuine colonial consensus . . . the extensive and costly empire remained a permanent object of discussion" (Wesseling 1997: 45, 25). In Britain, "public interest became evident only from 1894, and then it was a spasmodic reaction to specific overseas issues rather than a consistent expression of nationalist or racialist idealism" (Fieldhouse 1973: 75).

In an investigation of working-class attitudes toward imperialism, Henry Pelling assessed British working-class attitudes by focusing on the South African (Boer) War. He concluded that there was "no evidence of a direct continuous support for the cause of Imperialism among any sections of the working class." There was, however, some support among Ulstermen and Irish protestant immigrants to Britain, as well as from soldiers and sailors and shipbuilding workers. But the trade union leadership "always adhered to the 'little England' view" (Pelling 1968: 99).

Lenin's view was that the upper stratum of the working class was politically corrupted by imperialism (Lenin 1939a: 64, 67). Certainly, policies of exclusion and commercial restrictions, if they threatened other states with loss of potential markets, could, thus, become an interest of working people, as well as capitalists. But Pelling reports that, of the dozen trade union leaders who were in the House of Commons at the outbreak of the South African War, only one (Havelock Wilson) took the imperialist side. Of the nine trade union leaders in the new parliament elected in 1900, none supported the war (Pelling 1968: 82–83). In a later study, Richard Price concluded that Britain's empire mattered little to the working classes (1972, passim), and, in an earlier study, this was Alfred Williams's conclusion, as well (1911: 157).

Johan Galtung's characterization of imperialism (1971) is consistent with these findings. Galtung identifies imperialism as a system characterized externally by a harmony of interests and structural interconnection between the ruling classes in rich and poor countries and internally by a disharmony of interests between those classes and their own workers and peasants. This "structural theory of imperialism" contributes to our understanding of imperialism by drawing attention to what other perspectives tend to obscure: that workers and peasants, in both imperial and colonial countries, were victims of imperialism, and that elites, both in Europe and in colonial territories, accumulated wealth and power. As Barratt Brown notes, "the majority of the British people shared with the colonial people in the disadvantages of imperialist relations. They paid the taxes and manned the armies without sharing the dividends" (Barratt Brown 1970: x). Dependency and world systems theorists fail to recognize, first, that all capitalist development has been dependent development, and, second, that the dependency is class dependency, not state dependency.

It might be argued that immigration, by providing the unemployed and disaffected with "exit" rather than "voice," benefited the millions of people who left Europe permanently between 1800 and 1914. But the mass emigration out of Europe was not related to imperialism: the most important destination of the millions of people who left Europe permanently between 1800 and 1914 was not to the colonies but to the United States.[49] The jobs created by imperialism were for either cheaper slave or contract labor or for the sons of the upper classes – that is, the administrative and army posts that the expansion of the civil and military services provided for the graduates of Oxford and Cambridge.[50]

But if it was landowning and industrial elites that championed imperialist expansion, did they do so because they saw it as an alternative to internal expansion? Those who championed imperialism were the very elements that resisted reform at home and that declined to invest at home. Moreover, they emphasized imperialism as a means of offsetting the land hunger and poverty that resulted from their monopolization of assets and their exploitation of labor. When Germany's big landowners and large industrialists in the 1870s championed the cause of acquiring additional *Lebensraum* in order to offset the land hunger of the German masses, they were expressing a general

---

[49] Of the 32 million immigrants that the United States absorbed between 1820 and 1915, most were from Europe. Nearly a million people came from England, Scotland, and Wales, and 2 million people came from Ireland between 1820 and 1860. About 5.5 million Germans migrated to the United States between 1816 and 1914, most to escape the conditions of peasant life there. Over 4.5 million people came from the Austro-Hungarian Empire during the nineteenth century. The agricultural crisis of the 1880s drove millions of migrants of Eastern Europe and Southern Europe to the United States. Some 17 million Europeans entered the United States between 1880 and 1910.

[50] Employment for some 20,000 administrators and posts in the Army, Navy, and Air Force went to the second-class graduates of these institutions; the first-class graduates went into the Home Civil Service. Together, these posts "somewhat relieved the pressure of graduates at the employment exchanges" (Brown 1970: 146).

theme of landowners and industrialists everywhere in Europe. Everywhere
in Europe, imperialists stressed its value chiefly for immigration and as a
means of reducing the misery of the urban working classes and pacifying the
peasants.

It has been argued that imperialism was a means of defusing tensions at
home.[51] It was the conviction of many authors, Wesseling contends, that
the enviable level of prosperity and remarkable degree of political and social
stability found in the great colonial powers was connected with their overseas
possessions (Wesseling 1997: 41). Wehler (1969) has argued that Bismarck's
motivation in seeking colonies was to overcome internal tensions.

But by the eve of World War I, the extremes of wealth and poverty created
by dualistic economic expansion were generating more or less continual
conflicts (see Chapters 4 and 5). In 1913, less than 5 percent of Britain's
population over twenty-five years of age possessed over 60 percent of the
wealth of the country (Clough 1952: 672–73). Though the population of
Britain became on average nearly three and a half times richer between 1830
and 1914, "the range of incomes around the average did not significantly
diminish; the rich remained much richer than the average, the poor much
poorer. . . . up to a third of the population in 1914 had incomes which did
not provide them with sufficient food to sustain health throughout the year"
(Floud 1997: 15). Moreover, "while 30% lived below the margin, perhaps a
further 40% or even more lived so close to the margin that they could be, and
often were, forced below it by a variety of life events."[52] The impoverished
masses crowding the slums of London and other cities were so "stunted and
wizened by illness and poverty" as to appear "as another race to upper class
observers" (Floud 1997: 14). In 1914, Britain "was a divided country, in
which extremes of wealth and poverty coexisted, often in a state of mutual
fear and incomprehension" (Floud 1997: 7).

---

[51] This description of the circumstances that contributed to the revolutionary uprisings in
France in 1848 makes the point:

> When, because of the industrial crisis, a multitude of Parisian manufacturers and big
> traders could no longer do any business in the foreign market and were thrown onto
> the home market, the large establishments they set up ruined the small grocers and
> shopkeepers *en masse* leading to innumerable bankruptcies among this section of the
> Paris bourgeoisie, and hence their revolutionary action in February. (Marx 1952: 32)

[52] Floud 1997: 24. A number of investigators of working-class life showed that, in the decade
leading up to the First World War, a significant proportion of the population of England
and Wales was living in poverty without recourse to poor relief (Bell 1907; Davies 1909;
Rowntree 1913; Bowley and Burnett-Hurst 1915).

In his survey of London's East End in 1886, Charles Booth showed that over 30 percent
of the population had an income that was inadequate for their support (1889). Seebohm
Rowntree in his survey of York in 1899 found that 28 percent of the population was too
malnourished to work a normal day and their children could not be fed enough to grow
at a normal rate (1901: 86–87). Though wages rose sharply between 1905 and 1913, the
gain was offset by a strong increase in the cost of living and by a wide range of social and
economic factors (Perrot 1986: 104; Benson 1989: 56).

By the eve of World War I, tensions were rising not only within European states but among them, as well. Overseas expansion had helped to maintain the balance of power system in Europe by providing a compensatory mechanism. And in spite of the heavily militarized and competitive character of Europe's overseas expansion, diplomatic instruments were found to regulate it such that conflicts over territory were prevented from escalating to war.

However, as more and more countries began to pursue dualistic, externally oriented economic expansion, conflict over still unexploited territories in Africa and Asia increasingly threatened to lead to war. At the same time that overseas tensions were increasing, Europe itself became the focus of expansionist aims. Networks of British-built and -financed railroads already covered overseas territories, but, after 1870, an upsurge in European railway construction began: France built railroads in Russia, German steel and capital built the Baghdad Railway, and Italy and Austria-Hungary competed for railroad concessions in Southeast Europe so that, as 1914 approached, "there was something of a railroad war between Italy and Austria-Hungary in the Balkans" (Kurth 1979: 21). Rivalry and rising tensions in Europe led to the dissolution of the "Bismarckian System," and this, along with the antagonism created by German naval building, led to the reconfiguration and increasing polarization of interstate relations in Europe. The European balance of power and imperialist regimes began to dissolve. By 1914, war appeared to be the only means by which "national" capitals could improve the terms on which they were integrated into the world circuit of capital.

CONCLUSIONS: DUALISM AND "DEPENDENT DEVELOPMENT" IN EUROPE'S NINETEENTH-CENTURY INDUSTRIAL EXPANSION

Accommodations of various sorts forged at various times among aristocrats and industrialists in Europe produced a dualistic system of industrial expansion there that operated to a large extent on the basis of nonindustrial and anti-industrial social and political values and interests (Warwick 1985). The system expanded production and increased profits for a transnational landowning and industrial elite, but it also limited the geographic and sectoral spread of industrialization, mass mobilization for industrial production, and the rise of new classes at home. As a result, despite the massive population movements within and outside Europe, and the appearance of great flux and change over the entire surface of European life, traditional bases of social and political power remained intact. Thus,

the new society of the nineteenth century was not so new after all. A very ancient form of authority and social deference was given a new set of clothes. This in itself was quite a cataclysmic occurrence, one that left no individual fate untouched. But the individual was never liberated in the way that the apostles of the new age claimed (and later its critics believed). Bourgeois freedom is slavery for the vast majority, Marx declared in 1848: in reality bourgeois freedom never came into existence. (Reddy 1987: 4)

As late as 1912, Britain's Lloyd George could still declare a national land campaign to "break down the remnants of the feudal system" (Cannadine 1990: 70). It was not until World War I that processes of rapid and radical change set in motion the final "passing of feudalism" in Europe. As C. F. G. Masterman wrote a few years later, as a result of the war "the Feudal System vanished in blood and fire, and the landed classes were consumed" (1923: 48). It was only after World War II that there was a shift to a system of production oriented to the improvement of the standard of living of workers. It came, as it had previously come in the United States (in the 1860s)[53] and Russia (1917–22), as a result of protracted and bloody civil war among elites (the Europe-wide civil war of 1939–45) and the consequent breakdown of forces of resistance to social reform.

---

[53] In the United States, the demands of the slave owners limited the development of industry and retarded the growth of a home market. Slavery made it impossible for the plantation to reform itself and eroded possibilities for economic advancement. The ability to introduce new methods of restoring soil fertility – changing crops, altering the style of farming, or introducing new methods and organization – was barred by a commitment to the single-crop, staple agriculture most compatible with slavery. Effective reform required a smaller labor force and a new form of farm organization, and the release of capital locked up in slaves for machinery and fertilizers (Genovese 1965).

4

Europe's Century of War, 1815–1914

Karl Polanyi begins his survey of Europe's nineteenth-century market system in *The Great Transformation* by highlighting what he believed was one of its most striking features: "The nineteenth century produced a phenomenon unheard of in the annals of Western civilization," he wrote, "namely, a hundred years' peace – 1815–1914." Focusing on interstate conflict and, specifically, multilateral great power conflict, he noted that, apart from the Crimean War, England, France, Prussia, Austria, Italy, and Russia "were engaged in war among each other for altogether only eighteen months" (1944: 5).

Many scholars believe that nineteenth-century Europe was a relatively peaceful place.[1] However, fourteen wars were fought in Europe during that time between and among Britain, France, Germany, Spain, Russia, Denmark, Austria, Italy, Greece, and Serbia. Twelve wars were fought by Britain, France, Russia, and Austria against foreign populations in Europe. During that period, European states also were involved in some fifty-eight wars outside Europe.

Nonetheless, some scholars characterize Europe at that time as "relatively peaceful" because no war was fought in Europe itself during the century comparable in size to the Napoleonic Wars or to World War I and World War II. But could not this be said of most centuries of European history? Others assume, erroneously, that European states were involved in fewer conflicts during that century than during the previous one. Quincey Wright, however, found that there were *more* conflicts involving European states (both domestic and international) in the nineteenth century than in the eighteenth. According to Wright, the number and type of wars involving European states in the eighteenth and nineteenth centuries were as shown in Table 4.1.

---

[1] David Kaiser, for instance, in his book on war in modern European history, refers to "the long, only rarely interrupted period of European peace from 1815 through 1914" (1990: 271).

TABLE 4.1. *Comparison of European Wars, Eighteenth and Nineteenth Centuries (Number of Wars Fought)*

	1700–1800	1800–1849	1850–1900
Mainly in Europe.	31	15	14
Mainly outside Europe.	7	26	34
TOTAL.	38	41	48

	1700–1800	1800–1900	
Types of wars participated in by European states			
Balance of power.	23	20	
Civil.	10	17	
Imperial.	5	24	
TOTAL.	38	61	

Source: Wright 1965: 651.

It might be argued that if European states were involved in a larger number of conflicts in the nineteenth century than in the eighteenth, it was due to the set of Napoleonic Wars fought between 1805 and 1815. However, if we compare the whole of the eighteenth century with just the second half of the nineteenth, we still find that there were more wars fought by European states in the nineteenth century.

The "peace" that is thought by many to characterize nineteenth-century Europe applies only to regional multilateral great power conflicts. During the nineteenth century, there were few such wars because Europe's monarchs and aristocracies feared that another major conflict in Europe would call into use the mass armies that, during and immediately after the Napoleonic Wars, had triggered revolutionary upheavals and threatened to destroy the social order. But between the end of the Napoleonic Wars (1815) and the beginning of World War I (1914), European states were nonetheless continually engaged in conflict with their own populations, with other European states and populations, and with territories and states outside Europe. Thus, the notion that Europe enjoyed "a hundred years of peace" is misleading. Violent conflict was a fundamental dimension of Europe's industrial expansion in the nineteenth and early twentieth centuries: interstate and cross-border wars; ethnic and nationalist, religious and ideological conflicts; riots, insurrections, rebellions, revolutions, uprisings, violent strikes, and demonstrations; coups, assassinations, brutal repression, and terrorism were characteristic of European societies until 1945.

CONFLICT AND DUALISTIC INDUSTRIAL EXPANSION

The system of industrial expansion that began to operate in Europe beginning at the end of the eighteenth century generated recurring violent conflict. Political and economic restrictions on labor and minorities generated

TABLE 4.2. *Number and Intensity of European Wars, 1815–1914*

	No. of magnitude[a] 3+ wars[b]	% of magnitude 3+ wars in all wars	No. of magnitude 4+ wars
1815–65			
1815–19	1	8	
1820–29	15	54	
1830–39	14	26	
1840–49	9	13	
1850–59	18	80	
1860–65	9	13	
TOTAL	66	32	19
1866–1914			
1866–69	4	22	
1870–79	14	41	
1880–89	8	36	
1890–99	14	64	
1900–1909	10	32	
1910–14	25	48	
TOTAL	75	42	22

[a] Magnitudes represent the number of war dead, as follows: magnitude 7: 31,622,777–3,162,278; magnitude 6: 3,162,277–316,228; magnitude 5: 316,227–31,623; magnitude 4: 31,622–3,163; and magnitude 3: 3,162–317. The magnitudes are taken from Richardson (1960) and are rounded down (e.g., from 3.5 to 3.0) and up (e.g., from 3.6 to 4.0). The rest of the magnitudes are computed from numbers given in the sources indicated in Appendix 3.

[b] "Wars" here refer to small, medium, and large conflict events. These include regional and extraregional conflicts involving European states, as well as insurrections, rebellions, revolutions, uprisings, violent strikes, riots, and demonstrations in Europe. For the data on which this table is based, see Appendix 3. Percentages in this table are rounded to the nearest tenth.

labor, enfranchisement, and ethnic conflicts at home and, by blocking the expansion of the domestic market, led to imperialist conflicts abroad. Thus, between 1815 and 1914, conflicts fought by European states, both within and outside Europe, increased in number and intensity. Table 4.2 compares the number of high-casualty European conflicts and proportion of them in all European conflicts fought during the first and second halves of the period.

Because governments appeared to be allied with employers against workers, working-class activism was focused on both the marketplace and the political arena. As a result, the call for industrial reform tended, increasingly, to overlap and merge with that of political reform. Thus, it is not always possible to clearly distinguish between enfranchisement and labor struggles.[2] Both are class conflicts – conflicts between classes[3] over rights and privileges, including the right to vote, secure bread at an affordable price, organize, raise wages, shorten hours of employment, and work in safe conditions.

Labor struggles, whether waged in the marketplace or in the political arena, are struggles against proletarianization and the proletarian condition.[4] These struggles are often associated with or interpreted as nationalism.[5] Historically, workers are embedded in ethnic, national, and other communities and identities. Thus, the "banners" raised in struggles are often those of communal identification rather than specifically those of working-class identification. In some cases, the overlap between class and ethnicity/nationality/gender is so close that struggles taking place under a communal banner can be easily identified as labor unrest (Silver 1995: 16). In some places where class and ethnicity were overlapping social categories, class and minority (ethnic and religious) issues and conflicts were thoroughly intertwined.[6]

The structure of rights throughout the nineteenth century and everywhere in Europe tended to advantage and disadvantage the same groups. Everywhere in Europe the upper classes generally had the same privileges, and lower classes and ethnic minorities were, in general, subject to the same restrictions. Thus, the belligerents in labor, enfranchisement, and ethnic

---

[2] Most strikes and labor disputes were concerned with improving wages, hours, and working conditions. But many workers used the weapon of the strike as a means of demonstrating for the extension of the franchise. This became the case, increasingly, after the turn of the century. In Belgium in 1902, workers went out on strike in an attempt to force an extension of the franchise. In 1906, the Free Trade Unions and Social Democrats adopted the same weapon to combat a proposed restriction of the suffrage in Hamburg (Evans 1979). Authorities in various European countries routinely noted those strikes that they deemed to be "political."

[3] Classes represent locations, places in the social structure, defined in terms of structural relations of inequality with regard to some fundamental or central distributive value, that is, power, wealth, status, or some combination of these. Classes are sets of individuals that can be defined by certain common interests, by the fulfillment of certain functions and the holding of certain positions.

[4] Proletarianization: lacking ownership or control over the means of production and over the labor power of other workers.

[5] See, e.g., Ernest Gellner 1983; Eric Hobsbawm 1990; and Immanuel Wallerstein 1996. All argue, though based on different reasons and in different ways, that nationalism and class conflict are intimately related.

[6] In certain parts of Hungary, for instance, the landed gentry were Magyars, the urban middle class German-speaking, the peasants Croat or Slovak natives. In Galicia, landowners were Polish and the peasantry was Ruthenian. Thus, class and ethnicity were totally intertwined when in Austria-Hungary, Slovak, Ruthenian, and Roman serfs rose up against their Magyar and Polish lords in 1831. In the midst of an uprising of Polish nobles in Galicia in February 1846 against Austrian corvées, the mostly Ruthenian peasantry turned on their Polish landlords, killing some 2,000 of them. In 1910, Austrian troops violently suppressed the Ruthenian peasants in Galicia when they rebelled against the Polish nobility at election time (Jászi 1929).

conflicts belonged to transnational reference groups. In this situation, the outcome of a conflict in one state bore on the relations of power between members of the same groups living in other states.

During the nineteenth and early twentieth centuries, labor conflicts were matters of international concern. The Internationale, an organization feared by European elites far beyond the degree warranted by its actual strength, attempted to make socialism transnational.[7] However, as early as 1818, Robert Owen had urged the Great Powers (Russia, Prussia, Great Britain, Austria-Hungary, and France) meeting at Aix la Chapelle to take international steps for the improvement of labor conditions.[8] After World War I, as labor conflicts grew in strength and number, it was generally believed that conflicts involving labor were a threat to world peace.[9] During the interwar period, traditional and conservative elites organized against labor movements, domestically, through a variety of corporatist arrangements and, internationally, through support of Germany's rise as a bulwark against communism (see Chapter 7).

Enfranchisement conflicts were also a matter of international concern. After the French Revolution, it was an accepted fact that revolution in a single country could be a European phenomenon.[10] Thus, at the conclusion of the Napoleonic Wars, the kings and aristocracies of Europe formed an *internationale*, a "Concert of Europe" (concluded in 1815 among Great Britain, Russia, Austria, and Prussia, and, later, France) for the purpose of suppressing revolutionary uprisings throughout the region.[11] Austrian troops

---

[7] It was wrongly but nonetheless widely believed that the Internationale had instigated the Paris Commune of 1871, and its anarchistic contingent struck fear into the hearts of autocrats and aristocrats throughout the region.

[8] The first International Conference on Labor Protection was not convened, however, until 1890 (in Berlin). In 1876, a proposal by the Swiss Federal Council for a European Conference to consider the idea of international regulation had been formally rejected by Bismarck. In 1890, however, Bismarck resigned in a dispute with the Emperor Wilhelm II over abrogation of the anti-Socialist laws.

The record of opinions expressed at the Conference showed that European thought as a whole at that time was disinclined to favor such reforms as a minimum age for child labor; a maximum working day both for women and children; relieving women and children of night work; healthy and safe working conditions; and Sunday rest, holidays, and giving workers notice before dismissal (Garvin 1919: 332).

[9] According to the constitution of the International Labour Organisation set up by the League of Nations after World War I, "the establishment of universal peace... can be established only if it is based on social justice.... [C]onditions of labour exist involving such injustice, hardship, and privation to large numbers of people as to produce unrest so great that the peace and harmony of the world are imperilled" (in Zilliacus 1946: 234–35).

[10] "Never in European history and rarely anywhere else has revolutionism been so endemic, so general, so likely to spread by spontaneous contagion as well as by deliberate propaganda" (Hobsbawm 1962: 137). And in fact, there were waves of revolutions in Europe: in the 1820s, 1830s, 1840s, and 1900s.

[11] The English translation is in Hertslet 1891: i, 375, Article VI.

suppressed uprisings in Parma, Modena, Bologna, Ferrara, and Romagna in 1831. Italian risings elsewhere were suppressed by or with the support of Austria and France, and various risings were put down in parts of Germany (e.g., in the Palatinate in 1832 and in Frankfurt in 1833 and 1846). In 1848, Austria attempted to occupy Bologna in order to suppress an uprising there. French troops bombarded Rome when insurrection threatened the Pope in 1849. Russia invaded Hungary and Wallachia to put down rebellions, and Prussia occupied the Bavarian Palatinate and the Duchy of Baden to put down insurrections. Prussian troops restored order in Saxony and Hanover in May 1849. A joint force of Russians and Austrians crushed a revolt by Herzegovinians in 1862. France and Britain intervened in a rebellion in Crete, 1866–69. France and Lithuania intervened in the Russo-Polish War of 1918–20.

Concerned to defend their common way of life, Europe's owning classes of all nations joined together, fighting side by side with "foreign" class allies to suppress dissident and revolutionary elements from among their own countrymen. British and French forces backed Spanish conservatives in Spain (1820, 1821, 1823–33), Austrians fought with Piedmontese nobles in Naples (1820, 1848), British troops fought side by side with Portuguese royalists in Portugal (1829), German forces backed the Finnish right in Finland (1918), and Romanians and Hungarians put down a communist revolution in Hungary (1919). France, Britain, Czechoslovakia, Germany, the United States, Poland, and Japan fought with Russian conservatives to overturn the Bolshevik Revolution in Russia. Germany and Italy supported the antigovernment fascists in the Spanish Civil War of 1936–39. These cross-border military interventions in Europe helped to preserve the essential contours of local class structures throughout the nineteenth century.

Labor, enfranchisement, ethnic, and imperialist conflicts were all related to a pattern of development that, itself, was related to class interests and struggle. Political and economic restrictions led to labor and minority conflicts and struggles for and against the extension of the franchise. Inasmuch as external expansion was pursued by elites in order to consolidate their position in class struggles at home, it was also related to class struggles in Europe. Analytically, it is possible to discuss these separately, as they are below. Conflicts in which labor issues are clearly at the center of concern are discussed below as "labor conflicts" (see Table 4.3). These include numerous forms of resistance – violent strikes, industrial riots, bread, food, and housing riots – by wage workers as well as agricultural wage laborers and the unemployed;[12] as well as various types of government action against labor,

---

[12] Rioting was commonplace in the nineteenth century. Riots were not simply a reaction to transitory hardship; in the absence of institutionalized access to political power and economic resources, they represented a rational means of pressing demands. They were, in fact, "an

TABLE 4.3. *Intervention by European States in Class (Labor and Enfranchisement) and Ethnic Conflicts in Other Regional States*

Conflict	Type	Intervention by
Greece, 1821	Ethnic	France, Britain, Venice, Russia
Naples, 1820	Class	Austria
Spain, 1820	Class	France
Spain, 1821	Class	France
Portugal, 1826–33	Class	Spain, Britain, France
Belgium, 1830–33	Ethnic	Britain, France
Spain, 1833–40	Class	Britain, Portugal
German States, 1848	Ethnic	Prussia, Bavaria
Hungary, 1849	Ethnic	Russia
Crete, 1866–69	Ethnic	France, Britain, Greece
East Rumelia, 1885	Ethnic	Bulgaria
Russia, 1918–21	Class	France, Italy, Britain, Germany
Finnish civil war, 1918	Class	Germany, Russia
Hungary, 1919	Class	Romania
Spain, 1936–39	Class	Germany, Italy
Greece, 1944–46	Class	Britain, Yugoslavia, Bulgaria, Albania

including states of siege, coups d'etat, imposition of martial law, and police and military clashes in response to labor unrest. Those conflicts in which extension of the franchise was at issue are treated here as "enfranchisement conflicts." Conflicts involving ethnic minorities and largely concerned with nationalism, issues of nationality, or national rights, are called "ethnic conflicts." Conflicts involving the acquisition of territory or of indirect control over the political or economic life of other areas are called "imperialist conflicts."[13]

LABOR CONFLICTS

Starting in England at the end of the eighteenth century, and in Western continental countries around 1840, lack of land and work opportunities helped to make the conditions of life for labor worsen immeasurably. As a result, there was a marked increase in social conflict in Europe. While there may not be everywhere and at all times a link between misery (or poverty) and militancy, in nineteenth-century Europe it is possible to find many instances

essential part of the methods of struggle" of the early working class, an acknowledged form of 'political' behavior" (Peacock 1965: 13–14).

[13] That a country's involvement in a war was imperialistic can be shown with reference to the territories gained or sought (see discussion below and Appendix 2).

where these appear to have been linked and, in addition, reasons why this linkage might be found there and then.

First, it should be noted that poverty in Europe in the nineteenth century differed from that which existed in ages past in a number of crucial ways. Poverty in earlier periods had been "poverty of the unfortunate – the old, sick, lame, widowed, orphaned, demented, or temporary victims of local harvest or employment problems." But the reorganization of economic relations at the end of the eighteenth century "created a permanent group of able-bodied" individuals who were destitute because they were unable to find work or to make a living wage (Goldstone 1991: 254). Moreover, unlike past ages, the mass misery of nineteenth-century Europe arose within societies capable of producing an unlimited quantity of goods. The problem, thus, was not of production but of distribution.[14] Countless nineteenth-century writers, social scientists, reformers, and statesmen were acutely conscious of the social implications of the problem.[15]

While some scholars insist that real wages increased during the nineteenth and early twentieth centuries, as Chapter 3 argued, if we examine this increase by sector, we find that it was largely confined in Britain to a "labor aristocracy" consisting of a maximum of 15 percent, and probably less, of the work force. These workers were employed in the export sectors – those that were more mechanized and, consequently, required a more highly skilled work force. Wages throughout the rest of the economy were lower until after World War II.

There was a link between the timing and geographical spread of radical activity, on the one hand, and changes in real wages, on the other.[16] The revolutions of 1830 and 1848 were immediately preceded by economic depressions (1826–29 and 1846–48, respectively). Mass socialist working-class parties emerged all over Europe during the era of the Great Depression (1873–90). The depression also triggered an explosive rise in strike activity throughout Europe. Strikes also became far more numerous and violent

---

[14] Douglas Ashford notes:

> Socioeconomic interpretations of British poverty make a serious error in blaming British poverty on industrial capitalism. The history of British local taxation from 1834 onwards is about protecting landowners from taxation for local social needs, and the now abandoned grant system was initially devised in 1929 for the same reason. The outcry against Lloyd George's national insurance in 1911 was largely due to the imposition of a small land tax. (1992: 150n3)

[15] Hegel pointed out that "against nature man can claim no right, but once society is established, poverty immediately takes the form of a wrong done to one class by another" (*Philosophy of Right*, addition to 244).

[16] On this, see, e.g., Foster 1974: chap. 2; Hobsbawm 1964: 130–33; Charlesworth 1983: passim. Official and journalistic reports and inquiries often attributed labor violence to low wages (see, e.g., note 21 below).

between 1910 and 1914 when inflation threatened to erode working-class living standards (Geary 1981: 122–25).

During the Napoleonic Wars and despite the rapid rise in production within both industry and agriculture,[17] real wages declined in Britain. Those years saw "the largest outbreak of food disturbances to occur in England at any period" (Stevenson 1975: 65). During the wars, these began increasingly to overlap with strikes and wage riots (Archer 1990: 88). "By 1799, virtually every form of working-class association or collective action was illegal or licensable by the justices of the peace" (Munger 1981: 93). However, by the end of the wars, trade union activity had overtaken rioting in many places (Stevenson 1975: 63). Various forms of covert protest became widespread during the wars, as well.[18] Arson, the most widely feared of these, became a continuous form of rural protest in England during the nineteenth century,[19] provoking "prodigious fears" on the part of landowners and compelling them to regularly ask for troops "to patrol affected areas" (Wells 1990: 44–45).

Between 1793 and 1820, more than sixty acts directed at repression of working-class collective action were passed by the British Parliament. Waves of food and wage riots (1799–1801, 1809–10, and 1812–13) were vigorously suppressed during the wars by both regular and volunteer soldiers.[20] In 1811–12, it took 12,000 regular troops nearly a year to suppress a guerrilla campaign in England covering most of the north and midlands (Foster 1974: 40).

The end of the Napoleonic Wars brought no peace. Beginning in 1815, England experienced one of the most violent periods in her history. Just as the labor market was swollen by discharged soldiers and sailors, the introduction of threshing machines decreased demand for labor, and a postwar agricultural depression cut into farmers' profits and ruled out pay increases for laborers. In London, discussion of the Corn Bill set off several days of rioting. Rioting continued throughout 1815. Rioters protested the high price of bread in Bridport; the export of grain at Biddeford; unemployment in Birmingham, Walsall, and Preston; and the use of agricultural machines in Bury. A protest against starvation wages and intolerable working conditions

---

[17] Note that there was a substantially greater increase in exports than in imports.

[18] Overt protest by agricultural laborers endangered their claim to poor relief. See, for the period of the war, the partial listing of arson attacks in Wells 1990: 42–43.

[19] For a discussion of the debate on its scope and character, see Archer 1990. A *Times* "Inquiry into Incendiary Fires" (June 7, 1844) concluded that the widespread incendiarism in the southern agricultural counties was caused by exceptionally low wages; the decline of farm service; the enclosure of open fields, commons, and wastes; and antagonism to the New Poor law and the law's detrimental effect on employment (cited in Snell 1985: 104).

[20] The Volunteer Movement was created as an armed patriot party by the government to act both as a reserve in case of invasion and as a police force. The landowners and farmers played the major role in the movement.

was suppressed in Nottingham with a force greater than Wellington used in Spain (Droz 1967: 87). In 1816, there began a series of riots against agricultural machinery and low wages in Ely and Littleport. Colliers and others protested a reduction of wages at Methyr-Tydville and Newcastle-upon-Tyne; rioters plundered shops at Dundee in protest at the high price of bread (Peacock 1965: 12, 14–15; Stevenson 1975 : 62–63; Musket 1984: 2). Rural unrest increased by 1819. That year saw the Peterloo massacre in England and riots in Hamburg, Frankfurt am Main, Würzburg, and Karlsruhe.

Revolutionary uprisings swept through Europe during the 1820s. Agrarian protests continued throughout the decade, as, for instance, the riots in England in East Anglia in 1822 and the widespread and violent disturbances throughout the manufacturing districts of the north of England in 1826. Then, in 1830, there began a series of protests against farmers, landowners, magistrates, and the clergy that collectively came to be known as the "Swing Movement." Miners, colliers, and iron workers in Wales and Scotland rioted for higher wages. Other riots protested the Poor Law in England and church rates, tithes, and high rents in Wales (Williams 1955). A peasant rebellion known as the "Tithe War" broke out in Ireland in 1830. Similar conflicts erupted during the 1830s in other countries of Europe. There were riots in Naples and Sicily; antitax, antipolice, food, and worker's riots in many parts of Germany (e.g., in Saxony, Hessen, Braunschweig, and Hannover); and a revolt of Berlin journeymen in 1835. There were also violent demonstrations in Paris and a few other large cities in 1830 and 1832; attacks on machines in St. Etienne, Bordeaux, and Toulouse; and food riots in the east and southwest. In April 1834, there was a major uprising in Lyons, followed by an insurrection in Paris. In both places, national guards and troops suppressed the uprisings, killing and wounding many (see Appendix 3).

In 1840, the French military put down a strike of Paris tailors and workers in other trades that spread to other parts of the country. The following year there were tax rebellions in the southwest. There was a weavers' revolt in Silesia in 1844 and riots in Frankfurt in 1846. Serious and widespread food riots, known as the "potato war," broke out in the spring of 1847 in Berlin and other cities. Barricades were thrown up and troops were called out to quell the rioting. Then, in March 1848, some 300 workers were killed during an insurrection in Berlin. In 1846, widespread food riots and similar conflicts broke out in a semicircle around Paris. In June 1848, a workers' rebellion put Paris under a state of siege. There were demonstrations and riots in Palermo and Messina; in August 1848, an uprising in Livorno forced officials and troops to flee the city (see Appendix 3).

The 1850s saw the emergence of the strike as the weapon of choice of European working classes. Before 1850, strike activity outside England had been almost entirely defensive in nature, with workers uniting in hard times to defend themselves against wage cutting. However, after the 1850s, the strike became an offensive weapon for the improvement of wages and

TABLE 4.4. *Strikes in Britain in the 1870s*

Year	Number	Year	Number
1870	30	1875	245
1871	98	1876	229
1872	343	1877	180
1873	365	1878	268
1874	286	1879	308

Source: Bevan 1880: 37.

working conditions. By the 1870s and throughout Europe, the strike had become the "workers' preferred form of action."[21]

There was a sharp increase in strike activity in Europe as a result of the depression of the 1870s. The rise in numbers of strikes in Britain each year of that decade was indicative of the general trend (see Table 4.4). In Italy, there were a handful of strikes in the 1850s, 132 strikes in the 1860s, and 520 strikes in the 1870s. In the 1870s, there were violent strikes of agricultural workers in Lombardy and Emilia (1871, 1872, 1875) and of textile workers in Pisa (1873).

The decade began, in France, with the rising of the Paris commune in which Parisians led a movement to secede from France. Some 20,000 were killed or banished during the repression and reprisals. Working-class radicalism in France was effectively crushed until the turn of the century. In Germany there were massive, bloody riots in Frankfurt am Main in 1873, and in Tuscany there were bread riots in 1874.

There were numerous violent strikes in France in 1880 and in Italy strikes and demonstrations in the Cremona and Parma regions (1883), in the Verona region (1883), and in the Polesine region (1884). In Belgium, troops put down rioting miners in Liége and Charleroi and throughout the Borinage in 1886, and killed twelve during a general strike and an armed uprising of the mining population in 1893. In 1889, there were violent miners' strikes in the Ruhr

[21] Gillis 1983: 269. Though there were occasional strikes much earlier than this, "these seem to have played a far less important role in the broad array of popular protest and collective action" (Cronin 1989: 84–85). The gradual replacement of riots by strikes was noted by observers in the early 1870s (see, e.g., Potter 1870: 34–35; and 1871: 535).

The "meaning" of a strike is considerably different at different times and places. After World War II, the official strike became accepted as a normal bargaining tool in contract relations. "Strikes which occur in a time and place where they are illegal cannot be easily equated with strikes in a time and place where they have become legal, routine, and routinized" (Silver 1995: 21). Where strikes have become legal and routinized, they do not represent a significant form of struggle against the proletarian condition. Thus, the high level of strike activity in the United States during the 1950s and 1960s is not necessarily an indication of "labor unrest." A strike in Franco's Spain is not comparable in terms of measuring the degree of labor unrest with a strike in the United States in the 1990s.

and Silesia, and in 1890, there were large clashes between socialist workers and police in Berlin (see Appendix 3).

Troops were called in on numerous occasions to quell militant labor disputes in Switzerland during the 1890s. In Italy, there was a large strike of masons in Rome in 1890 and violent strikes of textile workers and agricultural workers in Lombardy and among day laborers in the Ravenna area. Clashes involved workers in France, Poland, and Spain (1891), as well as in Britain, Italy, and Belgium (1893).

After the turn of the century, industrial disputes reached unprecedented proportions. Bitter strikes swept France, Germany, Italy, Britain, Belgium, and Russia during the 1900s. In France, the years from 1892 to 1910 were the most militant in the history of the working class. There were over 1,000 strikes per year after 1906. In 1900–1901, there were insurrectionary strikes in Belfort, Montceau-les-Mines, Marseilles, and elsewhere in the country. The year 1902 saw the first effective industry-wide strikes. In 1905–6, violent strikes involved struggles with troops on numerous occasions. The first attempts to organize national stoppages came in 1906.[22] French troops killed twenty strikers and wounded 667 at Nantes in 1908 (Tilly, Tilly, and Tilly 1975). The number of industrial disputes escalated in Germany: from 1,468 strikes in 1900 to 2,834 in 1912 (Geary 1981: 105). There were bloody strikes in Berlin in 1910 and in the Ruhr in 1912. Between 1900 and 1914, labor conflict increased dramatically in Italy: strikes, strikers, and workdays lost were about eight times higher than in the 1880s (Bordogna, Cella, and Provasi 1989: 223–24). There were large, violent strikes both in agricultural (1901–6) and industrial areas (1906–7, 1910–13). In Britain, there were massive railway and dock strikes in 1911. Some 200 were wounded in the Liverpool riots in 1911. Also in 1911 and extending into 1912, miners, dockers, seamen, and railwaymen at Southampton, Liverpool, Hull, and Cardiff attacked trains, looted, set fire to buildings, and fought troops, of whom some 50,000 were used to break strikes and quell riots (see Appendix 2). In Belgium, there were massive strikes in 1902; eight strikers were killed that year at Louvain (Goldstein 1983: 264). There was a general strike in 1913.

In Russia, violence escalated throughout the first decade of the century. There were 155 interventions by troops in 1901; on 365 occasions, troops were used to crush the peasantry in 1902. In 1903, a force far greater than the army of 1812 was used for internal order (Stone 1983: 212–13). During that year, there were 322 interventions by troops, involving 295 squadrons of cavalry and 300 battalions of infantry, some with artillery. Troops were needed on 114,108 occasions in 1909. A total of 2,709,695 workers in 13,111 enterprises participated in strikes in 1905. In just one of these – a railway strike in Riga during October – 120 people were killed (Miliukov 1922). The total number of strikes rose from 466 in 1911, to 2,032 in 1912, and

---

[22] For a compilation of statistical data, see Shorter and Tilly 1974: appendix B.

TABLE 4.5. *Percent of European Population Enfranchised, 1910*

Finland	45	Austria	21
Norway	33	Sweden	19
France	29	United Kingdom	18
Spain	24	Denmark	17
Bulgaria	23	Portugal	12
Greece	23	Romania	16
Serbia	23	Russia	15
Germany	22	Netherlands	14
Belgium	22	Italy	8
Switzerland	22	Hungary	6

Source: Goldstein 1983: 241.

to 3,534 in 1913. Between 1912 and 1914, the incidence of strikes, mass protests, police arrests, and killings continued to increase to an alarming degree (Seton-Watson 1967: 541; Stone 1983: 257). By 1913, there were 100,000 arrests for "attacks on State power" (Stone 1983: 244). Not only in Russia but in all the capitals of Europe, labor violence was raising alarms on the eve of World War I.

ENFRANCHISEMENT CONFLICTS

Throughout the nineteenth and early twentieth centuries, enfranchisement conflicts were a constant feature of European societies. They were started either by lower classes protesting their exclusion from political life and opportunities for economic advancement or by upper classes resisting efforts to expand political participation and economic freedom.

Before 1945, European "democracy" was a severely limited form of representative government that excluded the great majority of adults from participation. Like democracy in the ancient world, it was really an "egalitarian oligarchy," in which "a ruling class of citizens shared the rights and spoils of political control" (MacIver 1932: 352). Universal adult suffrage would have enfranchised 40 to 50 percent of each country's population. In 1910, only some 14 to 22 percent of the population was enfranchised in Sweden, Switzerland, Great Britain, Belgium, Denmark, the Netherlands, and Germany. Where the suffrage included members of the poorer classes, three-class and other weighted and plural voting systems, as well as open balloting and restrictions on and biases against working-class organizations and parties, made it futile for poor people to vote.[23] Thus, the figures listed in Table 4.5 do not reflect the actual number of people who were permitted

[23] Until 1918, suffrage qualifications were so complicated in England that it was difficult to determine the number of qualified voters. Lodgers had to make an annual claim in order

to vote under the systems existing at the time. In nearly all states in Europe, the franchise remained highly restricted until after World War II. On the eve of World War I, Norway was the only country in Europe with universal and equal suffrage. It was only after World War II that universal, equal, direct, and secret suffrage became the norm throughout Western Europe.

Following the Napoleonic Wars, violent conflict erupted over efforts to expand or preserve the existing structure of rights within European societies. Enfranchisement conflicts erupted in Europe in every decade of the nineteenth century. In the 1820s, uprisings pitted royalists against republicans in Spain (1820, 1821) and pressed for democratic reforms in Italy (1820). Spanish royalists, aided by the French, fought against the liberal government and reinstated the absolutist rule of King Ferdinand (1823); liberals rebelled against the autocratic rule of Nicholas I in Russia (1825); nobles and clerics fought to put an end to the Portuguese constitution (1828–34).

In July 1830, French king Charles X refused to heed the verdict of an election and issued decrees dissolving the Chamber of Deputies and establishing a new electoral system that would shift even more electoral power to noble and landed proprietors and away from the professional, commercial, and industrial middle classes. Revolution started in Paris within a day. Two hundred soldiers and 2,000 citizens died in the fighting. The uprising had immediate repercussions in Nantes, Bordeaux, Toulouse, Nimes, and a few other places. Later, there were tax rebellions, food riots, workers' protests, and violent demonstrations in many parts of France. During the following year, there were major rebellions in Paris, minor ones in a number of other cities, food riots in the east and southwest, large Legitimist protests at several points in the south, and an even larger Legitimist insurrection through important parts of the west. In 1834, national guards and troops

---

to keep on the register. Claims and objections were heard and passed on by the revising barristers in the presence of party agents. This method of compiling the lists did not secure accuracy or completeness (Gosnell 1930). Though 88 percent of the adult male population should have qualified to vote in 1911 were it not for complications and limitations in the registration procedures that were biased against the working class, less than 30 percent of the total adult population of the United Kingdom was able to vote. Moreover, in 1911, half a million of the eight million voters were plural voters and, needless to say, not many of them were working class (Blewett 1965; Rueschemeyer et al. 1992: 97). In the Austrian Kurien and the Prussian three-class system, the weights of the votes given to the lower classes were infinitesimal in comparison with those of the established landed or financial elite. France did not introduce proportional representation until 1945; up until then, electoral practices ensured the overrepresentation of more conservative rural voters (Wright 1964). The Netherlands did not adopt proportional representation until 1917. In Hungary and Prussia as late as 1914, in Denmark until 1901, and in Austria until 1906, open balloting, usually by oral voting or by a show of hands, facilitated the use of pressure and manipulation by governmental officials and local elites, especially in rural areas (Goldstein 1983: 15–17). Plural voting and other electoral abuses survived in England until 1948 (O'Leary 1962).

massacred insurgents in uprisings in Lyons and Paris (*Annual Register* 1834: 350–52).

In Britain, insurrection, both in the cities and in the countryside, was prevented when the parliament passed the Reform Bill and admitted to political life the well-to-do elements of the middle class. By this concession the ruling landed interests enlisted the support of the most influential sector of the opposition, thus forestalling a real alliance between the upper middle class and the lower strata of the population in town and country.

In Germany, there was rioting, revolts, and rebellion in many parts of the country during August and November, including antitax, antiadministration, food, and worker's riots (1830–31), and a huge antiaristocratic demonstration in the Palatinate (1832). In Italy, insurrections in Romagna, Modena, and Parma demanded domestic reform (1831). There were civil wars in Spain and Portugal between conservatives and liberals (1828–40). In Spain, the Carlist Wars (1833–40) pitted conservatives and clerics for Don Carlos as absolute monarch against liberals for parliamentary government and the British government for constitutionalism. In Portugal, the "Miguelite Wars" pitted nobles and clericals against Portuguese liberals between 1828 and 1834. A revolt in Portugal in 1836 by the "Septembrists" forced Queen Maria II to promise the restoration of the Portuguese constitution of 1822.

A period of reaction followed these revolutions. The July monarchy of Louis Philippe was soon forced to become conservative. The rising in Bologna strengthened Austria's hold over the papacy. In reaction to the constitutions that had been proclaimed in Bavaria, Würtemburg, and Saxony, it was decided at the Federal Diet of 1832 that a German prince was bound to reject petitions that increased the power of the Estates at the expense of the power of the Sovereign. The Hanoverian Constitution of 1833 went down four years later.

In 1848, another wave of revolutions swept through France, all of Italy, the German states, and most of the Hapsburg Empire, triggering upheavals in Spain, Denmark, Russia, Romania, Ireland, Greece, and Britain. In France, a revolution secured the introduction of universal suffrage for departmental councils. In Italy, there were Republican insurrections in Pavia, Piacenza, Bologna, Volterra, Genoa, Lucca, Reggio, Carrara, and Milan. Insurrection in Rome caused the Pope to flee (November 1848) and led to the proclamation of a Roman republic (February 1849). In Austria, a movement for constitutional government and demands for democratic government drove the Emperor from Vienna, Prince Metternich, into exile. Emperor Ferdinand was compelled to accept the "March Laws" formulated by the Hungarian Diet. The population of Wallachia secured liberal concessions from the Turkish government. In Britain, there was a final flare-up of Chartism in April 1848, when news of the revolutions on the Continent led to serious riots in Glasgow and London, and in July, an insurrection in Ireland. An uprising against the English administration of the Ionian Islands broke out in Cephalonia in September 1848. Riots and demonstrations in Germany forced King Frederick William IV to call a constituent assembly. Uprisings broke out in May and June 1849 in the Rhineland. Marx, Engels, and other communists were expelled. In Dresden, the King fled the city and appealed to the Prussian government for military aid. An insurgence in the Bavarian Palatinate was put down by Prussian troops in June. Prussian occupation forces put down an insurgency in Baden, where radicals from all over Europe had gathered.

The coup d'etat of Louis Napoleon in December 1851 triggered an insurrection in Paris that left over 500 people killed or wounded. There was armed resistance to the coup in almost a third of France's departments (Langer 1969: 462). Throughout 1850 and 1851, there was much violence in the territories occupied by Prussian, Austrian, and Bavarian troops (Tilly 1975b). In 1854, a military insurrection in Spain issued demands for the amelioration of the election and press laws, the diminution of taxes, and advancement in the civil service according to merit. Feudal lords in Bosnia-Herzegovina and Montenegro rose in rebellion against liberal Ottoman reforms (1852, 1853, 1861–62); peasants in Bosnia-Herzegovina rebelled against feudal obligations in 1858. In 1859, Austrian-controlled rulers in Italy fought to maintain their autocracies. Liberals led by Garibaldi, Cavour, and Victor Emmanuel fought for democracy against the autocratic governments of Sicily, Naples, and the papal states. In the 1870s, Carlists fought for Church rights, absolutism, and local autonomy against the parliamentary Spanish governments of King Amadeo (1872), then of Republicans (1873), then of Alphonso XII (1874–85). In 1881, there was an uprising of Radical Republicans against the papacy. There were violent disturbances in Belgium over extension of the suffrage in 1899 and 1902 (Carstairs 1980: 55). In Hungary, 200,000 turned out for a suffrage demonstration in 1907. In May 1912, a huge suffrage protest and general strike in Hungary led to severe rioting after troops fired on demonstrators, killing six and wounding over 200. A revolution in Russia in 1905 was sparked by demands for representative government and universal and equal suffrage.

ETHNIC CONFLICTS

In Europe, lower classes and ethnic minorities often were similarly situated with respect to economic opportunities and rights of citizenship. Thus, the struggle of lower classes for extension of the franchise and for better living conditions merged with the struggle of ethnic minorities in Europe to secure equal rights. As elsewhere, minorities in Europe usually favored secularism and individual rights and were associated with the struggle for democracy. Thus, in opposing minorities, elites sought to contain demands for democracy. The absence of democracy in Europe prevented countries in Europe from becoming fully integrated nation-states in the nineteenth century. Thus, the task of nation building continued to be regarded as problematic for almost every European country up until World War II.

Britain was continually faced with rebellion in Ireland and anti-English feeling in the Scottish Highlands. Throughout the nineteenth century, not a single decade went by without some crisis over Ireland[24] where, in one of the most backward areas of Europe, large segments of the peasantry lived in abject misery. Regional traditions survived very strongly in France, most notably in Brittany and in the French Basque region. Catalan and Basque separatist movements remained active in Spain throughout the period. In the twentieth century, there was still an active Flemish movement in Belgium, Jurassic separatism in Switzerland, and an autonomist movement among the German-speaking Tyrolese in Italy. In Germany, the territorial duchies (e.g., Bavaria, Saxony, Swabia, and Franconia) remained the focus of patriotic sentiment throughout the century. Catholics rioted in 1836, 1864, 1866, and 1874. German control over part of Poland generated constant tension. There were anti-Semitic riots in eastern Prussia in 1881 and in Hamburg, Frankfurt am Main, Würzburg, Karlsruhe, and smaller places in 1919. During the 1920s, there were separatist movements in the Rhineland and in the Bavarian Palatinate.[25]

Nationalist uprisings in the Austro-Hungarian Empire and in the European provinces of the Ottoman Empire erupted in every decade of the nineteenth century. The Russian Empire included non-Russian regions that today are Finland, the Baltic States, and Poland. Russia put down uprisings in the portion of Poland under its control in 1831 and 1863. Anti-Jewish pogroms swept Belostok, Odessa, Nikolaev, Kiev, and some sixty-six other towns and villages from 1903 to 1905, leaving hundreds of Jews dead and thousands destitute (Urusov 1908: chaps. 4 and 5). In 1913, the Russian army sought to crush resentful ethnic minorities – Poles, Finns, Georgians, Latvians, Estonians, and Armenians – who were seeking to preserve concessions over "Russification" that they had obtained during 1905–6 (Seton-Watson 1967: 485, 607, 643). The disaffection of the major non-Russian nationalities was one of the principal factors contributing to the Revolution of 1917 in Russia. All the revolutionary parties of Russia counted among their leaders members of the educated classes of many nationalities.[26]

---

[24] Goldstein records a continual stream of agrarian uprisings and riots in Ireland throughout the century, as well as the crises these events engendered in London (1983: 229–30, 252, 257, 258–62).

[25] In September 1923, separatists seized Düsseldorf, and a month later, the "Rhineland Republic" was proclaimed at Aachen (October 21) and at Coblenz (October 25). Bonn, Wiesbaden, Treves, and Mainz were also occupied by separatist forces. The "Autonomous Government of the Palatinate" was proclaimed at Speyer on November 11, and was officially recognized by the French High Commissioner (Mowat 1927: 254–57; Benns 1930: 394–402).

[26] Aspaturian 1968: 143. Both Lenin and Stalin were specialists on the national question. Lenin was one of the chief and original expositors in the twentieth century of the principal

In Austria-Hungary, nine different racial groups were ruled over by Germans and Magyars, making the Empire the scene of recurring discontent and armed insurrection. The subordination of minorities was a significant factor in the events leading up to the First World War (Claude 1955: 10). In 1914, traditionalists and conservatives in the Empire attempted to end the drive of the Slavic peoples, who together comprised half the population of the Empire, for national autonomy.

With Franz Ferdinand's active support and encouragement, improved representation had been extended to non-German minorities in Austria by the Moravian Compromise of 1905, the Bukovina Compromise of 1910, and the Polish-Ruthenian Compromise of early 1914. His assassination in 1914 cleared the way for a conservative backlash against the liberalization that had taken place under his direction. During the Balkan Wars of 1912–13, all sections of the right in Austria had urged the government to invade Serbia in 1913. Now, with Franz Ferdinand dead, the balance of power within the Austrian government shifted (Williamson 1979).

IMPERIALIST CONFLICTS

As discussed in previous chapters, in order to expand production and increase profits while at the same time maintaining political and economic restrictions on other classes and on minorities, landed and industrial elites pursued imperial expansion in lieu of developing the home market. Expansionist and imperialist policies were proposed and advocated by elites as a means of increasing revenue and resources and alleviating land hunger without redistribution and reform. In Britain, elites championed imperial expansion as a means of reducing the misery of the metropolitan industrial proletariat and pacifying the peasants.[27] In Italy, Francesco Crispi's colonial policy gained support principally from the church and the landowning nobility.[28] In Germany, the big landowners and leaders of heavy industry in the Pan-German League were the most persistent and zealous champions of territorial expansion.[29]

---

of national self-determination, a concept that found its way into President Wilson's Fourteen Points some years after the Bolsheviks had incorporated it into their own political program.

[27] In their attempt to prove the material advantage of colonialism, British imperialists "stressed the value of the colonies chiefly as a market for emigration" (Burt 1956: 446).

[28] In the 1890s, in the midst of widespread rural violence throughout Sicily aimed at breaking up the big estates and distributing the land, Crispi conjured up the image of colonial lands to be exploited to appease the southern peasants demanding land (Gramsci 1971: 67n25).

[29] In the late 1870s, landowners and large industrialists in Germany attributed bottlenecks in the economy to a lack of *Lebensraum*, a doctrine that asserted the need to acquire "living space" in order to offset the excessive concentration of Germany's population on a restricted area of arable soil (the word "*Lebensraum*" was later given wide usage by Hitler

Throughout the nineteenth and early twentieth centuries, efforts to secure protected foreign markets generated imperialist conflicts. Imperialist exploitation of other states and territories, both within and outside Europe, also generated resistance from the affected populations. There was resistance during the establishment of the colonial system (wars), under colonialism (taxation and famine riots, peasant revolts, etc.), and at the end of it (wars of decolonization, military actions, pacifications).

The "Golden Age" of European imperialism began with the Napoleonic Wars and continued for some 150 years. During that period, European states – France, Great Britain, Russia, Austria-Hungary, Germany, Sweden, Belgium, the Netherlands, Italy, Spain, Portugal, Greece, Serbia, Bulgaria, Romania, and Poland – embarked on imperial expansion, annexing territories and engaging in imperialist rivalries and wars, both in Europe and outside the region.

As the century progressed, imperialism fused with nationalist movements: witness, during this period, the Great Germany crusade, Russian Pan-Slav Movement, and movements for a Greater Serbia, Greater Bulgaria, a Great Slav state, a Greater Greece, Greater Romania, Greater Macedonia, and Greater Croatia. In the early twentieth century, Polish nationalists sought the resurrection of the Polish Commonwealth; Lithuanians sought the resurrection of the Kingdom of Lithuania. Fascist Italy launched a crusade to recreate a Roman empire; Nazi Germany sought to create a vast German empire in the heart of Europe.

Beginning with the Napoleonic Wars, and throughout the nineteenth and early twentieth centuries, Europe itself was an arena of imperialist expansion and conflict. Napoleon, facing an annual deficit of hundreds of millions of francs, and having no more success in substantially raising direct taxes than had Louis XVI, had first confiscated the property of foreigners in France, and then extended his campaign of plunder to other countries. Confiscation of crown and feudal properties in defeated countries, spoils taken directly from the enemy's armies, garrisons, museums, and treasuries, and the imposition of war indemnities in money or in kind offset Napoleon's enormous military expenditures and produced considerable profits for France.[30]

---

and Himmler). The landowners wanted to expand eastward so as to lend added weight to the agrarian sector in the German economy and in the political sphere as a whole. In the east, they hoped to annex the Polish frontier districts and Russia's Baltic provinces as a "strategic bulwark" and "settlement area." Heavy industry wanted to annex the French iron ore districts, control Belgium, and acquire the Belgian Congo.

[30]   The sums acquired by the administrators of this *domaine extraordinaire* in the period of France's zenith were quite remarkable and in some ways foreshadow Nazi Germany's plunder of its satellites and conquered foes during the Second World War. Prussia, for example, had to pay a penalty of 311 million francs after Jena, which was equal

After 1803, Napoleon formed an economic combine of Continental Europe. His Continental System, which was directed against his own allies as well as Great Britain, worked to provide a large, protected market for France's historic luxury industries and her fledgling textile industry (Heckscher 1964). He incorporated Holland and the Hanseatic States into the French Empire as protected markets for French products and envisioned transforming the Kingdom of Italy (northern Italy) entirely into an economic dependency and a supplier of cotton for France's textile industry (Heckscher 1964: 297).

Sweden's Crown Prince Bernadotte (later to be known as King Charles XIV) launched a military attack against Norway and made it a subordinate unit in a personal union with Sweden. Finland, part of the Swedish Kingdom until 1809, was ceded to Russia in 1809 and remained a subordinate territory within the Russian Empire until 1917. Belgium was incorporated into France from 1795 to 1815 and dominated by the Dutch until 1830 (and by the Germans between 1914 and 1918). The northern part of Denmark's Duchy of Schleswig, ceded to Prussia from 1864, was part of Germany until 1920. In 1860, France acquired Savoy and Nice from Piedmont. Alsace and Lorraine were ceded to Germany from 1871 to 1918.

Russia fought wars to acquire Moldavia and Wallachia (1806–12, 1828, 1853–56), Finland (1808–9), and Bessarabia, and Austria-Hungary fought to retain control of Naples (1815, 1820), Piedmont (1821, 1848–49), Milan (1848), its possessions in Italy (1859), and Venetia (1866) and to acquire Schleswig-Holstein (1864) and Bosnia-Herzegovina (1878). Germany fought to acquire Schleswig-Holstein (1848–50, 1864) and the south German states (1866, 1870). Italy fought for control of northern Italy (1859), southern Italy (1860–61), and Venetia (1866). Montenegro fought to expand its boundaries (1852–53, 1858–59). Serbian and Bulgarian ambitions with regard to Bosnia and East Rumelia, respectively, led to war between those countries and the Ottoman Empire in 1876, 1878, and 1885.

The European chase to acquire Ottoman territories or spheres of influence both within and outside Europe was a focus of imperialist rivalries throughout the nineteenth and early twentieth centuries. The Great Powers worked to exploit ethnic divisions in the Balkans and in other Ottoman territories, making the expected (or hoped for) breakup of the Ottoman Empire (the "Eastern Question") a permanent cause of crisis in Europe throughout the century (starting with the Greek uprising in the 1820s). Britain and France exploited ethnic distinctions in the Ottoman Empire in their quest to control the sea and land routes to India. Austrian imperialist ambitions in

to half of the French government's ordinary revenue. At each defeat, the Hapsburg Empire was forced to cede territories and to pay a large indemnity. In Italy between 1805 and 1812 about half of the taxes raised went to the French. (Kennedy 1987: 132–33)

Bosnia-Herzegovina generated a series of conflicts from 1878 until the start of World War I. Britain sought to shore up Turkey against Russian expansion in order to protect the sea and land routes to India and her growing economic interest in the Empire.[31] In 1914, France supplied 45 percent of the foreign capital in the private sector of the Ottoman economy and 60 percent of the Ottoman public debt, and thus had an enormous stake in the empire's continued existence and vitality.[32] Russia sought to win the straits between Europe and Asia Minor that controlled its access to the Mediterranean. Russian imperialist ambitions with respect to Moldavia and Wallachia led to war with the Ottoman Empire in 1806–1812, 1828, 1853 (the Crimean War), and 1878. After 1866, Austrian interest in the Balkans as an area for expansion led to conflict with both Russia and Serbia, generating a series of conflicts from 1878 until the start of World War I.[33] Germany developed links with the Ottomans through arms sales and military aid.

Romanians and Bulgars disputed the Dobrudja; Serbs and Bulgars, the Pirot district; Bulgars and Greeks, Thrace; and Greeks and Albanians, Epirus. The Muslim Albanians were engaged in a bitter struggle against Greeks, Serbs, and Montenegrins. Serbia fought to acquire Bosnia (1876) and for other extensions of its territory (1878, 1885, 1912, 1913). Bulgaria also fought to expand its territory (1878, 1885, 1912, 1913). In Macedonia, the Bulgarians, Greeks, Serbs, and Romanians opened schools, extended their ecclesiastical influence, and instituted *comitadji* bands, who not only worked for revolution against the Turks but fought against each other and terrorized and massacred the adherents of the other national parties.

Imperialist wars in Europe often drew in additional regional actors seeking to advance their own imperialist aims. Britain intervened in the Russo-Turkish war of 1806; Denmark in the Russo-Swedish War of 1808–9; and Bulgaria in the Russo-Turkish war of 1828–29. France took part in the

---

[31] In 1914, Sir Mark Sykes, the Tory M.P. who was his party's leading expert on Turkish affairs, warned the House of Commons that "the disappearance of the Ottoman Empire must be the first step towards the disappearance of our own" (Sykes 1953: 207).

[32] Andrew and Kanya-Forstner 1981: 68. François Georges Picot argued in the Senate that it was in France's interest that the Ottoman Empire remain intact, for its "feeble condition" offered France "limitless scope" to expand her economic influence (Andrew and Kanya-Forstner 1981: 89).

[33] Austrian leaders such as Crown Prince Rudolf envisioned removing the Russian danger by a successful war and then forming a ring of client states in the Balkans. Because the Magyars opposed any further acquisition of Slavic territory, Austrian policy aimed at the commercial and political control of the Balkan states. Speaking to the eminent Belgian economist, Maurice de Laveleye, the German ambassador at Constantinople, described the Austrian viewpoint: "we do dream of conquests, but.... They are the conquests to be made by our manufacturers, our commerce, our civilization. But to realize them we must have railways in Serbia, Bulgaria, Bosnia, Macedonia; and above all, a junction with the Ottoman system, which will definitely connect East and West" (Laveleye 1887: 5; in Langer 1931: 324).

Crimean War (1854–56) in order to retain its influence in the Balkans, carried on a war with Austria in Italy (1859) for acquisition of Italian territory, and intervened in the Italo-Sicilian War of 1860–61. Greece (and France and Britain) intervened in an uprising in Crete in 1866–69. France attempted throughout the nineteenth and early twentieth centuries to extend its frontier up to the Rhine. Napoleon III had contemplated receiving compensation on the Rhine[34] in exchange for supporting Prussia in the Austro-Prussian War of 1866 and went to war against Prussia in 1870 when Prussia refused to grant it any territorial concessions. But France not only failed to gain new territories in this war, it lost to Germany the valuable French provinces of Alsace-Lorraine. Russia intervened in the Serbo-Montenegran-Turkish War of 1876. Lithuania (and France) intervened in the Russo-Polish conflict of 1918–20. France and Russia intervened in the Greco-Turkish War of 1919. Albania, Bulgaria, and Yugoslavia (and Britain) intervened in a civil war in Greece in 1944–46.

Outside Europe, Great Britain fought to acquire Arakan and Tenasserim and to control Assam (1823–26), Tasmania (1825–30), and Argentina (1836–52); to annex Sind to British India (1843); to acquire frontier land from the Sikhs (1845–46); to annex the Punjab (1848–49); to annex Pegu (1853); to prevent Russian influence in Afghanistan (1838–42); for dominance in Gwalior, India (1843); to secure property in South-East Africa (1850–52); to prevent the extension of Russian influence in Persia (1856–57); for trade and commercial privileges in China (1839–42, 1856–60); to secure control of Abyssinia (1867–68); to transfer authority from the East India Company to the British Crown in India (1857–59); and against the Ashantis in the Gold Coast (1821–26, 1873–74). Between 1814 and 1849, the size of the British Indian Empire increased by two-thirds of the subcontinent, as a result of a series of wars against Mahrattas, Nepalese, Burmans, Rajputs, Afghans, Sindis, and Sikhs.

France fought for control of Argentina (1836–52), Algeria (1839–47, 1871–72), and Senegal (1857); fought for trade concessions in China (1856–60); conquered Cambodia in 1863; and fought in Mexico (1861–67). Russia fought wars to acquire Georgia, Erevan, Armenia, Nakhitchevan (1825–28), Khiva (1839), Circassia (1859–64), and Samarkand and the Oxus (1865–68). The Netherlands fought for trade and dominion in Central Sumatra (1807–37), to secure control of Bali (1846–49); for control of coal mines in South Borneo (1859–63), and to secure control of South Celebes (1859–60). Spain fought to secure Spanish settlements in Morocco (1859–60) and to extend the area of her commercial exploitation (1810–24). Portugal fought to gain control of Zambesi and Delagoa Bay (1833–36).

---

[34] After the war, France suggested a variety of possibilities for compensation: the left bank of the Rhine, the frontier of 1814, Luxembourg, and Belgium. Bismarck rejected them all.

The Great Depression and the agrarian distress of 1873–86 launched a second great wave of European imperialism. The period beginning in the late 1870s was one of steady closure and constriction everywhere in Europe. As tariff walls went up, there were increasing pressures to transform areas not yet encapsulated into national markets into extensions of those that already were in the form of "spheres of influence" or imperial domains. After the 1870s and throughout Europe, there was a marked increase in both protectionism at home and imperialism abroad. These trends led to international tensions and to imperialist conflicts. At the same time, the new industrial nations began to seek outlets for surplus goods. Furthermore, the danger arose that the colonies, if they were let go, would fall into the hands of some other European power and would then be closed to general trade. The American Civil War in the 1860s had shown only too clearly how dangerous it was for a modern industrial state to be dependent on a foreign power for the supply of an essential raw material such as cotton (Langer 1931: 284).

During the new imperialism that began in the 1880s, France fought for control of Tunisia (1881), Madagascar (1894–1901), China (1882–85, 1899–1900), and Morocco (1912). Great Britain fought to advance the British frontier in Afghanistan (1878–80); to secure the boundaries of the Boer Republic of the Transvaal (1879, 1906); to annex Transvaal and the Orange Free State (1899–1902); for control of the Sudan (1881–85, 1885–95, 1896–1900); to annex Burma (1885–86); to maintain control of India's northwest frontier (1897–98), Uganda (1897–1901), and Cuba (1898); to extend control over Sierra Leone (1898); to secure trade and commercial privileges in China (1899–1900); and for control of Egypt (1882).

Other countries also fought to acquire additional territories and markets: Germany, to secure commercial privileges in China (1899–1900) and for colonization of South-West Africa (1903–8); Russia, for control of Transcaspia (1878–81), for commercial privileges in China (1899–1900), and with the Japanese over Korea and Manchuria (1904–5); Italy, for an extension of Italian territory in the Ottoman Empire (1885), to control Abyssinia (1894–96), for commercial privileges in China (1899–1900), to acquire the Dodecanese and Tripolitania (1911), and for expansion into Libya (1911–17); the Netherlands, for direct rule over the Achinese sultanate (1873–1908), and to extend direct rule over the Malay Archipelago (1891–94); Belgium, for control of the Congo (1892–94); Austria, for commercial privileges in China (1899–1900); Spain, to maintain control of Cuba (1898); and Greece, to acquire territory from Turkey (1896–97).

The new imperialism of the 1880s and 1890s was "a stupendous movement, without parallel in history" (Barraclough 1967: 63–64). By 1900, Britain was the center of an empire ruling over 13 million square miles, inhabited by 370 million people. Between 1884 and 1900, France annexed three and a half million square miles with nearly 40 million people. Germany acquired one million square miles and 17 million subjects. Belgium, in the Congo, obtained nearly one million square miles and 30 million people. Portugal gained an additional 800,000 square miles in Africa containing 9 million inhabitants (Cole and Postgate 1966: 391–92). Russia moved into Siberia, acquired Bokhara, Khiva, and other Asiatic states, and began the military occupation of Manchuria.

In 1876, not more than one-tenth of Africa had been brought under European control; by 1900, nine-tenths of the continent was controlled by European powers. In the last decade of the century, France laid claim to a quarter of the total area and nearly a fifth of the population of China; Britain asserted exclusive interests in the whole basin of the Yangtse, with well over half the population of the empire; while Russia set its sights on the vast northern province of Manchuria (Barraclough 1964: 61–62). Though there were still gains to be made in Africa and especially Asia, given the poverty of these countries and their low rates of growth, their demand for manufactures was limited. As the potentialities of overseas outlets diminished, imperialist ambitions focused increasingly on Europe.

The Balkan Wars in 1912 and 1913 unleashed an imperialist frenzy in Europe that continued unabated through 1918 and beyond. In 1914, when war broke out in the Balkans, France was plotting to reacquire Alsace-Lorraine and Germany was obsessed with keeping control of it; Russia was seeking to gain control of the Dardanelles for access to the Mediterranean; Britain, involved in an Anglo-German naval-building race, feared that Germany would gain control over the channel ports.

All the belligerents in World War I sought vast extensions of their territories. The Central Powers planned to divide Russian Poland between Austria-Hungary and Germany and that Serbia would be divided between Austria-Hungary and Bulgaria and planned to annex Montenegro to Austria-Hungary and give it control of Albania and of Venetia at least to the Tagliamento River (Meyer 1955: 135). Bulgaria was to get Macedonia; Germany was to acquire substantial territories in Eastern Europe, to retain some form of effective control of Belgium, and to annex the French coal region of Briey-Longwy.[35]

The Allies also sought vast extensions of their territories. Secret treaties concluded among the Allies[36] provided for the following territorial

---

[35] Letter to Count Czernin, August 17, 1917, cited in Mowat 1927: 98. Herr Michaelis, who succeeded Bethmann-Hollweg as chancellor in July 1917, agreed with Ludendorff that Germany could not give up Alsace-Lorraine, and that it must have some military and economic, if not political, power over Belgium and over Courland, Lithuania, and Poland, as well as economic influence in the French Briey-Longwy basin.

[36] These treaties were published in the official journal of the Soviets, and in the *Manchester Guardian*. A good summary is found in Bass 1920: chap. 2; and Baker 1922: vol. 1, chap. 2.

acquisitions at the conclusion of the war: (1) Great Britain: a "neutral" zone in Persia, Southern Mesopotamia, Baghdad, Haifa and Akka in Syria; and part of the German colonies; (2) France: Syria,[37] the Adana Vilayet, territory in Asia Minor, Alsace-Lorraine, the Saar Valley, territories on the left bank of the Rhine, and a part of the German colonies; (3) Romania: Transylvania, the Banat, and Bukovina; (4) Serbia and Montenegro: the Southern Dalmatian Coast, Spalato, Ragusa, Cattaro, San Giovanna di Medua in Albania, and the possible annexation of the Northern Albanian district; (5) Italy: Trentino, Southern Tyrol, Trieste, Country of Gorizia-Gradisca, Istria, Istrian Islands, Dalmatia, Dalmatian islands, Valona, Islands of the Aegean, Adalia and territory in Asia Minor, extension of colonies in Africa, a share in the war indemnity;[38] and (5) Russia: Constantinople, Bosphorus and Dardanelles, Sea of Marmora, Imbros and Tenedos in the Aegean, full liberty in Northern Persia, Ispahan and Yezd, Trebizond, Erzerum, Van and Bitlis, further territory in Asia Minor,[39] and those parts of Poland that were in 1914 under Prussia and Austria.[40]

[37] An elaborate network of understandings and agreements between the Allied Powers and notables of the Ottoman Empire provided for the dissolution of the Ottoman Empire and the rise of a separate Arab world in which Britain and France would have definite zones of predominant influence, while a corner was in some form to be set aside for the Jews. The rest of the Empire, apart from the Straits allotted to Russia in 1915, was divided into four sections: (1) a Russian sphere south of the Caucasus, abutting on (2) a French one, Cilicia, that was in turn adjacent in the south to the French portion of the Arab world; (3) next to the French sphere, to the west, roughly the southern half of the remaining part of Anatolia, including the city of Smyrna, was to be the Italian share. (4) The northern half alone was to remain unreservedly Turkish.

[38] In April 1915, Italy and the Allied Powers signed the secret London Treaty (sometimes called the Adriatic Treaty). It provided, among other things, that if France or Great Britain augmented their territories in Africa, Italy could claim equitable compensation, especially by the settlement in its favor of certain questions concerning the frontiers of the Italian colonies of Eritrea, Somaliland, and Libya (Article 13; *State Papers, British and Foreign*, 1919, pp. 973–77).

[39] Russia did not enter the war with the view of gaining Constantinople. In an offer dated August 16, 1914, the British, French, and Russian governments gave a guarantee of the independence and integrity of Turkey, on condition that it remain neutral. But after Turkey, rejecting the offer, attacked the Russians on October 28, 1914, Russia was free to revert to her ancient ambition. From the moment that Turkey entered the war on the side of the Central Powers, the Entente Powers began to take measures directed against the Straits. The result of this, in reasonable probability, would be the capture of Constantinople. The question naturally arose as to what to do with it. It could be restored to the Turks at the end of the war, but the Entente Powers naturally did not wish to have the risk always hanging over them of a closure of the Straits by the Porte, and there seemed to be no other Balkan state that could be put in charge of Constantinople. Accordingly, it was really impossible for France and Great Britain not to acknowledge the historic claims of Russia to Constantinople (Mowat 1927: 27–29).

[40] See Declaration of the Grand Duke Nicolas, August 15, 1914 (in Mowat 1927: 65).

CONCLUSIONS

Accounts of modern European development that downplay the role of conflict and violence in nineteenth-century Europe present an incomplete and misleading picture of how industrial capitalism and democracy developed there. The development of industrial capitalism in Europe was accompanied by a great deal more volatility and loss of life than conventional accounts report. And it was achieved much later than is generally assumed, and not gradually or peacefully, but within a short period of time and by means of wide-scale, massively destructive war (1914–45).

Landed and industrial elites in Europe attempted to monopolize gains from industrial expansion and to exclude other classes and ethnic groups from political and economic life. Elites blocked land reform and, through the creation of cartels and syndicates, monopolized trade and industry. Restrictions on suffrage, on parliaments and labor, and on the mobility of foreigners deprived labor and minorities of access to political and economic power. As a result, states were continually beset with domestic conflicts growing out of efforts to either challenge or defend these structures: for or against changes in property relations, higher wages, extension of the suffrage, and redistribution of the national product. As states pursued policies aimed at territorial expansion and the establishment of protected "spheres of influence," imperialist ambitions and rivalries gave rise to more or less continual conflict, both within and outside Europe. The following chapters show how and why these conflicts culminated in the world wars, and how and why Europe was transformed in the course of them.

5

World War I and the Postwar Retrenchment

Starting with the Great Depression and the agrarian distress of 1873–86, tensions increased within many European countries. At the same time, a second great wave of European imperialism began that increasingly focused European imperialist ambitions, once again, on Europe itself.

The resurgence of imperialist rivalries in Europe had profoundly dangerous implications. It had the potential to trigger a multilateral Great Power conflict in Europe that not only would bring massive dislocations and destruction, but, by threatening the territory and national survival of the belligerents, it would compel governments and ruling elites to mobilize the masses for war.

Mass mobilization during the Napoleonic era had strengthened radical forces throughout Europe, sustaining the "Great Fear" of 1789 throughout the French Revolutionary and Napoleonic wars and for decades beyond. This was not simply one among many events recorded in the collective memory of Europe's owning classes: it had shaped the socioeconomic and political institutions of European societies throughout the nineteenth century. The growth of union organization and socialist radicalism in the final decades of the century gave European elites even more immediate grounds to fear the consequences of mass mobilization.

But by the beginning of the twentieth century, with fewer possibilities for overseas expansion, and Europe itself becoming, once again, an arena of imperialist rivalry, ruling elites were confronted with the possibility of a major European war and, consequently, the necessity, once again, to mobilize the masses. This was precisely what a century of overseas imperialist expansion had been designed to prevent. However, elites resisted changes that would permit an expansion of domestic markets and production for mass domestic consumption rather than for markets abroad. In the absence of redistribution and reform, external expansion continued to play the central role in European economic expansion. Thus, in the years leading up to the 1914–18 war in Europe, the two central features of European industrial production – internal repression and external expansion – were rapidly coming into conflict.

IMPERIALISM AND WAR IN EUROPE

At the end of the nineteenth century, the scope and intensity of imperialist rivalries in Europe began to increase. There were a number of reasons for this.

First, landlocked or effectively landlocked European countries were beginning to expand production for export and sought sea and land routes that would provide them with outlets to international markets. It was largely to secure access to ports and waterways that compelled Russia (whose northern ports were frozen for most of the year) and the Austro-Hungarian Empire to engage in wars with the Ottoman Empire and with each other over the Balkans throughout the nineteenth century.

Russia depended on unimpeded freedom of passage through the straits of the Bosphorus and the Dardanelles for its grain export trade and for Western imports for the development of industry in the Ukraine. Russian ships had gained the right to travel freely through the Turkish Straits after 1774, making Odessa and other Black Sea ports an important outlet for massive exports generated by the expanding production of Ukrainian grainfields. In the nineteenth century, Russia endeavored to win control of the straits: for though the Straits were open to merchant ships of all nations, the Ottoman Empire controlled them and could close them at any time.

The Balkans were seen as the key to winning control of the straits, and to facilitate the extension of its influence there, the Russian government and ruling elite vigorously promoted pan-Slavism: the idea that Russia and the Slavic peoples of the Balkans formed a community of race and that all Slavs should be united under the aegis of Russia. A movement based on this idea took form in 1858 with the establishment of a Slavic Welfare Society in Moscow. In 1867, a meeting of representatives of all Slavs was held there and, in the three following years, branches of the society were opened in St. Petersburg, Kiev, and Odessa (Langer 1931: 67).

The Austro-Hungarian Empire was an obstacle to the realization of Pan-Slav aspirations. It controlled many of the smaller Slavic nations and controlled, as well, the entrance to the Balkans, the narrow pass between the Carpathian Mountains and the Black Sea.[1] Moreover, Austria also had

[1] The Panslavic group in Russia was filled with hatred of Austria, for the destruction of the Hapsburg Empire was a prerequisite for the union of all Slavs. Once this obstacle was removed, the Slavic world could be organized as a huge confederation under the leadership of Russia. Pan-Slav Russian writers such as Nikolai Danilevsky and Rostislav Fadeiev developed and popularized this view. Danilevsky's *Russia and Europe* (1871), which became the standard work of pan-Slavism, argued that Russia must create a Slav federation under her leadership and develop Slavic civilization, under the protection of this powerful political union, for the

interests in the Balkans. Expelled from Germany in 1866, and deprived by the Franco-Prussian War (1870–71) of any possibility of a restoration of its position in Central Europe, Austria saw the Balkans as the only region where there still remained a possibility for her to expand. Beginning in the 1870s, Austrian ambitions focused more exclusively and to a greater extent than ever on the Balkans.

As tensions were rising in the Balkans, a second area in Europe emerged as a focus of imperialist rivalry: Alsace-Lorraine. Germany had annexed these valuable French provinces after defeating France in the Franco-Prussian War of 1870–71. Alsace had long been one of the most progressive areas in Europe, home of the most modern segment of the French textile industry.[2] However, the famous Alsatian textile industry was not its only attraction. The region also boasted a wealth of raw materials. It had valuable iron ore deposits, particularly in the Lorraine region. Output in Lorraine had quadrupled between 1857 and 1869 (from 109,000 tons in 1857 to 420,000 in 1869), a growth far faster than that achieved in the Nord and Pas-de-Calais (Landes 1969: 168). These deposits would give German industry a massive boost, particularly after the 1880s when Lorraine's phosphoric iron ore was found to be ideally suited for the new steel-smelting techniques that emerged then. Unique potash deposits found around Strassfurt would help to fuel the growth of Germany's chemical industry. Salt, sulphur, and brown coal, found in abundance in the region, would also provide critical raw materials for German industry.

Germany's annexation of Alsace-Lorraine left a wound that prevented any normalization of Franco-German relations. No French government ever renounced publicly the idea of regaining the lost provinces. Right up to the outbreak of war in 1914, France's overriding concern was to wrest Alsace-Lorraine back from Germany. Germany, for its part, devoted its political energies to constructing a series of treaties designed to deprive France of the opportunity of acquiring allies to support this endeavor. The immediate aim of the treaties was to prevent a conflict from breaking out either between Austria and Russia in the Balkans or between Austria and Italy over the

---

benefit of all mankind. In the federation that he envisioned, Danilevsky included Russia (with Galicia, the Ukrainian parts of Bukovina and Hungary, and the Carpatho-Ukraine added), Yugoslavia, Trieste, Gorizia, Istria, the major part of Carinthia, Czechoslovakia, Romania, Hungary, Bulgaria, Greece, and Constantinople. Similar plans were proposed by Fedeiev in his *Opinion on the Eastern Question* (1871).

[2] Tipton and Aldrich 1987a: 19–20. The industry had a high percentage of plants in operation employing the most advanced technology available, particularly in the region around Mulhouse, where the cotton printing industry produced finished products of high quality. Fortunes accumulated in this field, plus funds advanced by Swiss capitalists, had enabled entrepreneurs to build large spinning and weaving mills. As early as the 1840s, Mulhouse had become "a center of mechanical invention and was exporting mules and looms in competition with Britain throughout Europe" (Landes 1969: 160–61).

Adriatic: for if tensions there escalated into armed conflict, French support for one or another of the belligerents might be exchanged for support in launching a war against Germany.

The treaties, the brainchild of Germany's Chancellor, Otto Von Bismarck, pledged German support for Austria and Russia except in the case that either began a war over the Balkans, and did the same with Austria and Italy over the Adriatic. By diffusing imperialist tensions between these two pairs of potential belligerents, and allying them all to Germany, these treaties created a relatively stable balance of power system during the 1870s and 1880s – historians call it the "Bismarckian System."

The centerpiece of the system was the Three Emperors League that Germany concluded in 1873 to patch up Russian and Austrian conflicts of interest in the Balkans. But the Russo-Turkish War of 1878 destroyed the fragile truce that it had constructed. As a result of the war, Russia secured some significant gains in the Balkans and, though Austria got some compensation – permission to "administer" Bosnia-Herzegovina – tensions between the two countries began to rise once again. This began the unraveling of the Bismarckian system. Its final dissolution came, however, when relations between Germany and Russia deteriorated and, finally, were decisively broken off. Russia then became available to France as a potential ally for prosecuting a war against Germany. The Franco-Russian alliance established a connection between the Balkan and Alsace-Lorraine conflict arenas. Thus, when conflict erupted in the Balkans in 1914, it would serve as a conduit enabling the conflict to spread and escalate into a Europe-wide war. This, of course, was France's great hope, and it set about reconstructing Russian military forces in preparation for a war to wrest Alsace-Lorraine back from Germany. Thus, Russia's desertion from the Three Emperor's League, by dissolving the Bismarckian System, brought about a reorganization of political relations in Europe that proved decisive in moving Europe toward a major European war.[3]

Intraclass conflict in Germany, according to Eckart Kehr's influential analysis (1975, 1977), was the key factor leading to Russia's decisive break with Germany at this crucial juncture in European politics. Conflict between the rising class of German industrialists, on the one hand, and the traditional agrarian landowning class (Junkers), on the other, compelled Bismarck to pass a number of measures that antagonized German relations with Russia, as well as with Britain. The Junkers, antagonistic toward their great agricultural competitor, Russia, demanded high tariffs against Russian rye. But German industrialists opposed these tariffs, because Russian rye provided

---

[3] For a good discussion of the Three Emperors League, the Bismarckian system, and how Russia's role in the breakdown of these alliances contributed to the causes and conditions of war in 1914, see Langer 1931: chaps. 12 and 13; Remak 1967: 1–38, 62–64; and Albrecht-Carrié 1973: chaps. 6–8.

cheaper food for the urban work force and, thus, allowed industrial employers to keep wages down. The industrialists were antagonistic not to Russia but to their major competitor in the industrial realm, Britain, and they wanted Germany to expand its naval-building program so as to better enable them to compete with British trade and industry.

Bismarck worked out a deal: industrialists agreed to high tariffs to keep out Russian rye, and in exchange, the agrarian landowners agreed to the expansion of the German naval fleet. The agrarian landowning class thus supported industry in its competitive struggle with Great Britain, while industry supported the agrarians against competition from Russian rye producers. Germany's subsequent naval buildup put a further strain on Anglo-German relations; the adoption of tariffs that closed the German market to Russian rye soured relations with Russia.

The dissolution of the Bismarckian System paved the way for the emergence of two camps in Europe: the Triple Alliance and the Triple Entente. This new structure heightened competition and tension and led to an accelerated arms race in Europe. In these conditions, the Balkans took on a new significance: for if either power combination made gains in the Balkans, it would achieve a decisive advantage over the other bloc. In 1914, it was this, many theorists argue, that motivated Germany's unconditional support for Austria and Russia's support for Serbia.[4] Backing a potential ally in a war to reacquire Alsace-Lorraine, France gave its support to Russia.

As the Bismarckian System was dissolving, tensions in the Balkans had continued to rise. Following the Russo-Turkish War of 1878, Romania, Serbia, and Montenegro were recognized as fully sovereign states; Bulgaria was given autonomy; Romania ceded Bessarabia to Russia but was compensated in the Dobrudja; and Montenegro received a new seaport on the Adriatic (Antivari). However, this left none of the newly independent or autonomous Balkan countries satisfied. Romania was aggrieved at the loss of Bessarabia and continued to covet Transylvania. Serbia, which contained only a fraction of the Serbian people, was aggravated by the Austrian military presence in Bosnia, Herzegovina, and the Sanjak. Bulgaria viewed Macedonia and Rumelia as *irredenta*. The Montenegrins and Albanians nearly went to war over the Adriatic coast.

A series of customs wars involving Austria-Hungary and Balkan states contributed to a further rising of tensions in the area: Austria-Hungary launched a customs war, first with Romania (1886–93), then with Serbia

---

4 This is the "balance of power" explanation favored by most realist and neo-realist International Relations theorists: that the war resulted when the dissolution of the Bismarckian system led to a breakdown of the balance of power in Europe. According to this view, the bipolar international structure that emerged after World War II and the presence of nuclear weapons reestablished the balance and accounts for the absence of Great Power war after World War II; see, e.g., Morgenthau 1948; Gulick 1955; Herz 1959; Claude 1962; Waltz 1979; Levy 1983; Mearsheimer 1990.

(1906–11), and finally with Bulgaria and Turkey (1908). An arms buildup in the area increased tensions even further. Bulgaria concluded treaties for the acquisition of artillery from France and munitions from Germany in 1904; a bitter struggle developed between France and Germany over Turkish military acquisitions; then Serbia sought military equipment from France, precipitating violent anti-Serbian reactions in Austria and the beginning of a customs war between the two countries (Djordjevic and Fischer-Galati 1981: 183–84).

Meanwhile, starting in the 1880s, Europe had launched a massive imperialist onslaught outside the region that had begun to seriously diminish the possibilities for overseas expansion. Thus, European imperialist ambitions and energies were becoming ever-increasingly focused on Europe itself, and, as they did, the tensions and rivalries that they generated moved Europe steadily toward war.

THE POST–WORLD WAR I RETRENCHMENT

The First World War was widely considered to be a turning point in history, even by contemporary observers.[5] The war brought about massive displacements in European societies.[6] Among the many changes it wrought, the one that was perhaps most widely noted and potentially far-reaching in its implications was the apparent decline of the aristocracy.[7] The ranks of the aristocracy had been drastically reduced as a result of the slaughter of their

---

[5] Lenin and others had seen as early as December 1914 that the war might well prove to be the beginning of a new epoch. John Maynard Keynes wrote: "An age is over... the earth heaves... it is... the fearful convulsions of a dying civilization" (1988: 4). In 1917, the German chancellor, in a speech in the Prussian Landtag, spoke of "the transformation of our political life, which in spite of all opposition must result from the experiences of the war" (in Chambers 1972: 348). German, Spanish, French, and English writers wrote of the decay of traditional European civilization.

[6] The Carnegie Endowment's survey of these changes occupies 150 volumes.

[7] Throughout the 1920s, diagnoses of upper-class anguish testified to a great sense of transition. The world war, according to one commentator in 1918, "has so profoundly overturned the conditions of life for the French bourgeoisie that it is undergoing a crisis whose gravity just cannot be exaggerated" (André Lichtenberger, "Le bourgeois," *Revue des Deux Monde*, November 15, 1921, p. 388; in Maier 1975: 39). Marcel Proust's masterpiece, *A la recherche du temps perdu* (published between 1913 and 1922), has been called the greatest obituary of the French nobility. Works of fiction too numerous to list chronicled the passing of traditional Europe, including those of Anton Chekhov, Henrik Ibsen, Thomas Mann, and Robert Musil.

Sorokin noted that between 1912 and 1927, many heads of government and hereditary dynasties were deposed or assassinated: those in Russia, Germany, Austria, Portugal, Turkey, Persia, Hungary, Greece, Bulgaria, Poland, China, Abyssinia, Afghanistan, Albania, and several states in Arabia and South America. "There are few epochs which rival our time in this respect," he wrote. "This 'wholesale' overthrow of monarchs and heads of the government means also the overthrow of a considerable group of the previous court aristocracy. With the deposition of their leaders they also lost their high position in the political

officer sons at the front. After the war, land sales by impoverished landowners in Western Europe and the land reforms in Eastern Europe worked to further weaken them.

The sense of aristocratic decline was, in part, a product of fear; it was, in any event, greatly exaggerated. The overthrow of tsarism in Russia, the dissolution of Austria-Hungary, the abdication of the German Kaiser, and the advent of revolution in the cities of Central, Eastern, and Southeastern Europe produced a consciousness, at least among the upper classes, that Europe had reached the end of an era.

Throughout Europe, the mobilization of urban working classes and peasant masses to fight the war had produced stronger, larger, more united, and better organized urban and rural labor movements, whose members believed and in some places had been promised that their sacrifices would gain for them a better way of life after the war. In Britain, the participation of the lower classes in the war effort had been "for the first time the critical condition of victory," and it had been "felt to be so by politicians, civil servants, trade unionists, and the press" (Abrams 1963: 46). Thus, after the war there were great expectations of far-reaching change, and increasingly forceful demands for it.

But though concessions were made to working-class demands, the expectations, hopes, and promises of a better way of life after the war remained largely unfulfilled. For however much the war had transformed Europe, there still remained in power, however precariously, a narrow elite with a massive share of land and national income, and this elite proved unwilling to make the concessions needed to transform the conditions of life for the mass of the population.

THE DECLINE OF THE ARISTOCRACY

After the war, an enormous transfer of land occurred throughout Europe as gentlemen farmers and great "feudal" families in Great Britain, France, Italy, Hungary, Austria, and Italy found it no longer profitable to maintain their country places. In the four immediate postwar years, one-quarter of the land of England changed hands, the biggest transfer of land since the Norman Conquest (Montagu 1970: 174). Land was purchased by financiers and merchants who had been enriched by war contracts[8] and by tenant farmers, or transferred to county and rural district councils and other public

---

pyramid" (1927: 481). Sorokin says that they then became "common laborers, artisans, servants, clerks," but this seems unlikely given the probability that they were wealthy men; being wealthy would have been a condition of their having held those positions, or a consequence of it.

[8] Not, in most cases, for the purpose of becoming full-fledged agriculturists but to satisfy their desire to own country seats and sporting properties (Ogg 1930: 646–47).

bodies.[9] Land sales in France accelerated as a result of heavy taxation on land values during and after the war; in Italy, the impetus was wartime inflation and postwar agrarian radicalism.

In Central and Eastern Europe, legislation began the breakup of large estates. In Austria, Romania, Yugoslavia, Czechoslovakia, Poland, Hungary, Latvia, Estonia, Bulgaria, Lithuania, and Finland, the masses of peasants who had been the backbone of the fighting armies in World War I demanded the abolition of the latifundia and the creation of peasant freeholds. Land redistribution schemes were introduced in Germany and Yugoslavia. In Poland, a total of 2.5 million hectares were redistributed between 1921 and 1937. By 1930, the king of Romania (impelled by fear of Bolshevik agitation spreading through the army) had redistributed over four million hectares of land. A more modest program came into force in Czechoslovakia. In Bulgaria, about 330,000 hectares of land were redistributed. In Greece, a total of 1,684 estates were broken up in the 1920s to provide land to families numbering about a million persons.[10]

However, the redistribution of land in Central and Eastern Europe after World War I was only partial and, in some places, was reversed. Germany's land reform had been mainly a paper one.[11] In Hungary, the Magyar elite prevented any land reform; thus, nearly half the land remained in large estates, leaving some three million peasants landless. In Yugoslavia, the peasants had begun to seize land in 1918 and 1919, but the actual redistribution that resulted was modest. Land reforms begun in other countries of Eastern Europe were halted and, in many places, reversed when right-wing governments came to power in the late 1920s and in the 1930s. The new republican government in Spain passed an agrarian statute in 1932 that allowed the expropriation of grandees' property without compensation, but the program

---

9   Because there were more estates offered for sale in Britain during the postwar years than there were buyers, considerable numbers of country places were converted into holiday resorts, boarding schools, and convalescent hospitals (Ogg 1930: 648).

10 A brief summary of the reforms in Romania, Bulgaria, and Yugoslavia can be found in Michael 1929: 22–34, 88–90, 138–41. For reforms in Hungary and Czechoslovakia, see Morgan 1969. A discussion of the reforms in Poland, Portugal, and Spain can be found in Tipton and Aldrich 1987a: 251–54; for Germany's reform, see Ogg 1930: 650–53. For the Greek land reform, see Lampe and Jackson 1982: 351–54.

11 An article incorporated into the republican Constitution of 1919 authorized the expropriation of landed property whenever necessary "to meet the needs of housing, for the furtherance of settlement on the land, and for the purpose of bringing it into cultivation, or for the encouragement of agriculture." This article was supplemented by various decrees and laws providing for the formation of associations of landlords for the disposal of their lands where more than 10 percent of the land in a district was in the hands of large owners. However, there was very little actual expropriation by public authority. In the relatively sparsely populated provinces of northeastern Germany where the great Junker estates were to be found, the demand for expropriation was exceedingly slight, while in sections such as Bavaria and the Rhineland, where land hunger was acute, only 2 or 3 percent of the holdings exceeded the statutory maximum of 100 hectares (Ogg 1930: 649–50).

had not been completely implemented before the beginning of the civil war in 1936. In Portugal, a proposal for rural reorganization and the parceling of private property in 1924–25 died with the fall of the left-wing government.

The aristocracy had seen the destruction of its wealth and savings as a result of the war. Income from land or building rents, fixed-interest securities, and stocks had declined as a portion of national products.[12] Thus, by 1929, a bank account in France and Germany that had remained untouched since 1913 was worth about 15 to 20 percent of its original value (Maier 1975: 45). But those who derived income from capital assets were not the only ones to suffer a decrease in income as a result of the war: the middle classes were battered by postwar inflation, the proletariat saw gains that they had made during the prewar decades wiped out, and the peasantry found themselves plunged into an immediate postwar rural depression as the war-stimulated markets for their goods dissolved. As a result, and despite the wartime profits made in some sectors and by some individuals, wartime and postwar conditions generally decreased wealth throughout the social structure.

Thus, all in all, and despite the human and material losses suffered by the aristocracy during the war and in the years immediately following it, Europe's prewar social structure survived. As a result, there was little change in the essential dynamics of European industrial expansion after the war. Restrictions on labor and minorities and reliance on imperialism as an engine of growth remained characteristic features of European societies. These conditions had worked to generate European conflicts throughout the previous century and a half, and they continued to do so throughout the interwar years.

LABOR

In the years leading up to the First World War, there had been a marked rise of socialist parties and a steady and dramatic increase in the number of their members, their candidates returned to representative bodies, and their share of the popular vote. By 1914, labor violence was raising alarms in all the capitals of Europe and social polarization and conflict was evident throughout the region. In Russia, the first half of the year had seen a marked rise in the intensity of both political and economic strikes.[13] A massive confrontation between employers' organizations and labor unions was looming on the horizon in Germany. The socialist leader, Jean Jaurès, was assassinated in

[12] The war turned Britain into the world's greatest creditor. The British lost about a quarter of their global investments during the war, which they had to sell in order to buy war supplies. The French lost about half of their investments (Hobsbawm 1996: 97).

[13] "Even the over-conservative estimates of the Factory Inspectors reported for this period a total of 1,254,441 strikes, of which 982,810 were listed as political." These calculations, which covered only the first six months of 1914, excluded for the first time the highly industrialized Warsaw guberniya (Haimson 1964: 628).

France. Britain seemed on the verge of actual civil war over the question of Irish home rule. For all governments and ruling elites, war in 1914 came at a time of particularly intense domestic difficulties.

Even as they declared war, European governments were unsure whether workers would voluntarily join the war effort or whether oppressive measures would be needed to induce them to participate. However, everywhere in Europe, they succeeded in inducting their industrial workers and peasant masses into national armies and molding them into effective fighting forces. In some places, working classes enthusiastically supported the war. In Britain, working-class volunteers flocked in droves to sign up before conscription was introduced in January 1916. South Wales and Clydeside, both of which had been centers of working-class unrest in the decades leading up to the war, provided greater quantities of soldiers relative to their populations than did the rest of the United Kingdom (Gill and Dallas 1985: 35). By the time volunteering ceased, nearly 30 percent of the men employed in industry had volunteered. Nearly five million industrial workers would enter the armed forces before hostilities ceased.

Many contemporary observers assumed that working-class participation in the war effort represented a victory of nationalism over socialist solidarity.[14] But this was decidedly not the case. Throughout the war, labor struggles continued unabated and, in many places, increased in both number and intensity. In 1917, millions of workers throughout Europe participated in massive strikes and demonstrations in solidarity with the Russian Revolution.[15] In fact, the war proved to be a watershed in the development of socialism and of organized labor as a force in Europe. At the end of the war, left-wing parties and movements emerged throughout Europe,[16] and trade union membership skyrocketed as unskilled and agricultural laborers and women joined the ranks of organized labor for the first time.[17] Thus, it seems reasonable to assume that when the working classes joined up with national armies, they did so to advance their own struggle for

---

[14] This is an assumption held by many of the historians and social scientists who have written about these events. For instance, Julius Braunthal asserts that "the spirit of international solidarity [was] superseded by a spirit of national solidarity between the proletariat and the ruling classes" (1967: 355). Joseph Schumpeter saw 1914 as "socialism at the crossroads" having "not stood the test" (1976: 353). See also Carr 1945: 20–21. For additional works that concur in this view, see Doyle 1997: 317–19, and esp. 318n9.

[15] See Chapter 6.

[16] Socialist parties came to power in Sweden (1920), Denmark (1924), and Norway (1927); the first Labor government took office in Britain at the end of 1923; the left triumphed in France in 1924; in Belgium and Holland, socialists entered the cabinet for the first time in 1939.

[17] Trade union membership doubled in Britain (from 4 to 8 million; Geary 1981: 151–55); in Italy, having doubled during the war, it nearly doubled again by 1920 (Maier 1975: 47). By 1920, Europe had 34 million trade unionists (Vandervelde 1925; Ogg 1930: 759–97).

economic and political rights.[18] It was widely acknowledged that the war could not be won if workers did not support it. Workers therefore had reason to believe that, through their patriotism and sacrifices, they might win the rights for which they had struggled for over a century. Their struggle continued, both during and after the war, and, ironic or contradictory as it might seem, socialist solidarity continued to be an important means of advancing it.

Workers were probably also motivated to join the war effort for the economic security of army pay as well. Sir Ian Hamilton had pointed out in 1911 that "each year about three fifth of the recruits of the Regular Army enlisted between October and March" when work was short in industries such as agriculture and building (in Benson 1989: 162). During the Boer War, the increasing willingness of working people to fight, one scholar notes, "was probably less a measure of their growing patriotism than of their growing poverty" (Benson 1989: 162). The same relationship between poverty and enlistment was observed by the *Western Daily Press* in Bristol at the start of World War I: "in this city, as elsewhere, there are a great many single fellows who are not in employment, and who would welcome the chance to be doing some real service" (in Benson 1989: 162).

By the end of the war, labor's wartime mobilization and participation had increased its relative power within European societies. As a result, and despite the fact that endeavors to reward labor for its wartime cooperation were, in general, provisional, partial, and half-hearted, it was nonetheless the case that labor achieved some real gains.

At the end of the war, labor in all the chief Allied countries demanded extensive reform by international arrangement as part of the peace settlement, and that it be undertaken by a Special Committee of the Peace Congress, with either labor representatives from every country or a Labor Congress sitting concurrently to frame resolutions. In the face of these demands, and to deter labor from setting up a rival workers' peace conference, European leaders appointed a commission to deal with international labor at the first plenary session of the Peace Conference (Temperley 1920: 2, 32–33) and subsequently devoted an entire part of the peace treaty (Part xiii) to the welfare of labor and to the setting up of an International Labor Office (ILO).[19] Labor's new power and the threat of social revolution also

---

[18] Eric Hobsbawm has argued this view persuasively (1990: esp. 120–30).

[19] The preamble to this Part declared that "universal peace" was dependent on "social justice" and called for, among other things, a maximum working week, prevention of unemployment, a living wage, protection against sickness, and provision for old age and injury. The league imposed on all its members the obligations of becoming members of the ILO and performing the duties involved by such membership. However, as a response to the demands of organized labor, the ILO was far from sincere. It was a "'stabilizing action" intended to induce the workers to content themselves with "positive promises for the future" instead of "achievement at the moment"' (Zilliacus 1946: 234–35).

impelled European leaders to accede to the establishment of the League of Nations.[20]

Locally, individual governments took seriously the threat of social revolution and the need for wide-ranging reform at home to deter it. In Britain, "Ministers had agreed again and again that the people, by their conduct during the war, had won the right to a better way of life" (Abrams 1963: 43). It was felt, in particular, "that the wives and children of men who had volunteered for the forces should not be subjected to the humiliation of poor relief."[21] In 1916, the government established a Reconstruction Committee to discuss plans for a new society, and the following year, a Ministry of Reconstruction was created. Under these two bodies, a host of subcommittees were set up to examine ways to provide for a rational system of public health, new educational opportunities, innumerable small-holdings, security of employment, and the building of working-class housing. Of these areas, advances were significant only in the provision of social insurance, and even here, the changes that were finally introduced and implemented only incompletely institutionalized a new system.

In 1914, there were the beginnings of a comprehensive insurance program in Britain, as well as in France, Denmark, Sweden, Italy, Austria, Russia, and some of the Balkan states. Social insurance programs for workers in Europe had begun in Germany in the 1880s. Social unrest and the increase in the numbers of votes cast for socialist candidates for seats in Germany's Reichstag in the 1870s led Bismarck and a small number of conservatives to the conviction that the establishment of obligatory insurance against workers incapacitated through accident or old age would ameliorate conditions that drove men to socialism. Thus, with the hope of bringing socialist agitation to an end and undercutting support for the socialist party, Bismarck introduced a series of social insurance bills beginning in 1883.[22] In 1884 and 1885, Sickness Insurance and Accident Insurance bills were put into effect for employees of railways, mines, and factories,[23] and an Old Age and

---

[20] That the League of Nations was born out of fears of the Russian Revolution is supported by the record of the succession of world conferences, speeches of the statesmen at Geneva, and their diaries and correspondence. See, e.g., Baker 1922.

[21] Rose 1971: 284–85. "For all the battering it had received at the hands of the Royal Commission, the nineteenth-century poor-law system stood, only slightly amended, on the eve of the First World War" (Rose 1971: 267).

[22] The socialists (particularly those of the Wagner-Schmoller "state socialist" school) were in a very real sense the authors of this program, "but to meet their more pressing demands, to allay discontent, and to prevent further triumphs [for revolutionary propaganda], Bismarck made the scheme his own" and contrived to "force the proposed reforms through a reluctant parliament." The immediate object was "to cut the ground from under the feet of the socialists" (Ogg 1930: 548–49, 551).

[23] Miners and railway workers made up a small fraction of the total work force in the 1880s. About a third of Germany's work force was employed in industry (Mitchell 1975: 54). However, most European industry throughout the nineteenth century continued to involve urban artisans and craftsmen working in small shops.

Invalidity bill took effect in 1891. Each of these measures was partial and provisional; however, between 1899 and 1903, they were extended to workers in other sectors and branches of industry. In 1911, the separate laws and numerous amending acts relating to each were drawn together in a centrally administered Workmen's Insurance Code in 1911. But it was not until 1914 that this code became operative.[24]

Other countries emulated Germany's example and, by 1914, had introduced legislation for the provision of social insurance. In most cases, these laws were applied to a small group of men, were voluntary rather than obligatory, and private rather than public (see Ogg 1930: 543–609). The war in 1914 brought about important changes and extensions to these provisions. Belgium introduced social legislation for the first time during the interwar years. Salaried employees in France had been covered by an old-age pension law starting in 1910, but after 1914, a system of sickness and accident insurance was put into action. A modest unemployment scheme was set up during the war, and after the war, it became permanent (and remained modest).

Britain's National Insurance Act of 1911 was applied to only certain sectors of the work force. However, with the onset of mass unemployment after the war,[25] features of the poor-law system – unconditional outdoor relief, relief scales, and relief in aid of wages – began to reappear. Unemployment Insurance Acts in 1920–22 set up the system of the dole for those out of work for longer than a month. But if a worker had any income or lived with relatives whom the government thought capable of supporting him, he was ineligible. The result, therefore, was to split apart families and increase overcrowding in tenements.

At the end of the war, there was a massive state initiative in house building in Britain with subsidies from the central government in order to build "houses fit for heroes." The need for public control and participation in building new housing had been recognized by all political parties in Britain during the war. Thus, the defeat of housing reform during the postwar years made it the issue of social reform that showed most clearly what would be the outcome of the general ideological collision between proponents of planning and a free market. Since the building industry was at the mercy of profiteering trade associations who were driving up building costs, implementation of proposed housing policies required economic controls on the building market. But, vast as the machinery of government was by prewar standards, it would not be the means of affecting such sweeping social reforms. Thus, in the 1920s, the wartime plans for social rebuilding were set aside (Abrams 1963).

---

[24] The English version of the complete text of the code is in *Bulletin of U.S. Bureau of Labor*, no. 96 (Sept. 1911), pp. 514–774.

[25] At the end of 1918, some 45,000 were receiving poor relief in England and Wales; by July 1921, that number had risen to nearly 1,500,000 (Rose 1971: 292).

During World War I, nationalization of industries in Britain, as well as limitation and taxation of profits and government control of labor relations, had been hailed by some sections of the labor movement as the beginning of socialism (Menderhausen 1943: 328–29). But following the armistice in 1918, the British government took a series of decisions that reversed the wartime trend toward state regulation of the economy.[26] The socialist and partly socialist governments that ruled in Britain during some years of the interwar period, like those in Germany, France, and Austria, were brought down before they were able to effect any change in capitalist institutions.[27]

In Britain, as in all Western European countries, leaders and ruling classes were committed to reestablishing the prewar status quo. As Philip Abrams points out, in Britain, the very term "reconstruction" reflected the ambiguity of official thinking in those years. Though "Ministers spoke by 1918 as though the word meant transformation . . . the original reconstruction committees had been set up . . . to restore the social and economic conditions of 1914" (Abrams 1963: 58). An early report of the Ministry of Reconstruction stated that its mandate was "to pick up the broken threads, to renew old habits and traditions, to go back as far as possible to the social and industrial situation as existed at the outbreak of the war" (Ministry of Reconstruction 1918). As Abrams rightly notes, those who endeavored to make major policy changes on behalf of social reform during the interwar years failed "to come to grips with the structure of British society" and to recognize "deeply rooted patterns of social conflict" (Abrams 1963: 57–58). For, despite the profound dislocations that it had brought, the war did not bring about a transformation of European society. Forces of resistance would prevent its breakdown until a second massively destructive war in Europe shifted the class balance still further and made restoration of the nineteenth-century system impossible.

DEMOCRACY BETWEEN THE WARS

After the war, J. L. Garvin, editor of the *Observer*, commented:

The workers in the mass had to be promised, and they were, not only that they would not be exploited after the war – they had to be assured a thousand times that in the event of victory of their freely-accepted discipline over the more forced and serf-like drill of the German system, unprecedented efforts would be made to raise the common people to an altogether higher level of intelligent, responsible,

[26] However, economic demobilization did not proceed as quickly as the government and private business had intended: the removal of food control was impeded by the persistence of acute shortages; but in 1921, control of flour mills, railroads, and coal mines was discontinued. In Germany, also, wartime controls on foodstuffs were retained in some regions until 1923 (Menderhausen 1943: 341).

[27] Thus, in Britain, "nationalization of mines, heavy industries, and other economic branches subsisted only at the margin of the economic system" (Menderhausen 1943: 340).

and well-conditioned citizenship. Those pledges must be kept not grudgingly, but amply and to epoch-making effect. Otherwise there will be revolutionary trouble.... Nothing can be as it was before the war. The whole *tempo* of the democratic movement must be quickened if nations are to avoid internal tumult and dislocation as unmatched in their magnitude as the war itself. (1919: 323–24)

In fact, the interwar years did see movement toward achieving democracy in Europe. However, the record of the interwar period was largely one of partial democratization in some countries, and reversals of democratic rule in many others. "Democracy" is a political system in which there are found (1) free and fair elections of representatives with universal and equal suffrage and (2) the institutionalization of opposition rights.[28] In this definition, it can be argued that democracy in most of Western Europe was not achieved until after World War II.

In Britain, the Representation of the People Act of 1918 nearly tripled the size of the electorate by simplifying the requirements for male voters and by extending the suffrage to some women thirty years and over. In 1928 the suffrage was extended to women on the same terms as men. However, plural voting and other electoral abuses still barred the operation of democratic politics (O'Leary 1962). Extra votes went to an elite minority represented by the "business vote" and the "university vote" (see Carstairs 1980: 189–98). It was not until 1948 that plural voting was abolished.

Parliamentary democracy was established in Germany after 1918. However, this was reversed in 1933 and not reinstated in West Germany until the defeat of the Third Reich in 1945. In 1920, Austria was a democratic and socialist republic, but this was only a temporary result of defeat in war. During the interwar years, increasing turmoil and violence culminated in civil war, and at its conclusion, all democratic rights in Austria were wiped out (Deutsch 1934: 11–13; MacDonald 1946). Austria's present-day democracy dates from 1955. In Italy, the vote was extended in 1918 to all men over twenty-one who had served in the armed forces during the war. However, the free exercise of full and equal voting rights was not established for either males or females until 1946.

In most of Europe, opposition rights were not institutionalized until after World War II. Thus, parties representing the working class were not permitted to participate in the parliamentary process on an equal basis. Throughout

---

[28] This definition borrows from Rueschemeyer et al. (1992: 43–44), who, however, include a third element in their definition: (3) responsiveness of the state apparatus to the elected parliament. This element is dependent on the first two: where there are important electoral abuses, unelected or highly restricted upper houses with absolute veto power over all legislation, and the exclusion of working-class organizations and parties from the political process, the state's responsiveness to the legislature can hardly be considered a measure of popular representation. Since such abuses, restrictions, and exclusions characterized European political systems until World War I and, in some places, beyond, this third element is largely irrelevant to the discussion.

Europe, the chief political objective for most conservative parties or interest groups during the interwar years was to exclude socialists from any decisive influence on the state. As Charles Maier describes the politics of the period,

> If the socialist left seriously presented its own economic objectives on the national level, alarmed conservatives fought back. They resorted either to decentralized but simultaneous boycotts of government bonds and money (as in France), or to concerted political opposition to taxation within the terms of coalition politics (as in Germany), or to extra-legal coercion (as in Italy). (Maier 1975: 581)

Thus, though labor parties participated in government in several countries before 1945, their presence was strenuously and sometimes violently resisted by the right. This was an important factor in the rise to power of authoritarian movements in France and Spain, as well as in Austria, Hungary, Poland, Bulgaria, Romania, and Portugal. Socialist parties were shut down by right-wing governments in Italy (PSI), Germany (SPD), Austria (SPÖ), and Spain (PSOE) and were outlawed in Portugal (1926), Hungary (1919), Poland (1926), and the Balkan countries (1923, 1926, 1929). Socialists did not participate in cabinets in Belgium and Holland until 1939. In most of Europe, socialist and communist parties did not become fully legitimate participants in the political process until after World War II.

The first Labor government took office in Britain in 1923, but fell two years later as a result of its failure to prosecute an alleged communist editor charged with sedition. During the election campaign that followed, a "red" scare was aroused by the Foreign Office and played a decisive role in Labor's defeat. The party made a comeback in 1929. But in 1931, in a bitter campaign, a coalition of Liberals and Conservatives that eventually formed the new government denounced Labor leaders for being Bolshevik fellow-travelers and convinced a majority of the voters that the Labor Party represented "Bolshevism run mad" (McHenry 1940: 16–17).

In November 1919, conservatives in France won their greatest electoral victory since 1871. They won every other postwar election as well, except the one in 1936. As a result, all French governments, except the one elected in 1936, were committed to retrenchment. The economic elite of major landowners, financiers, and businessmen and those in positions of state authority remained in control of the country and lived much as they did before the war. Conservative governments cut public spending and, after 1931, increased the proportion of taxation paid by the working classes. To protect the franc and avoid taxing the wealthy, they sold short-term bonds to wealthy members of the financial community.[29] Thus, when a

---

[29] Governments refused to consider tax increases as a way of financing reconstruction (Tipton and Aldrich 1987a). In France, the failure to impose taxation was notorious. Before the war, the aggregate French and British budgets, and also the average taxation per head, had been about equal. But in France no substantial effort was made to cover the increased expenditure. Taxes increased in Great Britain during the war, it has been estimated, from 95 francs per head

left-wing government was elected in 1936, the financial community was able to bring it down by threatening to pull its money out of government bonds.[30]

During the first decade of the interwar period, the German Social Democratic Party (SDP) and the German Federation of Trade Unions (ADGB) had worked to establish parliamentary democracy in Germany. The SDP leadership was fully committed to cooperation between socialists and nonsocialists. However, when the socialist parties entered into coalition governments during the Weimar Republic, nonsocialist parties, organized business interests, and the military refused to cooperate with them and, as a consequence, the Republic collapsed (Breitman 1981). After 1933, the houses, newspapers, and property of the SDP were seized and the party was dissolved as "subversive and hostile to the state."[31]

During the interwar years, commitment on the part of elites to democratic government was highly qualified. Regimes suspended parliaments, outlawed opposition parties, censored the press, and limited assemblies. In Britain, the use of the Official Secrets Acts against journalists, the passing of the Incitement to Disaffection Act in 1934, and the curtailment of the right of public meeting and procession represented a definitive movement toward a restriction of democratic liberties. Parliamentary democracy was destroyed in Hungary (1919), Italy (1922), the Balkan countries (1923, 1926, 1929), Belgium (1926, 1935), Portugal (1926), the Baltic states (1926), Poland (1926), Germany (1934), Austria (1934), the Netherlands (1935), Switzerland (1935), and Spain (1936).

In general, political institutions were designed to increase the power of traditional forces against the lower classes; in general, they were successful

---

to 265 francs, whereas the increase in France was only from 90 to 103 francs. The taxation voted in France for the financial year ending June 30, 1919, was less than half the estimated normal postbellum expenditure. The French Ministry of Finance made no plan or policy for meeting this deficit, except in expectation of receipts from Germany on a scale that the French officials themselves know to be baseless (Keynes 1988: 247).

[30] Backed by communists and radicals who feared for the Republic, Léon Blum, a socialist, became premier of France in 1936. But his unstable coalition proved unable to govern a nation polarized between left and right. Hoping for immediate benefits, workers led massive sit-down strikes. After carrying into law labor reforms that the wealthier classes regarded as revolutionary, Blum was denounced as an agent of Moscow (Carr 1947: 264). French capitalists sent their capital to safe havens abroad, warning Blum that they would aid the government only if he dropped his social legislation and cut government expenditure. When, in June 1937, French capitalists refused to purchase government bonds, Blum resigned.

[31] Carsten 1967: 156. Industrial workers were almost totally absent from the supporters of National Socialism. National Socialism was supported by racist, *völkisch*, and extreme right-wing groups and parties, some of which had existed in Germany for decades. The members of these groups came from among artisans, tradesmen, civil servants, and white-collar employers. Support also came from paramilitary organizations formed after the war, former soldiers, and students. See Carsten 1967: 130–32.

in achieving that end. Only after the Second World War did universal, equal, direct, and secret suffrage become the norm throughout Western Europe.

MINORITIES

During the interwar years, minorities everywhere were deprived of elementary political and economic rights. This facilitated the growth of both radicalism and imperialism in Europe throughout the interwar period.

The revision of frontiers and reshuffling of populations following the war left many problems relating to minorities unresolved and created numerous new ones.

The postwar settlement left Danes and Lusatian Serbs in Germany; Basques and Catalonians in Spain; Russians, Swedes, and Germans in the Baltic states; Russians in Poland; and Germans in Poland, Hungary, Czechoslovakia, Romania, Yugoslavia, southern Ukraine, and the Volga region. The Poles of German Upper Silesia and the Macedonians continued to hold minority status in states dominated by other nationalities. The civil war in Finland in 1918 left nationality problems between Finns and the Russian and Swedish minorities.

The post–World War I arrangements also converted large numbers of Hungarians, Germans, Jews, Ukrainians, Albanians, Bulgarians, Turks, Tartars, Russians, Serbs, and Poles into new national minorities.[32] More than 9 million Germans acquired minority status as a result of the treaties of Versailles and St. Germain and of the events that followed the conclusion of the peace (Schechtman 1946: 29). The greatly enlarged Romania had substantial new minorities.[33] The Banat, whose population consisted largely of Germans, Magyars, and Jews, was divided between Romania and Serbia, and Serbia was given, in addition to Macedonian territory she had previously lost, an additional district that was purely Bulgar.[34] The decisions of 1919 created

[32] These numbered 1.3 million Hungarians, 680,000 Germans, 536,000 Jews, 550,000 Ukrainians, 300,000 Bulgarians, 230,000 Turks and Tartars, 120,000 Russians, 48,000 Serbs, and 35,000 Poles (Seton-Watson 1934: 566–67). By the treaties of St. Germain and Trianon, Romania had been promised Transylvania, Bukovina, and the Banat of the Temesvar. At the close of the war, the retiring Austrian governor placed the administration of the Bukovina in the hands of the Ruthene majority, but the local Romanians proclaimed union with Romania and Romanian troops then occupied the country. The Supreme Council allowed Romania to retain the province. In the Dobrudja, the 1913 frontier was restored, thus leaving a large Bulgarian minority within the Romanian frontier.

[33] Before the war, its population of slightly less than 6 million was 92 percent Romanian and 8 percent non-Romanian; following the peace treaties, the total population of Romania rose to 18 million, of which 80 percent were ethnic Romanian and 20 percent were non-Romanian.

[34] Despite vigorous claims advanced by the Serbs and Greeks to the contrary, the majority of the population of Macedonia was Bulgarian, though much of it was still subject to the Greek Patriarchate and was therefore frequently referred to as Greek. Ethnological maps made by pan-Slav writers and other maps published by leading authorities in Western Europe agree that most of Macedonia was primarily inhabited by Bulgarians. The German

a Czechoslovak state that contained slightly less than 10 million Czechs and Slovaks and nearly half that number of other nationalities; among these, the largest by far was the Sudeten Germans (3,200,000). In the new state of Lithuania, approximately 2 million (16 percent) were minorities.[35] The new state of Latvia had, out of a total population of 1.6 million in 1920, a quarter of a million Russians, Lithuanians, Germans, and Jews (League of Nations 1926: 104–5). The Treaty of Neuilly assigned some 3 million Magyars to Czechoslovakia, Romania, and Yugoslavia. Thus, "Almost all twenty-eight states of postwar Europe – old, enlarged, or newly created – contained more or less sizeable groups of persons who differed widely from the ruling minority in race, language, or religion" (Schechtman 1946: 4). While the existence of these minorities need not have been an obstacle either to the political unity of these states or to peace among them, restrictions on minorities and their exclusion from political and economic life generated increasing tensions during the interwar years, both within states and among them.

In parts of Central and Eastern Europe, interethnic tensions emerged as a result of the discriminatory policies pursued by many governments. Agrarian reform acts, which had been passed in nearly all the new and enlarged states, were applied openly as a political means of weakening the position of the minorities.[36] Not only were the minority landowners expropriated more ruthlessly, and with less compensation, than the majority proprietors, but the redistribution of the expropriated land was often quite inequitable. As C. A. Macartney describes it, though in certain cases members of a minority shared in the benefits of these reforms, as a general rule the members of the majority received almost exclusive preference, far beyond what was warranted by their previous situation. "Particularly grievous to the minorities was the practice of 'colonization,' i.e. of bringing settlers from distant parts of the country and giving them land to the exclusion of the local, land-hungry peasantry. This practice, which caused great discontent, was largely adopted in frontier districts and regions of great political unrest, with the deliberate purpose of breaking up the solidarity of a politically unreliable minority and weakening its position" (Macartney 1934: 389).

The Peace Conference had inserted minority provisions in the treaties it concluded with defeated states (Austria, Hungary, Bulgaria, and Turkey). It had also required new or enlarged states (Poland, Czechoslovakia, Yugoslavia, Romania, and Greece) to conclude special treaties relating to the protection of minorities. States applying for membership in the League of

---

geographer Ritter reported 1,125,000 Bulgars, 360,000 Turks, 422,000 Serbs, Albanians, and Wallachians, and 60,000 Greeks in the territory (in Langer 1931: 349).

35 Of this 16 percent, 8 percent were Jews, 3 percent Poles, 2.5 percent Russians, and 2.5 percent others (League of Nations 1926: 106).

36 For instance, in Transylvania, Slovakia, Backa, and Banat, where landless Hungarian peasant laborers lived side by side with Romanian and Serbian peasants, Hungarian peasants were considered to be part of the "enemy nation" and received a less than equitable share of the lands of their former Hungarian masters (Seton-Watson 1945: 79, 297).

Nations (Albania, Lithuania, Latvia, and Estonia) were obliged to make a declaration to the Council of the League that was analogous to the minority treaties. However, Germany, and also Italy, which had acquired national minorities in the peace settlement, were exempted. Moreover, international intervention to protect minorities under the terms of these treaties and obligations was selective. Thus, attempts to enforce the system were applied only to the small states of Eastern and Central Europe, and these were partial and ineffectual. The system was essentially used as a means for the principal allied and associated powers to police new states and not to ensure liberal and just treatment of minorities. By preaching the principle of national self-determination and then only partially applying it, the Conference, in fact, served only to increase ethnic tensions.

Meanwhile, the powers penalized or ignored by Versailles (e.g., Germany, Hungary, and Bulgaria) set out deliberately to exploit the national minorities of Eastern Europe for the purpose of undermining the Versailles settlement. Hungary fostered Slovak discontent in the hope of fragmenting Czechoslovakia (a Magyar minority of 700,000 persistently pursued an irredentist policy, spurred on actively by the Hungarian government). Italy encouraged Croat separatism in the interests of disrupting Yugoslavia, Bulgaria promoted Macedonian agitation also to undermine Yugoslavia, and Germany sponsored the Prometheus Movement to undercut the Soviet Union.

These efforts, together with the treatment of minorities by their own state governments, helped to bring about a revival of imperialism in Europe at the very start of the interwar period. Throughout the interwar years, statesmen grounded demands for frontier changes on the argument that it was their national duty to rescue conational minorities from oppression by "alien" masters, and this became a key element in the propagandistic schemes used by governments and ruling classes to justify expansionist policies.

In Germany, National Socialist doctrine held that the mother country had a protective right (*Schutzrecht*) over minorities scattered throughout the world. This was a familiar tactic of imperialist expansion in the nineteenth century. Tsarist Russia had demanded that it be granted that role with respect to the Eastern Orthodox subjects of the Ottoman Empire. France had used the same tactic with respect to the Maronite Catholics of Mt. Lebanon in order to ensure access to raw silk supplies from the area for France's silk industry.

When Germany declared that it would serve as the guarantor and protector of Germans everywhere, this threatened to end the internal unity of any state having a sizable German minority. The postwar settlements had created on the borders of Germany four new countries that included nearly 12 million Germans,[37] and these became a major source of postwar instability in Central

---

[37] Among these were Austrian and Polish German minorities, Baltic Germans, and Bohemian Germans (Sudeten Germans).

Europe. The postwar settlements had deprived Germany not only of her over-seas colonies and trade but of her Central European economic interests, as well. The German minorities provided a lever for the reassertion of German influence in the area. Germans had played a leading role in Central and Southeastern Europe through the Hapsburg Empire; the governments in the successor states established in the area had taken over German economic in-terests. When, in the 1940s, Germany succeeded in gaining control of Central Europe, German minorities would become the ruling groups throughout the area.

In the 1930s, a group called the Movement for National Mutual Assistance of Germans in Romania was organized in Germany and became an important political force among the 750,000 Germans that, in 1919, had been incorpo-rated into Greater Romania. By 1935, a Sudeten Deutsche Partei had emerged in Czechoslovakia that, according to the 1935 election, commanded the alle-giance of some 70 percent of the Sudeten Germans and was in close contact with the German Nazis. The party originally demanded redress of specific grievances, but after the Anschluss it issued more far-reaching demands. The eight points of its Carlsbad program of April 1938 were tantamount to a de-mand for autonomy. Simultaneously, the German press began to take new interest in the "oppressed" Sudeten German brothers, and a plan was made ready in Germany for an attack on Czechoslovakia.

Like the German minorities in many states, Hungarians in Romania and Macedonians in Yugoslavia also colluded with revisionist states. In Yugoslavia, the Italian minority in Dalmatia provided a pretext for the asser-tion of Italian irredentist claims, and Italy exploited friction between Serbs and Croats in Yugoslavia for this purpose. Croatian terrorists, the Ustashi, found shelter and assistance in neighboring states, particularly Hungary and Italy, both of which entertained irredentist grievances toward Yugoslavia.

The fact that territory, rather than population, was the issue in these prob-lems can be illustrated by the case of Hungary. Throughout the interwar years, Hungarian statesman had expressed grief at being cut off from their conationals residing in other states. Yet after World War II, Hungary opposed the transfer of Hungarians from Romania because it preferred to bring about the transfer of land rather than simply of population and, for the same reason, adamantly refused to receive 200,000 Magyars whom Czechoslovakia pro-posed to transfer to Hungary (Claude 1955: 121, 130).

IMPERIALISM IN THE INTERWAR YEARS

Imperialism remained the basis of economic expansion after the war. Some imperialist activity continued in territories outside Europe: France fought for control of Syria (1920, 1925–26) and Morocco (1920–27, 1929–33), to maintain control of Indochina (1930–31), and to control Syria (1941). Britain fought for control of Iraq (1920–21) and Palestine (1940–47). Italy fought a war for expansion in Libya (1920–32) and to annex Ethiopia

(1935–37). However, Europe itself had, by this time, become the central focus of European imperialist ambitions. Two factors had facilitated the more
exclusively European focus of imperialism during the interwar years.

First, during the First World War, each side had endeavored to cut the other
off from the world's markets by means of an offensive economic war. As a
result, fully one-third of Europe was effectively blockaded during the war.
The Allies encircled the Central Powers in an increasingly tighter blockade;
the German government sought, by means of a commercial war fought with
U-boats, to isolate Britain economically.[38] However, until 1917, when the
German navy assumed the offensive with an unrestricted submarine campaign, the pressure on sea-borne trade was almost entirely from the Allied
side. In addition to the Allied blockade of German coasts, British naval
units controlled the approaches to the Mediterranean at Gibraltar and Suez;
French, and later Italian, warships blockaded the Austrian ports; and after
Bulgaria's entry into the war on the side of the Central Powers, the Allies
extended the official blockade to the Bulgarian littoral. With the U.S. entry into the war in 1917, the blockade around the Central Powers became
"impenetrable" (Hardach 1977: 28–30).

The war, it was widely thought, was to have been a short one. However,
the two sides "were so nearly equal that there was something like a deadlock
for the first three years." Thus,

The war became an affair of siege tactics; and on the whole it was the Central powers
who were besieged, and who vainly tried to break through the investing lines. In
such a war the endurance of the home populations was strained as well, and if the
endurance of the population of one side or another collapsed, the war would be over.
Consequently, it became one of the objects of the contesting nations to shut out all

---

[38] The high seas blockade whereby Allied naval forces controlled the approaches to the North
Sea and the Mediterranean was not a blockade within the meaning of the Declaration of
London, which was agreed in 1909 and which codified rules concerning economic warfare.
Thus, the term "blockade" was studiously avoided in official circles (Hardach 1977: 14).
Neither the British nor the French government ever declared a blockade of Germany. Though
they declared blockades of German East Africa (300 miles of coast) in February 1915 and
of Turkish, Bulgarian, and Greek coasts in the Mediterranean in 1915 and 1916, there was
no legal blockade declared concerning the German coasts in Europe. However, an order
of March 11, 1915, declared that no merchant vessel would be allowed to proceed to or
from a German port, and it was freely acknowledged by the British Foreign Office that this
amounted to blockade. Moreover, the term "blockade" often appeared in British official
papers during the war. The British Secretary of State wrote in diplomatic correspondence
that "the British fleet has instituted a blockade" (Grey to Ambassador Page, March 13, 1915;
quoted in Mowat 1927: 34n1). In 1918, a permanent Allied Blockade Committee was set
up for the better coordination of blockade policy and met for the first time in March of that
year in London.

   Basic material on the Allied blockade policy can be found in Bell 1937. This history of
the blockade was first published for official use only, and was made available to the general
public in 1961. The studies of Consett (1923) and Parmalee (1924) give a feel for how the
blockade was construed by contemporary observers and analysts.

supplies, whether of peaceful or warlike goods, from reaching their enemies. As the Entente powers had command of the sea, they had the best chance of starving out their opponents. (Mowat 1927: 33)

The war, therefore,

was as much a war of competing blockades, the surface and the submarine, as of competing armies. Behind these two blockades the economic systems of the two opposing groups of countries were engaged in a deadly struggle for existence, and at several periods of the war the pressure of starvation seemed likely to achieve an issue beyond the settlement of either the entrenched armies or the immobilized navies. (Salter 1921: 1; in Hardach 1977: 11)

After the war, many Germans held that the blockade had "starved" their country and had forced it to sue for peace. "The imputation was that the enemy had been able to win only by resorting to the 'unfair' method of the 'hunger blockade'" (Hardach 1977: 30). The result of the blockade was, therefore, to steer Germany after the war to a policy of expansion in Europe:

In a relatively free world German economic energies had expanded and were diffused in Weltpolitik. In an age of blockade these energies were intensified and concentrated on the Continent: in plans for mid-European integration, in the realization of the Fatherland Party's annexationist drives, in the straitjacket of totalitarian war and the Hindenburg Program. (Meyer 1955: 337–38)

The experience of the war inspired similar policies in other countries. In Britain, France, Germany, and Italy, there was a marked trend, both during and after the war, toward establishing imperial autarky based on colonial possessions or on dominating the raw materials and markets of smaller states that would be politically reliable in a crisis. Britain's empire had served as a market for her textile, coal, iron, steel, and shipbuilding industries throughout the nineteenth century. But in 1917, the Dominions were requested to enact legislation for the further development of intra-imperial trade. After 1919 colonial products were granted preferential reductions from the regular customs duties fixed by the British revenue acts.[39]

The postwar trend toward imperial autarky resulted in a division of the world into various trading blocs: a sterling bloc, based on British trade patterns and enhanced by "imperial preferences" agreed at the 1932 Ottawa Conference; a gold bloc, led by France; a yen bloc, dependent on Japan, in the Far East; a U.S.-led dollar bloc (after Roosevelt also went

[39] Beginning in 1916, the French government likewise put into effect a comprehensive policy of import restrictions. After continuing through most of 1919 the policy of import licensing, France returned progressively to a protective system based on specific duties, which could be multiplied by a so-called coefficient of two or three as determined at frequent periodic intervals by an interministerial commission. This provided a flexible arrangement for expeditiously levying higher rates on German and Austrian goods without recourse to a parliamentary overhauling of the tariff.

off gold); and Russia, now the Soviet Union, pursuing the seemingly independent development of "socialism in one country" (Kennedy 1987: 283).
The Nazis' theory of the "economics of large areas" (*Grosraumwirtschaft*)
was consistent not only with postwar trends but with German aspirations to compete with powers – the British Empire, the United States, and
the Soviet Union – who were able to draw on resources of continental
dimensions.

Before the war, agrarian congresses in Berlin (1880) and Budapest (1884)
had debated the issue of creating a Middle European customs union to expand and secure their markets by combining smaller areas within a uniform
tariff system.[40] The idea attracted the attention of theoretical economists,
and many wrote on the subject.[41] During the war, Friedrich Naumann refo-
cused attention on the issue. His book, *Mitteleuropa,* was the literary event of
1917, and translations were soon published in France, Britain, Italy, Sweden,
Switzerland, and the United States. Publications on *Mitteleuropa* and the
crescendo of discussion and writing on the subject aroused much apprehension in the West and remained a center of Entente attention to the end
of the war.[42] During 1916 the Allies met twice at Paris to consider the impending threat of an economic Mitteleuropa, and they agreed to continue
the economic war against the Central Powers even after the cessation of
hostilities.[43]

[40] Meyer 1955: 60. Enthusiasm for the customs union soon dissolved as Hungarian agrarians
fought Balkan imports and the Reich-German Junkers became very sensitive to imports from
the monarchy.
[41] Lujo Brentano in 1885 published an analysis indicating a strong trend in the world toward a
few huge economic regions, each dominated by a great power. He maintained that Germany's
only hope for securing ample markets and sources of raw materials lay in a customs union of
the two monarchies and the Balkans. L. Bosc, *Zollallianzen und Zollunionen* (Berlin, 1907),
311–57, gives a detailed account of these discussions. Most prominent were the Austrian-
German Alexander von Peez and the Reich-German Gustav Schmoller. Peez believed that the
states of the Triple Alliance could survive competition with the other Great Powers (Britain,
Russia, and the United States) only if they united to form their own economic region. Gustov
Schmoller, editor of the most important prewar German economic journal, also saw a definite
need for some type of mid-European "defense" against the other economic colossi. See "Die
Wandlungen in der Handelspolitik des 19. Jahrunderts," *Schmollers Jahrbuch* 24 (1900):
373–82.
[42] By early 1916, it was firmly believed in the high, policy-making circles of the Allies that a
German desire to create Mitteleuropa had been one of the fundamental causes of the war
and constituted the major objective of the German government. In May 1917, Lord Balfour
sent President Wilson a statement of remarks he had recently made to the Imperial Council;
among these was his stated belief that prewar German policy had tried to pave a land route
to India and that the wartime Mitteleuropa was the logical fulfillment of these earlier dreams
(cited in Meyer 1955: 251–52).
[43] A conference of Allied politicians met in Paris on March 27 and 28, 1916. Here it was
decided to convene an economic conference that would examine in detail inter-Allied economic cooperation in war and peace. This conference opened in Paris on June 14, 1916.
The chief result of its deliberations was agreement on closer cooperation in the blockade

The wartime blockade, the restrictive economic clauses of the peace treaties, and the burdens of reparations intensified German efforts to develop mid-European markets. However, during the interwar years, Germany embraced a new eastward orientation that made Osteuropa, rather than Mitteleuropa, the focus of German expansionism. This new orientation, as embodied in the program of General Ludendorff and his Reich Pan-German supporters, envisioned "colonial" land in Europe for a self-sufficient German future, "liberation" for the German kinsmen in Slavic lands, and a suitable area to carry out the "mission" of a superior race and culture (Meyer 1955: 315–16). In the *grossraum* they envisaged for Germany in the East, Nazi writers postulated a regional specialization of economic functions with corresponding racial types. The central industrial core inhabited by Aryans would be surrounded by extensive regions producing agricultural products and industrial raw materials and inhabited by Slavs. From the Nazi point of view, then, the East had the twin advantages of providing unlimited space and being occupied by inferior peoples.

A second factor contributing to imperialism in Europe after World War I was the disappearance of the Ottoman Empire. This created a Balkan zone of new states fiercely competing with each other for additional territory in Europe. There were border disputes between Serbians and Bulgarians, Russians and Romanians, Romanians and Magyars, and Greeks and Turks. Romania fought for territory in Hungary (1919). Greece fought to acquire territory from Turkey (1919–22). Frontier incidents between Greece and Bulgaria were frequent, and in October 1925, Greek troops crossed the border into Bulgaria.[44] Territorial disputes were a source of friction elsewhere in Europe after the war. Germans and Poles quarreled over Silesia; Poland sought expansion in Russia (the Russo-Polish War of 1918) and in Vilna (1920); Russia sought to acquire Constantinople in 1920; and Italy conquered Albania (1939). Europe, as Lloyd George observed during the interwar years, was "a seething cauldron of international hates" (1923: 38). In these circumstances, the minority problems that remained from prewar Europe, combined with the ones created by the postwar settlement, gave

of the Central Powers, on the exchange of natural resources, and on the protectionist measures to be adopted vis-à-vis German trade during the demobilization phase. A resolution was also adopted on the long-term prospects of economic cooperation after the war. Agreement was reached on two types of measures: tightening of the blockade, particularly by controlling trade of the neutral nations, and continued economic pressure on the Central Powers after hostilities ceased by cooperative resistance against German exports (abolition of most-favored-nation agreements) and by denying the mid-European powers access to raw materials under control of the Entente nations. These resolutions were passed over vigorous protests of the Russians, who stood to lose 40 percent of their prewar grain markets, and the mixed reactions of the British, who feared being forced off free trade (Great Britain, H.M.S. Stationary Office, Cd. 8271, *Recommendations of the Economic Conference of the Allies Held at Paris on June 14–17, 1916*; Nolde 1928: 57–58, 152–70).

[44] Following a Bulgarian appeal to the League of Nations, the Greeks consented to withdraw.

impetus not only to outward expansion but to its more exclusive and intensive focus on Europe itself.

Thus, the quest for empire in Europe continued throughout the interwar period. Germany annexed Austria in 1938 and gained, thereby, five divisions of troops, some iron ore and oil fields, a considerable metal industry, and $200 million in gold and foreign exchange reserves. In September, Czechoslovakia was forced to cede the Sudetenland (perhaps four-fifths German) to Germany, Ruthenia and part of southern Slovakia (three-fifths Hungarian) to Hungary, and Teschen (two-fifths Polish) to Poland. In March 1939, Germany seized the remainder of Czechoslovakia, along with gold and currency assets held by the Czech national bank, the large and profitable Czech arms industry, the aircraft, tanks, and weapons of the Czech army, and large stocks of ores and metals, and, as with Austria, Jewish firms and other local concerns, especially the banks (Kennedy 1987: 308, 340).

In September 1939, Germany annexed Western Poland, expelled some one million Poles, and replaced them, by 1943, with a nearly equal number of ethnic Germans from enclaves in Eastern Europe and Russia as well as from Germany itself; it also took some two million Poles to work as forced laborers in Germany. In April 1940, Germany invaded two countries, Norway and Denmark, for which it had devised long-term development plans.[45] In May, it invaded the Netherlands and Belgium, which were intended by the Nazis to form part of the Aryan heartland, and Luxembourg. It then invaded France, where it requisitioned huge quantities of raw materials, foodstuffs and industrial products, Jewish property that had been confiscated, and what would be the largest number of foreign males engaged in forced labor in Germany. In Hungary, Romania, Bulgaria, and the puppet state of Slovakia, bilateral arrangements obliged governments to deliver goods to Germany, which Germany paid for in blocked and therefore useless credits. However, both Hungary and Bulgaria regained territory lost after the First World War and Bulgaria annexed the bulk of Macedonia, as well as of Thrace. In April 1941, Yugoslavia was invaded and completely destroyed. Slovenia was partitioned between Germany and Italy.

CONCLUSIONS

Though the structure of European society was profoundly affected by the Great War, forces of resistance during the interwar years prevented its breakdown. However, forces of change had been unleashed as a result of the war.

Mass mobilization for war had worked to strengthen the unity and organization of labor and to shift the balance of power within European societies

---

[45] Germany envisaged gigantic industrial investments in Denmark and Norway. Installed horsepower, much of it in new power plants, increased in Denmark from 550,000 to 710,000 and in Norway from 2.2 to 2.4 million. However, as the military situation worsened, long-term development plans were increasingly relegated to the background (Tipton and Aldritch 1987b: 27).

somewhat in its favor. Working-class participation in the war had not marked the victory of nationalism over socialism or its demise as a force for change in Europe, as some accounts of the period contend. In fact, during the war, labor had developed a growing determination that a better standard of living for the masses must emerge with the coming of peace. At the end of the war, labor was stronger, better organized, and more unified, and in a position to back its demands with threats.

The social revolutionary turmoil that swept through Europe during and after the war compelled elites to make a number of concessions to labor in the early years of the interwar period. But by the 1930s, various measures, including corporatist and fascist institutions and structures, had been devised to prevent any further shift in the balance of power within European societies. As a result, the basic dynamics of internal repression and external expansion that had characterized European societies throughout the nineteenth century continued to shape developments in Europe between the wars. Political institutions in Europe were continually compromised and undermined by efforts to preserve privilege and to forestall the acquisition of power by subordinate groups and classes. Where liberal electoral politics were introduced, governments had difficulty in maintaining them for sustained periods of time. Constitutions and democratic civil liberties were continually thwarted by extralegal patronage systems, corruption, and violence. Parliaments were dissolved and election results were disregarded. Thus, the prewar order prevailed with respect to labor and minorities.

By 1918, the "final surge of land hunger" and "chase for 'spheres of influence' that have been called the New Imperialism" had left few opportunities for overseas expansion (Landes 1969: 240–41). The best markets abroad had already been formally annexed or informally integrated into European economies. However, European states continued to search for alternatives to the development of their domestic markets. Imperialism, a central feature of Europe's industrial expansion throughout the previous century, became crystallized, along with other aspects of Europe's nineteenth-century social system, in fascism. Thus, imperialism, now primarily focused on Europe itself, continued to be a focus of European energies throughout the interwar years.

All in all, the essential contours of Europe's nineteenth-century socioeconomic and political system were preserved after the war. As a result, conflicts involving labor and minorities were a constant feature of the interwar years, as were imperialist rivalries and conflicts. Europe remained, during the interwar years, a militarily dangerous and politically volatile region.

The next two chapters detail the domestic and interstate tensions of these years. They show how the increasing polarization of European society along class lines led, in 1939, to a second regional conflagration and, as a consequence of that war, to a decisive (though temporary) shift in the balance of class power in Europe.

II

THE INTERREGNUM

6

The Polarization of European Society, 1918–1939

Wandering between two worlds, – one dead,
The other powerless to be born.
> Matthew Arnold, *Stanzas from the Grande Chartreuse*

The crisis consists precisely in the fact that the old is dying and the new cannot be born; in this interregnum a great variety of morbid symptoms appear.
> Gramsci 1971: 276

During the expansion of industrial capitalism in Europe, attempts to maintain or eradicate restrictions on political rights and economic opportunities generated minority and class conflicts at home; efforts to secure protected markets abroad in lieu of developing internal markets generated imperialist conflicts abroad. These conflicts generated tensions that produced, in 1914, a massively destructive regional war.

During the interwar years, struggle between left and right in Europe was carried on in a more or less continuous round of violent strikes, demonstrations, riots, and street fighting, as well as coups, rebellions, and revolutions. As a result, over the course of the nineteenth century, the domestic and international relations of European states became increasingly polarized.

Before that, Europe had developed, over the course of several centuries, a three-fold social class structure: an upper class of noble landowners and administrators, a peasantry, and, set off from both of these by law (e.g., in Germany) or by custom (e.g., in England and France), an urban commercial and professional middle class. In much of Central and Eastern Europe (e.g., in Russia, Poland, Lithuania, Austria, Hungary, Bohemia, and Romania), the urban middle class was set off from the landowners and the peasantry nationally as well as legally.

In the eighteenth century, this class grew in size and strength as increases in colonial and domestic trade and the expansion of governmental activities swelled the ranks of lawyers, lesser magistrates, civil servants, men in commerce and trade, and nontitled property owners. As these classes grew, pressures for change grew, as well. However, as Chapter 2 argued, the struggle for change merged with a struggle for control over its nature and direction; for, with the growth of new classes and state autonomy, traditional elites in Europe sought to gain control of state institutions and, by this means, to control capitalist development and to restrict it in ways that would preserve the traditional bases of their political and economic power.

Many scholars assume, correctly, that the French Revolution was the result of pressures for change, but they assume, erroneously, that it marked the rise to power in Europe of a new capitalist bourgeoisie. Though the Revolution was begun by the French aristocracy, it was the wealthy elements of the urban bourgeoisie who, by charting an independent course, "gave rise to a vague awareness that a new order was in the making" (Tocqueville 1955: 1). However, the goal of this class was not to bring about a fundamental change in social structure but to be included in the ranks of the aristocracy.

During the nineteenth century, the interests of the traditional landed elite and of new wealthy elements fused, and these two classes became factions of a single dominant class. As the new urban bourgeoisie assimilated to the upper classes, the three-fold social class structure of previous centuries in many places in Europe was transformed. In its place, there emerged a social structure that increasingly came to be characterized by the split between a powerful landed and industrial elite, on the one hand, and urban working classes and peasant masses, on the other.

LIBERAL CHALLENGE, CONSERVATIVE RESPONSE: THE CLASS COMPROMISE OF 1848

Though the fusion of the landowning and industrial classes began in the early nineteenth century, it was not completed until much later. It was accelerated as a result of the 1848 revolutions and was completed during the Great Depression of the 1870s and 1880s. During the first half of the nineteenth century, the industrial and commercial classes attempted to wrest a share of political power from the traditional landowning classes. However, each attempt, whether successful or not, was followed by a period of conservative retrenchment.

Following the French Revolutionary and Napoleonic Wars, there was, everywhere in Europe, a period of restoration and reaction. In France, a "white terror" arose as royalist gangs, often led by nobles, murdered thousands of former Jacobins, Bonapartists, Protestants, and Jews. Some former revolutionaries and Bonapartists were executed, thousands were jailed, and over a third of all government officials were purged. A series of emergency laws suspended individual freedom in 1815; in 1820 there began a long period of Ultra reaction. England, in 1819, introduced martial law provisions (in the Six Acts). That year, Prussia halted reforms initiated by Napoleon, abrogated liberal constitutions, imposed strict press and publication censorship, and assigned government representatives to each university to rout out instructors, students, and secret societies of liberal persuasion (the Carlsbad Decrees). A revolt of the Guard at St. Petersburg in 1820 inaugurated the reaction in Russia. In Piedmont, a conservative and clerical reaction ensured the preservation of a despotic and militaristic monarchy (Droz 1967: 87).

The decade of the 1820s was filled with uprisings by the industrial and commercial classes against monarchs, royalists, nobles, and clerics. However, wherever they were successful in winning charters and constitutions, the Concert of Europe helped to bring about a swift and decisive conservative restoration. When an uprising in 1820 forced King Ferdinand to grant a charter, a mandate from the Concert authorized Austria to restore him to power. The Austrian army rendered a similar service to the king of Sardinia following a revolution in Turin in 1821.[1] France put down a revolution in Spain in 1820 and an uprising there in 1821. Under a mandate from the Concert, French troops went to Spain again in November 1822 after a liberal government had forced King Ferdinand VII to grant a constitution. The Austrian army crushed resistance in Piedmont in 1823. Britain and France (and Spain) intervened in the Portuguese Civil War of 1826–33.

Then, in the 1830s, elements from within the industrial and commercial classes showed themselves prepared to ally with the lower classes in order to achieve their objectives. To forestall this outcome, the landed upper class in France (1831 and 1833) and in Britain (1832) expanded the suffrage to include a small minority of the most highly taxed commercial and industrial elements. In France, the expansion of the suffrage created an electorate of some 200,000 out of a population of approximately 30 million. Thus, the regime remained largely what it had been under the Bourbons, one of mostly landowning notables (Cole and Campbell 1989: 43–44). In Britain, a rural uprising that in scale very nearly matched "The Great Fear" of 1789 impelled the English parliament to pass the Reform Bill of 1832 and admit to political life the well-to-do elements of the middle class. With this concession some 217,000 voters were added to the existing electorate of 435,000. This left 95 percent of the population of the country without democratic representation. The reform did little in subsequent years to change the social composition of the House of Commons. Thus, while the upper house remained the preserve of the landed aristocracy, the lower house continued as

---

[1] King Victor Emmanuel I had abdicated in favor of his brother Charles Felix, naming at the same time Charles Albert, the next in the line of succession, as regent. The latter, liberally inclined, proclaimed a constitution, but the Austrian intervention established Charles Felix in control.

before to be an assembly of the younger sons of the nobility and placemen of influential magnates (Gillis 1983: 124–25). During this decade, constitutions were proclaimed in Bavaria, Würtemburg, Saxony, and Hanover. However, in the restoration that followed, the German Confederation's Federal Diet declared that German princes were bound to reject petitions that decreased the power of the sovereign.

The revolutionary uprisings and upheaval of 1848 brought about a decisive and irrevocable fusion of landowning and capitalist interests. These uprisings led by liberals, socialists, and communists established the Second Republic in France; induced the rulers of Naples, Tuscany, and Piedmont, and the Pope, to grant constitutions; forced King Frederick William IV to agree to summon a Constituent Assembly in the German states; forced the Austrian emperor to consent to the convening of a Constituent Assembly;[2] and triggered a final flare-up of Chartism in Britain.

However, as before, the new order closed ranks against republicans and the left. Thus, like those of the 1820s and 1830s, the revolutions of 1848 were followed by a period of restoration and reaction. In elections held for the president of the French Republic and the assembly in 1849, Louis Napoleon won by more than five to one over his liberal opponents, then purged the government and army of republicans and disenfranchised some 3 million of those most likely to vote for the left (Cole and Campbell 1989: 45). Frederick William IV revised the Prussian constitution (granted in 1850) to give himself absolute power over the army and over all legislation, and an electoral system weighted in favor of wealthy landowners. Austria canceled previous liberal concessions and granted the Church more powers than it had enjoyed since the Counter-Reformation. In Italy, French influence, which had displaced Austrian, soon turned conservative as Louis Napoleon sought to enlist conservative Catholic support within France. Hungary's "March Laws" were withdrawn after Russian troops invaded the country. Wallachia's liberal movement was crushed when Russian troops invaded and occupied the country (see, e.g., Maurice 1887; Droz 1967).

Following the 1848 revolutions, Europe became increasingly polarized between conservatives and liberals, on the one hand, and all socialistic and working class elements, on the other. Liberalism, after all, was the ideology of the wealthy urban bourgeoisie seeking freedom from restrictions favoring landed wealth. Most of the middle-class liberal agitators in the Paris uprisings of 1848 were seeking to acquire for themselves the same rights as the propertied bourgeoisie and had no intention of allowing these rights to be extended to the lower classes. After 1848, liberalism became explicitly linked with the interests of the propertied classes: the defense of the institution of private property, the suppression of labor, and, above all, resistance to the

---

[2] The Austrian emperor also accepted Magyar rule over Hungarian lands (the "March Laws"). Notables in Wallachia won liberal concessions from the Turkish governor there.

pressure of the lower classes for a democratic system.[3] Democracy was the ideology of the working classes, and of some social reformers, seeking freedom from restrictions that prevented the lower classes from gaining a living wage and a decent standard of living. Most German liberals equated it with despotism. As Polanyi memorably wrote, "from Macauley to Mises, from Spencer to Sumner, there was not a militant liberal who did not express his conviction that popular democracy was a danger to capitalism" (Polanyi 1944: 226). In 1871, the revolutionary rising in Paris completed, decisively and violently, the parting of the ways between bourgeois republicans and socialist revolutionaries, and in the decades that followed, European society became increasingly polarized between a socialist left and an ultraconservative right.

During the 1880s and 1890s, falling prices, bad harvests, and cheap wheat imports brought about the largest transfer of land in Britain that had occurred for more than 200 years (Montagu 1970: 169). As would occur following the First World War, the new landowners adopted not only the landed estates but the habits of the old landowning elite as well. At the same time, the old landowners, there and everywhere in Europe, adopted industrial interests on a larger scale than ever before, spreading their assets by investing on the stock exchange. Thus, the great estate and the large corporation increasingly became bound together by overlapping and common economic interests. By 1896, more than one-quarter of the British peerage held directorships, most of them in more than one company (Montagu 1970: 170). The younger sons of the nobility went into the professions. In the 1880s, almost without exception, the most successful lawyers came from titled and landed families (Cannadine 1990: 250). In Hungary, a large part of the land-owning aristocracy was ruined by agricultural crisis during the 1870s and 1880s and found employment in the civil service and free professions. A similar process took place in Poland and elsewhere in Europe. Thus, with the depression of the 1870s and 1880s, Europe became more sharply divided into landowning and industrial elites, on the one hand, and working classes, on the other.

---

[3] There is a tendency to associate "liberals" with the struggle for democracy in nineteenth-century Europe. However, liberals and democrats had two quite distinct ideologies and aims. Liberals subscribed to an aristocratic theory of government that held that only a select few were possessed of sufficient intelligence, discipline, and character to govern. The leading French Restoration liberal-radical, Benjamin Constant, declared that only property owners had "sufficient leisure to develop the capability to exercise his political rights" (in Goldstein 1983: 7). Noting that "all the nations of Europe" that have representative government consider private property "the only proper indication of electoral capacity," liberals in Spain, in their 1837 electoral law, disenfranchised 98 percent of the population (in Goldstein 1983: 6). The Whig (liberal) historian and parliamentarian, Thomas Macauley, declared in 1842 that universal suffrage would be "utterly incompatible with the existence of civilization" (in Goldstein 1983: 3).

Democrats argued that with the proper education and environment, all (or most) citizens could share the responsibilities of governing (see Tussman 1960: chap. 4).

THE SOCIALIST THREAT

A meeting in St. Martin's Hall, Long Acre, London, on September 28, 1864, led to the founding of the First International, officially called the International Working Men's Association. During its first years, the aim of the English trade unionists who controlled the association was to extend the benefits of British trade unionism to the continent. Under their guidance, trade societies were created in Germany, France, Belgium, and Switzerland. Later, trade societies developed in Spain, Italy, Holland, Denmark, and Portugal.

The 1880s marked the rise throughout Europe of socialist parties the essential object of which was the reconstruction of society in the interest of the wage-earning classes. In the years leading up to the First World War, the number of their members, their candidates returned to representative bodies, and their share of the popular vote increased by leaps and bounds.

The Social Democratic Party (SPD) was founded in Germany in 1869. It polled 493,000 votes in 1877, some 1,427,000 in 1890, and 4,239,000 in 1912 (Palmer 1983: 265). By 1914, with over a million inscribed members and a budget of more than two million marks a year, the SPD "constituted something not far short of a state within a state" (Barraclough 1967: 135).

There were two principal socialist parties in France: the Parti Socialiste de France (composed of the Guesdists and, after 1901, the Blanquists);[4] and the Parti Socialiste Française (composed principally of the followers of Jaurès and the Independents).[5] The two parties fused in 1905 in the Parti Socialiste Unifié, and was designated officially as the French Section of the International Workingman's Association (Section Française de l'Internationale Ouvrière). At the elections of 1906, their candidates polled 1,000,000 votes, and won 250, or 38 percent, of the total seats in the Chamber (Ogg 1930: 519–20).

In the Netherlands, a Social Democratic Labour Party with a strictly socialist program was established in 1894. Its candidates polled 13,025 votes in 1897; 38,279 in 1901; and 65,743 in 1905 (Ogg 1930: 531). The Parti Ouvrier Belge was founded in Belgium in 1885 and became avowedly socialist in 1894. A Social Democratic Party was founded in Switzerland in 1888, and returned to the National Council from two to nine deputies (in a total of 167) after 1890 (Ogg 1930: 536). A branch of the Internationale was organized in Denmark in 1871, and a Danish Social Democratic Union was

---

[4] Louis Blanc (1811–82) was the first of the French socialists to propose to democratize the existing governmental system and to make of it the medium for the erection of a socialistic state, and he was the first who was able to recruit a considerable party and lead it to temporary triumph. In 1839, he founded the *Revue du Progrès*, which became the organ of the most advanced democrats. It was in this paper that his greatest socialistic work, the *Organisation du Travail*, appeared in 1840 (the text of this treatise is printed in Marriot 1913). The first proposal in Blanc's social program was that the state should be reconstituted on a broadly democratic basis. That done, the government should direct its energies to the emancipation of the proletariat.

[5] Jean Jaurès (1859–1914) was the outstanding socialist writer and orator of his time.

established six years later. Between 1906 and 1914, there were 24 socialist members in parliament (of a total of 114).

The Social Democratic Labour Party, founded in Sweden in 1889, returned four deputies to the Riksdag in 1902, and 64 (in a total of 230) in 1911. The Labor Party, organized in Norway in 1885, won four seats in the Storthing in 1903, and 23 (in a total of 123) in 1912 (Ogg 1930: 535). The United Socialist Party was established in Austria in 1888. The aggregate socialist vote in 1907 was 1,041,948, or almost one-third of the total, and the number of deputies elected to the Reichsrath was 87, of a total of 516. In the elections of 1911, some 80 deputies were returned (Ogg 1930: 536). In Italy, a socialistic workingmen's party, founded at Milan in 1885, polled 301,000 votes in 1904 (about one-fifth of the total number) and returned 26 members. In 1913, it polled a million votes and returned 79 candidates to the chamber (Ogg 1930: 538).

The Social Democratic Party (originally "the Democratic Federation") was established in Britain in 1880. In 1893, the Independent Labour Party was founded with the purpose of bringing about the election to parliament of men pledged to the party's strongly socialistic program. In the parliamentary elections of 1906, seven of its candidates and sixteen of its members were sent to the House of Commons. Around it, there was built up a more broadly based organization known simply as the Labour Party. The party, which began its existence in 1900, originally was nonsocialistic. Its first constitution, adopted in 1918, called for "the common ownership of the means of production, distribution and exchange."[6]

Beginning in the 1880s, Britain also "witnessed increasing class division. There was an explosive rise in strikes, as well as demonstrations, riots, and uprisings by urban and rural labor. Enmity grew between employers and workmen" (Meacham 1972: 1351). Party politics also became increasingly polarized, culminating in the great Whig secession of 1886 that concentrated the members of landowning families on one side of the House (Thompson 1977: 24).

The year 1889 opened a new era in labor relations in Britain, one that represented "a qualitative transformation of the British labor movement and its industrial relations" (Hobsbawm 1985: 15). Beginning in 1889, labor disputes in Britain were continuously connected to a nationwide campaign that revealed itself, thereby and definitively, as class struggle (see Chapter 1). That year, Britain experienced its first nationwide and national industrial disputes and collective bargains and the first interventions of central government in labor disputes, and it established the first government offices designed to address labor disputes (Hobsbawm 1985: 15–16). Unionism was extended to new industries and types of workers, helping to break down the localized and sectional form of collective bargaining that had been

---

[6] Labour Party, *Party Constitution and Standing Orders* (1918), 7.

dominant. Issues such as the eight-hour day and the principle of mechanization became, more definitively, national issues. The dock strike that year "precipitated permanent changes in attitude" among employers, politicians, and government administrators (Hobsbawm 1985: 17). After the strike, "effective and permanent employers" organizations were formed on a national scale" (Hobsbawm 1985: 15). By 1893, "even a simple wage reduction in the coalmines implied a simultaneous nationwide dispute, since the coalfields (outside Wales, Scotland, and the north-east) were now co-ordinated in the new Miners' Federation of Great Britain" (Hobsbawm 1985: 19). Moreover, the scale of such disputes was unprecedented.

Between 1910 and 1914, total membership in all unions in Britain rose by 66 percent; membership in the so-called new unions – dockers, seamen, and general laborers – increased by over 300 percent (Meacham 1972: 1344). Though working-class history in the nineteenth century had been marked by violence, disturbances in 1911 and after

seemed at the time, and contemporary descriptions make them seem now, to possess a quality of their own. Something – the ever-increasing numbers involved, the restless, never-ceasing pattern of agitations – fused them into an expression of mass dissatisfaction and mass uncertainty that was unprecedented and therefore alarming. (Meacham 1972: 1346).

Between 1910 and 1914, there were 3,165 strikes totaling 60 million mandays lost (Hobsbawm 1985: 17). The average number of strikes in England increased from 872 strikes per year in 1911 to 1459 in 1913 (Meacham 1972: 1344, 1347).

Large or newly federated employers launched a counterattack. A British Employer's Defense Union was formed to counter union activity. Members of the union observed in 1908 that workers' demands were transforming "commercial problems into class problems" (Clegg, Fox, and Thompson 1964: vol. 1, p. 433; in Meacham 1972: 1351). And, indeed, sharper class divisions were evident outside the factory, as well. "In matters of pay, dress, drink ... health, life, and death" the working and middle classes "appeared to be as far apart as they were in the 1840s and in some cases were further apart. The result was a heightened sense of class consciousness" (Meacham 1972: 1352). By 1914, labor unrest and socialist agitation on the left and the rise of an ultraconservative, nationalist and anti-Semitic right gave a violent cast to British society that the war in 1914 only temporarily relieved.

In France, the period following 1890 was characterized by the politics of "concentration" – the migration of bourgeois republicans to the right over economic and social issues (Hoffmann 1961). The "concentration" majorities during this period were preoccupied with tariff protection, labor unrest, antisocialism, and labor union organization. By 1910, even moderate Radicals ran on socially conservative platforms. The formation of Raymond

Poincaré's 1912 government, and his election to the French presidency a year later, signified the continued preoccupation of the "concentration" majority with labor unrest. Ultrapatriotic and royalist leagues such as the Action Française drew support from a wide range of elements: aristocrats, military officers, clergy, members of the religious teaching orders banned by the Republic, upper middle-class industrialists (especially those in war-related industries), small shopkeepers, and villagers from traditionally royalist areas. The goal of the Action Française, its founders declared, was a conservative revolution to restore premodern values and institutions (Weiss 1977: 103). The elections of 1914 pitted those who sympathized with these views against an alliance of the French Socialists (SFIO) and Radical Socialists.

In Germany, violent strikes in Berlin in 1910 and in the Ruhr in 1912 and a series of massive strikes and lockouts in 1914 centered on demands for recognition of unions, better pay, improved working conditions, and better representation and social legislation (Hardach 1977: 183). In Italy, there were violent strikes in 1898, 1901, 1902, and 1903, a general strike in 1904, another wave of industrial unrest that crested in 1906–7, and violent agricultural strikes in 1908. In 1914, a general strike in Rome in opposition to tax increases intended to pay for the looming war spread to other towns, some of which remained in the hands of strikers for a week or more (Tipton and Aldrich 1987a: 115).

Under the threat of revolution, the government of Russia had made a number of concessions in 1905, including freedom of association and assembly, but these were largely rescinded when the relevant legislation was introduced in 1906. Almost the whole of the trade union movement was forced into illegality after 1905. Official authorization was needed to set up a trade union, and labor disputes were attended by open and often brutal intervention by the military and the police on the side of the employers, investing all industrial disputes with a political quality irrespective of the motive behind them (Hardach 1977: 217–18). In 1912, a tremendous wave of strikes began, the orientation of which became increasingly political until, in the summer of 1914, they were deliberately aimed at creating a new revolutionary situation.

WORLD WAR I AND MASS MOBILIZATION

In 1914, European societies were divided and polarized. Thus, when the war came in 1914, it "came as a respite from crisis, a diversion, perhaps even as some sort of solution" (Hobsbawm 1968: 193). On the day war was declared (July 20 in the Russian calendar), there were antiwar demonstrations in Moscow, St. Petersburg, and a number of other industrial centers. Reservists in the provinces demonstrated with red flags, revolutionary songs, and cries of "Down with the war!" (Hardach 1977: 219). During August, two million Russians got married in order to avoid being drafted into the army (Kennedy 1987: 237). Social relations in Britain were delicately poised between national integration and class conflict. German transport workers had sent £5,000 to the London dockers during their 1912 strike. In 1913, the National Transport Workers Federation had passed a resolution demanding the general strike "in the event of national war being imminent."[7]

However, all across Europe the war brought about a social truce between the ruling classes and their native working classes. Trade union leaders, concerned to ensure that their organizations would continue to enjoy legality and recognition, opted for cooperation. Masses of workers hoped that participation in the war might win the rights for which they had fought for over a century. The truce, however, was short-lived. Early in the war, the threat from "the inner fronts of industrial warfare" reemerged.

On the outbreak of war the unions in Britain supported an industrial truce and recruitment for the armed forces. Both on patriotic grounds and because they believed that the war and the concomitant price rises would be of short duration, they also renounced an active wages policy. Later, they cooperated with the employers and the state in the mobilization of industry. But by the end of 1914, when it had become apparent that price rises had come to stay, the struggle for higher wages and a better standard of living resumed.[8] In the Clyde area, the "campaign against the war, against high prices and rents and for increased wages was in full blast" (Gallacher 1940: 32), and in February 1915, it acquired national importance (see Scott 1924; Pribicevic 1959; McLean 1975), as did the crisis that occurred over the question of dilution.[9] By the end of the war, workers were demanding higher wages, greater control at the workplace, the nationalization of coal

---

[7] National Transport Workers Federation, *Annual General Council Meeting*, 1913, p. 31.

[8] Members of the English working class had enjoyed a general increase in real wages during the second half of the nineteenth century. But although the general trend in incomes of workers was upward between 1850 and 1900, not all workers benefited. In general, improvements in material standards of living for workers in Britain before World War I were limited (Reid 1992: 25). Then, around 1900, real wages declined. According to the *Annual Report* of the Federation of Trades Unions for 1911, real wages rose by 1 percent between 1900 and 1908; however, during that period food prices in London rose by 9 percent, and profits rose by 12.5 percent (in Meacham 1972: 1350). At the same time that real wages were declining, the low rate of unemployment (no higher than 3.3 percent from 1911 to 1914) gave workers increased power to press their demands (Meacham 1972: 1350). Real wages caught up with the cost of living by 1914, but by that time the average worker was "exhausted and a good deal poorer than he thought he should be" (Meacham 1972: 1348).

[9] "Dilution" was the practice of reorganizing production so as to be able to use unskilled workers for jobs previously performed by skilled workers. After a great deal of bargaining between employers and workers, punctuated by strikes, the Shells and Fuses Agreement was concluded in March 1915. By its terms, the unions accepted dilution, while for their part the employers promised that skilled workers would suffer no material loss from the reorganization of production, that the terms would be valid only for the duration, that after the war the old conditions would be restored, and, above all, that the unions would be permitted to participate in the implementation of dilution in the various factories (Hardach 1977: 186).

and other industries, and a host of social reforms connected with housing, health, and employment.

In Germany, the lowering of wages and the simultaneous rise in the cost of living hit the workers particularly hard. Retail prices soared as a result of widespread panic buying. The shops were invaded by people anxious to lay in stocks of food and other articles, and the traders charged whatever the market would stand (Hardach 1977: 198). In the autumn of 1915, rising food prices and scarcities provoked food riots in the working-class districts of Berlin and riots, local disturbances, and protest meetings in many German towns. By 1916, food riots had begun to merge with political demonstrations and demands for peace (Carsten 1982: 42). In May 1916, infantry and cavalry units were moved into Leipzig during three days of riots, and a state of siege was proclaimed (Carsten 1982: 76). In August, the military was called in to Hamburg to reestablish order after a three-day food riot turned into a massive antiwar demonstration. In February 1917, six companies of infantry were required to restore order in Hamburg after two days of rioting. The army was called to restore order that month in the Rhineland. During the following months, violent mobs looted bakers' shops and battled with the police and, sometimes, cavalry units in Mainz, Düsseldorf, Stettin, Upper Silesia, Hindenburg, and Gleiwitz (Carsten 1982: 130, 132–35, 148–49). In 1915 an average of 1,000 workers were on strike each month; in 1916, the average was 10,000 (Hardach 1977: 183). In 1916, there were 240 strikes, affecting 124,000 workers; in 1917, there were more than twice as many strikes (562), involving more than four times as many strikers (651,000; Carsten 1982: 124–25).

By 1915, the steady deterioration in the standard of living and the demand for ever greater sacrifices had created a volatile situation in Russia. While wages had gone up by about 100 percent in 1914, food prices had risen by three to five times as much (Marwick 1974: 37). Terrible shortages developed in 1916 and 1917, in part as a result of disruption of transportation and distribution, but also due to speculation, hoarding, and profiteering.[10] Widespread industrial strikes were the result. In 1915, there were strikes involving half a million workers; in 1916, they involved more than a million workers.

In January 1917, a strike in St. Petersburg called to mark the anniversary of the 1905 revolution and protest the war escalated into demonstrations that drew 40 percent of the city's workers into the streets. During February, the strike movement spread. When army units stationed in the cities refused

[10] Russia was a country naturally rich in agriculture: the peasantry made up 80 percent of the population and cereals alone constituted half of her exports (Nove 1982: 20–25). The Turkish stranglehold on the Dardanelles cut the export trade off, making all the food formerly sent out of the country available to be consumed at home. Though there was a fall in the production of agricultural estates caused by the loss of labor to the army, more than enough food was produced to feed the country (Seton-Watson 1967: 704–5).

to fire on the strikers, a coalition of the Constitutional-Democrat Party (the "Cadets," or liberal bourgeois) and the moderate socialists secured the abdication of the tsar and formed a provisional government.

A wave of strikes swept through France, Spain, Britain, Italy, and Germany in the wake of the revolution in Russia. In France, a great wave of strikes shook the munitions industry and the armed forces in the spring of 1917. In Spain, strikes and rioting in industrial centers were suppressed by the military. In Britain, there were great strikes in Lancashire and the Midlands, and in May, a strike at Castleton near Manchester spread to Liverpool, Sheffield, Derby, and Coventry and then south to London, Southampton, and Bristol. The strike movement, which spread to some forty-eight towns in all and involved about 200,000 workers, threatened to paralyze the war industries. In Italy, a general strike and insurrection in Turin in 1917 involved some 50,000 workers in five days of street fighting, and led to hundreds of casualties (Tilly et al. 1975).

In Germany, the beginning of 1917 was marked by strikes in the North Rhine–Westphalian munitions industry and by food riots in a number of towns. News of the terms that the German High Command was demanding of Russia produced massive strikes in January. In February, a million munitions workers went on strike to demand peace with Russia and to express indignation with the German government's delaying tactics in negotiations with Russia at Brest Litovsk (begun on December 20, 1917, and not concluded until March 3, 1918). The strikers also demanded franchise reform (Ryder 1963: 207). On April 15, 1917, workers in Berlin and Leipzig struck in protest when it was announced that the bread ration would be cut. The following day, between 200,000 and 300,000 workers went on strike, closing down more than 300 armament works in Berlin (Carsten 1982: 124–25). In Leipzig, workers demanded better supplies of foodstuffs and coal, the conclusion of a peace without annexations, the ending of the state of emergency, the abolition of the Auxiliary Service Law, freedom of the press and of assembly, and universal and equal suffrage throughout the Empire (Hardach 1977: 183–84). Henceforward, there was an unbroken succession of protest strikes. June and July 1917 saw a great wave of strikes, centered mainly on the Ruhr and Upper Silesia.

In October 1918, thousands demonstrated in front of the parliament building in Berlin against the war and against the new government. Army units sent from the east to the western front unfolded red flags and demonstrated against the war. By the end of October, there was open mutiny. Near Metz, a whole division of the territorial army refused to go back to the front, and many thousands of soldiers did not return from their leave. At the end of the month, the German admiralty decided to launch a last desperate attack on the British navy. When sailors manning the battleships at Wilhelmshaven and other ports received orders to put to sea, they refused to weigh anchor. The mutiny spread to Kiel, where a naval patrol, sent ashore to bring mutineers back on board, opened fire on a crowd of demonstrators, killing eight men and wounding many more. On November 5, most of the ships in the harbor at Kiel hoisted the red flag. Officers who tried to resist were disarmed or thrown overboard. Dockyard workers struck in sympathy with the mutineers. Armed sailors with red flags marched to the military prison and freed incarcerated sailors. From Kiel, the revolution spread to the ports along the coast of the Baltic and the North Sea to Lübeck, Hamburg, Bremen, and Wilhelmshaven. Sailors, wearing red insignia, acted as the avant-garde of the revolution. On November 7, Kurt Eisner, the leader of the Independent Social Democratic Party, proclaimed the revolution in Munich. All the barracks were taken by the revolutionaries. The public buildings were occupied by armed detachments. That evening, the king and his family fled the city. Two days later, the revolution reached Berlin. The factories closed and the barracks emptied, as soldiers either joined the revolution or left for home. Political prisoners were freed from the civil and military prisons. Phillip Scheidemann, a Social Democratic Party (SPD) member of the government, proclaimed the German Republic from the balcony of the parliament.[11] Elections were held for representative assemblies in the local, state, and federal levels in early 1919. A coalition government was formed by members of the SPD, the Democrats, and the Catholic Center Party. However, as would eventually become apparent, in the German Republic, the old bureaucracy, the old judiciary, and the officer corps continued to hold sway.

POSTWAR REVOLUTIONARY CURRENTS AND THE FASCIST REACTION

The end of the war in 1918 brought no peace to Europe. The specter of revolution continued to haunt Europe's governments and ruling classes, and with the rise of the left following the war, European society became increasingly polarized between a newly powerful left and a resurgent, ultraconservative, and militant right.[12]

The Rise of the Left

Following World War I, Western states confronted, in addition to a Bolshevik revolution abroad, newly organized and more powerful labor movements at home. In 1919, a new revolutionary movement – the Third International – was formed under the auspices of Lenin and the Russian Bolsheviks; mass communist parties emerged in France, Germany, and Italy; and Hungary

---

[11] Carsten 1982 : 215–26. Soon after, Karl Liebknecht, a leader of the Spartacus Group, proclaimed the "German Socialist Republic" from the balcony of the royal palace.

[12] As Arno Mayer has noted, "whenever politics operates under the influence of the specter of revolution," as it did after March 1917, "societies become much more polarized" (1969: 4).

briefly became a communist country. In Britain, the red flag was raised on the town hall in Glasgow, and the British War Cabinet feared that a Bolshevik revolution was being attempted (Mayer 1967: chapter 5). In 1923, a year of communist riots in Germany culminated in an attempted communist revolution at Hamburg. The first Labor government took office in Britain in 1923,[13] and the left triumphed in France in 1924. Socialist parties came to power in Sweden in 1920, in Denmark in 1924, and in Norway in 1927. In Belgium and Holland, socialists entered the cabinet for the first time in 1939. Everywhere the left seemed to be on the rise.

Following the war, skilled and unskilled workers, workers of different occupations, anarchists and socialists, Social Democrats and Communists, revolutionaries and reformists, closed ranks.[14] By 1920, Europe had 34 million trade unionists.[15]

In 1870, the lower classes had constituted some 75 percent of European society, of which only about 15 percent were skilled workers (Gillis 1983: 268). But up until World War I, the great landed families and their allies had been successful in maintaining the social and political isolation of agrarian labor by exempting their resident tenants and other workers from labor legislation and preventing them from securing the right to organize.[16] Thus, unskilled labor had remained outside the ranks of organized protest almost everywhere before the First World War.[17]

Between 1914 and 1921, unskilled labor joined the ranks of organized labor; as a result, trade union membership doubled in Britain during the war, from 4 million to 8 million (Geary 1981: 151–55). In Germany, unskilled

---

[13] The immediate postwar elections in Britain had increased the socialists' electoral share to an average of 32 percent, and trade union organization two and a half fold (Rueschemeyer et al. 1992: 97).

[14] James Cronin observes that, before the war, the distinction within the working class "between 'rough' and 'respectable,' between the skilled and organized and the unskilled and unorganized," had been "very real to contemporaries and was reflected in many aspects of politics and collective action." Following the war, however, "a variety of technical, social and economic processes conjoined to produce a working class that was, if not more internally homogeneous, at least less sharply divided within itself, and also more culturally distinct from middle and upper class society than its Victorian analogue had been" (1982a: 139, 121).

[15] For Britain, France, Germany, Italy, and Czechoslovakia, see Ogg 1930: 759–97. For a review of general trends in Europe, see MacDonald 1921 and Vandervelde 1925.

[16] Peasants who were part-time artisans were often radical in politics. But peasants whose main contact with the outside world was the local church accepted the traditional order (Zeldin 1977: 127–39). Unlike liberal capitalists, the feudal lords had always felt an obligation toward their serfs in times of need (as Bismarck pointed out). Moreover, in those places where peasants could hope to buy land, the peasants saw the nobility as allies against the bourgeoisie in the competition for landownership.

[17] The July 1830 insurrection in Paris was staged by highly skilled workers in specialist trades (see Pinkney 1964). It was from the skilled workers, the top 15 percent of the working class, that the trade union leadership in Britain was recruited beginning in the 1860s (Gillis 1983: 269).

workers became active for the first time during the revolutionary upheavals of the postwar period. In Italy, the rapid expansion of heavy industry during the war and in the immediate postwar period drew the new factory working class into radical politics. They entered the political scene on a significant scale for the first time in France during the era of the Front Populaire in the 1930s. Revolutionary protests and strikes in the Balkans occurred only after World War I, and involved mainly urban unskilled labor in the railway, mining, tobacco, and textile industries (Seton-Watson 1945: 134–38; McClellan 1964: 275–96; Dedijer et al. 1974: 522; Djordjevic and Fischer-Galati 1981: 206–8). After World War I, revolutionary activity in Poland, Hungary, and Czechoslovakia was carried out mainly by unskilled urban labor and by peasants.

After World War I, peasant protest also emerged in new organizational forms throughout Europe. In 1919, the Confédération Nationale des Associations Agricoles was established in France – the first serious effort at peasant unity. But it was the Great Depression of the 1930s that ended the passivity of the peasantry. In 1934, for the first time in modern French history, an angry crowd of peasants converged on Paris to demonstrate on the Champs-Elysées, and the dairymen of the Paris region staged France's first successful producers' strike (Wright 1964: 42). In Germany, Austria, Romania, Yugoslavia, Czechoslovakia, Poland, Hungary, Latvia, Estonia, Bulgaria, Lithuania, and Finland, hordes of peasants who had fought in the war demanded the abolition of large estates and the creation of peasant freeholds. Thus,

Between 1918 and 1920, there was a sudden rise of peasant movements in every country of eastern Europe. Some of these were genuinely revolutionary movements, inspired by the Russian revolution; others had a more constitutional and parliamentary character. . . . All, however, were united by the common desire to end feudalism and to build up in its place a democratic society based on peasant ownership. Only the Czechoslovak Agrarian Party succeeded in remaining in power till 1938, in collaboration with other political parties. With this exception dictatorships put an end to the democratic regimes, in most cases identified with the peasant parties, in every country in south-eastern Europe. The process began with Hungary in 1918, and was continued in Bulgaria (1923), Poland (1926), Yugoslavia (1929), and Romania (1931–33). (RIIA 1944: 57, 60)

Though Germany's constitution of 1919 authorized expropriation of landed property whenever necessary to meet the needs of housing and to encourage cultivation, very little was expropriated. In Hungary, a land redistribution scheme was discussed but little actual change took place. Modest reforms were made in Yugoslavia, Bulgaria, and Czechoslovakia. In many countries of Eastern Europe, land reforms were halted and in many places reversed when right-wing governments came to power in the late 1920s and in the 1930s. Land reforms in Spain and Portugal were halted in the same way.

In Italy, Mussolini had promised to break up the large estates but never did so. The large landowners grew wealthier because of the rising price of wheat, thanks to government tariffs and subsidies, but the peasants' condition deteriorated. The possibility of emigration to America had provided some alternative before 1922; now, however, the United States drastically restricted immigration.[18] By the fall of 1919, the membership of the National Federation of Agrarian Workers had more than doubled to reach 475,000 militant members, and it increased to almost 900,000 a year later (Maier 1975: 47).

During the interwar years, trade failed to grow as fast as before, and European economies were plagued by persistent unemployment and an unprecedented degree of contraction (Landes 1969: 390–91). In Britain, there was widespread, almost chronic unemployment in industry and commerce. As industrial production fell and exports fell off sharply, unemployment rapidly increased. By 1919, unrest in Britain was widespread and persistent. In its *Survey of Revolutionary Feeling during the Year 1919*, the Home Office listed the causes of the unrest, in order of importance:[19]

1. Profiteering and high prices
2. Insufficient and bad housing accommodation
3. Class hatred, aggravated by the foolish and dangerous ostentation of the rich, the publication of large dividends, and distrust of a "government of profiteers"
4. Education by Labour Colleges, schools and classes and better circulation of literature on Marxian economics
5. Influence of extremist Trade Union Leaders – Mann, Cramp, Smillie, Godges, Bromley, Hill, Williams, Turner
6. Unemployment
7. Labor press, particularly the "Daily Herald," "The Workers' Dreadnought," and "The Worker"
8. External influences – Russia, Ireland, Egypt, India.

The year 1919 began an unparalleled series of strikes in Britain. The Forty Hours' Strike in January 1919 prompted a discussion at Cabinet level. Strikes in 1920 became decidedly political in nature as workers repeatedly came into conflict with the government over British support for Poland in the Polish-Russian War. In February 1920, Lloyd George raised with Sir Hugh Trenchard (the Chief of Air Staff) the question of the availability of the Royal Air Force to deal with labor unrest (McLean 1975: 237). On May 10,

---

[18] In 1920, some 350,000 Italians entered the United States, but in 1924 only 4,000 were admitted. Mussolini was also opposed to emigration and restricted the movement of the population (Tipton and Aldrich 1987a: 248).

[19] Basil Thomson, "Survey of Revolutionary Feeling during the Year 1919," pp. 4–5; in Cronin 1982a: 120.

dockers engaged in loading a freighter with munitions for Poland struck work with the support of their union and the coal-trimmers refused to coal the vessel. A week later the Dockers' Union put a general ban on the loading of munitions for use against Poland.[20] On July 21, British troops broke a strike of dockers at Danzig against the landing of munitions for the Poles. On August 7, Lord Curzon, the Foreign Secretary, sent a note threatening the Soviet government with war if the advance of the Red Army was not halted. The next day Labour Party headquarters telegraphed all local parties and trade union councils urging demonstrations against war with Russia. The result was nation-wide demonstrations.

In April 1921, mine owners reduced wages and the miners went on strike ("Black Friday"). When the mine owners once again demanded a cut in wages (13 percent) in 1925, the government agreed to subsidize the mines to preclude wage cuts. But in 1926, the mine owners asked again for a 13 percent wage cut, along with an increase in hours. The miners refused, and on April 30, mine owners locked out one million coal miners. Thereupon, the Trade Union Congress called for a "national strike." A "general strike" began at midnight on May 3, 1926, and the next morning 3.5 million workers refused to show up for their jobs in solidarity with the miners. The strike lasted until May 12. During these "nine days that shook Britain," the country was brought to a virtual standstill. Only a small number of nonunionized blue-collar workers continued to work; there was no transport, no factory work, no mining.[21]

The beginning of the interwar period also saw increasing numbers of strikes in other countries in Europe. In 1918, labor unrest culminated in a socialist uprising in the Netherlands. In France, there were attempted general strikes and national workers' demonstrations leading to fights with troops, police, and other workers in 1919–20 (Tilly 1975b). In Germany, there were strikes in Saxony, Hamburg, and the Ruhr in 1921 (Tilly 1975b). Huge strikes in the cities of Italy soon spread to the countryside, where the peasants tried to take over the land from the landowners. In Sweden, Norway, and Denmark, war profiteering at one end of the social scale and food scarcities at the other heightened class tensions. Strikes and riots in Sweden and Norway appeared genuinely revolutionary. In both countries,

---

[20] When the Poles, using the menace of Bolshevism as an excuse, invaded the Soviet Union in 1920 and annexed large areas in the east, the Allied powers supported them by sending shipments of munitions and numerous contingents of military advisers. Then, after a cease-fire was called, the powers sanctioned a new frontier that gave Poland a considerable amount of additional territory, despite the fact that these areas contained large numbers of minorities and were forcibly annexed.

[21] The general strike was a total defeat for the workers. Faced with threats of arrest and overwhelming opposition from the elite and the middle classes, the TUC called off the strike. The miners fought on, but were forced to return to work in November at substantially lower wages (Tipton and Aldrich 1987a: 39–240).

troops were used against strikers, with considerable loss of life in Sweden (Tipton and Aldrich 1987a: 279). In 1919, Switzerland had riots and threats of a general strike. In Italy, landlords recruited "squads" of men (as they had done before the war) to end land seizures and repress strikes. In early 1921, riots that pitted fascists against communists broke out in Florence. In 1922, fascists engineered coups against the city governments of Fiume, Bologna, and Milan. Conditions in Spain, Portugal, and Greece degenerated rapidly after the war to something approaching chaos (Parker 1969: 141).

The Great Depression, which eventually engulfed all of Europe except the Soviet Union, increased the gap between the rich and the poor and exacerbated fears of socialist revolution in Europe. However, it failed to steer European governments off the course they had charted for the previous 150 years. During the depression, the British government restricted foreign lending in the hope of stimulating investment generally; but it was only rearmament that began to absorb large numbers of unemployed industrial workers (Tipton and Aldrich 1987a: 172). In France, workers were cushioned from the effects of massive unemployment by the thousands of foreign workers in the country. In the 1920s, France had imported hundreds of thousands of workers for both agriculture and industry, largely from Eastern Europe.[22] With the depression, an estimated 600,000 were laid off and returned home. However, French industry recovered at a rate slower than that of any advanced nation, partly because conservative governments worsened matters by refusing to stimulate purchasing power through public spending. Instead, the salaries of lesser civil servants were cut as well as budgets for the few social services that existed (Weiss 1977: 135). In 1940, the French economy was still producing not much more than it had in 1913 (Tipton and Aldrich 1987a: 175). Germany ended unemployment by sending unemployed workers to compulsory labor camps to clear lands and build roads at subsistence wages (Weiss 1977: 161). In Spain, the depression added to the already bitter hostility between republican social reformers and conservative forces, and in 1936 the country was engulfed in an extraordinarily destructive civil war.

The Rise of the Right

The rise of socialist radicalism, and in particular the Bolshevik Revolution in Russia in 1917, tended to drive all of Europe's relatively privileged or well-to-do groups and elements into one antirevolutionary coalition. Bolshevism, which had not only laid Russia low but was spreading into central Europe; the unrest in Germany, the demise of the Hohenzollerns and the Hapsburgs,

---

[22] The largest number came from Poland. The value of the franc, which had been undervalued throughout the 1920s, was another factor reducing French unemployment and maintaining exports despite the depression (see Kindleberger 1973).

the communist regime in Hungary, and Lenin and Trotsky's appeals to workers everywhere to join in the revolutionary movement all contributed to a "great fear." Antagonisms between large and small landowners, between monopolistic and competitive business, between liberal bourgeois and reactionary feudal overlords, and between domestic and foreign interests were largely submerged by a common interest in staving off socialism. Frederick Schuman describes the coalition elements and their immediate motivations and goals:

The aristocracies, plutocracies, and priesthoods of the Continent – first in Italy, then in Germany, later ... in Austria, Poland, Portugal, Hungary, Spain and other states, sought refuge: the feudal gentry ... feared the pressure of land-hungry peasants; the great entrepreneurs ... feared the exactions of their wage-earners; the industrialists and financiers ... welcomed "protection" for Property against proletarian radicalism; the Clergy of the Church of Rome, and of some other churches as well ... brought "protection" for Religion against Marxist atheism; the peasantries who either believed promises of land distribution or merely rejoiced in a cause which vocalized their primitive folk-resentment against rationalism, urbanism, and the alien world of metropolitan culture. . . . The diplomats and strategists of the Western Powers caught in the fears and vacillations of the elites for whom they spoke, joined the parade. (Schuman 1942: 498)

Strong repressive actions were taken against the left. In Britain, special laws were passed to repress strikers (1927); troops and police were sent to put down strikers in France (1919, 1920), Yugoslavia (1920), and Switzerland (1932). In Sweden and Norway, troops were used against strikers. In Germany, the government used the remnants of the army and right-wing veterans groups to crush revolutionary activity (1922, 1923, 1929, 1931–1932); the Nazi government crushed the labor movement there in 1933. In Italy, both before the war (1898–1914) and after it, the strike movement was repressed by the police and military units extensively supplemented by armed "squads" hired by conservative landlords (Tipton and Aldrich 1987a: 115). In 1922, the government brought Mussolini's fascists to power in order to curb the workers and peasants by violent means (Jarman 1963: 153–55; Saladino 1966: 251–53; Gay 1970: 19–22); fascists destroyed Italian socialism in the 1920s. In Bulgaria, a right-wing government killed 10,000 to 30,000 leftists after seizing power in 1923. In the 1930s, fear of revolution and the growth of communism precipitated the growth of fascist parties and movements throughout Europe. In Germany, the National Socialist Party – originally a right-wing splinter group – had 800,000 members in 1932 and over 13.5 million votes.[23] In France, a wealth of ultraright and fascist groups

---

[23] Weiss 1977: 158. Nazi organizations were not comprised of lower-class rabble, as has been often alleged. The Nazi regime that came to power in Germany after 1933 showed little interest in radical modifications of the social structure of the country. The sons of aristocratic and upper middle-class families were highly overrepresented in the SS leadership, as well as

flourished in the 1930s, often taking Mussolini as their model.[24] When the government dismissed the right-wing head of the police in 1932, ultraconservative patriotic leagues, including members of the Action Française, took to the streets in massive riots. The battle, which raged for six hours in the center of Paris, resulted in the deaths of fourteen demonstrators and one policeman and led to the fall of the government. There continued to be large demonstrations of both left and right leading to frequent clashes among demonstrators, counterdemonstrators, and government forces (Tilly et al. 1975). In Austria, a united conservative-clerical fascist opposition defeated the labor movement in 1934.

With the outbreak of civil war in Spain in 1936, the struggle between fascism and Bolshevism took the form of an armed struggle in Western Europe. Italy and Germany backed the conservative forces, helping to ensure a victory for fascism in Spain; the Soviet Union backed the left. In Britain, the war sharply polarized British opinion:[25] K. W. Watkins claims that "probably not since the French Revolution had a foreign event so bitterly divided the British people" (1963: vii; see also 11). Both sides were convinced that the war was the result of an international conspiracy – either an international communist plot or an international fascist conspiracy (Watkins 1963: 32–33). In February 1939, even before the Madrid government had surrendered, Britain and France recognized the fascist government of General Franco.

Conflict between Left and Right

In 1918, a conflict between left and right in Finland escalated into full-scale civil war. As many as a quarter of Finland's working class may have been massacred or jailed during the White Terror unleashed by the upper classes (Serge 1972: 186–91). There was a peasant uprising in Bulgaria, a socialist

in the notorious murder squads, the Einsatzgruppen. The core of the old conservatism, the traditional backbone of the armed forces, remained unaltered, its standing and prestige little affected. Led by Hermann Göring, Nazi leaders aped the life-style of assorted princes, counts, and barons who were their preferred companions (Barraclough 1967: 135). In July 1944, just months before their final demise, representatives of the East Prussian Junker class sought to overthrow Hitler. In reaction, Hitler began the liquidation of the East Prussian nobility. Stalin completed the job.

[24] Besides the still influential Action Française, the most important of the many groups were Colonel de la Rocque's Croix de Feu, Jacques Doriot's Parti Populaire Française, Georges Valois's Faisceau, François Coty's Solidarité Française, Marcel Bucard's Francistes, Pierre Taittinger's Jeunnesse Patriotes, the terrorist Cagoulards ("hooded ones"), and Henri Dorgère's Défense Paysanne, whose "green shirts" attracted perhaps half a million peasants. Each expressed with variations ideals roughly similar to those of Mussolini's fascists: the warrior ethic, ultranationalism, the cult of virility, ruralism, patriarchy, imperialism, and anticommunism. Their supporters tended to come from the same classes and groups that supported European fascism in general (Weiss 1977: 137).

[25] The time of "not taking sides" was past, as Sir Curtis Keeble later noted (1990: 132).

uprising in the Netherlands, civil war in Russia, and a war between the Allies and the Bolshevik regime in Russia; in Germany, there was a revolution in Kiel, a socialist revolution in Munich, and a right-wing military putsch attempt in Berlin. In 1919, there were communist risings throughout Germany – a Spartacus revolt in Berlin, a general strike and street fighting both in Berlin and in the Ruhr (January), a communist revolution in Bavaria (March) – and a communist takeover in Hungary (March). In Romania, a general strike of workers and miners in the Jiu Valley spread to the oil workers of the Prahova Valley and ended after a massacre of workers by government forces. There was an uprising in Portugal; general strikes and national workers' demonstrations leading to fights with troops and police in France; a Greek military offensive against Turkey; huge strikes in the cities of Italy and massive rebellions in the countryside; railway strikes in Great Britain; and a civil war in East Galicia between Ruthenian peasants and Polish landlords.[26]

Violent conflicts occurred in every year of the following decade. In 1920, general strikes and national workers' demonstrations continued in France, leading to fights with troops and police. Strikes and rebellions also continued in Italian cities and rural areas. The Polish-Russian War began when the Poles invaded Vilna and fought, with the support of French officers, against Bolshevik troops. War also broke out between Poles and Lithuanians. A civil war erupted in Great Britain, with fighting in both southern Ireland and Ulster. That year, there was a revolt in Albania; miners' strikes in Great Britain; and riots and threats of a general strike in Switzerland. There was a massive railway strike in Bulgaria. Almost 400,000 workers participated in mass demonstrations in Romania. In Yugoslavia, some 30,000 miners and railwaymen clashed with police and military forces in Slovenia, Croatia, and Bosnia.

In 1921, there were strikes in the Soviet Union, and a massacre of (anticommunist) strikers in Kronstadt.[27] There were strikes followed by communist revolts in Saxony, Hamburg, and the Ruhr. In 1922, there were riots and political demonstrations all over Germany. In 1923, there was a coup in Spain (September); an attempted coup by the right in Munich; separatist riots in the Rhineland; and communist putsch attempts in Hamburg and Saxony (November). There was a coup by the right in Bulgaria followed by the execution of between 10,000 and 30,000 supporters of the leftist regime that had been overthrown. In 1924, there was a revolution in Albania, and communist uprisings in Estonia. In 1925, there was an attempted coup by the right in Portugal. In 1926, a military-led uprising toppled the government

---

[26] Carr maintains that this was not a nationalist conflict. It was fueled by the hostility of the peasants to the Poles as landlords, not as Poles (1959: 25).

[27] Among other things, the strikers called for "Soviets without Communists." See Mazour 1951: chap. 6.

in Portugal; there was a coup in Poland, a general strike in Great Britain that paralyzed the country, and a coup in Lithuania. In 1927, there was an uprising in Portugal. In 1928, there was a war in Bulgaria between the left and the right. In 1929, there were May Day riots in Berlin.

Class conflicts continued into the 1930s. In 1930, there were violent strikes in Germany in the Mansfield mining area; and massacres of Kulaks in the Soviet Union. In 1931 and 1932, there was street fighting, political demonstrations, and strikes all over Germany and especially in Berlin (Tilly 1975b). There were clashes between socialists and police in Switzerland, leading to the deaths of twelve people (Luck 1985). In 1933, a revolt began in Spain. In Romania, strikes among miners, oil workers, and railway workers culminated in the so-called Gravita uprising that was suppressed with heavy loss of life (Djordjevic and Fischer-Galati 1981: 208). In 1934, there was a civil war in Austria between conservatives and socialists; riots, street fighting, and demonstrations between the left and right in France; and civil violence in Germany (Tilly 1975b). In 1935, violence continued in France with large demonstrations of both left and right leading to frequent clashes, attempted general strikes, and violent meetings of peasant organizations. In 1936, there was an attempted coup in Greece. There were massive strikes and clashes between communists and extreme right-wing organizations in France. A civil war erupted in Spain between forces of the left and right. Massive purges were carried out by Stalin in the Soviet Union.[28] In 1937, violence continued in France between the left and the right. In 1938, tens of thousands of workers went on strike in France. A planned general strike was thwarted by government mobilization of workers into the army, the arrest of hundreds of labor leaders, and the firing of thousands of workers. Premier Édouard Daladier spoke of having saved France from Bolshevism (Schuman 1942: 464).

THE POLARIZATION OF EUROPEAN SOCIETY

Throughout the interwar years – before, during, and after the years of the Great Depression – a struggle between left and right in Europe was carried on in a more or less continuous round of violent strikes, demonstrations, riots, and street fighting, as well as coups, rebellions, and revolutions. Table 6.1, which shows *all* the conflicts that occurred during these years, reveals the degree to which this was, in fact, the case. Throughout the interwar period, violent conflict erupted continually; all of it, except for a handful or events, testified to the growing polarization of European societies along class lines.

---

[28] Stalin's purges of the party hierarchy, beginning in 1928, targeted bourgeois, intelligentsia, and other upper-class elements and replaced these with peasants and workers. See Fitzpatrick 1979, 1982.

TABLE 6.1. *Social Polarization in Europe during the Interwar Years*

1918
Allies vs. Bolsheviks in Russia
Russian civil war
Civil war in Finland between the left and right
Socialist uprising in the Netherlands
Revolution in Kiel
Socialist revolution in Munich
Right-wing military putsch attempt in Berlin
Peasant uprising in Bulgaria

1919
Communist risings throughout Germany
Communist takeover in Hungary
War between Romania and communist Hungary
General strike in Romania ends with a massacre of workers by government forces
Spartacus revolt in Berlin
General strike and street fighting in Berlin and in the Ruhr
Communist revolution in Bavaria
Royalist uprising in Portugal
General strikes and national workers' demonstrations in France crushed by troops
    and police
In Italy, huge strikes in the cities and massive rebellions in the countryside
General strike in Switzerland
Ruthenian uprising against Polish landlords in East Galicia[a]

1920
General strikes and national workers' demonstrations in France crushed by troops
    and police
Strikes and rebellions in Italian cities and rural areas
Miners' strike in Great Britain
Riots and threats of a general strike in Switzerland
Massive railway strike in Bulgaria
Mass demonstrations of Romanian workers
Miners and railwaymen clash with police and military forces in Yugoslavia
Revolt of Catholics in Albania

1921
Communist revolts in Saxony, Hamburg, and the Ruhr
Massacre of anticommunist strikers in Kronstadt

1922
Riots and political demonstrations throughout Germany

1923
Coup in Spain
Attempted coup by the right in Munich

(continued)

TABLE 6.1 *(continued)*

Separatist riots in the Rhineland
Communist putsch attempts in Hamburg and Saxony
Coup by the right in Bulgaria; 10,000 to 30,000 supporters of the former leftist
    government are executed

1924
Communist uprisings in Estonia
Revolution in Albania

1925
Attempted coup by the right in Portugal

1926
Military-led uprising topples the government in Portugal
Coup in Poland
Coup in Lithuania
General strike in Great Britain

1927
Uprising in Portugal

1928
War in Bulgaria between the left and the right
Massive purges in the Soviet Union

1929
May Day riots in Berlin

1930
Violent strikes in Germany
Massacres of Kulaks in the Soviet Union

1931
Street fighting, demonstrations, and strikes throughout Germany

1932
Street fighting, demonstrations, and strikes throughout Germany
Clashes between socialists and police in Switzerland
Riots in France

1933
Leftist revolt in Spain
Strikes in Romania culminate in the Gravita uprising

1934
Civil war in Austria between conservatives and socialists
Riots, street fighting, and demonstrations between the left and right in France
Civil violence in Germany

1935
Frequent violent clashes in France between left and right

1936
Massive strikes, and clashes between communists and extreme right-wing
  organizations in France
Coup in Greece
Civil war begins in Spain between the left and the right

1937
Violence continues in France between the left and the right
Civil war continues in Spain

1938
Civil war continues in Spain

---

[a] Carr maintains that this was not a nationalist conflict, but was fueled by the hostility of
the peasants to the Poles as landlords, not as Poles (1959: 25).

CONCLUSIONS

The liberal challenge in Europe at the end of the eighteenth century was
followed by a conservative response at the beginning of the nineteenth. In
1848, however, when liberals joined with the masses in a Europe-wide ex-
plosion that threatened monarchs and governments throughout the region,
the upper classes extended political rights to the upper reaches of industrial
and commercial wealth. Thereafter, both classes closed ranks to prevent the
lower classes from gaining institutionalized political or economic power. By
the end of the nineteenth century, the rise of labor organization and of socialist parties had polarized European society along class lines. World War I and
the revolutions of 1917–22 further increased the socialist threat and, during
the interwar years, this threat precipitated a Europe-wide fascist reaction.

On the eve of World War I, the labor movement had become a major
political force in mining and industry. During the interwar period, there was
an explosive rise of trade union membership, peasant organization, socialist
parties, and socialist radicalism. In reaction, there formed a counterrevolutionary coalition of all relatively privileged or well-to-do groups and elements
in European societies. As a result, during the interwar years the domestic and
international relations of European states became increasingly polarized. A
more or less continuous round of demonstrations, riots, violent strikes, and
street fighting, as well as coups, rebellions, and revolutions, swept through
France, Britain, Germany, Italy, Switzerland, and Eastern and Southeastern
Europe. As Europe's ruling classes became increasingly preoccupied with
the threat of socialism at home and Bolshevism abroad, the concern with
stopping the spread of communism became inextricably bound up with the
preservation and defense of the traditional structures of European society.
As the next chapter shows, British and French appeasement policies were a
reflection of this preoccupation, and led to World War II.

7

The Politics of Appeasement and Counterrevolution

International Relations in Europe, 1918–1939

Speaking before the House of Commons in 1938, Sir Harold Nicolson reminded his audience that "for 250 years at least the great foundation of [British] foreign policy, what Sir Eyre Crowe called 'a law of nature,' has been to prevent by every means in our power the domination of Europe by any single Power or group of powers" (in Gilbert and Gott 1963: 7).* For centuries, Britain had been committed to a policy of preventing a hostile power from completely dominating the continent of Europe. Britain, historically, had played the role of the "balancer" in Europe, seeking safety by making itself the linchpin of coalitions against threatening aggressors: Philip II of Spain, the France of Louis XIV and Napoleon, and Wilhelmine Germany. But after World War I, British policy took a sharply different turn: throughout the 1920s and 1930s, Britain sought, against all reason and historical experience, to appease rather than to balance the power of a threatening aggressor.

This chapter argues that the central constellation of forces and threats shaping international relations throughout the interwar years was social and not territorial, as standard studies assume. The overriding concern of European statesmen during this period was not German territorial ambitions and aggression but the rise of the left in Europe and the westward spread of Bolshevism from the Soviet Union. This concern, which preoccupied Britain from the very beginning of the interwar period and continued without interruption until the outbreak of World War II, overrode concerns with preserving the existing territorial order. Thus, instead of balancing German power by allying with the Soviet Union, Britain, fearing that a strong Soviet Union would advance the cause of socialists and communists at home and that

---

* An earlier version of this chapter was published as "The Politics of Appeasement: The Rise of the Left and European International Relations during the Interwar Years," in David Skidmore, ed., *Contested Social Orders and International Politics* (Nashville: Vanderbilt University Press, 1997).

a weak Germany would lead to the establishment of communist regimes in Central and Eastern Europe, chose, instead, to ally with the fascist powers in the Four Power Pact and to encourage and aid in the revival and expansion of German power. Even after Britain and France declared war on Germany in 1939 to warn her against further aggression (the "phony" war), their first act was to prepare for war not against Germany but against the Soviet Union in Finland.

BRITISH APPEASEMENT POLICIES

Standard interpretations of British appeasement of Germany are based on three seriously flawed assumptions about British foreign policy during the interwar period: they assume that Britain (1) appeased Germany, (2) was concerned to prevent war in Europe at all costs, and (3) had no other option for preventing war but to appease Germany. "Appeasement" may be defined as "a foreign policy that seeks to propitiate an aggrieved rival by making concessions over matters otherwise likely to lead to war" (Palmer 1983: 25). The term has been applied to the attempts of the British and French governments to satisfy Hitler's demands between 1936 and 1939 by reaching direct agreements with both Germany and Italy. It is not true that Britain attempted to "appease" Germany during the interwar years. Britain actively aided and encouraged the revival and expansion of German power in Europe during the interwar period. As Frederick Schuman has pointed out, every effort was made to assist or condone the aggrandizement of the fascist states and to subvert all attempts on the part of their victims or rivals to offer collective resistance (1942: 332). The British "were often closer adherents to German expansionist policy than the Germans themselves" (Gilbert and Gott 1963: 35). The formal presentation of British proposals endorsing an expansion of German military and political power was preempted on two occasions when Hitler reintroduced conscription in the Reich and remilitarized the Rhineland (Medlicott 1969). The demilitarization of the Rhineland had been one of the decisive limiting factors to German rearmament, for this was its main industrial region, with 80 percent of its coal production. Germany could not build up a great armaments industry until this vital industrial base was secure (Medlicott 1963: 240). German rearmament was also facilitated through various economic concessions made by Britain (Medlicott 1969: chapters 11 and 13; Macdonald 1972). Proposals put forward by Lothian, Ashton-Gwatkin, Jebb, and, for a while, Eden recommended not only conceding economic superiority in Central and Southeastern Europe to Germany, but also alleviating its shortage of foreign currency and raw materials (Schmidt 1986: 88). After Hitler came to power, Britain rescheduled debts, rolled over loans, and enabled Germany to openly and rapidly build a powerful military machine (see, e.g., Bonnell 1940: 64–66; Einzig 1942: 74–78, 116–19; Schmidt 1986: 88–89; and further discussion below).

Standard accounts of interwar international relations fail to recognize, let alone explain, this essential fact of British policy.

Nor is it true that Britain was concerned with preventing war in Europe at all costs: though Britain consistently sought to avoid war with Germany (even after Germany invaded Poland), at least twice during the interwar years (1918–20 and 1939), Britain chose war rather than accommodation and negotiation with the Soviet Union. Britain also encouraged Poland in its war of aggression against the Soviet Union in 1920, despite the fact that the Soviets made numerous pleas for a settlement of differences by negotiation. Most accounts neither recognize nor explain the fact that Britain seemingly preferred "appeasement" to war with respect to Germany (e.g., in 1936, 1938, and 1939), but not with respect to the Soviet Union (e.g., in 1918, 1920, and 1939).

As with Britain, France dreaded war "not *per se* but because this war would have to be fought against Fascism [in the name of the People's Front] and in alliance with Moscow. It would therefore have to be fought at home against the '200 families,' the financial oligarchy, the corrupt magnates of the press, the great industrialists, and the reactionary remnants of aristocracy" (Schuman 1942: 458). The concern was to avoid at all costs a war "in alliance with Bolshevism and against the self-appointed Fascist saviors of property, religion, and the family" (Schuman 1942: 458). Such a war would have had disadvantageous consequences for the moneyed elite, and advantageous consequences for the left and for workers and peasants, who would gain a stronger strategic position in the Republic.

Finally, to argue that Britain allowed a threatening aggressor to rearm and to gain control of additional territories and resources as a means of preventing war suffers from an inherent lack of logic and plausibility and is wholly inconsistent with British policy over the centuries. At any point during the interwar years Britain had the option of forming an alliance with the Soviet Union in order to halt German aggression. This option was rejected before, during, and after the Munich crisis, and even after the German invasion and subjugation of Poland, Norway, Denmark, Belgium, the Netherlands, and France. Conventional accounts fail to adequately explain Britain's refusal to ally with the Soviet Union.

Territorial versus Social Orders

Two threats faced Europe after World War I. The first was German imperial ambitions in Europe, the second was the rise of the left in Europe, represented by Bolshevism abroad and socialism at home. Both threatened the European status quo. German ambitions threatened Europe's territorial order, while Bolshevism "aimed at the destruction of the [existing] social order" (*The Times*, April 13, 1922). Those who saw German ambitions as the greater of the two threats advocated an alliance with the Soviet Union against Germany.

Those who saw Bolshevism as the greater threat advocated an alliance with Germany against the Soviet Union (the "appeasers"):[1]

Churchill wrote that after the first world war "A new and more terrible cause of quarrel than the imperialism of Czars and Kaisers became apparent in Europe. The Civil War in Russia ended in the absolute victory of the Bolshevik Revolution.... Germany and Italy nearly succumbed to Communist propaganda and designs. Hungary actually fell for a while under the control of the Communist dictator, Bela Kun... European civilization trembled in the post-war years. (Churchill 1948: 13)

Bolshevism, wrote *The Times* in 1926, aimed at "the ruin of British trade, the overthrow of the British Constitution and the destruction of the British Empire" (in Keeble 1990: 103). "Of the two evils threatening Europe – German aggression and communism," wrote one influential appeaser, Lord Lothian, "communism is the worse evil" (letter to *The Times*, August 29, 1937). Thomas Lamont, who was the most powerful partner of the Morgan Bank in 1934, wrote, following the Italian conquest of Ethiopia: "I must say I prefer, of two foul evils, the fascists who make war, to the communists who seek to overthrow our governments" (in Chernow 1990: 403). De Gaulle observed that, after the German invasion of Poland, "some circles were more inclined to see Stalin the enemy than Hitler. They were much more concerned with the means of striking at Russia, whether by aiding Finland or bombarding Baku or landing at Istanbul, than how to cope with the Reich" (1954–59: vol. 1, p. 28; in Richardson 1973: 140).

Much of what appear puzzling and inexplicable in standard accounts of the interwar years becomes coherent and logical if we assume that the threat with which British statesmen were concerned throughout the period was not German power but the rise of the left in Europe and the westward spread of Bolshevism from the Soviet Union. Motivated by this concern, Britain chose to sacrifice the existing territorial order of Europe to German ambitions in order to better defend the existing social order from the threat of Bolshevism.

Europe's preoccupation with the spread of Bolshevism from the Soviet Union began in 1917 and continued without interruption until the outbreak of World War II. During the Paris Peace Conference, attention was riveted on the Allied war against the Bolsheviks in Russia and on communist revolutions in Germany and in Hungary. Decisions taken at the conference regarding Germany, Polish border disputes, political arrangements in the Baltic, and settlement of the "Eastern Question" were shaped by concerns about the spread of Bolshevism from the Soviet Union.

[1] A third way in which these challenges could be met, and a fond hope of many in Europe, was that Germany and the Soviet Union would destroy each other. This hope engendered bitter outrage when, in 1922 and 1939, Germany and the Soviet Union concluded treaties (though these were, at best, marriages of convenience). The British government reacted to the German-Soviet Pact by ordering the Chiefs of Staff to consider possible military action by Britain against the Soviet Union (Keeble 1990: 163).

It might be argued that it is impossible to square the existence of a pro-fascist, anti-Bolshevik alliance among the powers during this time with the several trade agreements and treaties that were concluded in the interwar years among Great Britain, France, Germany, and the Soviet Union (the Anglo-Soviet trade agreements of 1921 and 1924, the German-Soviet trade agreement of 1922, the Franco-Soviet Pact of 1935, and the German Soviet Pact of 1939). But as is shown below, these treaties were measures undertaken to meet critical economic or security needs or to forward imperial ambitions, that they were uneasy alliances, highly divisive domestically that, ultimately, did not exert decisive influence over the dominant trends of the period.

The Peace Conference

The threat of Bolshevism dominated the minds and shaped the decisions of the Paris Peace Conference. The attitudes of top policy makers in the peace negotiations betrayed a more or less continuous preoccupation with the threat of Bolshevism. As Ray Stannard Baker, one of President Wilson's assistants at the Peace Conference pointed out, the Bolsheviks, "without ever being represented at Paris at all...were powerful elements at every turn."[2]

Attention at the peace conferences was riveted on the Allied war against the Bolsheviks in Russia (1918–20). In August 1918, British forces occupied the various Transcaucasian republics, French troops occupied Odessa, and a Czech force made up of deserters from the Austrian army, along with Japanese and American contingents, began operations in Siberia. When Churchill took Lloyd George's place at the Peace Conference in February 1919, he pressed vigorously for a large allied army to crush the Bolsheviks. By the end of the year, the Allies were forced to leave Odessa. Churchill continued to lobby the conference for Allied implementation of a grand anti-Bolshevik strategy (Dockrill and Goold 1981: 123). However, President Wilson refused to commit any more American soldiers to Russia, and Lloyd George insisted that such an enterprise would drive the Russian people into the arms of the Bolsheviks (Thompson 1966: 207). The Allies continued their military support of the anti-Bolshevik White Armies until 1920.[3] Military and political missions maintained political liaison with the Russian generals and their embryo governments, and a blockade of Russia was maintained in the Baltic. In July, the British Cabinet decided that a state of war existed

---

[2] Baker 1922: 64. The anti-Bolshevik groups were represented at the Conference of Paris. Though the Soviet government was prepared to send representatives to the conference on condition that the powers refrain from "interference in Russian internal affairs," the anti-Bolsheviks and the French government were unwilling. See Temperley 1920–24: vol. 6, p. 313; Mowat 1927: 280–81; Dockrill and Goold 1981: 122–23.

[3] For a history of these events, see Maynard 1928; Graves 1931; Ironside 1953; Denikin 1973.

between Britain and Bolshevik Russia and authorized British naval forces to engage the enemy (Keeble 1990: 56–57).

In March 1919, there was a communist revolution in Bavaria, and communists seized power in Hungary. The threat of Bolshevism to Central and even Western Europe became a constant preoccupation. David Lloyd George, in his famous Fontainebleu memorandum of March 1919, discerned "a spirit of revolution" in every country of Europe, including his own.[4] "We are sitting upon an open powder magazine and some day a spark may ignite it," wrote Colonel House (Baker 1922: vol. 2, p. 64; Callwell 1927: 148; Seymour 1926–28: vol. IV, p. 405). The conference considered military action against Hungary, but while the conference debated the matter, a Romanian army invaded the country and smashed the communist regime.[5] Sir Charles Hardinage feared that Bolshevism would spread from Hungary into Austria and Czechoslovakia.[6]

The fear of Bolshevism spreading from Russia to the west dominated the minds of the Allied statesmen and was the main argument for granting lenient terms to Germany (Baker 1922: vol. II, p. 64). Germany's Social Democrat Party was the greatest Marxist political organization in the world outside the Soviet Union. It was in Germany that the preconditions for the transition from capitalism to socialism, as Marx had defined them, seemed to be furthest advanced. Germany had a highly developed industry and a politically conscious and mature proletariat. Sir Henry Wilson noted: "Our real danger now is not the Boches but Bolshevism." Lloyd George argued that a more moderate peace would prevent Bolshevism from swallowing up Germany. His views were echoed by Sir Henry Wilson, who warned that unless the French-dictated peace terms were mitigated, Europe would succumb to Bolshevism (Lloyd George 1938: 403–16). Clemenceau argued that British rejection of a revision of German frontiers would, by leaving the national aspirations of the Central and Eastern European peoples unsatisfied, be more likely to open Central Europe to Bolshevism (Lloyd George 1938: 416–20).

When the Poles, using the menace of Bolshevism as an excuse, invaded the Soviet Union in 1920 and annexed large areas in the east,[7] the Allied powers supported them by sending shipments of munitions and numerous contingents of military advisers. The Soviets had made numerous pleas for a

---

4 "Some Considerations for the Peace Conference before They Finally Draft Their Terms," *Memorandum Circulated by the Prime Minister on March 25, 1919*, Cmd. 1614 (1919), cited in Mayer 1967: 581–83. On the revolutionary situation in Europe, see Bertrand 1977; also Kendall 1969 and Cronin 1982a, 1982b.
5 The next concern of the Peace Conference became the refusal of the Romanians to evacuate Budapest and their seizure of Hungary's industrial and agricultural assets. However, the decision was made not to take any action against the Romanians.
6 "Minute by Sir Charles Hardinage," March 1919, British Foreign Office, 608 series, 11.
7 See the statement in Paton 1924–27: 414–19.

settlement of differences by negotiation. Instead, Marshal Pilsudski launched an offensive that ended with the Polish capture of Kiev. When the Bolsheviks mounted a counteroffensive, the Allies sent munitions and advisers to support the Polish army. In Britain, there was a bitter struggle between the Labour Party, which favored the Soviet side in the Polish-Russian War, and the conservatives, who favored the Poles. During the summer, dockers actually succeeded in preventing the departure of certain shiploads of munitions for Poland. German dockers at Danzig also refused to allow shipments to pass through Germany to Poland (Kennan 1960: 167). After a cease-fire was called, the conference gave its sanction to a new frontier that gave Poland a considerable amount of additional territory, despite the fact that these areas contained large numbers of minorities and were forcibly annexed (Kennan 1966: 160–61).

The conference's handling of the power vacuum in the Baltic was also shaped by its concern with the Bolshevik menace. The conference had ordered German troops to remain in Latvia, Lithuania, and Estonia, which German troops had occupied following the collapse of Russia in 1917, because this seemed the only alternative to a Bolshevik takeover. At the end of 1918, the Bolsheviks overran part of Estonia, then occupied Latvia. After the Royal Navy, militias of White Russians, Swedes and Finnish volunteers, and a German brigade ejected the Bolsheviks from Estonia and Latvia, the German brigade then proceeded to overthrow the Latvian government (Dockrill and Goold 1981: 118–19).

The resolution of the "Eastern Question," the problem of what to do with Turkey, was inextricably bound up with fears on the part of policy makers in London, Paris, and Versailles concerning Bolshevik influence in the former Asian territories of the Ottoman Empire. The new rulers in postwar Turkey, Afghanistan and Persia, had each negotiated a treaty with the Soviet Union as its first move in foreign policy. Britain resolved to make the rest of the region a bulwark against the spread of Bolshevism (Dockrill and Goold 1981: chapter 5; and Fromkin 1989, esp. chaps. 53–55). Lord Curzon proposed the creation of "a Moslem nexus of states" in the Middle East as a shield to ward off Russian expansion (Morgan 1979: 119; see also Dockrill and Goold 1981: chap. 5; Fromkin 1989: chaps. 53–55). In 1920, he claimed that "the Russian menace in the East is incomparably greater than anything else that has happened in my time to the British Empire" (in Darwin 1981: 214). There was a growing conviction that Bolshevik Russia was involved in a far-reaching conspiracy that had incited rebellion throughout the Middle East (Fromkin 1989: chap. 53).

While Britain and France concluded peace treaties with Germany at the Paris Peace Conferences, they remained, nominally, in a state of war with the Soviet Union. No definite treaty of peace was made between these powers and Soviet Russia, nor did they recognize the Soviets as the de jure Russian government.

The Years 1920–1932

In 1920, Britain and France abandoned the war against Soviet Russia, but they continued to wage an anti-Bolshevik campaign throughout the interwar years. The hills and troughs that marked this campaign generally followed the alternation of liberal and conservative governments in Britain and France. In 1920 and 1921, the Labour Party maintained that the way to rehabilitate British trade and industry and combat Britain's rapidly increasing unemployment was to resume trade with Russia (and to abolish unproductive expenditures on anticommunist military "adventures" in the Near and Far East). But until the collapse of the British economy in 1921, the Liberals and Conservatives blocked the adoption of all proposals reflecting these views and denounced the Labour leaders for being Bolshevik fellow-travelers. In 1921, when prices collapsed, exports slumped, companies went out of business, and the country was gripped by mass employment on a scale never known before (Benns 1930: 476), an Anglo-Soviet trade agreement was finally pushed through by Lloyd George over strenuous Conservative opposition.[8] Six months after the conclusion of the treaty, the Conservatives defected from the ruling coalition, Lloyd George resigned, and a new, more conservative government was formed that blocked all efforts to turn the Anglo-Soviet agreement into a reality. When a governmental "Interdepartmental Committee on the Bolshevik Menace to the British Empire" (established in 1923) purported to find evidence of a Soviet breach of assurances embodied in the agreement that it would not engage in hostile activities in Asia, the Conservative government issued an ultimatum demanding that the Soviet Union recall its representatives in Persia, Afghanistan, and India. When it refused, Britain abrogated the agreement.

In the winter of 1922, the idea arose of convening an international economic conference of all the countries of Europe with a view to the reconstruction of the European economy. The conference was convened in Genoa in April 1922. It was widely believed that Europe's recovery would not be possible without the reintegration of the Russian economy into that of Europe as a whole (Kennan 1960: 202–3). But though Lloyd George proposed to invite the Soviet Union to the conference in order, among other things, to secure the Soviet recognition of its inherited debt liability and the need for comprehensive safeguards for Western European private interests in Russia (Keeble 1990: 86), French intransigence and British parliamentary opposition made any accommodation to Soviet proposals at the conference impossible, and "equality among the participants was no more than nominal"

---

[8] In presenting the trade agreement to Parliament, the prime minister was at pains to point out that it was "purely a trading agreement," not a treaty of peace. He insisted that commercial relations would "convert" them and "put an end to their wild schemes" (in Keeble 1990: 80).

(Keeble 1990: 86). Thus, a week after the opening of the conference, the German and Russian delegations slipped off to Rapallo and signed their own trade agreement. For Germany, it was a first step toward regaining the primacy in the Russian market it had previously enjoyed. The Soviet Union obtained most favored nation status for trade and diplomatic recognition.

The British and French were outraged by this "unholy alliance" and condemned the Weimar Republic's "open defiance and studied insult to the Entente powers."[9] For the Western allies, the Soviet-German agreement represented the loss of Germany as a partner in "a united Western approach to the problem of Russian communism" (Kennan 1960: 211). When the treaty was ratified in the Reichstag with the aid of the Social Democrats, the Nationalist ministers resigned in protest. In 1925, the Weimar Republic also concluded an economic treaty with Russia, and in 1926 it signed a treaty in which the two countries promised neutrality in the event of the other being a victim of aggression and not to join others in financial or economic boycotts. These treaties gained for Germany a resumption of the trade relations that had been so valuable before the war (Benns 1930: 414–16).

In 1921, British Foreign Secretary Lord Curzon warned that recognition of the Soviet Union would be used by the Soviet government "to spread the tentacles of their poisonous influence throughout the world" (*The Times*, March 17, 1921). However, when the first Labour government took office in Britain at the end of 1923, one of its first acts was to extend de jure recognition to the Soviet government and to invite the Soviet Union to send a delegate to London to draw up the preliminary basis of a complete treaty. This invitation was accepted, and a conference was opened in April 1924 in London. Two draft treaties – a General and a Commercial Treaty – were signed the following August. However, when the Conservative Party was returned to Parliament the following year, the new government refused to ratify the treaties and in 1926 severed all relations with the Soviet Union (Benns 1930: 591–92; Keeble 1990: 69–70, 82–83, 92, 107). The Labour government fell because of its failure to prosecute an alleged communist editor charged with sedition. During the election campaign that followed, the notorious "Zinoviev Letter" was produced. It was purported to be from the Communist International to the British Communist Party urging them to promote revolution. The authenticity of the letter has never been established, but it was published in the British press four days before the general election, and played a decisive role in the defeat of the Labour Party (McHenry 1940: 12–14).

During 1925 the enmity of the Conservatives toward the Soviet Union was increased by the discovery of close connections between the Bolshevik Third

---

[9] As the *Sunday Times* put it; in Kennan 1960: 210. The permanent nightmare of Western statesmen during the first decade after the Armistice was an alliance of Germany with Russia (Seton-Watson 1945: chap. 9).

International and the Communist Party of Great Britain. During the general strike of 1926, relations between the two governments were further strained when it was learned that Russian funds had been sent to subsidize British strikers. The government also believed that Britain's loss of trade in China was due to Russian propaganda being carried on there. In 1927, the Conservative government accused the Soviets of conducting military espionage in Great Britain. Though the government's attempts to produce evidence in support of this charge were unsuccessful, the Parliament voted, nevertheless, to sever all relations with the Soviet Union (Benns 1930: 490–91).

Aided by the deepening trade depression, the Labour Party made a comeback in 1929. But it was short-lived. Spokesmen for the coalition of Liberals and Conservatives that eventually formed the new government convinced a great majority of the voters that the Labour Party represented "Bolshevism run mad" (McHenry 1940: 16–17).

In France, as in Great Britain, a shift in policy occurred when control of the government shifted from the parties of the right to those of the left. When conservative governments were in power, French policies were driven by fear of Bolshevism. This fear united the conservative parties in a national bloc that won a decisive victory in the parliamentary elections of 1919. In 1922, under an extreme nationalist, Raymond Poincaré, France became the prime exponent of the policy of Russian containment, advocated under the name of "*cordon sanitaire.*" Under left governments, France extended de jure recognition to the Soviet Union (1924) and signed a nonaggression pact with Russia (1932) and a Franco-Soviet treaty (May 1935).

In the 1920s, France's apprehension about its security drove it to combat Germany's efforts to conclude trade agreements with the countries of Eastern Europe and to close its capital and money markets to new German and Austrian borrowing. As time went on, Britain became increasingly irritated by French efforts to keep Germany down. In December 1922, after the Reparations Commission resolved that Germany's failure to make certain deliveries in kind (timber and telegraph poles) constituted a German default, the French used this default as a pretext to move troops into the Ruhr. The Ruhr episode strained the Franco-British Entente to the breaking point.[10] The British government believed that not merely Germany but Europe as a whole was being ruined by the Ruhr occupation and by the crumbling of the German economic and political system (Mowat 1927: 250).

British views on Germany eventually prevailed. In 1925, Italy, France, Belgium, and Great Britain concluded treaties with Germany (the Locarno treaties). In September 1926, Germany was admitted to the League of Nations and was given a permanent seat on the council along with France, Great Britain, Italy, and Japan. By the end of the 1920s, relations between the

---

[10] Mr. J. R. Macdonald in the House of Commons, March 6, 1923; in *Hansard*, 5th Series, vol. 161, p. 318.

Western powers and Germany had grown much stronger. They would grow stronger still after the National Socialists took power in Germany in 1933.

The Years 1933–1939

Germany under Hitler based its foreign policy on opposition to Bolshevism and sought to make common cause with the Western powers against the Soviet Union. In 1933, Hitler withdrew Germany from the League of Nations after it refused to accede to Hitler's demand for an increase in German rearmament. The five permanent members of the council of the League – Britain, France, and the three fascist powers (Germany, Italy, and Japan) – then joined together in two new overlapping associations: the Four Power Pact (1933)[11] and the anti-Comintern Pact (1936). With Britain and France now engaged in an alternative grouping with the fascist powers, and with the strength and prestige of the League fatally diminished, the League ceased to play any effective role in European affairs. The anti-Comintern Pact, formed by Germany and Japan in 1936 (Italy joined in 1937), declared the hostility of its signatories to international communism and formalized opposition to communism as the basis of German foreign policy.

Germany, formally allied with France and Great Britain, and with their acquiescence, now began to openly and rapidly rearm. In 1935, the year Germany declared itself a bulwark against Bolshevism, the German government reintroduced conscription. This was the first formal repudiation of a clause of the peace treaty. The British and French governments did nothing more than issue protests. From then on, German rearmament was a fully open matter and was carried out with vigor and speed. Hitler ended the restrictions placed on Germany by the treaty by the end of 1937.

In March 1935, and in the face of rapid German rearmament, a left government in France signed an agreement with the Soviet Union that guaranteed mutual assistance in the face of aggression over a period of five years. A few days after formal ratification of the pact (March 1935), Hitler, naming the pact as his excuse, reoccupied the Rhineland with German troops. Churchill pressed for the League of Nations to take action. "On every side of Geneva," he wrote at the time, "stand great nations armed and ready, whose interests as well as whose obligations bind them to uphold, and in the last resort enforce, the public law. This may never come to pass again. The fateful moment has arrived for choice between the New Age and the Old" (Churchill 1948: 182). The French wished to resist the German move by military action, but

---

[11] The Four-Power Pact, concluded in Rome in 1933, provided that Britain, France, Italy, and Germany, as the four great powers of Europe and on the basis of equality among themselves, should be responsible for the organization of Europe and the preservation of peace.

the British dissuaded them (Kennan 1960: 286). Three months later, Britain signed a naval agreement with Germany.

In 1936, polarization between left and right in Western Europe escalated into armed conflict with the outbreak of the civil war in Spain. Italy and Germany backed the conservative forces; the Soviet Union backed the left. Britain and France remained on the sidelines, while Italy and Germany helped to ensure a victory for fascism in Spain. Spain became the symbol of a global struggle between democracy and social revolution on the one side, and "a uniquely uncompromising camp of counter-revolution or reaction," on the other (Hobsbawm 1996: 157). The news and editorial pages in *The Observer* characterized the war in Spain as a "historic crusade" against World Communism. The outbreak of civil war in Spain in 1936 sharply polarized British opinion (Keeble 1990: 132). Harold Nicholson observed in his diary on August 8, 1936, that the conflict emphasized "the division of Europe between left and right" (Nicholson 1966: 270). From his study of British opinion toward the Spanish Civil War, K. W. Watkins concluded, "Probably not since the French Revolution had a 'foreign event' so bitterly divided the British people..." (1963: vii; in Thompson 1971: 115). The British ruling classes, conservative politicians, and most of the British diplomats, consuls, and other officials in or near Spain immediately were sympathetic to the rebels and opposed to the "Reds." The British Embassy moved from Madrid to Biarritz, where the Marquis Merry del Val represented Franco; the Duke of Alba established himself in London as Franco's agent.

With the outbreak of the Spanish Civil War, France faced the possibility of having a fascist dictator on a third French frontier. However, the prospect of fascist encirclement was apparently not an alarming one to the French right. The Paris correspondent for the Manchester Guardian reported:

Fantastic as it may seem, the greater part of the French Right-Wing press . . . wished the rebels complete victory. The arguments that this would mean Fascist encirclement of France, that it would turn France into a vassal state of Germany . . . and that it would reduce France to the position of a second or a third class Power in Europe, did not seem to embarrass them in the least. They felt on the contrary, that it would be all to the good; for then French public opinion – so the argument ran – would be forced to realize that in the circumstances only a Fascist or semi-Fascist Government in France would be in a position to "speak" on equal terms to France's Fascist neighbors. Thus a Fascist encirclement of France presented itself to the French Fascist element as a much-to-be-desired opportunity to overthrow the Popular Front Government, or any normal democratic Government for that matter. (in Watkins 1963: 74)

France and Britain barred the export of arms to Spain. In February 1939, even before the Madrid government had surrendered, they extended full diplomatic recognition to Franco's fascist government. Spain, that year, joined the anti-Comintern.

During the time that Germany carried on the struggle against Bolshevism in Spain (July 1936 to April 1939), it also invaded Austria and absorbed it into the German Reich (March 1938), annexed the Sudetenland (September 1938), and then annexed the rest of Czechoslovakia (March 1939). Three months after France's Prime Minister Chautemps and Foreign Minister George Bonnet indicated to German Chancellor Franz von Papen that France might be willing to accept German dominance in Eastern Europe (Albrecht-Carrié 1973: 519), Germany invaded Austria (March 1938) and absorbed it into "Greater Germany." In 1919, because socialists held a majority of the seats in Austria's Assembly and were part of a coalition government in Weimar Germany, the Allies had forbidden the union of the two countries because it would have strengthened the socialists in both countries. In 1938, however, when the two countries were under fascist governments, their union created, instead, a formidable anti-Bolshevik fortress in the center of Europe.

In September 1938, the members of the Four Power Pact – Britain, France, Germany, and Italy – agreed at Munich that Czechoslovakia should be made to surrender the Sudetenland to Germany, implementing a proposal that Mussolini had made to the members of the alliance in 1933. Six months later, in March 1939, they acquiesced when the whole of the state of Czechoslovakia was occupied by German troops. Mussolini, seeking compensation, landed troops in Albania, and was quickly able to add the Albanian crown to those of Italy and Ethiopia.

In August 1939, a Nazi-Soviet Pact was concluded. This is generally considered to have been, at best, a marriage of convenience (Albrecht-Carrié 1973: 44). Despite their ideological differences, Hitler and Stalin both needed to make a deal. Stalin's overwhelming concern was to buy time and to avoid a war. The Soviets, according to Churchill, were very much aware of the peril to them of a German takeover of Poland (Churchill 1948: 348). "[T]heir vital need was to hold the deployment positions of the German armies as far to the west as possible so as to give the Russians more time for assembling their forces from all parts of their immense empire" (Churchill 1948: 351). In the words of the French ambassador in Berlin, the Soviet Union "preferred to partition rather than to defend Poland" (in Churchill 1948: 330). By late July 1939, Hitler had come to the conclusion that Britain and France would fight to save Poland, and that the way to prevent this was to bring Russia over to the German side (Sontag 1971: 367, 377). Hitler sought to neutralize the Soviet Union and, at the same time, increase the pressure on the Western nations to abandon Poland (Kennedy 1987: 339). Though Hitler viewed negotiating with the Soviet Union "with the deepest distaste," an agreement with the Soviet Union provided a means for achieving these objectives (Kennan 1960: 302, 306). It was, in fact, a few months after concluding the German-Soviet Pact, in December 1939, that the German government took the decision to proceed with Operation Barbarossa, the attack on the Soviet Union.

The "Phony War" and the Fall of France

Immediately following the German conquest of Czechoslovakia, Poland came under increased pressure from Germany to make territorial concessions and to join formally the anti-Comintern. German territorial ambitions appeared now to be weakening the *cordon sanitaire* protecting the West from the spread of Bolshevism, for Poland, during the interwar years, had been "a spearpoint of anti-Bolshevism." Those in London who had argued all along that Germany must be stopped – Churchill, Anthony Eden, and other malcontent Conservatives, as well as Labourites – succeeded in passing a resolution to offer guarantees to Poland (Wrench 1955: 393). However, the guarantee to Poland "was conceived as a deterrent and given in haste," and no strategy was devised to implement it if it failed to deter (Keeble 1990: 141). When Hitler invaded Poland in September 1939, Britain and France declared war on Germany. But following this declaration of war, neither France nor Britain attempted an offensive against Germany. In what became known as the "phony war," "the western front lay in a state of strange unreal inactivity" (Kennan 1960: 361). The French armies, "their mobilization completed ... remained motionless along the whole front." The British dropped pamphlets "to rouse the Germans to a higher morality. This strange phase of the war astounded everyone," Churchill recalls. "France and Britain remained impassive while Poland was in a few weeks destroyed or subjugated by the whole might of the German war machine" (1948: 376).

It is generally thought that appeasement ended after Germany, violating assurances made at Munich, occupied the rest of Czech lands in March 1939. With the German annexation of Bohemia and Moravia, support in Britain for appeasement collapsed overnight (Sontag 1971: 358). Thus, the British government was compelled to adopt a posture of resistance to German aggression. As Eric Hobsbawm has pointed out,

Western states declared war, not because their statesmen wanted it, but because Hitler's own policy after Munich cut the ground from under the appeasers' feet.... the German occupation of Czechoslovakia converted British public opinion to resistance, [and so] forced the hand of a reluctant government.... (1994: 155)

Actually, for two days after the German invasion of Poland, Britain and France tried to avoid declaring war. Under immense pressure from the House of Commons, the British government finally declared war seventy-two hours after the German attack on their ally, Poland. But neither Britain nor France attempted an offensive against Germany. Though Britain and France, separately and together, were in a position to take action against German forces, neither came to Poland's aid, and Germany proceeded unimpeded with its conquest of Poland.

In fact, up until the summer of 1940, Britain pursued a policy of exploring the possibility of peace with Germany. The main advocates of this policy were the Foreign Office and its two ministers, Lord Halifax and Rab Butler, and Neville Chamberlain. During the autumn of 1939, the British government tried officially at least five times to explore possible peace terms with Germany. In October, some five weeks after Britain had declared war on Germany, Neville Chamberlain's private secretary declared, "Communism is now the great danger, greater even than Nazi Germany . . . we should . . . not destroy the possibility of uniting, if necessary, with a new German government against the common danger" (quoted in Ponting 1989: 47). In November 1939, Butler said that Germany would not be required to withdraw from Poland before negotiating an end to the war (Ponting 1989: 99). It was not until July 1940, and only after Germany refused further negotiations, that British leaders ceased their attempts to come to terms with Germany over Poland.

During the months of inactivity that are recorded in history as the "Phony War" with Germany, Britain and France were actively engaged in preparations for war against the Soviet Union. Following the German invasion of Poland, the Soviet Union had moved to block the lines of entry into the Soviet Union from the West. One of these lines led through Finland to a point that lay just twenty miles away from the suburbs of Leningrad. The allies had used this route to threaten Leningrad in 1919. Even the White Russian Government of Colonel Kolckak had informed the Peace Conference in Paris that bases in the Baltic States and Finland were necessary to protect the Russian capital. In 1939, with German troops in Poland, Stalin made the identical claim. He demanded that the Finnish frontier be moved back so that Leningrad was outside artillery range and that Russia be allowed to lease the Port of Hango at the entrance of the Gulf of Finland for use as a naval and air base. Negotiations between the Soviet Union and Finland over these demands broke down, Finland began to mobilize, and, two days later, the Russians attacked Finland.

With the outbreak of the Russo-Finnish War at the end of November 1939, the conservative leadership of both Britain and France suddenly became warlords and sought to forestall any negotiated settlement between Finland and the Soviet Union.

On February 15, 1940, the Anglo-French Supreme War Council agreed that Britain and France would each land 15,000 troops at the Norwegian port of Narvik, from which they would advance into Finland. Britain began to assemble its force for this purpose. Two British divisions, British bombers, 50,000 French "volunteers," and 100 French bombers were readied to send to Finland. On March 2, without consulting Britain, Premier Daladier cabled Helsinki that 50,000 French troops along with 100 bombers and other military equipment would arrive in Finland at the beginning of April (Richardson 1973: 136; Schachtman 1962: 153). The French and British plans for getting supplies and Allied troops to Finland were thwarted because of Swedish and Norwegian opposition to the passage of Allied forces through their territory. The collapse of Finnish resistance in March rendered useless any further plans for intervention. In a secret session of the French Chamber of Deputies on March 19, Prime Minister Daladier was severely criticized for his failure to save Finland. Deputy Pierre Etienne Flandin was cheered and applauded when he castigated Daladier for losing the support of "all the forces of the world who consider Bolshevism the principal enemy" (in Richardson 1973: 147–48). At the end of March 1940, a fortnight after the Russo-Finnish peace treaty, the Supreme War Council, meeting in London, considered detailed plans for an air attack on the Soviet oilfields at Baku on the Caspian Sea.[12] Meanwhile, with the war in Finland now at an end, French General Gamelin, rather than sending his troops on to Norway to counter the German offensive, dispersed his troops instead.

While Britain and France were occupied with preparing for war against the Soviet Union, Germany completed its subjugation of Poland and then proceeded with an attack on Norway. Observers at the time recalled Britain's "lack of rapid and vigorous initiative" in countering the German attack on Norway (Wrench 1955: 411). Two weeks before the Norwegian defeat, and while the Norwegians were fighting valiantly against the invading German forces, the British Royal Navy had not yet engaged with Nazi battle cruisers and Britain had not yet lost a man in its supposed war against Germany (Wrench 1955: 413). Instead, Britain was busy sending aircraft and other critical war material, including armored divisions, to aid the Finns in their fight against the Soviet Union. The first outbreak of serious fighting with the Germans in Norway did not occur until April 1940. British pilots were not allowed to attack German-held aerodromes in Denmark and Norway until April 11, and then initially only with machine guns, not bombs. British pilots were not given permission to bomb the Ruhr until May 15 (Amery 1953: 332; in George 1962: 213).

Among the many mysteries that conventional studies have failed to solve concerning the interwar period is the fall of France. The German army that invaded France in 1940 was a "badly equipped, ramshackle force." Expansion had brought with it enormous problems in training and equipping the new army. There was a lack of trained officers and NCOs. Half the German army depended for transport on requisitioned civilian vehicles and the rest

---

[12] The argument was advanced that this would cut off critical oil supplies to Germany. However, oil imports to Germany from the Caucasus amounted to barely 3 percent of Germany's war needs. Evidence of this was reported in *Paris soir* on April 15, 1940 (Ponting 1989: 48).

relied on 500,000 horses for mobility (Ponting 1989: 79). The success of the army against France, as well as against Poland and Norway, has thus been attributed to its use of a new form of warfare: the "blitzkrieg," a term first used by a journalist to describe the German campaign in Poland in September 1939. But the rapid Polish defeat was the result not of a new form of warfare but of the weakness of Polish defenses: the Polish decision to use a thin linear defense all along its 3,000-mile border with Germany and its decision to keep troops in reserve to thwart an expected Soviet invasion (Ponting 1989: 78–79).

In France, there was only "sporadic and local resistance" to the German invasion. "In a state of disorganization," French troops retreated before the German armies. In the end, the French army was cast back by a few thousand armored vehicles (Albrecht-Carrié 1973: 546–47; Keegan 1989: chap. 3). Conservative leaders, including Pierre Etienne Flandin, Georges Bonnet, and Pierre Laval, had for years advocated the policy of surrender in the event of a German invasion. Many of the "Two Hundred Families" tended to favor the idea. They feared that a fight to the bitter end would lose them their fortunes and privileges; they believed that surrender would allow them to hold on to their wealth. They thought that the result of Hitler's victories would be merely the establishment of new regimes in the conquered countries and that Germany wished only to assure that the regimes of all countries it conquered should be identical with that of Germany (Einzig 1940: 14–15). Many treat the history of the Vichy government of 1940–44 as though it had been a brief, unhappy departure from republicanism, and that collaboration had been the work of a tiny minority. But 1940 was not a radical departure in French politics. It was the fact that French society was deeply polarized that accounted for the ease of the transition to a divided France.

Throughout 1940, Hitler tried to "make peace" with Britain. To the very end, some Nazi leaders still hoped for a separate peace with the Western powers as the prelude to a joint crusade against the Soviet Union (Tipton and Aldrich 1987b: 45). In the face of Britain's continued refusal to come to terms, Germany began bombing British supply routes, airfields, shipping, and, finally, canal towns. But Hitler still "clung to the hope of winning Britain's cooperation, rather than beating her into subjection" (Keegan 1989: 128). In October 1940, Germany ceased its assault on Britain's coastal defenses, and German forces turned eastward, invading Yugoslavia and Greece in April 1941 and then, in June 1941, invading the Soviet Union. The following month, Britain's new coalition government signed an Anglo-Soviet agreement that allied Britain and the Soviet Union against Germany. This wartime alliance between Britain and the Soviet Union was fraught with friction throughout. The bond between the two countries, insofar as it existed, depended on the common enemy and dissolved at the end of the war (Keeble 1990: 158).

THE "APPEASERS"

Appeasement was a Conservative policy.[13] In Britain, conservatives were in power with large majorities for seventeen of the twenty years between the wars. Appeasement was supported by Conservative Ministers of Cabinets, members of Commons, peers of the Lords, respected journalists, and leaders of society who equated their own class interests with the "honor and vital interest" of their country.[14] Its propagandists were the conservative press: *The Times* (Geoffrey Dawson, editor), the *Daily Mail* (owned by Lord Rothermere), the *Daily Express* (owned by Lord Beaverbrook), and the *Observer* (owned by Lord Astor).

A very big proportion of Conservative M.P.s belonged to the class of the extremely wealthy.[15] A large proportion of Conservative M.P.s were also employers of labor and captains of industry (at least 44 percent). While only 0.1 percent of the population were company directors, 44 percent of Conservative M.P.s were company directors. Moreover, all Conservative M.P.s (with possibly a few rare exceptions) were large shareholders, and thus represented the interests of the employing class (Haxey 1939: 35).

Britain's interwar governments in large part came from the business world. Big business had shifted to Conservatism toward the end of the nineteenth century. With a few exceptions (e.g., Halifax, Londonderry), cabinet ministers during the interwar years had emerged from industrial and commercial families (George 1962: 17–18).

The Soviet Union was European capitalism's public enemy number one. On the other hand, Germany after World War I offered British capitalists

[13] Liberal support for "appeasement" was indirect and "pursued by way of omission rather than commission." It was based on opposition to war and to the machinations at Versailles and began to dissolve after 1933. It is clear, from representative Liberal journals, that Liberals did not concur with the assumptions on which Conservative appeasement was based. But before 1933, Conservative fear of war and Liberal pacifism appeared, from time to time, to place Conservatives and Liberals in the same camp with respect to appeasement. After 1933, the term "appeasement" changed its meaning: it ceased to be connected to considerations of morality and justice and became wholly bound up with upper-class fear and expediency (see Morris 1991). In the course of 1936, appeasers disappeared from the Labour Party. Thereafter, the left agreed that Hitler must be countered by alliances and arms (Taylor 1957: 191, 195).

[14] John Thompson disputes the notion that there was any significant Conservative opposition to appeasement. Such opposition, he argues, is "rather like a mirage: the more it is studied the less substantial it appears.... " What emerges on closer examination "is a picture of sporadic and discontinuous dissent, of individual critics and small cliques but no cohesive group. Until Anthony Eden's resignation as Foreign Secretary in February 1938, there was no group at all; and even after Eden's retirement... there was only a loose collection of private M.P.s who shared a common concern about the direction of foreign affairs but who were unable to agree on policy or tactics" (Thompson 1971: 2).

[15] From reports in *The Times*, Simon Haxey compiled figures on the estates left by 33 of the 43 Conservative M.P.s who died between 1931 and 1938. The 33 Conservative M.P.s left an average fortune of £218,516. See Haxey 1939: 28–29.

tempting investment opportunities, with high interest and profit rates. A number of important bankers and businessmen favored a rapprochement with Germany for purely self-interested business considerations: their firms were doing profitable business with Germany and they favored policies that facilitated such transactions. For these, the personal benefits derived from good relations with Germany outweighed the fact that their activities assisted Germany in her rearmament. Other bankers and businessmen were pro-German because they feared that another war would bring socialism to Great Britain (Einzig 1941: 22–23).

Montagu Norman, elected governor of the Bank of England by the bank's board of directors in 1929, had a "well known phobia about Bolshevism" that could be activated by profit-seeking British financiers who argued that a prosperous Germany was a non-communist Germany and a bulwark against the domination of Europe by the Soviet Union (George 1962: 155–58). After meeting with Norman in July 1934, a partner at J.P. Morgan and Company in New York, Robert Leffingwell, wrote in a letter that

Monty says that Hitler and Schacht are the bulwarks of civilization in Germany and the only friends we have. They are fighting the war of our system of society against communism. If they fail, communism will follow in Germany, and anything may follow in Europe. (Chernow 1990: 398)

Many British statesmen believed that Bolshevism had been a serious alternative in German domestic politics in 1930–32 and that "the appropriate provision of credit facilities was to counteract the recurrence of such a situation" (Schmidt 1986: 88). Lord Lothian (Under-Secretary of State for India, 1931–32), Frank Trelawney Ashton-Gwatkin (Foreign Office), Gladwyn Jebb (Private Secretary to Alexander Cadogan), and Anthony Eden (Foreign Secretary, 1936–38) put forward proposals for alleviating Germany's shortage of foreign currency and raw materials. For them, finance was to be used for stabilizing German and other strongly anti-Bolshevik regimes. Norman and the bank became more interested in Germany as a partner after the Nazis "stabilized" Germany in 1933 (George 1962: 157). And Norman gave his support to financial reconstruction in Austria, Hungary, Bulgaria (German allies in World War I), the free City of Danzig (essentially a German city), and Greece (which had restored the pro-German regime of King Constantine after the war). Other countries, in as great a need of assistance for financial reconstruction – for example, Poland, Romania, and Yugoslavia – were unable to secure the bank's assistance.

Various London banks provided Nazi Germany with short-term commercial credits, all of which went into armaments. The Bank of England could have stopped these transactions but did not. In 1934, after using millions of pounds of loan capital on public works and rearmament, Germany defaulted on its commercial debts. Norman came to the rescue of the Reichsbank and the Hitler regime by granting a credit sufficient to tide Germany over the difficulties. No attempt was made to use German financial difficulties as a means of moderating German foreign policy (Einzig 1941: 75–76; see also Schmidt 1986: 88–89).

All available foreign exchange was used to amass stocks of raw materials for the eventuality of war. Government orders for armaments increased the need for foreign raw materials. Reichsbank reserves could not long support an import surplus. Rising world prices for raw materials further complicated matters. Germany financed rearmament with the sterling obtained from her considerable trade surplus with Britain. Part of the sterling proceeds of German exports could have been seized for the benefit of British creditors. But the Bank of England was strongly opposed to "exchange clearing," even at a time when it was employed with success by a large and increasing number of countries. Under forced clearing Germany could not have realized *devisen* (claims of one economy against another) from exports to creditor countries until debts were settled. Since Germany needed raw materials, she could not risk forced clearings. "Had Germany been compelled to relinquish some foreign exchange in favor of her foreign creditors as a result of strong pressure, there would have been less foreign exchange available for raw materials for rearmament purposes. Consequently it is possible that Hitler's aggressive moves might have been delayed" (Einzig 1942: 74).

Instead, in June 1934, at a time when it was generally known that Germany was rearming rapidly, Britain concluded a Payments Agreement with Germany that provided for the settlement of the commercial arrears. But within months it was on the verge of breakdown. It would have been easy at this point either to financially strangle the Nazi regime or to compel Germany to adopt a more moderate foreign policy. Instead, the Bank of England stepped in and granted a credit to the Reichsbank in order to save the agreement and to thus obviate the necessity for imposing exchange clearing on Germany. Germany thus continued to collect sterling from her export surpluses. These surpluses amounted to some £55,466,000 between October 1934 and March 1939, out of which only some £20 million was used for the service of Germany's various debts to Great Britain; the rest was used to subsidize German rearmament (Einzig 1942: 74–75). In addition, Germany was permitted to maintain favorable trade balances with other countries in Northern and Western Europe as a result of Britain's willingness to accept unfavorable trade balances with them. Britain could have compelled them to spend the proceeds of their exports to Britain on British goods, thus causing a contraction of German exports and a consequent slowdown in her rearmament. Instead, Britain's trade partners were allowed to spend a large part of the proceeds from exports to Britain in Germany.

In 1938, the Federation of British Industries entered into discussions with Germany's Reichsgruppe Industrie toward the end of concluding an agreement that would provide Germany with additional foreign exchange resources. A few days after the opening of negotiations in Düsseldorf, German troops entered Czechoslovakia in violation of Hitler's pledge at Munich. After consultation with London, the British delegates "astonished their German colleagues by announcing their intention of proceeding with the matter" and signing the preliminary agreement (Einzig 1942: 116). One clause of the agreement stated that one of the objects of the agreement was to enable Germany to increase her foreign exchange resources. At the moment when Germany was completing its conquest of Czechoslovakia (and Hungarian and Romanian armies were mobilizing against a widely expected German march through these countries and into the Balkans), "British politicians and industrialists were engaged in devising a scheme by which to enable Germany to accelerate her rearmament through increasing her foreign exchange resources" (Einzig 1942: 116–19).

German withdrawal from the League of Nations (1933), the return of the Saar (1935), the reoccupation of the Rhineland (March 1936), denunciation of the German war guilt thesis by Hitler (fall 1936), intervention in Spain (1936–39), the establishment of the Rome-Berlin Axis (October 1936), and conclusion of an anti-Comintern pact (November 1936) "foreshadowed a vigorous German foreign policy for the years following" (Bonnell 1940: 74). But the Bank of England abstained from bringing pressure on Germany's London banking creditors to induce them to cut their losses and liquidate at least part of their commitments, as French, Dutch, and Swiss banking creditors began doing when the nature of Hitler's foreign policy became increasingly obvious.

Not only did British banking creditors fail to liquidate old credits, but a number of London banks continued to issue new credits to this defaulting debtor during 1936 and 1937 for the purpose of facilitating the import of raw materials by Germany for rearmament requirements.[16] The government did not express any objection to the granting of new credits to Germany by various London banks, though the matter was repeatedly raised in Parliament. However, in 1937, persistent criticism in Parliament and the press caused a discontinuation of the practice of granting new credits.

In March 1938, the Bank of England promptly surrendered Austria's gold and foreign assets to Germany after the German absorption of Austria (Anschluss). The government made no move to prevent this or the surrender of privately owned sterling assets to Germany. Foreign creditors could have exercised some pressure on the German government by threatening to adopt forced clearing or to attach Austrian assets. Instead, Britain concluded a new Payments Agreement and a Transfer Agreement regarding the Austrian obligations. "In view of the fact that the only effective pressure that could

---

[16] Where they were not used directly for that purpose, they made it possible for resources that would otherwise have been used to meet civilian needs to be used for rearmament. In some cases, firms directly engaged in Germany's rearmament, e.g., I. G. Farbenindustrie, obtained new credits from London banking houses (Einzig 1942: 77–78).

have been placed upon Germany at the time would have been the joint pressure of all guarantors to the loans [Britain, France, Belgium, Czechoslovakia, Denmark, Holland, Sweden, and Switzerland], the action of the British in attempting bilateral negotiations with the Germans was criticized. The German press gloated over the fact that the creditors' front had been broken. Subsequently arrangements were negotiated by the other creditors with Germany" (Bonnell 1940: 65–66).

Nazi Germany as a "Bulwark against Bolshevism"

The Soviet Union represented a new class enemy committed to the ultimate destruction of interclass and international relations of which the conservative oligarchy was the beneficiary. This enemy had emerged as the ruler of the largest, most populous, and potentially most powerful of the Great Powers, and at a time when landowners increasingly feared the pressure of land-hungry peasants and industrialists feared the growth of proletarian radicalism. The fear of peasant or proletarian revolt became a determining factor in the political behavior of European aristocrats and industrialists and of the diplomats and strategists who became caught up in the fears of the elites for whom they spoke. The conditions in which the masses lived made this fear well founded. No efforts were made to remove the sources of mass misery and thus to diminish the potential appeal of communism, because the wealthy classes were unwilling to make the sacrifice of wealth and privilege that this would entail. Instead, they first attempted to squash the Bolshevik menace through military means: starving and slaughtering millions of Russians by means of blockade, intervention, and subsidized civil war (1918–20). The fear of social revolution at home impelled them to abandon this effort, but the rise of fascism – first in Germany, Italy, and Japan, later in Austria, Poland, Portugal, Hungary, Spain, and other states – offered the aristocrats and industrialists of Western Europe a second line of attack against the Bolshevik menace. Britain and France supported Japan's drive to "save China from Bolshevism" in 1927, Nazi Germany's quest to secure mastery of Central Europe, fascist Italy's attempts to strengthen itself in Africa and the Mediterranean, and the defeat of the Spanish Republic.

By the start of the twentieth century, Germany was the most industrialized nation in all Europe, and the first powerful industrial state dominated by institutions and values that stemmed from the pre-liberal and pre-industrial past (Kennedy 1987: 214). "This in itself revived what had been the declining power of European conservatives, for it demonstrated that the forces of nationalism and industrialism need not always favor liberals" (Weiss 1977: 73). The fascist state, with its elimination of factious party politics, its "corporatist" planning for the economy in place of disputes between capital and labor, and its commitment to government action, seemed to offer an alternative to the model being offered by the Bolsheviks (Kennedy 1987: 292).

Throughout Europe, princes, politicians, and generals looked to Germany to save them from revolution. In Germany, "Hitler was brought to power by Junkers and industrialists. His advent was welcomed consequently among their opposite numbers in Great Britain, who hailed him as the savior of Germany from Communism" (Schuman 1942: 69). Conservative M.P. Sir Thomas Moore, in an article in the *Daily Mail* (April 25, 1934) entitled "The Blackshirts Have What the Conservatives Need," described a fascist rally in Albert Hall: "There was little if any of the policy which could not be accepted by the most loyal follower of our present Conservative leaders... surely there cannot be any fundamental difference of outlook between the Blackshirts and their parents the Conservatives..." (in Haxey 1939: 24).

Conservatives argued that Nazi Germany should be supported as a bulwark against the westward spread of Bolshevism from the Soviet Union. That Nazi Germany was a "bulwark against Bolshevism" was repeated over and over again in that influential organ of conservative opinion, *The Times*, and became a stock phrase in its editorials (George 1962: 144). Lloyd George argued:

In a very short time, perhaps in a year or two, the Conservative elements in this country will be looking to Germany as the bulwark against Communism in Europe.... Do not let us be in a hurry to condemn Germany. We shall be welcoming Germany as our friend. (in Schuman 1942: 340)

J. L. Garvin argued, "The creation of a strong Middle Europe under German leadership would provide an effective bulwark against the expansion of Communist Russia" (*Observer*, March 21, 1937; in Thompson 1971: 34).

ALTERNATIVE INTERPRETATIONS

International relations theorists explain British foreign policy between the wars in terms of either the nature of the multipolar structure of the international system or of processes of hegemonic transition.

Some international relations theorists argue that the multipolar distribution of power that characterized the period increased the potential for miscalculation and misperception. Under these conditions, for instance, states may "pass the buck" and count on third parties to bear the costs of stopping a rising hegemon, thereby failing to form balancing alignments in time to stem the rise of a hegemon. Kenneth Waltz believes that buck passing explains the alliance behavior of Britain and France between the wars: "As the German threat grew, some British and French leaders could hope that if their countries remained aloof, Russia and Germany would balance each other off or fight to the finish" (Waltz 1979: 165; see also Christensen and Snyder 1990). Britain and France thought they could pass the buck: stand aside and intervene only "if and when the initial belligerents showed signs of having exhausted themselves" (Christensen and Snyder 1990: 147).

But most international relations theorists, including those just cited, believe that the international system was multipolar from the end of the Napoleonic Wars (1815) to the end of World War II. Thus, assumptions about the greater instability of multipolarity do not help to explain why Britain was suddenly, massively, fatally, and inexplicably afflicted by misinformation, miscalculation, and misperception in the conduct of its relations with Europe during the interwar years. Britain, after all, was a world power. It had managed to expand from its small island base to hold sway over one-fifth of the earth's surface and, more to the point, had for centuries played a leading role in European affairs.

Other international relations theorists view the interwar years as a period of hegemonic transition. In this view, Britain, though still playing a central role in European politics, was a declining hegemonic power – an economically weakened, strategically overstretched empire faced with threats in the Far East, the Mediterranean, and in Europe. By the 1930s, Britain's position was being challenged by Italy, Japan, and Germany. In the background, the United States remained by far the most powerful manufacturing country in the world, and the Soviet Union was quickly transforming itself into an industrial superpower. Britain thus faced the problem of how to fight off the challenge presented by Japan, Italy, and Germany without weakening its own power in the process. Britain's solution was to appease Hitler so as to reduce the number of threats and increase its ability to meet the remaining ones (Kennedy 1987).

Numerous analyses of the interwar period have argued that Germany's vast military-industrial strength left Britain no choice but to pursue policies of appeasement toward her (e.g., Barnett 1972; Howard 1972; Watt 1975; Hyde 1976; Bialer 1980; Bond 1983; Murray 1984). But this argument ignores the politics that led appeasers to propagate inflated estimates of German power, and policy makers to accept them. Estimates of German military power were grossly and deliberately inflated (see, e.g., Barnett 1972: 505–7; Kennedy 1981: 291–93; Murray 1984) and were disputed by many at the time. Churchill disputed inflated estimates of German military power, calling them "far from the truth" and "an undue appeal to the fear motive" (Churchill 1948: 332). During the late 1930s, a succession of envoys from the German army, fearing that Germany would suffer defeat if there were a war, came to London seeking British support for a coup against Hitler. These envoys were in a position to know the disposition of German military strength, and repeatedly they put this knowledge at the disposal of the British government (Rowse 1947: 81). Arguments concerning the decline of British power ignore the politics that foreclosed both a British rearmament effort to meet the challenge of German power and an alliance with the Soviet Union as a counterweight to German power.

Some analysts argue that Britain failed to undertake an adequate rearmament effort after World War I because of financial constraints imposed by the treasury (Dunbabin 1975; Parker 1975, 1981; Peden 1979, 1983). But as Paul Kennedy has pointed out, Britain did not lack the necessary financial resources to meet the challenge of German power during the interwar years. With $19.5 billion invested overseas, equaling some 43 percent of the world's foreign investments, "there was no question that [Britain] could pay for even a large-scale, expensive war if the need arose" (1987: 236). Other analyses argue that increased military spending would have had dangerous economic consequences for Britain (Peden 1979; Wendt 1983; Schmidt 1986). But these analyses are based on a consideration of the rapid buildup undertaken after 1938 (McKeown 1991). They tend to ignore what impact an earlier and more measured buildup would have had and the politics that foreclosed that course of action. In the 1920s, Churchill was concerned that the dislocative effects of a naval buildup would ensure "the return of the Socialist Administration" (in Ferris 1989: 161–62). Measures that might have mitigated these effects (e.g., exchange controls, wage and price controls, and rationing of supplies of labor) were ruled out because business groups, on whose support Conservatives depended, opposed them (McKeown 1991: 271–72). The reason for this was that arms production, which usually required a higher proportion of skilled labor than civilian products, often increased unemployment among the mass of the unskilled. This was an outcome Conservatives wished to avoid.[17] The future of the Conservative Party seemed to depend on the success of the "National Government" in persuading voters to believe that economic recovery since 1931 was its work and that Conservative government brought safely growing prosperity, falling unemployment, and improved conditions of life, in contrast to the alleged follies of Labour in power (Parker 1993: 276).

Analyses pointing to other aspects of British defense weakness, such as the need to maintain British forces in substantial numbers in India and other locations (Howard 1981; Meyers 1983; Kennedy 1986; Friedberg 1988: chap. 5), also tend to ignore the politics involved. As already noted, Britain resolved to make the Asian territories of the former Ottoman empire a bulwark against the spread of Bolshevism by creating "a Moslem nexus of states" in the Middle East as a shield to ward off Russian expansion (Morgan 1979: 119). If British forces were needed in substantial numbers abroad, it was because Britain deemed Bolshevism to be a greater threat to the empire than Germany was to Europe.[18]

---

[17] The left opposed rearmament before 1933. However, the rise of Hitlerism brought about a complete reversal of Liberal opinion toward rearmament. After the spring of 1935, all the Liberal journals recognized the need for British rearmament; after Munich "they all clamored for 'massive' rearmament, especially in the air. Even the Quaker-edited *Spectator* tardily joined the rearmament lobby" (Morris 1991: 176).

[18] Darwin 1981: 214; Fromkin 1989: chap. 3. "India" was a codeword for "the left will take over" (i.e., the Communist Party of India), and was a part of a discourse that was understood and recognized by the left.

Arguments concerning defense weaknesses, economic constraints, and extra-European obligations leave unanswered the question of why Britain, faced with these limitations, refused to ally with the Soviet Union in order to balance German power. At any point the British had the option of allying with the Soviet Union as a means of overcoming any real or perceived weaknesses relative to Germany. "The critical issue," as Timothy McKeown pointed out recently, "is the failure of Britain and France to fashion an alliance with the Soviet Union" (McKeown 1991: 268). The combined strength of the Soviet Union and Great Britain, at any point during the interwar years, could have been used to stop Germany. German aircraft production in 1941 was significantly smaller than that of Britain. The German surface fleet was in no position to take on the Royal Navy, despite occasional raids into the North Atlantic. Germany's production of artillery pieces, self-propelled guns, and tanks was considerably less than Russia's, let alone the combined Allied totals (Kennedy 1987: 341, 353). The Allied powers during World War II possessed at least twice the manufacturing strength, three times the "war potential," and three times the national income of the Axis powers, even when the French shares are added to Germany's total (Goldsmith 1946). German aircraft production in 1939 was about 675 a month, no more than that of Great Britain or of Russia; her tank production was less (Medlicott 1963: 241). In the war that eventually ensued between Germany and Britain, Germany exhibited myriad weaknesses and vulnerabilities. Mismatched equipment and vehicles were gathered from all over Europe, and no provisions made for repair or replacement (Tipton and Aldrich 1987b: 21). Italy, Germany's ally, proved unable to make a sustained contribution to the war effort. In fact, Italy's complete dependence on German supplies of coal led to shortages in Germany and severely restricted any increase in Italian industrial production (Tipton and Aldrich 1987b: 25). The German air force failed to secure air superiority over Britain and broke off its assault on Britain's coastal defenses before they had been destroyed. The Blitzkrieg failed in Russia.

The Soviet Union had expressed willingness to cooperate with Britain and France in deterring German aggression (Churchill 1948: 245–46, 272–73; Gilbert and Gott 1963: 135–38). However, British and French leaders were unwilling to have the Soviet Union as a military ally. It has been argued that Britain refused to ally with the Soviet Union against Germany because Soviet military capability was such as to render the value of a Soviet military alliance negligible (e.g., Herndon 1983). This was patently not the case.

The year after Hitler came to power in Germany, the Soviet Union began a military reorganization and expansion that by 1935 had increased the strength of the Soviet Red Army from 562,000 to 1,300,000 (Erickson 1962: 763). In 1936, representatives of the international military community were invited to observe Soviet military maneuvers. These excited a good deal of interest and stimulated efforts on the part of the British, French, German, and Italian armies to catch up with the Soviet Union by developing paratrooper units and the capacity to airlift tanks (Erickson 1962: 327). In addition, British military observers reported that the performance of the Soviet cavalry and mechanized infantry and armor was "well ahead of similar types" in the British service. The House of Lords was informed that while the British had about 100 medium tanks, the Soviets had 5,000 to 6,000, and the Soviet BT tank was "at least twice as good" as the latest British experimental model. Soviet fighters and medium bombers were judged "well-armed, fast, and maneuverable." The Soviet military was described as "lavishly" equipped; the officers were young and enthusiastic, and the rank and file were "magnificent physically, with high morale" (Herndon 1983: 302–3). British officials who observed the performance of Soviet equipment in action against German and Italian material during the Spanish civil war rated Soviet fighters and bombers of "very high quality," the Soviet light and medium tanks as generally better than the German, and Soviet pilots better than their German and Italian counterparts (1983: 304).

James Herndon argues that the purge of Soviet military personnel in June 1937 left the British government during the Czechoslovakian crisis "no alternative... but to discount the USSR as a military factor in its policy formulation" (1983: 308). But when Britain rejected Soviet proposals for concerted action to prevent a German takeover, Churchill found it "astonishing" that these proposals "by one of the greatest powers concerned" should not have played a part in the conduct of the crisis, and repeatedly protested against his government's continued rejection of "the indispensable aid of Russia" (Churchill 1948: 272–73, 336). Churchill, who at the time had urged the creation of a Franco-British-Russian alliance as the only hope of checking Germany, wrote that "no one would be so foolish to suppose that huge country, with its vast population and enormous resources, would be a negligible factor in such a situation as that with which we are confronted" (1948: 334). Instead, the Soviet offer was treated with "indifference" and "disdain." What doubts arose at the time concerning Soviet military capability were, as Anthony Eden later conceded, "exaggerated" (in Herndon 1983: 306). In fact, after Munich, "[f]requent favorable reference was made to the size of the Red Army and the Soviet air force, and the need for an Anglo-Soviet accord was increasingly advocated in parliamentary debates" (Herndon 1983: 308). British leaders had a high enough regard for the Soviet Union's military capability after 1937 to fear that if war broke out in Central and Western Europe, the Soviet Union would step in triumphantly at the last as *"tertius gaudens."*[19]

In fact, Soviet military capability was never at issue during the interwar years. At issue was the domestic political cost of an alliance with the Soviet

---

[19] *"Tertius gaudens"*: a third party. Sir Anthony Eden, June 1, 1937, *Foreign Relations of the United States (FRUS)*, 1937, vol. 1, p. 318; Neville Chamberlain, September 21, 1938, *FRUS* 1938, vol. 1, p. 632.

Union. Conservative opinion in Britain held that any relationship with the Soviet Union would strengthen the left at home and abroad. Conservatives were opposed even to British *recognition* of the Soviet Union. As previously noted, *The Times*, an influential organ of conservative opinion, warned that de facto recognition would be used by the Soviet government "to spread the tentacles of their poisonous influence throughout the world" (March 17, 1921). Conservatives opposed making common cause with the French against the Germans during the Rhineland crisis in 1936 because that year France had concluded a pact with the Soviets; to support France would thus "draw [Britain] in on the side of Russia" (Rowse 1947: 39). Similarly, at Munich, Chamberlain's one fear, according to Leopold Amery, was that Britain would "drift into a Franco-Soviet combination" against Mussolini and Hitler (in Rowse 1947: 74). In May 1939, after Germany had begun to accelerate its pressure on Poland for territorial concessions, an alliance with the Soviet Union was discussed by First Lord of the Admiralty Earl Stanhope in a letter to Lord Halifax (president of the Cabinet): "The military advantages [of an alliance with the Soviet Union] only arise if we eventually come to war [with Germany]. If we assume that somehow or other we are going to avoid this, I feel that more than ever the political disadvantages outweigh the possible military advantages."[20]

Between the German absorption of Sudetenland (September 1938) and the German occupation of Prague (March 1939), French Air Minister Philip Cot wrote in *L'Oeuvre* (October 8, 1938) that France, Britain, and Czechoslovakia alone had more planes than the Reich and that with only half of the Soviet fleet added to their forces they would command squadrons outnumbering those of Italy and Germany combined (cited in Schuman 1942: 469). In fact, on October 26, Lloyd George acknowledged that Britain had "handed over a little Democratic State in Central Europe to a ruthless dictator." He dismissed that argument over armaments that had been used to affect this end: "I know something about armaments. The French army is today the best army in Europe, and the Russian army is the greatest army in the world so far as numbers are concerned and so far as its air force is concerned" (in Schuman 1942: 469).

On April 18, 1939, the Soviet Union proposed a triple alliance of Britain, France, and itself. A few days earlier (April 13, 1939) a dozen speakers in the House of Commons, including Labour and Liberal ministers as well as Churchill, had called for an alliance with the Soviet Union (Parker 1993: 222–23). Anthony Eden, who had resigned as Foreign Secretary in February 1938, and Lloyd George also supported the alliance. Gallup opinion polls in June 1939 gave 84 percent "yes" replies to the question, "Do you favor a military alliance between Britain, France, and Russia?" (Parker 1993: 233). But Chamberlain, supported by Halifax, remained steadfastly opposed to

[20] CAB 21/551: Stanhope to Halifax, May 25, 1939, pp. 1–2, 5; in Herndon 1983: 310.

the alliance. On April 19, Chamberlain succeeded in persuading the Foreign Policy Committee to reject the Soviet proposal. At the end of May 1939, the Cabinet finally decided to accept an alliance with the Soviet Union. But a new set of proposals and counterproposals failed to bring the representatives of the two countries into agreement on the terms of an alliance.

In the summer of 1939, Alexander Cadogan (then permanent Under-Secretary of State) argued that the purged Red Army was so enfeebled, the Soviet navy was so weak, and Russian aviation was so out of date that though "Russia may be good for the defence of her territory," she could not offer "useful active assistance outside her frontiers." The only reason for seeking Soviet support, he asserted, had been "to placate our left-wing in England," rather than to obtain any solid military advantage (Parker 1993: 225). In August 1939, the Soviet Union abandoned attempts to secure the British alliance.[21]

All governments maintain permanent diplomats, consuls, military, naval, and air attaches, and widespread intelligence services for the purpose of assessing the military strength of other states. Arguments based on ignorance, miscalculation, or misperception are really without foundation. Clearly, false estimates of the relative strengths of Germany and the Soviet Union were deliberately propagated in order to cause millions of Britons to believe that policies of appeasement were necessitated by German invincibility and Soviet weakness.

In sum, Britain could have redressed a real or perceived military weakness relative to Germany either by rearming or by forming an alliance with the Soviet Union. Rearmament was ruled out because Conservatives feared that government measures that would cushion its economic effects would lose them the support of business and that rearmament undertaken without these measures would swell the ranks of the socialists. Alliance with the Soviet Union was ruled out because Conservatives feared that any relationship with the Soviet Union would enhance its stature and increase the power of socialists at home.

Some accounts of the period assert that appeasement was essentially a policy derived from moral principles and idealism, a British reaction against the harsh terms imposed on Germany by the Versailles Treaty (Carr 1964; Gilbert 1966; Lentin 1984). But appeasers were not deceived as to the moral character of Hitler's regime. After the "Night of the Long Knives" (June 30, 1934), Lord Lothian, Under-Secretary of State for India (1931–32) and subsequently British Ambassador to the United States (1939–40), exclaimed: "We can't have any dealings with these people; they are nothing but a lot of gunmen" (quoted in Rowse 1961: 31). Arthur Salter, the director of the Economic Section of the League of Nations (1919–20, 1922–31), warned against "dealing with gangsters" (quoted in Rowse 1961: 43). Chamberlain, who,

---

[21] An account of the negotiations is in Parker 1993: 224–45.

it is often asserted, was blinded by idealism and thus misperceived Hitler's aims, refers to Hitler in his diaries and letters as "half mad," "lunatic," and untrustworthy (Feiling 1946: 350, 354, 357, 360). Anyway, Hitler's aims were in print for all to read (*Mein Kampf*) and were publicly and regularly repeated before massive rallies in Germany and broadcast on German radio. It is unlikely that moralism or idealism played a role in appeasement of Germany or that Chamberlain and other appeasers misperceived Hitler's aims.

One line of argument contends that Britain's appeasement policy was the work of Neville Chamberlain and the product of his particular psychology. For instance, Larry Fuchser argues that Chamberlain had a problem with authority, stemming from his relationship with his father, that made it impossible for him to work cooperatively with others. Thus, Britain at a crucial juncture fell victim to his autocratic style of decision making.[22] But Chamberlain's policies did not differ in any essential aspect from British policy toward Germany under other Conservative governments during the period. His policies were certainly consistent with Baldwin's as well as with a strong current of influential conservative opinion at the time. There is no reason, therefore, to scrutinize Chamberlain's psychological makeup in order to explain what was clearly a more general phenomenon.

CONCLUSION

When one examines the period from 1918 to 1939 in its entirety, it becomes clear that during those years, the threat of Bolshevism to the social order overrode concerns about German threats to the territorial order. France had more to fear than Britain from German territorial ambitions, but eventually even in France, fear of Bolshevism triumphed over fear of German power. A strong and very influential current of conservative thought in both countries held that an alliance with the Soviet Union against Germany would strengthen the Soviet Union and advance the cause of socialists and communists at home. On the other hand, a Germany made stronger by an alliance with Britain would be less likely to fall victim to a communist insurrection and would also provide a bulwark against the westward spread of Bolshevism from the Soviet Union. In a domestic and international environment increasingly polarized by conflict between left and right, the concern with stopping the spread of communism became inextricably bound up with the preservation and defense of the traditional structure of European society.

On the eve of twentieth century, Vilfredo Pareto had warned that "slowly but surely the socialist tide is rising in almost every country of Europe" (Pareto 1966: 162). By 1918, communists had overthrown the tsarist regime in Russia and now controlled the vast resources of the Russian Empire. The left was on the rise throughout Europe. The rising tide of socialism made

[22] See Fuscher 1982: esp. chap. 1; and the bibliography of works offering similar arguments.

these dangerous times for the wealthy classes in Europe. Rather than balancing German aggression with countervailing power, the classic balance-of-power game, European governments chose instead to gamble that Germany's drive for empire in Europe would stop short of destroying them and at the same time enable them to defeat communism at home and abroad.

Just as the "ideas of 1789" became potent when they were identified with the power of France, so the association of communism with the power of the Soviet Union transformed it from the doctrine of a small subversive minority into a world movement, backed, as time passed, by an increasingly formidable economic and military power. The supreme object of the great powers after 1815 had been to prevent another French Revolution or a general European revolution on the French model. After 1917, the supreme object of the powers became to contain the spread of Bolshevism in Europe.

After Hitler came to power, Germany began step by step to dismantle the restrictions placed on it by Versailles. At each step of the way, an alliance between the Western powers and the Soviet Union could have put a halt to the resurgence of German power in Europe. At each step this option was rejected. Instead, Britain and France allowed Germany to reoccupy the Rhineland and to openly rearm after 1934. Between 1936 and 1939 they allowed the fascist powers a free hand in the Spanish civil war. In 1938, they acquiesced to the union of fascist Germany and fascist Austria, though they had in 1919 and during the 1920s refused to allow a union of Austria with the German Weimar Republic when it was proposed by a socialist-dominated Austrian government. In 1938, the powers refused to make common cause with the Soviet Union against Hitler's demands regarding the Sudetenland. They took no action when Nazi Germany then proceeded to absorb the whole of Czechoslovakia. The following year, even before the civil war in Spain had drawn to a close, they extended full diplomatic recognition to the fascist regime. When Hitler invaded Poland, they declared war on Germany but took no action whatever. Instead, while Germany was allowed to defeat Poland, and then to proceed unopposed with the invasion and subjugation of Norway, Britain and France were busy preparing to fight a war with the Soviet Union in Finland, though Soviet aims in Finland were known to be limited and purely defensive in nature. The war in Finland ended before the first shots were fired between the Allies and the Soviet Union. But it was a war with the Soviet Union that the Allies were readying their forces to fight in 1939, and not war with Germany. Germany proceeded virtually unimpeded with its conquest of Poland, Norway, Denmark, Belgium, and the Netherlands. France itself capitulated with hardly a struggle. It was only after Britain was left to face Nazi Germany all alone that she finally entered into an alliance with the Soviet Union.

Clearly, Europe's leaders throughout the interwar period were primarily concerned not with Germany but with the rise of the left at home and abroad.

This is the conclusion drawn by A. L. Rowse:

They would not listen to warnings, because they did not wish to hear. And they did not think things out, because there was a fatal confusion in their minds between the interests of their social order and the interests of their country. They did not say much about it, since that would have given the game away, and anyway it was a thought they did not wish to be too explicit about even to themselves, but they were Anti-Red and that hamstrung them in dealing with the greatest immediate danger to their country, Hitler's Germany. (Rowse 1961: 117)

Thus, "a class in decadence" and, particularly, "eminent specimens of it, be-ribboned and be-coroneted, with the best will in the world, well-nigh ruined their country" (Rowse 1961: 118).

III

THE GREAT TRANSFORMATION

8

The Post–World War II Order

> Thrones have been overthrown, ancient and entrenched aristocracies have been dispersed, feudal dominions shattered, old privileges abolished; statesmen and politicians who had dominated events have disappeared into retirement, exile, or the grave; the old parties have split, coalesced, transformed themselves, died out or blossomed exceedingly; new men, new parties, new ideas have emerged from the coulisses of history and filled the centre of the stage.... The habits and traditions of a millennium have been revolutionized in a decade.
>
> Betts 1950: 196

Europe's nineteenth-century market system collapsed in the course of the world wars. Karl Polanyi tracks its collapse through the dissolution of its central institutions. He begins with the dissolution of the balance-of-power system. Europe, he assumed, had enjoyed an unprecedented one hundred years' peace as a result of this system. After 1900, however, it began to dissolve, and when, in 1914, it finally broke down, it unleashed a war of monumental proportions. But as Polanyi rightfully points out, this would not be the war to end all wars. World War I was part of the old nineteenth-century system, "a simple conflict of powers unleashed by the lapse of the balance-of-power system" (1944: 30). It did not, as World War II would, form "part of the world upheaval" that marked the great transformation. The end of the international political system nonetheless set the stage for the demise of the other institutions of Europe's nineteenth-century market system. During the interwar years, the international economic system collapsed; but even before its definitive end with the demise of the gold standard system in 1933, the threat of its collapse began to erode the other institutions of Europe's market system. Thus, "[t]he liberal state was in many countries replaced by totalitarian dictatorships, and the central institution of the century – production based on free markets – was superseded by new forms of economy" (1944: 29).

Contemporary analyses of the world wars, though they rarely give as full an account of the interconnection of international and domestic political and economic institutions, offer a somewhat similar explanation of the wars. In common with Polanyi's account, most contemporary explanations of the wars focus first and foremost on the collapse of the balance-of-power system. Their explanation for the relative peace that Europe enjoyed after 1945 follows logically from this: it was due to the reestablishment of international stability with the emergence of a bipolar balance-of-power system after World War II.[1]

Previous chapters have argued that Europe did not enjoy a century of peace before 1914. They have shown that a more or less continuous round of recurring social conflicts characterized nineteenth-century Europe and that these conflicts became increasingly frequent and violent in the early twentieth century. These wars culminated and came to an end in the two-phased world war that began in 1914. War ensued from the breakdown of the European balance-of-power system in 1914, but both were the result of the extreme polarization of European society along class lines.

After 1945, there was a sharp decline in the number of conflicts in Europe. This chapter argues that the recurring social conflicts that characterized nineteenth- and early twentieth-century Europe came to an end when the structures that had generated them were destroyed in the world wars. The breakdown of the existing structure of social power in Europe, and of the class, land, and income structures on which it had rested, brought peace and prosperity to Europe. The elimination of sharp political and economic inequalities and the consequent reorientation of development to foster a more balanced and internally oriented growth, along with the radical alteration of the ethnic map of Europe, sharply reduced the incidence of conflict in Europe and laid the foundation for an era of unprecedented prosperity there.

EUROPE'S POST–WORLD WAR II SOCIAL PEACE AND PROSPERITY

All of Europe, both East and West, experienced phenomenal growth after 1945. In the 1950s, the growth of output and consumption, productivity, investment, and employment in Europe surpassed any recorded historical experience (Maddison 1964: 25). Western Europe's greatest boom, by any statistical definition, began with the end of the war and proceeded without interruption until 1967 (Milward 1984: 477). During the 1950s and early 1960s, and in common with "the advanced industrial countries of the Western world," Western Europe enjoyed an extended period of prosperity for which it is impossible to find a precedent. The growth of production "was extremely rapid ... much faster and less interrupted, than in any previous

---

[1] The relevant works are cited in Chapter 5, note 4.

period" (Schonfield 1965: 61). Between 1850 and 1913, output per head in the most advanced countries of Western Europe had grown by not more than 1.5 to 2 percent a year; between 1950 and 1973, it grew in those same countries by 3 to 4 percent per year (Lewis 1978b: 33). In most of Western Europe, industrial production surpassed prewar levels by 1947 (France, Austria, Italy, and the Netherlands were the exceptions; Aldcroft 1978: 148). In France, where the entire economy had been reshaped "in a way that was almost revolutionary," national income tripled from 1938 to 1970.[2] Between 1950 and 1970, total output increased at 3.5 percent each year in Belgium, 4.2 percent in Switzerland, and 5 percent in Austria and the Netherlands. Industrial production increased by an average annual rate of 8.3 percent in the period 1949–63 (Ricossa 1973: 291).

The benefits of this prosperity were very widely diffused (Schonfield 1965: 61). There is near unanimity that in Britain, income after World War II was distributed more equally than in 1938 (see also Seers 1949; Cole 1955; Marsh 1958; Paukert 1973; Westergaard and Resler 1975). The income tax system consistently worked to reduce the share of after-tax income received by the top 1 percent. As a result, between 1949 and 1976–77, the share of before-tax income received by this top 1 percent of earners fell dramatically. The decline of the Gini coefficient – a measure of distributional equality – of both before- and after-tax income between 1949 and 1976–77 shows that the distribution became more equal over time, and the fact that for each year the after-tax Gini coefficient was always below the before-tax figure shows that the income tax system was consistently redistributive (Johnson 1994: 313–14). Before the First World War (1911–13), the top 5 percent of the population owned 87 percent of personal wealth, the bottom 90 percent, 8 percent; just before the Second World War (1936–38), 79 percent and 12 percent; and in 1960, 75 percent and 17 percent (Hobsbawm 1968: 274).

A large number of factors have been held responsible for Western Europe's phenomenal growth after World War II. The most common ones include U.S. aid to Western Europe, the creation of institutions to coordinate and facilitate regional development, the influx of foreign labor, trade liberalization, war-induced institutional and technological changes, learning (i.e., new ideas), and the reorganization of production impelled by the "Second Industrial Revolution."

Many scholars assume that Europe's phenomenal postwar growth is attributable to the $9.4 billion of U.S. aid made available to Western European countries between the end of 1947 and June 1950 through the Marshall Plan. But while Marshall funds played a prominent role in Western Europe's postwar recovery, they do not explain the phenomenal growth that it experienced after the war. Western European countries before World War II had not been

---

[2] It had barely doubled from the best year of the *belle époque*, 1900, to the best year of the *après-guerre* period, 1929 (Fohlen 1973: 73).

in need of outside investment capital. In fact, Britain, France, Germany, and Austria made available enormous amounts of capital to each other and to other European countries before 1945.

Moreover, Eastern Europe, which did not receive Marshall funds, also experienced an unprecedented period of rapid industrial development and increasing affluence from the early 1950s until around 1970. Beginning in 1945, the income gap between the Eastern countries and the more advanced countries of the West began to narrow noticeably for the first time since the eighteenth century. By 1947, Eastern European countries had surpassed their prewar industrial production levels, in some cases by a large margin.[3] By the late 1960s "it had become clear that the Eastern European economies had grown extraordinarily rapidly, and that the boom in the east shared important characteristics with the boom in the west" (Tipton and Aldrich 1987b: 113). By 1970, the eight Eastern European countries accounted for some 30 percent of world industrial output, as against 18 percent in the early 1950s (Aldcroft 1978: 215, 219).

Rapid changes in Eastern Europe *did* share important characteristics with those that occurred in Western Europe, as is discussed further below. They did so because they experienced social and economic changes similar to those that occurred in the West. Eastern Europe's phenomenal growth and the similarities of changes in social structures across East and West shows that the existence or absence of Marshall funds cannot be used to explain developmental outcomes, either in Europe or elsewhere in the world. In fact, there was an unprecedented inflow of foreign investment into Latin America after 1955 that, despite the abundant human and material resources of the countries involved, failed to bring about a transformation similar to the one that occurred in Europe. Enormous amounts of U.S. aid went to countries in various parts of the world throughout the post–World War II period, and in most cases, as in Egypt, these funds failed to stimulate dynamic, broad-based growth.

Some arguments focus on the role of regional and international organizations as the key element in Europe's postwar prosperity. Regional trading blocs existed before World War II: the British Empire's system of imperial preferences, the French Union's "franc bloc," as well as Japan's Greater East Asian Co-Prosperity Sphere are prominent examples. If Western Europe's postwar growth was the result of such institutions, what conditions enabled these institutions to operate so differently and so much more effectively after the war? More specifically, what prevented them from bringing about a return to the protectionist regionalism of the 1930s?

The earliest of these regional organizations was the European Coal and Steel Community, established in 1951 to form a free-trade zone uniting the heavy-industry regions that spanned the French-German border. The

---

[3] Except for East Germany, where reconstruction plans were delayed until 1949 (Aldcroft 1978: 158).

European Economic Community was established in 1957 with the aim of ensuring free trade and the free flow of capital and labor in the coal, iron, and steel industries of West Germany, Belgium, the Netherlands, France, Luxembourg, and Italy. Britain did not join but established, instead, the European Free Trade Area among itself, Norway, Denmark, Sweden, Switzerland, Austria, and Portugal. However, by the time these organizations had abolished trade restrictions among their members, the postwar takeoff in these countries was well under way. In fact, the changes that had occurred in these countries by that point, and which are generally attributed to the creation of regional institutions, were the *preconditions* for, rather than the results of, their success. Certainly, in Asia, Latin America, and elsewhere, the creation of regional trade compacts has failed to produce the results attributed to them in the Western European case. The Association of South East Asian Nations (ASEAN) is a case in point. Established in 1967 with the objective of developing cooperation among its member states, ASEAN, after thirty-six years of existence, has yet to achieve this objective to any significant degree.

Some accounts of Western Europe's postwar growth focus on international institutions and, in particular, the General Agreement on Tariffs and Trade (GATT), which was established in 1947 to reduce tariffs and quantitative restrictions (the Organization for European Economic Cooperation was created in 1948 for the distribution of American aid, but it also reduced quantitative restrictions on trade among its sixteen members in the 1950s). According to these accounts, Europe's postwar growth was a product of the trade liberalization that was undertaken with the encouragement of international bodies. However, Edward Denison (1967) argues that the contribution of trade liberalization to the growth in production in Western Europe amounted to between 1 percent and 6 percent in its member countries, with a weighted average of 2 percent. This means that 98 percent of Western Europe's growth can be explained by other factors. Moreover, as Paul Bairoch shows, free trade is not necessarily associated with high growth. Between 1889 and 1913, economic growth in Great Britain, which had remained faithful to free trade, was slower than on the Continent, which had turned protectionist: 0.9 percent and 1.5 percent, respectively, in terms of per capita GNP (Bairoch 1993: 167).

Some explanations for Europe's postwar prosperity focus on the availability of large supplies of labor after the war. For instance, Charles Kindleberger (1967) has argued that the rapid advance of Europe's economy was due to the availability of a large supply of labor – the result of a high rate of natural increase, immigration, the presence of unemployed workers, and transfers from agriculture to industry.[4] However, an examination of growth

---

4 With the exhaustion of Europe's excess supply of labor, the rates of economic growth fell: instead of an annual increase of 6 to 8 percent, a yearly growth of 2 to 4 percent became more common.

in employment and output in Western Europe shows that these were not always associated (Aldcroft 1978: 141). Besides, Western European countries
did not suffer from insufficient labor before 1945. In fact, Western Europe
experienced persistent unemployment, even during the boom of the 1920s
(Landes 1969: 390–91). Moreover, foreign workers were available in large
numbers before 1945 and were used in significant numbers in industrial areas (Strikwerda 1993: 1122). More than two-thirds of the labor force in
the industrial area of French Lorraine was foreign (Vignes 1913: 685–86).
Germany employed approximately a million foreign workers (Bade 1985:
133). By 1910, at least one-quarter of Ruhr miners were Polish, and many
others were Italian and Dutch (Herbert 1990: 21).

Some people believe that Europe's postwar growth rates were affected by
war-induced changes in technology and institutions (see, e.g., Simon Kuznets,
discussed below). Growth in the 1950s was a matter of "catching up" in the
double sense of recovering the actual material losses sustained during the
war and compensating for the failure during the war to exploit the technological and other advances made elsewhere in the world. Some argue that
a more effective exploitation of these advances was made possible after the
war because of war-induced changes in beliefs and attitudes about economic
organization and policy, and departures during the wars by some countries
from established economic practices that were successful in terms of increasing output. For instance, Simon Kuznets argues that after the war there was a
"greater consensus of society in accepting active responsibility for economic
growth" and a greater "readiness to weigh critically, and even discard, long-
established notions that may have retarded economic growth in the past"
(1964: 108–9). In particular, there were changed views on the feasibility of
unrelieved economic competition.

Kuznets also focuses on the changed role of government. The goal of
deliberately shaping economic and social institutions to enhance economic
growth became, in many countries, "a more clearly accepted responsibility
of government than it was before" (1964: 84). Governments had been unable
to carry on the war simply by collecting and spending funds and leaving the
organization of industry to private individuals. No nation had entrusted its
war effort to a market economy directed and stimulated solely by financial
means. Governments demanded restrictions of the market through control
of profits, prices, and wages. These institutional changes, Kuznets argues,
would have emerged in the course of time without the world wars: "the war
accelerated trends but did not create them" (1964: 85).

This argument is that the changes that occurred after World War II were
the result of "learning." According to this argument, governments previously
had not known how to industrialize on the basis of the internal market. More
specifically, they did not know how to create the mass demand necessary for
industrialization to proceed on the basis of the internal market. The economic
knowledge was not there.

But government-induced demand creation was not a twentieth-century invention. It was a key feature in Europe's nineteenth-century industrial expansion. Almost universally, national governments in Europe were involved in weapons procurement, building railways and ports, and the expansion and control of credit institutions. Government demand (and foreign inputs) substituted for missing developmental "prerequisites" such as capital, skills, and a home market for industrial goods (Morris and Adelman 1988: 123–24).

The British state was active in the advancement of navigation and trade and in the regulation of colonial economies, and promoted through protectionist legislation the growth of new and rising industries (Mathias 1983: chaps. 3–5). The French state organized and supported a major expansion of the French steel industry and French railroads, under the Second Empire of Napoleon III (1852–70) and under the Third Empire (e.g., the Freycinét Plan of 1878). In Germany, the economic role of the Steurräte and Fabrikinspektoren and the Bismarckian policy of economic and industrial expansion continued a line of state activity in the development of domestic industries begun by Frederick the Great's policies of public aid and investment benefiting textile and chemical factories (Henderson 1958; Pounds 1959; Supple 1973: 311, 317, 327–29; Price 1981: 159–68). The German government's procurement of explosives was important to the development of its chemical industry. Italy's steel industry constructed in the 1890s depended on state contracts and guarantees. The industrial takeoff of tsarist Russia was accomplished by state agencies, which not only established infrastructure and banking institutions, but also worked to encourage investment via fiscal policy (Gerschenkron 1962: 119–52). The same is true of industrial development in the Scandinavian countries (Jörberg 1973). The "American Model" had been available for export by the 1870s. By the end of 1914, the machinery of government had vastly expanded in Britain. It was nationalizing industries, raising taxes, limiting profits, controlling labor relations, and imposing rationing and price controls to effect equitable distribution. During the interwar period, and particularly during the years of the Great Depression, the Soviet Union had demonstrated that central governments could in fact control economic development effectively. During the Depression, at a time when unemployment in the West had reached frightening proportions and industrial production in the principal capitalist countries had declined below the level of 1913, the West had observed that the Soviet Union, which had suffered severe unemployment in the period of the New Economic Policy, was faced with a shortage of labor at a time that its industrial production had increased almost fourfold (Barraclough 1967: 208–9).

Moreover, if the shift that oriented investment and production toward the domestic market after World War II was the result of learning, that is, of gaining a better or different understanding of demand management, then why has this learning not benefited growth in the contemporary developing world? Why are the countries of Asia, the Middle East, Africa, and Latin America not expanding and integrating their domestic markets? Some comparative historical reflections are in order, both for clarifying the nature of Europe's postwar growth and laying the foundation for an alternative explanation for it.

Liberal historiography tends to define a sharp distinction between the West and the rest of the world. Among other things, this tends to obscure the fact that Europe's growth in the nineteenth century was not spectacular relative to the rest of the globe. Between 1870 and 1913, per capita national income in Colombia, Brazil, and Mexico grew faster than in Britain and France and in much of Central and Southeast Europe (Furtado 1963: 162–65; Lewis 1978a: 216; see Halperin 1997a: statistical appendix, tables 10 and 11). In fact, on the eve of World War I, the richest Latin American countries were as rich as the richest European countries, and the poorest European countries were poorer than the poorest Latin American countries. In fact, according to Arthur Lewis (1978a), Argentina, Chile, and Uruguay had a standard of living that was well in excess of that of Europe. In these countries, average export levels in 1913 were above those of France, Germany, and Sweden (Banks 1971: 171–205). In Brazil, Colombia, Venezuela, and Cuba, agricultural exports grew just about as fast as industrial production in the leading industrial countries. In those countries that took advantage of this, output per head grew as rapidly as in Western Europe before 1914.[5] In the decades before World War I, the annual rate of growth of exports of Argentina, Brazil, Ecuador, Peru, Colombia, Mexico, and Uruguay was greater than that of Belgium, France, and Great Britain (see Halperin 1997a: statistical appendix, tables 1, 7–10). In sum, on the eve of World War I, and despite its earlier start, Europe as a whole had achieved a level of economic development and well being about equal with that of Latin America.

It was the world wars that divided the fortunes of Europe and what today we call the third world. After the world wars a gap opened up between Europe and the third world. But *not* because Latin American growth slowed; it did not. In fact, its rate of growth increased. Between 1913 and 1950, the annual average GDP growth for Latin America as a whole was 3.5 percent (as against only 1.9 percent for the countries that today are the advanced capitalist countries; Maddison 1991: 17). Between 1945 and 1955, total output rose at an annual rate of about 4.9 percent and output per capita by 2.4 percent (United Nations, Department of Economics and Social Affairs, 1956: 3; see also Kuznets 1971: 30–31; Bairoch 1975: 184). But though the rate of Latin American growth increased, it simply could not keep up with the

---

[5] Stover 1970: 62; Lewis 1978a: 223. Argentina, Chile, Brazil, Columbia, Cuba, Venezuela, and Mexico contain 66 percent of the region's population.

phenomenal and unprecedented surge of growth experienced by European countries following World War II.[6]

Many of the factors regarded as the chief obstacles to economic development in third world countries – lack of savings, shortage of entrepreneurs and skilled labor, inflation – do not explain the lag in Latin American development relative to European growth after 1945. There was an unprecedented inflow of foreign investment into Latin America after 1955. Its rate of savings was not very much below that of the advanced Western countries. Its entrepreneurs were sufficiently numerous and talented to have increased its production of goods and services by 60 percent between 1945 and 1958. The labor force was sufficient to allow the manufacturing industry to expand its production by 90 percent during that period. Monetary instability was not an obstacle: inflation-ridden countries, such as Brazil, developed at a rapid rate, while fairly stable ones, such as Cuba, progressed slowly (Ahumada 1963: 115).

World systems and dependency theories attribute underdevelopment in Latin America to its incorporation into the world economy as a raw material producing area (e.g., Wallerstein 1974: 392; Cardoso and Faletto 1979: 16– 21, 23–24). But many of today's advanced capitalist countries followed this route (e.g., the United States, Canada, Denmark, Sweden, and Australia), and Latin American countries had as much opportunity to industrialize with the revenues from staple exports as they did. In fact, those Latin American countries that participated in the world economy through the export of primary products experienced a rapid internal accumulation of capital and the growth of productive forces. The question, then, is why did raw material production and export and the internal accumulation of capital not "spur the growth of domestic industry"? (Zeitlin 1984: 17). Though Latin American countries were just as capable of developing an industrial complex of skills, institutions, and ideas, they did not do so. The growth of exporting offered Latin American countries the opportunity to strengthen their infrastructure, increase productivity in food, and move toward industrialization for home and export markets, but they did not do so.

In Latin America, as in Europe before the world wars, power was concentrated in the hands of landed classes, who benefited from cheap imports and saw no reason to develop an internal market, widen the geographic and sectoral spread of economic growth, and support the emergence of new classes (Lewis 1978b: 11). There, as in Europe, success in exporting motivated entrenched groups and classes dependent on the export trade *not* to industrialize but to monopolize resources and to block reforms that favor the emergence of new classes. As a result, foreign investment and aid to Latin America has failed to bring about the changes that, some argue, occurred

---

[6] Exports from developing countries rose at an average annual rate of 4.8 percent, but in the industrialized countries it rose 7.9 percent (Lord and Boye 1991: 121).

in Western Europe as a result of Marshall aid after World War II. Nor have regional organizations and trade liberalization there, or in Asia, Africa, and elsewhere, had the impact attributed to them in the Western European context. In these regions, the internal restructuring that occurred in European countries *prior* to the investment of funds and the establishment of regional institutions has yet to occur.

The difference between today's advanced industrial countries and Latin America is that, in the former countries, there was a change in the balance of class forces. This change did not come about gradually over the course of centuries, but within a short period of time and as a result of much violence and destruction. In the United States, where a strong landowning class developed in the south, a struggle between landowners and industrialists culminated in civil war and the victory of the industrial capitalist bourgeoisie. As a result, smallholder patterns of land ownership evolved there. The balance of class forces changed in Russia, as a result of the civil war of 1917–22, and throughout the rest of Europe in the course of the world wars. In Japan, a massive and spectacularly successful land reform, imposed by the Allied powers after World War II, brought about a transfer of political power and the transformation of its economy and society.[7] In Australia, Canada, and New Zealand, the landowning classes were circumscribed from the start, and so revenues were not used solely to enrich a traditional landowning class and their allies, as they were in Europe and in Latin America.[8] These were the countries that were able to participate fully in the historically unprecedented boom of the 1950s and 1960s.

Latin American countries, meanwhile, have neglected to expand and integrate their domestic markets not because they failed to learn lessons learned in the West but because they did not experience the massive slaughter and destruction that Europe suffered as a result of the two world wars. Crises arose there during the Great Depression and the era of the world wars, but these led only to a retrenchment of traditional structures. Corporative arrangements were introduced that perpetuated the traditional order on a renewed basis and turned urban laborers into industrial serfs. As a result, the developmental trajectories of the two regions began rapidly to diverge. As many analysts have pointed out, the issues that are central to development are not technical issues but political ones. The full mobilization of domestic

---

[7] Before the reform, 54 percent of the cultivated land was owner-operated; after the reform 92 percent was owned by farmers. Between 1947 and 1949 the government bought and resold 5.8 million acres of land. Three years after the beginning of the reform, approximately three million peasants had acquired land. On the Japanese land reform, see United Nations Economic Commission for Asia and the Far East, *Economic Survey of Asia and the Far East* (New York, 1950), pp. 188–89; and U.S. Department of Agriculture, *Agricultural Geography of Europe and the Near East* (Washington, D.C., September 1951), pp. 187–89.

[8] In these countries, there was no preexisting landed elite, and the colonists displaced, overwhelmed, or destroyed prior inhabitants.

labor (full employment) leads to rising wages and a shift in the distribution of profit to productive capital and to labor. That is why government spending to maintain full employment encounters political obstacles. As Michael Kalecki argued, "the assumption that a government will maintain full employment in a capitalist economy if it only knows how to do it is fallacious" (1971: 138).

Explanations that attribute Europe's postwar growth to evolutionary developments and learning are consistent with the assumptions of liberal historiography and, in particular, with its key assumption: that positive change in every realm can be explained with reference to the progress of modernization and economic growth or to the logic of industrial development. Explanations of the "origins" and "development" of the welfare state after World War II are based on the same assumption.[9] What these explanations imply, as Asa Briggs notes, is that the history of the nineteenth and twentieth centuries led "inevitably and inexorably along a broad highway with the 'welfare state' as its destination" (Briggs 1962: 221, 222). This, Briggs rightfully points out, represents an attempt to rewrite history. They ignore the fact that, as Chapter 2 argued, welfare systems had existed well before the advent of industrialization, and so were neither a concomitant of it nor a result of a process of evolution during the course of it. Such arguments also misunderstand the nature of the changes that occurred throughout Europe following World War II. These changes, as Schumpeter and others have pointed out, represented not a further evolution of nineteenth-century trends but "a massive capitulation" to social democracy.

The abolition of the poor law systems and the shift to universalist, tax-financed benefit systems following World War II was not the culmination of trends set in motion by Bismarck's social welfare schemes of the 1880s. These schemes had had as their goal the subordination of labor to the state. Their goal was not the equality of labor but its subservience through dependence on the state (Briggs 1962: 249). A "welfare state" is

a state in which organized power is deliberately used (through politics and administration) in an effort to modify the play of market forces in at least three directions – first by guaranteeing individuals and families a minimum income irrespective of the market value of their work or their property; second, by narrowing the extent of insecurity by enabling individuals and families to meet certain "social contingencies" (for example, sickness, old age, unemployment) which lead otherwise to individual and family crises; and third, by ensuring that all citizens without distinction of status or class are offered the best standards available in relation to a certain agreed range of social services. (Briggs 1962: 228)

The welfare state emerged as a result of the world wars and because the victor in those wars was the social democracy of noncommunist labor movements.

[9] See, e.g., Bruce 1966; Gilbert 1966; Wilensky 1975; De Swaan 1988.

The welfare state bore the mark of these movements in both its goals and its policy instruments.

After World War II, every country in Europe adopted the principle of a planned economy. This, and the radical changes in the structure of European economies that followed from it, owed much, as E. H. Carr pointed out, to "the Soviet example" (Carr 1947: 44). Following World War II, the policies of the Bolsheviks became the model for the changes instituted throughout Europe, both in the East and in the West. Virtually every European nation introduced some form of economic planning during the postwar period.[10] All agreed that economic development could and should be "planned" and that social policy could and should both foster economic development and minimize its possible negative effects.

In addition to a planned economy, Britain implemented, at least in part, key elements of the social democratic agenda between 1945 and 1951: substantial nationalization, socialized medicine, the extension of welfare, the dismantling of empire, and the narrowing of income differentials. The government nationalized the coal industry, electricity and gas, railways and road transportation, iron and steel, and the Bank of England. By the late 1960s, government provision, subsidy, contract, and regulation had become pervasive.

In France, government officials and business executives adopted the opinion, long held by labor leaders and widespread in the Resistance, that some form of planning was required to overcome the continual economic crises of the preceding decades. The need for a more interventionist state – state planning, nationalization, big public investments, "economic and social democracy," state control over cartels, prices or capital movements – one of the main planks of Resistance platforms, was accepted by postwar governments. The state began to promote measures of income redistribution and showed concern for social welfare on a scale unknown before (Hoffmann 1961: 49–50).

What could have compelled this massive capitulation to social democratic reforms that previously had been so strenuously and often violently resisted? As Schumpeter and many others observed, a decisive shift in the balance of class power had occurred throughout Europe as a result of World War II, and this explained not only the transformation that had taken place there but its apparent permanence:

The business class has accepted "gadgets of regulation" and "new fiscal burdens, a mere fraction of which it would have felt to be unbearable fifty years ago. . . . *And it does not matter whether the business class accepts this new situation or not. The power of labor is almost strong enough in itself* – and amply so in alliance with the other groups

[10] For the influence of the Soviet example on "planning," see Hobsbawm 1996: 96–97. Of course, the type and extent of planning varied considerably, and not all changes in all countries evolved from a study of the Soviet example.

that have in fact, if not in words, renounced allegiance to the scheme of values of the private-profit economy – *to prevent any reversal* which goes beyond an occasional scaling off of rough edges.[11]

As Schumpeter observed, a shift in the balance of power meant that the changes that had occurred following World War II would not be reversed. Previous regional conflagrations had been followed by restorations (e.g., the Napoleonic Wars, the revolutions of 1830 and 1848, and World War I). After World War I, despite government promises to reward labor for its wartime cooperation, the attempt by Britain's Ministry of Reconstruction and its host of subcommittees to make good on those promises, to create new systems of land tenure, social insurance and public health, education, and employment, came to naught. Instead, forces of resistance had worked "to restore the social and economic conditions of 1914" (Abrams 1963: 58). However, after World War II, a shift in the balance of social power and consequent changes throughout the class structure made restoration impossible. Instead, a thoroughgoing reconstruction took place on the basis of redistributive policies that, before the world wars, had been effectively blocked. Throughout Western Europe, conservative parties were as committed to the welfare state and to government action to ameliorate social problems as their leftist opponents. Returned to power in 1951, the British Conservatives ruled for the next fifteen years, but did not attempt to dismantle the welfare provisions introduced by the Labour governments of the reconstruction period. British Conservative leader Harold Macmillan argued for "the Socialist remedy" wherever "private enterprise had exhausted its social usefulness, or where the general welfare of the economy requires that certain basic industries and services need now to be conducted in the light of broader social considerations than the profit motive will supply" (Marwick 1974: 198).

A number of influential studies have argued that, while a shift in the balance of social forces transformed Europe, it did not primarily involve an increase in the power of labor. Rather, the shift that occurred was within the capitalist class and as a result of *intra*class struggles over different methods of production. It was this that was determinative of the transformation that took place in the course of the wars (see, e.g., van der Pijl 1984, 1998).

---

[11] 1976: 419–20; emphasis added. With the elements of post–World War II economic orthodoxy accepted by the business class and by a large number of economists after the war, he noted, "we have traveled far indeed from the principles of laissez-faire capitalism" (1976: 418). These new gadgets, according to Schumpeter (1976: 218), included the following:

  1. a large amount of public management of business situations;
  2. the desirability of greater equality of incomes and, in connection with this, the principle of redistributive taxation;
  3. a rich assortment of regulative measures;
  4. public control over the labor and money markets;
  5. indefinite extension of the sphere of wants that are to be satisfied by public enterprise;
  6. all types of security legislation.

An intraclass division began to open up during the interwar period as a result of World War I. In Britain, this was evident by the chasm that by 1939 divided Chamberlain and Churchill. Confronted with more powerful and militant working classes as a result of the war, elements of capital began to recognize the limits of the system. It became apparent that far more dire social externalities might be produced by a continuing dependence on methods of increasing absolute surplus value than those that the U.S. model showed might be produced by a shift to relative surplus value production. The narrowing prospects for increasing overseas markets and the escalating costs it entailed also must have become increasingly apparent. Moreover, a "Second Industrial Revolution" was occurring, made up of the electrical, chemical, and auto industries, comprised of relatively large firms with capital-intensive processes. These industries

were bound to look upon good labour relations and high and steady levels of production as more important than low wages and mere cheapness. Since their products and production runs demanded a more homogeneous market of high-income consumers, they were also more interested in the domestic and Dominion markets than with those of India and the less developed world or even Europe. (Boyce 1987: 11)

That elements of Britain's capitalist class were beginning to consider the possibilities of the U.S. model was apparent from discussions of the U.S. experience during the 1920s and, in light of that experience, the importance of the home market for British manufacturers and the need to reconsider Britain's approach to foreign lending and its reliance on overseas markets (see, e.g., Boyce 1987: 102–5).

However, though there were differences among fractions of capital during the interwar years, the revolutionary currents unleashed by World War I increasingly polarized European societies and, in this way, worked effectively to keep the capitalist class unified. As a result, the continuing prominence of the traditional elite was evident in 1939 and later.

The mobilization of the masses for war in 1914, for the first time since the Napoleonic Wars, had vastly increased the organizational strength and power of the working classes. The need for mass mobilization again in the 1940s was decisive in increasing the political power of workers relative to that of capital.

Many scholars have argued that alterations in class structures are brought about in just this way, that is, by participation in war efforts "by formerly underprivileged social groups."[12] Participation in areas of work and social life usually barred to them strengthens the market position of disadvantaged classes and imbues them with a new sense of status (Marwick 1974: 12–13). As Chapter 5 has shown, an important effect of World War I was

---

[12] Marwick 1974: 10; see also Titmuss 1958: 86; Andreski 1968: 33–38; Marwick 1980: chap. 11.

to stimulate a much more aggressive consciousness and pattern of activity among the working class. Massive numbers of workers took part in the labor upheavals during and after the war. The industrial strife of these years continued without cessation throughout World War II. The number of days lost due to strikes steadily rose during each year of the war. In 1945, it was double what it had been in 1939 (Marwick 1974: 158).

Moreover, the need for their participation induces governments to buy or reward their support for the war effort by direct government action.[13] During World War I, workers were promised that their sacrifices would be rewarded with a better standard of living after the war. These promises remained unfulfilled. In World War II, governments once again called for the support of labor. This time, however, the demand for labor compelled a political accommodation with the working-class movement:

Trade unions were recognized as the accredited agents of the working class, their officials were recruited to government advisory committees to ensure that labor, an increasingly scarce commodity, was used fully and effectively for the purpose of prosecuting the war and they were drawn into decision-making processes from which they had traditionally been excluded.[14]

In World War II, the experience of full employment and of equitable distribution effected through taxation, rationing, and price control led to strong popular demands for a postwar society free from unemployment and inequality of opportunity. During the war, "the knowledge that large sums of money, raised through taxation at a level without precedent, were being used to wage war led without difficulty to the conclusion that smaller sums of money could produce a 'welfare state' in times of peace" (Briggs 1962: 227). World War II could not be won "unless millions of ordinary people ... were convinced that we had something better to offer than had [their nation's] enemies – not only during but after the war" (*The Times*, July 1, 1940). The war, after all, was being fought in alliance with the Soviet Union to defeat the fascist "bulwark against Bolshevism." Capitalists needed their cooperation not only in the war against fascism but also, after the defeat of fascism, in order to resume the war against socialism. Thus, in Britain, it was "an imperative for war strategy" for the authorities to concern themselves with that elusive concept "civilian morale" (Titmuss 1958: 82). As a result, even before the end of the war, preparations were under way to meet the demands of workers for social justice, for the abolition of privilege, for a more equitable distribution of income and wealth, and for drastic changes in the economic and social life of the country.

---

[13] In Britain, the "price" of Labour's support for the war, wrote Harold Laski in 1940, was to be the construction of "a more equal society" (Laski 1940: 145).

[14] Waites 1987: 29. Under Asquith, Arthur Henderson entered the Cabinet as president of the Board of Education; under Lloyd George he was admitted into the War Cabinet, and George Barnes was appointed Minister of Pensions.

In response to trade union pressure, the British government appointed a committee in May 1941 to study "existing national schemes of social insurance and allied services" and to work out a comprehensive plan of social security. Sir William Beveridge, who was appointed by parliament to head this committee, expressed his belief in a central tenet of social democratic thought: that "private control of the means of production, with the right to employ others at a wage in using those means, cannot be described as an essential liberty of the British people" and that "full employment and social security for all are the aims which the country will expect its government to achieve, whatever sacrifices are entailed."[15]

Beveridge's blueprint for a "universalist" welfare state envisioned the state as maintainer of full employment and provider of free health service and family allowances. In contrast to most of the prewar social services, all citizens irrespective of income or class were to contribute and were to be entitled to benefits. The report that he put forward in 1942 recommended a comprehensive social insurance system for the entire nation and suggested that there was a need for a national health service, avoidance of mass unemployment, child allowances, and enlightened national policies for housing and education. While the government's reception of the Beveridge Report was cool, it became a matter of public debate and widespread enthusiasm (Marwick 1974: 158). Three White Papers of 1944 entitled "Social Insurance," "Full Employment," and "A National Health Service" established the model of postwar welfare services. Labor's victory in the general election of 1945 ensured their adoption.

In Britain, the wartime demand for labor compelled a political accommodation of the working-class movement. Trade unions were drawn into decision-making processes from which they had traditionally been excluded. Moreover, fascism and the sacrifices entailed in defeating it effectively discredited the old right throughout Europe.[16] Thus, even where workers were not mobilized for the war effort as, for instance, in France, the balance of political power after the war shifted in their favor. In France, a restoration in 1945–46 brought back parties discredited in 1940 and political institutions close to those of the Third Republic. But the old right was sufficiently discredited by Vichy to enable power to fall into the hands of groups who for one reason or another did not belong to or had become separated from the former "stalemate society" (Hoffmann 1961). Until its dissolution

---

[15] *The Economist*, July 18, 1942, pp. 66, 67; and August 8, 1942, p. 166; in Menderhausen 1943: 331.

[16] The widespread discrediting of the old right can be seen in the strategic realignment of the Catholic Church. Before the war, the Church had generally allied with the right in European politics. After the war, and in varied contexts, the alliance of Catholicism and the old right ended. It withdrew from explicit politics altogether (steering clear, especially, of the politics of a restorationist right) and generally became an advocate of the welfare state.

in 1958, the Fourth Republic bore characteristics of the Third, but the political personnel of the Third Republic never succeeded in regaining its former power.

SOCIAL STRUCTURE AND DEVELOPMENT IN POSTWAR EUROPE

The world war era represents a great divide in modern European history. Though revolutions in Europe in 1789, in the 1820s and 1830s, and in 1848 had given a stronger position to industrialists and bankers, weakened the landlords' influence, and, in places, partly replaced the political personnel, they failed to bring about a thoroughgoing transformation of social structures. Except in Russia after 1917, the traditional social structure of Europe remained essentially intact up until 1945. The suffrage was expanded, and legislatures and local governments were reformed, but economic and social structures remained essentially the same. In the course of the wars of 1914 and 1939, this social, economic, and political world was swept away.

Though the structure of European society was profoundly affected by the Great War, forces of resistance in the years that followed delayed the final breakdown of traditional society. Thus, despite the massive destruction of the First World War and the enormous changes that took place during the course of it and immediately following it, it was the Second World War that was the great watershed in modern European history. This was by far the most destructive of all wars. The scale of destruction and disruption of European economic life and the extent of the damage and loss of production was far greater than that which Europe had experienced in the First World War.[17]

Social Structures

World War II brought about a thoroughgoing breakdown of the old class structure of Europe. As a result, since World War II, "structural changes in almost all aspects of economic and social life have been greater than during the previous 200 years" (Bairoch 1993: 175). Large-scale changes took place throughout the class structure after the war. The role of the property elite in the economic field was limited by the development of state-owned enterprises, the introduction of a capital-gains tax, and the growth of managerial power (Aron 1950: 129). In Britain, country houses were demolished; taxes and death duties rose to unprecedented heights; and urban estates that had survived the interwar period were put up for sale (Cannadine 1980: 417–20). In the political sphere, the monopoly of power of the upper class was

[17] See the *General Report of the Committee of European Economic Cooperation*, Paris, September 1, 1947.

broken. In Great Britain, Germany, and the Scandinavian countries, access to power of the social democratic parties and their predominantly middle-class leadership changed the composition of the political elite. In France, a return to the former "stalemate society" became impossible (Hoffmann 1961). In Eastern Europe, the Communist Party dislodged the former upper classes and recruited new elites from among the lower and middle ranks.

Increasing job opportunities in the service sector swelled the ranks of the middle class. The expansion of the service sector, the development of new technologies, and the availability of consumer products to large proportions of the population also decreased the difference between the middle and working classes, and greater access to education opened up the path to middle-class status.[18] The blue-collar working class, those employed in mining, manufacturing, transport, building, and artisanal trades, lost its primacy as the largest segment of the work force in many European societies. By the 1980s, Romania was the only country in which the tertiary sector employed less than 30 percent of the active population.[19]

The provision of health care, education, and other social services, the revival of trade unions, and, following their nineteenth-century intentions, their provision of facilities and institutions for the working class[20] improved the minimum standard of living for the working class. Lower paid and least skilled workers gained through a narrowing of pay differentials. In Western Europe, the average level of real earnings of industrial or manual workers in 1948 was almost a fifth higher than in 1938 (Milward 1984: 486). In the German Democratic Republic, real wages more than tripled in this period; in Bulgaria, Yugoslavia, and Romania, they rose by over 150 percent (Aldcroft 1978: 212–15). Lower paid workers also benefited from the lowering of housing rents and the greater security of employment compared with before the war.

During the nineteenth century and until the beginning of the 1950s, manufacturing productivity in Western Europe had increased at a rate almost twice as fast as that of agriculture. Since the 1950s the converse has been true. Between 1850 and 1950, productivity increased annually by 1.8 to 2 percent in industry, compared with 1.1 to 1.3 percent in agriculture. Between 1950 and 1990, this increase was 3.4 to 3.5 percent in industry and 5.4 to 5.6 percent in agriculture (Bairoch 1993: 151, 175; see also Bairoch 1989).

---

[18] Middle-class status generally implies work that is not manual labor, a minimal level of education, payment by salary rather than by hourly wages, and a number of the comforts of consumer society.

[19] Tipton and Aldrich 1987b: 173. By 1980, the tertiary sector accounted for at least 60 percent of employment in Belgium, Denmark, Norway, the Netherlands, Sweden, and Switzerland, and at least 50 percent in Austria, Finland, France, Luxembourg, and the United Kingdom.

[20] One major West German union, for example, owned the fourth largest bank in Germany, the largest insurance company, the largest property development firm, and one of the three largest travel agencies (Tipton and Aldrich 1987b: 178).

This is important, since before 1914 almost half of Western Europe's working population was employed in agriculture (including fishing and forestry). By 1955, the farming population represented only 24 percent of the total (Laqueur 1992: 179). Employment in agriculture declined dramatically in France (from 5.2 million in 1954 to 3.9 million in 1962) and in West Germany (from 5.1 million in 1950 to 3.6 million in 1961). In Italy, agricultural employment fell from 8.3 million to 5.6 million and industrial employment rose from 6.3 million to 7.9 million between 1951 and 1961. During the 1960s, Spain began to follow along the same path.

By the late 1970s, nowhere in Europe did agricultural workers account for a majority of the labor force, and only in Greece, Poland, and Portugal did they make up a quarter of the workers. Most European countries had less than 10 percent of their work force in agriculture (Tipton and Aldrich 1987b: 114, 173).

All countries in Eastern Europe underwent a political and social revolution in the postwar period involving a complete change in the system of property relationships and the emergence of the state as the main agent of economic activity. In Romania, Bulgaria, and Hungary, military defeat brought the collapse of the old order; in Poland, Czechoslovakia, and Yugoslavia, the old order collapsed with the overthrow of German and quisling governments. In Czechoslovakia, where alone of all the Eastern European countries there was a large organized body of industrial workers, two large socialist parties (the Communists and the Social Democrats) gained a majority of votes and seats in elections held in 1946 (the Communists won 38 percent and the Social Democrats won 12 percent of the vote). Communists came to power through free elections in Romania in November 1946 (Hammond 1971). The former upper classes were dislodged from government bureaucracies, and new elites from among the lower and middle ranks were recruited.

Before WWII, the countries that are now part of Eastern Europe were the most economically backward, except Czechoslovakia, Poland, and Hungary. Except for Czechoslovakia, every Eastern European country was predominantly rural; industrial workers were a minority in Poland, Hungary, Romania, Yugoslavia, and Bulgaria. From 1950 to 1970, unprecedented and rapid economic and especially industrial growth throughout Eastern Europe shifted a majority of labor and capital into nonagricultural activities within one generation (Lampe and Jackson 1982: 576). In percentage terms the structural transformation of East Germany nearly matched that of West Germany, and in Bulgaria the share of agriculture in the labor force declined from 80 percent in 1950 to 40 percent in 1970.

The agrarian policies of the new regimes in Eastern Europe generally followed those of the Soviet Union. In the first phase, large estates were "confiscated from the former owners without compensation and redistributed free among the peasants, with the state retaining a part for its own purposes" (Aldcroft 1978: 170). The outcome of this phase by 1950 was described as follows:

Generally speaking, throughout central and eastern Europe the principle applies that
the land belongs to those who work it, and there is everywhere a maximum area of
land which can be owned by one person, 100 hectares (250 acres) or 50 hectares.
This does not mean that the majority of the peasants owns anything like so much,
especially in those countries which have a surplus peasant population, but it does
mean that many small holdings have been increased beyond starvation size. (Betts
1950: 201)

The most important of the postwar land reforms was the Hungarian.
According to a 1945 survey, 0.8 percent of the total number of holdings
(holdings of more then 100 Hungarian acres) possessed 48 percent of the
land, while 93 percent of the holdings (those of less than 20 acres) possessed
only 32 percent. As a result of the land reform begun in 1945, holdings
above 100 acres were reduced to 20 percent of the total holdings; the
share of holdings under 20 acres increased to 65 percent. The state retained
42 percent of the confiscated land; 26 percent of this was forest land,
7 percent was pasture land, and 9 percent was put to miscellaneous use.
Some 58 percent of the confiscated land was redistributed to landless
laborers and smallholders with too little land to support their families
(Seton-Watson 1951: 265–66). In Czechoslovakia, 1,650,000 hectares of
arable land were confiscated. Of this, 1,300,000 were distributed to new
owners, two-fifths of which were landless laborers and smallholders with
too little land to support their families (Seton-Watson 1951: 266).

In Albania before the war, one-third of the fertile land of the country
belonged to 200 landowners. In 1945, the communist regime confiscated
all holdings of over 20 hectares. Private forest land was taken by the state,
and some arable land was given to state farms and agricultural schools.
Some 320,000 hectares were divided among 60,000 peasant families (Seton-
Watson 1951: 267). In Romania, the great estates had been broken up by
land reforms in 1918. However, in the following twenty years, land had
again changed hands, so that in 1944 there existed once again a substantial
class of big landowners. The new land reform in 1945 confiscated 1,423,145
hectares. Of this, 329,048 hectares were used for various state agricultural
enterprises; 1,094,097 were given to 828,853 landless laborers and peasant
smallholders (Seton-Watson 1951: 267).

In Yugoslavia, about four million acres of land, much of it belonging to
the Catholic Church, the banks, and the *Volkdeutsche*, were expropriated
by the state; about half of it was redistributed to the peasants (Warriner
1950: 136). In Poland, 9,327 large rural estates (covering approximately six
million hectares) were expropriated and were given to more than a million
peasant families, 76 percent of whom were formerly landless and 24 percent of whom were smallholders. In addition, 10,662 industrial and 2,252
commercial enterprises were nationalized (Vaughan 1971: 322).

This phase of postwar agrarian policy resulted in "an extreme fragmentation of holdings." The next step, therefore, was to organize "the cooperative pooling of farm units" (Aldcroft 1978: 170). This was accomplished during the course of the 1950s. By the beginning of the 1960s, agricultural production had largely been collectivized.[21]

Planning

The restructuring of social elites made possible the expansion of the powers and responsibilities of central governments. Most governments were committed not just to rebuilding economies but to changing the economy's method of functioning. In Britain, there was large-scale expenditure by government in support of research. The Industrial Reconstruction Corporation helped reconstruct and accelerate growth of companies. A Prices and Incomes Board was established with varying powers over price and income changes. There were monopoly laws to encourage efficiency and investment incentives to encourage capital formation. By the early 1970s, the government became responsible for approximately 35 percent of investment expenditure (56 percent if the nationalized industries are included) and for some 16 percent of consumption expenditure (Youngson 1973: 175).

The goals of France's First Economic Plan (Monnet Plan) for the period 1947–50 were to develop and modernize the coal, electricity, iron and steel, cement, and transport sectors in order to eliminate existing bottlenecks. Though no production quotas were established as in the Soviet planning system, the plan established for each sector aimed at a 25 percent increase in 1929 in industrial and agricultural output and a substantial rise in the standard of living. The Second Plan (1952–57) and Third Plan (1958–61) sought to accelerate industrial productivity (6 percent per year) and specialization, to improve outlets for agricultural produce, and to ensure full employment. Guidelines were laid down for channeling investment into areas where it was most needed. A Fourth Plan (1962–67) concentrated on improving the lot of low-income wage earners and farmers and on developing backward regions (Fohlen 1973: 96–97).

In 1960, the nationalized sector of the Austrian economy employed 30 percent of the labor force and produced nearly a third of total exports. The ratio of public sector outlays to gross national income exceeded 50 percent in Scandinavia and the Netherlands in the 1970s (Aldcroft 1978: 186). In Switzerland, the government controlled massive flows of investment in public utilities and housing, and in those fields exercised a substantial influence on other sectors as well (Tipton and Aldrich 1987b: 122).

In the Netherlands, a body with responsibility for planning economic policy, the Centraal Planbureau, was created in 1945. The primary aims of

[21] Poland and Yugoslavia were exceptions.

economic policy in the late 1940s were full employment, stable prices, and equilibrium in the balance of payments; economic growth and a just distribution of rewards became policy aims in the 1950s (De Vries 1973: 43). The West German government inherited extensive industrial interests from the Nazi regime that it organized into two massive holding companies. After the war, there was an intensification of existing economic controls of production and consumption. A mixed system, combining the market principle and central guidance, characterized the economy after 1948 (Hardach 1973). At the end of the war, Italy possessed large state-owned enterprises. After the war, state intervention in the economy was broadened and reinforced by means of public concerns operating in the sectors of the industry, transport and communications, credit, and so on. In 1957, the Ministry of State Holdings was established with the purpose of guiding and coordinating public concerns. Through holding companies, the Italian government controlled fully one-third of the economy (Tipton and Aldrich 1987b: 201).

Though industrial expansion had been encouraged during the war in many East European countries in order to support the German war effort, Germany had had no interest in developing large new industries in Eastern Europe. After the war, however, it was Soviet economic policy to develop industry in Eastern Europe as a cure for the rural overpopulation and poverty that characterized the area before the world wars (Seton-Watson 1951: 262–63).

In Eastern Europe, central governments had controlled much of the heavy industrial sector even before the war. The state had owned important industrial enterprises, and there had been state agencies with wide powers in agriculture, trade, and finance. This inheritance derived not only from the experiences of the Depression, rearmament, and the Second World War, but also from the long-standing legacy of governments more powerful than any private sector of the economy, industry in particular (Lampe and Jackson 1982: 573–74).

What was new, however, was the commitment of Soviet-style planning and a new Communist set of top managers to an overriding emphasis on heavy industry and balanced growth, with capital for almost all investment coming directly from the state budget. Governments imposed Soviet-style central planning and used it, with the state budget as the financial means for assembling savings, to distribute investment and spread technological skills. The coalition governments and later socialist regimes eventually nationalized all economic activity, instituting a system of planning directed by central agencies modeled on those of the Soviet Union. All decisions affecting the economic process were planned and determined centrally. Centrally drawn up plans set out in detail targets to be met in different sectors of the economy. The functions were carried out in each case by State Planning Commissions or Offices. By 1949, most major branches of economic activity apart from agriculture were owned and operated by the state. By 1952, only traces of private enterprise remained outside agriculture.

After World War II, governments in Western Europe tended increasingly to consult organized interests outside parliament regarding legislation and administration. Consultation with industrial and labor organizations lay at the heart of the French style of "indicative" planning and was implicit in the extensive government shareholdings in private corporations in West Germany and Italy. In Switzerland, the legislative process continued to incorporate the "consultation of interests." In the Low Countries, successive coalition governments attempted to achieve consensus by cooperating with the major interest groups such as the Netherlands Federation of Labor and its Social-Economic Council and through the creation of government bodies such as the Belgian National Investment Corporation. In Austria, the process of balance and compromise reached such an advanced stage that virtually all legislation was passed unanimously when it finally appeared before the parliament. Corporatism was most completely developed in the Nordic countries under the leadership of the socialist parties and in the socialist countries of Eastern Europe.

The networks of public-private relations that evolved in Great Britain, France, Germany, Sweden, Italy, Belgium, and Holland bore a strong resemblance to the ideologies of the conservative regimes of the interwar period, especially Mussolini's fascist "corporations." However, these corporatist arrangements differed from prewar corporatism in two crucial ways: their inclusion of the working class and their elimination, rather than support, of monopoly and other restrictive policies and practices characteristic of the prewar era.

The Aims of Planning

In contrast to prewar economic policies, postwar policies were designed to expand domestic markets through increased production, rather than to divide up and exploit national markets through restrictive practices; to encourage competition rather than cartellization; to raise the level of earnings and of welfare of the working class; and to increase and regulate domestic investment. After 1945, policies were designed to produce sustained growth characterized by a more equitable distribution of income as well as rising income per head. Very large wage increases were conceded by many governments as one of their first acts following the war. In addition, raising the level of employment was treated as a very high priority in the formulation of development strategies and plans and in the laying down of investment criteria.[22] Governments focused on sustained investment, balanced growth, the elimination of monopoly, and the production of higher levels of welfare for the population.

---

[22] On the investment criteria debate of the 1950s, see Galenson and Leibenstein 1955; Dobb 1960; Sen 1960.

Investment. One of the major aims of government economic policy following the war was to raise the level of domestic investment. During the nineteenth century, the two largest foreign investors, Britain and France, had failed to invest adequately at home. In both countries, considerable surplus capital had gone into industrial investments elsewhere. After the war, however, all governments in Europe made every effort to boost domestic investment through cheap and easy credit, favorable tax provisions, and measures to stimulate savings.[23] The government itself became the largest single investor either directly in its own public enterprises or through intermediary channels.

Postwar French investment policy was representative of trends throughout Europe. After 1946, the French government regularly instituted a series of major investment plans that, among other things, defined targets for public and private investment and for housing. In addition to fostering private investment through loans, subsidies, and guarantees, the state itself was an important investor: between 1947 and 1951, some 30 percent of all investment came from government sources. New investment accounted for an average of 19 percent of each year's GNP between 1950 and 1960.[24]

As a result of government policies, private domestic investment increased. High levels of investment throughout Europe after 1945 were due not to reconstruction and replacement investment but to new investment and industrial expansion; in some cases, replacement investment was postponed so as not to impede new investment (see Milward 1984: 37–38, 478–85).

Increased domestic investment, steep increases in real earnings in most countries, and the great increase in the total volume of earnings in many opened up the prospect of a rapid growth in consumer goods markets (Milward 1984: 485). As a result, high rates of accumulation, which had seemed likely to end with the end of the postwar reconstruction, continued due to the growth of domestic consumption (Marglin and Schor 1990: 51).

There was a strong growth of the volume of exports after the war. However, until the mid-1960s, the proportion of resources devoted to exports (measured by the current price ratio of exports to GDP) declined in Europe. Production for international trade did not absorb an increasing proportion of labor within the advanced countries until the end of the 1960s. As Marglin and Schor point out, "in this sense the golden age of growth could be regarded as primarily domestically based" (1990: 51).

---

[23] German investment had averaged only 14 percent of gross national product from 1914 to 1949, but the average rate of investment rose to 27 percent from 1950 to 1970, while the total capital stock of West Germany's manufacturing sector doubled during the 1950s and doubled again during the 1960s (Tipton and Aldrich 1987b: 121). Investment figures for other countries in Europe are in Milward 1984: 36.

[24] Aldcroft 1978: 151. In other countries, the proportion was as high as one-half. Investment in Britain, however, has been a lower proportion of GDP than in the other countries of Western Europe. It was 17 percent of GDP in the early 1950s and 22 percent in the mid-1960s and early 1970s (Cairncross 1981: 379).

Regional Development. Another aim of postwar economic policy was to reverse the dualism of European economies by bringing regional developments more into balance. As a result of the dualistic expansion of the nineteenth century, rising disparities in regional income had become typical of many European countries. Regional inequality had become increasingly severe from the 1860s to World War I, and it remained prominent in most European countries until the end of World War II (Williamson 1965). Once-prosperous regions became backward, among them Brittany, parts of central and southeastern France, eastern Finland, and Transylvania. A regressive "devolution" took place in some rural areas of Germany, the Netherlands, and Scandinavia. Southern Italy and the Slav areas of Austria-Hungary became increasingly backward in relation to more advanced areas (Riggs 1964: 24–26; Badie and Birnbaum 1982: 25–64).

At the end of World War II, Britain's midlands and south were relatively prosperous, while large sectors of its Celtic periphery (Wales, Scotland, and Ireland) remained depressed and nonindustrial. In France, enormous regional disparities had emerged after the 1870s. Industrial activity became concentrated in the north and northeast, while most of the Midi, Brittany, the center-east mountainous areas, and the southeastern and southwestern margins of the Paris basin became characterized by archaic agriculture, low levels of commercialization, the survival of only residual industry, and demographic decline (Price 1981: 237–38). In 1945, Jean-Francois Gravier described France as an "island" of prosperity, centered on Paris, surrounded by "the French Desert" (Gravier 1947). In 1945, Germany was still a country where large sectors of the economy were characterized by landless peasants and impoverished shopkeepers. Belgium's economic expansion had taken place mainly in the Walloon section of the country. The Flemish-speaking areas, which had earlier been the center of Belgium's economic life, became economically backward and were characterized by extreme poverty during the nineteenth century (Davin 1969; De Vries 1973: 29; Mokyr 1976: 239). In the course of the nineteenth century, the southwest regions of Finland had experienced a relatively rapid and successful commercialization, while industry in eastern Finland had stagnated. Dualism was also characteristic of Norway, Sweden, and Denmark (Osterud 1978: 111–12; Alapuro 1979: 351).

Between the 1930s and the immediate postwar period, many countries throughout Europe experienced tremendous changes toward reduced regional disparity; all of them experienced significant convergence in regional income levels (Williamson 1965: 23). Regional inequality in France and Germany began to decrease (Williamson 1965: 30). In Belgium, refineries and petrochemical plants established in the port area of Antwerp and industrialization along the Ghent-Terneuzen Canal accelerated the growth of Flanders; in 1967, per capita national income in the Flemish region exceeded that of Wallonia for the first time (Davin 1969; De Vries 1973: 29). In Italy, the government created the Cassa per il Mezzogiorno, or Southern

Development Fund, to finance the rebirth of the south, and undertook a major land reform and massive direct investment in the south (Ricossa 1973: 306). Regional inequalities were also reduced in Britain, Norway, Sweden, and the Netherlands.

Government policies to reduce regional inequalities were reinforced by the European Economic Community (EEC), which from its inception concerned itself with the development of regions within its member countries that were areas of relative poverty, underdevelopment, and outward migration. One of the expressed objectives of the Treaty of Rome was to promote "balanced expansion," by reducing the difference between the various regions and mitigating the backwardness of the "less favored."[25]

Monopoly. Government policies that had tolerated and encouraged cartelization and restrictive trade policies before the war were reversed. In Britain, a Monopolies Commission was established in 1948 to deal with monopoly and restrictive practices. An Act of 1956 required the registration of all restrictive trade agreements and set up a Restrictive Practices Court with powers to require the abandonment of any restrictive agreement not proved to be in the public interest. The Resale Prices Act of 1964 and the Mergers Act of 1965 strengthened the general move against monopoly. In West Germany, the breaking up of the cartels began under the direction of the Allied Occupation authorities. An anticartel law was passed in 1957 and strengthened in 1971. Anticartel legislation was also passed and carried out in France and the Netherlands.

The prevention of the recurrence of cartels and tariffs in the coal, iron, and steel industries of West Germany, France, the Netherlands, Belgium, and Italy became a central task of the European Coal and Steel Community (ECSC). The organization sought to modernize and rationalize production in the member countries and ultimately to ease the difficulties of a shift out of these "declining" industries. The guiding principle for the ECSC was the elimination of tariffs, quotas, discrimination on prices or freight charges, special privileges, and subsidies. To this end, the agreement called for an end to cartel arrangements in restraint of trade, substituting in effect the one gigantic cartel of the community itself. Unlike private cartels, however, this one aimed not at maintaining the status quo and preserving the

[25] These backward regions initially fell into two principal categories: (1) underdeveloped peripheral agricultural regions typified by the Mezzogiorno of Italy and southwest France, and (2) industrialized regions where traditional industries are in decline, such as some of the assisted areas of the United Kingdom and parts of northern France and Belgium. With the enlargement of the European Economic Community, whole countries – Ireland, Greece, Portugal – were considered as falling into the former category, which is characterized by per capita incomes markedly below the average for the community as a whole. See Commission of the European Communities, *Report on the Regional Problems in the Enlarged Community* (Brussels: The Commission, 1973).

members from the pains of competition but at expanding and rationalizing the industry. This required the closing of marginally inefficient enterprises and a substantial reallocation of resources.[26]

Articles 65 and 66 of the Treaty of Rome, which set up the ECSC, were what Jean Monnet called "Europe's first anti-trust law." Article 65 deals with cartels and bans agreements between enterprises and concerted practices that distort competition by sharing markets, fixing prices, or restricting production, investment, and development. In the first ten years of the community, 214 cases were investigated under Article 65: of these, twenty-seven were authorized (Curtis 1965: 135–36). Article 66 of the treaty allows the High Authority (created by the treaty as a supranational body) to authorize new mergers and to veto them if they are large enough to determine prices, control production or distribution, or restrict competition in the market.

Social Services. It was not until the postwar era that social security brought about a massive transfer of income in favor of lower income groups (Postan 1967: 353). After World War II, all governments in Europe extended the range of social services available to their citizens. In Britain, the comprehensive set of proposals put forward by the Beveridge Report of 1942 became the basis for the reorganization and extension of unemployment, sickness, and disability benefits, workmen's compensation, pensions and benefits for widows and orphans, maternity benefits, and funeral grants. These were enacted in a series of acts passed in 1945 and 1946. In France, De Gaulle's provisional government "quite unambiguously, put into effect the main features of the Program of the C.N.R. of March 1944 of the French Resistance" (Marwick 1974: 198). The program called for the institution of a "true economic and social democracy" and the removal from the direction of society of the "great economic and financial feudalisms." Specifically, it called for the right to work, a guaranteed wage that would ensure for each worker and for his wife security, dignity, and the opportunity for a full life, and the recreation of an independent trade union movement, this time with a large say in the organization of economic and social life. Agricultural workers were to obtain the same rights as industrial workers. A comprehensive social security program, as laid down by the CNR, was inaugurated in October 1945 and

---

[26] The French government was temporarily permitted to maintain various subsidies designed to facilitate competition with Germany, on condition that it cooperate in closing the high-cost mines of the Centre. The European Economic Community offered similar concessions to Italy and Belgium, always on a terminal basis, while contributing its own resources to the indemnification of those displaced or unemployed by the process of rationalization. By February 1958, the last of these breaches of free competition disappeared, except for the special status accorded the Belgian coal mines. There the purge required was too big, the political implications too serious for an unconditional application of the principles of economic rationality. In 1960, the community had to admit temporary defeat and segregate the Belgian mines from the rest of the West European market. See Milward 1984.

has remained unchallenged ever since. Belgium introduced a comprehensive social security system.

In the Netherlands and in the Scandinavian countries, social security measures were adopted almost immediately after the war. The standard of living of most people in the Eastern European countries improved substantially between 1950 and 1970 and in some cases by appreciable amounts. The supply of free or nearly free social services was at least equal to those in the West. The new socialist regimes, adopting Russian models, insisted that childcare, education, medical treatment, and support in old age should be provided to all equally, as a matter of individual right and public responsibility. The state increased the numbers of schools and teachers and made vastly increased provision for adult education. Where education was still in the hands of the churches, it was secularized. The state widened the basis of admission to the universities and provided an undifferentiated education to all up to the age of fifteen.

PEACE IN EUROPE

The social transformation effected in the course of the world wars eliminated the conditions that had generated recurring conflict throughout the nineteenth and early twentieth centuries in Europe. Because the world wars shifted the balance of class power in Europe, states were able to place their economies on an entirely different footing and to pursue goals related to a more balanced and internally oriented development. A thoroughgoing reconstruction took place on the basis of redistributive policies that before the world wars had been effectively blocked. After 1945, growth centered on the home market. It was this that made possible the widespread prosperity and stable democratic politics of post–World War II Western Europe.

With rapidly expanding internal markets, states in Europe were relatively free of external and internal claimants to power; their international relations occurred on the basis of the securely established sovereignty of each state over its territory and population. A radical change in the number and status of minorities overdetermined this outcome by bringing the ethnic map of Europe into closer agreement with the political map. As a result, after 1945, Europe also enjoyed relative stability. There was a sharp drop in the number of class and minority conflicts in Europe. There was also a sharp drop in wars involving European states.

The year 1968 is generally seen as representing a turning point in the post–World War II order. Events during that year appeared to mark the reemergence of flux, uncertainty, and more intense conflict in political life in Europe, in both the East and the West. At the same time, in both parts of Europe, it was possible to discern the formation of a new class structure, with features reminiscent of nineteenth-century European society and, as a result, a resurgence of nationalism and class conflict. These events and the beginning of a general reversal of the post–World War II order are taken up in Chapter 9. The following discussion, therefore, focuses on European conflicts during the first twenty-five years of the postwar era.

Class and Enfranchisement Conflicts

Workers became a powerful organized force following World War II. Parties representing labor became legitimate participants in the political process in most countries of Western Europe and the dominant power in Eastern Europe. These parties had participated in government in several countries before 1945, but their presence in government had been strenuously and sometimes violently resisted. It was only after 1945 that socialist and labor party participation in European governments was treated as fully legitimate. New trade unions were organized, and unions, which before the war had been hindered by police repression, acquired significant numbers of new members and were reorganized.

By the end of the 1950s, workers in Western Europe "had become pretty confident" that by "using the ordinary weapons of bargaining at their disposal" they "would be able to increase their wages each year in line with the growth of the national product" (Schonfield 1965: 8). This, of course, was not true of all countries at all times. A notable exception is Germany during the early 1950s and France during the late 1950s. However, as Schonfield points out, "in these cases, the period which followed showed a tendency for wages to move up more quickly than the growth of national product" (Schonfield 1965: 8). Nevertheless, there was a significant decrease in class conflicts following the war. Among those that occurred, the most notable were the insurrectionary strikes throughout France and frequent rioting and conflicts with police during 1947–48; strikes in Belgium in 1960 and in Spain in 1962; and bombings and political murders in Italy in the 1960s.

In both Western and Eastern Europe, redistribution had taken place as a result of the world wars. But in Eastern Europe it became associated with "foreign rule" or Soviet-backed communist rule, and required political repression to bring it about and to maintain it. In 1956, there were riots in Poland. The Soviet Union intervened forcibly to halt a reform process initiated by the communist party of Hungary that year. Soviet troops were sent to Czechoslovakia to crush reforms in 1968. In both cases, Soviet troops engaged in street battles with students.

Though there was no democracy in Eastern Europe, the social structural changes that had been imposed from above eventually enabled it to achieve democracy by means of a "velvet revolution." This stands in stark contrast to the experience of many countries in the third world, where the transition from authoritarianism to some sort of political pluralism has been only partial and accompanied by much violence. There, the absence of the social structural changes that occurred throughout Europe after World War II and the Cold War crusade against communism worked effectively to block the growth of reformist and progressive elements and currents that, in Europe and elsewhere, supported and encouraged struggles for democracy and the democratization of national politics. Thus, while the prospects for democracy look fairly good in the former communist countries of Eastern Europe, they look fairly dim in regions such as the Middle East, where authoritarian regimes and ruling groups, with the support of Western powers, eliminated the social forces and conditions needed to produce and maintain democracy.

Ethnic and Nationalist Conflict

There was a sharp drop in the number of ethnic conflicts in Europe after 1945. Genocide, expulsion, flight, and border shifts between 1912 and 1948 radically altered the ethnic map of Europe and brought it into much closer agreement with its political divisions. Despite this, many minorities remained within European countries. The social, political, and economic changes that took place after World War II, however, changed the status of minorities and eliminated the conditions that had previously fueled ethnic and nationalist conflicts.

Massive population transfers in Europe – the largest since those associated with the breakup of the Roman Empire – began during the Balkan Wars of 1912–13 and continued throughout the 1940s. During the Balkan Wars, thousands of Turks, Bulgars, Greeks, and Muslims fled before Balkan, Greek, and Turkish armies. In 1914, some 265,000 Greeks were expelled from Turkey, and 85,000 deported to the interior; 115,000 Muslims left Greece, and 134,000 left the other Balkan states for Turkey. During World War I, about 1,600,000 Armenians were massacred or expelled from Turkey. After the Armistice, about 240,000 Greeks returned to East and West Thrace and Asia Minor, but nearly all these had to flee again in 1922, with the balance of the Armenians (Pallis 1925a; Ladas 1932). Post–World War I conventions between Greece and Bulgaria and between Greece and Turkey "confirmed or caused" the displacement of more than two million people (Ladas 1932: 3). These movements had the effect of profoundly modifying the racial geography of Macedonia, Thrace, and Anatolia.

Forced population transfers initiated by the Nazis during World War II also resulted in a consolidation of the various national groups. During the early years of World War II, Hitler conducted a large-scale transfer of German minorities from Central and Eastern Europe to Germany. Three and a half million Germans in Eastern and Southeastern Europe were transferred, by various means, to Germany (Kulischer 1948: chap. 10).

After the war, a massive migration removed all but a tiny minority of Germans from Central and Eastern Europe.[27] Between ten and twelve million

---

[27] The bulk of the German population of the South Tyrol remained under Italian rule, and some small German communities remained elsewhere.

Germans – four million from Poland, three million from Czechoslovakia, two million from the Baltic states, and smaller numbers from Hungary, Yugoslavia, Romania, and Russia – were forced into Austria, East Germany, and West Germany (Wiskemann 1956: 118). Some ten million Soviet citizens displaced eastward by the war moved from central and eastern Russia toward the west and northwest. Five million Poles left western Russia and eastern Poland to resettle within the new Polish boundaries. Nearly 200,000 Czechs and Slovaks moved from eastern to western Czechoslovakia, 160,000 Turks were expelled from Bulgaria, and 400,000 persons moved from southern to northern Yugoslavia, where they replaced some 300,000 Italians and an equal number of Germans (Wiskemann 1956: 213). This simplification of ethnic boundaries "solved" some of Europe's most intractable problems.

By expelling the Germans from its newly acquired western territory, while losing its essentially Ukrainian and Byelorussian districts to the Soviet Union, Poland became one of the world's more homogeneous states. Millions of Germans were expelled from Czechoslovakia and Hungary, making the territories contained within these three countries almost ethnically homogeneous for the first time since the Middle Ages. During World War II, the Soviet Union deported seven nationalities to Siberia and Central Asia, a policy that was officially denounced in the late 1950s (Conquest 1976: 102–7). The Soviet Union concluded formal agreements with Czechoslovakia in 1945 and 1946 for the reciprocal transfer of minorities.

The combined effects of wartime deaths, minority territorial compaction, frontier revision on a massive scale, and wholesale population transfer halved the prewar minorities' proportion of the population, bringing the post-1945 level down near 10 percent of the total (see Table 8.1).

TABLE 8.1. *Minorities in Europe, 1910–1930*
(percent of total population)

	1910	1930	1950
Austria	67	3	1
Hungary	52	8	5
Germany[a]	7	1	
German Democratic Republic			0.1
Poland		31	3
Bulgaria	26	12	12
Romania	7	25	13
Albania		9	4
Greece		12	8
United Kingdom	12	6	6

[a] In German Upper Silesia, 42 percent of the population was made up of minorities (Macartney 1934: 517).
Source: Krejci and Velimsky 1981: 66.

TABLE 8.2. *Europe's Magnitude 3 + Wars, 1945–1990 (extraregional wars are in brackets)*

War	Date	Magnitude	Source
[Algeria/France]	[1954–62]	5	Singer and Small 1972: 75
[Congo/Belgium]	[1960–64]	5	SIPRI 1969: table 4a.1
[Afghanistan/USSR]	[1979–88]	5	Leger-Sivard 1989
[Yemen/Britain]	[1962–64]	5	Paget 1969: 264
Greek civil war	1946–48	4	Richardson 1960: 50
[Kenya/Britain]	[1953]	4	Carver 1990: 43
[Indochina/France]	[1947–54]	4	Wright 1965: 1544
[Angola/Portugal]	[1962–63]	4	SIPRI 1969: table 4a.1
[Madagascar/France]	[1947]	3	Singer and Small 1972: 125
[Indonesia/Netherlands]	[1947–49]	3	SIPRI 1969: table 4a.1
[Malaya/Britain]	[1947–52]	3	Wright 1964: 1544
[Palestine/Britain]	[1948]	3	Singer and Small 1972: 126
[Tunisia/France]	[1952–54]	3	SIPRI 1969: table 4a.1
Cyprus War	1955–59	3	SIPRI 1969: table 4a.1
Hungarian Revolution	1956–57	3	Singer and Small 1972: 126
[Suez/Britain, France]	[1956–57]	3	Singer and Small 1972: 127
[Lebanon/Britain]	[1958]	3	SIPRI 1969: table 4a.1
[Malaysia/Britain]	[1963]	3	Carver 1990: 97
Cyprus War	1963–64	3	Wright 1965: 1544
Northern Ireland	1969–82	3	Kende et al. 1982: 355
Cyprus War	1974	3	SIPRI 1969: table 4a.1
[Falkland Islands/Britain]	[1982]	3	Carver 1990: 289

Not all minority problems were eliminated. Hungary opposed the transfer of Hungarians from Romania and from Czechoslovakia, hoping to bring about the transfer of land rather than simply of population (Claude 1955: 121, 130). Ethnic conflict continued in Belgium, Spain, and Northern Ireland. Tensions emerged between the Flemish and the Walloons in Belgium in 1966 and in 1968. The Basque Euskadi Ta Ezkatasum separatists assassinated numerous high-ranking Spanish officials, including Spain's prime minister in the 1970s, and Northern Ireland remained a continual battleground.

Imperialist Conflicts

World War II marks the beginning of the end of European empire. Great Britain granted independence to the Indian subcontinent in 1947 and to Ceylon and Burma in 1948. Indonesia became independent from the Dutch in 1949; Libya from Italy in 1949. Egypt became fully independent of Britain in 1952. Laos, Cambodia, and North Vietnam gained independence from the French in 1954; Malaysia from the British in 1957. By 1965, Britain had granted independence to its African colonies (except for Southern Rhodesia), and Tunisia, Algeria, and Morocco had gained independence from France. Britain relinquished control of Aden in 1967. By 1974, Portugal had granted independence to Angola and Mozambique.

Some wars involving European states were related to the Cold War as, for instance, British involvement in civil wars in Lebanon (1958) and in North Yemen (1962–67). However, most of the wars that involved European states after 1945 resulted from the attempts on the part of European states to hold on to colonial possessions. These decreased rapidly, however. (See Table 8.2 for Europe's post–World War II wars.)

CONCLUSIONS

After the end of World War II, the class structures of the states of both Western and Eastern Europe were radically changed. These changes in class structures made possible the establishment of a new economic and political order in the region on the basis of interest groups, parties, unions, and other organizations linked to sectors of the economy that had been formerly excluded from power.

The integration of labor into the political process and changes in laborers' status and level of welfare ended the labor and enfranchisement conflicts that had recurred more or less continually throughout the nineteenth and early twentieth centuries. Changes in the status and number of minorities put an end to nationalist strife. Increased domestic investment and the rising real wages of the work force altered the structure of demand for domestic goods and services. The resulting expansion of domestic markets put an end to the pursuit of profit through colonialism and imperialism. Processes of accumulation that lead not only to an expansion of the economic surplus but to its wider distribution generate sustained growth. Those that lead to an expansion of the economic surplus but not to its wider distribution generate crisis.

In Europe, the maldistribution of taxes and income and the monopolization of economic resources and opportunities created a social structure of accumulation that was so distorted from a welfare point of view that it ran into ever-recurring bottlenecks and became socially and politically intolerable.[28] By 1914, monopoly, poor use of resources, maldistribution of

[28] Accumulation processes are critically dependent on social relations and institutions. David M. Gordon (1980) introduced the term "social structure of accumulation" to describe the interdependence of social relations and accumulation. The social structure of accumulation is comprised of those institutions whose stability is necessary for rapid accumulation of capital. Accumulation and social structures are mutually interdependent: tendencies toward economic crisis are likely to generate corresponding crisis in the social structure of accumulation; internal contradictions of the social structure of accumulation can reinforce or even trigger general tendencies toward economic crisis.

income, and inequitable tax systems had combined to produce a crisis in Europe.

A "crisis" is not a mere oscillation but a set of tensions and strains that affect the basic structures of the system. Though the vulnerability that they create frequently brings on external challenges (e.g., invasion or war), they are essentially internally generated. Thus, changes in the prevailing social relationships are necessary to bring the crisis to an end. Those changes may not necessarily be progressive.[29] The economic contraction that invariably accompanies crises leads to social struggle for the control of diminishing resources and shapes the terms of resolution of the crisis. The nature of the social transformation embodied in the new social structure will depend on the balance of class forces that engage in struggle during the crisis.

The radical transformation of social structures through crisis and conflict appears to be a process recurring throughout history. The balance of class forces that emerges from these crises sets the path of development thereafter – until the next crisis. The socially progressive synthesis that emerged in Europe following World War II reflected a new balance of class forces. The new synthesis unleashed productive forces on an unprecedented scale.

Elites try to monopolize the gains generated by technological change and changes in productive forces. They work to preserve the structures and institutions of society that allow them privileged access to the gains resulting from these changes. These efforts effectively block the development of human resources. Progress is also checked because elites block the application of new techniques and the rational distribution of resources in order to protect their monopoly position and to avoid the revamping of class relationships that these changes might entail. The resulting rigidity generates crisis and conflict. The outcome of the crisis may be the breakdown of traditional structures and a widening of access to valued goods, followed eventually by another cycle of closure and greater openness. Alternatively, the outcome of crisis may be retrenchment and political reaction, leading to stagnation.

Where there is change, there will be struggle, by already privileged elements within societies, for control over its tempo and direction and, above all, for control over the distribution of its costs and benefits. The problems of conflict and change today are essentially the same as those that confronted societies in the past; they are likely to be the same in the future.

---

[29] Crises, according to the Chinese ideograph, are "phases of danger and opportunity." Crises can stimulate either progress or regress.

9

The Great Transformation and the Eternal Return

"Globalization" Reconsidered

The world, even if it is no longer a God, is still supposed to be capable of the divine power of creation, the power of infinite transformations; it is supposed to consciously prevent itself from returning to any of its old forms; it is supposed to possess not only the intention but the means of avoiding any repetition. . . .

The recently attained preponderance of the scientific spirit over the religious, God-inventing spirit leads us to the belief that the world, as force, may not be thought of as unlimited, that the world lacks the capacity for eternal novelty. By rejecting the belief in the "beyond," the limitless, the transcendental, we reject also the belief in the capacity for eternal novelty.

Friedrich Nietzsche, *The Eternal Recurrence*[1]

If the French Revolution were to recur eternally, French historians would be less proud of Robespierre. But because they deal with something that will not return, the bloody years of the Revolution have turned into mere words, theories and discussions, have become lighter than feathers, frightening no one. There is an infinite difference between a Robespierre who occurs only once in history and a Robespierre who eternally returns, chopping off French heads.

Milan Kundera, *The Unbearable Lightness of Being*[2]

Karl Polanyi assumed that the demise of the unregulated market system would bring about a "great transformation" both in the nature of the international system and in its constituent states. However, soon after the publication of *The Great Transformation*, it became clear that this expectation would not be fulfilled (Polanyi 1947). Though the free market and the laissez-faire state gave way, in varying degrees, to regulated markets and interventionist states, the liberal international order survived. The hybrid system that this

---

[1] In *The Will to Power*, trans. William Kaufmann (New York: Vintage Books, 1967), pp. 544–50, 546.
[2] Trans. Michael Henry Heim (New York: Harper and Row, 1984), p. 2.

created has been characterized as one of "embedded liberalism" (Ruggie 1982).

Polanyi's analysis in *The Great Transformation* was the inspiration for the notion of markets as "embedded" and "disembedded."[3] Polanyi argued that before the rise of the unregulated market system at the end of the eighteenth century, exchange relations were governed by principles of economic behavior (reciprocity, reallocation, and householding) that were embedded in society and politics. At the end of the eighteenth century, however, states began to institute changes that formed the basis of the disembedded capitalist development that characterized Europe's nineteenth-century industrial expansion.

For Polanyi, it was the commodification of land and labor that was the substance of the disembedded economic relations in the nineteenth century. But as previous chapters have shown, European economies were disembedded in another sense, as well. Throughout the nineteenth century, European economies grew through the expansion and integration of external markets, while home markets remained underdeveloped. This dualism was evident everywhere in Europe. Even in the most protectionist and interventionist states, external markets were developed in lieu of internal ones. Capital was largely invested either abroad or in home production that was chiefly for export. It was chiefly in this sense that economic relations were disembedded in the nineteenth century, and it is in this sense, too, that today, through "globalization," they are becoming disembedded once again.

The collapse of the nineteenth-century system and the conclusion of a compromise between capital and labor led to the reembedding of European economies after 1945. Welfare reforms partially decommodified labor, and by means of market and industry regulation, investment and production were made to serve the expansion and integration of national markets. Now, however, a campaign to promote the dispersal of capital investment and production to foreign locations – the current "globalization" campaign – is seeking to reverse the post–World War II compromise and to disembed national markets once again.

In the history of capitalism, then, there have been phases of nationally embedded and global free market capitalism – periods when capital is relatively more and relatively less free from national state regulation. Markets were embedded until the end of the eighteenth century; after that, and throughout the nineteenth century, they were disembedded; then, after the nineteenth-century system collapsed in the course of the world wars, a compromise was

---

[3] John Ruggie popularized the term, arguing that the postwar international system was one of economic "multilateralism...predicated upon domestic intervention," which he termed "embedded liberalism" (1982: 393).

concluded that resulted in markets being reembedded. Today, proponents of globalization are endeavoring to reverse this compromise and to return, once again, to the disembedded capitalism that characterized nineteenth-century Europe.

Globalization, then, is not, as Francis Fukuyama (1992) and others have argued, the end point of an evolutionary process (nor, as is argued, is it one that is working to move all societies in the direction of liberal democracy). Globalization is neither a radical and absolute break with the past nor the result of an evolutionary process but a recurring phenomenon within capitalism.

A similar campaign to free capital from restrictions imposed by local communities was launched at the end of the eighteenth century. As with the current campaign, it worked to reconfigure the structure of political power by means of a broad-based, far-reaching, and all-encompassing ideological assault on what was depicted, and rapidly came to be seen, as the "old order." Previous chapters have explored this earlier chapter in the history of capitalist globalization. It examined the disembedding of markets that accelerated capitalist globalization at the end of the eighteenth century and the conditions that made possible the reembedding of capital in the course of the world wars at the beginning of the twentieth century.

This chapter endeavors to bring this history to bear on what may be the beginning of another iteration of a recurring process of accelerated capitalist globalization. It does so by addressing two questions: What, historically, have been the context and conditions for the disembedding and reembedding of capital? And to what extent can this history provide insight into the social conditions, relations, interests, and forces driving and resisting efforts to dismantle the post-1945 order and to disembed capital today? More specifically, are the causes and conditions of the class compromise that reembedded capital after World War II relevant today?

The following sections explore these questions by linking the historical account developed in previous chapters to globalization. The first section reviews the arguments and evidence on which that account was based and considers them in relation to both the strengths and the weaknesses of Polanyi's analysis in *The Great Transformation* and to development theory. The second section begins the exploration of globalization by focusing on the turning point of the 1970s and the return to "unfettered markets." The third section addresses the "incommensurability thesis": that the accelerated globalization of capital that took place during the nineteenth century is irrelevant for understanding today's "globalization." After elaborating arguments that affirm its relevance, the chapter concludes by drawing from the history of capitalist globalization lessons for the future.

NINETEENTH-CENTURY INDUSTRIAL EXPANSION: THE "GREAT
TRANSFORMATION" REVISITED

The historical account of Europe's nineteenth-century industrial expansion
presented in the previous chapters rests on a number of claims (these are
italicized below). Two claims were advanced and elaborated in Chapter 1.
Chapter 1 argued, first, that *the balance of social class power determines the
nature of development.* It argued, second, that *shifts in the balance of class
power bring about the transformation of social orders.* Subsequent chapters
detailed the shift in the balance of class power that gave rise to Europe's
nineteenth-century market system. They focused, first, on the configuration
of social power that emerged at the end of the eighteenth century (Chapter 2)
and how, thereafter, this configuration shaped and was reproduced by the
system of industrial expansion that predominated in Europe throughout the
nineteenth century (Chapter 3). It then described the conflicts that were
generated by this system (Chapter 4) and how these conflicts increasingly
began to shift the balance of class power in Europe (Chapters 5 and 6).
Finally, they showed how mass mobilization for the First World War and
the polarization of Europe's internal and international relations during the
interwar years led to World War II and, once again, to a shift in the balance
of class power in Europe (Chapters 7 and 8).

A number of subsidiary claims were advanced along the way. Among the
first of these is that *the Industrial Revolution and the expansion of industrial
production did not bring about the demise of traditional classes.* Though this is
an aspect of Europe's modern history that has been noted by a large number of scholars (cited in Chapters 1–3), its implications have not been fully
drawn in conventional analyses and histories of modern European development and are not reflected in the various theoretical perspectives based
on them.

As Chapter 2 shows, the rise of Europe's nineteenth-century market system was the result not of the rise of new classes but of a decisive shift in
the balance of power between "absolutist" monarchs and aristocracies, in
favor of the latter. This shift was institutionalized by the national states
and governments that replaced absolutist states and monarchs in Europe.
Thus, contrary to conventional accounts, the emergence of nation-states did
not bring about the demise of traditional landowning and aristocratic elites.
Rather, it enabled them to gain control of capitalist development and to
channel it into noncompetitive, ascriptive, and monopolistic forms. As a result, *industrial expansion operated to a large extent on the basis of nonindustrial
and anti-industrial social and political values and interests.*

The social power of traditional landowning and aristocratic elites was
reproduced in and through the social relations of surplus extraction and
production that predominated in nineteenth-century Europe. Chapter 3
shows, specifically, how local relations of production (political, social, and

economic) restricted the home market for producer goods and articles of mass consumption while, at the same time, expanding markets for capital and goods among a network of wealth owners, ruling groups, and governments within and outside Europe. As a result, industrial expansion in Europe was shaped not by a liberal, competitive ethos, as is emphasized in most accounts of European industrial development, but by feudal forms of organization, by monopolism, protectionism, cartelization, and corporatism. Domestic economies remained limited and weakly integrated, while strong linkages were forged between their expanding sectors and those of foreign economies. While production expanded and profits increased for a transnational landowning and industrial elite, the geographic and sectoral spread of industrialization remained limited, as did mass mobilization for industrial production and the rise of new classes at home. Production expanded primarily through the intensification of labor, in both agriculture and manufacturing. In sectors producing for export, the productivity of labor increased by means of technological improvements. Even here, however, mechanization was introduced far later and less completely than is generally thought. In the rest of the economy, methods of increasing absolute surplus production predominated: extending the length of the working day, intensifying work, and decreasing the standard of living of the labor force. As a result, despite the massive population movements within and outside Europe, and the appearance of great flux and change over the entire surface of European life, *traditional bases of social and political power remained intact throughout the nineteenth and early twentieth centuries.*

Europe's system of industrial expansion was made possible by the operation of state-created and -supported local and international institutions. State and police power made possible the increase in absolute surplus value production at home and the aggressive pursuit of markets abroad. Thus, *Europe's industrial expansion was characterized not by a separation of political (state) and economic power but by their fusion.* This fusion was evident in systems of political rights that everywhere in Europe were based on wealth rather than citizenship.

Because political and economic power were fused, maintaining the subordination of labor to capital required that elites become increasingly wealthy, not only in absolute terms but relative to the mass of workers. The restriction of mechanization and skilled labor to sectors producing for export reduced the mass of workers entirely to a factor of low-skilled production, keeping masses of unskilled labor "in reserve" and the overall market position of labor weak. *Throughout the nineteenth and early twentieth centuries, the mass of workers remained poor, unskilled, uneducated, unorganized, and in excess of demand.*

The social structures and relations of power maintained and reproduced by Europe's system of industrial expansion generated social conflicts and wars throughout the nineteenth and early twentieth centuries. *Recurring*

European conflicts, both in Europe and throughout the world, characterized Europe's industrial expansion. Chapter 4 shows that these conflicts involved a recurrent set of issues, actors, and alliances relating to industrial expansion and were continually replayed or fought continuously but intermittently over long periods of time. Of these conflicts, 379 were domestic. The majority, 221 conflicts, were bread and wage riots and strikes or demonstrations over the conditions of work or the distribution of property. Of the 161 conflicts fought by European states against other states or other populations, the reasons for fighting in the majority of cases involved rivalry for access to markets or natural resources; barriers to trade such as embargoes, boycotts, and tariffs; the attempt by one belligerent group to seize the land or territory of another group; irredentist claims; boundary disputes; and autonomist or secessionist motives. There were in all some 537 conflicts fought by or in European states between 1789 and 1945. Thus, contra Polanyi, it can be said that *for Europe, the nineteenth century was a century not of peace but of war.*

The power of labor increased, not through its mobilization for industrial production but through mobilization for war. As Chapter 5 showed, mass mobilization for World War I brought about a substantial increase in the organizational power of working classes. Far from marking the defeat of socialism by nationalism and its demise as a force for change in Europe, as some accounts contend, the war strengthened the unity and organization of labor.

World War II was the result of the growing polarization of European society. Chapter 5 discusses how and why European societies became increasingly polarized along class lines after World War I. During the interwar years, there was an explosive rise of trade union membership, peasant organization, socialist parties, and socialist radicalism. A counterrevolutionary coalition of all relatively privileged or well-to-do groups and elements in European societies formed in reaction. Chapter 6 shows that between 1918 and 1939, there was a more or less continuous round of violent strikes, riots, demonstrations, and street fighting, as well as coups, rebellions, and revolutions. As Chapter 7 shows, the struggle between left and right in Europe increasingly polarized international as well as domestic relations.

War (also plague and invasion) *is a principal means of bringing about shifts in the balance of class power.* As Chapter 8 argues, the nature and the irreversibility of the changes instituted throughout Europe following World War II were indicative of a shift in the balance of power within European societies. Just as the use of massive and expensive professional or mercenary armies in the seventeenth century worked to increase the power of wealthy classes (by draining state revenues and making the British monarchy reliant on London merchants and the commercialized gentry and aristocracy allied with them), the use of mass citizen armies in the world wars of the twentieth century and the consequent reliance of states on working-class cooperation increased the power of labor in European societies. It was the shift in the balance of class power that, after World War II, brought about a transformation of European societies.

Some have argued that, while the wars may have accelerated the changes that took place after 1945, these changes would have emerged in the course of time without the wars (e.g., Kuznets 1964). Others attribute these changes to a shift in the balance of power not of labor and capital but among different fractions of capital. They argue that the political and military costs of developing and defending foreign markets made Keynesianism attractive not only to labor but to productive capital, as well, and they argue that it was the increase in the power of this fraction of capital that resulted in the postwar changes. But, as Chapter 8 argued, given the resistance to state planning and comprehensive welfare reform before World War II, and the vigorous resistance of the United States to "national capitalism" after the war, it is unlikely that a massive capitulation to social democratic reforms and the expansion and consolidation of nationally embedded capital formations would have occurred in Europe had not the wars vastly increased the power of labor. Moreover, this increase occurred in the context of a war against socialism. Thus, capitalists, needing both to "keep workers away from Communism and create an army of consumers" (Lipietz 1992: 10), were willing to commit some portion of their profits to wage increases and home investment.

The account of the rise and demise of Europe's nineteenth-century market system developed in previous chapter suggests that prosperity, stability, and peace are associated with a relatively more equal dispersion of wealth. It shows that a more equal distribution of wealth was a key factor in producing the social peace, growth, and prosperity of Britain in the eighteenth century and of Europe as a whole following World War II.[4]

The post–World War II class compromise reinstated the state welfare and regulatory functions that had been relinquished in the nineteenth century.[5] Throughout Europe, labor was partially decommodified through

---

[4] As Tawney observed in 1931, an "unstable compound" is created by the conflict between the claims of common men to live their lives on the plane that a century of scientific progress has now made possible and the reluctance of property to surrender its special privileges. The result is a struggle that, while it lasts, produces paralysis, and that can be ended only by the overthrow of either economic and social privilege or political equality (1952: 193). Matthew Melko, having reviewed the history of fifty-two societies that at some time between 2650 B.C. and A.D. 1973 experienced a century of internal peace (i.e., had no civil war over approximately the fourth magnitude), concluded that these societies were on the whole uncommonly prosperous, with their prosperity fairly well distributed (1973: 113–15).

[5] Most historical accounts of Western development treat the welfare provisions of the post–World War II "welfare state" as the outcome of progressive developments achieved in the course of industrial capitalist development, as a modern and enlightened era that is immeasurably superior to anything that went before. But studies have shown that, in Britain, transfer payments to the elderly (see, e.g., Thomson 1984) and to single-parent families (see, e.g., Snell and Millar 1987) were significantly less under Britain's post–World War II welfare system than under the old poor law.

state-provided health care and education, housing subsidies, and child-care allowances. States expanded domestic markets by increasing and regulating domestic investment, and this, in turn, increased production and raised the level of earnings and welfare of the working class. The reembedding of European economies led to a more balanced and internally oriented development and to an era of unprecedented growth and relative peace and stability. Although there was a strong growth of the volume of exports after the war, the expansion of domestic markets for domestic goods and services ensured that the proportion of resources devoted to exports (measured by the current price ratio of exports to GDP) declined. "It was not until the end of the 1960s that production for international trade absorbed an increasing proportion of labor within the advanced countries" (Marglin and Schor 1990: 51).

The territorial coincidence of production and consumption and the resulting expansion of domestic markets brought to an end, for a time, intense social conflicts and the great movements of colonialism and imperialism. The integration of workers and minorities into the political process and changes in their status and level of welfare ended the labor and minority conflicts that had recurred throughout the nineteenth and early twentieth centuries. The reduction of protection and monopoly increased domestic investment, and the rising real wages of the work force altered the structure of demand for domestic goods and services. The resulting expansion of domestic markets[6] ended the pursuit of profit through colonialism and imperialism.

Polanyi's "Great Transformation"

The account presented in previous chapters points to a number of ways in which Polanyi's analysis misleads. In particular, it challenges his conceptions of society and the state and his arguments concerning the "double movement" of European industrial development and Europe's century of peace. The analysis of previous chapters begins by tracing the social and economic interests that gave rise to the unregulated market. Polanyi recognizes these interests and their relation to the state, but does not draw the implications either for class politics or for the nature of the state in nineteenth-century Europe.

In fact, Polanyi does not offer a detailed analysis of the "first transformation" that, at the end of the eighteenth century, brought about the rise of the unregulated market system. A closer look at this chapter in Europe's

---

[6] Tariffs and various other controls had enabled a narrow elite to monopolize domestic markets and international trade, obstructing rising entrepreneurs and limiting the expansion of industry at home. In contrast, postwar policies focused on expanding domestic markets through increased production rather than dividing up and exploiting national markets through restrictive practices.

industrial expansion shows that the dismantling of market regulations and systems of national welfare prevailing at that time in Britain, France, and elsewhere in Europe was evidence not of the rise of new liberal commercial interests but of the continuing power of rural, pre-industrial, and autocratic structures of power and authority.

States were not autonomous actors, either in these changes or in the consolidation and maintenance of the system to which they gave rise. "National" political revolutions ensured that states would remain aligned with Europe's dominant landed and industrial classes throughout the nineteenth century. In Britain, France, Germany, Sweden, Russia, and elsewhere, this alignment was encouraged by the social integration of top state personnel with the upper classes, especially the landed upper class. In some places, aristocrats directly performed the role of governing and administering (e.g., in Germany); in other places, a separate bureaucratic elite filled this role (e.g., in France, at times); in many cases, the role was filled by some combination of the two. In all cases, however, the governing elite of national states proved either unwilling or unable to successfully challenge the power of traditional elites and to effect meaningful reforms over their opposition. In fact, they typically developed or strengthened a variety of corporate structures that provided dominant classes with privileged access to the state.

State legislation advanced the interests of dominant landed and industrial classes throughout the nineteenth and early twentieth centuries. As a result, landowners did not experience significant political setbacks with respect to tariffs, labor legislation, land reform, state allocations, tax policy, or internal terms of trade until after World War II. The absence of agrarian reform, the social and political isolation of agrarian labor, low agricultural land taxes (which offset price controls and taxes on agricultural exports when they were unavoidable), and the monopolization of domestic industry and international trade through the creation of cartels and syndicates revealed the close association of state policies with the immediate interests of landowning elites. States also made possible the pursuit of aggressive external expansion on which Europe's system of dualistic industrial production depended.

Polanyi's notion of a "double-movement" – the unfettering of the market, on the one hand, and the search for protection by all groups within society, on the other – is also misleading. It is for two reasons. First, markets were not unregulated in the nineteenth century. Second, not all groups within society were threatened by the expansion of markets, and not all groups sought protection from it. State regulations made possible the expansion of industrial production through absolute surplus value production at home and the acquisition of markets abroad, the restriction of domestic markets and expansion of external ones, the monopolization by a narrow transnational elite of the profits generated by industrial expansion, and the creation and reproduction of a circuit of exchange that, while enriching elites, bypassed the mass of the populations of the trading countries. If elites were threatened by the expansion of markets, it was because of their potential to increase social mobility and promote the growth of new commercial classes. In response to this threat, elites ensured their social and economic domination over lower classes and ethnic minorities by shaping industrial capitalist development in ways that limited competition and social mobility. Not everyone was hurt by the expansion of the market. As Polanyi himself points out, industrialists demanded from the state that their property be protected not from the market but "from the people" (1944: 225). Clearly, some elements within society sought not protection from harm but monopoly. Polanyi observed that in the late eighteenth and early nineteenth century,

The traditional unity of a Christian society was giving place to the denial of responsibility on the part of the well-to-do for the conditions of their fellows. *The Two Nations were taking shape.* To the bewilderment of thinking minds, unheard-of wealth turned out to be inseparable from unheard-of poverty. (Polanyi 1944: 102; emphasis added)

However, Polanyi failed to draw the implications of this observation. If "Two Nations" were taking shape in Europe, then, clearly, European societies in the nineteenth century were not organic unities. In fact, as we have seen, social divisions led to continual conflict in Europe.

Europe's supposed "Hundred Years' Peace" was the starting point for Polanyi's analysis because it was the basis for his arguing that Europe's nineteenth-century market system represented the victory of liberal interests and values and of free trade, free markets, and the liberal, noninterventionist state. But, as we have seen, industrial expansion in Europe produced not a hundred years of peace but a century of social conflict and war. These were the result of societies increasingly divided by the structures and processes of dual economic expansion.

It was possible for Polanyi to treat society as an organic unity only by ignoring the social conflicts that persisted and increased throughout the century. Polanyi maintained that class antagonism in Europe began only in the 1920s. But, as Chapter 2 showed, it began, in fact, in the last decades of the eighteenth century. Thereafter and throughout the nineteenth century, Europe experienced more or less continual conflict over the distribution of resources and the terms and conditions under which market forces operated. As Chapter 4 showed, conflicts involving labor became a continuous source of tension, leading to recurring outbreaks of violence nearly everywhere in Europe. As the century progressed, these struggles increasingly overlapped with enfranchisement struggles and nationalist conflicts. Conflict erupted for or against changes in property relations, higher wages, extension of the suffrage, redistribution of the national product, shorter hours of employment, and the right to secure bread at an affordable price, to organize, and to work in safe conditions. Workers, in other words, were not simply clamoring for protection but struggling against monopoly and greed.

Development and Underdevelopment Reconsidered

While challenging many key tenets of liberal theory, dependency and world systems theories never challenged conventional liberal accounts of the nature of the societies that emerged in the West as a result of Western industrial capitalist development. In common with Polanyi's analysis, they tend to focus on social wholes and, thus, to treat development and underdevelopment as conditions that apply to whole societies, rather than to classes within and across societies. However, development and underdevelopment correspond not to a vertical division among nations or among regions but to a transnational and horizontal one among classes. Development and underdevelopment recur throughout history, often in the same regions. Moreover, their causation is essentially the same: processes of class formation and class and intraclass struggle that tend to occur, in any mode of production, with the opening up of new sources of wealth and with advances in the means of production.

World systems and dependency theories claim that underdevelopment in third world regions was the result of a global division of labor that required them to be incorporated into the world capitalist economy as raw-material producing areas. But many countries in the core were also incorporated into the system as raw material producers (e.g., Denmark, Sweden, the United States, Canada, and Australia), and as previous chapters argued, core and peripheral development before the world wars was generally more similar than dissimilar.

Dependency theory is concerned with the monopolization of productive assets by foreign elites and the growing income gap between developed and less developed countries that is thought to result from this. But local elites also monopolize resources, and the historical record suggests that the monopolization of productive assets by these elites is as detrimental to development as the monopolization of assets by foreign groups. The gap between rich and poor countries is significant, as both liberal and neo-Marxist approaches emphasize, but elites in the third world enjoy the same level of income and standard of living as elites in the developed countries (Sunkel 1973: 150), and the gap between them and the poor masses within third world countries is at least as significant as that between countries.

Whatever the role of foreign states and groups, it is local elites who are decisive in bringing about external reliance, in translating it into structural "distortions," and in determining how the benefits of collaboration with foreign capital are distributed and used. States that are fully independent and able to capture a large share of global product do not necessarily distribute their gains more equitably or use them more productively, internally. It is local dominant classes that dictate the form, substance, timing, and pace of change and determine whether and how economic development and its benefits spread across sectors and regions.[7]

Economic development (as opposed to growth) cannot take place without a progressive and radical social transformation. In particular, it requires improving agricultural productivity and widening access to land. As many scholars have emphasized, this depends, in turn, on the reorganization of agriculture and the revamping of class relationships (e.g., Moore 1966). But landowning elites, like all privileged classes, tend to resist measures that require them to relinquish their privileges. There is, as Rueschemeyer et al. point out, a "near-universal tendency of the powerful to preserve their position" (1992: 60). In consequence, radical social transformation rarely (if ever?) takes place in the absence of war or natural disaster.[8] Economic development also requires a change in the structure of employment: workers must be assured of an increasing share in the productivity increments that take place in each sector, but privileged classes also resist measures that would ensure this – such as those that enable trade unionism to develop as an effective instrument of working-class representation.

Today's advanced industrial countries are those in which the balance of power among classes permitted a broadening of the distribution of wealth sufficient to raise the standard of living of the mass of workers and increase the wealth of those countries as a whole relative to others. This occurred in countries that (1) never had an entrenched landed elite (e.g., Canada and Australia); (2) saw a significant decline in the power of landowners as a result of civil war (e.g., the United States and Russia); (3) experienced a breakdown of their traditional social structures and massive land reforms as a result of either invasion and external forces (e.g., Japan) or devastating wars (e.g., most of Europe).

In Europe, the destruction of the traditional class structure as a consequence of the world wars strengthened the working class and weakened the

---

[7] Robert Packenham asks, "What were the powerful egalitarian elements in the Brazilian tradition that were being smothered by foreign pressures?" Elitism, tolerance for massive socioeconomic disparities, capitalism, and authoritarianism "are powerful and authentic national traditions" (1992: 147). In fact, as Alejandro Portes notes, domestic owners, managers of multinational subsidiaries, and top administrators of public enterprises "are united by their common position relative to subordinate groups and their interest in preserving the status quo." They "have coalesced in supporting the rise of conservative governments and have joined forces in opposing the various forms of populism and socialism in the region" (1985: 10–11). Morris and Adelman concluded in their study of developing countries that "domestic dominance of government policy did not assure widely beneficial economic growth" (1988: 210).

[8] As Jorge Ahumada notes, "there is nothing inherent in the structure and dynamic of the Latin American economy . . . that can be expected to lead spontaneously . . . to a narrowing of . . . the glaring discrepancies in the distribution of private income" (1963: 116).

upper classes.[9] New trade unions were organized, and unions that before the war had been hindered by police repression were reorganized. For the first time, parties representing labor became legitimate participants in the political process. As a result, after World War II, Europe enjoyed rapid growth, broadly based prosperity, and relative peace.

The contrast with Latin America is instructive. As Chapter 8 showed, on the eve of World War I, Latin America had achieved a level of economic development and well being about equal with that of Europe. But Latin America did not experience the massive slaughter and destruction that Europe suffered as a result of the two world wars. Most of Latin America (including Brazil) avoided extensive participation in the world wars. As a result, Latin America never experienced the large-scale transformation of landholding and class structures that occurred in Europe. It was not, like Japan and the "Asian tigers," part of the geostrategic encirclement and containment of the Soviet Union, and so did not have a massive land reform imposed on it. While it continued to experience economic growth, it did not participate in the historically unprecedented boom of the 1950s and 1960s and, instead, became part of the third world. As a result, while Europe achieved sustained growth based on a more equitable distribution of income, development in Latin America after World War II continued, as before, to be in general limited to areas tied to its main export sectors.

GLOBALIZATION: THE "GREAT TRANSFORMATION" REVERSED?

In Europe, the demand for labor and need for its cooperation during World War II compelled a political accommodation of working-class movements. The accommodation was sustained after the war by the need for working-class cooperation in resuming the fight against socialism. The struggle against socialism had been interrupted when Germany's invasion of France and attack on Britain had forced the nonfascist capitalist countries to enter into a temporary alliance with the Soviet Union. These countries had been successful in containing the spread of socialism between 1917 and 1939. But following the interruption of World War II, and within a period of a few years, socialism made huge gains. Social democratic reforms were institutionalized in varying degrees throughout Europe, the crusading anticommunist old right in Europe was suppressed, and the communist pattern of organization had spread to much of Eastern Europe, as well as to China. To prevent it from spreading still farther and wider – to the colonial areas in Africa and Asia that had become independent from European powers – the struggle against the Soviet Union that had commenced with the

[9] One indicator of the change in class power was the swell in labor organization after World War I from an average prewar level of 9 percent of the labor force to a postwar peak of 30 percent (Rueschemeyer et al. 1992: 91–92).

Bolshevik revolution in 1917 was resumed after World War II and continued unabated until 1989.

The class compromise concluded in Europe after World War II was based on Keynesian and social democratic goals and policy instruments. It required that social democrats consent to private ownership of the means of production and that capitalists use the profits they realized from this to increase productive capacity and partly for distribution as gains to other groups (Przeworski 1979: 56). The state administered the compromise by resuming the welfare and regulatory functions that it had relinquished in the nineteenth century.

The Keynesian social democratic compromise in Europe, like the Fordist compromise in the United States, took place "within the wider context of the struggle against Communism" (Lipietz 1992: 6). Keynesian policies in Europe provided "a real third alternative" between old-style capitalism and Marxism, "the absence of which...had driven many into the Communist camp" (Winch 1969: 349). Employers had to grant wage increases in order to "keep workers away from Communism and create an army of consumers" (Lipietz 1992: 10). Given the strength of the left and the labor movement throughout Western Europe, "[t]o resist wage demands strenuously...would have invited a further radicalization of the working class and raised the specter of revolution" (Block 1977: 77–78).

The United States had already adopted Fordism during the Great Depression. Fordism increased mass production on the basis of higher mass consumption. It also reworked the technical division of labor in such a way as to fully develop relative surplus value production and, simultaneously, deskill labor (see Chandler 1977; Aglietta 1979). After World War II, Fordism became permanent. The participation of U.S. workers in the war effort during World War II transformed the position of labor unions. U.S. unions were never granted the role that British union leaders were, but union leaders were put on the War Production Board and other tripartite committees, and in exchange for a no-strike pledge, they gained guarantees that increased their membership and enhanced their financial security. In 1933, one-tenth of the work force had belonged to trade unions (3.5 million workers); in 1946, more than one-third of American workers had joined unions (Macshane 1992: 79).

However, the Fordist compromise in the United States required far less of a concession by capital than did the Keynesian social democratic compromise in Europe. The United States had already made the shift to mass production and consumption when it adopted Fordism. It had poured its steel into its own railroads and then into automobiles,[10] and it had enjoyed

---

[10] In 1914 in the United States there was about one car per thirty-five persons, a level not reached by European countries until the 1960s. By the 1920s, 30 percent of American steel

a higher level of domestic investment and had grown faster than Western European economies (Schonfield 1965: 5–6). U.S. industry had few competitors, so the higher wages conceded as part of the Fordist compromise could be paid for by higher prices. With few competitors, industry could also add capacity relatively cheaply. Moreover, Keynesian policies delivered benefits to the monopoly sector by functioning as a welfare program for the mass production of armaments that, in the United States, had begun in the 1860s and thereafter had become an increasingly important part of the U.S. economy.

For a time, governments of advanced industrial countries pursued more internally oriented policies that centered production and services on local and national needs. In the 1960s, however, the competitive advantage enjoyed by U.S. industry began to erode;[11] as international competition from Europe and Japan intensified, profit margins in the United States began to narrow. Business blamed the narrowing profitability on wage increases.[12] Wage increases previously had been paid for by higher prices. But when international competition began to act as a constraint on pricing in the 1970s, capitalists were caught in a profit squeeze between labor keeping wages high and foreign competitors holding prices down (Cox 1987: 280; see also Rupert 1995: 177–78). Tight labor markets in the United States had pushed up wages and compressed wage structures through the late 1960s. But reducing wages was precluded by labor militancy and by the political radicalism engendered by mass conscription for the Vietnam War.

High levels of inflation[13] and slow growth, surplus capacity, and low investment characterized the 1970s. Governments first responded with, among other measures, tighter foreign exchange controls and closer restrictions on foreign direct investment.[14] Business promoted a strategy to protect short-term profitability by keeping wage increases below productivity growth and pushing down domestic costs. Growth depended on increasing investment, and this, it was argued, could be had only by increasing profit margins

---

went into automobiles. This had been an important factor in American "isolationism" before World War II (Kurth 1979: 27–28).

[11] A decline in the U.S. share of world manufactured exports and an intensification of import competition in the U.S. home market began in the 1960s. For a discussion, see Rupert 1995: 176–77; Coates 2000: 28–32.

[12] Cox 1987: 279–80. For a discussion of the debate on trade union power, see Coates 2000: chap. 4.

[13] Inflation in the industrialized capitalist countries grew from an average of 5.3 percent annually (1970–72) to 10 percent annually (1974 to the end of the 1970s; Cox 1987: 274).

[14] Other measures included controls on prices and wages, interstate and state intervention in energy markets, bailing out (in some cases through nationalization) loss-making firms and industries, and illiberal forms of trade protection including in particular (so-called) voluntary export restraint agreements.

through wage restraint and a radical restructuring of production to reduce costs – a more technology-intensive production using fewer permanent and skilled workers.

But in the United States, business was also concerned to escape the implications of class compromise in a "sealed-off domestic context."[15] It renewed its attack on state regulatory policies. It engaged in concerted political action to get states to deregulate industry and markets, privatize their assets, and curtail their welfare functions.[16]

In response, states began to dismantle the restrictions and barriers on capital mobility that they had imposed after World War II and to restructure or eliminate regulatory agencies and social welfare programs. In 1978, the United States introduced far-reaching measures of deregulation; the following year marked the beginning of a series of measures that moved the United Kingdom in the same direction.[17] The shift in the other Organization for Economic Cooperation and Development countries and the European Community began in the early to mid-1980s. The consequence has been (1) a return to methods of absolute surplus value production at home and (2) the expansion of export-oriented growth.

In the 1970s and early 1980s, U.S. manufacturing capital went searching overseas for areas of redundant labor supply and labor cheaper than they could be found at home. Labor-intensive industries such as garment assembly and textiles and the labor-intensive portions of the newly emerging electronics industry moved to low-wage export processing zones in Asia and Mexico.[18]

The increase in capital mobility and foreign investment and the ability to move production to low-wage areas forced workers to compete with

---

[15] Van der Pijl 1998: 119. Van der Pijl dates this development from the emergence of U.S. hegemony at the end of World War II. In his account, it was not in the 1970s but much earlier that America's "Fordist mode of accumulation and the class compromises on which it rested were extrapolated to the international level" (Van der Pijl 1984: 94).

[16] In the United States, the problem of poverty has been treated, once again, as arising from individual defects rather than structural causes. Consistent with this are initiatives in the United States for "faith-based" welfare – which relies on religious morality to judge who is worthy of charity.

[17] Changes in direction took place in France (1982–83), Australia (1983), Canada (1984), and New Zealand (1984). Among the developing countries, the first major program of reform was that launched by the Pinochet government in Chile in the mid-1970s. China's historic new departure began in 1978.

[18] "Light" industries such as textile production and semi-automated food processing are highly labor-intensive, but other industries are as well. The electronics industry remains highly labor-dependent, with labor accounting for about half of its costs of production (Mandel 1978: 206).

It might be argued that, while some manufacturing jobs moved south, many more service ones were created. Coates argues, however, that "It is not the loss of manufacturing employment that is currently threatening U.S. living standards so much as the concentration of those displaced workers in low productivity service provision" (2000: 29).

low-wage labor elsewhere. This reduced the bargaining power of labor relative to capital in negotiations that determined wages and working conditions, not only in industries experiencing capital outflow but in related industries, as well (Crotty and Epstein 1996: 131). The methods of absolute surplus value production returned: intensifying work regimes; reducing real wages; cutting health, pension, and social safety net protections; and eroding job security by restructuring employment away from full-time and secure employment into part-time and insecure work.

There has also been a return to export-oriented expansion. As Herman Schwartz notes, the U.S. capital exports that mark this expansion differ in a number of ways from those that characterized the outflow of U.S. "productive" capital to Europe and elsewhere after World War II. Before the 1970s, U.S. capital exports were relatively small (British capital exports in the nineteenth century had amounted to 10 percent of GDP; at their peak, those of the United States had been around 2 percent of GDP). U.S. firms invested in Europe because it was the only way to access European markets, given "[t]he sharp drop in the trade share of GDP that occurred in Europe subsequent to the depression, the persistence of capital and currency controls, and the presence of substantial non-tariff barriers...." Moreover, these investments had supported an overall system of welfare, income equality, and higher wages at home. "While firms fought for market share overseas, they did so in ways that boosted workers' incomes and domestic demand rather than suppressing those incomes" (Schwartz 2002–3: 340–41).

The U.S. capital exports that began in the late 1970s, however, are part of an overall shift that involves downsizing work forces and resetting corporate activity "at ever lower levels of output and employment" (Williams, Williams, and Haslam 1989: 292). In fact, despite the tendency to refer to current trends collectively as "neo-liberal" globalization, the expansion underpinning globalization has been essentially *anti*liberal in nature. Like that which underpinned Europe's nineteenth-century expansion, it is characterized by increasing concentration and monopoly. Large firms are tending increasingly to buy existing assets through mergers and acquisitions rather than to build new ones. The purpose of these, as Jonathan Nitzan argues, is to avoid creating new capacity so as to prevent glut and falling profit and to augment the power of large firms (Nitzan and Bichler 2001: 241). Nitzan argues that firms tend to pursue "differential accumulation": a faster rise of profit than the average so as to make their distributive share bigger.[19] The most important and effective path to differential gain, and the one to which large firms most incline, is through mergers and acquisitions. "Once the national scene has been more or less integrated, the main avenue for further expansion [through differential accumulation] is across international

[19] For implications and applications of the concept of "differential accumulation," see Nitzan 1998, 2002; Nitzan and Bichler 2001.

borders, hence the current *global* merger wave" (Nitzan and Bichler 2001: 245). Nitzan predicts that "far from contributing to growth," this wave of mergers "is likely to further exacerbate stagnation and unemployment" (Nitzan 2002: 261).

An economic development process involves accumulation of capital and the employment of more personnel to increase productive capacity. This can be achieved either by expansion – a simple multiplication of the capacity at a given moment – or by intensification, that is, an improvement in production techniques. Before World War II, economic development in Europe proceeded principally by means of lateral gains, through the acquisition of spheres of interest, rather than intensive gains, through improved organization or productivity. Similarly, U.S. expansion today is proceeding not through the creation of additional capacity but by lateral gains: by squeezing other countries' firms out of their markets, restructuring those markets and integrating them into U.S. commodity chains; and, increasingly, through buying existing assets through mergers (Nitzan 2001). As was pointed out previously, adding capacity is cheap when you are without competitors. Once there is competition, there is the threat of glut and declining profit. Thus, key players are concerned with keeping overall capacity from growing too fast.

The position of the United States following World War II was similar to that of Britain at the end of the Napoleonic Wars (another, earlier world war). Britain had emerged from the Napoleonic Wars with an economy that was far stronger than those of its nearest competitors. Its takeoff to industrial development prior to the war had occurred on the basis of the expansion of its domestic market (for this argument, see Chapter 2). The United States emerged from World War II with an economy that, like Britain's in 1815, was far stronger than those of its nearest competitors. The United States had industrialized, as had Britain, on the basis of the expansion of its domestic market. However, its growth has come to depend, as had Britain's, on the global integration of cross-national commodity chains, the acquisition of cheap labor abroad, and a backflow of cheap goods to keep wages down at home.

The "taproot" of U.S. expansion today and that of Britain in the nineteenth century is also similar. Just as Hobson argued that the taproot of Britain's nineteenth-century imperialism was a politically created maldistribution of income in the British domestic economy, the taproot of U.S.-driven globalization today, it can be argued, is located in a politically created maldistribution of income in the U.S. domestic economy.[20]

---

[20] This argument, sketched out below, is based on Schwartz 2002–3. Schwartz traces the "taproot of U.S. informal imperialism in Asia" to the maldistribution of income in the U.S. domestic market. For more on this argument, see below.

GLOBALIZATION REDUX? THE INCOMMENSURABILITY
THESIS EXAMINED

The Incommensurability Thesis I: The Nature of "Globalization" Today

Hobson argued that, in the nineteenth century, a politically created mal-distribution of income in the British domestic economy had led, first, to underconsumption and, second, to the export of capital. This was not, he argued, a necessary outcome of capitalist development. If the domestic distribution of income was shifted from *rentiers* toward workers, a raise in domestic demand would create new and profitable opportunities for investment at home and obviate the need for aggressive external expansion.

After World War II, there was a dramatic shift in wealth and income away from the top of the income/wealth spectrum. Political mechanisms redistributed productivity gains to workers, ensuring rising domestic demand to accommodate the rising output that resulted from rationalization and economies of scale. The result in the developed economies was rapid and intensive growth, full or near full employment, and an increase in the standard of consumption of the working class.

However, in the late 1970s, substantial exports of financial capital reemerged and, thereafter, grew rapidly. Herman Schwartz argues that, despite the fact that Britain was an "under-consumptionist capital exporter" in the nineteenth century, while the U.S. today is an overconsumptionist capital exporter, the underlying dynamic fueling both British expansion in the nineteenth century and U.S. expansion today is the same. The "inversion of over and under-consumption," he argues, "is simply the surface manifestation of a more important underlying phenomenon that is consistent with Hobson's analysis (2002–3: 349)." Consistent with Hobson's analysis of British imperial expansion as generated by a politically created maldistribution of income in the British domestic market, Schwartz traces "the taproot of U.S. informal imperialism in Asia" to the politically created maldistribution of income in the U.S. domestic market.

The structure of British imperial finance, Schwartz reminds us, rested not just on exports of British capital but also on imports of capital into Britain. Most non-British banks kept large, low-interest, short-term deposits in London banks. As long as sterling was the international reserve currency of choice and virtually all international transactions cleared in London, Britain could borrow short-term at extremely low interest rates and then loan that money long-term at higher interest rates. The Bank of England aggressively raised short-term interest rates when capital flowed out of London, to avoid maturity mismatches and also to profit from arbitraging between different interest rates.

Schwartz argues that the structure of U.S. lending after 1971 parallels Britain's in the nineteenth century. Beginning in the 1970s, enormous flows of long-term capital from the United States produced, in turn, enormous imports of short-term capital back into the United States. As in Britain, in the United States, holders of capital issue fixed income securities and invest the proceeds in higher yielding equities and productive investments. In this way, Asian and European holdings of liquid U.S. financial assets finance the continued expansion of the U.S. economy by creating additional purchasing power in the U.S. domestic market and financing continued investment by U.S. firms in real productive capacity.[21] It also creates more fictitious capital,[22] permitting U.S. firms to continue to invest at home and abroad with a low cost of capital.

As was the case with Britain, consumers of U.S. investment goods tend to have stunted domestic markets and hyperextended export sectors. If Asian states released the trade surpluses that are parked in U.S. financial instruments into Asian domestic economies, domestic consumption and imports would surge. Instead, they constrict local consumption through fairly strict control over labor unions and workers[23] and, thus, make their economies increasingly reliant on a narrow range of exports to the U.S. economy.

The 1990s investment wave made Asia even more structurally reliant for growth on exports to the U.S. market.[24] These investments produced extensive growth in low-priced Asian textiles, toys, and household goods, as well as low-end electronics, cars, and car parts. This increased output flowed into the U.S. market.

The huge increase in Asian and especially Chinese production had exactly the effects that Hobson predicted. Hobson argued:

Once encompass China with a network of railroads and steamer services, the size of the labour market to be tapped is so stupendous that it might well absorb in its development all the spare capital and business energy that the advanced European countries and the United States can supply for generations. . . . the pressure on the working-class movements in politics and industry in the West can be met by a flood of China goods, so as to keep down wages and compel [labor discipline]. . . . (Hobson 1902: 313, in Schwartz 2002–3: 346–47).

The difference, Schwartz argues, is that these effects have been largely felt by Asian workers and not, immediately, by U.S. ones. The "huge reservoir

---

[21] By November 2001, the Asian economies had huge holdings of U.S. Treasury and other passive foreign assets: Japan, $404 billion; China, $196 billion; Taiwan, $122 billion; Hong Kong, $111 billion; Korea, $103 billion; Singapore, $77 billion (Hong Kong Monetary Authority 2002; in Schwartz 2002–3: 345).

[22] Credit, shares, debt, speculation, and various forms of paper money.

[23] This as well as "appeals to national pride, 'Asian values' and a general sense that Asia's century had arrived were used to gloss over substantial dislocation of peasant populations and worker unrest" (Schwartz 2002–3: 345–46).

[24] There is a high level of intra-Asian exports in comparison to other developing regions. In 2000, for example, 38 percent of Asian (excluding Japan) exports went to other Asian economies. But external demand remains critical for growth (Schwartz 2002–3: 345–46).

of purchasing power" that U.S. workers retain has prevented the emergence of the underconsumptionist dynamic that Hobson described. In the United States, "real wages remained essentially flat from 1980 and 2000, permitting valorization of overseas investments in basic goods" (2002–3: 345). But U.S. investment in mass-consumption articles made with cheaper foreign labor keeps U.S. wages down in *all* sectors and compels labor discipline. This will eventually erode working class power and lead, again, to a withdrawal of "rights" previously held (power over wages and prices).

Overall, the circuit of capital that underpins U.S. expansion redounds to the benefit of those who hold U.S. equities and to the detriment of overseas workers and those in the United States who work in basic manufacturing and/or pay the taxes that fund the U.S. public debt. The circuit, as Greg Albo points out, is leading to

> an unstable vicious circle of *"competitive austerity"*: each country reduces domestic demand and adopts an export-oriented strategy of dumping its surplus production, for which there are fewer consumers in its national economy given the decrease in workers' living standards and productivity gains all going to the capitalists, in the world market.... So long as all countries continue to pursue export-oriented strategies, which is the conventional wisdom demanded by IMF, OECD, and G7 policies and the logic of neo-liberal trade policies, there seems little reason not to conclude that "competitive austerity" will continue to ratchet down the living standards of workers in *both* the North and the South. (1994: 147)

The globalized integration of cross-national commodity chains, together with the process of increasing enclosure and deepening commodification of all possible aspects of daily life, leads inevitably toward the depression of working conditions and wages in the core.

With the emergence of these changes, tensions within European societies began to increase. Beginning in the 1960s, a reappearance of more intense social conflict in Europe, in both the East and the West, became apparent. At the same time, in both parts of Europe, observers began to discern the emergence of class structures reminiscent of nineteenth-century European society and, as a result, a resurgence of nationalism and class conflict.

The post–World War II order is generally considered to have reached a turning point with the events of 1968. Street battles between students and riot police in Paris in May of that year were followed by a general strike that involved ten million workers and closed down most businesses in the country. In Italy, demonstrations that month at the Universities of Milan and Trento spread and eventually paralyzed the Italian university system. Soviet troops sent to Prague to crush reforms engaged in street battles with students. Italian troops fought with left- and right-wing guerrillas in 1970. In 1973, there was a wave of militant strikes in West Germany in the summer of 1973, and government troops in Greece killed thirty-four student demonstrators in street battles in Athens.

In the post–World War II period, millions of people from the rural under-developed south of Europe – Portugal, Spain, southern Italy, Yugoslavia, and Greece – and from Turkey and Algeria, Pakistan, and India have moved into the factories of industrial Europe – France, Germany, north-ern Italy, Switzerland, Britain, and other countries (Castles 1984: 146–48). The proportion of immigrant workers is considerable today in France and Germany; in Switzerland they comprise about one-third of the total labor force, and almost the whole of the manual working class.

By the 1960s, this massive import of foreign workers had begun a process of new class formation in Western European societies. Today, they represent a new "subproletariat." For the most part, they work at the least attractive and worst paid manual jobs. Their rates of unemployment are higher than those of indigenous workers, and in periods of recession, their unemploy-ment rises faster (Castles 1984: 149). Unrepresented in the government and unorganized, they are unable to bring effective pressure on either employer or government for higher wages, shorter hours, or better working conditions. Foreign workers played a leading role in the events of May 1968 in Paris and elsewhere (Castles 1984: chap. 1). Other waves of strikes in Western Europe since then have been led by these workers (e.g., a wave of militant strikes in West Germany in the summer of 1973 that involved mainly foreign workers). The immigrant groups, particularly those from poorer lands, are often content with or resigned to less space and comfort than older workers, creating, as David Landes observes, "a situation reminiscent, in small, of the industrial slums of the early 19th century" (1969: 501). Immigrants and their descendants are forming new ethnic minorities in Europe. Racism is on the upsurge in all the countries of immigration, expressed in media campaigns against immigrants, racist attacks, the growth of neo-Nazi organizations, and the emphasis on racial problems in the policies of major political parties (Castles 1984: chap. 1).

After the 1960s, there were also changes in Eastern Europe and in the Soviet Union reminiscent of pre-1945 Europe. The relative decline in the material and social standing of the proletariat and the corresponding ad-vancement of the new white-collar professions has resulted in a class strat-ification system in Eastern Europe that became by the end of the 1960s in many ways similar to that of Western capitalism (Parkin 1969: 255–74). Reforms introduced in nearly all Eastern European countries beginning in the 1960s that aimed at instituting greater market freedom widened income differentials (Parkin 1969: 361–64). Yugoslavia, which instituted market re-forms earlier and far more radically than the other socialist countries (Landy 1961) became also the most politically volatile and the scene of the greatest communal violence.

At the end of the 1970s, the economies of Eastern Europe began to slow dramatically. The East had overinvested in heavy industrial sectors while not introducing technological advances rapidly enough. Eastern European governments sought therefore to increase the efficiency of their economies in the 1970s by importing advanced technology from the West. But the high prices of this technology and the low quality of Eastern European manufactured goods meant that these countries had to borrow from Western banks, governments, and international agencies. The slow growth of the world economy in the late 1970s and 1980s made it difficult to repay these loans, and the burden of debt contributed to severe economic crises in Poland, Romania, and Yugoslavia and to increasingly difficult conditions throughout the East (Tipton and Aldrich 1987b: 248–52).

Demonstrations and strikes took place throughout the final years of the 1980s in the Soviet Union. In 1989, a wave of demonstrations swept through Eastern Europe – in Poland, Czechoslovakia, the German Democratic Republic (GDR), Romania, Bulgaria, Albania, and Yugoslavia. These were the prelude to relatively peaceful "revolutions" that that year brought about a change of government in Poland, Czechoslovakia, the GDR, Romania, and Bulgaria.

The revolutions of 1989 were aimed at accelerating the marketization begun in the 1960s. They were initiated by those elements within the increasingly deproletarianized communist parties (see, e.g., Taborsky 1961: 32–37; Von Lazar 1966) best able to take advantage of marketization and capitalist forms of ownership. The revolutionaries were members of the old nomenklatura seeking a future in new "market" fiefdoms (see, e.g., Tismeneanu 1989: 31; Lipski 1989–90: 19–21). It was this element of the ruling elite in Eastern Europe that was in the best position to take advantage of marketization and capitalist forms of ownership and that sought to accelerate the conversion of East European economies to market systems. Following the revolutions, there was a marked increase in class conflict in Eastern Europe. Societies became much more visibly stratified. There has been a further decline in living standards. For the first time in the post–World War II order within Eastern Europe, armies of the unemployed have emerged alongside the new entrepreneurial classes. The reemergence of inequality in Eastern European societies is already much in evidence, as are class tensions and, perhaps, the early beginnings of a process of class struggle.

The Incommensurability Thesis II: The Nature of Labor Today

The discussion of the preceding chapters suggests that the trends that collectively we term "globalization" can be halted by politically mobilizing labor together with other social forces to secure concessions from capital. But are we at a historical juncture that precludes this remedy? Many people characterize the historic class compromise concluded between labor and capital following World War II as a "positive" class compromise, since both parties (capital and labor) gained something from expanding aggregate demand through Keynesian policies (Lipietz 1992; Glyn 1995; Brecher 1997;

Wright 2000). Nationally regulated capitalism in 1945 offered capitalists a trade-off: while the compromise required that they concede to higher labor costs and restrictions on hiring and firing, it also provided them with stable commodities markets and labor markets.

But some analysts have argued that a nationally based positive class compromise is no longer possible. While nationally regulated capitalism in advanced industrial countries offered capitalists *some* advantages up until around 1975, after the mid-1970s the development of countries in other parts of the world and the possibilities for significantly expanding commodities and labor markets increasingly eroded the conditions on which these advantages were based (see Table 9.1). The development of a world market for commodities means that the sale of commodities no longer depends on the purchasing power of those workers who produce them. Thus, Keynesian demand management solutions no longer have the same appeal. Capitalists do not have to treat labor as a factor of consumption. They sell to other states and wealthy groups within other states.

If nationally regulated capital no longer provides advantages for capitalists, it follows that the only compromise by which labor might gain concessions from capital is a *negative* class compromise, that is, one in which both sides give up something. This requires an increase in the power of labor relative to that of capital. Many contend, however, that because

TABLE 9.1. *Advantages for Capitalists of Capitalism That Is Nationally Embedded and Disembedded, 1950–1975 and 1975–2000*

Interests of capitalists	1950–1975		1975–2000	
	Embedded	Disembedded	Embedded	Disembedded
• Minimize labor costs		X		X
• Hire and fire labor at will		X		X
• Sell all commodities produced	X		X	
• Have a particular mix of skills in the labor market	X		X	
• Have predictable and adequate supplies of labor	X		X	

increased heterogeneity and inequality within labor markets have irrevocably eroded the economic conditions for labor solidarity (Teeple 1995; see also Wright 2000), the conditions for negative compromise no longer exist either (e.g., Teeple 1995; Standing 1997). The post–World War II compromise created "a new, fragmented proletariat, that is parcellized and interchangeable" (Buci-Glucksman 1979: 226). Moreover, with globalization, an industrial pattern has emerged that, by combining high technology in some phases of production with labor-intensive manual production in others, has further fragmented the labor process between automated parent plants and labor-dependent assembly plants located in low-wage areas.

However, the assumption that these are new and insurmountable conditions facing labor is erroneous. Industrial development in Europe before the world wars was largely carried out by atomized, low-wage, and low-skilled labor forces. Labor became largely permanent and full-time only as a *result* of the postwar compromise. The compromise was concluded at a time when labor was neither permanent nor full-time nor represented by national industrial unions. Moreover, since capitalists were free to take their capital elsewhere, the conditions for forging labor solidarity internationally were no more favorable than they are today. In the nineteenth century, competition of goods produced by lower wage European workers and threats by employers to replace striking workers with Europeans were as much a bar to winning British workers to the cause of international labor solidarity as the analagous situation is for workers in the United States today (Collins and Abramsky 1965: 39).

The attempt to create working-class internationalism by means of the labor Internationale and as a response to capitalist globalization ultimately proved ineffective. The International Working Men's Association, founded in 1864, established regular contacts between labor leaders of different countries and, in many countries, inspired trade union organization and helped to formulate some of the ideas that later became the basis of the demands of organized labor. But it failed to organize the unskilled majority of the working class.[25] Though the Second Internationale (1889–1914) was much larger than its predecessor, labor internationalism ultimately proved "unable to move beyond the exchange of information and a reinforcement of national union identities."[26] It was mobilization for war in 1914 that, by driving unskilled labor into the ranks of organized labor for the

---

[25] It was hardly "the powerful, well administered, smoothly functioning organization of current legend" (Collins and Abramsky 1965: v–vi).

[26] "Unions looked increasingly towards the state as the source of economic and social protection. . . . Far from the workers having no country, that was almost all they had, including the transferred allegiance to another country, claimed as the workers' state, the Soviet Union" (Macshane 1992: 47).

first time (between 1914 and 1921), created a unified and powerful labor force.[27]

CONCLUSIONS: LESSONS FROM HISTORY

In current discourses, "globalization" tends to be misrepresented in two ways. First, it is wrongly represented as either a radical and absolute break with the past or the result of an evolutionary process. Second, it is treated as impelled by macroeconomic forces and the technological evolution of capitalism. Globalization is not new; capitalism "globalized" from the start.[28] Moreover, the processes currently working to *accelerate* capitalist globalization are, first and foremost, *political* and *national* rather than macroeconomic. A broad-based political campaign is endeavoring to accelerate the globalization of capital today. While it is being waged on many fronts, it is specifically aimed at reversing the postwar social settlements that tied capital to the development of national communities by shifting power from labor to capital *within states* and undermining democratic national governments.

Throughout its history, the globalization of capital has been driven by processes that are largely national and political.[29] In the eighteenth century, the acceleration of capitalist globalization was made possible by a shift in the overall balance of class power in favor of *capital*. The overall balance of class power shifted in favor of *labor* after the world wars, forcing capitalists to concede to nationally regulated capital in order to maintain their position in relation to labor.

Two factors in particular helped to bring about an increase of working-class political power relative to that of capital. First, World War I forced governments and ruling groups to mobilize the masses for war for the first time since the Napoleonic Wars. This was decisive in increasing the organizational strength, unity, and political power of labor. Second was the participation of labor in broad-based social movements in which struggles for democracy, for workers' and minority rights, and for protection against the market merged. Today the role of unions in these struggles in various parts of the world is seen as representing a new form of labor politics and is called "social movement unionism."

[27] Unskilled workers became active in Germany for the first time after World War I. Revolutionary protests and strikes in the Balkans, Hungary, and Czechoslovakia after World War I involved mainly urban unskilled labor and peasants (Seton-Watson 1945: 134–38; McClellan 1964: 275–96).

[28] That globalization is the *necessary* product of capital's expansion was asserted in 1848 by Marx and Engels in the *Communist Manifesto*: "The need of a constantly expanding market for its products chases the bourgeoisie over the whole surface of the globe."

[29] This, I have argued elsewhere (Halperin 1997a), is as true for the periphery as for the core: it is local dominant classes that are decisive in bringing about external reliance and in determining how the benefits of collaboration with foreign capital are distributed and used.

But working-class activism in nineteenth- and early twentieth-century Europe was always part of a broad social movement. Labor struggles were waged in both the marketplace and the political arena, and because those who participated in them were embedded in ethnic, national, and other communities and identities, class and minority (ethnic and religious) issues and conflicts were often thoroughly intertwined. Mass mobilization for war and the increasing strength of social movement unionism in national arenas were both products of a system of dualistic industrial expansion that generated social conflicts at home and rivalries and tensions among the advanced capitalist countries.

With the reembedding of capital after 1945, unions became more narrowly based and focused, and, as a result, national union federations came to represent a declining and often minor part of the working population (Norway and Sweden are exceptions). After World War II, states ceased to raise citizen armies and to mobilize mass populations to fight wars. The Vietnam War ended the use of citizen armies in the United States. Since then, the Cold War fight has depended on the use of anticommunist mercenary armies wherever possible (the Contras in Nicaragua, Renamo in Mozambique, Savimbi's forces in Angola), selective military engagement, and occupation of strategic chokepoints (both geographically and institutionally). As was the case with nineteenth-century European imperialism, the deployment of military force to secure and defend capitalist globalization today is being carried out by professional armies. Overall, this has weakened the bargaining position of workers and strengthened the position of capital.[30]

Recent changes in the organization of production are not being driven by the logic of technological development, markets, or international capital. Production processes, as Alfred Sohn-Rethel (1978b) has pointed out, are designed in part to consolidate and maintain the basic relation of capital – the subordination of labor to capital. These changes are, therefore, never politically neutral. Globalization is fundamentally political in nature. States and interstate regimes have played a key role, today as in the past, in defining and guaranteeing through state policies, military action, and international treaties the domestic and global rights of capital.

The mobilization of opposition in local and national arenas has played a key role in opposing capitalist globalization. International solidarity ties have helped, too, but they cannot provide an effective alternative to national

---

[30] "The replacing of mass conscript armies with professional armed forces," as Joachim Hirsch has argued, "is incompatible with maintaining the principles of citizenship. Universal liability for military service has historically been inseparable from democracy" (1999: 309). What would be the consequence, in the current context of widespread antiglobalization sentiment, if governments depended on mass citizen armies to advance and defend through military means the further globalization of capital?

mobilization. It was mobilization in national arenas not internationally and not for industry but for war that succeeded in bridging the divide between urban and rural, skilled and unskilled labor and increasing labor's relative power within European societies.

Karl Polanyi treats the emergence of the unregulated market system as unprecedented, and its demise as inevitable. But Europe's nineteenth-century market system was not a once-and-for-all occurrence. It was part of a struggle over the distribution of costs and benefits of industrial capitalism that began centuries ago and that continues today. It is most likely the *recurrence* of unregulated markets that is inevitable; most likely their demise is not. The "double movement" that Polanyi places at the center of his analysis suggests that unregulated markets, by inevitably triggering a protective reaction from all sectors of society, will inevitably be destroyed. But if, as I have argued, the balance of social forces determines who gets protection and when and if change occurs, then the notion that a Polanyian double movement has emerged or will inevitably emerge to bring about the reembedding of capital may engender a complacency that is unwarranted.

Appendix 1

Europe Defined

Geographers are not agreed as to precisely which lands are to be regarded as included in or lying outside Europe. There is a difference of opinion concerning several islands in the Atlantic and the Mediterranean. Here, Great Britain and Ireland; Iceland; the Faeroe, Channel, and Frisian Islands; Madeira and Heligoland; Cyprus, the Ionian, Balearic, and Aegean Islands; Corsica and Sardinia, Sicily, Malta, and Crete will all be included as part of "Europe."

There are also difficulties in classifying the Ottoman Empire and Russia, which, in terms of their histories and geographical location, straddle two regions.

Some or all of both entities should be considered as part of Europe. Russia actively participated in the Napoleonic Wars that were fought during the period with which this study begins. After 1815, Russia played a major political role in Europe. Russia, together with Great Britain, Austria, and Prussia, formed a Quadruple Alliance that provided for collective security against a renewal of French aggression and a "Concert of Europe" to facilitate major power cooperation in keeping order. Russia, with its "Army of Europe," and Austria led the Concert in intervening to put down uprisings in Spain and Italy (1820s), in Poland (1830), in Hungary (1848–49), and in Herzegovina (1862). The Ottoman Empire was also intimately involved in the affairs of Europe. It was weighed in the balance of Europe throughout the nineteenth and early twentieth centuries. The "Eastern Question" was a European problem of central importance throughout that period and had critical implications for the balance of power in the region. The Powers of Europe formally recognized the Ottoman Empire as a member of the Concert of Europe at the Congress of Paris in 1855.

Russia and the Ottoman Empire are commonly divided into a European part (Russia west of the Urals, the Ottoman provinces on the European continent) and an Asiatic part (in Russia, from the Urals eastward to the Pacific, and the parts of the Ottoman Empire lying on the Asian continent).

297

European Russia is treated here as part of "Europe." During the period covered by this study, Russia officially recognized the crest of the Urals and the Caucasus as her European limits, though the boundaries of the Russian administrative divisions bore no relation to these. These areas were considered by other states to be part of Europe and were claimed and fought over by Romania, Czechoslovakia, Germany, Poland, and Finland. On the other hand, areas of Asian Russia in contention among European powers were considered as part of Asia and thus as potential colonial acquisitions rather than as a division of European territory. Asian Russia, including Transcaucasia, is therefore treated as lying outside the region, and the conflicts that occur there are recorded in the data as "extraregional wars."

Similar considerations are applicable to the classification of the European and Asian parts of the Ottoman Empire. The provinces of the Ottoman Empire that lie on the continent of Europe are treated as part of Europe in this study; the provinces of the Ottoman Empire on the Asian continent are treated as lying outside the region, and the conflicts that occur there are recorded in the data as extraregional wars. An exception is made for Smyrna, which is included here in "Europe"; its history during the nineteenth and early twentieth century was continually bound up with European populations and movements and with regional politics. The European provinces of the Ottoman Empire were part of Europe prior to the fourteenth century, and the populations of those areas considered themselves and were considered by Europeans to be European. The European provinces were bound up with European movements and events; the Asian provinces were largely or totally unaffected. The revolutions of 1830 and 1848 reverberated throughout the Ottoman Empire's European provinces, but had no impact elsewhere in the Empire. Balkan nationalist movements were among the first to appear on the continent following the French Revolution; the rest of the Empire was indifferent to nationalism until the twentieth century.

It would make very little difference to the data or the argument presented here if conflicts in Asian Russia and Asian Turkey had been included in my data for Europe. In the nineteenth century, uprisings in Asian Russia and Asian Turkey remained limited in scope and did not lead to general revolt. By including the wars of Asian Russia and the Asian Ottoman Empire, three additional wars would have been included as regional wars, rather than as extraregional wars in the data on "Europe's Wars": the Caucasian Campaigns (1829–40), the war in Circassia (1859–64), and the war in Turkestan in 1916 (the wars in Syria and Iraq in the 1920s occurred after the dissolution of the Ottoman Empire, and thus would be considered extraregional wars either way).

Appendix 2

A Sample of Europe's Class, Ethnic, and Imperialist Conflicts, 1789–1945

Some of these conflicts are discussed in Chapter 4. More details on all of them can be found in Appendix 3.

A SAMPLE OF CLASS CONFLICTS IN EUROPE, 1789–1945

These are conflicts over rights and privileges, including the right to vote, secure bread at an affordable price, organize, raise wages, shorten hours of employment, and work in safe conditions. They include violent strikes, industrial riots, and bread, food, and housing riots by urban and agricultural wage laborers, the unemployed, peasants, and soldiers, as well as enfranchisement struggles.

1789	French Revolution
1790	Peasant uprising in Bohemia
	Peasant uprising in Saxony
1791	Priestly riots in Birmingham
1793–95	Uprising in Silesia
	Uprising in Zurich
1798–99	Peasant uprising in Silesia
1800	Lancashire riots
1807	"Rebellion of Tica"
	"Rebellion of Djak"
1808	Lancashire weavers' strike in England
1809–10	Bread and wage riots in Britain
1811–13	Food and wage riots throughout Britain
1815–16	Corn Bill riots
1816	East Anglia (Ely and Littleport) riots in England
1818	Strikes in Lancashire, England
1819	Peterloo massacre in England
	Riots in Hamburg, Frankfurt am Main, Würzburg, and Karlsruhe

1820	Strike in Glasgow
	Revolt in Spain
1822	East Anglian riots
1825	Decembrist revolt in Russia
1826	Peasant uprisings and rebellions in Russia
1830	"Swing" riots in England
	"Tithe War" in Ireland
	Wage riots in Wales
	Insurrections in Germany
	Paris revolt
1830–32	Rebellion in Bosnia (nobles against economic reform)
1831	Insurrection in Russia
	Peasant uprising at Novgorod, Russia
	Colliers' riots in Derbyshire, England
	Wage riots in Glamorgan, Ireland
	Uprisings in Lyons and elsewhere in France
	Uprisings in Rome, Parma, Modena, and Bologna
	Riots in Saxony, Hessen, and Hannover
	Insurrection in Göttingen, Germany
1832	Demonstrations in the Palatinate, Germany
	Uprisings in Paris and elsewhere in France
1834	Uprising of silk workers in Lyons, France
	Insurrection in Paris
1835	Poor Law riots in England
	"Fireworks Revolt" of Berlin journeymen
1838	Rebecca riots in Wales
1839	Insurrection of the Seasons in France
	Chartist demonstrations in England
1840	Strikes in Paris
1841	Tax rebellions in the southwest of France
1842–43	"Rebecca Riots" (peasant uprising) in Wales
1844	Uprising of Silesian weavers
	Uprising of textile and railway workers in Prague
1845	Strike of woolen workers in Lodève, France
	Rimini revolt in Romagna, Italy
1846	Frankfurt riots in Germany
1846–47	Food riots outside Paris
1847	Food riots, the "potato war," in Berlin
	Peasant uprising in Bulgaria
	Revolt of serfs in Russia
Feb. 1848	Uprising of workers in Paris
March 1848	Uprising in Vienna
	Uprising in Pesth
	Uprisings in Posen and Silesia

	Uprising of workers in Berlin
	Insurrections in German states
April 1848	Insurrection in Baden
May 1848	Uprising in Vienna
	Riots in Milan
June 1848	Paris uprising
	Uprising in Wallachia
Nov. 1848	Uprising of workers in Paris
June 1849	Insurrections in Baden, the Rhineland, Dresden, and Bavaria
	Insurrection in Paris
	Insurrection in Lyons
1850	Riots in Prussia
1851	Paris insurrection
1854	Insurrection in Madrid
1860	Uprising and attacks on landlords in Sicily
1861	Peasant uprisings in Italy
1862	Riots and demonstrations in Sicily
1865	Riots in Palermo
1866	"Seven and a Half Revolt" in Palermo
	Riots in Germany
1868	Macinato revolt in Italy
	Revolution in Spain
1868–69	Demonstrations and riots throughout Italy
1869	Labor violence throughout Germany
1869–70	Violent strikes in St. Etienne and Aubin in France
1870	Insurrection in Pavia, Piacenza, Bologna, and Genoa
1871	Paris Commune
1871–72	Violent agricultural strikes in Lombardy
1873	Violent textile strike in Pisa
	Riots in Frankfurt am Main
1874	Bread riots in Tuscany and Emilia-Romagna
	Insurrection in Bologna-Taranto
1877	Insurrection in Benevento-San Lupo, Italy
1878	Insurrection in Mote Labro (Tuscany)
1882	Strikes and demonstrations in Cremona and Parma
1883	Strikes and demonstrations in Verona region of Italy
1884	Strikes and demonstrations in Polezine, Italy
1885	"La Boje" revolt in Mantovano, Italy
1886	Trafalgar Square riots in England
1889	Violent miners' strikes in Ruhr and Silesia
1889	Violent strikes in Lombardy
1889	London dock strike
1890	Violent strike in Ravenna area of Italy
	Clash between socialists and police in Berlin

1893	General Strike in Belgium
	Revolt in Sicily
1896	Demonstrations in Milan
April 1898	Violent demonstrations in Milan and Florence
1900–1901	Insurrectionary strikes at Belfort and Marseilles
1902	Strikes at Leuven, Belgium
1903	Uprising in Bulgaria
	Strikes in the Netherlands
1905	Peasant/worker uprisings in Russia
1906	Strikes of tobacco workers in Bosnia
	Strikes of railwaymen in Bulgaria
1907	Strikes in Belgrade, Serbia
1908	Strikes at Nantes, France
1909	General strike in Spain
	Strikes at Salonika, Macedonia
1910	Violent strikes in Berlin
1911	Liverpool riots in Great Britain
	Uprising in Galicia
1912	Violent strikes in the Ruhr
1913	General strike in Belgium
1914	General strike in Rome
	Strikes in Germany
	Strikes in Russia
	Strikes in Britain
1915	Strike in South Wales
1917	Russian Revolution
	Bread riots in Bavaria, Silesia, Stettin, and Düsseldorf
	Strikes in Germany
	Strike of munitions workers in Germany
	General strike in Italy
1918	Strike in Germany
	Civil war in Finland
	Revolution in Kiel; socialist revolution in Munich; right-wing military putsch attempt in Berlin
1918–19	Strikes in Andalusia suppressed by troops
1918–20	Russian upper classes vs. Bolshevik Revolution
1919	General strike in Switzerland
	Strikes in Bulgaria
	Strikes in Britain
	General strike in Germany
	Spartacist revolt in Berlin
	Communist coup d'etat in Hungary
	Communist revolution in Bavaria

1919–20	Strikes and demonstrations in France
	Strikes in Romania
	Strikes in Italy
1919	Royalist uprising in Portugal
1920	Strike in Bulgaria
	Strikes in Yugoslavia
	Kapp Putsch in Germany
1921	Strikes and communist revolts in Germany
	207 killed, 819 wounded in fascist attacks in Italy
	Kronstadt massacre in Russia
1922	Riots and demonstrations in Germany
1923	Nazi beer hall putsch
	Bulgarian Repression
1926	General Strike in Britain
1927	Riot in Vienna
	Leftist uprising in Portugal
1929	May Day riots in Berlin
1930	Violent strikes in Mansfeld mining area, Germany
1930–34	Massacre of Kulaks, USSR
1931	Strikes in Spain
1932	Riots in France
1933	Revolt in Aragon, Spain
	Uprising in Romania
1934	Civil war in Austria
	Rioting in Paris
	Uprising in Andalusia, Spain
	Four-week general strike in Sargossa
1936–37	Strikes in France
1936–39	Spanish civil war
1938	General strike in France

A SAMPLE OF ETHNIC CONFLICTS IN EUROPE, 1789–1945

These are conflicts involving ethnic minorities that are largely concerned with nationalism, issues of nationality, and national rights, or the ethnicity of those who are the target of the attack.

1798	Uprising in Ireland
1804–13	Serbian uprising
	Insurrection in Bosnia
1808	Insurrection in Portugal
1809	Rebellion in Bosnia
	Uprising in Tyrol

1814	Rebellion in Serbia
1815	Uprising in Serbia
1819	Anti-Jewish riots in German states
	Anti-Prussian riots in German states
1820	Uprising in Piedmont
	Massacre of Turkish population at Petras, Greece
1821	Piedmont revolt
	Insurrection in the Danubian Principalities
1821–30	Greek uprising
1821	Romanian uprising
1830	Uprising in the Netherlands (Belgian Revolution)
1830–31	Bosnian revolt
	Uprising in Poland
1831	Uprising of Slavs against Magyars in Hapsburg lands
	Rebellion in Albania
	Uprising in Hungary
	Uprising in Bulgaria
	Uprising in the Danubian Principalities
	Uprisings in Rome, Parma, Modena, and Bologna
1832	Sonderbund rising in Switzerland
	Nationalist uprising in the palatinate
1832–35	Rebellion in Albania
1832–42	Rebellion in Montenegro
1833	Rebellion in Serbia
1833–40	Basque uprising
1834	Rebellion in Bosnia-Herzegovina
1835	Uprising in Turnovo, Bulgaria
1837	Catholic riots in Rhineland, Westphalia, and Posen
1841	Insurrection in Crete
	Insurrection on the Ionian Islands
	Insurrection in Nis, Serbia
1844	Insurrection in Italy
1845	Rimini revolt in Romagna, Italy
1846	Uprising in Galicia
	Uprising in Denmark
1847	Civil war in Switzerland
	Riots in Milan and Palermo
Sept. 1847	Riots in Messina
Jan. 1848	"Smoking riots" in Milan
	Uprising in Palermo
Feb. 1848	Uprising in Naples
March 1848	Milan uprising
	Piedmont-Austrian War
	Uprising in Vienna

	Uprising in Pesth
	Uprising in Posen and Silesia
	Uprising in Venice
May 1848	Uprising in Vienna
	Riots in Milan
	Serbo-Hungarian civil war
June 1848	Uprising in Wallachia
July 1848	Insurrection in Tipperary, Ireland
Aug. 1848	Uprising in Livorno
Sept. 1848	Insurrection in the Ionian Islands
1848–49	Hungarian insurrection
1849	Insurrection in the Ionian Islands
March 1849	Insurrection in Naples
1850	Insurrection in Bulgaria
1852–53	Revolt in Herzegovina
1853	Turco-Montenegrin War
1857–58	Uprising in Herzegovina
1858	Uprisings in Bosnia
1861–62	Insurrection in Herzegovina
1862	Serbian uprising
	Uprising in Bulgaria
	Montenegrin uprising
1863–65	Polish uprising
1866	Revolt in Epirus
1866–67	Crete insurrection
1868	Uprising in Albania
1872–76	Uprising of minorities in Spain
1872	Catholic riots in Germany
1874–75	Catholic riots in Germany
1875–76	Uprisings in Bosnia-Herzegovina
Sept. 1875	Insurrection in Bulgaria
1876	Bulgarian massacre
	Serbia and Montenegro vs. Turkey
May 1876	Rebellion in Macedonia
1876–78	Insurrection in Crete
1877–1878	Insurrection in Thessaly
1878	Uprising in Bosnia-Herzegovina
1878–79	Rebellion in Macedonia
Oct. 1880	Rebellion in Macedonia
Jan. 1881	Rebellion in Albania
1881	Dalmatian revolt
	Anti-Semitic riots in Pomerania, Germany
1882	Uprising in Herzegovina
1885	Rumelian struggle

1894–96	Armenian massacres in Turkey
1896–97	Insurrection in Crete
1900	Revolt in Albania
	Riots in Bulgaria
1901	Polish riots in Posen, Germany
1903	Uprising in Macedonia
	Uprising in Bulgaria
	Rebellions in Albania
1903–1905	Pogroms in Russia
1905	Rebellion in Kroya and Argirocastro, Albania
1906–7	Insurrection in Elbasan, Albania
1908	Revolt in Macedonia
1909	Armenian massacres in Turkey
1910–12	Insurrection in Albania
1911	Uprising in Galicia
Nov. 1913	Anti-Prussian riots in Zabern, Alsace
1915	Armenian massacres in Turkey
1916	Uprising in Turkestan
	Rebellion in Ireland
1917	Flemish separatist movement in Belgium
1917–22	War of the Russian Nationalities
1919	Rebellion in East Galicia
1919–22	Rebellion in Ireland
1920	Revolt in Albania
1924	Revolution in Albania
1928–34	Internal Macedonian Revolutionary Organization in Bulgaria
1938	Revolt in Crete
1938–1939	Czechs vs. Sudeten-German Czechs
1940s	Jews expelled and massacred throughout Europe
1943	Massacres in Yugoslavia

A SAMPLE OF EUROPE'S IMPERIALIST CONFLICTS, 1789–1945

These are conflicts involving the acquisition of territory or of indirect control over the political or economic life of other areas.

Imperialist Conflicts in Europe

French Revolutionary Wars (1792–1802)	France, for territory
Napoleonic Wars (1803–15)	France, to restore its colonial empire

Ottoman Empire vs. Serbians (1806)	Ottoman Empire, to maintain control
Russia vs. Turkey (1806–12)	Russia, to acquire Moldavia and Wallachia
Russia vs. Sweden (1808–09)	Russia, to annex Finland
Austria vs. Naples (1815)	Former King Murat of Naples for Naples
Uprising in Naples (1820)	Austria, to maintain control of Naples
Uprising in Piedmont (1821)	Austria, to maintain control of Piedmont
Russia vs. Turkey (1828)	For Moldavia and Wallachia
Revolt in Milan (1848)	Austria, to maintain control
Piedmont-Austria (1848–49)	Austria, to maintain control
Prussia-Denmark (1848–50)	Prussia, for Schleswig-Holstein
Crimean War (1853–56)	Russia, for Moldavia and Wallachia
Turko-Montenegrin War (1852–53)	Montenegro, for expanded boundaries
Turko-Montenegrin War (1858–59)	Montenegro, for expanded boundaries
Italy-Austria (1859)	Italy and Austria, for Italy
Italy-Sicily (1860–61)	Piedmont, for Italy
Prussia-Denmark (1864)	Prussia, for Schleswig-Holstein
Italy-Austria (1866)	Italy and Austria, for Venetia
Austro-Prussian War (1866)	Prussia, for south German states
Franco-Prussian War (1870)	Prussia, to acquire south German states
Serbia and Montenegro vs. Turkey (1876)	Serbia, to acquire Bosnia
Russo-Turkish War (1878)	Russia, to reacquire Bessarabia; Serbia and Bulgaria, for expansion
Austria vs. Bosnia-Herzegovina (1878)	To occupy Bosnia-Herzegovina
Bulgaria vs. Turkey (1885)	For acquisition of East Rumelia
Serbia vs. Bulgaria (1885)	For territorial compensation; Piedmont, for territory
Greco-Turkish War (1896–97)	Greece, to acquire territory
Italy vs. Turkey (1911)	For Dodecanese and Tripolitania
First Balkan War (1912)	Bulgaria and Serbia vs. Turkey, for territory
Second Balkan War (1913)	Serbia vs. Bulgaria, for division of territorial spoils
Russo-Polish War (1918)	Poles, for expansion
Hungaro-Romanian War (1919)	Romania, for territory
Greco-Turkish War (1919–22)	Greeks, for expansion
Vilna (1920)	Poles, for expansion
War in Anatolia (1920)	Russia, for Constantinople

Germany annexes Austria
  (1938)
Germany annexes
  Czechoslovakia (1939)
Italy conquers Albania (1939)
Germany occupies Poland
  (1939)
Russia occupies East Poland
  (1939)
Russia vs. Finland (1939)   Russia, for territory near Leningrad
Germany invades Norway,
  Denmark, Luxembourg,
  and Romania (1940)
Russia occupies Lithuania,
  Estonia, Latvia, and
  Bessarabia (1940)
Bulgaria annexes part of
  Dobruja (1940)
Hungary annexes part of
  Transylvania (1940)
Germany occupies Bulgaria
  and Hungary (1941)

Extraregional Imperialist Conflicts Involving European Powers

Egyptian Expedition   France, for control
  (1798–1801)
Mysore Wars (1789–99)   British, for supremacy in southern India
British Maratha War   British, for territory
  (1803–5)
Invasion of St. Domingo   Napoleon, to establish control
  (1804)
Battles for La Plata (1807)   British vs. Spain, for control
Central Sumatra (1807–37)   Dutch, for trade and dominion
Spanish-American War   Spain, for commercial exploitation
  (1810–24)
Anglo-American War   Britain, to blockade U.S. ports, ban U.S.
  (1812–14)   trade with France
Gurkha War (1814–16)   Britain, to maintain control
Revolt of the Padries   Dutch, for territory
  (1819–22)
War on the Gold Coast   Britain, for control
  (1821–26)

Military operations in Sumatra (1823)	Dutch, for control
Burmese War (1823–26)	Britain, to acquire Arkan and Tenas; Serim, control over Assam
Persia (1825–28)	Russia and Armenians, for Georgia
Tasmania (1825–30)	Britain, to secure control
Caucasian Campaigns (1829–40)	Russia, against raids and for control
Zambesi and Delagoa Bay (1833–36)	Portugal, to gain control
War in La Plata (1836–52)	France and Britain, to control Argentina
British-Afghan War (1838–42)	Britain, to prevent Russian influence in Afghanistan
First Opium War (1839–42)	Britain to open Shanghai, Canton, Amoy Foochow, and Ningpo to trade
Khivan (1839)	Russia, for expansion
Conquest of Algeria (1839–47)	France, for expansion
Gwalior, India (1843)	Britain, for dominance and order there
Conquest of Sind (1843)	Britain, to annex Sind to British India
British-Sikh War (1845–46)	Britain, to acquire land from the Sikhs
Bali (1846–49)	Dutch, to secure control
British-Sikh War (1848–49)	Britain, to annex the Punjab
South-East Africa (1850–52)	Britain, to secure property
Burma (1853)	Britain, to annex Pegu
Anglo-Persian War (1856–57)	Britain, fearing Russian influence
"Opium War" (1856–60)	Britain and France, for trade
Senegal (1857)	France, to control Senegambia
India (1857–59)	Britain, to transfer authority from East India to British Crown
Spain vs. Morocco (1859–60)	To extend the boundaries of Spanish settlements
South Celebes (1859–60)	Dutch, to secure control
South Borneo (1859–63)	Dutch, for control of coal mines
War in Circassia (1859–64)	Russia, for expansion
Mexican Expedition (1861–67)	French, Spaniards, and British, for control
Bokhara (1865–68)	Russia, for Samarkand and the Oxus
British-Abyssinian War (1867–68)	Britain, to secure control
Algeria (1871–72)	France, to maintain control
Ashanti (1873–74)	Britain, for free trade
War in Achin (1873–1908)	Dutch, for direct rule over the Achinese sultanate

British-Afghan War   Britain, against Russian influence, and to
  (1878–80)   advance the frontier at Pishin
Sieges of Geok Tepe   Russia, for expansion
  (1878–81)
Zulu War (1879)   Britain, about a disputed boundary
Tunisia (1881)   France, to govern Tunisia
Revolt of the Mahdi   Britain, for control
  (1881–85)
Egypt (1882)   Britain, for control
Tongking War (1882–85)   France, for trade route to China
Britain vs. Burma (1885–86) Britain, to complete annexation
Sudanese Independence   Britain, for reconquest
  (1885–95)
Malay Archipelago (1891–94) Dutch, to extend direct rule
Eastern Congo War   Belgium, for ownership
  (1892–94)
Italo-Abyssinian War   Italy, for control
  (1894–96)
Conquest of Madagascar   France, to annex
  (1894–1901)
Sudan Campaigns   Britain for establishment of an "Anglo-
  (1896–1900)   Egyptian Sudan"
Northwest Frontier of India Britain, to maintain control
  (1897–98)
Uganda (1897–1901)   Britain, to maintain control
Sierra Leone (1898)   Britain, to affirm and extend control
Spanish-American War (1898) Spain, to control Cuba
Chinese Boxer Rising   Russia, Britain, France, Germany, Italy,
  (1899–1900)   and Austria for commercial privileges
South African War   Britain, to annex Transvaal and the
  (1899–1902)   Orange Free State
South-West Africa (1903–8)   Germany, for colonization
Russo-Japanese War (1904–5) Russia, concerning rival interests
Zulu Revolt (1906)   Britain, to maintain control
War in Libya (1911–17)   Italy, for expansion
Morocco (1912)   France, to maintain control
War in Turkestan (1916)   Russia, for colonization
Morocco (1916–17)   France, to maintain control
Syria (1920)   France, for control of its Mandate
Iraq (1920–21)   Britain, for control of its Mandate
Northern Morocco (1920–27)   France, for control
War in Libya (1920–32)   Italy, for expansion
Syria (1925–26)   France, for control of its Mandate
Morocco (1929–33)   France, to extend control

Indochina (1930–31)	France, to maintain control
Ethiopian War (1935–37)	Italy, to annex
Britain in Palestine (1940–47)	For control
Vichy French vs. British in Syria (1941)	For control
Algeria (1945)	France, to reestablish control
France in Lebanon (1945)	For control

Appendix 3

European (Regional and Extraregional) Wars, Insurrections, Rebellions, Revolutions, Uprisings, Violent Strikes, Riots, and Demonstrations, 1789–1945

Note: Magnitude 3+ events are in boldface; extraregional wars are in brackets.

Case no.	Event	Date	Magnitude	Actors and reasons for fighting	Explanation	Result	Source
1	[Mysore Wars]	1789–99	4	British for supremacy in southern India vs. Mysoris in defense	The British sought to gain for the British East India Company areas in southern India. To do this they had to win several battles: first, against Hyder Ali (allied with the Nizam and the Marathas); then against his son, Tipu Sultan, a leading Indian power.	The British annexed Kanara, Coimbatore, Wynad, and Dharpouram besides the entire seacoast of Mysore.	Harbottle 1971: 155, 229, 232, 256–57
2	French Revolution	June 1789– Nov. 1795	4	Aristocrats and middle class elements against "absolutism" and for an extension of their	The revolution began with the proclamation of the National Assembly in June 1789 and ended with the	A series of changes were made in political, social, and economic structures of France.	Wheatcroft 1983: 22

No.	Event	Date	Parties in conflict	Events	Outcome	Source
			privileges; the laboring poor, small craftsmen, shopkeepers, and artisans for egalitarian society vs. the Bourbon monarchy and royalists		establishment of the government of the Directory, under the Constitution of the Year III in November 1795.	
3	Uprising in Bohemia	1790	Peasants protesting seigniorial demands and privileges vs. landlords	Peasants refused to do labor service and stormed manor houses.	Landlords suppressed the uprising and inducted rebels into the army.	Blum 1978: 342
4	Uprising in Saxony	March 8–Sept. 1, 1790	Peasants for elimination of seigniorial obligations vs. landowners	When bad weather had reduced the food supply, peasants demanded the thinning of game animals and compensation to peasant fields. Protest spread from one manor house to cover 5,000 sq. km.	Some landowners reduced obligations, some took no action, and still others increased their flocks at the expense of the peasants. Some 158 were imprisoned.	Blum 1978: 337–38
5	Priestly riots in Birmingham	1791	Antirevolutionary gangs in England vs. reformers	Loyalist mobs burned down dissenting chapels and destroyed the laboratory of the Radical Unitarian chemist Joseph Priestly (discoverer of oxygen) and the homes of less well-known reformers. The authorities made no attempt to interfere.	Antirevolutionary violence, encouraged by landowners and the clergy, continued in England for several years.	Stevenson 1975

Case no.	Event	Date	Magnitude	Actors and reasons for fighting	Explanation	Result	Source
6	French Revolutionary Wars	April 1792–March 1802	6	France against absolutism and feudalism and to acquire "natural frontiers" vs. Austria, Prussia, England, Spain, Netherlands, Sardinia, Turkey, United States, Russia, Naples, Portugal, and Sweden resisting the spread of French revolutionary ideas and expansion	The Wars consisted of four overlapping wars: the War of the First Coalition, Feb. 1792–Oct. 1797; the Egyptian Expedition, July 1798–1801; the American naval war with France, 1789; and the War of the Second Coalition, April 1799–March 1802.	Turkey and Britain concluded peace treaties with France. Russia withdrew from the coalition before the conclusion of hostilities. Austria and Portugal were defeated by France.	Kinder and Hilgemann 1978: 25; Levy 1983: table 4.1
7	Uprising in Silesia	1793–95		Rural weavers, landless peasants, and urban artisans vs. employers and landowners	Peasants expected the new Prussian legal code to free them from seigniorial obligations and suspected lords and bureaucrats of hiding these provisions from them.	Troops put down the protests, but the disturbances continued until the end of the decade	Blum 1978: 339
8	Uprising in Zurich	1794–95		Spinners and weavers for voting rights and right to participate in commerce vs. urban elites	Unrest emerged among spinners and weavers inspired by the egalitarian doctrines of the French Revolution.	Soldiers suppressed the uprising.	Blum 1978: 344
9	Uprising in Silesia	1798–99		Peasants resenting seigniorial exactions vs. landlords	Disorders that had recurred during this decade, and which were exacerbated by	Military force was used to restore order.	Blum 1978: 339

		Dates		Antagonists and issue	Description	Outcome	Source
10	Uprising in Ireland	May to Aug. 1798	4	Irish vs. English overlords	restrictions on linen exports, reached a peak during these years. Major battles took place at Dungannon, Castlebar, and Ballinsloe.	Almost 30,000 people were killed.	Pakenham 1969; Goldstein 1983: 117; Wheatcroft 1983: 30–33
11	Napoleonic Wars	1803–15	6	France to acquire German and Italian lands vs. Austria, England, the Netherlands, Sweden, Russia, Prussia, Sardinia, and Spain	Fighting followed the Peace of Amiens (1802) and French attempts to restore its colonial empire. Defying the Treaty of Basle, France occupied Hanover (1803). Seven wars against Napoleon resulted.	Resulting wars were: (1) Third Coalition (1803), (2) France against Prussia and Russia (1806–7), (3) Peninsula War (1809–14), (4) Franco-Austrian War (1809), (5) Russian Expedition (1812), (6) War of Liberation (1813–14), and (7) Hundred Days' War (1815).	Levy 1983: table 4.1
12	[British Maratha War]	1803–05	3	British to increase the territory of British India vs. Maratha clans opposed to British control	The East India Company used divided Maratha clans to their advantage. By restoring Baji Rao II to the Peshwarship, the British secured a treaty allowing inter alia permanent British forces. The treaty was unacceptable to the Bhosales and the Sindhias.	The Bhosales and the Sindhias were defeated. The influence of the East India Company was extended. British forces were stationed in the territories of the Sindhia and Bhosale.	Harbottle 1971: 17, 30, 43, 142

Case no.	Event	Date	Magnitude	Actors and reasons for fighting	Explanation	Result	Source
13	[Invasion of St. Domingo]	1804		Native islanders under Toussaint for independence	Fearing that governor-general Toussaint Louverture would lead the colony toward independence and pressurized by French planters who had been disenfranchised by the liberation of the slaves, Napoleon launched an invasion aimed at establishing control.	The black army definitively defeated the French, declared their independence, and established the republic of Haïti on the western third of the island.	*Annual Register* 1806
14	Serbian uprising	1804–13		Nobles to control tax revenues and autonomy vs. Jannissaries; reacting to terrorism of the Jannissaries, Serbian rebels vs. Jannissaries (Dahiis) vs. Ottoman troops for control	Jannissaries precipitated an uprising by forcibly taking over the province's fiscal regime. The uprising culminated in the massacre of scores of Serb nobles, which triggered an uprising involving about 30,000 Serbian peasants.	The peasant uprising developed into a movement for independence that, over the course of the subsequent ten years, involved Turkish troops in repeated attempts to regain control of the area. The uprising was not crushed until 1813.	Djordjevic 1967; Lampe and Jackson 1982: 110; Djordjevic and Fischer-Galati 1981: 69–70; Goldstein 1983: 132

#	War/rebellion		Dates	Objectives	Description	Outcome	Source
15	**Russo-Turkish War**	5	Dec. 1806–Aug. 1812	Russia to acquire Moldavia and Wallachia, and Britain and Russia to coerce Turkey into joining a coalition against France vs. Turkey	Without a prior declaration of war, a Russian army marched into Moldavia and Wallachia, overrunning it speedily, entering Bucharest, and preparing to cross the Danube. The British fleet sailed through the Dardanelles into the Sea of Marmora.	Russia acquired Bessarabia.	Russell 1877; *Annual Register* 1812: 183; Levy 1983: table 4.1
16	"Rebellion of Tican" in Srem, Austria		1807	Peasants against oppression by feudal landlords and bureaucratic abuses by Austrian authorities	The rebellion was part of the general ferment throughout the Balkans unleashed by the Serbian uprising of 1804 and was tied directly to it by the involvement of several Serbian insurgents who had actively participated in events in Serbia.	The rebellion was crushed by Austrian forces.	Djordjevic and Fischer-Galati 1981: 72
17	"Rebellion of Djak" in the Banat		1807	Peasants against oppression by feudal landlords and bureaucratic abuses by Austrian authorities	A rebellion in the Banat village of Krusica was part of the general ferment of rebellion throughout the Balkans unleashed by the Serbian uprising of 1804.	The rebellion was crushed by Austrian forces.	Djordjevic and Fischer-Galati 1981: 72
18	[War in central Sumatra]	3	1807–37	Dutch for trade and dominion vs. Padris	One of a series of battles between Dutch troops and the Padries.	Dutch gained control of central Sumatra.	Richardson 1960: 78

Case no.	Event	Date	Magnitude	Actors and reasons for fighting	Explanation	Result	Source
19	Insurrection in Bosnia	1807		Bosnians and Serbs for independence	The Serbian uprising (1804) against Ottoman control generated aspirations for independence in other southern Slav lands. Serbian insurgents led by Karadjordje staged an insurrection in the Bosnian Podrinje, which helped to recruit Bosnian insurgents.	Ottoman armies in Bosnia retained control.	Djordjevic and Fischer-Galati 1981: 71–73
20	[Battles for La Plata]	June–Oct. 1807		British vs. Spanish for control of Buenos Aires and Montevideo	The involvement of 10,000 townspeople prevented the defeat of the Spanish.	Britain was defeated and withdrew.	Annual Register 1806
21	Lancashire weavers' strike	1808		Weavers vs. employers	Widespread and violent strikes and a great wave of protests.	The disturbances were terminated by massive repression.	Munger 1981: 80, 94
22	Russo-Swedish War	Feb. 1808–Nov. 1809	4	Russia to annex Finland and to extend control of the Baltic vs. Sweden	Finland had been united with Sweden since the early Middle Ages. A Russian invasion in 1808 converted Finland into a Grand Duchy within the Russian Empire.	Finland became an autonomous part of Russia.	Levy 1983: table 4.1
23	Insurrection in Portugal	June–Aug. 1808		Lisboners protesting Spanish-imposed pro-French governor of the city, aided by British	Uprising spread to the whole northern part of Portugal.	The authority of the Prince Regent was reestablished. The British sent French troops back to France.	Annual Register 1808: 219

				troops, *vs.* French occupying force		
24	Rebellion in Bosnia	1809		Peasants with tribesmen from Herzegovina and northern Albania *vs.* Turks	A rebellion in Bosnia supportive of the uprising in Serbia.	The rebellion was suppressed by Turkish troops.	Djordjevic and Fischer-Galati 1981: 73
25	[Spanish-American War]	1810–24	4	American-born Spaniards for sovereignty and against social and economic inequality *vs.* Peninsular Spaniards for economic exploitation and the divine right of kings	At a time when Napoleon had upset the Spanish monarchy, American-born Spaniards, Indians, and others sought to establish their sovereignty as Bolivians, Ecuadorians, Venezuelans, Colombians, Argentinians, Uruguayans, Chileans, Peruvians, and Mexicans.	Ten independent states were formed.	Richardson 1960: 51
26	Riots in Britain	1811–12		Unemployed rural workers against mechanization	Increases in industrial production triggered anti-industrial riots by machine breakers (Luddites).	Machine breaking continued in parts of Britain into the 1820s.	Charleswath et al. 1996: 32–34; Hobsbawm 1964
27	[Anglo-American War]	1812–14	3	Britain for the right of British ships to blockade continental ports against American vessels *vs.* the United States with France	British ships seized sailors and forced them to join the British Navy and blockaded U.S. ports to prevent American trade with Napoleon. In June 1812 the United States declared war on Britain.	A peace treaty signed in December 1814 restored relations between the two countries.	Harbottle 1981:181

Case no.	Event	Date	Magnitude	Actors and reasons for fighting	Explanation	Result	Source
28	[Gurkha War]	1814–16	3	British to maintain the territory under the control of the British East India Company vs. Gurkhas to regain territories lost to the company	The Gurkhas, a tribe of the Western Himalayas, had conquered territories in the Nepal valley including Bhutwal, which had been under the control of the East India Company. Bhutwal was regained by the company, but in 1814 Gurkhas sought to take it back.	After defeating the Gurkhas and reaching the Katmandu Valley, British forces effectively took control of Nepal.	Harbottle 1981: 132
29	Rebellion in Serbia	Sept. 1814	3	Serbian rebels for independence vs. Turkish forces for control	A revolt in September 1814 was quickly suppressed by Turkish forces and was followed by the torture and murder of several hundred Serbs by Turkish troops.	Violence continued in Serbia.	Goldstein 1983: 132
30	Corn Bill riots	1815–16		Unemployed workers against the Corn Bill	Riots erupted with the introduction of the Corn Bill. Rioters protested the high price of bread, exportation of grain, and reduction of wages.	Violence continued throughout the decade.	Peacock 1965: 12
31	Austro-Neapolitan War	1815	3	Former King Murat of Naples for Naples vs. Austria	Murat, who aspired to the crown of Italy, supported Napoleon against Austria, but he was defeated by	Murat was defeated by Austria. Ferdinand I became "King of the Two Sicilies."	Berkeley 1932; Levy 1983: table 4.2

					Austria at the Battle of Tolentino.		
32	**Rebellion in Serbia**	April–Oct. 1815	3	Serb nobles to control tax revenues vs. Turkish troops	A revolt in April 1815 ended six months later with an agreement signed by Serbian leader Milos Obrenovic and the Ottoman Empire.	Turkey agreed to grant substantial autonomy to Serbia. The main economic provision was the restoration of tax collection by the Serbian notables.	Goldstein 1983: 132–33
33	White Terror in France	June 18–Aug. 15, 1815		Royalists vs. Jacobins and Bonapartists	Napoleon's defeat at Waterloo unleashed a "white terror" in southern France in which 200 people suspected of Jacobin and Bonapartist loyalties were killed, and several thousand others were jailed.	Election of the ultra-royalist "Chambre introuvable."	Goldstein 1983: 111
34	Riots in England	1816		Workers against low wages and rise in prices vs. shopkeepers and millers	Food and wage riots in East Anglia, incendiarism and machine breaking triggered by unemployment and economic hardship as a result of a poor harvest, lack of markets for manufacturers, and reduced demand for iron.	One killed by troops, five executed, and dozens were transported.	*Annual Register* 1816: 93; Peacock 1965: 14–15; Stevenson 1975: 62–63; Muskett 1984: 2

Case no.	Event	Date	Magnitude	Actors and reasons for fighting	Explanation	Result	Source
35	Food riots in France	1816–17		Rioters against grain shortages and high prices	Food riots erupted in the face of grain shortages and high prices in Grenoble in mid-1816 and at Lyons in June 1817.	Twenty-eight rioters were executed.	Goldstein 1983: 112
36	[Algiers War]	1816	4	British with the help of Dutch troops for the abolition of Christian slavery vs. the bey of Algiers seeking to retain slavery in his dominions	British forces bombarded the forts of Algiers. Casualties amounted to 885 of the allies, and over 6,000 of the Algerines were killed.	The forts, along with a large part of the city, were destroyed. Slavery was abolished in Algiers.	Harbottle 1981: 17
37	[British Maratha War]	1817–18	4	Marathas led by the Peshwa Baji Rao II opposed to British administration of the Maratha States vs. British for control	After the Peshwa was forced to sign the humiliating Treaty of Poona in June 1817, he sacked and burned the British Residency at Poona and then attacked the British forces at Khirki with about 27,000 men.	The Peshwa was completely defeated. The office of the Peshwa was abolished by the British and the Peshwa's possessions in Poona were incorporated in the Bombay Presidency.	Harbottle 1981: 64, 132, 134, 154, 247
38	Strikes in Lancashire, England	1818		Textile workers vs. employers	A wave of strikes racked the Lancashire textile industry. Large-scale, county-wide strikes by mule spinners and handloom weavers were accompanied by	By the end of this extremely violent decade, labor protests had become increasingly interconnected and nationwide.	Munger 1981: 86–87

39	[Revolt of the Padries]	1819–22	"considerable violence" by strikers against scab workers. Some 20,000 Padries vs. 500 Dutch and 13,000 Malays.	Dutch vs. Padries for territory and protection of allied tribes	Malays deserted and Dutch subdued Padries.	Annual Register 1823: 171
40	Anti-Jewish riots, Germany	1819	Anti-Jewish uprisings expelled Jews from Hamburg, Frankfurt, Wurtzburgh, Meiningen, and other German towns.	German townspeople against the protection of Jews by German sovereigns vs. Jews	Order was restored. The local magistrates, who had taken no action to repress the risings, were harshly rebuked by the sovereigns and threatened with the loss of their positions.	Annual Register 1819: 190–91; Tilly 1975b
41	Peterloo massacre	Aug. 16, 1819	In 1819, armed yeomanry attacked some 10,000 workers gathered at St. Peter Fields near Manchester. Fifteen people were killed and 400 injured by being trampled or slashed with sabres.	Workers demanding the repeal of the Corn Laws, the enactment of the minimun wage, and parliamentary reform vs. armed yeomanry	The "Ultra Tories" passed the "6 Acts" limiting freedom of press and assembly.	Thompson 1966; Munger 1981: 74
42	**Revolt in Spain**	Jan.– March 1820 3	Troops, enraged at the idea of submitting to the constitutionalists, opened fire on a crowd celebrating the proclamation by King Ferdinand of the 1812 Constitution.	Troops protesting the proclamation of a constitution vs. celebrants	Some 400 people were killed and an equal number were wounded.	Annual Register 1820: 223–31; Marx and Engels 1939: 77–84

Case no.	Event	Date	Magnitude	Actors and reasons for fighting	Explanation	Result	Source
43	Strike in Glasgow	April 1, 1820		Workers for political rights vs. soldiers	Two small bands of about 100 people attempted to turn a strike in Glasgow into a general uprising. The dissidents struggled with a band of soldiers before the rebellion was suppressed.	Three of the leaders were executed. The idea of the revolutionary strike was introduced and became familiar in radical circles.	Prothero 1974: 167; Goldstein 1983: 116
44	Uprising in Naples and Sicily	July 1820–21	3	King Ferdinand I for divine right of kings vs. Carbonarists for constitution	An uprising in Naples forced King Ferdinand I to grant a constitution when the army refused to oppose the rebels.	Ferdinand's powers were restored.	Richardson 1960: 74
45	[Filipino uprising]	Oct. 9–10, 1820		Filipinos against foreigners vs. government troops	Filipinos rose against French, British, Americans, and Chinese in Manila believing they poisoned the water, food, and air.	Some 125 were killed.	Annual Register 1821: 314
46	[War on the Gold Coast]	1821–26	3	British vs. Ashantis	One of a number of conflicts over British commercial exploitation of the area.	The Ashantis were defeated and had to pay 600 ounces of gold.	Richardson 1960: 75
47	Riots in Spain	Feb. 6–9, 1821		Protesters vs. monarchists	Mob seiged barracks of the king's bodyguards for three days and two nights.	Revolt was suppressed and King Ferdinand restored as the "absolute" ruler.	Annual Register 1821: 174

48	Greek uprising	March 25, 1821– Feb. 1830	4	Greeks for independence vs. Turks	The Hetairia Philiké, a secret revolutionary society organized in Odessa in 1814, began a war of independence with a revolt in Moldavia and the Morea. The revolt turned into a series of "civil wars" or factional struggles between powerful local leaders.	An agreement among the Powers of Europe (London Protocol of February 3, 1830) established an independent state of Greece with a Bavarian prince, Otto I, as its king.	Richardson 1960: 52; Goldstein 1983: 136
49	**Revolt in Piedmont**	March 1821	3	King Charles Felix and Austrians for autocracy vs. Carbonarists, liberal nobles for a constitution	King Victor Emmanuel I abdicated, naming Charles Felix and Charles Albert regent. When Charles Albert proclaimed a constitution, a combined Austrian and Sardinian force attacked.	Piedmontese were defeated. Charles Felix's powers were restored.	Richardson 1960: 74
50	Romanian uprising	March 1821		Romanian peasants vs. Phanariot Greeks, Boyars, and Turks for reforms with Greek troops under Ypsilanti for expansion of the Greek revolt	Romanian peasants under the leadership of Tudor Vladimirescu called for the replacement of Phanariots by native Romanian classes, a national assembly of representatives, organization of a national army, fiscal reform, and a tax moratorium.	Insurrection failed after Russia refused to intervene. Greek forces were decimated by Ottoman troops in the summer of 1821.	Djordjevic and Fischer-Galati 1981: 80–82

Case no.	Event	Date	Magnitude	Actors and reasons for fighting	Explanation	Result	Source
51	Protests in Madrid	May 3–4, 1821		Masses demanding death of Canon Vinvesa	Protesters stormed the prison and killed Canon Vinvesa.	Municipality restored order.	*Annual Register* 1821
52	Uprising in Pomerania	June 1821		Monarchists vs. antimonarchists	Some 600 people were involved in a plot to kill supporters of the monarchy.	The military crushed the plot, and there was an increase in press censorship.	*Annual Register* 1821
53	Protests in London	Aug. 1821		Londoners protesting the treatment of Queen Caroline of Brunswick vs. troops	Troops used sabres to clear a path when the queen's funeral procession was barred by protesters using stones torn from a park wall as missiles.	Protesters injured soldiers. Troops fired on crowd, killing two.	*Annual Register* 1821
54	Protests in Madrid	Aug. 20, 1821		Masses vs. royal bodyguards and military	Morillo dispersed a crowd gathered in front of the prison with rumored plans to kill royal bodyguards inside. The following day, 10,000 people gathered to protest his supposed use of a sabre against civilians.	Morillo resigned and crowds calmed down.	*Annual Register* 1821: 188
55	Demonstrations in Spain	Sept. 1821		Protesters for the return of the king of Madrid, expulsion of French ambassador, and Assembly of Cortes	Mass demonstrations in Madrid.	The demonstrations were a prelude to a bloody revolt (Dec. 1821–April 1823).	*Annual Register* 1821: 191

#	Event	Date		Parties	Description	Outcome	Source
56	Uprisings in Ireland	Oct.–Dec. 1821		Irish against taxes and tithes	Protesters in Limerick, Mayo, Tipperary, and Cavan counties resisted the payment of taxes and tithes and engaged in plunder and murder.	Troops killed at least 19 rebels.	*Annual Register* 1821: 129
57	[Uprising in Brazil]	Nov. 1821		Native troops demanding departure of Prince Don Pedro and European troops vs. Portuguese troops	"Great numbers" of native Brazilian troops were killed at Bahia and Para in an uprising against the Portuguese.	Portuguese troops suppressed the uprising.	*Annual Register* 1821: 220
58	**Revolt in Spain**	Dec. 1821–April 1823	4	Republicans for constitution vs. royalists and French troops	A further outbreak of violence following the 1820 Revolution, in which French troops intervened of behalf of conservatives and helped to consolidate the forces of reaction.	King Ferdinand became an "absolute" ruler.	*Annual Register* 1821; Small and Singer 1982: 223
59	East Anglian agrarian riots	Feb.–Aug. 1822		Agricultural laborers against mechanization	Threshing machines were broken, dismantled, and stopped from operating. Large-scale rioting and other incidents of machine breaking and incendiarism took place throughout the following six months.	Some 123 men were brought before the courts in connection with the disturbances.	Muskett 1984: 5–9

Case no.	Event	Date	Magnitude	Actors and reasons for fighting	Explanation	Result	Source
60	[Military operation in Sumatra]	1823		Dutch government officials vs. Padries	Dutch troops attempted to drive the Padries from their villages in the neighborhood of the Dutch colony of Samawang.	Some 21 Dutchmen were killed and 139 wounded. Padries were expelled.	*Annual Register* 1823: 171
61	Franco-Spanish War	April-Nov. 1823	3	France with and for the deposed Bourbons vs. Spain's liberal government	French forces seized Madrid and the fortress of Trocadero and remained in occupation while forces loyal to the king expected severe retribution.	The powers of Ferdinand VII were restored.	Clarke 1906; Artz 1934; Levy 1983: table 4.1
62	["First" Burmese War]	Sept. 1823-Feb. 1826	4	Britain against encroachments and atrocities in Assam vs. Burma against pirates and fugitives	In 1824, the threat of a Burmese invasion of Bengal led to the dispatch of a British military expedition, which captured Rangoon in 1826.	Burma was forced to cede territory in the south, renounce its claims on Assam, and pay the British £1 million.	Richardson 1960: 51
63	[War in Tasmania]	1825-30	3	Britain to secure control and against murders vs. Tasmanians against executions	Part of the consolidation of British control that established Tasmania as one of four British colonies in Australia.	Tasmanians nearly exterminated.	Richardson 1960: 76
64	[War in Persia]	1825-28	3	Russia and Armenia vs. Persia to regain Georgia	Part of a series of Russian campaigns between 1801 and 1864 to annex the whole of the Caucasus.	Persia ceded Erivan, Armenia, and Nakhitchen to Russia and paid £3 million.	Richardson 1960: 75

#	Name	Dates		Parties	Description	Outcome	Sources
65	Rebellion in Serbia	1825		Serbian dissidents for socioeconomic reform and the end of Milo's rule	A rebellion involving 50,000 dissidents lasted ten days. The rebellion ended when troops intervened.	The leader of the rebellion was shot, followed by murders, beatings, and jailings.	Goldstein 1983: 133–34
66	[Insurrection in Java]	July 23, 1825– March 28, 1830	5	Javanese against Dutch commercial control vs. Dutch for trade and control	Javanese under Dipa Negara opposed Dutch commercial controls imposed with the help of the Court of Jokjakarta.	After repeated Dutch losses to the Javanese, reinforcements were sent from Europe. Rebellion was suppressed.	Annual Register 1827: 265
67	Revolt in Spain	Aug. 16, 1825		Spanish ultramonarchists against liberalism of King Ferdinand's ministers	Three regiments went to Madrid to free the king from his ministers. They were joined by others on the way.	Troops suppressed the disturbances and shot eight of the leaders.	Annual Register 1825: 170–71
68	[Insurrection in Java]	Aug. 1825		Javanese rebels against the oppressive administration vs. Dutch troops	An uprising of some 12,000 Javanese rebels against the Dutch administration.	More than 100 Europeans were killed.	Annual Register 1825: 152
69	[Siege of Bharatpur]	Dec. 1825– Jan. 1826	4	Britain for boy-rajah vs. Jat Hindus	Bharatpur was stormed and looted by the British Sepoys, ghurkas, when the Jat Hindus showed defiance.	Rajah became subject to British control.	Richardson 1960: 52
70	Decembrist revolt in Russia	Dec. 14, 1825		Nobles to end czarist absolutism vs. Czar	Czar Nicholas I had loyal troops fire on 3,000 mutineers in Petersburg, killing 60 or 70. A revolt in the south was suppressed with little difficulty.	Corruption and poor enforcement of laws was reduced, but Nicholas I's distrust of any ideas connected with liberalism was confirmed.	Annual Register 1825: 162; 1826: 272; Mazour 1937; Goldstein 1983: 131

Case no.	Event	Date	Magnitude	Actors and reasons for fighting	Explanation	Result	Source
71	Massacre of the Janissaries, Turkey	1826	5	Sultan Mahmoud II for reform and control vs. Janissaries and provincial authority	The Sultan's troops exterminated the Janissaries, first in Constantinople and then throughout the Ottoman provinces.	The Sultan was released from all armed opposition within his territories.	Richardson 1960: 44; Kinross 1977: 456–57
72	Uprisings in Russia	1826–49		Peasants vs. masters	There were 1,904 disturbances and 381 troop interventions between 1826 and 1849.		Masaryk 1967: I; Langer 1969; Blum 1978: 333
73	Spanish-Portuguese War	Nov. 1826–1827		Portuguese for Don Miguel as king, aided by Spain, vs. Portuguese for Queen Maria and the constitution	Portuguese opposed to the constitution, with Spanish assistance, proclaimed Don Miguel king.	Tensions remained. (See Miguelite Wars below.)	Annual Register 1846, 1847; White 1909
74	Peasant uprising in Spain	1827	3	Peasants under Carlist influence vs. King Ferdinand	A major peasant revolt.	Uprising was savagely put down. Some 300 people were executed.	Goldstein 1983: 128
75	Rising at Cilento	1828		Liberals for reform vs. Austrian troops for control	A revolt at Cilento in the Two Sicilies.	The revolt was violently crushed. The heads of its leaders were paraded from town to town in iron cages.	Goldstein 1983: 124

#	Name	Dates		Issue / parties	Description	Outcome	Sources
76	Miguelite Wars in Portugal	1828–May 1834	4	Nobles and clerics for Don Miguel as absolute king vs. liberals in the name of Queen Maria led by Don Pedro	Don Pedro gave Portugal a British-type constitution and his infant daughter Maria was to become queen. Don Miguel, acting as regent, abolished the charter, purged liberals, and restored feudal rights.	Liberals reinstated Queen Maria.	White 1909; Richardson 1960: 54; SIPRI 1969: table 4a.1
77	Russo-Turkish War	May 1828–Sept. 1829	5	Russia to protect Christians and to acquire Wallachia and Moldavia vs. Turkey	During the war of Greek independence (1821–29), the Turks, indignant over the loss of their fleet at Navarino (1827), came into intense conflict with Russia in Moldavia and Wallachia.	Russia received the mouth of the Danube and the right to protect Greece. Moldavia and Wallachia became almost independent of Turkey.	Russell 1877; Richardson 1960: 44
78	Caucasian campaigns	1829–40	4	Russia against raids and for control vs. Circassians for independence		Russians were unsuccessful.	Allen and Muratoff 1953; Richardson 1960: 54
79	Otmoor disturbances	1830–35		Farmers against enclosures	Demonstrations during which some 1,000 people took possession of the moor were triggered by a court case in 1830 that was interpreted by local farmers as invalidating the enclosures.	Military detachments were sent to the moor and remained stationed there for two years, and afterward were replaced by police detachments.	Dunbabin 1974: 20

Case no.	Event	Date	Magnitude	Actors and reasons for fighting	Explanation	Result	Source
80	Riots in Wales	1830		Miners for wages			Rudé 1967
81	Uprising in Austro-Hungarian Empire	1830		Slovak, Ruthenian, and Roman peasants vs. Magyar lords	A devastating cholera epidemic combined with long-standing grievances to trigger a massive peasant uprising.	The uprising was harshly suppressed. Political controls were further tightened.	Goldstein 1983: 154
82	Swing movement	1830–31		Farmers and laborers for higher wages and against threshing machinery vs. clergy and landowners	A protest movement engulfed the south of England. It involved some 1,500 incidents, including 400 cases of machine breaking, 300 cases of arson, and 250 riots for higher wages and other demands.	Nineteen people were executed and hundreds were exiled or jailed.	Hobsbawn and Rudé 1973
83	Revolt in Bosnia-Herzegovina	1830–32	3	Bosnian nobles and Albanians against economic reforms vs. Ottoman sultan and Herzegovinians	The efforts of Selim III (1789–1807) and Mahmoud II (1808–39) to institute reforms aimed at curbing the power of local notables triggered violence.	The revolt was crushed. The reform movement went into higher gear after 1839, triggering recurring violence.	Stojanovic 1939: 12–27; Richardson 1960: 77

#	Event	Date		Parties	Background	Outcome	Source
84	Tithe War in Ireland	1830–33		Peasants vs. tithe agents	Rural violence against high rents, lack of security against evictions, and compulsory title payments to support the Church of England.	The government set up a special fund to pay the tithe. A stiff new Coercion Act was passed.	Goldstein 1983: 156–57
85	**Revolt in Paris**	July 1830	3	Middle-class elements and workers vs. the government of Charles X	King Charles X refused electoral results and then attempted to shift more electoral power to nobles and landed elites and away from the middle class. The rebellion spread, triggering tax, food, and workers' rebellions in other parts of France.	Some 200 soldiers and 2,000 citizens died. Charles was exiled and succeeded by Louis Phillipe.	Richardson 1960: 76; Hobsbawm 1962
86	**Revolution in Belgium**	Aug. 1830–1833	3	Belgium for independence vs. Dutch	A rising in Brussels expelled a Dutch garrison; independence was sought by Belgium. The Dutch king appealed to other legitimate brother rulers. British proposed an international conference, which established Belgium, but Belgians and the Dutch king objected.	Anglo-French cooperation enforced the decision of the Concert of Europe. An independent state of Belgium was established.	Pirenne 1900–1926; Richardson 1960: 77

Case no.	Event	Date	Magnitude	Actors and reasons for fighting	Explanation	Result	Source
87	Insurrections in Germany	Aug.–Nov. 1830		Workers and peasants vs. employers and landlords	There were riots, revolts, and rebellion in many parts of the country during August and November 1830, including antitax, antiadministration, food, and workers' riots, especially in Saxony, Hessen, Braunschweig, and Hannover.	Seven people were killed during labor riots.	*Annual Register* 1830: 278–79; Maurice 1887; Goldstein 1983: 66
88	Insurrection in Poland	Nov. 1830–Sept. 1831	4	Russian tsar for control vs. Poles for autonomy	The tsar's mobilization of the Polish army for possible intervention in the Belgian revolution triggered an uprising. The Russian viceroy was expelled. The czar's refusal to compromise led to a declaration of independence.	Harsh suppression of revolt and the Polish grievance had greater justification after than before the abortive uprising. Thousands emigrated to other European countries, where the emigrés kept up active and intense propaganda.	Leslie 1969; SIPRI 1969: table 4a.1
89	[War in Syria]	1831–33	4	The Turkish sultan, with help from Russia, France, and Britain, to retain his overlordship of Syria vs. Egypt for control	Mehmet Ali, viceroy of Egypt, sought to extend his power and rule and launched an attack on Syria in the hope of adding the province to his dominions.	The Egyptians were victorious and Syria was subsequently governed from Egypt.	Richardson 1960: 53

90	Riots in England	1831	Lower classes for the extension of the suffrage	Rioters in London, Derbyshire, Bristol, Nottingham, Bilton, and Staffordshire protested the Reform Bill of 1831, which disenfranchised boroughs below a minimum population.	There were looting, jail breaks, and attacks on warehouses, and homes were damaged.	*Annual Register* 1831; Rudé 1967
91	Riots in Ireland	1831	Workers for wages *vs.* employers	Iron workers rioted in Glamorgan.		Rudé 1967
92	Riots in Germany	1831		Antitax and antipolice demonstrations in Saxony, Hessen, Braunschweig, Hannover, and Gottingen.	Troops disbanded the protesters.	*Annual Register* 1831: 416; Tilly 1975b
93	Uprisings in Italy	Feb. 3–March 26, 1831	Austria for control *vs.* Italians for independence	Riots in Rome, Parma, Modena, Bologna, Ferrara, and Romagna were suppressed by Austrian troops.	Austrian power was reaffirmed in Central Italy. To balance this power, a French regiment occupied Ancona, where it remained for the next six years.	Mowat 1923; *Annual Register* 1931: 451
94	Uprising in Danubian Principalities	April 1831	Hungarian peasants *vs.* Russians	Some 60,000 peasants in Hungary rose in political protest against the introduction of the Organic Statutes.	Cossacks crushed the revolt.	Blum 1978: 342

Case no.	Event	Date	Magnitude	Actors and reasons for fighting	Explanation	Result	Source
95	Demonstrations in France	Feb. 1831		Workers vs. employers, the state, and the clergy	Violent demonstrations in Paris and other large cities. Attacks on machines in St. Etienne, Bordeaux, and Toulouse. In Paris, mobs broke up a memorial service for the Duc de Berry, sacked the convent of St. Germain l'Auxerrois, and destroyed the archbishop's palace.	Strikes, riots, and demonstrations throughout the 1830–34 period.	*Annual Register* 1831: 334; Tilly 1975b
96	Uprising in Wales	June 1831		Workers for higher wages vs. soldiers	An uprising of workers lasting for three days (June 2–4).	Troops killed twenty-three.	*Annual Register* 1831: 78
97	Uprising in Russia	June–Oct. 1831		Peasants vs. troops	Peasants protested conditions in the military colonies at Poltava, Chernigov, and Mogilev, which were ravaged by cholera.	Major troop action was needed to suppress the uprising. Some 3,000 peasants were punished, but the camps were gradually disbanded.	Blum 1978: 348
98	Frankfurt riots	Oct. 24, 1831		Government troops vs. workers	Troops opened fire on workers in Frankfurt protesting an attack on their liberties.	Three were killed and many wounded.	*Annual Register* 1831: 168

No.	Event	Date		Parties	Description	Source
99	Uprising in Lyons, France	Nov. 1831	3	Workers vs. troops	A violent uprising of striking textile workers erupted when troops, attempting to block a march into the city, killed eight marchers. The rising was suppressed by 20,000 troops at a cost of 600 military and civilian casualties.	Goldstein 1983: 67, 147
100	Riots in Ireland	Nov.–Dec. 1831		Protesters vs. the police	A riot followed the arrest of some who rebelled against the tithe. Some 40 people were killed.	*Annual Register* 1831: 326–27
101	Demonstration in Germany	May 1832		Liberals and radicals for press freedom and a united German Republic	Huge anti-aristocratic demonstration in the Palatinate. Troops were sent into the Palatinate to enforce martial law.	Goldstein 1983: 149
102	Rebellion in Montenegro	1832–42		Montenegrins for expansion of their territory vs. Ottoman troops	Native rebel forces assisted by Christian tribes of northern Albania assaulted numerous towns and defeated the Ottomans at Mastinic. Confrontations continued until 1842. The frontier of Herzegovina was redrawn to Montenegrins' satisfaction.	Djordjevic and Fischer-Galati 1981
103	Rebellion in Albania	1832–35		Albanian notables vs. Ottoman troops	Albanian beys and *bayraktars* (notables) opposed recruitment in the regular army (*nizam*) and performance of military service outside Albania. It was not until 1835 that forces loyal to the sultan crushed the rebellion.	Frasheri 1964

Case no.	Event	Date	Magnitude	Actors and reasons for fighting	Explanation	Result	Source
104	Sonderbund uprising in Switzerland	March 1832–1833		Liberal cantons for reforms vs. Catholic cantons for the authority of the Church	Conflict between liberal and Catholic cantons over the authority of the clergy and state control of education and marriage.	The Catholic Sonderbund was dissolved by the Diet. Reformers sought to reduce authority of the clergy. However, tensions continued despite several changes in government. (See civil war in 1847.)	Bonjour, Offler, and Potter 1952
105	Revolt in France	June 1832	3	Republic sympathizers vs. troops	A demonstration of some 25,000 in Paris on the occasion of the funeral of General Lamarque, a popular liberal figure, developed into a serious insurrectionary outburst.	Several hundred died.	Rudé 1967; Langer 1969
106	[Portuguese War in East Africa]	1833–36	3	Portuguese for rule vs. Manikusa for control of their territory	Manikusa, son of the Swazi chief Gaza, made himself master of the country as far north as the Zambezi and captured the Portuguese posts at Delagoa Bay, Inhambane, Sofala, and Sena. The Portuguese reoccupied their posts, but held them with great difficulty.	Manikusa were successful in thwarting the Portuguese.	Richardson 1960: 78

107	Strike in Spain	1833	Agricultural workers	An agricultural workers' strike in Jerez in the early summer was crushed by troops.	Nine strike leaders were executed.	Goldstein 1983: 290–91
108	[War between France and Annam]	1833–39 3	France and Christian converts vs. Annamese		Christians were massacred.	Richardson 1960: 79
109	Insurrection in Serbia	April–May 1833	Serbs for territory vs. Ottomans	A peasant uprising began in the district of Krusevac, which the Porte had confiscated from Serbia in 1813. The uprising rapidly spread to other regions. The 12,000–15,000 peasants who took part in the uprising were armed entirely by Serbia.	Porte conceded and Serbia was enlarged by one-third.	Petrovich 1976
110	Insurrection in Frankfurt	April 3, 1833	Republicans vs. national guardsmen	Students attacked main guard houses and attempted to free political prisoners. They were joined by townspeople. Troops attacked and many were killed and wounded.	Political prisoners were freed. Austrians restored order.	*Annual Register* 1833: 280–81

Case no.	Event	Date	Magnitude	Actors and reasons for fighting	Explanation	Result	Source
111	Riots in Rhenish Bavaria	May 18, 1833		Republicans vs. troops	Revelers celebrating the anniversary of a liberal festival clashed with troops.	At least one was killed and 8–60 wounded.	*Annual Register* 1833: 281
112	**First Carlist War, Spain**	Oct. 1833–40	4	Conservatives and clerics for Don Carlos as monarch vs. liberals for constitution and Isabella as queen; Britain for constitutionalism and Basques for autonomy	King Ferdinand tried to ensure that his daughter Isabella would succeed him. Ferdinand's brother, Don Carlos, supported by conservatives, sought to gain the throne for himself. Queen Christina as her daughter's regent sought support among liberals.	Carlists were defeated and the parliamentary government was restored but remained unstable. Basque privileges were confirmed.	Richardson 1960: 55
113	Strike in Derby	1834		Silk-weavers vs. employers for the "right to resist repression"	Workers, disappointed with the 1832 Reform Bill and the "Liberal" victories of 1832 and 1834, turned increasingly to labor organization.	The defeat of the strike "produced great bitterness against employers as a class" and aroused sympathy and enthusiasm for trade unionism.	Prothero 1974: 167
114	Insurrection in Bosnia-Herzegovina	1834		Bosnians vs. Ottomans for control	In the Kraina, a rebellion broke out, the so-called Rebellion of Masic.	Severe reprisals and emigration of Bosnians to Serbia and Austria.	Djordjevic and Fischer-Galati 1981: 92–93

	Event	Date		Actors	Description	Outcome	Source
115	Uprising in Paris	Feb. 1834		Workers	Seventeen died and over 2,000 wounded in an uprising in Paris.	Violence continued in France throughout the year.	Tilly 1975b
116	Uprising in France	April 1834	3	Silk workers against reductions in piece prices paid to textile workers and others against making political associations illegal	A major uprising in Lyons was followed by an insurrection in Paris. For two days, "national guards and troops literally massacred the ill-prepared insurgents."	Some 329 were killed and 2,000 arrested and imprisoned or deported.	Annual Register 1834: 350–52
117	Insurrection in Albania	Dec. 1834–Sept. 1835		Albanian rebels vs. Turkish troops	An Albanian insurrection in the southern part of the province together with an uprising in Scutari took a year to suppress. Porte blockaded the coast of Albania with a fleet sent from Constantinople. Troops sent in August attacked rebels in September.	The Porte removed from office the unpopular Pasha of Scutari.	Annual Register 1835: 496–97
118	Revolt in Germany	1835		Journeymen	"Fireworks Revolt" of Berlin journeymen.	Riot laws were enacted in Prussia.	Tilly 1975b
119	Riot in England	April 1835		Paupers against the new Poor Law vs. authorities	A crowd of between 200 and 300 protested a provision of a new poor law statute, which authorized the giving of relief in food and clothing rather than money.	Riots continued over the next few years, contributing in 1838 to the campaign for a "People's Charter" (Chartism).	Dunbabin 1974: 39

341

Case no.	Event	Date	Magnitude	Actors and reasons for fighting	Explanation	Result	Source
120	Uprising in Bulgaria	May 1835		Peasants vs. Turkish troops	The "Velchova Rising" in Turnovo was part of a series of peasant rebellions in northwestern Bulgaria.	Rebellions continued to break out over the next two years.	Djordjevic and Fischer-Galati 1981
121	Uprising in Serbia	Dec. 1835		Serbians for a constitution vs. the governor	Rebels ousted the governor and gave power to his son and regent.	The governor yielded to all demands and delivered a constitution within a month.	*Annual Register* 1835: 497
122	Revolt in Portugal	1836		The "Septembrists" for restoration of 1822 constitution vs. Queen Maria II	The "Septembrists," led by Sa da Baniera, forced Queen Maria II to promise the restoration of the constitution of 1822.	The queen promised the restoration of the constitution of 1822, but a compromise charter emerged.	*Annual Register* 1836
123	[War in La Plata]	1836–52	4	Argentine unitarians allied with French and British troops, Uruguay, and Brazilians vs. Argentine federalists under Rosas	A conflict between Buenos Aires and provinces that had been united in 1816 as the "United Provinces of South America."	Argentina was unified under Rosas.	Richardson 1960: 58
124	Riots and insurrec-tion in Naples and Sicily	1837		Liberals vs. the government	Cholera epidemic disorders led to an attempted takeover by liberals in Naples (Cosenza, Salerno, and Avellino) and Sicily (Syracuse, Catania, and Messina).	The liberals were unsuccessful.	Tilly et al. 1975: 304

125	Riots in Germany	1837–39	Catholics against government interference in church affairs	Catholics rioted against government intervention in church affairs in Rhineland, Westphalia, and Posen.	Tensions between Catholics and the government remained.	Tilly 1975b
126	[First British-Afghan War]	Oct. 1838– Sept. 1842	4	Britain for defense of India and suspicious of Persian and Russian influence in Afghanistan vs. Afghans against invasion	Britain attempted armed intervention in the internal affairs of Afghanistan with a view toward setting up a pro-British government in Kabul.	The attempt ended in failure, although the British occupied Kabul from Aug. 1839 to Jan. 1842.	Richardson 1960: 56
127	[War in Syria]	1839–41	4	Mehmet Ali, viceroy of Egypt, for expansion vs. Ottoman Porte, and British and Austrian troops in defense	British and Austrian troops helped the Turks to oust Mehmet Ali from Syria with the help of Maronites and Druse.	The quest to expand Egyptian power against the Ottoman Porte was halted.	Richardson 1960: 54
128	[War between Russia and Khivan]	1839	4	Russia for expansion vs. Khivans in defense	Part of Russia's search for a "border" in Central Asia and warm-water ports.	Russia was unsuccessful.	Richardson 1960: 79
129	Riots in Wales	1839–44		Workers against church rates, tithes, high rents, the Poor Law, and the activities of insensitive agents and clerical magistrates	The "Rebecca Riots" were part of a series of insurrectionary outbursts that generated alarm in the government.	The unrest precipitated a general roundup of Chartist leaders.	Williams 1955

Case no.	Event	Date	Magnitude	Actors and reasons for fighting	Explanation	Result	Source
130	[First Opium War]	Nov. 1839–Aug. 1842	4	Britain for trading facilities vs. Chinese against opium	The Chinese confiscated opium at Canton that belonged to British merchants. The British government maintained that Chinese courts could not authorize the seizure of their property. The Chinese refused demands for reparations and fired on British warships.	China ceded Hong Kong and opened Shanghai, Canton, Amoy, Foochow, and Ningpo to British trade.	Richardson 1960: 56
131	[Conquest of Algeria]	Nov. 1, 1839–Dec. 23, 1847	5	France for expansion vs. the Moroccan government, Algerians, and Moors in defense	French efforts in North Africa were aimed at acquiring influence in Egypt.	The French obtained control of the coastal region of Algeria.	Richardson 1960: 57
132	Uprising in England	Nov. 4, 1839		Chartists and workers vs. troops	A band of some 2,000 coal and iron workers marched on Newport, Monmouthshire, and was fired on by troops.	Fifteen men were killed and 50 were wounded.	*Annual Register* 1839: 316; Goldstein 1983: 160
133	Strikes in France	1840		Workers	A major strike wave involving 20,000 workers. A tailors' strike in Paris was quickly joined by workers in other trades and began to spread to the provinces.	The strikers were suppressed by troops. Hundreds of leaders were arrested, tried, and transported.	*Annual Register* 1840: 175; Goldstein 1983: 173

134	Rebellions in France	1841	Tax rebellion in the southwest.	Tilly 1975b
135	Insurrection in Baden	1841	Republicans	Maurice 1887
136	Insurrection in Crete	1841	Greek Cretans vs. Ottomans	First of a series of insurrections aided by the Athens-based Central Committee of Cretans.	*Annual Register* 1841
137	Bulgarian uprising	1841	Peasants vs. Turkish troops	A peasant uprising in Nis on the Serbian frontier was crushed by Turkish troops. Many Bulgarians were massacred. Scores of villages were burned, and caravans of women and children were sold as slaves. Some 10,000 Bulgarians fled to Serbia.	Goldstein 1983: 173
138	Serbian insurrection	April 1841	Peasants for reform vs. nobles	One of the more significant peasant insurrections was triggered by the refusal of the nobles to accept reforms promulgated by the sultan in 1839. Protests against autocratic rule continued until September 1842.	Petrovich 1976
139	Insurrections in Italy	1841–45	Liberal nationalists for reform and independence vs. autocrats and Austrians	An attempted insurrection in Savigno, Romagna, in 1843; revolts in the Kingdom of Sicily in 1841 and 1844 and in the Papal states in 1843 and 1845. The revolts failed, but they attracted considerable attention and sympathy elsewhere in Europe.	Tilly et al. 1975: 304; Goldstein 1983: 175

Case no.	Event	Date	Magnitude	Actors and reasons for fighting	Explanation	Result	Source
140	Peasant insurrection in Kazan, Russia	1842		Peasants vs. landowners	Major peasant insurrection in the Kazan province of Russia involving about 130,000 serfs.	The insurrection was suppressed by troops.	Goldstein 1983: 173
141	Riots in England	Aug. 1842		Workers for a fair wage vs. masters	Industrial distress led to severe rioting, paralyzing most of the northern and central industrial regions of England and affecting industrial centers in Scotland and southern Wales as well.	Workers returned to work at the same wage. Chartist leaders were prosecuted.	Rose 1957: 112; Goldstein 1983: 172
142	[War in Gwalior, India]	1843	3	British for dominance and order vs. Sindhiale family against intrusion		Gwalior was defeated. British officers were appointed as part of the Gwalior army.	Richardson 1960: 80
143	Riots in Bohemia-Moravia	1843–44		Textile and railway workers vs. employers	A number of riots took place, part of an upsurge of working-class unrest throughout the more advanced industrial areas of Europe.	Unresolved tensions made the area a center of uprisings during the 1848 Europe-wide revolutions.	Goldstein 1983: 172

144	Coup in Greece	1843		Military coup in opposition to King Otto	Opposition to King Otto culminated in a coup by military units in Athens and the demand for a constitution.	A constituent assembly promulgated a constitution in March 1844 that established a lower legislative chamber elected by universal male suffrage. However, the king had veto power over legislation.	Goldstein 1983: 177–78
145	[Conquest of Sind]	Jan.–June 1843	4	British to annex Sind vs. Baluchis in defense	Part of the quest to establish British domination throughout the subcontinent.	Sind annexed to British India.	Richardson 1960: 56
146	Insurrection in Spain	July 1843		Liberal and radical parties against General Espartero's conservative social policies vs. the government	An armed insurrection began in Madrid and the insurrectionary movement swept the country.	The regent and head of government, General Espartero, fled the country.	Goldstein 1983: 179
147	Uprising in Cosenza	1844		Liberals against the authoritarian rule of General Ramon Narvaéz	An uprising by liberal plotters in Cosenza (Calabria).	The uprising inspired a Bandiera expedition later that year.	Tilly et al. 1975: 304
148	Riots in Prussian Silesia	June 1844		Workers against industrial mechanization	An uprising of about 5,000 starving linen handloom weavers unable to compete against machine-made cotton fabrics.	Troops put down the rising, killing thirty-five workers.	Reichert 1969: 31
149	Hussar uprising in Hapsburg Empire	Oct. 1844		Serbian exiles vs. the Hapsburg government	A pro-Obrenovic uprising was launched by Serbian exiles in the Hapsburg Empire.	The uprising was suppressed with great severity.	Goldstein 1983: 177

Case no.	Event	Date	Magnitude	Actors and reasons for fighting	Explanation	Result	Source
150	Strike in France	1845		Workers	A strike of wool workers occurred in Lodeve.		Shorter and Tilly 1974
151	[First British-Sikh War]	Dec. 1845– March 1846	4	British to annex Punjab vs. Sikhs	Part of the quest to establish British domination throughout the Indian subcontinent.	British took some frontier land and sold Kashmir to Gulab Singh.	Richardson 1960: 56
152	[War in Bali]	1846– 49	3	Dutch for control vs. Balinese for independence		Dutch gained control.	Richardson 1960: 81
153	Riots in France	1846– 47		Workers and the unemployed	Food riots in and around Paris occurred when the most terrible crop failures of the nineteenth century resulted in higher food prices and famine, and the depression of 1847 had brought widespread unemployment.	Social and political unrest culminated in revolution a year later.	Tilly 1975b
154	Uprising in Poland	Feb. 1846	3	Peasants for an end to feudal dues and service vs. the Polish nobility	Attempts by Polish revolutionaries to stir up a general uprising against the Austrian administration in Galicia ended up triggering a peasant uprising against	The uprising inspired peasant unrest throughout the Hapsburg Empire. Over 5,000 troops were needed to force Galician peasants to resume labor services.	Goldstein 1983: 181

						the Polish nobility. About 2,000 members of the Polish landowning class were slaughtered.	
155	**Uprising in Krakow**	March 1846	3	Poles *vs.* Austrians and Russians	An insurrection in the independent city of Krakow in early March was crushed by Austrian and Russian troops. Eleven Poles were sentenced to death.	Austria annexed Krakow in violation of the 1815 Treaty of Vienna.	Goldstein 1983: 181
156	Uprising in Denmark	April 1846		German nationalists against female succession *vs.* King Christian VIII	When it became evident that the Danish king would not have a male heir, a dispute arose. When King Christian VIII announced (1846) that succession by females was to apply to Schleswig as well, there was violent opposition among German nationalists.	Prussian forces occupied Schleswig-Holstein. The response to the truce in the Frankfurt Parliament triggered the Frankfurt riots in September. Frederick VII, who succeeded Christian, declared the complete union of Schleswig with Denmark in 1848.	Harbottle 1971: 85
157	Insurrection in Germany	Sept. 1846		Baden Republicans *vs.* federal troops	The Baden Republicans gathered for action following the Frankfurt riots. The leadership of the movement fell to Struve, who now proclaimed the Republic from the Town Council House in Lörrach.	Federal troops were sent against the insurgents, who were at the first collision easily defeated. The insurrection was remembered as the Struve Putsch.	Maurice 1887

Case no.	Event	Date	Magnitude	Actors and reasons for fighting	Explanation	Result	Source
158	Riots in Frankfurt	Sept. 1846		Liberals vs. the King of Prussia	A dispute in the Frankfurt Parliament over concessions to the King of Prussia led to a walkout by Democrats and the left and insurrectionary activity in the streets. The ministry requested help, and Bavarian, Prussian, and Austrian generals responded.	A state of siege was declared.	Maurice 1887: 375
159	Riots in Germany	1847		Workers for food and work	Exceptionally serious and widespread food riots known as the "potato war" broke out in the spring of 1847 in Berlin and other cities.	Troops were called in to suppress the riots.	Tilly 1975b
160	Uprising in Bulgaria	1847		Peasants	Peasant uprising in the Kula region.		*Annual Register* 1847
161	Revolt in Russia	1847		Peasants, disappointed in their hopes of employment	Some 10,000 peasants in Vitebsk, who were decimated by hunger and drought, revolted.	Troops suppressed the protestors and meted out harsh punishments.	Blum 1978: 346

162	Demonstrations and riots in Italy	1847		Liberals for reform	Demonstrations and riots in Palermo, Milan, Messina, Naples, and elsewhere led to bloody clashes with police.	Press censorship was eased.	Goldstein 1983: 184
163	Civil war in Switzerland	1847		Liberals *vs.* Catholics and conservatives	A vote in the Diet for the dissolution of the Sonderbund resulted in civil war. The liberal victory was possible due to the nonintervention of the powers, for which British Foreign Secretary Lord Palmerston was mostly responsible. With his influence, he restrained Metternich.	The victorious liberals reorganized the state and drafted a new constitution in 1848 to replace the existing statute of 1815.	Maurice 1887: 159, 214
164	[Second British-Sikh War]	1848–49	4	British for control *vs.* Sikhs for independence	A British-Indian force completed the conquest of the Punjab and put an end to the Sikh state.	British annexed Punjab.	Richardson 1960: 57
165	Uprising in Italy	Jan.–Aug. 1848		Neopolitans for changes in proposed constitution and Sicilian peasants for reforms	Uprising in Naples, followed by Palermo and other Sicilian cities. The Palermo rising triggered a widespread agrarian rebellion among the Sicilian peasantry that featured the burning of property records and attacks on the property of the rich.	Troops crushed the revolts.	*Annual Register* 1848; Tilly 1975b

Case no.	Event	Date	Magnitude	Actors and reasons for fighting	Explanation	Result	Source
166	Uprising in France	Feb. 1848	4	Workers	A protest in Paris on Feb. 22 and 23 became revolutionary when troops fired on marchers, killing or wounding about 80 people. Barricades went up. Louis Philippe abdicated in favor of his grandson, but a provisional government proclaimed France a republic.	There was continued rioting and agitation up to the June days: attacks on machines and railroads, resistance to tax collectors, anti-Semitic violence, and attacks on convents and chateaux throughout many parts of France.	Tilly 1975b; Grenville 1976: 103
167	Uprising in Germany	March 1848	3	Workers (artisans and journeymen) for constitutional government, responsible ministry, and withdrawal of troops	A revolutionary uprising occurred after troops opened fire on demonstrators in Prussia.	After some 230 civilians and 20 soldiers had died, the king ended press censorship, promised a meeting of the Diet, and granted a constitution and the establishment of a civil guard.	Langer 1969: 392; Goldstein 1983: 187
168	Piedmont-Austrian War	March 1848–49	3	Piedmont to annex Austrian Lombardy-Venetia and the independent duchies of Modena and Parma vs. Austria to maintain control	The Italian states became a major center of revolutionary activity during the 1848 Europe-wide revolutions.	Some 960 Italians were executed for political offenses by the Austrian authorities.	Cantimori 1948; Singer and Small 1972: 92; Goldstein 1983: 190

169	Uprising in Vienna	March 1848	Students, artisans, and workers vs. the government	Students and artisans marched on the Assembly of the Estates of Lower Austria, seeking the removal of Metternich, freedom of press and of religion, responsible government, and connection with Germany.	Metternich was dismissed. Forced labor and other manorial obligations were abolished, simultaneously compensating landlords by mainly taxing peasants. The emperor granted a constitution for Austrians and made Hungary virtually independent.	Maurice 1887: 234
170	**Revolt in Milan**	March 1848	3	Milan for independence vs. Austria to maintain control	The Milanese appealed to Piedmont for help against Austria, but Charles Albert was reluctant to throw in his lot with the revolutionary committee in control of Milan.	The viceroy of Milan promised reforms and dismissed some troops from Milan.	*Annual Register* 1848: 318; Maurice 1887; Smith 1971: 15
171	**German-Danish War**	April 1848– July 1850	5	Denmark for closer integration of Schleswig-Holstein vs. Prussia for the Germanic people and maintaining status quo	Schleswig-Holstein, resisting closer integration into Denmark, caused a revolt, which brought in Danish troops. German national feeling was aroused; Prussia was trusted to resist Danish encroachment. Swedish and Norwegian troops responded to Danish appeals.	Prussian troops retreated after pressure from Russia and Britain, but Denmark renounced this armistice. The second armistice was concluded with the intervening assistance of Britain, Russia, and Sweden.	Langer 1969; Small and Singer 1982: 82

Case no.	Event	Date	Magnitude	Actors and reasons for fighting	Explanation	Result	Source
172	Rebellion in England	April 1848		Chartists	News of revolutions on the continent led to riots in Glasgow and London. Disturbances in the north went on for several months.	The disturbances gave the authorities a pretext for arresting most of the leaders of Chartism.	Langer 1969: 70–71
173	**Revolution in Hungary**	April 1848–Aug. 1849	4	Hungarians for independence vs. Austrians and Croats	The Hungarian Diet declared Hungary a republic. Russia and Austria combined their efforts to preserve Austrian integrity. The Hungarians appealed to Britain for assistance without success. The Croats wanted to be freed from Hungarian subjection.	Hungary remained part of the Austrian Empire.	Maurice 1887; Fejtö 1948
174	Serbo-Hungarian civil war	May 1848		Serbs against efforts of the Hungarian government to "Magyarize" them vs. the Hungarian government	Proclamation by Voivodina Serbs and their alliance with Croatia, Slavonia, and Dalmatia resulted in civil war. Aid and donations were sent to the insurgents from the Serbs of Dalmatia, Trieste, and Vienna.	The "nationalities," though they had supported the cause of the imperial center against the Hungarians, fared no better in the 1848 revolutions.	Langer 1969: chaps. 11, 14

175	**Paris uprising**	June 23–26, 1848	3	Workers protesting government abolition of national workshops vs. troops	Several days of bloody street fighting following the government closure of the national workshops set up by the previous government.	As many as 1,500 insurgents and soldiers were killed. Some 3,000 insurgents were executed after the uprising.	Langer 1969: 349–50; Goldstein 1983: 68
176	Revolution in Wallachia	June 1848		Boyars vs. Turks	A nationalist revolution broke out in Wallachia in June 1848. Russian troops moved into the rebellious province and remained in occupation until 1853.	After 1853, Austrian troops replaced the Russian troops in the province with Turkish consent until 1883.	Maurice 1887
177	Insurrection in Ireland	July 1848		Revolutionaries for reform and independence vs. troops and police	Insurrection occurred in Tipperary.	The insurrection was quickly put down and harsh repressive measures were imposed.	Bury 1948
178	Uprisings in Livorno	Aug. 1848		Workers for more land, reduced obligations to landlords, higher wages, public works to generate employment, and restrictions on the introduction of machinery vs. landlords and officials	An uprising in Livorno in August forced officials and troops to flee the city.	Workers were too disorganized to assume power.	Cantimori 1948; Langer 1969

Case no.	Event	Date	Magnitude	Actors and reasons for fighting	Explanation	Result	Source
179	Uprising in Livorno	Aug. 1848		People of Bologna against Austrian occupation of the city vs. Austrian troops for control; unemployed workers vs. property owners and employers	An uprising in Bologna occurred in August when Austrian troops attempted to occupy and hold the city. Austrian troops were forced to retreat. For weeks the city was at the mercy of unemployed workers, who pillaged, murdered, and tyrannized the population.	Eventually an Austrian government emissary backed by Swiss mercenaries succeeded in restoring order.	Cantimori 1948; Langer 1969
180	Insurrection in the Ionian Islands	Sept. 1848–49		Ionians for reform	Under the pressures of 1848, the British administration of the Ionian Islands initiated a program of belated reforms that were, however, insufficient to stem the insurrection that broke out in Cephalonia in September 1848.	After the insurrection of 1848, the British attempted to revive the Constitution of 1817. This failed to restore the peace, and a new insurrection broke out in 1849.	Miller 1936: 83–90
181	Insurrection in Baden, Germany	Sept. 1848		Republicans for independence vs. federal troops	Following the Frankfurt riots, Baden Republicans proclaimed the republic.	Federal troops suppressed the insurrection.	Maurice 1887: 377–78

	Event	Date	Parties	Description	Outcome	Source
182	Insurrection in Rome	Nov. 1848	Romans for a republic vs. federal troops	In Rome, agitation flared up into insurrection in November 1848, forcing the Pope to flee to Gaeta.	A constituent assembly proclaimed a Roman republic three months later.	Langer 1969: 432–36
183	Insurrection in France	1849	Radicals for socialist reforms vs. the French government	Radical elements called on the people to throw up barricades in Paris following the assembly election of 1849.	The insurrection was suppressed. Some 200 people died in the fighting. Martial law and other repressive measures were put in place in Paris and Lyons.	Langer 1969: 451–52
184	**Roman Republic War**	March–July 1849	Romans for a republic vs. Austria and France for the restitution of the Pope	After being forced to flee Rome, Pius IX appealed for help from France, Naples, and Austria.	French troops entered Rome in July 2. The Pope was restored.	Langer 1969: 436–50; Small and Singer 1982: 82
185	Revolutions in Germany	May–June 1849	Lesser bourgeoisie, artisans, journeymen, and factory workers in support of the Frankfurt Constitution	The "Second German Revolution" in Rhineland, Baden, Dresden, and Bavaria. In Dresden, a chief center of the insurgency, the king fled the city and appealed to the Prussian government for military aid. Radicals all over Europe gathered in Baden.	Insurrections were put down by Prussian troops. Marx, Engels, and communists were expelled.	Maurice 1887

Case no.	Event	Date	Magnitude	Actors and reasons for fighting	Explanation	Result	Source
186	Insurrection in Bulgaria	1850	3	Peasants against oppressive taxes, corruption, and extortion vs. Turkish landlords and officials	Peasant unrest in 1849 was evident in the region of Vidin, and by 1850 the unrest had escalated into a major peasant insurrection. In June 1850, the insurrection spread to the regions of Kula, Belgradcik, and Lom.	The rebels were defeated. About 700 peasants and 15 Turkish troops were killed in the fighting. Turkish troops slaughtered over 2,000 civilians in Belgradcik after suppressing the uprising.	Djordjevic and Fischer-Galati 1981: 109–10; Goldstein 1983: 214
187	[War in southeast Africa]	1850–52	3	Britain against cattle raiding and to secure property vs. Kaffirs and Basutos		Kaffirs were worn down and the Basutos made peace.	Richardson 1960: 82
188	Riots in Germany	1850–51		Radicals vs. troops	Violent outbreaks in territories occupied by Prussian, Austrian, and Bavarian troops.	A wave of arrests of radicals, especially in Prussia, took place.	Tilly 1975b
189	Coup and insurrection in France	Dec. 1851	3	Louis Napoleon for control vs. dissidents and protestors	In the aftermath of the coup d'etat of Louis Napoleon in December 1851, insurrection erupted in Paris. There was armed resistance to the coup in almost a third of France's départements.	Over 500 people were killed or wounded.	Langer 1969: 462; Tilly 1975b; Mergadout 1979

	Name	Dates		Issues	Description	Outcome	Sources
190	Insurrection in eastern Herzegovina	1852		Feudal lords and Montenegrins against reforms vs. the Ottoman Sultan	An insurrection in eastern Herzegovina brought the intervention of the Montenegrin Prince Danilo and led to open warfare against the Ottomans.	The Montenegrins were saved from annihilation by the intervention of the Great Powers.	Djordjevic and Fischer-Galati 1981: 109
191	Turko-Montenegrin War	Dec. 1852–March 1853	4	Ottoman troops vs. Montenegrins	Ottoman forces under Omer Pasha attacked Montenegro in retaliation for its role in an insurrection in Herzegovina during 1852.	The Montenegrins were saved from annihilation by the intervention of the Great Powers.	Gopcivic 1887; Singer and Small 1972: 73; Djordjevic and Fisher-Galati 1981: 109
192	[War in Burma]	1853	3	Britain to annex Pegu vs. Burma for independence	Britain engaged in a series of battles in order to complete the annexation of Burma in 1886.	Britain annexed Pegu.	Richardson 1960: 82
193	Crimean War	Oct. 1853–March 1856	5	Russia for principalities and to protect Orthodox Christians in the Ottoman Empire vs. Ottomans, Britain, France, and Austria to limit Russian influence; Piedmontese with the British and French in order to extend their influence in the Ottoman Empire	Russia occupied the principalities to pressurize the sultan. Britain and France declared war on Russia. Austrian mobilization caused Russia to evacuate the principalities. When Great Power proposals were rejected by Russia, war broke out in the Crimea.	Russia accepted the Four Points of Vienna. Except for Russia losing access to the Danube, the antebellum status quo was restored. Eliminating a privileged Russian position in the Ottoman Empire was a setback for Russia. The Ottoman Empire became part of Concert of Europe.	Russell 1877; Allen and Muratoff 1953; Richardson 1960: 44

Case no.	Event	Date	Magnitude	Actors and reasons for fighting	Explanation	Result	Source
194	Insurrection in Thessaly	1854		Greeks to annex Epirus and Thessaly vs. Ottoman Empire and French troops to maintain Ottoman control	During the Crimean War, the crossing of the Prut River by Russian armed forces was regarded by Greek nationalists as the signal for the invasion of Epirus and Thessaly. Greek volunteers led by officers of the regular army were sent to Epirus and Thessaly.	The Porte aided by the French and other anti-Russian powers defeated the rebel forces. In the Treaty of Parsi, the Great Powers guaranteed the integrity of the Ottoman Empire, thwarting Greek plans of liberation and annexation of Epirus and Thessaly.	Djordjevic and Fischer-Galati 1981: 115–16
195	Insurrection in Madrid	June 1854	3	Military for reforms vs. loyalist troops	A military insurrection demanded the removal of the camarilla, the rigorous observation of the fundamental laws, the amelioration of the election and press laws, the diminution of taxes, and the advancement in the civil service according to merit.	At least 3,000 were killed in an insurrectionary movement led by generals disaffected by the corruption of the camarilla and the queen mother. A new government was formed.	*Annual Register* 1854: 406–11; Marx and Engels 1939: 88–113
196	[Anglo-Persian War]	1856–57	3	British against Persian attack on Herat vs. Persian troops	A Persian attack on Herat raised British fears that Persian encroachments in Afghanistan would facilitate Russian penetration of the area.	Persia abandoned claims on Herat.	Richardson 1960: 83

197	[Second Opium War]	1856–60	4	Britain and France to compel the Chinese emperor to grant trade concessions vs. Chinese against Westerners and opium	Resistance to the thriving opium trade and to British and French residency and trade resulted in a second war. China again was defeated.	The Treaty of Tientsin opened new Chinese ports to trading, allowing foreigners to travel in the interior. Christians could spread their faith and hold property, another way for Western penetration. The United States and Russia gained the same privileges separately.	Richardson 1960: 59
198	Uprisings in Madrid and Barcelona	July 1856	3	Spanish rebels vs. government troops	Protesting O'Donnell's accession to power.	About 800 rebels and 100 government troops were killed.	Goldstein 1983: 213
199	Uprising in Spain	1857		Artisans and day laborers vs. landowners	Quasirepublican uprising of about 200 artisans and day laborers at El Arahal near Seville. Land records and landowners' houses were destroyed.	Fifty perpetrators were executed.	Goldstein 1983: 213
200	[War in Senegal]	1857	3	France for control vs. Fula Muslims	France fought a series of wars for expansion into and control of Senegalese regions.	France gained control of Senegambia.	Richardson 1960: 83

Case no.	Event	Date	Magnitude	Actors and reasons for fighting	Explanation	Result	Source
201	[Indian Mutiny]	1857–59	4	"Bengal" army against annexations vs. British	An army of disbanded soldiers and dispossessed princes and landlords fought against British-trained Indian troops and Nepalese state troops.	The revolt was crushed. Authority was transferred from the East India Company to the British Crown.	Richardson 1960: 58
202	Insurrection in Herzegovina	Nov. 1857–April 1858		Herzegovinian tribal chiefs for territory and Montenegro for independence vs. Ottomans	An insurrection in Herzegovina aided by Montenegro spread to the tribes on the Montenegrin frontier. Despite Austrian efforts, the revolt continued as the rebels, aided by Montenegrin volunteers, repulsed Turkish attacks in January 1858.	The Turkish army was defeated by Montenegrins at Grahovo late in April 1858. Only action by the Great Powers, which redrew the Montenegrin-Ottoman borders and granted recognition to Montenegro's independence, led to the pacification of Herzegovina.	Djordjevic and Fischer-Galati 1981: 117–18
203	Turko-Montenegrin War	1858–59	3	Montenegrins for pan-Slavism and expanded boundaries vs. Ottomans for control	Montenegrin resistance to Ottoman overlordship erupted throughout the first half of the nineteenth century.	Ottomans were defeated by Montenegrins. The Great Powers redrew Montenegrin-Ottoman borders and recognized Montenegro's independence.	Richardson 1960: 84

204	Uprising in Bosnia	Jan.–July 1858		Peasants against feudal obligations vs. nobles	Uprisings in Sava and Kraima started during the Crimean War when the peasants refused to abide by their feudal obligations. By the beginning of 1858, armed revolts were recorded in the regions of Gradacac, Bosanski Samac, and in the Trebava mountains.	Uprising was suppressed by Ottoman troops.	Djordjevic and Fischer-Galati 1981: 117–18
205	[War in South Celebes]	1859–60	3	Dutch to secure control and Aru Palaka claiming the throne of Boni vs. Boninese for independence	Dutch had acquired dominion over South Celebes in 1825, but Boninese "arrogance" and "insults" triggered a Dutch effort to consolidate its control.	Aru Palaka became the overlord of Boni and feudal to the Dutch.	Richardson 1960: 84
206	[War in South Borneo]	1859–63	3	Dutch for control of coal mines vs. Banjermasinese for independence	Part of the struggles involved in establishing control in the Dutch East Indies.	Dutch secured control over Banjermasin.	Richardson 1960: 85
207	War in Circassia	1859–64	3	Russians for expansion vs. Circassia in defense	Part of Russia's search for a "border" in Central Asia and warm-water ports.	Russia was victorious. Many Circassians emigrated to Turkey.	Richardson 1960: 86

Case no.	Event	Date	Magnitude	Actors and reasons for fighting	Explanation	Result	Source
208	Italian-Austrian War	April-Nov. 1859	4	Piedmontese, led by Cavour and Victor Emmanuel for Italian unification, vs. Austria and Austrian-controlled rulers for autocracy and France for liberation of Lombardy and for compensation	Democratic Italian unification was resisted by Austria, despots in Italy, and the papacy.	Lombardy, Emilia, and Tuscany were united with Piedmont. Savoy and Nice went to France.	Rose 1905; Richardson 1960: 59; Smith 1971
209	[Spanish-Moroccan War]	Oct. 1859–April 1860	4	Spain to extend boundaries of settlements and to suppress Moroccan plunderers vs. Moroccans resisting Spanish encroachments	Part of Spanish efforts to consolidate control and add Morocco to Spain's African possessions.	By the Treaty of Fez, the boundaries of Spanish settlements were extended. Morocco was required to pay £4 million sterling and admit Spanish missionaries.	Richardson 1960: 59
210	Revolt in Italy	1860		Workers and peasants vs. employers and landowners	Food protests in Carrara, a revolt in Palermo, and attacks on landlords in Sicily.	Tensions continued to increase and soon after helped to fuel civil war.	Smith 1971
211	Italian-Sicilian War	May 1860–March 1861	3	Piedmont for unified Italy vs. Sicilians and Rome for independence	Uprising in Sicily led to Piedmontese intervention and victory, later moving on to Naples, Rome, and Venice.	Italy was unified except for Rome and Venice.	Trevelyan 1919; Richardson 1960: 84

212	Italian Civil War	1861–69	4	Southern Italians against northern domination and peasants against economic discrimination by the government and landlords	A series of civil wars were fought in the south. Bourbonists and Papalists exploited the wish for autonomy and the hatred of northern conscription and taxes. Economic discrimination by government and landlords kept the peasantry as a revolutionary force.	The casualties in this civil war were probably as many as those lost in all the wars fought against Austria for national independence.	Smith 1971: 36
213	Insurrection in Herzegovina	1861–Sept. 1862		Herzegovinian feudal lords and Montenegrins against Ottoman reforms	Continuing unrest caused by strained feudal relationships led to a new rebellion in Herzegovina. The insurrection had the support of Montenegro and quickly spread beyond the Montenegrin-Herzegovinian frontier. The Great Powers intervened with the Porte.	In 1862, Prince Nikola of Montenegro formally joined the conflict against the Turks, only to be defeated. Nikola accepted an ultimatum issued by Omer Pasha Latas in September 1862.	Djordjevic and Fischer-Galati 1981: 118
214	[Mexican Expedition]	1861–69	4	France, Spain, and Britain for control vs. Mexicans	French set Archduke Maximillian as Emperor of Mexico in 1864. When French troops were withdrawn in 1867, Maximillian was defeated by Juarez.	Juarez became president.	Richardson 1969: 60

Case no.	Event	Date	Magnitude	Actors and reasons for fighting	Explanation	Result	Source
215	**Rebellion in Sardinia**	1861–63	4	Separatists *vs.* Sardinia	A separatist rebellion occurred in Sardinia. Some 120,000 troops (almost half of the Italian army) were dispatched to suppress the revolt.	By 1863, some 1,038 had been summarily shot for possession of arms and 2,413 had been killed in the fighting.	Goldstein 1983: 219
216	Demonstrations in Russia	March 1861		Peasants *vs.* the government	When the terms of the emancipation of the serfs were proclaimed by Alexander in March 1861, a massive wave of violent protest convulsed rural Russia.	Troops were called out in 500 instances. At Bezda, nearly 100 peasants were killed.	Goldstein 1983: 226
217	Demonstrations in Warsaw	April 8, 1861		Polish peasants *vs.* Russian administrators	Troops opened fire on a crowd protesting the dissolution of the Agricultural Society, which had criticized the terms of the emancipation decree freeing the serfs.	As many as 200 people were killed.	Goldstein 1983: 227

218	[Franco-Mexican War]	1862–63	4	French vs. Mexicans	In May 1862, French troops in a battle with Mexican forces were ousted from La Plata. In March 1863, some 25,000 French troops besieged the Fort of San Xavier, then laid siege in May to La Puebla. The Mexican forces surrendered.	The French put Archduke Ferdinand on the throne.	Harbottle 1981: 141
219	Rebellion in Montenegro	1862	3	Christian Montenegrins and Herzegovinians vs. Turks	An uprising of Montenegrins and Herzegovinians was suppressed by Turkish troops. Several hundred people may have been killed.	Scutari restricted arms flows into Montenegro.	Richardson 1960: 85; Djordjevic and Fischer-Galati 1981: 118
220	Uprising in Serbia	1862	3	Serbs for greater autonomy vs. Turks	Serbs, led by Michael, rose against the Turkish garrison in Belgrade. The uprising left 300 people dead.	A compromise was enforced by the Great Powers.	Richardson 1960: 85; Djordjevic and Fischer-Galati 1981: 118
221	[Maori War]	1863–66	4	British for colonization vs. Maoris for holding their land	The third of four wars of British colonization of the area.	The Maoris were defeated.	Richardson 1960: 87

Case no.	Event	Date	Magnitude	Actors and reasons for fighting	Explanation	Result	Source
222	Uprising in Poland	Jan. 1863–Aug. 1864	3	Poles for independence vs. Russia for control	The virtual restoration in 1862 of the 1815 arrangement won the tsar some support, but the radical Polish party was not content with anything less than complete independence, which precipitated violence. England, France, and Austria protested diplomatically.	For largely domestic reasons, Napoleon warned the tsar and proposed rearrangements in Poland, gaining some British support. Britain did not wish joint action. Ultimately, the Poles were deceived in their hopes of Western assistance. The revolt was crushed.	Richardson 1960: 87; Leslie 1980
223	[Spanish operations against Chile and Peru]	1864–65	3	Peruvians and Chileans for sovereignty vs. Spaniards for control	The murder of Basque workmen and other acts of resistance to Spanish commercial exploitation prompted a settling of scores by Spanish naval power.	Spanish warships bombarded Valparaiso, La Serena, and Callao.	Richardson 1960: 87

#	Name	Date		Parties	Description	Outcome	Reference
224	**Prussia/ Denmark**	April– June 1864	4	Denmark vs. Austria and Prussia	King Fredric VII's efforts to assimilate the Duchies of Schleswig, Holstein, and Lauenburg into his domain led to a joint Austrian-Prussian attack. Prussian troops defeated Denmark and seized lands containing sizable German populations.	Denmark was defeated and surrendered Schleswig and Holstein. Fearing both Prussian aggrandizement and German unity under Prussian leadership, Austria was easily manipulated into war (Austro-Prussian War of 1866).	Steefel 1932; Harbottle 1971: 19, 85, 139
225	Riots in Turin	Sept. 1864		Protestors against the transfer of the Italian capital to Florence vs. the government	Antigovernment riots occurred.	Troops killed 197 people and wounded hundreds more.	Martin 1969: 670
226	[War in Bokhara]	1865–68	3	Russians for territory vs. Bokharians	Part of Russia's quest to establish a border in Central Asia and acquire warm-water ports.	Russians took Samarkand and the Oxus.	Richardson 1960: 89
227	Uprising in Bucharest	Aug. 1865		Boyars, liberals, and peasants vs. the Cuza government	A popular rising in Bucharest was suppressed with 20 deaths and hundreds of arrests.	Cuza was overthrown in a bloodless coup six months later.	Goldstein 1983: 235
228	Riots in Germany	1866		Prussians against conscription	Universal military service had been compulsory in Prussia since 1813, but on the eve of the Austro-Prussian war (1866), a territorial army corps was more fully developed.	The riots were suppressed.	Tilly 1975b

Case no.	Event	Date	Magnitude	Actors and reasons for fighting	Explanation	Result	Source
229	Uprising in Palermo	1866		Armed bands vs. the government	Dozens of armed bands with grievances against the government seized Palermo for a week.	The city was shelled into submission by the navy and then occupied by 10,000 troops.	Goldstein 1983: 219
230	Italian-Austrian War	1866	4	Italians for the liberation of Venetia vs. Austria	The conflict between Austria and Prussia in 1866 and French support enabled Italy to acquire Venetia from Austria.	Italy acquired Venetia, but by the Peace of Vienna gave up its claims (for a time) to South Tyrol and Istria.	Smith 1971: 23–32; Small and Singer 1982: 85
231	Rebellion in Crete	1866–67	4	Cretans for union with Greece vs. Turks	The revolt had various background causes, including national and liberation activities supported by Greece. Crete proclaimed unilaterally a union with Greece, which helped the insurrection by organizing insurrections in Epirus, Thessaly, and Macedonia.	The insurrections failed, leaving more than 600 villages destroyed. Some 50,000 refugees fled to Greece, and the Ottoman forces lost some 20,000 men. The Convention of Halepa in 1868 promised certain liberties to the Cretans.	Arnakis 1966: 108; Stillman 1966

232	Austro-Prussian War	April–Aug. 1866	5	Prussians for leadership of the German states with Italy to acquire Venetia vs. Austrians, Bavarians, Saxons, and Hanoverians	Prussia and Italy fought against Austria and the smaller German states over the disposal of Schleswig and Holstein. The Prussian army defeated the Austrians in a few weeks, and those German liberals who earlier opposed Bismarck became his admirers.	Prussia acquired both provinces, forced the Hapsburgs out of German affairs, and established the North German Confederation under her own leadership. Italy was rewarded for her participation by the acquisition of Venetia.	Richardson 1960: 45; Grenville 1976
233	Riots in Amsterdam	July 25–26, 1866			Antipolice riots killed twenty-six.		Kossman 1978: 31
234	Strike in Belgium	1867		Coal miners vs. Belgian troops	Troops were called in to suppress a coal miners' strike.	Troops shot and killed many strikers and arrested others, including the leading members of the Belgian Section of the Internationale.	Goldstein 1983: 239
235	[British-Abyssinian War]	1867–68	3	Britain to gain control vs. Abyssinia	After British were taken captive and imprisoned, British troops launched an attack.	Abyssinia was defeated. King Theodore shot himself.	Richardson 1960: 88

Case no.	Event	Date	Magnitude	Actors and reasons for fighting	Explanation	Result	Source
236	Macinato revolt in Italy	1868–69		Protesters against the national milling tax	Demonstrations and riots against the Macinato, the national milling tax, involved more Italians than any previous cluster of industrial violence, took place in very many places, and involved attacks on municipal buildings and mills.		Tilly 1975b
237	Uprising in Spain	1868		Army officers for Queen Isabella's abdication	In 1868, an army revolt led by exiled officers determined to force Isabella from the throne brought General Juan Prim, an army hero and popular progressive leader, to power.	Queen Isabella fled and was deposed. The dispute over Isabella's successor set the stage for the Franco-Prussian War.	Payne 1967; Clarke 1906
238	Riots in Italy	Dec. 1868–Jan. 1869		Protesters against a new tax on foodstuffs	Riots protesting a new tax on foodstuffs were suppressed by troops.	Some 257 people were killed and 1,100 wounded.	Neufeld 1961: 167–74; Goldstein 1983: 238–39

239	Uprising in Albania	1869	Albanians against legal reforms vs. the Ottoman Porte	Rebellions that had erupted throughout the 1830s emerged again.	Albania remained a focus of tension within the Ottoman Empire's European territories.	Frasheri 1964
240	Strikes in France	1869–70	Workers vs. troops	Strikes led to battles with the police and troops, especially in St. Etienne and Aubin.	These years marked an upsurge in strike activity. Strikes increased in number throughout the 1870s.	Tilly 1975b
241	Violence in Germany	1869	Workers vs. employers	Labor conflicts erupted throughout Germany.	Labor violence increased in Germany throughout the 1870s as a result of the depression.	Tilly 1975b
242	Insurrection in Austro-Hungarian Empire	1869	Nobles against the abolition of feudal privileges	An insurrection by nobles broke out in Austrian territory, the Boka Kotorska, and was aided by Herzegovina and Montenegro. This rebellion was caused by opposition to Austro-Hungarian measures seeking to abolish ancient privileges and tribal autonomy.	The insurrection was crushed by Austrian forces.	Djordjevic and Fischer-Galati 1981: 119

Case no.	Event	Date	Magnitude	Actors and reasons for fighting	Explanation	Result	Source
243	Insurrection in Alsace	1870–71		Alsatians against German occupation and opposed to annexation of Alsace to Germany vs. German occupiers for control	German national feeling held that Alsatians were German and that Alsace should be part of Germany. The common Alsatian speech is Germanic, and French possession of Alsace was relatively recent. The people of Alsace, however, were opposed to annexation.	By the Treaty of Frankfurt that formally ended the Franco-Prussian War of 1870–71, France ceded to Germany the whole of Alsace as well as a part of Lorraine. This became a source of tension in Europe up until World War I.	Tilly 1975b
244	Insurrection in Italy	1870		Republicans vs. conservatives	Multiple republican insurrections took on a scale previously unprecedented except in 1848. The republican insurrections or attempts took place in Pavia, Piacenza, Bologna, Volterra, Genoa, Lucca, Reggio, Carrara, and Milan.	The insurrection was suppressed.	Tilly 1975b

245	Franco-Prussian War	July 1870–May 1871	6	Prussia to unify southern and northern German states *vs.* France bitter over Sadowa	In the aftermath of French diplomatic victory over the Spanish throne, France demanded too much from Germany, and Bismarck manipulated France into declaring war. Russia and Italy were looking for benefits from the war.	France ceded to Germany the whole of Alsace and a part of Lorraine. Germany emerged as the most powerful state on the continent, and Rome became the Italian capital.	Mowat 1923; Richardson 1960: 45; Grenville 1976; Bond 1983: 16
246	Insurrection in Paris	1871	4	Members of the Commune of Paris (mostly dominated by working-class and lower-middle-class delegates) *vs.* the Versailles government	An insurrection in Paris in opposition to the newly elected National Assembly (sitting in Versailles rather than Paris) was brutally repressed. Some 25,000 Parisians were killed by government troops.	The event fostered fears of lower-class radicalism throughout Europe.	Goldstein 1983: 249
247	[War in Algeria]	1871–72	3	France to maintain control *vs.* Algerians		French control was reestablished.	Richardson 1960: 89
248	Strikes in Italy	1871–73		Agricultural and textile workers *vs.* employers	Violent strike of agricultural workers in Lombardy and Emilia (1871, 1872) and of textile workers in Pisa (1873).	The agricultural crisis and depression of the 1870s helped to make Italy a focus of labor violence throughout the decade.	Tilly 1975b
249	Rebellion in Austria-Hungary	Oct. 1871		Croats for independence	A rebellion occurred in Rekovica, which was the only genuine revolt launched by Croats in the nineteenth century.		Jelavich 1967

Case no.	Event	Date	Magnitude	Actors and reasons for fighting	Explanation	Result	Source
250	Third Carlist War, Spain	April 1872–Feb. 1876	4	Carlists for church rights, Carlos as a king, and local autonomies vs. parliamentary governments of King Amadeo, the Republicans, and Alphonso XII	One of a series of conflicts between moderates and liberals, on the one hand, and conservatives and circles, on the other, over the issue of absolute monarchy vs. constitutionalism.	Some Carlists accepted Alphonso, others were defeated. Basque local autonomy was abolished.	Richardson 1960: 60
251	[War in Ashanti]	1873–74	3	Britain for free trade vs. Ashanti for rent for port of Elmina	One of a number of conflicts over British commercial exploitation of the Gold Coast.	Ashanti renounced the port of Elmina and promised indemnity and free trade.	Richardson 1960: 89
252	Riots in Germany	1873		Protesters against high beer prices vs. local dispensers	Massive bloody riots protesting beer prices occurred, especially in Frankfurt am Main.	The riots were suppressed.	Tilly et al. 1975: 311
253	[War in Achin]	1873–1908	5	Dutch for direct rule and against piracy vs. Achinese for independence	Ended a series of struggles in Sumatra that helped establish Dutch control in the East Indies.	Dutch destroyed the Achinese sultanate and governed the country directly.	Richardson 1960: 47
254	[First Tonkin War]	1873–74	3	French against obstacles to trade vs. Tonkinese in defense	One of a series of struggles to establish French commercial privileges in Indochina.	The French were defeated and withdrew. Native Christians were massacred.	Richardson 1960: 90
255	[War in Annam]	1873		France for control vs. Annamese in defense	One of a series of struggles to extend French influence in Indochina.	A treaty signed in 1874 promised the toleration of French missionaries.	Fieldhouse 1973

No.	Event	Date		Conflict	Description	Outcome	Reference
256	Riots in Germany	1874–75		Catholics vs. the government	Catholics rioted against the Prussian Kulturkampf.	The Kulturkampf continued until 1879.	Tilly et al. 1975: 311
257	Insurrection in Italy	1874			Bakunin-inspired insurrection took place in Bologna-Taranto.	Further insurrections of this type occurred later in the decade.	Tilly 1975b
258	Riots in Italy	1874			Bread riots in Tuscany and Emilia-Romagna.		Tilly 1975b
259	Massacre in Montenegro	Oct. 1874		Ottomans for control vs. Montenegrin revolutionaries	A massacre of Montenegrins by Ottoman forces over a conflict in Podgorica.	The already tense political situation was further aggravated.	Djordjevic and Fischer-Galati 1981: 148
260	Strikes in Italy	1875		Workers vs. landlords	Strike by agricultural workers in Lombardy.	Strike activity increased throughout the decade as the depression of the 1870s put increasing pressure on the lower classes.	Tilly 1975b
261	Serbo-Montenegrin War against Turkey	1875–July 1876	3	Serbia and Montenegro for unification with Bosnia vs. Turks	The insurrection in Bosnia-Herzegovina put pressure on Serbs and Montenegrins to intervene militarily. After beginning military attacks, Ottoman troops invaded Serbia. Battles continued until the following fall.	Russian diplomatic intervention prevented total defeat of Serbia and Montenegro. The Serbs were obliged to disband all revolutionary organizations.	Stojanovic 1939: 78–94; Djordjevic and Fischer-Galati 1981: 155

Case no.	Event	Date	Magnitude	Actors and reasons for fighting	Explanation	Result	Source
262	Rebellion in Bosnia-Herzegovina	July 1875–April 1876		Herzegovinians, Montenegrins, and Bosnian Serbs for autonomy vs. Ottomans	In July 1875, an uprising of the Christian population took place in the province of Herzegovina and spread, obtaining international support. The Ottomans sent 30,000 men to crush the rebellion. An estimated 156,000 refugees were created.	Rioting spread to Constantinople, where Sultan Abdul Aziz was found dead in circumstances suggesting murder. Apparently, high Austrian officials were responsible for the outbreak of the insurrection.	Langer 1931; Stojanovic 1939: 12–27
263	Insurrection in Crete	1876–March 1878		Cretans for autonomy vs. Ottomans	An insurrection broke out when the leadership asked the Porte for autonomy. The uprising gained momentum in 1878 as Greek troops entered Thessaly.	A provisional Cretan government, which sought complete autonomy for the island, continued the fight until an ill-kept armistice was concluded between the rebel and Ottoman forces.	Miller 1936; Kofos 1975
264	Uprising in Bulgaria	April–May 1876	4	Peasants against overlords vs. Turks	Peasants protesting feudal exactions and seeking possession of land slaughtered unarmed Turks. The authorities, who were outnumbered, armed the Muslim population.	Many villages were burned and plundered.	Langer 1931: 85; Djordjevic and Fischer-Galati 1983: 152; Jelavich 1983: 346–47

378

265	Rebellion in Macedonia	May 1876–Sept. 1878	Macedonian rebels vs. local authorities	Rebellion started in Razlog, where Ottoman troops cut rebels off, who retreated to mountains until a new rebellion erupted in Kreshna.	The rebellion proved to be but a prelude to the violent insurrections that occurred later in 1878 and 1880.	Stavrianos 1958
266	Insurrection in Italy	1877		Bakunin-inspired insurrection took place in Benevento-San Lupo.		Tilly 1975b
267	Insurrection in Thessaly	1877–78	Greeks in the Ottoman province of Thessaly for independence	Pursuing territorial gains, Greece had fomented anti-Turk rebellions in the provinces of Epirus and Thessaly. The Russian declaration of war (1877) against Turkey offered opportunities for rebellion against Turkish rule and for Greek irredentism.	Greece acquired most of Thessaly as a result of the Convention of May 1881.	Kofos 1975
268	Romanian War of Independence	1877–78	Romanians for independence	The Ottoman provinces of Wallachia and Moldavia became autonomous following the Treaty of Adrianople in 1829 and formed Romania in 1868. Assisted by Russia, Romania declared independence from the Ottoman Empire at the outset of the Russo-Turkish War in 1877.	Romania's independence was confirmed in the Treaty of Berlin in 1878.	Rose 1905

Case no.	Event	Date	Magnitude	Actors and reasons for fighting	Explanation	Result	Source
269	**Russo-Turkish War**	April 1877–78	5	Russia to enforce the joint Protocol of the Powers joined by Serbians, Montenegrins, Bulgarians, and Romanians vs. Turkey	After the war between Serbia and Montenegro against Turkey, Turkey rejected the joint Protocol of the Powers drafted in London. Russia declared war on Turkey, and Serbians, Montenegrins, Bulgarians, and Romanians joined Russia.	Turkey was defeated, and Russia exchanged some territory gained with Romania and reacquired Bessarabia. Serbia and Montenegro were enlarged and, like Romania, freed of the last dependencies on the sultan. Bosnia-Herzegovina was to become autonomous.	Rose 1905: 244–56; Stojanovic 1939: 145–183
270	Rebellion in Albania	1878		Albanians opposed to giving land to Montenegro vs. Ottomans and Great Powers	Albanian nationalists opposed the transfer of the districts of Gusinje and Plava to Montenegro as provided by the Treaty of Berlin following the conclusion of the Russo-Turkish War.	Montenegro received only half of the territory granted to it.	Swire 1929; Skendi 1953
271	Riots in Italy	1878			Anticlerical riots occurred in Rome.		Tilly 1975b
272	[Sieges of Geok Tepe]	1878–81	4	Russians against raids and for expansion vs.	As part of Russia's southward imperial	Russia controlled Transcaspia.	Rose 1905: 419–23;

No.	Name	Date		Participants	Description	Outcome	Source
				Tekke Turcomans with British officers for their homes	movement, Russia attempted to gain control of Turcoman territory. A series of campaigns were fought against Tekke Turcomans beginning in 1878.		Richardson 1960: 62
273	[Second British-Afghan War]	1878–80	4	Britain for defense of India against possible Russian aggression through Afghanistan vs. Afghans	After the Russians sent an embassy to the Kabul government, the British demanded that a mission from India should also be received at Kabul. The Afghan government refused. Two costly campaigns and the loss of many lives followed.	The Amir consented to accept a British residency, and the British frontier was advanced at Pishin.	Richardson 1960: 62
274	Insurrection and riots in Italy	1878		Agricultural workers, inspired by the Lazzaretti movement, vs. carabinieri	A Lazarettist insurrection in Monte Labro, Tuscany, led to clashes between agricultural workers and Carabinieri. The workers were inspired by a messianic movement that emerged in the 1870s calling for a republic and in Tuscany led by Davide Lazzaretti.	The carabinieri were successful in stamping out the movement.	Tilly 1975b

Case no.	Event	Date	Magnitude	Actors and reasons for fighting	Explanation	Result	Source
275	**Rebellion in Bosnia-Herzegovina**	June–Oct. 1878	4	Austrians to occupy Bosnia vs. Bosnian Muslims desiring to join Serbia instead	Austria fought for occupying Bosnia-Herzegovina as arranged by the Congress of Berlin of 1878 against Muslims in the provinces wishing to join Serbia. The Muslims and Serbians collaborated in resisting the Austrians, leading to an armed confrontation.	The Austrians ultimately prevailed, and the total occupation of Bosnia was accomplished by the end of October 1878.	Richardson 1960: 61; Djordjevic and Fischer-Galati 1981: 158–59
276	Insurrection in Macedonia	Oct. 1878–April 1879		Macedonians for independence vs. Ottomans	Insurrection broke out in Kresna and spread quickly. Turkish armies staged an offensive and despite fierce resistance captured Kresna.	The insurrection was completely crushed in April 1879. About ten villages were burned and some 25,000 inhabitants were forced to emigrate to Bulgaria.	Djordjevic and Fischer-Galati 1981: 163–64
277	[**Zulu War**]	1879	4	British over disputed boundary vs. Zulu	The ruler of the state of the Zulus on the border of the British colony of Natal armed and organized a disciplined army. The British demanded that the	The Zulu ruler, Cetewayo, was sent to St. Helena. Four years later, he was allowed to return. Zululand became a part of the British colony of Natal.	Richardson 1960: 61; Morris 1973: 282, 587

	Event	Date	Actors / goals	Description	Outcome	Source
				army be disarmed. When the Zulus refused, imperial troops quickly crushed the Zulu army.		
278	Insurrection in Bosnia-Herzegovina	Aug. 1879	Bosnians and Herzegovinians against denationalization and for religious autonomy vs. Austrians	The Russo-Turkish War of 1877 gave to Austria-Hungary the administration of Bosnia-Herzegovina. The agrarian problem and the denationalization policies of the Austrian authorities were causes of discontent in the provinces and led to armed insurrection.	Austria-Hungary retained control of the provinces. Nationalist agitation continued there until 1914.	Djordjevic and Fischer-Galati 1981: 165
279	Strikes in France	1880		Numerous violent strikes.		Tilly 1975b
280	[Basuto War, South-East Africa]	1880–83	British to maintain control vs. Basutos for independence	Basutoland was governed from London instead of Cape Town.		Richardson: 1960: 91
281	Insurrection in Macedonia	Oct. 1880	Macedonians against increased Muslim colonization	An insurrection broke out in October 1880 in western Macedonia as a consequence of increased Ottoman-Islamic colonization.	The uprising was crushed as the rebels, lacking support from neighboring Balkan states, were unable to resist the superior Ottoman forces located in central Macedonia.	Anastasoff 1938

Case no.	Event	Date	Magnitude	Actors and reasons for fighting	Explanation	Result	Source
282	Montenegro-Albanian League conflict	Nov. 1880		Montenegro for territory vs. Albanian tribes opposing their transfer to Montenegro	Turkey was reluctant to make the territorial concessions to Montenegro and Greece that had been provided for in the Treaty of Berlin. This included the transfer of some Albanian tribes to Montenegro that the tribes, the so-called Albanian League, opposed.	A Turkish force subdued the forces of the Albanian League, which threatened to become dangerous for the Turkish government itself. Dulcigno was then handed over to the Montenegrins.	Langer 1931
283	[War in Tunisia]	1881	3	France to govern Tunisia and to forestall Italian and British expansion vs. Tunisians in defense	At a time when French and Italian commercial interests were increasingly coming into conflict in Tunisia, and the country's debt (mostly held by French creditors) was undermining the rule of the bey, Britain and Germany at the Congress of Berlin conceded to France a free hand in Tunisia. French efforts to consolidate its control of the country met with resistance.	France governed Tunisia.	Richardson 1960: 91
284	Riots in Germany	1881			Anti-Semitic riots occurred in eastern Prussia, especially in Pomerania.		Tilly 1975b

#	Name	Date		Parties	Description	Outcome	Source
285	**Revolt in Dalmatia**	1881	3	Southern Dalmatians against military service and for autonomy vs. Austro-Hungarian Empire	Disturbances triggered by the civil administration established in the area by Austria-Hungary after 1878 spread from Dalmatia over the frontier into Herzegovina.	Austrian troops restored order.	Richardson 1960: 91
286	Rebellion in Albania	Jan.–March 1881		Various Albanian opposition groups vs. the Ottoman Porte	Rebellion began in Prizen and spread.	Turks defeated the rebels and occupied Kosovo and southern Albania.	Djordjevic and Fischer-Galati 1981: 168
287	Revolt and insurrection in Bosnia-Herzegov-ina	June 1881–Nov. 1882		Bosnians against Austrian Landwehr law	A revolt began as a response to the enforcement of the Austrian Landwehr law and spread, resulting in the proclamation of martial law. This action provoked a further insurrection, which also spread and reached its height in February 1882.	The Bosnian government proclaimed the rebellion over and pardoned the rebels, but rebellion lingered in eastern Herzegovina until November 1882.	Djordjevic and Fischer-Galati 1981: 168, 171–73
288	Uprising in Rome	July–Nov. 1881		Radical Republicans against the papacy	Radicals organized a movement to abolish the Italian guarantee of the Pope's position, and some advocated atrocities against the Vatican. The anti-papal outbreak demonstrated the Pope's exposure to humiliation. Some papal advisers urged him to voluntary exile.	The issue of whether the Pope should leave Rome and where he should go became the focus of complications among Italy, France, Germany, and Austria.	Langer 1969: 232–35

Case no.	Event	Date	Magnitude	Actors and reasons for fighting	Explanation	Result	Source
289	Pogroms in Russia	1881–82		Russian peasants for plunder vs. Jews	At Elisabetgrad, Balta, Kiev, and elsewhere, Jewish quarters were pillaged and burned.	Jews fleeing Russian pogroms contributed to their concentration in German and Austrian towns and cities and to their persecution in those countries in the early twentieth century.	Rose 1905: 304–5
290	[Revolt of the Mahdi]	Aug. 1881–May 1885	4	British and Egyptians for control vs. Sudanese for a revived religion and against taxes and foreigners	The Sudan, never completely under British control, broke into revolt after a religious leader proclaimed himself to be a mahdi, or savior. A force of Egyptian soldiers and a small British force were slaughtered.	Britain abandoned its ambitions in the Sudan until 1896.	Richardson 1960: 62
291	Strikes in Italy	1882–84		Rural and urban workers vs. landowners and employers	Starting in 1882, violent agricultural strikes and demonstrations took place in Cremona and Parma, 1882; Verona, 1883; and Polesine, 1884.	Labor violence continued into and through the 1890s and beyond.	Tilly et al. 1975: appendix B.

292	[British occupation of Egypt]	1882	3	British against extravagance and bankruptcy vs. Egyptians wanting "Egypt for the Egyptians"	In 1882, the Khedive of Egypt asked for British help in suppressing a rebellion. With the arrival of British troops in Egypt, Egyptian sovereignty came to an end. British troops remained in Egypt until 1954.	Richardson 1960: 92
293	[Second Tonkin War]	March 1882– June 1885	4	French colonial troops for control vs. the natives of Annam in defense and China for control	The treatment of French missionaries afforded an opportunity for France to extend its imperial control in Indochina. A protocol signed in April 1885 gave France a protectorate in Tonkin.	Richardson 1960: 63
294	Revolt in Spain	1883			Military revolted.	Clarke 1906
295	Strikes in Italy	1883		Workers vs. landowners	Violent agricultural strikes in Verona. Strikes continued throughout the 1880s in unprecedented numbers.	Tilly 1975b
296	[Madagascar]	June 1883– Dec. 1885	3		French troops bombarded Tamatave and Majunga in Madagascar.	Banks 1978: 34
297	Strikes in Italy	1885		Workers vs. landowners	Violent agricultural strikes in Mantovano.	Tilly 1975b
298	[Russian operations in Afghanistan]	1885	3	Russians for expansion vs. Afghans with British political officers in defense	Russia's efforts to establish the demarcation of the Russian-Afghan frontier consistent with Russian interests met with opposition from Britain. Britain resisted the encroachment by Russia on its position in Afghanistan. Russia defeated the Afghans. Britain nearly went to war against Russia.	Richardson 1960: 92

Case no.	Event	Date	Magnitude	Actors and reasons for fighting	Explanation	Result	Source
299	Revolt in Italy	1885			The "La Boje" revolt occurred in Mantovano.		Tilly 1975b
300	[War for Sudanese Independence]	May 1885–95	4	Britain and Egypt for reconquest with Italians for ownership of Kassala vs. Sudanese for independence		The Sudanese maintained their independence.	Richardson 1960: 64
301	Serbo-Bulgarian War	Sept. 1885–April 1886	3	Bulgaria for control of East Rumelia vs. Serbia for territorial compensation	Bulgaria was disappointed at not acquiring "Greater Bulgaria" and proclaimed a union with East Rumelia when insurrection broke out there. Serbia, demanding compensation, declared war.	Serbia was saved from complete defeat by Bulgaria by Austria's diplomatic intervention.	Mijatovich 1917; Richardson 1960: 93
302	[Third British-Burmese War]	Nov. 1885–86	4	British for control vs. Burmese	One of a series of wars for British control of Burma.	Britain completed the annexation of Burma.	Richardson 1960: 93
303	Strike in Belgium	1886			Troops were used to suppress a strike.	About a dozen people were killed. Martial law was declared.	Goldstein 1983: 60
304	Trafalgar Square riots	Feb. 1886		Unemployed workers	Riots over unemployment occurred.	The event created widespread alarm among the wealthier classes.	Rose 1905: 32

	Event	Date		Parties	Description	Outcome	Source
305	[First Italian-Abyssinian War]	1887	3	Italians vs. Abyssinians	Italy, in endeavoring to establish a colonial empire in Africa, occupied in 1885 two points on the littoral of the Red Sea, Beilul and Massowa. In protest, an Abyssinian force killed 500 Italian soldiers at Dogali.		Bakeless 1972: 79
306	Demonstrations in London	Nov. 13, 1887		London residents vs. troops	A huge rally of 50,000 people occurred in Trafalgar Square.	The demonstrators were dispersed by troops with considerable violence.	Goldstein 1983: 258
307	Strikes in Italy	1889		Workers vs. employers	Violent strikes of textile and agricultural workers occurred in Lombardy.		Tilly et al. 1975: appendix B. Tilly 1975b
308	Strikes in Germany	1889		Workers vs. employers	Violent strikes of mine workers occurred in Ruhr and Silesia.		
309	London dock strike	1889		Workers vs. employers	The strike shut down Britain's largest port. The strike was extraordinary at the time because the dock workers were believed to be too impoverished and demoralized to be capable of collective action.	The strike succeeded in winning most of the concessions that the workers demanded.	Lovell 1985
310	[Senegal]	1890–91	3	France for expansion vs. Senegalese in defense	One of a series of wars to impose French control.	France controlled upper Senegal.	Richardson 1960: 94
311	[Upper Niger]	1890–98		French for expansion vs. Chief Samory in defense	Chief Samory was captured and exiled.	The French ruled.	Richardson 1960: 96

Case no.	Event	Date	Magnitude	Actors and reasons for fighting	Explanation	Result	Source
312	Clashes in Germany	1890		Workers vs. the police	Street clashes in Berlin between socialists and the police.		Tilly 1975b
313	Strikes in Italy	1890		Workers vs. employers	A large strike of masons occurred in Rome; violent strikes of textile workers and agricultural workers in Lombardy (Upper Milanese, Como, and Varese); and a large violent strike among day laborers in the Ravenna area.		Tilly 1975b
314	[War in Malay Archipelago]	1891–94	3	Dutch for order and lest other Europeans should intervene, and Sasaks vs. Balinese	One of a series of struggles for defense of Dutch interests in the East Indies.	Dutch took Lombok and part of Bali under direct rule.	Richardson 1960: 95
315	Riots in Poland	May 6–10, 1891		Workers vs. employers	Labor riots in Lodz in the Russian part of Poland.	Some 46 people were killed.	Leslie 1980: 57
316	Demonstrations in France	May 1, 1891		Police vs. socialists	Disturbances arose from strikes on May Day at Fourmies, a textile center in Nord, France.	A deadly fusillade was used to put an end to the disturbances. Ten people were killed.	Goldstein 1983: 64
317	General strike in Barcelona	May 1, 1891		Workers vs. employers and the police	A general strike on May Day led to clashes with the police.	Martial law was imposed.	Goldstein 1983: 294

318	[Eastern Congo War]	1892–94	Belgians against slave raiding and for ownership vs. Arabs for ivory and slave trades	Belgians took control from Arabs.	Richardson 1960: 63
319	[Spanish Morocco]	1893	Spanish troops for control vs. Berber tribesmen	Spanish forces attacked when Berber tribesmen menaced the port at Melilla.	Banks 1978: 34
320	Miners' strike in Britain	1893	Miners vs. employers	Two miners were killed when troops fired on rioters in Leeds. A miners' strike in South Wales led to a pitched battle with haulers. The strikes were defeated.	Gilbert 1968: 88
321	Strikes and demonstrations in Sicily	1893	Peasants and workers protesting exploitation by businessmen, landlords, and officials	Economic distress, a sharp drop in prices, and continued exploitation spurred a wave of land seizures and attacks on communal and tax offices in dozens of rural Sicilian towns. Police and troops killed 92 demonstrators and wounded hundreds more.	Tannenbaum 1977: 293–94; Goldstein 1983: 316
322	General strike in Belgium	1893	Workers demanding suffrage reform	A general strike for suffrage reform erupted in April 1893 to protest the constituent assembly's rejection of universal and equal male suffrage. Troops killed 20 demonstrators. The constituent assembly adopted a scheme for universal male suffrage that gave extra votes to the wealthy and well educated, thus allowing about 30 percent of the electorate to cast a majority of the votes.	Goldstein 1983: 263

Case no.	Event	Date	Magnitude	Actors and reasons for fighting	Explanation	Result	Source
323	[Tuareg War]	1893–1904		French for control of Timbuktu and natives for security vs. Tuareg nomads for loot	The Tuareg, Berber-speaking pastoralists inhabiting parts of Algeria, Libya, Mali, and Niger, were suppressed when Timbuktu was invaded and occupied by the French during 1893–94.	The French controlled Timbuktu.	Richardson 1960: 98
324	[Conquest of Madagascar]	1894–1901	4	French for expansion and against British influence vs. Hovas in defense		France annexed Madagascar.	Richardson 1960: 65
325	Armenian massacres	1894–96	5	Turkish troops and Kurds vs. Armenians	Sultan Abdul Hamid suspected the loyalty of the Armenian community and a danger to the empire. He systematically disarmed Armenians while arming the hostile Kurds. In 1894, Kurds and regular Turkish troops began a series of attacks against the Armenians.	The attacks lasted two years and culminated in three days of slaughter of between 5,000 and 8,000 Armenians in Constantinople from August 26 to 29, 1896. About 300,000 Armenians were killed during the two-year period.	Richardson 1960; SIPRI 1969; Bryce 1972; Arlen 1975; Snyder 1982
326	Demonstrations in Hungary	1894		Peasants vs. landlords	Peasant demonstrations in central Hungary.	Demonstrations were suppressed with considerable bloodshed and the imposition of martial law.	Goldstein 1983: 298

392

#	Name	Date		Participants	Description	Outcome	Source
327	Attacks against peasants in Galicia	1894		Landowners vs. peasants	Peasants were attacked in the 1894 elections in Galicia, Austria.	Over 40 peasants were killed or wounded.	Goldstein 1983: 23
328	[Italian-Abyssinian War]	July 1894–Oct. 1896	4	Italians for control vs. Abyssinians in defense		Italy recognized the independence of Abyssinia.	Richardson 1960: 64
329	[Cuban insurrection]	1895–98	4	Unemployed laborers vs. Spain	An insurgency against Spain by unemployed laborers escalated into a war of independence. When Spanish troops brutally suppressed the revolt, the United States intervened militarily.	Spain lost Cuba, which was taken under U.S. protection.	Richardson 1960: 46
330	[Ashanti War]	1895–96		Britain for control of the Gold Coast vs. Ashantis for freedom	The new Ashanti king Prempah, perhaps to prop up his kingdom, sent raiding parties into British territory. Fearful that the French in Ivory Coast or the Germans in Togo might move in, London decided to bring the Ashantis under British control.	The British forced Prempah to accept protectorate status.	Banks 1978: 34
331	Attacks in Hungary	1896		Hungarian dissident voters vs. troops	Troops attacked dissident voters during elections.	About 100 people were killed or wounded.	Goldstein 1983: 23

Case no.	Event	Date	Magnitude	Actors and reasons for fighting	Explanation	Result	Source
332	Insurrection in Crete	1896–98		Cretans for union with Greece vs. Ottoman troops for control	Another in the series of insurrections aided by Athens-based groups (1841, 1866–67, 1876–78), this one triggering war between Greece and Turkey (Greco-Turkish War of 1896–97). The revolt continued after the war between Greece and Turkey had concluded.	After a high commissioner for Crete was appointed by the Concert of Europe and had taken up his post (November 1898), Admiral Noel of the British Navy had the ringleaders hung, and the revolt ended.	Wright 1965: table 40
333	[British bombardment of Zanzibar]	1896	3	Zanzibaris for autonomy vs. British for control	The death of the sultan of Zanzibar started a struggle for the throne there. Despite British objections, Khalid bin Barghash occupied the palace and took control of the harbor, the dhow fleet, and most of the capital city. The Royal Navy bombarded the city.	Britain's candidate for sultan was put on the throne.	Gallagher and Robinson 1981
334	[Sudan campaigns]	1896–1900	4	British to establish a "Cape to Cairo" route vs. Sudanese for independence	General Sir Herbert Kitchener (afterward Lord Kitchener of Khartoum) was sent into the Sudan with	The "Anglo-Egyptian Sudan" was established.	Richardson 1960: 64

No.	Name	Dates		Parties	Description	Outcome	Source
335	Insur- rection in Crete	March 1896– 97		Cretans for union with Greece	20,000 troops to reconquer it for the Khedive of Egypt. Two years of fighting ensued. Insurrection by the Greek population of Crete was supported by Greece. The Great Powers forced the withdrawal of the Greek forces. The island was blockaded as the Powers proclaimed its independence under Ottoman suzerainty and European protection.	Governorship of Crete was given to Greece's Prince George but under Ottoman suzerainty. Union with Greece, the principal aim of the Cretan nationalists, was frustrated through this dictated solution by the Powers.	Miller 1936
336	[War in Uganda]	1897– 1901	3	British to maintain control vs. their own mercenary Sudanese troops and Ugandans	A mutiny by mercenary Sudanese troops used by Britain in its Uganda Protectorate was only barely suppressed after transporting units of the Indian army to Uganda at considerable expense and more than two years of fighting.	The Buganda Agreement of 1900, which rewarded the Buganda chiefs for their support, granted the leading chiefs a large measure of autonomy and self-government within the larger protectorate. Uganda settled down under British rule.	Richardson 1960: 98
337	[War on northwest frontier of India]	1897– 98	3	British to retain control vs. Muslims objecting to British penetration		Afridis agreed to pay fines and to surrender their rifles.	Richardson 1960: 97

395

Case no.	Event	Date	Magnitude	Actors and reasons for fighting	Explanation	Result	Source
338	Strikes, demonstrations, and riots in Italy	1897–98		Workers vs. employers and the police	A wave of strikes, land seizures, demonstrations, and bread riots spread through Italy, frequently leading to bloody clashes with the police.	In April-May 1898, military governments replaced civilian rule in 30 of Italy's 59 provinces.	Tilly et al. 1975: 150–55; Goldstein 1983: 317
339	Strikes in Hungary	1897–98		Agrarian workers vs. the rural police	Clashes in Hungary involving tens of thousands of strikers and rural police forces.	Some 51 people were killed and 114 were wounded.	Goldstein 1983: 317
340	Election disorders in Croatia	1897			In Bosnjaci, Croatia, during the election of 1897.	Some 28 people were killed.	Gazi 1973: 200
341	[War in southwest Nigeria]	1897	3	British vs. Benin		Benin was added to the neighboring British protectorate.	Richardson 1960: 96
342	Greco-Turkish War	April–Dec. 1897	3	Greeks for the annexation of Crete vs. the Ottoman Empire	Greeks sought union of Greek areas, leading Turkey to declare war. Turkish armies entered Thessaly, occupied Larissa and Volos,	Turkey won back portions of Thessaly that had been ceded to Greece in 1881.	Richardson 1960: 96; Papadopoulos 1969

					and defeated Greek forces in the battle of Domoko and in Epirus. The Great Powers intervened and saved Greece from total defeat.	
343	[War in Sierra Leone]	1898	3	British against slavery and the murder of missionaries vs. inland tribes	British control was affirmed and extended.	Richardson 1960: 97
344	[Spanish-American War]	1898	5	Spain to maintain control vs. the United States and Cubans for independence	The United States intervened militarily when Spain tried to suppress an insurrection in Cuba. Spain ceded Puerto Rico, Guam, and the Philippines to the United States. Cuba was taken under U.S. protection.	Richardson 1960: 46
345	Demonstrations in Milan	May 1898		Workers protesting police repression	After the police killed the son of an opposition member of Parliament in Pavia, they arrested Milanese workers distributing leaflets protesting the incident. Bloody clashes ensued between demonstrators and the police. Troops killed some 80 civilians. A wave of indiscriminate repression followed. A state of siege was declared. Thousands of political dissidents were arrested.	Smith 1959: 192; Goldstein 1983: 317

Case no.	Event	Date	Magnitude	Actors and reasons for fighting	Explanation	Result	Source
346	[Chad]	1899–1901		French for control vs. Rabeh Zobeir, a follower of the Sudanese Mahdi, and his sons and followers in opposition to the French invasion	French forces continued their conquest of the Sahara by moving into the area of Lake Chad, razing villages and forcing compliance with Paris rule. In 1900, French troops defeated Rabah.	Rabeh and, later, his sons were killed. Other native leaders and tribes continued resistance to the French invasion. Territory southwest of Lake Chad was partitioned between France, Britain, and Germany.	Richardson 1960: 98
347	[Chinese Boxer Rebellion]	1899–1901	4	Chinese vs. foreigners in China	The Boxer society, organized in protest against foreign activities in China, tortured and killed missionaries and Christian converts in large numbers and laid siege to the foreign legations in Peking.	Chinese granted greater foreign penetration. The rebellion was suppressed.	Richardson 1960: 65
348	[War in British Somaliland]	1899–1904	3	British for order vs. Mullah		The Mullah was driven into Italian territory.	Richardson 1960: 99
349	[Boer War]	1899–1902	5	British for political power to British miners in Transvaal vs. Transvaal and Orange Free State Boers for independence		Some 35,000 were killed, and Britain annexed the Transvaal and the Orange Free State.	Richardson 1960: 65; Gilbert 1968: 94

350	Demonstrations in Bulgaria	1900	Protesters against the tithe vs. government troops	Antitax demonstrations in Trusenik and Doran Kulak in the northeast of the country led to clashes between peasant protesters and troops.	Some 94 people were killed.	Bell 1977: 43–46
351	Strikes in France	1900–1901	Miners for higher pay vs. industrialists and company-organized union	Insurrectionary strikes in Belfort, Montceau-les-Mines, Marseilles, and elsewhere.	The strikes were suppressed by the government.	*Annual Register* 1901: 244; Tilly 1975b
352	[Gold Coast]	1900	British vs. Ashantis	An uprising by Ashantis in the Gold Coast.	The uprising was suppressed by British troops.	Banks 1978: 34
353	Student protests in Naples	1900	Students vs. the government	Disagreements between the faculties and students of the university and the government led to street protests.	The university was closed.	*Annual Register* 1900: 275
354	Anti-Semitic disturbances in Germany	1900	Residents of Konitz vs. Jews	Residents blamed death of a school boy on Jews, thinking that Jews sought Christian blood for ritual use.	Disturbances were quelled by troops, but rioters later attacked Jewish homes and destroyed the synagogue.	*Annual Register* 1900: 295–96
355	Strikes in France	June–Aug. 1900	Workers vs. employers	There were strikes, some extremely violent, in seaports of Havre, Marseilles, Cette, Bordeaux, and Dunkirk.		*Annual Register* 1900: 267

Case no.	Event	Date	Magnitude	Actors and reasons for fighting	Explanation	Result	Source
356	Riots in Poland	1901		Poles against Germanization	Polish rioted against Prussian school policies in Posen, Leipzig, Breslau, Griefsswald, Halle, Darmstadt, Karlsruhe, and Wreschen.	Children were flogged, students arrested, and parents imprisoned for protesting.	*Annual Register* 1901; Tilly 1975b
357	Strikes in Italy	1901–7		Workers vs. landowners	There were large and violent agricultural strikes in Sardinia (1901–6) and violent strikes in industrial areas (1906–7).		*Annual Register* 1901; Tilly 1975b
358	Attacks on dissident voters in Hungary	1901		Dissident voters vs. troops	Troops attacked dissident voters in elections that year.	About 25 casualties were reported.	Goldstein 1983: 23
359	[Uprising in Angola]	1902		Portuguese troops vs. rebels in Angola	An uprising against Portuguese rule.	The uprising was suppressed by Portuguese troops.	Banks 1978: 35
360	Atrocities in Albania	1902		Muslims vs. Bulgarians and Christians	Protesters sought to prevent Russian consul from taking office and strengthening pro-Slavism and Orthodox Greek doctrine in the country.		*Annual Register* 1902

361	Strike in Belgium	1902		Workers for proportional representation	There was a general strike in Louvain, involving some 350,000 workers, after the government defeated a measure calling for proportional representation.	Troops killed eight people. Protests continued.	Goldstein 1983: 264
362	General strike in Barcelona	Feb. 1902		Workers vs. the government	A week-long general strike of 80,000 workers.	The government responded with massive repression.	Goldstein 1983: 294
363	[War in northern Nigeria]	1903	3	Muslim rulers of Kano and Sokuto for independence vs. British for expansion	The high commissioner Frederick Lugard attempted to conquer the entire region and obtain recognition of the British protectorate by its indigenous rulers. Where diplomacy failed, Lugard's campaign systematically subdued local resistance with armed force.	The chiefs of northern Nigeria accepted British supremacy.	Richardson 1960: 98
364	Macedonian uprising	1902–3		EMRO (External Macedonian Revolutionary Organization) raids into Macedonia across the Bulgarian-Macedonian border triggered an uprising.	War was narrowly avoided between Bulgaria and Turkey, and also between Bulgaria and Romania. Turkey remained sovereign in Macedonia.	Anastasoff 1938

Case no.	Event	Date	Magnitude	Actors and reasons for fighting	Explanation	Result	Source
365	Coup in Serbia	1903		Serbian nationalists vs. Milos Obrenovic	A coup in 1903 replaced the "Austrian" party with the "nationalists," who coveted Bosnia and Herzegovina and looked to Russia for support. King Milos Obrenovic and members of his court were murdered. A member of a rival family was placed on the throne.	An expansionist, anti-Austrian course was set.	Goldstein 1983: 308–9
366	Rebellion in Albania	1903		Albanian Christians against reforms	The Mirditë rebelled and blocked the route from Scutari to Prizren.	As a protest movement directed against the Mürzsteg reform program of the powers, Vucitrn in Kosovo was occupied, and an armed attack was launched against the Ottoman garrison at Mitrovica.	Djordjevic and Fischer-Galati 1981: 170
367	Strikes in the Netherlands	1903		Workers for higher wages and against replacing strikers with nonunion workers.	Workers in transport companies in Amsterdam striking for higher wages were replaced by nonunion workers. Other unions struck in support. Trains were completely stopped in Amsterdam; two people were killed.	The government introduced a law forbidding rail strikes.	*Annual Register* 1903: 331

368	[Revolt in South-West Africa]	1903–8	5	Germans for colonization vs. Hottentots against loss of land	A revolt by the Bondelzwart natives caused the German governor to strip Damarland of troops, thereby giving the Herero natives their opportunity for a long-planned revolt. The Hereros murdered German settlers and destroyed their farms.	Hottentots and others were killed or suppressed.	Richardson 1960: 47
369	Pogroms in Russia	1903–5	3	Peasants vs. Jews for plunder	Under the banner of a "Battle for the Fatherland and Orthodoxy," a tide of pogroms swept the country. The most serious were in Belostok, Odessa, Nikolaev, and Kiev. Hundreds of Jews were murdered and thousands were left destitute.	Some 66 towns and villages were affected by anti-Semitic violence.	Urusov 1908: chapters 4, 5; Richardson 1960: 99
370	Uprising in Macedonia	Feb.–Oct. 1903	3	Internal Macedonian Revolutionary Organization (IMRO) for autonomy vs. Ottomans	The revolution was seen as the means for attracting European attention to Macedonia and its eventual annexation to Bulgaria. The IMRO insurrection led to brutal Ottoman reprisals: 9,000 homes burned and 30,000 forced to emigrate.	The Turkish brutality in crushing the rebellion brought the Macedonian issue to the fore internationally. Committees for Macedonian aid were established in London, New York, Boston, Paris, Italy, and in the Balkan countries.	Pearson 1983: 90; Crampton 1987

Case no.	Event	Date	Magnitude	Actors and reasons for fighting	Explanation	Result	Source
371	Strikes in Russia	March 1903			Strikes in Zlatoust.	Some 69 people were killed.	Crankshaw 1976: 315
372	[Russo-Japanese War]	1904–5	5	Russia vs. Japan	Rival interests in Manchuria and Korea brought war between Japan and Russia.	Japan acquired Port Arthur, the lease of the Liao-Tung Peninsula, the Russian railways in lower Manchuria, and half of Sakhalin Island.	Richardson 1960: 47
373	[Insur-rection in Cameroon]	1904		Germans vs. Cameroonian rebels	An insurrection against German rule.	The insurrection was suppressed by German troops.	Banks 1978: 35
374	Railroad strike in Croatia	1904		Railroad workers vs. employers	A railroad strike was crushed with troops and conscripted workers.		Goldstein 1983: 300
375	[British in Tibet]	1904	3	British aided by Nepalese to secure trade relations for Britain vs. Tibetans	Britain invaded Tibet in order to suppress resistance to trade relations.	The Dalai Lama fled to Mongolia. A trade agreement was concluded and the invaders withdrew.	Richardson 1960: 99
376	General strike in Milan	Sept. 1904		Workers vs. employers and municipality	A general strike in Milan culminated three years of violent strikes throughout Italy.	The strike, which pitted workers from the full range of trades against employers and the municipality, was the first of its kind anywhere.	Tilly 1989: 11
377	Rebellion in Albania	1905			A rebellion in Kroya and Argirocastro.		Frasheri 1964

378	Strikes in Russia	1905		Workers vs. employers	Nearly 3 million workers in 13,000 enterprises struck in 1905. In a railway strike in Riga, 120 were killed.		Mazour 1951
379	**Demonstration in Petersburg**	Jan. 9, 1905	3	The police vs. demonstrators for social reforms and civil liberties, including political amnesty; freedom of speech, press, and assembly; and a constituent assembly elected by secret, universal, and equal suffrage	Police fired on peaceful demonstrators in Petersburg; 130 demonstrators were killed.	The event began a wave of violence, which culminated in revolution later in the year and inspired mass suffrage demonstrations in Austria and Germany.	Goldstein 1983: 660
380	**Revolution in Russia**	1905	3	Dissidents vs. the tsar	Nicholas II's refusal to establish constitutional government, the suffering of both peasants and industrial workers, and the defeats of the Russo-Japanese War combined to trigger strikes, demonstrations, and mutinies.	After a general strike paralyzed European Russia, the tsar granted a constitution and appointed a prime minister.	Mazour 1951; Richardson 1960: 99; Blum 1977; Goldstein 1983: 282–84
381	Strike in Ruhr	Jan.– Feb. 1905		Workers for higher pay and better treatment vs. employers	Some 100,000 coal miners struck in the Ruhr. Most of the ironworks in Westphalia and Rhenish Prussia were closed.	A bill was passed reforming conditions in mines.	*Annual Register* 1905: 281

Case no.	Event	Date	Magnitude	Actors and reasons for fighting	Explanation	Result	Source
382	Rebellion in Crete	March–Nov. 1905		Cretan rebels for union with Greece vs. Ottoman Empire	Some 600 riflemen defeated troops sent against them at the outset, and rebellion spread throughout the island. The Great Powers threatened with intervention if violence continued.	Rebels attacked and killed Muslims. There were also several French, Russian, and rebel deaths.	Annual Register 1905: 332
383	[Maji-Maji Rebellion]	July 1905–Jan. 1907	5	Germans vs. Wangoni		German authority was extended.	Richardson 1960: 47
384	Insurrection in Albania	1906–7			An insurrection in Elbasan.		Swire 1929
385	Industrial unrest in Italy	1906–7		Workers vs. employers	Violent strikes in northern industrial areas.		Tilly et al. 1975: 307
386	Strikes in Italy	1906–7		Agricultural workers vs. landlords	Violent strikes took place in Italy.	Official repression by the police and military units was extensively supplemented by armed squads hired by the landlords.	Goldstein 1983: 219
387	Terrorist attacks in Russia	1906–7	4	Government vs. rebels	About 4,000 people were killed in terrorist attacks.	About 1,000 were executed after trials in special summary tribunals between	Goldstein 1983: 285

No.	Event	Date		Parties	Description	Outcome / Notes	Source
388	Strikes in Bosnia	1906		Workers vs. employers	Tobacco workers struck in Bosnia.	August 1906 and April 1907.	Djordjevic and Fischer-Galati 1981: 207
389	Strikes in Bulgaria	1906		Workers vs. employers	Railwaymen struck in Bulgaria.		Goldstein 1983: 307
390	Strikes in France	1906–7		Workers vs. troops	Many violent strikes in Nord and Pas de Calais involving miners and, in other cities, builders, excavators, railwaymen, and postmen.	Troops were called to suppress the strikes.	Annual Register 1903: 270–71; Tilly 1975b
391	Strike in Germany	1906		Workers vs. the police	Some 300,000 metalworkers were locked out. Bloodshed occurred after collision with the police in Breslau, Offenbach, Berlin, and Dresden.	The strike was defeated.	Annual Register 1906: 289
392	[Zulu Revolt]	1906	4	Britain to maintain control vs. Zulus against poll tax		The rebellion was crushed.	Richardson 1960: 66
393	Riots in Hamburg	Jan. 17, 1906		Protesters against a revision of the local suffrage law vs. the police	Riots erupted after police tried to prevent 30,000 protesters from marching in town after a revision of the local suffrage law.	The protest was brutally suppressed by the police. Two men were killed and many more were injured.	Annual Register 1906: 284; Goldstein 1983: 64

Case no.	Event	Date	Magnitude	Actors and reasons for fighting	Explanation	Result	Source
394	Massacre of Jews	June 14–16, 1906		Peasants and the police vs. Jews	Peasants and the police attacked Jews and looted a Jewish quarter in Bialystok after officials circulated rumors that Jews had killed two priests and several children in a corpus christi procession.	Several hundred Jews were killed.	*Annual Register* 1906: 321
395	**Peasant uprising in Romania**	1907	4	Peasants vs. landowners	A peasant uprising resulting from ruthless exploitation of the masses by landowning aristocracy in Moldavia, where some Jewish tenants exploited peasantry with rented land. Spreading south, the revolt lost anti-Semitic character, and was generally against landowners.	The repression by the government was savage. An army of 120,000 regulars was put in the field, and several villages in the immediate vicinity of Bucharest were razed by artillery fire. Some 10,000 peasants were killed in fighting or were executed afterward.	Mitrany 1931: 42–92; Seton-Watson 1945: 62; Eidelberg 1974: 23–64
396	[Italian operations in Somaliland]	1908		Somali tribesmen led by religious leader Muhammad ibn Abd Allah for independence vs. Italian occupiers for control	After Italy assumed direct administration of Italian Somaliland, Muhammad ibn Abd Allah, having been given portions of the country by Britain, Italy, and Ethiopia in exchange	Attacks on Italian settlers continued for the next 20 years.	Gallagher and Robinson 1981

for an end to his guerrilla war against them, reopened the war.

397	Strikes in France	1908		Workers vs. employers	At Nantes.	French troops killed 20 strikers and wounded 667.	Tilly 1975b
398	Revolt in Macedonia	July 1908			In July 1908, the Turkish army forces, which were sent to put down an uprising, tended instead to fraternize with the insurgents. The sultan, deciding that opposition was futile, yielded to the demands of the Young Turks.	The sultan restored the constitution momentarily granted in 1876, which thus became the Turkish constitution of 1908.	Djordjevic and Fischer-Galati 1981: 194–95
399	[Spanish-Moroccan War]	1909–10	4	Spain to protect investments vs. Riffs for control of their territory	Spaniards took action against raids on railwaymen and to protect mines.	Moroccans were made to pay 65 million pesetas. Spain took control of the provinces of Guelia and Quebdana.	Richardson 1960: 66
400	Uprising in Albania	1909–Nov. 1912		Albanians for independence vs. Ottoman Empire	An Albanian nationalist uprising began in Kosovo and spread throughout Albania.	An independent Albania was proclaimed in 1912.	Djordjevic and Fischer-Galati 1981: 200–201
401	Strike in Greece	1909		Workers vs. employers	A strike of workers in the harbor of Salonika led to the closing of the harbor for a time.		Djordjevic and Fischer-Galati 1981: 207

Case no.	Event	Date	Magnitude	Actors and reasons for fighting	Explanation	Result	Source
402	Armenian massacres	1909	4	Turkish troops vs. Armenians	The 1909 or Adana massacre was the second of a series of large-scale massacres of Armenians in the Ottoman Empire.	An estimated 30,000 Armenians were killed, devastating the Armenian community in Cilicia.	SIPRI 1969: table 4a.1.
403	Coup in Greece	March 1909		Military leaders and middle-class elements for a new government	Massive demonstrations by socialists, craftsmen, and students paved the way for a military coup.	A prime minister more favorable to middle classes and the army was installed.	Papacosma 1979
404	Strikes in Russia	March 1909		Workers vs. employers	Strikes occurred in Zlatoust, Russia.	Some 69 people were killed.	Crankshaw 1976: 315
405	Uprising in Barcelona	July 1909		Catalan reserves against the war in Morocco and anarchists vs. the police and government troops	The government called up reservists to replace losses in Morocco, which triggered a general strike by anarchists in Barcelona that spread to other Catalan cities. All forces opposed to the central government took to the streets.	About 30,000 protesters controlled the streets of Barcelona, raised barricades, burned and sacked about 80 Catholic churches, monasteries, and welfare institutions, and murdered several clerics. Troops and police killed 104 civilians and wounded 300.	Goldstein 1983: 295–96
406	Strike in Bulgaria	1910		Railway workers vs. employers			Bell 1977
407	Coup in Portugal	1910		Republicans vs. the monarchy and loyalist military forces	The monarchy was overturned by moderate republicans in an uprising	Little social reform was undertaken by the new regime.	Goldstein 1983: 293

408	Strike in France	1910		Railway workers vs. employers	led by military elements and with considerable popular support. One of the most violent strikes in European history. Over 1,400 incidents of sabotage were reported, including 11 attempted bombings and 82 attempted train derailments.		Goldstein 1983: 61
409	Attacks on dissident voters in Hungary	1910		Troops vs. dissident voters	Troops attacked dissident voters in elections.	About a dozen people were killed.	Goldstein 1983: 23
410	Strikes in Italy	1910–13			Violent strikes in the Po valley and northern industrial area.		Tilly et al. 1975: 307–8
411	[War in Morocco]	Oct. 1910–1911	3	French for control vs. tribes around Fez in revolt	Moulai Hafid became sultan of Morocco in 1908, deposing Abd el-Aziz, who ruled as sultan of Morocco from Fez. The new sultan with his French protectors had to put down a revolt of tribes loyal to the deposed sultan.	French control was increased.	Richardson 1960: 100
412	Strikes in Germany	9/1910		Workers vs. employers	Violent strikes took place in Berlin as unionists protested against the use of nonunion replacements.	The strikes lasted two days and caused many injuries on both sides.	*Annual Register* 1910: 308; Tilly 1975b

Case no.	Event	Date	Magnitude	Actors and reasons for fighting	Explanation	Result	Source
413	Protests in Greece	March 1910		Peasants for land reform	Unarmed peasants demanded land reform.	Five were killed and 35 wounded when troops opened fire.	Goldstein 1983: 310–11
414	Rebellion in Bosnia	Aug.–Oct. 1910			A rebellion took place in Grbavci.	It took two months for the police and troops to restore order.	Vicinich 1967
415	Strikes in Russia	1911–13		Workers vs. employers	The total number of strikes rose from 466 in 1911 to 3,534 in 1913, and the number identified by the police as "political" in motive from 24 to 2,401. Workers' demands tended to become more extreme, and radical parties were supported.	Strikes and labor violence continued into World War I and contributed to the Revolution of 1917.	Tipton and Aldrich 1987a: 122
416	Strikes in England	1911–12		Workers vs. employers	Violent strikes and riots took place in Southampton, Liverpool, Hull, and Cardiff.	Some 50,000 troops were used to quell riots and break the strikes. Some 200 were wounded. Two were killed by police.	Gilbert 1968: 97
417	[War in Libya]	1911–17	4	Italians for expansion vs. Turks in defense with Sanusi beduin	During the Turko-Italian War of 1911–12, Italy conquered north Tripoli, but by the Treaty of Ouchy, which ended the war,	Italy was forced to undertake a long series of wars of pacification against the Sanusi and their allies.	Richardson 1960: 67

	Event	Magnitude	Date	Parties	Description	Consequence	Source
418	Attacks of peasants in Austria		1911	Polish nobles against voting rights for peasants	Attacks on peasants occurred during the 1911 elections in Drohobyz, Austria.	Some 28 peasants were killed and 86 were seriously wounded.	Goldstein 1983: 23
419	Strikes in England		Aug. 5–19, 1911	Porters and railwaymen vs. the police and troops	Porters protesting slow grievance resolution by conciliation boards. Some 75,000 others joined the strike after 200 were injured and two were killed in conflict with the police.	The strike spread to railwaymen outside Liverpool.	*Annual Register* 1911: 205
420	**Italian-Turkish War**	4	Sept. 1911–Oct. 1912	Italy for the acquisition of Dodecanese and Tripolitania vs. Ottomans	Turkey granted Tripoli and north Libya autonomy. The Libyans continued to fight the Italians, but by 1914 Italy had occupied much of the country. Turkey closed Dardanelles in response to Italian bombardment and fearing Russian influence.	Turkey was defeated. Libya became autonomous, but the disposition of Dodecanese was unresolved.	Askew 1942; Levy 1983: table 4.1
421	[Uprising in Morocco]		1912	French for order vs. Makhzen troops in revolt	A mutiny of native troops took place over reduction of pay and use of knapsacks.	The revolt was suppressed.	Richardson 1960: 101
422	Strikes in Germany		1912	Workers vs. employers	Violent strikes took place in the Ruhr involving some 200,000 workers.		*Annual Register* 1912: 329; Tilly 1975b

Case no.	Event	Date	Magnitude	Actors and reasons for fighting	Explanation	Result	Source
423	Protests, strikes, and demonstrations in Russia	April 12–22, 1912		Workers vs. the state	The news of the Lena goldfields massacre triggered a massive outburst of public protest. Some 250,000 workers went on strike throughout the country, 100,000 workers in Petersburg alone.	Labor violence continued into World War I.	Haimson 1964: 626
424	Lena goldfields massacre	April 4, 1912		Workers vs. employers	A work stoppage in the Lena goldfields provoked government troops to shoot striking workers.	Some 170 people were killed, sparking a massive wave of strikes and disorders over the next two years.	Goldstein 1983: 67
425	Strikes and demonstrations in Russia	May 1, 1912		Workers vs. the state	Nearly a half million workers were involved in a May Day political strike and demonstration, the largest number of protesters since 1905.		Haimson 1964: 626
426	Demonstrations in Hungary	May 23, 1912		Protesters for the vote	Suffrage demonstrations turned violent after troops shot and killed six and wounded 200.		Goldstein 1983: 302
427	[War in south Morocco]	Oct. 1912–May 1913	3	France and sultan Moulai Youssef for order vs. El Hiba		El Hiba was defeated, but rose again in 1916.	Richardson 1960: 101

428	First Balkan War	Oct. 1912– May 1913	5	Bulgaria, Greece, Serbia, and Montenegro to oust Ottomans from Europe and to partition Albania	In October 1912, Montenegro declared a war against Turkey. The Balkan League shortly after followed with its own declaration of war against Turkey. Russia and Austria began to mobilize, but British and German diplomacy came to the rescue.	The nationalisms of the small states were satisfied at Ottoman expense, and the Straits and Constantinople remained under Turkish sovereignty as agreed in London in 1913.	Helmreich 1938; Richardson 1960: 47
429	[British operation in Somaliland]	1913–20		British for control vs. native Somalis to end British occupation	In 1887, Britain made Somalia a British protectorate, naming it British Somaliland. Initially a dependency of Aden, it was placed under the administration of the colonial office in 1905. By 1913, uprisings had forced the British to the coastal regions.	The uprisings ended in 1920 after British air attacks.	Richardson 1960: 103
430	General Strike in Belgium	April 14– May 1, 1913		Workers, socialists for manhood suffrage	The Chamber of Deputies created a commission to reform the suffrage system.	*Annual Register* 1913: 360

Case no.	Event	Date	Magnitude	Actors and reasons for fighting	Explanation	Result	Source
431	**Second Balkan War**	June–July 1913	4	Greece, Serbia, Romania, Turkey, and Bulgaria for a favorable division of the spoils from the First Balkan War	Other nations resented Bulgarian gains from the First Balkan War. However, Bulgaria took the offensive but was brought to its knees by Serbia, Romania, Greece, and Turkey.	Although an independent Bulgaria remained with a minor port of the Aegean, Bulgaria lost considerable territory and was dissatisfied and bitter.	Helmreich 1938; Richardson 1960: 66
432	Riots in Germany	Nov. 1913		Alsatians for independence vs. Germany	Anti-Prussian riots in Zabern, Alsace.	The government of Alsace resigned.	*Annual Register* 1914: 306
433	Demonstrations in Germany	1914		Socialists against the war	Massive antiwar demonstrations by socialists in many cities.	Antiwar violence continued throughout the war.	Tilly 1975b
434	Insurrection in Albania	1914		Albanians against the rule of William of Weid vs. Italy	The neutral and independent Kingdom of Albania was to be ruled by William of Weid, but when he landed to assume the Albanian throne, insurrection broke out. He was confined to Durazzo until September 1914, when he abandoned the country.	Italian troops occupied Valona in Albania.	Zavalani 1969

#	Event	Date		Issue / Parties	Description	Outcome	Source
435	General strike in Rome	1914		Workers vs. the government	A strike in Rome against tax increases intended to pay for the looming war spread to towns outside Rome, and some remained in the strikers' hands for a week or more.	The army repressed the strike movement with the assistance of groups of armed men sponsored by conservative property owners.	Tipton and Aldrich 1987a: 115
436	[War in the Middle Atlas Mountains]	1914–17	3	French and Moroccans vs. Zaians		The Zaians were partly submitted to the French.	Richardson 1960: 101
437	World War I	1914–18	7	European powers for and against the revision of the distribution of territory and resources	Austria-Hungary declared war on Serbia on July 28, 1914. Germany declared war on Russia on August 1 and on France on August 3. Britain declared war on Germany on August 4. Germany and Austria-Hungary were joined by Turkey and Bulgaria.	Prewar domestic and international tensions remained unresolved.	Richardson 1960: 33
438	Strikes in Russia	July 1914		Workers for union recognition and better pay and conditions	Some 200,000 workers went out on strike.	The revolutionary movement was temporarily checked when war was declared on Germany.	Hardach 1977: 218–19

Case no.	Event	Date	Magnitude	Actors and reasons for fighting	Explanation	Result	Source
439	Massive strikes in Russia	July 4, 1914		Workers vs. Cossacks and police detachments	Workers in Petersburg struck in protest against the brutal suppression of a strike of the Putilov workers.	According to official estimates, 110,000 workers joined the strike by July 7. Almost all factories and businesses in the working-class districts were closed. Thousands of workers clashed in pitched battles with Cossacks and police detachments.	Haimson 1964: 640–41
440	Strikes in Clyde	1915		Workers for wage claims vs. employers	Workers went on strike under the pressure of the rising cost of living.	The ad hoc strike committee composed of workers and shop stewards remained after the strike was over and constituted itself into a permanent organization known as the Clyde's Workers' Committee.	Scott 1924; Pribicevic 1959; McLean 1975
441	Armenian Massacres	April 1915	6	Turks vs. Armenians	The Turkish massacre of Armenians began with the deportation and murder first of men, then of women and children. The slaughter "was a deliberate, systematic attempt to eradicate the Armenian	One million Armenians were killed.	Bryce 1972; Arlen 1975; Pearson 1983: 140

population throughout the Ottoman Empire."

#	Name	Date		Issue	Outcome	Source
442	Strike in South Wales	July 1915		Miners vs. employers and the government	In a wage dispute in Cardiff, 10,000 miners went on strike	The government gave way and agreed to most of the strikers' demands.	Hardach 1977: 188
443	[War in Russian Turkestan]	1916	4	Turkmen against encroachments and military service vs. Russia for colonization	Turkmen resented losing their grazing land and in 1916 joined a Muslim uprising throughout Russia's Central Asian territory.	The insurgents massacred the Russians and then fled to Chinese territory.	Richardson 1960: 67
444	[War in Morocco]	1916–17	3	French to maintain control vs. El Hiba	Recurrence of the 1912–13 conflict.	El Hiba was defeated.	Richardson 1960: 101
445	Rebellion in Ireland	April 24–May 1, 1916	3	Sinn Feiners for Irish independence vs. the British government	Armed men occupied Stephen's Green, the post office, City Hall, and Law Courts. The Sinn Feiners called on the Irish people to support the provisional government. The British government rushed reinforcements to Dublin and proclaimed martial law.	The British suppressed the rebellion at the cost of 600 British troops, but Sinn Fein remained active, declaring the republic of Ireland and a constitution and electing a president, who was arrested by the British.	Chambers 1972: 264
446	Wars of the Russian Nationalities	1917–22	5	Finns, Ukrainians, Latvians, Estonians, Lithuanians, Poles, and others in Asia for independence vs. the Bolshevik government		Nationalities had varying degrees of success: revolts in Ukraine, Georgia, and Asian Russia were crushed, but Poles, Finns, Latvians, Estonians, and Lithuanians gained independence.	Hrushevsky 1941; Carr 1950–53; Singer and Small 1972: 75

Case no.	Event	Date	Magnitude	Actors and reasons for fighting	Explanation	Result	Source
447	Riots in Germany	1917			Bread riots took place in Bavaria, Silesia, Stettin, and Düsseldorf.		Tilly 1975b
448	Coup in Portugal	1917			A pro-German officer led the coup and named himself president-dictator.	The coup leader was assassinated a year later, but the military remained dominant through 1926.	Nowell 1952: 228–29
449	Massive strikes in Germany	Jan. 1917		Workers against terms that the German High Command was demanding of Russia	In Germany, news of the terms that the German High Command was demanding of Russia produced massive strikes involving a million workers.	Violence continued throughout the war.	Marwick 1974: 40–41
450	Strike of munition workers in Germany	Feb. 1917		Workers for franchise reform, better food, and abolition of the state of siege	Strikers' initial demand was for peace with Russia and an end to the German government's delaying tactics in negotiating the peace at Brest Litovsk (Dec. 20, 1917–March 3, 1918).		Ryder 1963: 207
451	Strikes in Germany	April–June 1917		Workers vs. employers and the government	Under the influence of the Russian Revolution, at least 300,000 workers in Berlin and Leipzig participated in demonstrations and strikes. In Leipzig, the strike was led by a workers' council that		Ryder 1963: 207; Chambers 1972: 498; Marwick 1974: 31

452	General strike and insurrection in Italy	Aug. 1917		Workers vs. employers	In Turin, "Fatti de Agosta" strikes and insurrection over high bread prices and bread shortages occurred, involving some 50,000 workers in five days of street fighting... presented political as well as economic demands.	Hundreds of casualties were the result.	Tilly 1975b
453	**Russian Revolution**	Nov. 1917–1918	3	Workers and Bolsheviks against the war for social justice	The Russian government was blamed by the public for the failure of the Carpathian campaign of 1915. In the summer of 1917, Bolsheviks were the only party to take up the demands of the workers, peasants, and soldiers and to uphold them with any consistency.	The uprising led to the tsar's abdication and a provisional republican government, but it ignored the concerns of the masses, which the Bolsheviks took up. Civil war raged through 1918 between the "Reds" and the "Whites" and was complicated, for example, by Allied intervention.	Miliukov 1922; Carr 1950–53; Richardson 1960: 102
454	Civil war in Russia	Dec. 1917–20		Counterrevolutionary armies ("Whites"), with British, French, Czech, Japanese, and American troops vs. the Bolsheviks and their Red Army	Various counterrevolutionary movements were supported by troops sent by European governments. The fighting was complicated by national groups who with varying degrees of success sought autonomy or independence.	The "Whites" and their allies were defeated. The Red Armies were able to retain most of the territories the Empire had held in 1914. However, they did not win back Finland, the Baltic states, or Poland.	Carr 1950–53

Case no.	Event	Date	Magnitude	Actors and reasons for fighting	Explanation	Result	Source
455	Allied intervention in Bolshevik Revolution	1918–20	5	Russian nobles and bourgeois with Czechoslovakia, Britain, France, Japan, Italy, and the United States against property seizures and to overthrow Bolsheviks with Ukraine for independence	A coordinated effort to oust the Bolsheviks took a military form. The Allies, especially France, continued their support of the White armies. However, one by one these were defeated until the Bolshevik regime was in control of the entire country.	The Bolsheviks consolidated their control and the USSR was created.	Coates 1935; Richardson 1960: 41; Brinkley 1966
456	Riots in England	1918		Soldiers in solidarity with Russian workers	Soldiers rioted at Kinmel Park, raised the Red Flag, burned down the "Tin Town" at Witley, and stormed the Epsom Police Station.	Five people were killed and 21 wounded.	Cole and Postgate 1966: 534
457	Russo-Polish War	1918–20	4	Poles for expansion with French officers against communism vs. Bolsheviks in defense	Poles drove Bolsheviks out of Lithuania and proposed a union of the two countries. Lithuanians refused and fighting erupted. At the same time, the war between Poland and Russia continued.	The Red Armies were driven out of Poland, who gained land including 4 million Russians.	Mazour 1951; Richardson 1960: 68
458	Strike in Germany	Jan. 24, 1918		Workers for alleviation of food restrictions, an amnesty for political	Some 250,000 workers came out in Berlin, and proportionate numbers in	General stoppage of munitions industry.	Chambers 1972: 499

No.	Event	Date					
				offenders, the restoration of the right of assembly, peace on the basis of "no annexations and no indemnities," and the participation of workers' delegates at the peace negotiations	Bremen, Hamburg, Essen, Leipzig, and elsewhere.		
459	Civil war in Finland	Jan.–April 1918	4	"Reds" and Russians for Marxism vs. "Whites" for private property with Germans allied by Treaty of Brest-Litovsk	A communist revolt started in Helsinki and spread and was aided by Russian Bolsheviks. The Germans aided the bourgeoisie in fighting revolt.	The "Whites" won and Finland remained independent.	Serge 1972: 186–89
460	Uprising in Bulgaria	Sept. 1918		Peasants	An uprising led by the left-wing socialists, who in 1919 formed the Bulgarian Communist Party and the Agrarian Union.	The head of the Agrarian Union, Aleksandr Stamboliski, assumed power and became the head of a legally elected government in October 1919.	Djordjevic and Fischer-Galati 1981: 218
461	Kiel revolt	Oct. 28, 1918		Sailors, factory workers, and soldiers for abdication of the Hohenzollerns, abolition of the state of siege, equal suffrage for men and women, and the liberation of political prisoners	Sailors at Wilhelmshaven on the North Sea began demonstrations and strikes when they refused to obey orders for a final battle with Britain. In street demonstrations, sailors made revolutionary speeches and rioted.		Ryder 1963: 211

Case no.	Event	Date	Magnitude	Actors and reasons for fighting	Explanation	Result	Source
462	Revolution in Bavaria	Nov. 6, 1918		Bavarians vs. Allies	A demonstration in Munich on November 6 was followed by a march in which the public buildings were occupied. Bavaria was declared a republic.	A government of majority socialists and independent socialists was formed under Kurt Eisner and independent socialists.	Ryder 1963: 212
463	Revolution in Germany	Nov. 1918			Revolution started in Kiel and spread throughout Germany. A socialist revolution took place in Munich. A provisional government suppressed a right-wing putsch attempt in Berlin.		Tilly 1975b
464	Sailors' revolt in Germany	Dec. 21, 1918		Sailors vs. the government	Sailors refused to obey a government order to evacuate the royal palace in which they were quarrered. They marched to the Chancellery and arrested Friedrich Ebert, chairman of the Social Democratic Party, and his colleagues.	The army appeared in force and shelled the palace. About 30 people were killed.	Ryder 1963: 221

465	**Rebellion in Ireland**	1919–22	Irish for independence vs. British	Sinn Fein declared independence anew. The British tried to suppress the movement but compromised by setting up Parliaments for Protestant counties and allowing Irish deputies into Westminster. Civil war began after Sinn Fein boycotted British legislation.	In December 1922, the Irish Free State was officially declared. Ulster, however, remained part of the United Kingdom, a status that continued to be the main point of contention and source of frequent violence between Britain and the Sinn Fein.	Richardson 1960: 104; Gilbert 1968
466	Uprising in Portugal	Jan. 1919	Royalists vs. the government and the regular army	Royalist forces under Paiva Couceiro seized Oporto, Braga, Viseu, Coimbra, and Aveiro in northern Portugal. Officers of the regular army deserted to join the royalists. In Lisbon, a portion of the garrison raised the monarchist flag.	About 14,000 people were arrested, dozens of murders and executions were carried out, and over 5,000 rebels fled the country.	Nowell 1952: 228
467	General strike in Switzerland	1919	Workers vs. employers			Bonjour et al. 1952

Case no.	Event	Date	Magnitude	Actors and reasons for fighting	Explanation	Result	Source
468	Uprising in East Galicia	1919	3	Poles led by Pilsudski for expansion vs. Ukrainians to retain territory	In Oct.–Nov. 1918, Ukrainian units of the rapidly disintegrating Austrian army occupied the city of Lwow in Galicia, proclaiming it a part of a Socialist Ukrainian Republic. Polish army units invaded and pushed back the Ukrainians beyond the Zbrucz River.	The Poles kept East Galicia.	Richardson 1960: 103
469	Strikes in Bulgaria	1919		Workers vs. employers	The first major test for the Stamboliski government was a transport strike that lasted from December 1919 until February 1920. The strike was organized by the communists and the social democrats and involved urban workers and middle-class Bulgarians.	The strike was harshly suppressed by the army and the Orange Guard, a quasimilitary force that Stamboliski formed to counter mass demonstrations by parties of the left.	Djordjevic and Fischer-Galati 1981: 207
470	Strikes and demonstrations in France	1919–20		Workers vs. employers	An attempted general strike and workers' demonstrations led to fights with troops, the police, and other workers.		Tilly 1975b

471	General strike in Romania	1919–20	Workers, miners, and oil workers vs. employers	A general strike of workers and miners in Jiu Valley soon engulfed the oil workers of the Prahova Valley. By 1920, almost 40,000 workers were participating in mass demonstrations.	Weber 1965b
472	[Afghanistan]	1919	3	British and Nepalese state troops expelled Emir Amanullah's Afghani supporters from India.	Richardson 1960: 103
473	Strikes in Britain	Jan. 2, 1919	Workers for a shorter work week vs. employers	The Clyde and Belfast engineers struck defying their unions for a forty- and forty-four-hour week, respectively. Pitched battles with the police occurred in Glasgow. The secretary of commerce called the situation a "Bolshevist rising."	McLean 1975: 231
474	Sparticist rising in Berlin	Jan. 1919	Communists and other leftists vs. the government	The "Spartacus revolt" occurred in Berlin. In addition, there were communist revolts in many German cities, and a general strike and street fighting against military putsch both in Berlin and in the Ruhr. The Sparticist leaders, Karl Leibknecht and Rosa Luxemburg, were arrested and then murdered while on their way to prison at Moabit.	Ryder 1963: 224; Tilly 1975b

Case no.	Event	Date	Magnitude	Actors and reasons for fighting	Explanation	Result	Source
475	General strikes in Germany	Feb. 1919	3		General strikes broke out in many districts, including Berlin, where street fighting followed.	Some 1,200 people lost their lives.	Ryder 1963: 225
476	Revolution in Bavaria	March–April 1919		Radical socialists vs. federal troops	Following the assassination of the government head in Bavaria, leftist socialists gained control and proclaimed a soviet republic. Federal troops intervened, defeated the Bavarian radical government, and installed their own supporters in power.	The incident left many tensions in Bavaria, traditionally a conservative, Catholic area of Germany. Again in 1923, Munich would be the site of an attempted coup, this one a right-wing attempt to take power led by General Ludendorff and Adolf Hitler.	Benns 1930
477	Violent strikes in Italy	April 1919– Sept. 1920	3	Workers and peasants vs. employers and landlords	Economic distress, the deterioration of the peasants' condition, and restrictions on possibilities for emigration combined to produce huge strikes in the cities and massive rebellions in the countryside. These were violently repressed.	More than 320 workers were killed by police in the course of violent strikes.	Parker 1969: 141

478	[Rebellion in Amristar, India]	April 1919	3	British vs. Sikhs	A small British force in the Indian city of Amritsar, the holy city of the Sikhs, opened fire on a group of people, who had assembled in a public park for a political meeting.	Some 379 people were killed.	Fromkin 1989: 422
479	Hungaro-Romanian War	April–Nov. 1919	3	Romanians to suppress communism in Hungary and for territory vs. Hungarian communists	Bela Kun, a socialist, came to power and initiated communist reforms. Romanians invaded and occupied much of eastern Hungary, including Budapest. Kun quarreled with trade unions; strikes broke out and peasant uprisings began in the countryside.	Kun resigned and left Hungary, bringing to an end the Hungarian Soviet Republic. A conservative government took power. After the Supreme Council's ultimatum from Paris, the Romanian army evacuated Hungary. Romania acquired territory and towns.	Richardson 1960: 104; Seton-Watson 1962; Jászi 1969
480	Greco-Turkish War	May 1919–Oct. 1922	4	Greeks for expansion around Smyrna and Armenians for independence vs. Turks against dismemberment of Turkey	Greeks saw their position in Asia Minor threatened by the newly renascent Turks under Kemal Atatürk. A Greek offensive in 1921 aimed ultimately – at least in the eyes of extreme nationalists – at the reconquest of Constantinople, the old Byzantine capital.	A Turkish counteroffensive led to the total defeat of the Greeks in 1922. The Kemalist Turks drove out or massacred the civil populations of Armenians and Greeks. The Lausanne Treaty in 1923 gave Turkey better conditions than the Sèvres Treaty.	Richardson 1960: 49; Shaw and Shaw 1977: 348

Case no.	Event	Date	Magnitude	Actors and reasons for fighting	Explanation	Result	Source
481	War over Vilna	1920	3	Poles for expansion vs. Lithuanians	Polish and Lithuanian troops clashed in Vilna. The League of Nations intervened and in October an armistice was signed, but the Poles occupied Vilna. The league made preparations to send an international force but failed to do so.	The Polish government held a general election in the Vilna district for a Constituent Assembly, which voted that Vilna should form part of the Polish Republic. In March 1923, the Conference of Ambassadors accepted the fait accompli.	Benns 1930: 603–4, 607; Richardson 1960: 104
482	Strikes in Yu-goslavia	1920		Mine and railway workers vs. employers	A strike of some 30,000 miners and railwaymen led to clashes with the police and military forces in Slovenia, Croatia, and Bosnia.		Dedijer et al. 1974: 522
483	Strikes in Italy	1920		Workers vs. employers and landlords	A strike movement spread through the Italian countryside. In Turin, some 450,000 strikers were involved, mainly metalworkers. Landlords recruited squads of men to repress the strikes.	The event contributed to growing tensions between the left and the right.	Bordogna et al. 1989: 228

No.	Name	Date		Parties	Outcome	Reference
484	Strike of railway-men in Bulgaria	1920		Railway workers vs. employers	Facilitated the assumption of power by Stamboliski.	Bell 1977
485	[War in northern Morocco]	1920–27	4	Spain, France, and Moors for control vs. Riffs for an independent state	Morocco was partitioned between France and Spain.	Richardson 1960: 69
486	[War in Syria]	1920	4	France for control of its mandate vs. Arabs for independence	Syria became a French mandate.	Richardson 1960: 68
487	Revolt in Albania	1920		Albanians against Italian occupation and Yugoslavs in defense of Albanian Christians	A revolt of the Mirditë (Catholic Mirdita) was organized by the Committee of National Defense in the district of Vlora in 1920 against Italian occupiers of several Albanian districts. The Yugoslav army backed the revolt.	Swire 1929; Frasheri 1964; Zavalani 1969
488	[War in Libya]	1920–32	5	Italians for expansion vs. Sanusi beduins in defense	Italy governed Libya until driven out in World War II.	Richardson 1960: 50

Case no.	Event	Date	Magnitude	Actors and reasons for fighting	Explanation	Result	Source
489	Rebellion in Germany	March 1920		General von Lüttwitz, with irregular military *Freikorps* recently disbanded after fighting in the Baltic provinces, against the "Bolshevism" of the Weimar Republic vs. the German government	The "Kapp Putsch" was engineered by right-wing nationalists opposed to the Weimar Republic. Von Lüttwitz seized Berlin on March 13 and proclaimed a new nationalistic government with the right-wing journalist Wolfgang Kapp as chancellor.	The legitimate government fled Berlin and called a general strike. The putsch failed, in general, to gain the active support of the officer corps and was opposed by security police and workers, resulting in a failed coup.	Palmer 1983: 213
490	[War in Iraq]	June 1920– Feb. 1921	3	British for control of its new mandate vs. Shi'i Moslem Arabs for independent Iraq	The British suffered 2,000 casualties, including 450 dead.	A British mandate was established with a Sunni Muslim Arab king.	Richardson 1960: 104; Kleiman 1970: 57; Busch 1971: 408–9
491	Nation-wide demon-strations in Britain	Aug. 1920		Workers against war with Russia vs. the government	The British Foreign Secretary sent a note to the Soviet government threatening war if the advance of the Red Army was not halted. The Labour Party urged workers to protest against the war with		Zilliacus 1946: 281

492	[Moplah Rebellion, southwest India]	1921–22	Hindus and British for suppression of violence vs. Muslim Moplahs	Russia, resulting in nationwide demonstrations. Muslims reacted violently when they learned of the defeat of their caliph, the sultan of Turkey.	The rebellion was suppressed by British troops allied with Hindus.	Richardson 1960: 68
493	Strikes and revolts in Germany	1921	Workers and communists	Strikes and revolts occurred in Saxony, Hamburg, and the Ruhr.		Tilly 1975b
494	Fascist attacks in Italy	Jan.–May 1921	Fascists vs. communists	Fascist attacks involving burning, beating, and murdering 207 and wounding 819 in a "one-sided civil war." Fascists were able to use trucks belonging to the army or the carabinieri. Arms were widely provided for fascists by police and military.	Violence continued.	Parker 1969: 148
495	Kronstadt massacre in Russia	March 1921	Workers and sailors vs. employers	Petrograd workers struck and sailors at the Kronstadt naval base issued a list of demands in solidarity with the Petrograd strikers.	Under government orders, the military repressed the strike and moved against the Kronstadt sailors, killing hundreds and wounding thousands.	Wexler 1989: 48

Case no.	Event	Date	Magnitude	Actors and reasons for fighting	Explanation	Result	Source
496	Coup in Italy	1922		Fascists vs. city governments and the state of Italy	A wave of fascist attacks and violence throughout central and northern Italy. Fascists threatened to direct their civil war against the state, with a fascist "march on Rome," unless the state was handed over to them.	The government surrendered and King Victor Emmanuel III summoned Mussolini to become president of the council of ministers.	Parker 1969: 148–53; Tilly et al. 1975: 176–87
497	Riots in Germany	1922			Nazi disturbances occurred in Bavaria, riots and demonstrations all over Germany.		Tilly 1975b
498	Riots in Germany	1923		Rhinelanders and left vs. right	There were separatist riots in the Rhineland, the Nazi "Beer Hall Putsch" in Munich, and communist putsch attempts in Hamburg and Saxony.		Tilly 1975b
499	**Coup and repression in Bulgaria**	June 1923	4	Macedonians, the army, and conservatives against land reforms vs. the left	Republic headed by the peasant leader Stamboliski won elections in 1923, dissolved the large estates, and reorganized the legal and taxation systems. Macedonians, the army, and	Between 10,000 and 30,000 supporters of the progressive regime were executed. Government reverted to the conservatives and eventually to those further on the right.	Oren 1971; Bell 1977; Bulgaria Academy of Science 1985: 219

No.	Name	Date	Mag.	Parties	Description	Outcome	Source
					the bourgeois staged a coup, which was followed by repression of the left.		
500	Occupation of Corfu	Aug. 1923		Italy vs. Greece	Italian warships bombarded Corfu.	Mussolini ordered the occupation of the town.	Albrecht-Carrié 1973
501	Coup in Spain	Sept. 1923		Military	Led by General Miguel Primo de Rivera.	Primo de Rivera became the new ruler.	Payne 1967
502	Violence on Greco-Bulgarian frontier	Oct. 1923		Bulgaria vs. Greece	After firing occurred on the Greco-Bulgarian frontier, regular troops became engaged. Bulgarians and Greeks occupied each other's territory. The Greek General Staff sent out the Third Army.	Greek troops withdrew from Bulgarian territory. Bulgaria evacuated the Greek posts, which it had seized.	Albrecht-Carrié 1973
503	Revolution in Albania	June 1924		A coalition headed by Fran Noli vs. Ahmet Zog	A political revolution in June 1924 was directed against Ahmet Zog and his ruling "Zogist clique" by Fran Noli, with the cooperation of regional military commanders.	Zog proclaimed a republic the following year and served as its president until, in 1928, he was proclaimed King Zog I.	Frasheri 1964
504	[War in Syria]	July 1925–July 1926	4	French for its mandate vs. Druses and Arabs		The French mandate was upheld.	Richardson 1960: 105
505	Uprising in Portugal	1926		Military vs. the government	A military-led uprising took over the government.		Nowell 1952: 332

Case no.	Event	Date	Magnitude	Actors and reasons for fighting	Explanation	Result	Source
506	General strike in Britain	April 1926–May 1926		Miners protesting the cutting of wages and increasing hours and other workers in solidarity vs. employers	Mine owners demanded a cut in wages (13 percent) along with an increase in hours. After refusing, about one million miners were locked out by the mine owners. The next morning 3.5 million workers refused to work, demonstrating solidarity with the miners.	Britain came to a virtual standstill. The miners were forced to return to work in November at substantially lower wages.	Tipton and Aldrich 1987a: 239–40
507	Coup in Poland	1926		Military	Josef Pilsudski, a former socialist turned conservative nationalist, left office in 1922, partly from dissatisfaction with a new constitution that limited the president's powers, but returned in 1926 in a military coup.	The Polish Parliament was dissolved and opposition outlawed.	Seton-Watson 1962
508	Riot in Vienna	July 15, 1927		Workers vs. the government	An enormous outburst from workers occurred after the acquittal of men charged with shooting to death some workers in Burgenland. From all districts of the city, workers marched in protest	The police were ordered to shoot, and 90 people died.	Canetti 1982: 244–45

509	IMRO conflict in Bulgaria	1928–34	3	to the Palace of Justice and set fire to it. Internal Macedonian Revolutionary Organization (IMRO) warfare.	Barker 1950: 43–63
510	[War in Morocco]	1929–33	3	France for control vs. tribes for independence	French control was extended.	Richardson 1960: 107 Tilly 1975b
511	Riots in Germany	1929			May Day riots occurred in Berlin.	
512	Massacre of the Kulaks, USSR	1930–34	7	Soviet government vs. Kulaks	Opposition and resistance to collectivization by the Kulaks, former peasants who became proprietors of medium-sized farms after the reforms of 1906, led Stalin to decree the "liquidation of the Kulaks as a class." Rebellious villages were machine-gunned, and survivors were sent to unpopulated regions of Siberia. It is estimated that 10 to 15 million people perished.	Dallin and Breslauer 1970: 63; Conquest 1973, 1986; Palmer 1983: 226
513	Strikes in Germany	1930			Violent strikes occurred in the Mansfield mining area.	Tilly 1975b
514	[War in Indochina]	1930–31	3	France for control vs. nationalists and communists against exploitation	A mutiny of native troops at a French garrison in North Vietnam was brutally crushed by the French. The leader of the Vietnamese Nationalist Party (VNQDD) and 12 cohorts were arrested and beheaded. The VNQDD was virtually destroyed. Many from VNQDD joined the Indochina Communist Party, which fomented serious peasant uprisings. French forces reestablished control. Hundreds of Vietnamese were slain and thousands imprisoned. Disturbances continued against French rule.	Richardson 1960: 106

Case no.	Event	Date	Magnitude	Actors and reasons for fighting	Explanation	Result	Source
515	Violent strikes in Spain	1931		Anarchist militants vs. government troops	In July and August, anarchist militants (in the Confederación Nacional del Trabajo) set off a series of violent strikes, including a general strike in Barcelona and Seville, where government troops used artillery against the militants, killing 30 people.		Parker 1969: 198
516	Conflict in Germany	1931–33			Violence, street fighting, political demonstrations, and strikes occurred throughout Germany, especially in Berlin.		Tilly 1975b
517	Uprising in Romania	1933		Miners, oil, and railway workers vs. employers	Strikes of miners, oil workers, and railway workers culminated in the so-called Gravita uprising of 1933.	The uprising was suppressed.	Djordjevic and Fischer-Galati 1981: 208
518	Coup attempt in Austria	1934		Nazis vs. the government		Coup failed.	Macdonald 1946

						Tilly 1975b
519	Demonstrations in France	1934–35		Right vs. left	Large demonstrations of both left and right led to frequent clashes among demonstrators, counterdemonstrators, and forces of order. Attempted general strikes and violent meetings of peasant organizations also occurred.	
520	Asturian revolt and strikes in Spain	Jan. 1933–Oct. 1934	3	Anarchists, Communist syndicates, and other left-wing factions, miners, and ironworkers vs. government troops	In Jan. 1933, leftists learned that the Lerroux government would include ministers considered to be fascists, resulting in revolt and strikes throughout Spain. In June 1934, mining areas in Asturias were governed by workers' committees and a Red Army was set up. General Franco launched a full-scale campaign. Some 1,000 to 5,000 workers lost their lives in the fighting, and in the campaign of suppression following the fighting, 40,000 people were imprisoned. In Oct. 1934, Catalonia declared itself independent.	Benns 1930: 538–39; Parker 1969: 198–99, 200–201
521	Civil War in Austria	Feb. 1934	3	Left vs. clerics; right against land reform	The preservation of Austria required, internally, the cooperation of her clerical and democratic forces, but the tension between the left in Vienna and clerics dominating the countryside led to civil war. Socialists were defeated and suppressed. The government was reorganized along Italian lines.	Deutsch 1934; Macdonald 1946; Richardson 1960: 107

Case no.	Event	Date	Magnitude	Actors and reasons for fighting	Explanation	Result	Source
522	Riots in France	Feb. 1934		Rightists	When the rightist head of police was dismissed, rightists erupted in massive riots against the socialist-supported government.	Some 17 people were killed and 600 wounded. The riots were a sign of revival of the radical right.	Werth n.d.: 146–48, 150–52, 159
523	Conflict in Germany	June–July 1934	3	Hitler's Nazi supporters vs. Hitler's Nazi rivals for more socialism	The threat of a "second" socialist "revolution" was ended with the murder without trial of the chief-of-staff of the S.A., Eric Röhm, and the S.A. leadership devoted to him.	A month later, after Hitler assumed the office of the president, the armed forces were sworn in to him personally.	Richardson 1960: 107; Carsten 1967
524	[War in Ethiopia]	1935–37	4	Italians for expansion vs. Abyssinians in defense	Having penetrated Ethiopian territory, an Italian expeditionary force clashed with an Ethiopian force, suffering casualties. In quest of an East African Italian empire and ignoring the League of Nations, Mussolini used this as an excuse to invade Ethiopia.	Sanctions imposed by the League of Nations failed to deter the Italian invasion and defeat the annexation of Ethiopia by Italy	Richardson 1960: 71

525	**Purges in the USSR**	1936–39	6	Stalin to consolidate his control vs. those he considered possible rivals to his leadership and dissidents	Stalin purged opposition leaders and political enemies.	The purge shifted the socioeconomic character of the Communist Party and the Soviet leadership.	Hough and Fainsod 1953; Conquest 1973: 73
526	Strikes in France	1936–37		Left vs. right	When Blum gained office in 1936, massive sit-down strikes occurred, which were led by workers hoping for immediate benefits. French capitalists sent their capital abroad to safe havens.	Blum was warned by the financial community that they would aid the government only if he dropped his social legislation and cut government expenditures.	Tilly 1975b; Weiss 1977
527	Coup in Greece	1936		Royalists vs. republicans	Conflict between republicans and royalists brought General Ioannis Metaxas to power in a coup.	Metaxas imposed martial law and established a fascist-type dictatorship.	Woodhouse 1952
528	Riots in Spain	Feb. 1936		Peasants vs. landowners	With the victory of the Popular Front, the peasants joined together in land riots, attacking the houses of landowners and destroying their cattle and crops.	Tensions continued.	Carr 1966

Case no.	Event	Date	Magnitude	Actors and reasons for fighting	Explanation	Result	Source
529	Spanish Civil War	July 1936– April 1939	6	Republicans for parliamentary government and local autonomy with Russians for communism and volunteers from France, Britain, and the United States vs. Falangists and Irish volunteers for Church and landlords with Italians and Germans for fascism	The war began with a revolt of military commanders in Spanish Morocco disgruntled with the growing socialist and anticlerical tendencies of the Popular Front republican government of President Azana. Contending European ideologies and interests battled.	The republicans were defeated, and Franco organized an authoritarian government.	Richardson 1960: 42; Payne 1967; Kennedy 1987: 326
530	Revolt in Crete	1938			Suppressed inflation led to shortages and revolt.	The regime survived until the German invasion in 1941.	Albrecht-Carrié 1973
531	Italian occupation of Albania	Nov. 7, 1938		Italy vs. Albania	Mussolini, who had been given no prior warning of the German coup in Prague in 1938, endeavored to compensate for it by acting in similar fashion in Albania. Italian troops landed in Albania.	King Zog took flight, and Mussolini became the crown head of Albania.	Albrecht-Carrié 1973
532	General strike in France	Nov. 20, 1938		Workers vs. employers	Tens of thousands of workers all over France occupied factories or	Hundreds of labor leaders were arrested. Thousands of workers lost their jobs.	Schuman 1942: 464

					walked out of them on strike. A general strike ordered for November 30 was broken in many industries by mobilizing workers into the army.	Daladier spoke of having saved France from Bolshevism.	
533	**World War II**	1939–45	7	Germany vs. Poland, Denmark, Norway, Netherlands, Belgium, Britain, France, Yugoslavia, Greece, the United States; Germany, Finland, Italy, Hungary, and Romania vs. USSR; Italy vs. Tunisia, Ethiopia, Egypt, Britain, the United States; Japan vs. the United States, Mexico, Britain, and other countries	German invasion of Poland pushed Britain and France to declare war. Germany occupied Poland, Denmark, Norway, Belgium, Holland, and France; bombed Britain; and invaded Yugoslavia, Greece, and Russia. By the end of 1941, some 45 states were involved. Civil war in Yugoslavia and Greece.	See Chapter 8.	Bond 1983: 97; Palmer 1983: 310–11
534	**Russo-Finnish War**	Nov. 1939–March 1940	5	Soviet Union for territory and strategic bases fearing German influence vs. Finland in defense	French, British, and Swedish volunteers fought on the Finnish side. Russia gained territory around Leningrad and further protection for the Leningrad to Murmansk railway.	Soviets gained some territory and were expelled from the League of Nations.	Coates 1941; Richardson 1960: 50

Case no.	Event	Date	Magnitude	Actors and reasons for fighting	Explanation	Result	Source
535	Massacres in Yugoslavia	1943	6	Ustasha movement against all non-Croats	In the 1940s, the fascist Ustasha movement declared a "holy war" of "purification" on all non-Croats. The Ustashi systematically liquidated Serbs and gypsies.	Some 1,800,000 were killed.	Pearson 1983: 196
536	Greek civil war	1944–45	5	Communists and left vs. right	Leftist and rightist resistance groups turned on each. The ensuing civil war caused perhaps more destruction than the invasion and occupation. U.S. military and economic aid ensured an anticommunist victory and a basis for economic recovery.	The defeat of the communists in the civil war left Greece in the Western camp, but the war also left Greece with fratricidal recriminations. Large numbers of Greeks emigrated, and opponents of the victorious regime were imprisoned.	Richardson 1960: 50; O'Ballance 1966
537	[Algeria/ France]	1945	3	The French to reestablish control in the face of Muslim nationalist agitation	Social unrest in the winter of 1944–45 fueled partly by a poor harvest, shortages of manufactured goods, and severe unemployment culminated on May Day 1945 with demonstrations in 21 towns across the country and marchers demanding independence.	French control was reestablished.	Richardson 1960: 108

Works Cited

Abel, W. 1980. *Agricultural Fluctuations in Europe from the Thirteenth to the Twentieth Centuries.* London: Methuen.

Abraham, D. 1981. *The Collapse of the Weimar Republic: Political-Economy and Crisis.* Princeton, N.J.: Princeton University Press.

Abrams, I. 1944–45. The Austrian Question at the Turn of the Twentieth Century. *Journal of Central European Affairs* 4: 186–201.

Abrams, P. 1963. The Failure of Social Reform: 1918–1920. *Past and Present* 24: 43–64.

Abu-Lughod, J. L. 1987–88. The Shape of the World System in the Thirteenth Century. *Studies in Comparative International Development* 22: 3–25.

Abu-Lughod, J. L. 1989. *Before European Hegemony: The World System A.D. 1250–1350.* New York: Oxford University Press.

Adelman, M. A. 1966. Monopoly and Concentration: Comparisons in Time and Space. In A. Gabiotti, ed. *Essays in Honor of Marco Fanno*, vol. 2: *Investigations in Economic Theory and Methodology.* Padova: Edzioni Cedam.

Adler, J. 1989. *The Jews of Paris and the Final Solution: Communal Response and Internal Conflicts, 1940–1944.* New York: Columbia University Press.

Aglietta, M. 1979. *A Theory of Capitalist Regulation: The U.S. Experience.* London: New Left Books.

Aguet, J.-P. 1954. *Les Grèves sous la monarchie de juillet, 1830–1847: contribution À l'étude du mouvement ouvrier français.* Geneva: E. Droz.

Ahumada, J. 1963. Economic Development and Problems of Social Change in Latin America. Pp. 115–47. In Egbert De Vries and José Medina Echavarria, eds., *Social Aspects of Economic Development in Latin America*, vol. 1. Paris: UNESCO.

Akzin, B. 1964. *State and Nation.* London: Hutchinson.

Alapuro, R. 1979. Internal colonialism and the regional party system in Eastern Finland. *Racial and Ethnic Studies* 2, no. 3 (July): 341–59.

Alavi, H. 1982. The Structure of Peripheral Capitalism. In H. Alavi and T. Shanin, eds., *Introduction to the Sociology of Developing Societies.* New York: Monthly Review Press.

Albo, G. 1994. "Competitive Austerity" and the Impasse of Capitalist Employment Policy. In R. Miliband and L. Panitch, eds., *Between Globalism and Nationalism, Socialist Register 1994*. London: Merlin Press.

Albrecht-Carrié, R. 1973. *A Diplomatic History of Europe since the Congress of Vienna*. Revised ed. New York: Harper and Row.

Alcock, A. E. 1970. *The History of the South Tyrol Question*. London: Michael Joseph.

Aldcroft, D. H. 1978. *The European Economy, 1914–1970*. London: Croom Helm.

Allen, W. E. D., and P. Muratoff. 1953. *Caucasian Battlefields*. Cambridge: Cambridge University Press.

Allison, J. M. S. 1926. *Thiers and the French Monarchy*. Boston: Houghton Mifflin.

Althusser, L., and E. Balibar. 1971. *Reading Capital*. London: New Left Books.

Amery, L. S. 1953. *My Political Life*, vol. 3: *The Unforgiving Years, 1929–1940*. London: Hutchinson.

Amin, S. 1974. *Accumulation on a World Scale*. New York: Monthly Review Press.

Amin, S. 1976. *Unequal Development: An Essay on the Social Formation of Peripheral Capitalism*, trans. B. Pearce. New York: Monthly Review Press.

Amsden, A. 1990. Third World Industrialization: "Global Fordism" or a New Model? *New Left Review* 182:5–31.

Amsden, A., J. Kocanowicz, and L. Taylor. 1995. *The Market Meets Its Match: Restructuring the Economies of Eastern Europe*. Cambridge, Mass.: Harvard University Press.

Amuzegar, J. 1966. Nationalism versus Economic Growth. *Foreign Affairs* 44: 651–61.

Amuzegar, J., and M. Ali Fekrat. 1971. *Iran: Economic Development under Dualistic Conditions*. Chicago: University of Chicago Press.

Anastasoff, C. 1938. *The Tragic Peninsula: A History of the Macedonian Movement for Independence since 1878*. St. Louis, Mo.: Blackwell Wielandy.

Anderson, E. N., and P. R. Anderson. 1967. *Political Institutions and Social Change in Continental Europe in the Nineteenth Century*. Berkeley and Los Angeles: University of California Press.

Anderson, F. M. 1904. *The Constitutions and Other Select Documents Illustrative of the History of France, 1789–1901*. Minneapolis, Minn.: H. W. Wilson.

Anderson, P. 1974. *Passages from Antiquity to Feudalism*. London: Verso.

Anderson, P. 1979. *Lineages of the Absolutist State*. London: Verso.

Andreski, S. 1968. *Military Organization and Society*, Foreword by A. R. Radcliffe-Brown. Berkeley and Los Angeles: University of California Press.

Andrew, C. M., and A. S. Kanya-Forstner. 1981. *The Climax of French Imperial Expansion, 1914–1924*. Stanford, Calif.: Stanford University Press.

Annual Register. Various years. London: Baldwin, Craddock and Joy.

Appleby, J. 1976. Ideology and Theory: The Tension between Political and Economic Theory in Seventeenth Century England. *American Historical Review* 81: 499–515.

Apter, D. E. 1965. *The Politics of Modernization*. Chicago: University of Chicago Press.

Archer, J. E. 1990. The Wells-Charlesworth Debate: A Personal Comment on Arson in Norfolk and Suffolk. In M. Reed and R. Wells, eds., *Class, Conflict and Protest in the English Countryside, 1700–1880*. London: Frank Cass.

Arendt, H. 1958. *The Origins of Totalitarianism*. New York: Meridian.

Arlen, M. J. 1975. *Passage to Arafat*. New York: Farrar, Strauss and Giroux.

Armeson, R. B. 1964. *Total Warfare and Compulsory Labour: A Study of the Military-Industrial Complex in Germany during World War I.* Den Haag: Nijhoff.

Arnakis, G. G. 1966. *American Consul in a Cretan War – William J. Stillman,* revised edition of William J. Stillman, *The Cretan Insurrection 1866–7–8* (New York: Henry Holt, 1874). Austin, Texas: Center for Neo-Hellenic Studies.

Arndt, E. M. 1810. *Das Deutsche Volkstum.* Lübeck: Niemann und Comp.

Aron, R. 1950. Social Structure and the Ruling Class. *British Journal of Sociology* 1, no. 2: 126–43.

Art, R. J., and Robert Jervis, eds. 1973. *International Anarchy.* Boston: Little, Brown.

Artigues, D. 1971. *El Opus Dei en España, 1928–1962.* Paris: Ruedo Ibérico.

Artz, F. B. 1934. *Reaction and Revolution, 1814–1832.* New York: Harpers.

Ashford, D. E. 1986. *The Emergence of the Welfare State.* Oxford: Basil Blackwell.

Ashford, D. E. 1992. The Construction of Poverty. In R. Torstendahl, ed., *State Theory and State History.* London: Sage.

Ashton, T. S. 1955. *An Economic History of England: The 18th Century.* London: Methuen.

Askew, W. C. 1942. *Europe and Italy's Acquisition of Libya, 1911–1912.* Durham, N.C.: Duke University Press.

Aspaturian, V. V. 1968. The Non-Russian Nationalities. In A. Kassof, ed., *Prospects for Soviet Society.* New York: Praeger.

Aston, T., ed. 1967. *Crisis in Europe, 1560–1660.* New York: Doubleday.

Augé-Laribé, M. 1955. *La révolution agricole.* Paris: A. Michel.

Azrael, J. 1968. The Party and Society. In A. Kassof, ed., *Prospects for Soviet Society.* New York: Praeger.

Bade, K. 1985. German Immigration to the United States and Continental Immigration to Germany in the Late Nineteenth and Early Twentieth Centuries. In Dirk Hoerder, ed., *Labor Migration in the Atlantic Economies: The European and North American Working Classes during the Period of Industrialization.* Westport, Conn.: Greenwood Press.

Badie, B., and P. Birnbaum. 1982. *The Sociology of the State.* Chicago: University of Chicago Press.

Bairoch, P. 1975. *The Economic Development of the Third World since 1900.* London: Methuen.

Bairoch, P. 1981. The Main Trends in National Income Disparities since the Industrial Revolution. In P. Bairoch and M. Levy-Leboyer, eds., *Disparities in Economic Development since the Industrial Revolution.* London: Macmillan.

Bairoch, P. 1982. International Industrialization Levels from 1750 to 1980. *Journal of European Economic History* 11: 269–334.

Bairoch, P. 1989. Les Trois Révolutions agricoles du monde développé: Rendements et productivité de 1800 à 1985. *Annales,* E.S.C., no. 2 (March–April): 317–53.

Bairoch, P. 1993. *Economics and World History: Myths and Paradoxes.* London: Harvester.

Bakeless, J. 1972. *The Economic Causes of Modern War: A Study of the Period 1878–1918.* New York: Garland.

Baker, D. N., and P. J. Harrington, eds. 1980. *The Making of Frenchmen: Current Directions in the History of Education in France 1679–1979.* Waterloo, Ontario: Historical Reflections Press.

Baker, R. S. 1922. *Woodrow Wilson and World Settlement*, 3 vols. New York: Doubleday.

Balch, R. 1978. The Resigning of Quarrels: Conflict Resolution in the Thirteenth Century. *Peace and Change* 5: 33–38.

Baldwin, F. E. 1926. *Sumptuary Legislation and Personal Regulation in England*. Baltimore: Johns Hopkins University Press.

Baldy, E. 1922. *Les Banques d'affaires en France depuis 1900*. Paris: Librairie générale de droit & de jurisprudence.

Banks, A. 1971. *Cross-Polity Time-Series Data*, Cambridge, Mass.: MIT Press.

Banks, A. 1978. *A World Atlas of Military History, 1860–1945*. New York: Hippocrene Books.

Baran, P. A. 1970. On the Political Economy of Backwardness. In R. I. Rhodes, ed., *Imperialism and Underdevelopment*. New York: Monthly Review Press.

Baran, P. A., and P. M. Sweezy. 1966. *Monopoly Capital*. New York: Monthly Review Press.

Barany, G. 1969. Hungary: From Aristocratic to Proletarian Nationalism. In P. F. Sugar and I. J. Lederer, eds., *Nationalism in East Europe*. Seattle: University of Washington.

Barker, E. 1950. *Macedonia, Its Place in Balkan Power Politics*. London: Royal Institute of International Affairs.

Barnett, C. 1972. *The Collapse of British Power*. New York: Morrow.

Barraclough, G. 1955. *History in a Changing World*. Norman: University of Oklahoma Press.

Barraclough, G. 1967. *An Introduction to Contemporary History*. Harmondsworth: Penguin.

Barratt Brown, M. 1970. *After Imperialism*, revised ed. London: Merlin Press.

Bass, J. F. 1920. *The Peace Tangle*. New York: Macmillan.

Bayley, C. A. 1989. *Imperial Meridian: The British Empire and the World, 1780–1830*. London: Longman.

Becker, G. 1969. *Human Capital*. New York: Columbia University Press.

Beetham, D. 1974. *Max Weber and the Theory of Modern Politics*. London: George Allen and Unwin.

Bell, A. C. 1937. *A History of the Blockade of Germany, Austria-Hungary, Bulgaria, and Turkey, 1914–1918*. London: H. M. Stationary Office.

Bell, J. D. 1977. *Peasants in Power: Alexander Stamboliski and the Bulgarian Agrarian National Union, 1899–1923*. Princeton, N.J.: Princeton University Press.

Bell, L. F. E. 1907. *At the Works*. London: Arnold.

Bendix, R. 1977. *Nation-Building and Citizenship*. Berkeley: University of California Press.

Bendix, R. 1978. *Kings or People*. Berkeley: University of California Press.

Benewick, R. 1969. *The Fascist Movement in Britain*. London: Allen Lane.

Benns, L. 1930. *Europe since 1914*. New York: F. S. Crofts.

Benson, L. 1989. *The Working Class in Britain, 1850–1939*. London: Longman.

Berend, I. T., and G. Ranki. 1976. *Economic Development in East-Central Europe in the 19th and 20th Centuries*. New York: Columbia University Press.

Berger, S., and M. Piore. 1980. *Dualism and Discontinuity in Industrial Societies*. Cambridge: Cambridge University Press.

Berghahn, V. R. 1971. *Der Tirplitz-Plan: Genesis und Verfall Einer Innenpolitischen Krisenstrategie Unter Wilhelm II.* Düsseldorf: Droste Verlag.

Berghahn, V. R. 1994. *Imperial Germany, 1871–1914: Economy, Society, Culture, Politics.* Providence, R.I.: Berghahn Books.

Berkeley, G. F. H. 1932. *Italy in the Making, 1815–1846*, vol. 1. Cambridge: Cambridge University Press.

Bernard, M. 1997. Ecology, Political Economy and the Counter-Movement: Karl Polanyi and the Second Great Transformation. In S. Gill and J. H. Mittelman, eds., *Innovation and Transformation in International Studies.* Cambridge: Cambridge University Press.

Bersdahl, R. M. 1972. Conservative Politics and Aristocratic Landholders in Bismarckian Germany. *Journal of Modern History* 44: 1–20.

Bertrand, C., ed. 1977. *The Revolutionary Situation in Europe, 1917–1922: Germany, Italy, Austria-Hungary.* Montreal: Centre Interuniversitaire d'Études Européennes.

Betts, R. R. 1950. The Revolution in Central and South East Europe, 1945–1948. In R. R. Betts, ed., *Central and South East Europe, 1945–1948.* London: Royal Institute of International Affairs.

Bevan, G. P. 1880. On the Strikes of the Past Ten Years. *Journal of the Royal Statistical Society* 43: 35–54.

Bialer, U. 1980. *The Shadow of the Bomber: Fear of Air Attack and British Politics, 1932–1939.* London: Royal Historical Society.

Bigo, R. 1947. *Les Banques françaises au cours de XIXe siècle.* Paris: Sirey.

Binchy, D. A. 1941. *Church and State in Fascist Italy.* London: Oxford University Press.

Binder, L. 1964. *The Ideological Revolution in the Middle East.* New York: John Wiley.

Binder, L., et al. 1971. *Crises and Sequences in Political Development.* Princeton, N.J.: Princeton University Press.

Bisson, T. N. 1977. The Organized Peace in Southern France and Catalonia, ca. 1140–ca. 1233. *American Historical Review* 82: 290–311.

Black, A. 1993. Classical Islam and Medieval Europe: A Comparison of Political Philosophies and Cultures. *Political Studies* 41: 58–69.

Black, C. E. 1943. *The Establishment of Constitutional Government in Bulgaria.* Princeton, N.J.: Princeton University Press.

Blackbourn, D., and G. Eley. 1984. *The Peculiarities of German History: Bourgeois Society and Politics in Nineteenth-Century Germany.* Oxford: Oxford University Press.

Blainey, G. 1973. *The Causes of War.* New York: Free Press.

Bland, A. E., P. A. Brown, and R. H. Tawney. 1914. *English Economic History, Select Documents.* London: G. Bell & Sons.

Blaut, J. M. 1976. Where Was Capitalism Born? *Antipode: A Radical Journal of Geography* 8: 1–11.

Blewett, N. 1965. The Franchise in the United Kingdom, 1885–1918. *Past and Present* 32: 27–65.

Bloch, M. 1931. *Les Caractères originaux de l'histoire rurale française.* Cambridge, Mass.: Harvard University Press.

Block, F., and M. Somers. 1984. Beyond the Economistic Fallacy: The Holistic Social Science of Karl Polanyi. In T. Skocpol, ed., *Vision and Method in Historical Sociology.* New York: Cambridge University Press.

Block, F. L. 1977. *The Origins of International Economic Disorder*. Berkeley and Los Angeles: University of California Press.

Blum, J. 1957. Rise of Serfdom in Eastern Europe. *American Historical Review* 62: 807–36.

Blum, J. 1977. Russia. In D. Spring, ed., *European Landed Elites in the Nineteenth Century*. Baltimore: Johns Hopkins University Press.

Blum, J. 1978. *The End of the Old Order in Rural Europe*. Princeton, N.J.: Princeton University Press.

Bociurkiw, B. R. 1973. Church-State Relations in Communist Europe. *Religion in Communist Lands* 1, no. 4/5 (July/October).

Bociurkiw, B. R., and J. W. Strong. 1975. *Religion and Atheism in the U.S.S.R. and Eastern Europe*. London: Macmillan.

Boeke, J. H. 1953. *Economics and Economic Policy of Dual Societies*. New York: Institute of Pacific Relations.

Boltho, A. 1982. *The European Economy: Growth and Crisis*. New York: Oxford University Press.

Bonacich, E. 1972. A Theory of Ethnic Antagonisms: The Split Labor Market. *American Sociological Review* 5: 533–47.

Bond, B. 1983. *War and Society in Europe, 1870–1970*. London: Clarendon Press.

Bonjour, E., H. S. Offler, and G. R. Potter. 1952. *A Short History of Switzerland*. Oxford: Clarendon Press.

Bonnell, A. T. 1940. *German Control over International Economic Relations, 1930–1940*. Urbana: University of Illinois Press.

Booth, C. 1889. *Life and Labour of the People of London*, vol. 1. London: Williams and Norgate.

Bordogna, L., G. P. Cella, and G. Provasi. 1989. Labor Conflicts in Italy before the Rise of Fascism, 1881–1923: A Quantitative Analysis. In L. Haimson and C. Tilly, eds., *Strikes, Wars, and Revolutions in an International Perspective: Strike Waves in the Late Nineteenth and Early Twentieth Centuries*. Cambridge: Cambridge University Press.

Born, K. E. 1976. Structural Changes in German Social and Economic Development at the End of the Nineteenth Century. In J. J. Sheehan, ed., *Imperial Germany*. New York: New Viewpoints.

Bottomore, T. B. 1965. *Classes in Modern Society*. London: Allen & Unwin.

Botzaris, N. 1962. *Visions balkaniques dans la préparation de la révolution grecque (1789–1821)*. Geneva and Paris.

Boutruche, R. 1947. *La Crise d'une sociètè*, vol. 2. Paris: Belles Lettres.

Bouvier, J. 1961. *Le Crédit lyonnais de 1863 à 1882, les annàes de formation d'une banque de dépots*. Paris: S.E.V.P.E.N.

Bowley, A. L., 1930. *Some Economic Consequences of the War*. London: Thornton Butterworth.

Bowley, A. L., and A. R. Burnett-Hurst. 1915. *Livelihood and Poverty*. London: Bell.

Boyce, R. W. D. 1987. *British Capitalism at the Crossroads, 1919–1932*. Cambridge: Cambridge University Press.

Bozeman, A. B. 1960. *Politics and Culture in International History*. Princeton, N.J.: Princeton University Press.

Bracher, K. D. 1964. Problems of Parliamentary Democracy in Europe. *Daedalus* (Winter): 179–88.

Braudel, F. 1972. *The Mediterranean and the Mediterranean World in the Age of Philip II.* New York: Collins.

Braudel, F. 1979. *The Perspective of the World,* vol. 3: *Civilization and Capitalism, 15th–18th Century.* New York: Harper and Row.

Braudel, F. 1982. *The Wheels of Commerce,* vol. 2: *Civilization and Capitalism, 15th–18th Century,* trans. S. Reynolds. New York: Harper and Row.

Braunschwig, H. 1960. *Mythes et rèalitiès de l'impèrialisme colonial français, 1871–1914.* Paris: Colin.

Braunthal, J. 1967. *History of the International,* vol. 1: *1864–1914,* trans. H. Collins and K. Mitchell. New York: Praeger.

Brecher, J. 1997. *Strike!,* rev. ed. Cambridge, Mass.: South End Press.

Bredin, J.-D. 1986. *The Affair: The Case of Alfred Dreyfus.* New York: G. Braziller.

Breitman, R. 1981. *German Socialism and Weimar Democracy.* Chapel Hill: University of North Carolina Press.

Brenner, R. 1976. Agrarian Class Structure and Economic Development in Pre-Industrial Europe. *Past and Present* 70: 30–75.

Brenner, R. 1977. The Origins of Capitalist Development: A Critique of Neo-Smithian Marxism. *New Left Review* 10: 25–92.

Brenner, R. 1982. The Agrarian Roots of European Capitalism. *Past and Present* 97: 16–113.

Brentano, L. 1885. Über Die Zukünftige Politik Des Deutschen Reiches. *Schmollers Jahrbuch* 9: 1–29.

Brentano, L. 1929. *Das Wertschaftsleben der Antiken Welt.* Jena: G. Fischer.

Brewer, J., and J. Sayles. 1980. Introduction. In J. Brewer and J. Sayles, eds., *An Ungovernable People: The English and Their Law in the Seventeenth and Eighteenth Centuries.* New Brunswick, N.J.: Rutgers University Press.

Briggs, A. 1956. Middle Class Consciousness in English Politics, 1780–1846. *Past and Present* 9: 65–74.

Briggs, A. 1960. The Language of "Class" in Early Nineteenth Century England. In A. Briggs and J. Saville, eds., *Essays in Labour History.* London: CroomHelm.

Briggs, A. 1962. The Welfare State in Historical Perspective. *Archives euròpàenes des sociologie* 2: 221–58.

Brinkley, G. A. 1966. *The Volunteer Army and Allied Intervention in South Russia, 1917–1922: A Study in the Politics and Diplomacy of the Russian Civil War.* Notre Dame: University of Notre Dame Press.

Brinkley, R. 1935. *Realism and Nationalism, 1852–1871.* New York: Harper.

British and Foreign State Papers. 1919. London: Harrison & Sons and Her Majesty's Stationary Office.

Brown, B. E. 1970. *The French Revolt: May 1968.* New York: McCaleb-Seiler.

Brown, E. H. P. 1968. *A Century of Pay.* London: Macmillan.

Brown, M. E. 1993. Causes and Implications of Ethnic Conflict. In M. Brown, ed., *Ethnic Conflict and International Security.* Princeton, N.J.: Princeton University Press.

Bruce, M. B. 1966. *The Coming of the Welfare State,* rev. ed. New York: Schocken.

Brundage, A. 1974. The English Poor Law of 1834 and the Cohesion of Agricultural Society. *Agricultural History* 48: 405–17.

Brundage, A. 1979. *The Making of the New Poor Law.* New Brunswick, N.J.: Rutgers University Press.

Bruneau, T. C. 1976. Church and State in Portugal: Crises of Cross and Sword. *Journal of Church and State* 18: 463–90.

Bryant, C. G. A., and E. Mckrzycki. 1994. *The New Great Transformation?: Change and Continuity in East-Central Europe.* London: Routledge.

Bryce, V. J. 1972 [1916]. *The Treatment of the Armenians in the Ottoman Empire 1915–1916: Documents Presented to the Secretary of State for Foreign Affairs by Viscount Bryce.* Beirut: G. Doniguiana & Sons.

Brzezinski, Z. 1970. *Between Two Ages.* New York: Viking Press.

Brzezinski, Z., and S. P. Huntington. 1964. *Political Power US/USSR.* New York: Viking Press.

Buci-Glucksman, C. 1979. State, Transition and Passive Revolution. In Chantal Mouffe, ed., *Gramsci and Marxist Theory.* Pp. 207–36. London: Routledge.

Bulgaria Academy of Science, ed. 1985. *A Short Encyclopedia of the People's Republic of Bulgaria.* Oxford: Pergamon Press.

Burt, A. L. 1956. *Evolution of the British Empire and Commonwealth.* Boston: Heath.

Bury, J. P. T. 1948. Great Britain and the Revolution of 1848. In F. Fejtö, ed., *The Opening of an Era: 1848.* New York: Grosset and Dunlap.

Busch, B. C. 1971. *Britain, India, and the Arabs, 1914–1921.* Berkeley: University of California Press.

Butchman, W. 1939. *The Rise of Integral Nationalism in France, with Special Reference to the Ideas and Activities of Charles Maurras.* New York: Columbia University Press.

Cain, P. 1979. Capitalism, War and Internationalism in the Thought of Richard Cobden. *British Journal of International Studies* 5: 229–47.

Cain, P. J., and A. G. Hopkins. 1993. *British Imperialism, Innovation and Expansion 1688–1914.* London: Longman.

Cairncross, A. 1981. The Postwar Years, 1945–1977. In R. C. Floud and D. N. McCloskey, ed., *The Economic History of Britain since 1700,* vol. 2: *1860 to the 1970s.* Cambridge: Cambridge University Press.

Cairncross, A. K. 1953. *Home and Foreign Investment, 1870–1914.* Cambridge: Cambridge University Press.

Callahan, W. J. 1984. *Church, Politics, and Society in Spain, 1750–1874.* Cambridge, Mass.: Harvard University Press.

Callwell, C. E. 1927. *Field-Marshal Sir Henry Wilson,* vol. 2. London: Cassell.

Cameron, R. 1961. *France and the Economic Development of Europe, 1800–1914.* Princeton, N.J.: Princeton University Press.

Canetti, E. 1982. *The Torch in My Ear,* trans. J. Neugroschel. New York: Farrar Straus Giroux.

Cannadine, D. 1980. *Lords and Landlords: The Aristocracy and the Towns, 1774–1967.* Leicester: Leicester University Press.

Cannadine, D. 1990. *The Decline and Fall of the British Aristocracy.* New York: Doubleday.

Cantimori, D. 1948. Italy in 1848. In F. Fejtö, ed., *The Opening of an Era: 1848.* New York: Grosset and Dunlap.

Cardoso, F. H. 1973. Associated-Dependent Development: Theoretical and Practical Implications. In A. Stepan, ed., *Authoritarian Brazil: Origins, Policies, and Future.* New Haven: Yale University Press.

Cardoso, F. H., and E. Faletto. 1979. *Dependency and Development in Latin America.* Berkeley: University of California Press.

Carnoy, M. 1984. *The State and Political Theory.* Princeton, N.J.: Princeton University Press.

Carr, E. H. 1942. *The Conditions of Peace.* London: Macmillan.

Carr, E. H. 1945. *Nationalism and After.* London: Macmillan.

Carr, E. H. 1947. *The Soviet Impact on the Western World.* New York: Macmillan.

Carr, E. H. 1950–53. *The Bolshevik Revolution, 1917–1923.* London: Macmillan.

Carr, E. H. 1959. *International Relations between the Wars.* London: Macmillan.

Carr, E. H. 1964. *The Twenty Years' Crisis, 1919–1939.* New York: Harper and Row.

Carr, R. 1966. *Spain, 1808–1939.* Oxford: Clarendon Press.

Carstairs, A. M. 1980. *A Short History of Electoral Systems in Western Europe.* London: George Allen & Unwin.

Carsten, F. L. 1967. *The Rise of Fascism.* Berkeley and Los Angeles: University of California Press.

Carsten, F. L. 1982. *War against War: British and German Radical Movements in the First World War.* Berkeley and Los Angeles: University of California Press.

Carver, M. 1990. *War since 1945,* rev. ed. London: Ashfield Press.

Cassirer, E. 1946. *The Myth of the State.* New Haven: Yale University Press.

Castlereagh, V. R. S. 1853. *Correspondence, Despatches, and Other Papers of Viscount Castlereagh,* vol. 10, ed. Charles Vane, Marquees of Londerry, third series. London: J. Murray.

Castles, S. 1984. *Here for Good: Western Europe's New Ethnic Minorities.* London: Pluto Press.

Cecil, Lamar. 1970. The Creation of Nobles in Prussia, 1871–1918. *American Historical Review* 75: 757–95.

Chabad, F. 1975. *A History of Italian Fascism.* New York: H. Fertig.

Chambers, F. D. 1972. *The War Behind the War: A History of the Political and Civilian Fronts.* New York: Arno Press.

Chan, S. 1984. Mirror, Mirror on the War ... Are the Freer Countries More Pacific? *Journal of Conflict Resolution* 28: 617–48.

Chandler, A. D., 1977. *The Visible Hand: The Managerial Revolution in American Business.* Cambridge, Mass.: Harvard Belknap.

Charlesworth, A. 1983. *An Atlas of Rural Protest in Britain 1548–1900.* London: CroomHelm.

Charlesworth, A., D. Gilbert, A. Randall, H. Southall, and C. Wrigley. 1996. *An Atlas of Industrial Protest in Britain, 1750–1990.* London: Macmillan.

Charques, R. 1965. *The Twilight of Imperial Russia.* London: Oxford University Press.

Chartres, J. A. 1977. *The Internal Trade of England, 1500–1700.* London: Macmillan.

Checkland, Sydney. 1985. Part IV: Industrial Maturity and the Ending of Pre-eminence, 1874–1914. In *British Public Policy 1776–1939: An Economic, Social and Political Perspective.* Pp. 163–258. Cambridge: Cambridge University Press.

Chernow, R. 1990. *The House of Morgan: An American Banking Dynasty and the Rise of Modern Finance.* New York: Touchstone.

Chirot, D. 1977. *Social Change in the Twentieth Century*. New York: Harcourt Brace Jovanovich.

Chomsky, N., et al. 1997. *The Cold War and the University: Toward an Intellectual History of the Postwar Years*. New York: New Press.

Christensen, T. J., and J. Snyder. 1990. Chain Gangs and Passed Bucks: Predicting Alliance Patterns in Multipolarity. *International Organization* 44: 137–68.

Churchill, W. S. 1948. *The Gathering Storm*. London: Houghton Mifflin.

Ciano, G. 1948. *Ciano's Diplomatic Papers*. London: Odhams Press.

Cipolla, C. M. 1968. The Economic Decline of Italy. In B. Pullan, ed., *Crisis and Change in the Venetian Economy*. London: Methuen.

Cipolla, C. M. 1969. *Literacy and Development in the West*. Baltimore, Md.: Penguin Books.

Cipolla, C. M. 1980. Introduction. In C. M. Cipolla, ed., *Before the Industrial Revolution: European Society and Economy, 1000–1700*, 2nd ed. New York: Norton.

Clark, G. Kitson. 1966. "The Nobility and Gentry – Old Style" and "The New Politics and the New Gentry." In *The Making of Victorian England*. Pp. 206–74. London: Methuen.

Clark, J. C. D. 1985. *English Society, 1688–1832*. New York: Columbia University Press.

Clark, J. C. D. 1986. *Revolution and Rebellion: State and Society in England in the Seventeenth and Eighteenth Centuries*. New York: Cambridge University Press.

Clark, R. P. 1979. *The Basques: The Franco Years and Beyond*. Reno: University of Nevada Press.

Clark, S. 1979. *Social Origins of the Irish Landed War*. Princeton, N.J.: Princeton University Press.

Clarke, H. B. 1906. *Modern Spain, 1815–1898*. Cambridge: Cambridge University Press.

Clarke, S. 1978. Capital, Fractions of Capital and the State: Neo-Marxist Analysis of the South African State. *Capital and Class* 5: 32–77.

Claude, I. L. 1955. *National Minorities: An International Problem*. Cambridge, Mass.: Harvard University Press.

Claude, I. L. 1962. *Power and International Relations*. New York: Random.

Clegg, H. A., A. Fox, and A. F. Thompson. 1964. *A History of British Trade Unions since 1889*, 3 vols. Oxford: Clarendon Press.

Clough, S. B. 1930. *A History of the Flemish Movement*. New York: Richard R. Smith.

Clough, S. B. 1952. *Economic History of Europe*, 3rd ed. Boston: D. C. Heath.

Coates, D. 2000. *Models of Capitalism: Growth and Stagnation in the Modern Era*. Cambridge: Polity.

Coates, W. P. 1935. *Armed Intervention in Russia, 1918–1922*. London: Victor Gollancz.

Coates, W. P., and Z. Coates. 1941. *The Soviet-Finnish Campaign*. London: Eldon.

Cobban, A. 1968. *Aspects of the French Revolution*. New York: G. Braziller.

Cole, A., and P. Campbell. 1989. *French Electoral Systems and Elections since 1789*. Aldershot: Gower.

Cole, G. D. H. 1955. *Studies in Class Structure*. London: Routledge.

Cole, G. D. H., and R. Postgate. 1966. *The Common People, 1746–1938*. 4th ed. London: Methuen.

Cole, W. H. 1981. Factors in Demand, 1700–80. In R. C. Floud and D. N. McCloskey, eds., *The Economic History of Britain since 1700*, vol. 1: *1700–1860*. Pp. 36–65. Cambridge: Cambridge University Press.

Collas, H. 1908. *La Banque de Paris et des pays-bas*. Dijon: Barbier-Lèon Marchal.

Collins, H., and C. Abramsky. 1965. *Karl Marx and the British Labour Movement*. New York: Macmillan.

Collins, I. 1963. Liberalism in Nineteenth-Century Europe. In W. N. Medlicott, ed., *From Metternich to Hitler: Aspects of British and Foreign History*. New York: Barnes and Noble.

Connor, W. 1973. The Politics of Ethnonationalism. *Journal of International Affairs* 27: 1–21.

Conquest, R. 1973. *The Great Terror: Stalin's Purges of the Thirties*, rev. ed. New York: Macmillan.

Conquest, R. 1976. *Soviet Nationalities Policy in Practice*. London: Bodley Head.

Conquest, R. 1986. *The Harvest of Sorrow: Soviet Collectivization and the Terror-Famine*. New York: Oxford University Press.

Consett, M. W. W. P. 1923. *The Triumph of Unarmed Forces (1914–1918)*. London: Williams & Norgate.

Cox, H. 1922. Changes in Land Ownership in England. *Atlantic Monthly* 129: 556–62.

Cox, R. 1987. *Production, Power, and World Order: Social Forces in the Making of History*. New York: Columbia University Press.

Crafts, N. F. R. 1984. Patterns of Development in Nineteenth Century Europe. *Oxford Economic Papers* 36: 438–58.

Craig, Gordon. 1956. *The Politics of the Prussian Army, 1640–1945*. Oxford: Oxford University Press.

Crampton, R. J. 1987. *A Short History of Modern Bulgaria*. New York: Cambridge University Press.

Crankshaw, E. 1976. *The Shadow of the Winter Palace: Russia's Drift to Revolution, 1825–1917*. New York: Viking Press.

Cronin, J. E. 1982a. Coping with Labour, 1918–1926. In J. E. Cronin and J. Schneer, eds., *Social Conflict and the Political Order in Modern Britain*. New Brunswick, N.J.: Rutgers University Press.

Cronin, J. E. 1982b. Labor Insurgency and Class Formation: Comparative Perspectives on the Crisis of 1917–1920 in Europe. In J. E. Cronin and C. Sirianni, eds., *Work, Community and Power: The Experience of Labor in Europe and America, 1900–1925*. Philadelphia: Temple University Press.

Cronin, J. E. 1989. Strikes and Power in Britain, 1870–1920. In L. Haimson and C. Tilly, eds., *Strikes, Wars, and Revolutions in an International Perspective: Strike Waves in the Late Nineteenth and Early Twentieth Centuries*. Cambridge: Cambridge University Press.

Cross, C. 1961. *The Fascists in Britain*. London: Barrie and Rockliff.

Crotty, J., and G. Epstein. 1996. In Defence of Capital Controls. In L. Panitch, ed., *Are There Alternatives? Socialist Register 1996*. London: Merlin Press.

Crowley, H. E. J. 1970. The Peace and Truce of God in the Eleventh Century. *Past and Present* 46: 42–67.

Crump, G. C., and E. F. Jacob, eds. 1926. *The Legacy of the Middle Ages*. Oxford: Oxford University Press.

Cueva, A. 1982. *The Process of Political Domination in Ecuador*, trans. Danielle Salti. New Brunswick: Transaction Books.

Cumings, B. 2002. Boundary Displacement: The State, the Foundations, and Area Studies during and after the Cold War. In H. D. Harootunian and Masao Miyoshi, eds., *Learning Places: The Afterlives of Area Studies*. Durham, N.C., and London: Duke University Press.

Curtis, M. 1965. *Western European Integration*. New York: Harper and Row.

Curtis, R. E. 1931. *The Trusts and Economic Control*. New York: McGraw-Hill.

Da Silva, M. M. 1975. Modernization and Ethnic Conflict: The Case of the Basques. *Comparative Politics* 7: 227–51.

Dahrendorf, R. 1959. *Class and Class Conflict in Industrial Society*. Stanford, Calif.: Stanford University Press.

Dahrendorf, R. 1967. *Society and Democracy in Germany*. New York: Doubleday.

Dakin, D. 1973. *The Greek Struggle for Independence 1821–1833*. Berkeley and Los Angeles: University of California Press.

Dallin, A., and G. W. Breslauer. 1970. *Political Terror in Communist Systems*. Stanford, Calif.: Stanford University Press.

Dalton, H. 1957. *The Fateful Years, 1931–1945*. London: Muller.

Dangerfield, G. 1961. *The Strange Death of Liberal England*. New York: Putnam.

Daniels, R. V. 1971. Soviet Politics since Kruschev. In J. W. Strong, ed., *The Soviet Union under Brezhnev and Kosygin*. New York: Van Nostrand Reinhold.

Danilevski, N. 1871. *Rossiia I Europa*. St. Petersburg: Obshchestvennaia pol'za.

Daphnas, G. 1955. *Greece between the Wars, 1923–1940*. Athenai: Ikaros.

Darwin, J. 1981. *Britain, Egypt and the Middle East: Imperial Policy in the Aftermath of War, 1918–1922*. New York: St. Martin's Press.

Davies, J. C. 1962. Toward a Theory of Revolution. *American Sociological Review* 27: 5–18.

Davies, J. C. 1969. The J-Curve of Rising and Declining Satisfactions as the Cause of Some Great Revolutions and a Contained Rebellion. In H. D. Graham and T. R. Gurr, eds., *Violence in America*. New York: Signet Books.

Davies, M. F. 1909. *Life in an English Village*. London: Unwin.

Davin, L. E. 1969. The Structural Crisis of a Regional Economy: A Case-Study: The Walloon Area. In E. A. G. Robinson, ed., *Backward Areas in Advanced Countries*. Pp. 113–43. London: Macmillan.

Davis, L. E., and R. A. Huttenback. 1988. *Mammon and the Pursuit of Empire: The Economics of British Imperialism, 1860–1912*. New York: Cambridge University Press.

De Azcárate, P. 1945. *League of Nations and National Documents*. Washington: Carnegie Endowment for International Peace.

De Benoist, A. 1996. Confronting Globalization. *Telos* 108: 117–38.

De Gaulle, C. 1954–59. *Memoires de guerre*, 3 vols. Paris: Plon.

De Laveleye, E. 1887. *The Balkan Peninsula*. London: T. F. Unwin.

De Swaan, A. 1988. *In Care of the State: Health Care, Education and Welfare in Europe and the USA in the Modern Era*. New York: Oxford University Press.

De Vries, J. 1973. Benelux 1920–1970. In Carlo M. Cipolla, ed., *The Fontana Economic History of Europe*, vol. 6: *Contemporary Economies*. Glasgow: William Collins Sons.

De Vries, J. 1976. *The Economy of Europe in an Age of Crisis, 1600–1750*. London: Cambridge University Press.

Deane, P. 1979. *The First Industrial Revolution*, 2nd ed. Cambridge: Cambridge University Press.

Deane, P., and W. A. Cole. 1967. *British Economic Growth, 1688–1959: Trends and Structure*, 2nd ed. Cambridge: Cambridge University Press.

Dedijer, V., I. Bozic, S. Cirkovic, and M. Ekmecic. 1974. *History of Yugoslavia*. New York: McGraw-Hill.

Denikin, A. I. 1973. *The White Army*. Westport: Hyperion Press.

Denison, E. F. 1967. *Why Growth Rates Differ: Postwar Experience in Nine Western Countries*. Washington: Brookings Institution.

Deutsch, J. 1934. *The Civil War in Austria*, trans. D. P. Berenberg. Chicago: Socialist Party, National Headquarters.

Diamond, S. 1992. *Compromised Campus: The Collaboration of Universities with the Intelligence Community*. New York: Oxford University Press.

Dill, S. 1906. *Roman Society from Nero to Marcus Aurelius*. London: Macmillan.

Disraeli, B. 1950. *Sybil, or the Two Nations*. New York: AMS Press [1845].

Djilas, M. 1966. *The New Class: An Analysis of the Communist System*. London: Allen & Unwin.

Djordjevic, D. 1967. The Serbs as an Integrative and Disintegrative. In *History Yearbook III*, vol. II.

Djordjevic, D., and S. Fischer-Galati. 1981. *The Balkan Revolutionary Tradition*. New York: Columbia University Press.

Dobb, M. 1960. *Economic Growth and Planning*. New York: Monthly Review Press.

Dobb, M. 1963 [1947]. *Studies in the Development of Capitalism*, rev. ed. New York: International Publishers.

Dobb, M. 1965. The Discussion of the Twenties on Planning and Economic Growth. *Society Studies* 17: 198–208.

Dockrill, M. L., and J. D. Goold. 1981. *Peace without Promise: Britain and Peace Conferences, 1919–1923*. Hamden: Archon Books.

Dopsch, A. 1937. *Economic and Social Foundations of European Civilisation*. New York: Harcourt, Brace.

Dorwart, R. A. 1971. *The Prussian Welfare State before 1740*. Cambridge, Mass.: Harvard University Press.

Dos Santos, T. 1970. The Structure of Dependence. *American Economic Review* 60: 235–46.

Downing, B. M. 1997. *The Military Revolution and Political Change in Early Modern Europe*. Princeton, N.J.: Princeton University Press.

Doyle, M. W. 1997. *Ways of War and Peace: Realism, Liberalism, and Socialism*. New York: W. W. Norton.

Droz, J. 1957. *Les Revolutions allemande de 1848*. Paris: Presses Universitaires de France.

Droz, J. 1967. *Europe between Revolution, 1815–1848*. Ithaca, N.Y.: Cornell University Press.

Duby, G. 1980. *The Three Orders: Feudal Society*. Chicago: University of Chicago Press.

Dumas, S. 1922. *Losses of Life Caused by War*. London: Oxford University Press.

Dunbabin, J. P. D. 1974. *Rural Discontent in Nineteenth Century Britain*. London: Faber and Faber.

Dunbabin, J. P. D. 1975. British Rearmament in the 1930s: A Chronology and Review. *Historical Journal* 18: 587–609.

Durkheim, E. 1975. *Textes*, vol. 3. Paris: Éditions de Minuit.

Duveau, G. 1965. *1848*. Paris: Gallimard.

Eckstein, H. 1965. On the Etiology of Internal Wars. *History and Theory* 4: 133–63.

Edelstein, M. 1981. Foreign Investment and Accumulation, 1860–1914. In R. C. Floud and D. N. McCloskey, eds., *The Economic History of Britain since 1700*, vol. 2: *1860 to the 1970s*. Cambridge: Cambridge University Press.

Edward, R. D. 1983. *An Atlas of Irish History*. London: Methuen.

Eichengreen, B. J. 1992. *Golden Fetters: The Gold Standard and the Great Depression, 1919–1939*. Oxford: Oxford University Press.

Eidelberg, P. G. 1974. *The Great Romanian Peasant Revolt of 1907, the First Modern Jacquerie*. Leiden: E. J. Brill.

Einzig, P. 1940. *Europe in Chains*. London: Penguin.

Einzig, P. 1942. *Appeasement, before, during and after the War*. London: Macmillan.

Eisenstadt, S. N. 1966. *Modernization: Protest and Change*. Englewood Cliffs, N.J.: Prentice-Hall.

Eisenstein, E. 1965. Who Intervened in 1788? A Commentary on the Coming of the French Revolution. *American Historical Review* 71: 77–103.

El Guindi, F. 1999. *Veil: Modesty, Privacy, Resistance*. Leamington Spa, Warwickshire: Berg.

Elliot, J. H. 1963. *The Revolt of the Catalans*. Cambridge: Cambridge University Press.

Elvin, M. 1973. *The Pattern of the Chinese Past*. Stanford: Stanford University Press.

Engels, F. 1894. La Futura rivoluzione italiana e il partito socialista. *Critica Sociale* 4, no. 2 (February): 35–36.

Engels, F. 1951. *Violenza ed economia formazione del nuovo impero tedesco*. Rome.

Engels, F. 1964. Introduction. In K. Marx, ed., *Class Struggles in France, 1848–1850*. New York: International Publishers.

Engels, F. 1968. The Origin of the Family, Private Property and the State. In K. Marx and F. Engels, eds., *Selected Works*. London: Lawrence & Wishart.

Engels, F. 1969. *Germany: Revolution and Counter-Revolution*. New York: International Publishers.

Engels, F. 1971 [1889]. The Abdication of the Bourgeoisie. In K. Marx and F. Engels, eds., *Articles on Britain*. Moscow: Progress Publishers.

Engerman, S. 1994. Reflections on "The Standard of Living Debate": New Arguments and New Evidence. In J. James and Mark Thomas, eds., *Capitalism in Context*. Chicago: University of Chicago Press.

Englander, D. 1983. *Landlord and Tenant in Urban Britain*. London: Clarendon Press.

Erickson, J. 1962. *The Soviet High Command: A Military-Political History, 1918–1941*. New York: St. Martin's Press.

Evans, E. L. 1981. *The German Center Party, 1870–1933*. Carbondale and Edwardsville: Southern Illinois University.

Evans, P. 1979. *Dependent Development*. Princeton, N.J.: Princeton University Press.

Evans, P., D. Rueschemeyer, and T. Skocpol. 1985. *Bringing the State Back In*. New York: Cambridge University Press.

Evans, R. J. 1979. Red Wednesday in Hamburg: Social Democrats, Police, and Lumpenproletariat in the Suffrage Disturbance of 17 January 1906. *Social History* 4: 1–31.

Eversley, D. E. C. 1967. The Home Market and Economic Growth in England, 1750–1780. In E. L. Jones and G. E. Mingay, eds., *Land, Labour, and Population in the Industrial Revolution*. London: Arnold.

Fadeiev, R. 1871. *Opinion on the Eastern Question*. London: E. Stanford.

Feiling, K. 1946. *Life of Neville Chamberlain*. London: Macmillan.

Fejtö, F. 1948. Hungary: The War of Independence. In F. Fejtö, ed., *The Opening of an Era: 1848*. New York: Grosset and Dunlap.

Feldman, G. D. 1966. *Army, Industry, and Labor in Germany, 1914–1918*. Princeton, N.J.: Princeton University Press.

Ferris, J. R. 1989. *Men, Money, and Diplomacy: The Evolution of British Strategic Foreign Policy, 1919–1926*. Princeton, N.J.: Princeton University Press.

Ferro, M. 1973. *The Great War, 1914–1918*. London: Routledge and Kegan Paul.

Fichte, J. G. 1834–35. Der Patriotismus und Sein Gegenteil: Patriotische Dialoge. In I. H. Fichte, ed., *Fichtes nachgelassene Werke*, 3 vols. Bonn: Adolph-Marcus.

Fichte, J. G. 1922. *Addresses to the German Nation*, trans. R. F. Jones and G. H. Turnbull. London: Open Court.

Fieldhouse, D. K. 1973. *Economics and Empire, 1830–1914*. London: Weidenfeld and Nicolson.

Finer, Samuel. 1975. State and Nation-Building in Europe: The Role of the Military. In Charles Tilly, ed., *The Formation of National States in Western Europe*. Pp. 84–163. Princeton, N.J.: Princeton University Press.

Finlay, G. 1877. *A History of Greece, from Its Conquest by the Romans to the Present Time, B.C. 146 to 1864*, vol. 5. Oxford: Clarendon Press.

Fischer, D. H. 1996. *The Great Wave: Price Revolutions and the Rhythm of History*. New York: Oxford University Press.

Fischer, F. 1961. *Griff Nach der Weltmacht: Die Kriegzielpolitik des Kaiserlichen Deutschlands, 1914–1918*. Düsseldorf: Droste Verlag.

Fischer, W. 1966. Social Tensions at Early Stages of Industrial Development. *Contemporary Studies in Social History* 9: 64–83.

Fisher, G. 1958. *Russian Liberalism, from Gentry to Intelligentsia*. Cambridge, Mass.: Harvard University Press.

Fitzpatrick, S. 1979. Stalin and the Making of the New Elite, 1928–1939. *Slavic Review* 38, no. 3: 377–402.

Fitzpatrick, S. 1982. *The Russian Revolution, 1917–1937*. New York: Oxford University Press.

Floud, R. 1981. Britain 1860–1914: A Survey. In R. C. Floud and D. N. McCloskey, eds., *The Economic History of Britain Since 1700*, vol. 2: *1860 to the 1970s*. Pp. 1–26. Cambridge: Cambridge University Press.

Floud, R. 1997. *The People and the British Economy, 1830–1914*. New York: Oxford University Press.

Fogerty, M. P. 1957. *Christian Democracy in Western Europe, 1820–1953*. London: Routledge and Kegan Paul.

Fohlen, C. 1973. France 1920–1970. In Carlo M. Cipolla, ed., *The Fontana Economic History of Europe*, vol. 6: *Contemporary Economies*. Glasgow: William Collins Sons & Co.

Foster, J. 1974. *Class Struggle and the Industrial Revolution*. London: Weidenfeld.

Fraenkl, E. 1941. *The Dual State: A Contribution to the Theory of Dictatorship*, trans. E. A. Shils. New York: Oxford University Press.

Frank, A. G. 1967. *Capitalism and Underdevelopment in Latin America*. New York: Monthly Review Press.

Frank, A. G. 1970. The Development of Underdevelopment. In Robert I. Rhodes, ed., *Imperialism and Underdevelopment*. New York: Monthly Review Press.

Fraser, D. 1981. The English Poor Law and the British Welfare State. In W. J. Mommsen, ed., *The Emergence of the Welfare State in Britain and Germany*. London: CroomHelm.

Frasheri, K. 1964. *The History of Albania*. Tirana: Naim Frasheri.

Freedman, M. 1976. *Labor Markets: Segments and Shelters*. Montclair, N.J.: Allenhold, Osmun.

Freeman, C., and L. Soete. 1997. *The Economics of Industrial Innovation*. London: Pinter.

Friedberg, A. L. 1988. *The Weary Titan: Britain and the Experience of Relative Decline, 1895–1905*. Princeton, N.J.: Princeton University Press.

Friedrich, C. J., and Z. Brzezinski. 1956. *Totalitarian Dictatorship and Autocracy*. Cambridge, Mass.: Harvard University Press.

Fröbel, F., J. Heinrichs, and O. Kreye. 1980. *The New International Division of Labor: Structural Unemployment in Industrial Countries and Industrialization in Developing Countries*, trans. P. Burgess. Cambridge: Cambridge University Press.

Fromkin, D. 1989. *Peace to End All Peace: The Fall of the Ottoman Empire and the Creation of the Modern Middle East*. New York: Avon Books.

Fukuyama, F. 1992. *The End of History and the Last Man*. New York: Free Press.

Fuscher, L. W. 1982. *Neville Chamberlain and Appeasement*. New York: W. W. Norton.

Gagliardo, J. G. 1967. *Enlightened Despotism*. New York: Thomas Y. Crowell.

Galbraith, J. K. 1954. *The Great Crash, 1929*. Boston: Mariner Books.

Galenson, W., and H. Leibenstein. 1955. Investment Criteria and Economic Development. *Quarterly Journal of Economics* 69: 343–70.

Gallacher, W. 1940. *Revolt in the Clyde: An Autobiography*. London: Lawrence & Wishart.

Gallagher, J., and R. Robinson. 1953. The Imperialism of Free Trade. *Economic History Review* 2: 1–15.

Gallagher, J., and R. Robinson. 1962. The Partition of Africa. In *New Cambridge Modern History*, vol. 10. Cambridge: Cambridge University Press.

Gallagher, J., and R. Robinson. 1981. *Africa and the Victorians: The Official Mind of Imperialism*, 2nd ed. London: Macmillan.

Galtung, J. 1971. A Structural Theory of Imperialism. *Journal of Peace Research* 8, no. 2: 81–117.

Gardner, M. M. 1971. *Adam Mickiewicz: The National Poet of Poland*. New York: Arno Press.

Garvin, J. L. 1919. *The Foundations of Peace*. London: Macmillan.

Gaskell, P. 1833. *The Manufacturing Population of England: Its Moral, Social, and Physical Conditions, and the Changes Which Have Arisen from the Use of Steam Machinery; with an Examination of Infant Labour.* London: Baldwin and Cradock.

Gay, P. 1970. *Weimar Culture: The Outsider as Insider.* New York: Harper Torchbooks.

Gazi, S. 1973. *A History of Croatia.* New York: Philosophical Library.

Geary, D. 1981. *European Labour Protest, 1848–1939.* London: CroomHelm.

Geffre, C., and J.-P. Jossua. 1989. *1789: The French Revolution and the Church.* Edinburgh: T. & T. Clark.

Gehrlich, P. 1973. The Institutionalization of European Parliaments. In A. Kornberg, ed., *Legislatures in Comparative Perspective.* New York: D. McKay.

Gellner, E. 1983. *Nations and Nationalism.* Ithaca and London: Cornell University Press.

Genovese, E. D. 1965. *The Political Economy of Slavery: Studies in the Economy & Society of the Slave South.* New York: Pantheon.

George, H. 1962 [1879]. *Progress and Poverty.* New York: Robert Schalkenbach Foundation.

Gerschenkron, A. 1962. *Economic Backwardness in Historical Perspective.* Cambridge, Mass.: Harvard University Press.

Gerschenkron, A. 1965. *Agrarian Policies and Industrialization: Russia 1861–1917*, Cambridge Economic History of Europe. Cambridge: Cambridge University Press.

Gerth, H. H., and C. Wright Mills. 1946. *From Max Weber: Essays in Sociology.* New York: Oxford University Press.

Gestrin, F. 1962. Economie et société en Slovénie au XVIe Siècle. *Annales E.S.C.* 17, no. 4 (July–August): 663–90.

Giddens, A. 1972. *Politics and Sociology in the Thought of Max Weber.* London: Macmillan.

Gilbert, A. D. 1980. *The Making of Post-Christian England: A History of the Secularization of Modern Society.* London: Longman.

Gilbert, B. B. 1966. *The Evolution of National Insurance in Great Britain: The Origins of the Welfare State.* London: Michael Joseph.

Gilbert, M. 1966. *The Roots of Appeasement.* London: Weidenfeld and Nicolson.

Gilbert, M. 1968. *An Atlas of British History.* London: Dorset Press.

Gilbert, M. 1972. *An Atlas of Russian History.* London: Dorset Press.

Gilbert, M., and R. Gott. 1963. *The Appeasers.* Boston: Houghton Mifflin.

Gill, D., and G. Dallas. 1985. *The Unknown Army.* London: Verso.

Gill, S. 1995. Theorizing the Interregnum: The Double Movement and Global Politics in the 1990s. In B. Hettne, ed., *International Political Economy: Understanding Global Disorder.* London: Zed.

Gill, S. 1997. Transformation and Innovation in the Study of World Order. In S. Gill and J. H. Mittelman, eds., *Innovation and Transformation in International Studies.* Cambridge: Cambridge University Press.

Gillis, J. 1968. Aristocracy and Bureaucracy in 19th Century Prussia. *Past and Present.* 41.

Gillis, J. R. 1983. *The Development of European Society, 1770–1870.* Boston: Houghton Mifflin.

Gilpin, R. 1981. *War and Change in World Politics.* Cambridge: Cambridge University Press.

Glasman, M. 1994. The Great Deformation: Polanyi, Poland, and the Terrors of Planned Spontaneity. *New Left Review* 205: 59–86.

Glyn, A. 1995. Social Democracy and Full Employment. *New Left Review* 211: 33–55.

Gochman, C. 1990. The Geography of Conflict: Militarized International Disputes since 1816. Paper delivered at 31st Annual Convention of the International Studies Association, Washington, D.C.

Gold, D. A. 1977. The Rise and Decline of the Keynesian Coalition. *Working Papers on the Capitalist State* 6: 129–61.

Goldsmith, R. W. 1946. The Power of Victory: Munitions Output in World War II. *Military Affairs* 10: 69–80.

Goldstein, R. J. 1978. *Political Repression in Modern America: From 1870 to the Present.* Cambridge, Mass.: Schenkman.

Goldstein, R. J. 1983. *Political Repression in Nineteenth Century Europe.* London: CroomHelm.

Goldstone, J. A. 1991. *Revolution and Rebellion in the Early Modern World.* Berkeley and Los Angeles: University of California Press.

Goldthorpe, J. H. 1964. Social Stratification in Industrial Society. *Sociological Review Monograph*, no. 8: 97–122.

Golob, E. O. 1944. *The Méline Tariff: French Agriculture and Nationalist Economic Policy.* New York: Columbia University Press.

Gooch, G. P., and H. Temperley, eds. 1928. *British Documents on the Origins of the War.* London: H. M. Stationary Office.

Gopcivic, S. 1887. *Le Montènègro et les montenegrins.* Paris: Plon.

Gordon, D. 1972. *Theories of Poverty and Underdevelopment: Orthodox, Radical, and Dual Labor Market Perspectives.* Lexington: Lexington Books.

Gordon, D. M. 1980. Stages of Accumulation and Long Economic Cycles. In Terence K. Hopkins and Immanuel Wallerstein, eds., *Processes of the World System.* Pp. 9–45. Beverly Hills, Calif.: Sage.

Gosnell, H. F. 1930. *Why Europe Votes.* Chicago: University of Chicago Press.

Gouldner, A. W. 1977–1978. Stalinism: A Study of Internal Colonialism. *Telos* 34: 5–48.

Gourevitch, P. 1978. The Second Image Revisited: The International Sources of Domestic Politics. *International Organization* 32: 881–911.

Graff, H. J., ed. 1981. *Literacy and Social Development in the West: A Reader.* New York: Cambridge University Press.

Gramsci, A. 1949. *Il Risorgimento.* Turin: Einaudi.

Gramsci, A. 1971. *Selections from the Prison Notebooks of Antonio Gramsci,* ed. and trans. Q. Hoare and G. Nowell Smith. New York: International.

Granshof, F. 1970. *The Middle Ages: A History of International Relations.* New York: Harper and Row.

Graves, W. S. 1931. *America's Siberian Adventure, 1918–1920.* New York: J. Cape & Smith.

Gravier, J.-F. 1947. *Paris et le desert français.* Paris: Le Portulan.

Gray, J. 1998. *False Dawn: The Delusions of Global Capitalism.* London: Granta.

Gray, R. 1981. *The Aristocracy of Labour in Nineteenth Century Britain, 1850–1914.* London: Macmillan.

Greenfeld, L. 1992. *Nationalism: Five Roads to Modernity*. Cambridge, Mass.: Harvard University Press.

Greenfield, K. R. 1918. *Sumptuary Law in Nürnberg: A Study in Paternal Government*. Baltimore: Johns Hopkins University Press.

Greenleaf, W. H. 1985. *The British Political Tradition*. London: Methuen.

Gregor, A. J. 1979. *Italian Fascism and Developmental Dictatorship*. Princeton, N.J.: Princeton University Press.

Grenville, J. A. S. 1976. *Europe Reshaped, 1848–1876*. Ithaca, N.Y.: Cornell University Press.

Grieco, J. M. 1988. Anarchy and the Limits of Cooperation: A Realist Critique of the Newest Liberal Institutionalism. *International Organization* 42: 485–507.

Griffin, P. E., and L. Ellington. 1995. The Origins of Capitalist Markets: Transition in Poland with Comparison to East Asian Capitalism. *Journal of Economic Issues* 29: 585–91.

Griffiths, F. 1971. A Tendency Analysis of Soviet Policy-Making. In H. Gordon Skilling and F. Griffiths, eds., *Interest Groups in Soviet Politics*. Princeton, N.J.: Princeton University Press.

Groh, D. 1973. *Negative Integration und Revolutionärer Attentismus: Die Deutsche Sozialdemokratie am Vorabend des Ersten Weltkrieges*. Frankfurt am Main: Ullstein.

Gulick, C. A. 1940. *Austria from Hapsburg to Hitler*, vol. 2. Berkeley: University of California Press.

Gulick, E. V. 1955. *Europe's Classical Balance of Power*. Ithaca, N.Y.: Cornell University Press.

Gurr, T. R. 1968a. A Causal Model of Civil Strife: A Comparative Analysis Using New Indices. *American Political Science Review* 62: 1103–24.

Gurr, T. R. 1968b. Psychological Factors in Civil Violence. *World Politics* 20: 245–78.

Gurr, T. R. 1970. *Why Men Rebel*. Princeton, N.J.: Princeton University Press.

Gurr, T. R., and R. D. Duvall. 1973. Civil Conflict in the 1960s: A Reciprocal Theoretical System with Parameter Estimates. *Comparative Political Studies* 6: 135–69.

Gurr, T. R., and C. Ruttenberg. 1967. *The Conditions of Civil Violence: First Tests of a Causal Model*, Center of International Studies, Princeton University, Research Monograph no. 28. Princeton, N.J.: Princeton University Press.

Guttsman, W. L. 1954. Aristocracy and the Middle Classes in the British Political Elite, 1886–1916. *British Journal of Sociology* 5: 12–32.

Guttsman, W. L., ed. 1969. *The English Ruling Class*. London: Weidenfeld and Nicolson.

Haas, E. 1966. *International Political Communities*. Garden City, N.Y.: Anchor Books.

Haas, M. 1968. Social Change and National Aggressiveness, 1900–1960. In J. David Singer, ed., *Quantative International Politics*. New York: Free Press of Glencoe.

Haas, M. 1974. *International Conflict*. Indianapolis: Bobbs-Merrill.

Haimson, L. 1964. The Problem of Social Stability in Urban Russia, 1905–1917. *Slavic Review* 23: 619–42.

Haimson, L., and C. Tilly, eds. 1989. *Strikes, Wars, and Revolutions in an International Perspective: Strike Waves in the Late Nineteenth and Early Twentieth Centuries*. Cambridge: Cambridge University Press.

Halévy, E. 1930. *The World Crisis of 1914–1918: An Interpretation*. Oxford: Clarendon Press.

Hall, J. A. 1985. Religion and the Rise of Capitalism. *Archives euròpàenes des sociologie* 26: 193–223.

Hall, J. A., and G. J. Ikenberry. 1989. *The State*. Minneapolis: University of Minnesota Press.

Halperin, J. 1973. The Transformation of Switzerland: Prelude to Revolution. In F. Fejtö, ed., *The Opening of an Era: 1848*, vols. 50–66. New York: Grosset & Dunlap.

Halperin, S. 1993. Nationalism and the Autonomous State in 19th Century Europe. In R. Palan and B. K. Gills, eds., *Transcending the State-Global Divide: The Neo-Structuralist Agenda in International Relations*. Boulder: Lynne Rienner Publishing.

Halperin, S. 1996. *Polanyi's "Double Movement" and European Historiography: Free Markets and Protection in Comparative Perspective*, Working Paper no. 33. New York: New School for Social Research.

Halperin, S. 1997a. *In the Mirror of the Third World: Industrial Capitalist Development in Modern Europe*. Ithaca, N.Y.: Cornell University Press.

Halperin, S. 1997b. The Politics of Appeasement: The Rise of the Left and European International Relations during the Interwar Years. In D. Skidmore, ed., *Contested Social Orders and International Politics*. Nashville: Vanderbilt University Press.

Hammond, T. 1971. *The Anatomy of Communist Takeovers*. New Haven: Yale University Press.

Hankey, L. 1963. *The Supreme Control at the Paris Peace Conference, 1919: A Commentary*. London: Allen and Unwin.

Harbottle, T. 1981. *Dictionary of Battles*, 3rd rev. ed. New York: Van Nostrand Reinhold.

Hardach, G. 1977. *The First World War, 1914–1918*. Berkeley: University of California Press.

Hardach, K. 1973. Germany, 1914–1970. In C. M. Cipolla, ed., *The Fontana Economic History of Europe*, vol. 6: *Contemporary Economies*. Glasgow: William Collins Sons.

Harrison, R. 1965. *Before the Socialists: Studies in Labour and Politics, 1861–1881*. London: Routledge and Kegan Paul.

Harvey, B. F. 1991. Introduction: The "Crisis of the Early Fourteenth Century." In Bruce M. S. Campbell, ed., *Before the Black Death: Studies in the "Crisis" of the Early Fourteenth Century*. Manchester: University of Manchester Press.

Hausner, J. 1995. Imperative vs. Interactive Strategy of Systemic Change in Central and Eastern Europe. *Review of Political Economy* 2: 249–66.

Havinden, M. A. 1962. Agricultural Progress in Open-Field Oxfordshire. *Agricultural History Review* 9: 73–83.

Haxey, S. 1939. *Tory M.P.* New York: Harrison-Hilton.

Hechter, M. 1975. *Internal Colonialism: The Celtic Fringe in British National Development, 1536–1966*. Berkeley and Los Angeles: University of California Press.

Hechter, M., and W. Brustein. 1980. Regional Modes of Production and Patterns of State Formation in Western Europe. *American Journal of Sociology* 85: 1061–85.

Heckscher, E. F. 1964. *The Continental System*. Gloucester, Mass.: Peter Smith.

Hedley, B. 1977. *The Anarchical Society: A Study of Order in World Politics*. New York: Columbia University Press.

Hejeebu, S., and D. McCloskey. 1999. The Reproving of Karl Polanyi. *Critical Review* 13: 285–316.

Helmreich, E. C. 1938. *The Diplomacy of the Balkan Wars, 1912–1913*. Cambridge, Mass.: Harvard University Press.

Helms, C. M. 1984. *Iraq: Eastern Flank of the Arab World*. Washington: Brookings Institution.

Henderson, W. O. 1958. *The State and the Industrial Revolution in Prussia: 1740–1870*. Liverpool: Liverpool University Press.

Herbert, U. 1990. *A History of Foreign Labor in Germany, 1880–1980: Seasonal Workers, Forced Laborers, Guest Workers*, trans. William Templer. Ann Arbor: University of Michigan Press.

Herndon, J. S. 1983. British Perceptions of Soviet Military Capability, 1935–9. In W. Mommsen and L. Kettenacker, eds., *The Fascist Challenge and the Policy of Appeasement*. London: George Allen & Unwin.

Herr, R. 1977. Spain. In D. Spring, ed., *European Landed Elites in the Nineteenth Century*. Baltimore: Johns Hopkins University Press.

Hertslet, S. E. 1891. *The Map of Europe by Treaty*. London: Harrison and Sons.

Hertz, F. 1947. War and National Character. *Contemporary Review* 171: 274–81.

Herz, J. H. 1959. *International Politics in the Atomic Age*. New York: Columbia University Press.

Hettne, B. 1999. Globalisation and the New Regionalism: The Second Great Transformation. In B. Hettne, A. Inotai, and O. Sunkel, eds., *Globalisation and the New Regionalism*. London: Macmillan.

Hexter, J. H. 1961. The Myth of the Middle Class in Tudor England. In J. H. Hexter ed., *Reappraisals in History*. Chicago: University of Chicago Press.

Heyer, F. 1969. *The Catholic Church from 1648 to 1870*. London: Adam & Charles Black.

Hickling, M. 1973. Worse Church-State Relations Feared in Yugoslavia. *British Weekly*, April 27.

Hilferding, R. 1910. *Finance Capital: A Study of the Latest Phase of Capitalist Development*, edited with an introduction by T. Bottomore from a translation by M. Watnick and S. Gordon. London: Routledge.

Hill, C. 1981. A Bourgeois Revolution? In J. G. A. Pocock, ed., *Three British Revolutions: 1641, 1688, 1776*. Princeton, N.J.: Princeton University Press.

Hill, D. J. 1905. *A History of Diplomacy in the International Development of Europe*, vol. 1: *The Struggle for Universal Empire*. New York: Longmans, Green.

Hilton, R. 1975. *English Peasantry in the Later Middle Ages*. Oxford: Oxford University Press.

Hilton, R. 1976. A Comment. In P. Sweezy et al., eds., *The Transition from Feudalism to Capitalism*. London: NLB.

Hilton, R. H. 1951. Y-eut-il une crise gènèrale de la fèodalitè? *Annales E.S.C.* 6: 23–30.

Hinsley, F. H. 1967. The Concept of Sovereignty and the Relations between States. *Journal of International Affairs* 21, no. 2: 242–52.

Hintze, O. 1962. The Emergence of the Democratic Nation-State. In H. Lubasz, ed., *The Development of the Modern State*. New York: Macmillan.

Hintze, O. 1975. Military Organization and the Organization of the State; and the Formation of States and Constitutional Development. In F. Gilbert, ed., *The Historical Essays of Otto Hintze*. New York: Oxford University Press.

Hirsch, J. 1999. Globalisation, Class, and the Question of Democracy. In L. Panitch and C. Leyes, eds., *Global Capitalism versus Democracy, Socialist Register 1999*. London: Merlin Press.

Hirschman, A. O. 1973. The Changing Tolerance for Income Inequality in the Course of Economic Development. *Quarterly Journal of Economics* 87: 543–66.

Hirslaire, R. 1945. Parties. In J.-A. Goris, ed., *Belgium*. Berkeley and Los Angeles: University of California Press.

Hirst, F. W. 1905. *Monopolies, Trusts and Kartells*. London: Methuen.

Hobbs, D. A. 1973. *Mass Political Violence*. New York: Wiley-Interscience.

Hobsbawm, E. 1962. *The Age of Revolution 1789–1848*. New York: Mentor.

Hobsbawm, E. 1964. *Labouring Men: Studies in the History of Labour*. London: Weidenfeld and Nicolson.

Hobsbawm, E. 1968. *Industry and Empire*. London: Weidenfeld and Nicolson.

Hobsbawm, E. 1985. The "New Unionism" Reconsidered. In W. J. Mommsen and H.-G. Husung, eds., *The Development of Trade Unionism in Great Britain and Germany, 1880–1914*. London: George Allen & Unwin.

Hobsbawm, E. 1990. *Nations and Nationalism since 1780: Programme, Myth, Reality*. Cambridge: Cambridge University Press.

Hobsbawm, E. 1996. *The Age of Extremes*. New York: Pantheon.

Hobsbawm, E., and G. Rudé. 1973. *Captain Swing*. Harmondsworth: Penguin.

Hobson, J. A. 1902. *Imperialism: A Study*. London: Allen and Unwin.

Hodgkin, T. 1956. *Nationalism in Colonial Africa*. London: Frederick Muller.

Hodgson, G. 1994. The Evolution of Socioeconomic Order in the Move to a Market Economy. *Review of Political Economy* 1: 387–404.

Hoffman, W. G. 1955. *British Industry, 1700–1950*, trans. W. O. Henderson and W. H. Chaloner. Oxford: Basil Blackwell.

Hoffmann, S. 1961. The Effects of World War II on French Society and Politics. *French Historical Studies* 2: 28–63.

Holborn, H. 1951. *The Political Collapse of Europe*. New York: Alfred A. Knopf.

Holborn, L. W. 1943, 1948. *War and Peace Aims of the United Nations*, 2 vols. Boston: World Peace Foundation.

Holland, S. 1979. Dependent Development: Portugal as Periphery. In D. Seers, B. Shaffer, and M.-L. Kiljunen, eds., *Underdeveloped Europe: Studies in Core-Periphery Relations*. Sussex: Harvester Press.

Holloway, J., and Sol Picciotto, eds. 1978. *State and Capital: A Marxist Debate*. Austin: University of Texas Press.

Horowitz, D. 1983. Dual Authority Politics. *Comparative Politics* 14: 329–50.

Hough, J. F. 1972. The Soviet System: Petrification or Pluralism? *Problems of Communism* 25–45.

Hough, J. F., and M. Fainsod. 1953. *How the Soviet Union Is Governed*, rev. ed. Cambridge, Mass.: Harvard University Press.

House, E. M. 1928. *The Intimate Papers of Colonel House*, vol. 4. Boston: Houghton and Mifflin.

Howard, M. 1961. *The Franco-Prussian War: The German Invasion of France, 1870–1871*. London: Rupert Hart-Davis.

Howard, M. 1972. *The Continental Commitment: The Dilemma of British Defense in the Era of the Two Wars*. London: Temple Smith.

Howard, M. 1981. British Military Preparations for the Second World War. In D. Dilks, ed., *Retreat from Power: Studies in Britain's Foreign Policy of the Twentieth Century*. London: Macmillan.

Hrushevsky, M. 1941. *A History of the Ukraine*. New Haven: Yale University Press.

Hudson, M. 1968. *The Precarious Republic: Political Modernization in Lebanon*. New York: Random House.

Hudson, M. C. 1977. *Arab Politics: The Search for Legitimacy*. New Haven: Yale University Press.

Hufton, O. H. 1974. *The Poor of Eighteenth-Century France, 1750–1789*. Oxford: Clarendon Press.

Hume, D. 1975. *The History of England*, abridged by R. Kilcup. Chicago: University of Chicago Press.

Hume, M. A. S. 1900. *Modern Spain*. London: Fisher Unwin.

Humphries, S. C. 1969. History, Economics, and Anthropology in the Thought of Karl Polanyi. *History and Theory* 8: 165–212.

Hunt, A. 1996. *Governance of the Consuming Passions: A History of Sumptuary Law*. Basingstoke: Macmillan.

Huntington, S. P. 1968. *Political Order in Changing Societies*. New Haven: Yale University Press.

Hyde, H. M. 1976. *Air Policy between the Wars, 1918–1939*. London: Heinemann.

Iliffe, J. 1979. *Modern History of Tanganyika*. Cambridge: Cambridge University Press.

Inkeles, A. 1950. Social Stratification and Mobility in the Soviet Union: 1940–1950. *American Sociological Review* 15: 465–79.

Inkeles, A. 1968. *Social Change in Soviet Russia*. Cambridge, Mass.: Harvard University Press.

Ironside, S. E. 1953. *Archangel, 1918–1919*. London: Constable.

Jackson, R. H. 1990. *Quasi-States: Sovereignty, International Relations and the Third World*. New York: Cambridge University Press.

Janics, K. 1975. Czechoslovakia's Magyar Minority. *Canadian Review of Studies of Nationalism* 3: 34–44.

Jankowski, J. P. 1979. Nationalism in Twentieth Century Egypt. *Middle East Review* 12: 37–48.

Jarman, L. 1963. *A Short History of Twentieth Century England*. New York: Mentor.

Jászi, O. 1929. *Dissolution of the Habsburg Monarchy*. Chicago: University of Chicago Press.

Jászi, O. 1969. *Revolution and Counter-Revolution in Hungary*. New York: H. Fertig.

Jelavich, B. 1983. *History of the Balkans*, vol. 1. London: Cambridge University Press.

Jelavich, C. 1958. *Tsarist Russia and Balkan Nationalism: Russian Influence on the Internal Affairs of Bulgaria and Serbia, 1879–1886*. Berkeley: University of California Press.

Jelavich, C. 1967. The Croatia Problem in the Habsburg Empire in the Nineteenth Century. *Austrian History Yearbook* 3: 83–115.

Jemolo, A. C. 1960. *Church and State in Italy, 1850–1950*. Oxford: Basil Blackwell.

Jessop, B. 1982. *The Capitalist State: Marxist Theories and Methods*. New York: New York University Press.

Jessop, B. 1990. *State Theory: Putting the Capitalist State in Its Place*. University Park: Penn State University Press.

Jevons, W. S. 1914. *The State in Relation to Labor*, 4th ed. London: Macmillan.

Johnson, A. A. 1979. *The Disappearance of the Small Landowner*. Fairfield, N.Y.: A. M. Kelly.

Johnson, C. 1966. *Revolutionary Change*. Boston: Little, Brown.

Johnson, P. 1994. The Welfare State. In R. C. Floud and D. N. McCloskey, eds., *The Economic History of Britain since 1700*, vol. 3: *1939–1992*. Pp. 284–317. Cambridge: Cambridge University Press.

Joll, J. 1955. *The Second International, 1889–1914*. London: Weidenfeld and Nicolson.

Jones, E. L. 1974. *Agriculture and the Industrial Revolution*. New York: Wiley.

Jones, G. S. 1975. Class Struggle and the Industrial Revolution. *New Left Review* 90: 35–69.

Jörberg, L. 1973. The Industrial Revolution in the Nordic Countries. In C. M. Cipolla, ed., *The Fontana Economic History of Europe*, vol. 4, part 2: *The Emergence of Industrial Societies*. Glasgow: William Collins Sons.

Jorgenson, D. W. 1966. Testing Alternative Theories of the Development of a Dual Economy. In I. Adelman and E. Thornbecke, eds., *The Theory and Design of Economic Development*. Baltimore: Johns Hopkins University Press.

Joyce, P. 1980. *Work, Society and Politics: The Culture of the Factory in Later Victorian England*. New Brunswick, N.J.: Rutgers University Press.

Kaelble, H. 1985. *Social Mobility in the 19th and 20th Centuries*. Leamington Spa, Warwickshire: Berg.

Kaiser, D. 1990. *Politics and War: European Conflicts from Philip to Hitler*. Cambridge, Mass.: Harvard University Press.

Kalecki, M. 1971. Political Aspects of Full Employment. In M. Kalecki, *Selected Essays on the Dynamics of the Capitalist Economy*. Pp. 138–45. Cambridge: Cambridge University Press.

Kantorowicz, E. H. 1957. *The King's Two Bodies*. Princeton, N.J.: Princeton University Press.

Karamzin, N. M. 1959. *Karamzin's Memoir on Ancient and Modern Russia*, ed. R. Pipes. Cambridge, Mass.: Harvard University Press.

Katkov, G. 1967. *Russia 1917: The February Revolution*. New York: Harper and Row.

Katznelson, I. 1986. Working-Class Formation: Constructing Cases and Comparisons. In I. Katznelson and A. R. Zolberg, eds., *Working-Class Formation: Nineteenth-Century Patterns in Western Europe and the United States*. Princeton, N.J.: Princeton University Press.

Katznelson, I. 1997. The Subtle Politics of Developing Emergency: Political Science as Liberal Guardianship. In N. Chomsky et al., eds., *The Cold War and the*

University: Toward an Intellectual History of the Postwar Years. Pp. 233–58. New York: New Press.

Katznelson, I., and Martin Shefter, eds. 2002. *Shaped by War and Trade: International Influences on American Political Development.* Princeton, N.J.: Princeton University Press.

Kautsky, J. H. 1980. *The Political Consequences of Modernization.* Huntington, N.Y.: Robert E. Krieger Publishing.

Kautsky, K. 1970 [1914]. On Imperialism. Reprinted in *New Left Review* 59: 41–46.

Kedourie, E. 1960. *Nationalism.* London: Hutchinson.

Keeble, S. C. 1990. *Britain and the Soviet Union, 1917–89.* New York: St. Martin's Press.

Keegan, J. 1989. *The Second World War.* Harmondsworth: Penguin.

Kehr, E. 1975. *Battleship Building and Party Politics in Germany.* Chicago: University of Chicago Press.

Kehr, E. 1977. *Economic Interest, Militarism, and Foreign Policy: Essays on German History,* ed. G. A. Craig. Berkeley: University of California Press.

Kelly, G. A., and C. W. Brown, eds. 1970. *Struggles in the State: Sources and Patterns of World Revolution.* New York: John Wiley and Sons.

Kendall, W. 1969. *The Revolutionary Movement in Britain, 1900–1921.* London: Weidenfeld and Nicolson.

Kende, I., et al. 1982. Wars since World War II until May 1982. *Transaktie* 2, no. 4.

Kennan, G. 1960. *Russia and the West under Lenin and Stalin.* New York: Mentor Books.

Kennedy, P. 1980. *The Rise of the Anglo-German Antagonism, 1860–1914.* London: Allen & Unwin.

Kennedy, P. 1981. *The Realities behind Diplomacy: Background Influences on British External Policy, 1865–1980.* Glasgow: William Collins & Co.

Kennedy, P. 1986. Appeasement. In G. Martel, ed., *The Origins of the Second World War Reconsidered: The A. J. P. Taylor Debate after Twenty-Five Years.* Boston: Allen and Unwin.

Kennedy, P. 1987. *The Rise and Fall of the Great Powers: Economic and Military Conflict from 1500–2000.* New York: Vintage.

Keohane, R. O., and R. Nye. 1972. *Transnational Relations and World Politics.* Cambridge, Mass.: Harvard University Press.

Kern, R., ed. 1973. *The Caciques: Oligarchical Politics and the System of Caciquismo in the Luso-Hispanic World.* Albuquerque: University of New Mexico Press.

Kerr, C. 1954. Balkanization of Labor Markets. In W. Bakke et al., eds., *Labor Mobility and Economic Opportunity.* New York: Wiley and Sons.

Kesselman, M. 1973. Order or Movement? The Literature of Political Development as Ideology. *World Politics* 26: 139–54.

Kettle, M. 1981. *The Allies and the Russian Collapse, March 1917–March 1918.* London: André Deutsch.

Keynes, J. M. 1988 [1920]. *The Economic Consequences of the Peace.* Harmondsworth: Penguin.

Kieniewicz, S. 1948–1949. The Social Visage of Poland in 1848. *Slavonic and East European Review* 27: 91–105.

Kiernan, V. 1957. Foreign Mercenaries and Absolute Monarchy. *Past and Present* 11 (April): 66–86.

Kimche, J. 1968. *The Unfought Battle*. New York: Stein and Day.

Kinder, H., and W. Hilgemann. 1978. *The Anchor Atlas of World History*, vol. 2. Garden City, N.Y.: Anchor Books.

Kindleberger, C. 1964. *Economic Growth in France and Britain, 1851–1950*. Cambridge, Mass.: Harvard University Press.

Kindleberger, C. 1967. *Europe's Postwar Growth: The Role of Labor Supply*. Cambridge, Mass.: Harvard University Press.

Kindleberger, C. 1984. *Financial History of Western Europe*. London: Allen and Unwin.

Kindleberger, C. P. 1973. *The World in Depression, 1929–1939*. Berkeley: University of California Press.

King, B. 1899. *A History of Italian Unity*, 2 vols. London: J. Nisbet.

Kinross, L. P. B. 1977. *The Ottoman Centuries: The Rise and Fall of the Turkish Empire*. New York: Morrow Quill.

Kirchheimer, O. 1966. The Transformation of the Western European Party Systems. In J. Lapalombara and M. Weiner, eds., *Political Parties and Political Development*. Princeton, N.J.: Princeton University Press.

Kitchen, Martin. 1968. *The German Officer Corps, 1890–1914*. Oxford: Clarendon.

Kjekshus, H. 1996. *Ecology Control and Economic Development in African History: The Case of Tanganyika, 1850–1950*. London: James Currey.

Kleiman, A. 1970. *Foundations of British Policy in the Arab World: The Cairo Conference of 1921*. Baltimore: Johns Hopkins University Press.

Kochanowicz, J. 1993. Transition to Market in Comparative Perspectives: A Historian's Point of View. In K. Poznanski, ed., *Stabilization and Privatization in Poland: The Economic Analysis of Shock Therapy*. Boston: Kluwer.

Koenig, H. C. ed. 1943. *Principles for Peace*. Washington: N.C.W.C.

Kofos, E. 1975. *Greece and the Eastern Crisis 1875–1878*. Thessaloniki: Institute for Balkan Studies.

Kohn, H. 1932. *Nationalism and Imperialism in the Hither East*, trans. M. Green. London: George Routledge and Sons.

Kohn, H. 1955. *Nationalism: Its Meaning and History*. Princeton, N.J.: Princeton University Press.

Kohn, H. 1961. *The Habsburg Empire, 1804–1918*. Princeton, N.J.: Van Nostrand.

Kokoschka, O. 1974. *My Life*. London: Thames & Hudson.

Korbonski, A. 1970. Theory and Practice of Integration: The Case of Comecon. *International Organization* 24: 942–77.

Kosminsky, E. A. 1956. *Studies in the Agrarian History of England in the Thirteenth Century*, ed. R. H. Hilton, trans. R. Kisch.

Kossman, E. H. 1978. *The Low Countries, 1780–1940*. London: Oxford University Press.

Krasner, S. D. 1977. *Defending the National Interest*. Princeton, N.J.: Princeton University Press.

Krejci, J., and V. Velimsky. 1981. *Ethnic and Political Nations in Europe*. London: CroomHelm.

Krey, A. C. 1922. The International State of the Middle Ages: Some Reasons for Its Failure. *American Historical Review* 28, no. 1: 1–12.

Kuczynski, J. 1944. *A Short History of Labour Conditions under Industrial Capitalism*, vol. 2. London: F. Muller.

Kulischer, E. M. 1948. *Europe on the Move: War and Population Changes, 1917–47*. New York: Columbia University Press.

Kumar, K. 1983. Pre-Capitalist and Non-Capitalist Factors in the Development of Capitalism: Fred Hirsch and Joseph Schumpeter. In A. Ellis and K. Kumar, eds., *Dilemmas of Liberal Democracies*. London: Tavistock.

Kurth, J. R. 1979. The Political Consequences of the Product Cycle. *International Organization* 33: 1–34.

Kuznets, S. 1964. *Postwar Economic Growth: Four Lectures*. Cambridge, Mass.: Belknap Press of Harvard University Press.

Kuznets, S. 1966. *Modern Economic Growth*. New Haven: Yale University Press.

Kuznets, S. 1971. *Economic Growth of Nations: Total Output and Production Statistics*. Cambridge, Mass.: Harvard University Press.

Labrousse, E. 1933. *Esquisse du mouvement des prix et des revenus en France au xviiie siècle*, vol. 2. Paris: Librairie Dalloz.

Ladas, S. P. 1932. *The Exchange of Minorities: Bulgaria, Greece and Turkey*. New York: Macmillan.

Laeyendecker, L. 1972. The Netherlands. In H. Mol, ed., *Western Religion*. The Hague: Mouton.

Laird, R. D. 1970. *The Soviet Paradigm*. New York: Free Press.

Lammers, D. N. 1966. *Explaining Munich: The Search for Motive in British Policy*. Stanford: Hoover Institute.

Lampe, J. R., and M. R. Jackson. 1982. *Balkan Economic History, 1550–1950*. Bloomington: Indiana University Press.

Landes, D. S. 1954. Social Attitudes, Entrepreneurship and Economic Development: A Comment. *Explorations in Entrepreneurial History* 6, no. 4 (May): 245–72.

Landes, D. S. 1969. *The Unbound Prometheus: Technological Change and Industrial Development in Western Europe from 1750 to the Present*. Cambridge: Cambridge University Press.

Landy, P. 1961. Reforms in Yugoslavia. *Problems of Communism* (Nov.–Dec.).

Lane, D. 1971. *The End of Inequality? Social Stratification under State Socialism*. Harmondsworth: Penguin.

Langer, W. L. 1931. *European Alliances and Alignments, 1871–1890*. New York: Alfred A. Knopf.

Langer, W. L. 1969. *Political and Social Upheaval 1832–1852*. New York: Harper Torchbooks.

Laquer, W. 1992. *Europe in Our Time*. Harmondsworth: Penguin.

Laski, H. 1940. *Where Do We Go from Here?* New York: Viking.

Lasswell, H. D. 1958. *Politics: Who Gets What, When, How*. New York: Meridian Books.

Laveleye, E. de. 1887. *The Balkan Peninsula*. London: T. F. Unwin.

League of Nations. 1926. *Health Organization Handbook Series No. 6: Official Statistics of the Scandinavian Countries and the Baltic Republics*. Geneva: United Nations.

League of Nations. 1946. *Raw Materials Problems and Policies*. Geneva: United Nations.

Lefebvre, G. 1974. *The Coming of the French Revolution*, trans. R. R. Palmer. Princeton, N.J.: Princeton University Press.

Leger-Sivard, R. 1989. *World Military and Social Expenditures 1987–88*. New York: Public Affairs Committee.

Leitzel, J. 1997. Lessons of the Russian Economic Transition. *Problems of Post-Communism* 44: 49–57.

Lenin, V. I. 1939a. *Imperialism, the Highest Stage of Capitalism: An Outline*. New York: International.

Lenin, V. I. 1939b. *Lenin on Britain: A Compilation*, introduction by H. Pollitt. New York: International.

Lenin, V. I. 1967 [1899]. *The Development of Capitalism in Russia*. Moscow: Progress.

Lenski, G. E. 1966. *Power and Privilege: A Theory of Social Stratification*. New York: McGraw-Hill.

Lentin, A. 1984. *Guilt at Versailles: Lloyd George and the Pre-History of Appeasement*. Leicester: Leicester University Press.

Leslie, R. F. 1963. *Reform and Insurrection in Russian Poland, 1856–1865*. London: Athlone Press.

Leslie, R. F. 1969. *Polish Politics and the Revolution of November 1830*. Westport: Greenwood Press.

Leslie, R. F. 1980. *The History of Poland since 1863*. Cambridge: Cambridge University Press.

Levy, H. 1927. *Monopolies, Cartels and Trusts in British Industry*. London: St. Martin's Press.

Levy, J. S. 1983. *War in the Modern Great Power System, 1495–1975*. Lexington: University Press of Kentucky.

Lévy, M. 1951–52. *Historie èconomique et sociale de la France depuis 1848*. Paris: Les Cours de Droit, Institut d'Etudes Politiques.

Lewis, W. A. 1972. The Historical Record of International Capital Movements to 1913. Pp. 27–58. In J. H. Dunning, ed., *International Investment: Selected Readings*. Harmondsworth: Penguin.

Lewis, W. A. 1978a. *Growth and Fluctuation, 1870–1913*. London: George Allen & Unwin.

Lewis, W. A. 1978b. *The Evolution of the International Economic Order*. Princeton, N.J.: Princeton University Press.

Lichtheim, G. 1975. *A Short History of Socialism*. London: Fontana.

Lie, J. 1991. Embedding Polanyi's Market Society. *Sociological Perspectives* 34: 219–35.

Lie, J. 1993. Visualizing the Invisible Hand: The Social Origins of "Market Society" in England, 1550–1750. *Politics & Society* 21: 275–306.

Liefmann, R. 1933. *Cartels, Concerns and Trusts*. New York: E. P. Dutton and Company, Inc.

Linden, C. A. 1966. *Kruschev and the Soviet Leadership, 1957–1964*. Baltimore: Johns Hopkins University Press.

Linz, J. J. 1970. An Authoritarian Regime: Spain. In E. Allardt and S. Rokkan, eds., *Mass Politics: Studies in Political Sociology*. New York: Free Press.

Lipietz, A. 1985. *Mirages and Miracles: The Crisis of Global Fordism*. London: Verso.

Lipietz, A. 1992. *Towards a New Economic Order: Postfordism, Ecology and Democracy*. London: Polity Press.

Lipski, J. J. 1989–90. In Defence of Socialism. *Across Frontiers* (Fall/Winter): 19–21.

Lis, C., and H. Soly. 1979. *Poverty and Capitalism in Pre-Industrial Europe.* Sussex: Harvestor Press.

Liska, G. 1957. *The International Equilibrium.* Cambridge, Mass.: Harvard University Press.

List, F. 1885. *The National System of Political Economy: International Commerce, Commercial Policy, and the German Customs Union*, trans. S. S. Lloyd. London: Longmans, Green.

Livermore, H. V. 1947. *A History of Portugal.* Cambridge: Cambridge University Press.

Lloyd George, D. 1923. *Where Are We Going?* New York: George H. Doran.

Lloyd George, D. 1938. *The Truth about the Peace Treaties*, vol. 1. London: Victor Gollancz.

Lobanov-Rostovsky, A. 1933. *Russia and Europe, 1789–1825.* New York: Macmillan.

Lord, M. J., and G. R. Boye. 1991. The Determinants of International Trade in Latin America's Commodity Exports. In Miguel Urrutia, ed., *Long-Term Trends in Latin American Economic Development.* Pp. 117–56. Washington, D.C.: Inter-American Development Bank.

Lot, F. 1931. *The End of the Ancient World and the Beginning of the Middle Ages.* New York: Alfred A. Knopf.

Lovell, J. 1985. The Significance of the Great Dock Strike of 1889 in British Labour History. In W. J. Mommsen and H.-G. Husung, eds., *The Development of Trade Unionism in Great Britain and Germany, 1880–1914.* London: George Allen and Unwin.

Luck, J. M. 1985. *A History of Switzerland.* Palo Alto: SPOSS.

Luke, H. 1955. *The Old Turkey and the New: From Byzantium to Ankara.* London: G. Bles.

Lutz, R. H. 1934. *The Causes of the German Collapse in 1918.* Stanford, Calif.: Stanford University Press.

Luxemburg, R. 1913. *The Accumulation of Capital*, introduction by J. Robinson, translated by A. Schwartzchild. New York: Monthly Review Press.

Luxemburg, R. 1976. *The National Question: Selected Writings by Rosa Luxemburg*, ed. H. B. Davis. New York: Monthly Review Press.

Lyashenko, P. I. 1949. *History of the National Economy of Russia to the 1917 Revolution.* New York: Macmillan.

Lyttelton, A. 1973. *The Seizure of Power: Fascism in Italy, 1919–1929.* London: Weidenfeld and Nicolson.

Macartney, C. A. 1934. *National States and National Minorities.* London: Oxford University Press.

Macartney, C. A. 1968. *The Habsburg Empire, 1790–1918.* London: Weidenfeld and Nicolson.

Macdonald, C. A. 1972. Economic Appeasement and the German "Moderates," 1937–1939. *Past and Present* 56: 105–35.

Macdonald, M. 1946. *The Republic of Austria, 1918–1934: A Study in the Failure of Democratic Government.* London: Oxford University Press.

Macdonald, W. 1921. The Growth of Trade Unionism since 1913. *International Labour Review.*

MacIver, R. M. 1932. *The Modern State.* London: Oxford University Press.

Mackenzie, D. 1984. *Russia: On the Eve of War and Revolution*. Princeton, N.J.: Princeton University Press.

Mackinder, H. J. 1904. The Geographical Pivot of History. *Geographical Journal* 23: 421–44.

Macshane, D. 1992. *International Labour and the Origins of the Cold War*. Oxford: Clarendon Press.

Maddison, A. 1964. *Economic Growth in the West*. New York: Twentieth Century Fund.

Maddison, A. 1983. A Comparison of Levels of GDP per Capita in Developed and Developing Countries, 1700–1980. *Journal of Economic History* 43: 27–41.

Maddison, A. 1989. Measuring European Growth: The Core and the Periphery. In E. Aerts and N. Valerio, eds., *Growth and Stagnation in the Mediterranean World in the 19th and 20th Centuries*. Leuven: University of Leuven Press.

Maddison, A. 1990. *The World Economy in the Twentieth Century*. Paris: Development Centre Studies.

Maddison, A. 1991. Economic and Social Conditions in Latin America, 1913–1950. In Miguel Urrutia, ed., *Long-Term Trends in Latin American Economic Development*. Pp. 1–22. Washington, D.C.: Inter-American Development Bank.

Madison, J. 1961. *The Federalist*. New York: New American Library.

Magdoff, H. 1960. *The Age of Imperialism*. New York: Monthly Review Press.

Maier, C. 1975. *Recasting Bourgeois Europe: Stabilization in France, Germany, and Italy in the Decade after World War I*. Princeton, N.J.: Princeton University Press.

Maier, C. 1978. The Politics of Productivity: Foundations of American International Economic Policy after World War II. In P. Katzenstein, ed., *Between Power and Plenty*. Madison: University of Wisconsin Press.

Mallinson, V. 1963. *Power and Politics in Belgian Education 1815 to 1961*. London: Heinemann.

Mandel, E. 1962. *Marxist Economic Theory*, vol. 2. New York: Monthly Review Press.

Mandel, E. 1978. *Late Capitalism*. London: Verso.

Mandel, E. 1986. *The Meaning of the Second World War*. London: Verso.

Mann, M. 1988. European Development: Approaching a Historical Explanation. In J. Baechler, J. A. Hall, and M. Mann, eds., *Europe and the Rise of Capitalism*. Oxford: Basil Blackwell.

Manning, B. 1965. The Nobles, the People, and the Constitution. In T. Ashton, ed., *Crisis in Europe, 1560–1660: Essays from "Past and Present."* London: Routledge & Kegan Paul.

Maoz, Z. E., and N. Abdolali. 1989. Regime Types and International Conflict, 1916–1976. *Journal of Conflict Resolution* 33: 3–36.

March, J., and J. Olson. 1984. The New Institutionalism: Organizational Factors in Political Life. *American Political Science Review* 78: 734–49.

Marglin, S. A. 1974. What Do Bosses Do? The Origins and Functions of Hierarchy in Capitalist Production. *Review of Radical Political Economy* 6: 33–60.

Marglin, S. A., and J. B. Schor. 1990. *The Golden Age of Capitalism: Reinterpreting the Postwar Experience*. Oxford: Clarendon Press.

Marriot, J. A. R. 1913. *The French Revolution of 1848 in Its Economic Aspect*, vol. 1: *Louis Blanc's Organisation du travail*. Oxford: Clarendon.

Marsh, D. C. 1958. *The Changing Social Structure of England and Wales, 1871–1951*. London: Routledge.

Martin, C. 1969. *The Red Cross Shirt and the Cross of Savoy: The Story of Italy's Risorgimento*. New York: Dodd, Mead.

Martin, D. 1978. *A General Theory of Secularization*. New York: Harper and Row.

Martin, H.-P., and H. Schumann. 1997. *The Global Trap*. London: Zed.

Marwick, A. 1974. *War and Social Change in the Twentieth Century: A Comparative Study of France, Germany, Russia and the United States*. New York: St. Martin's Press.

Marwick, A. 1980. *Image and Reality in Britain, France and the U.S.A. since 1930*. London: Collins.

Marx, K. 1952. *Class Struggles in France, 1848–1850*. Moscow: Progress Publishers.

Marx, K. 1963. *The Eighteenth Brumaire of Louis Bonaparte*. New York: International.

Marx, K. 1964. *Class Struggles in France, 1848–1850*. New York: International.

Marx, K. 1967. *Communist Manifesto*. London: Penguin.

Marx, K. 1968. Wages, Price, and Profit. In K. Marx and F. Engels, eds., *Selected Works*. London: Lawrence & Wishart.

Marx, K. 1970. *A Contribution to the Critique of Political Economy*. Moscow: Progress.

Marx, K. 1990. *Capital*, vol. 1. London: Penguin.

Marx, K. 1991. *Capital*, vol. 3. London: Penguin.

Marx, K., and F. Engels. 1939. *The Revolution in Spain*. New York: International.

Marx, K., and F. Engels. 1968. *Selected Works*, vol. 3. London: Lawrence & Wishart.

Masaryk, T. G. 1967. *Spirit of Russia: Studies in History, Literature, Philosophy*, vol. I, trans. Eden Paul and Cedar Paul. London: Allen and Unwin.

Masterman, C. F. G. 1923. *England after the War*. New York: Harcourt, Brace.

Masters, R. D. 1964. World Politics as a Primitive System. *World Politics* 16 (July): 595–619.

Mather, F. C. 1975. The General Strike of 1842: A Study in Leadership, Organisation and the Threat of Revolution during the Plug Plot Disturbances. In R. Quinault and J. Stevenson, eds., *Popular Protest and Public Order*. London: St. Martin's Press.

Mathias, P. 1983. *The First Industrial Nation: An Economic History of Britain, 1700–1914*, 2nd ed. New York: Methuen.

Mattingly, G. 1955. *Renaissance Diplomacy*. Baltimore: Penguin Books.

Maurice, C. E. 1887. *The Revolutionary Movement of 1848–9 in Italy, Austria-Hungary, and Germany*. London: George Bell and Sons.

Maxwell, C., ed. 1923. *Irish History from Contemporary Sources*. London: Allen and Unwin.

Mayer, A. J. 1967. *Politics and Diplomacy of Peacemaking: Containment and Counter-revolution at Versailles, 1918–1919*. New York: Alfred A. Knopf.

Mayer, A. J. 1969. *The Political Origins of the New Diplomacy, 1917–1918*. New York: H. Fertig.

Mayer, A. J. 1981. *The Persistence of the Old Regime: Europe to the Great War*. New York: Pantheon.

Maynard, C. C. 1928. *The Murmansk Venture*. London: Hodder and Stoughton.

Mazour, A. 1937. *The First Russian Revolution, 1825. The Decembrist Movement: Its Origins, Development and Significance*. Berkeley: University of California Press.

Mazour, A. 1951. *Russia: Past and Present*. New York: Van Nostrand.

Mazower, M. 1998. *The Dark Continent: Europe's Twentieth Century*. London: Penguin.

Mazzini, G. 1877. Mazzini on the Eastern Question. *Fortnightly Review* 21: 559–79.

McCahill, M. 1981. Peerage Creations and the Changing Character of the British Nobility, 1750–1830. *English Historical Review* 96: 259–84.

McClellan, W. D. 1964. *Svetozar Markovic and the Origins of Balkan Socialism*. Princeton, N.J.: Princeton University Press.

McCloskey, D. N. 1981. *Enterprise and Trade in Victorian Britain: Essays in Historical Economics*. London: Allen and Unwin.

McHenry, D. E. 1940. *His Majesty's Opposition: Structure and Problems of the British Labour Party, 1931–1938*. Berkeley: University of California Press.

McKendrick, N., J. Brewer, and J. H. Plumb. 1982. *The Birth of a Consumer Society: The Commercialization of Eighteenth Century England*. London: Europa.

McKeown, T. J. 1991. The Foreign Policy of a Declining Power. *International Organization* 45: 257–79.

McLean, I. 1975. Popular Protest and Public Order: Red Clydeside, 1915–1919. In R. Quinault and J. Stevenson, eds., *Popular Protest and Public Order*. London: St. Martin's Press.

McMichael, P. 1996a. *Development and Social Change: A Global Perspective*. California: Pine Forge Press.

McMichael, P. 1996b. Globalization: Myths and Realities. *Rural Sociology* 61: 25–55.

McMillan, C. H. 1973. Factor Proportions and the Structure of Soviet Foreign Trade. *Association for Comparative Economic Studies Bulletin* 15: 57–81.

McNeill, W. H. 1974. *The Shape of European History*. London: Oxford University Press.

Meacham, S. 1972. "The Sense of an Impending Clash": English Working-Class Unrest before the First World War. *American Historical Review* 77: 1343–64.

Mearsheimer, J. 1990. Why We Will Miss the Cold War. *Atlantic Monthly* (August): 35–50.

Mearsheimer, J. 1994–95. The False Promise of International Institutions. *International Security* 19: 5–49.

Medlicott, W. N. 1963. The Coming of War in 1939. In W. N. Medlicott, ed., *From Metternich to Hitler: Aspects of British and Foreign History, 1814–1939*. New York: Barnes and Noble.

Medlicott, W. N. 1969. *Britain and Germany: The Search for Agreement 1930–1937*. London: Athlone Press.

Megaro, G. 1930. *Vittorio Alfieri: Forerunner of Italian Nationalism*. New York: Columbia University Press.

Meier, G. E., ed. 1970. *Leading Issues in Economic Development*. London: Oxford University Press.

Melko, M. 1973. *52 Peaceful Societies*. Ontario: CPRI Press.

Menderhausen, H. 1943. *The Economics of War*, rev. ed. New York: Prentice-Hall.

Mendras, H. 1970. *The Vanishing Peasant*. Cambridge, Mass.: Harvard University Press.

Meranto, P., O. Meranto, and M. Lippman. 1985. *Guarding the Ivory Tower: Repression and Rebellion in Higher Education*. Denver, Colo.: Lucha.

Meredith, H. O. 1904. *Protection in France*. London: P. S. King.

Mergadout, T. W. 1979. *French Peasants in Revolt: The Insurrection of 1851*. Princeton, N.J.: Princeton University Press.

Meyer, E. 1924. *Kleine Schriften*, vol. 1. 2nd ed. Berlin: Cotta.

Meyer, H. C. 1955. *Mitteleuropa in German Thought and Action, 1815–1945*. The Hague: Martinus Nijhoff.

Meyers, R. 1983. British Imperial Interests and the Appeasement Policy. In W. J. Mommsen and L. Kettenacker, eds., *The Fascist Challenge and the Appeasement Policy*. London: Allen and Unwin.

Meynial, E. 1926. Roman Law. In G. C. Crump and E. F. Jacob, eds. *The Legacy of the Middle Ages*. Oxford: Oxford University Press.

Michael, L. G. 1929. *Survey of Europe: The Danubian Basin*, Part 2: *Romania, Bulgaria and Yugoslavia*. Technical Bulletin no. 126. Washington, D.C.: U.S. Department of Agriculture.

Michel, H., and B. Mirkine-Guetzewitch, eds. 1954. *Les Idées politiques et sociales de la résistance*. Paris: Presses Universitaires de France.

Michelet, J. 1846. *The People*, trans. C. Cocks. London: Longman, Brown, Green.

Michels, R. 1914. *Probleme der Sozialphilosophie*. Leipzig and Berlin: B. G. Teubner.

Michels, R. 1949. *Political Parties*, trans. Eden Paul and Cedar Paul. Glencoe: Free Press.

Mickiewicz, A. 1833. *The Books of the Polish Nation and the Pilgrimage of the Polish Nation*, trans. L. Szyrma. London: J. Ridgeway.

Midlarsky, M. 1975. *On War: Political Violence in the International System*. New York: Free Press.

Mijatovich, C. 1917. *The Memoirs of a Balkan Diplomat*. London: Cassell.

Miliukov, P. N. 1917. The Representative System in Russia. In J. D. Duff, ed., *Russian Realities and Problems*. Cambridge: Cambridge University Press.

Miliukov, P. N. 1922. *Russia Today and Tomorrow*. New York: Macmillan.

Miller, M. B. 1994. *Shanghai on the Métro: Spies, Intrigue, and the French between the Wars*. Berkeley and Los Angeles: University of California Press.

Miller, W. 1936. *The Ottoman Empire and Its Successors*. Cambridge: Cambridge University Press.

Milner, H. 1991. The Assumption of Anarchy in International Relations Theory. *Review of International Studies* 17 (January): 67–85.

Milosz, C. 1968. *Native Realm*. New York: Doubleday.

Milward, A. S. 1984. *The Reconstruction of Western Europe, 1945–1951*. Berkeley and Los Angeles: University of California Press.

Ministry of Reconstruction. 1918. *Reconstruction Problems*, no. 1, Report of the Machinery of Government Committee. London: H. M. Stationary Office.

Mitchell, B. R. 1975. *European Historical Statistics 1750–1970*, abridged ed. New York: Columbia University Press.

Mitrany, D. 1931. *The Land and the Peasant in Romania*. New Haven: Yale University Press.

Mitrany, D. 1936. *The Effect of the War in Southeastern Europe*. New Haven: Yale University Press.

Mizsei, K. 1991. The "Small Transformation": The Historical Process of Reform in Eastern Europe. In M. Mendell and D. Salée, eds., *The Legacy of Karl*

Polanyi: Market, State and Society at the End of the Twentieth Century. New York: St. Martin's Press.

Mokyr, J. 1976. *Industrialization in the Low Countries, 1795–1850.* New Haven: Yale University Press.

Mommsen, W. J. 1973. Domestic Factors in German Foreign Policy before 1914. *Central European History* 6, no. 1 (March): 3–43.

Montagu, L. 1970. *More Equal Than Others: The Changing Fortunes of the British and European Aristocracies.* London: Michael Joseph.

Moody, J. N., et al., eds. 1953. *Church and Society: Catholic Social and Political Thought and Movements 1789–1950.* New York: Arts.

Moore, B. J. 1958. *Political Power and Social Theory: Six Studies.* Cambridge, Mass.: Harvard University Press.

Moore, B. J. 1966. *Social Origins of Democracy and Dictatorship: Lord and Peasant in the Making of the Modern World.* Boston: Beacon.

Morgan, K. O. 1979. *Consensus and Disunity: The Lloyd George Coalition Government, 1918–1922.* Oxford: Clarendon Press.

Morgan, O. S., ed. 1969. *Agricultural Systems of Middle Europe.* New York: AMS Press.

Morgenthau, H. J. 1948. *Politics among Nations: The Struggle for Power and Peace.* New York: Alfred A. Knopf.

Morris, B. 1991. *The Roots of Appeasement: The British Weekly Press and Nazi Germany during the 1930s.* London: Frank Cass.

Morris, C. T., and I. Adelman. 1988. *Comparative Patterns of Economic Development, 1850–1914.* Baltimore: Johns Hopkins University Press.

Morris, C. T., and I. Adelman. 1989. Nineteenth-Century Development Experience and Lessons for Today. *World Development* 17, no. 9: 1417–32.

Morris, D. R. 1973. *The Washing of the Spears.* London: Cape.

Morris, R. J. 1979. *Class and Class Consciousness in the Industrial Revolution, 1780–1850.* London: Macmillan.

Morse, E. L. 1971. Transnational Economic Processes. *International Organization* 25: 373–97.

Morse, E. L. 1976. *Modernization and the Transformation of International Relations.* New York: Free Press.

Mosca, G. 1939 [1896]. *The Ruling Class,* trans. H. D. Kahn. New York: McGraw-Hill.

Motlmann, J. 1986. Church and State in Germany: West and East. *Annals of the American Academy of Political and Social Science* 483: 110–18.

Mouzelis, N., and M. Attaldes. 1971. Greece. In M. Scotford Archer and S. Giner, eds., *Contemporary Europe: Class, Status, Power.* London: Weidenfeld and Nicolson.

Mowat, R. B. 1923. *A History of European Diplomacy, 1815–1914.* London: Edward Arnold.

Mowat, R. B. 1927. *A History of European Diplomacy, 1914–1925.* New York: Longman, Green.

Munger, F. 1981. Contentious Gatherings in Lancashire, England, 1750–1830. In L. A. Tilly and C. Tilly, eds., *Class Conflict and Collective Action.* Beverly Hills, Calif.: Sage.

Munting, R. 1982. *The Economic Development of the USSR*. London: CroomHelm.

Murray, W. 1979. Munich, 1938: The Military Confrontation. *Journal of Strategic Studies* 2: 282–302.

Murray, W. 1984. *Change in the European Balance of Power*. Princeton, N.J.: Princeton University Press.

Muskett, P. 1984. The East Anglian Agrarian Riots of 1822. *Agricultural History Review* 32: 1–13.

Musset, L. 1965. *Les Invasions: Les Vagues germaniques*. Paris: Presses Universitaires de France.

Musson, A. E. 1972. *British Trade Unions, 1800–1875*. London: Macmillan.

Musson, A. E. 1974. *Trade Union and Social History*. London: Frank Cass.

Nadal, J. 1973. The Failure of the Industrial Revolution in Spain 1830–1914. In C. M. Cipolla, ed., *The Fontana Economic History of Europe*, vol. 2: *Emergence of Industrial Societies*. Glasgow: William Collins Sons.

Nader, Laura. 1997. The Phantom Factor: Impact of the Cold War on Anthropology. In N. Chomsky et al., *The Cold War and the University: Toward an Intellectual History of the Postwar Years*. Pp. 107–46. New York: New Press.

Nagel, J. 1974. Inequality and Discontent: A Nonlinear Hypothesis. *World Politics* 26: 453–62.

Nagy-Talavera, N. M. 1970. *The Green Shirts and the Others: A History of Fascism in Hungary and Rumania*. Stanford, Calif.: Stanford University Press.

Nairn, T. 1981. *The Break-up of Britain*, 2nd ed. London: New Left.

Naschold, F. 1981. The Future of the Welfare State. In W. J. Mommsen, ed., *The Emergence of the Welfare State in Britain and Germany*. London: CroomHelm.

Naumann, F. 1916. *Mitteleuropa*. Berlin: G. Reimer.

Neale, R. S. 1968. Class and Class-Consciousness in Early Nineteenth-Century England: Three Classes or Five? *Victorian Studies* 12, no. 1: 5–25.

Neale, R. S. 1972. *Class and Ideology in the Nineteenth Century*. London: Routledge.

Neale, W. C. 1991. Society, State, and Market: A Polanyian View of Current Change and Turmoil in Eastern Europe. *Journal of Economic Issues* 25: 467–74.

Nelson, R. R., and G. Wright. 1995. The Erosion of US Technological Leadership as a Factor in Postwar Economic Convergence. In W. Baumol, R. R. Nelson, and E. N. Wolff, eds., *Convergence of Productivity: Cross-National Studies and Historical Evidence*. London: Oxford University Press.

Neufeld, M. F. 1961. *Italy, School for Awakening Countries: The Italian Labor Movement in Its Political, Social, and Economic Setting from 1800 to 1960*. New York: Cornell University Press.

Neumann, F. 1944. *Behemoth: The Structure and Practice of National Socialism, 1933–1944*. London: Oxford University Press.

Nicholson, H. 1966. *Diaries and Letter, 1930–1939*, ed. Nigel Nicholson. New York: Atheneum.

Niedhart, G. 1983. British Attitudes and Policies Towards the Soviet Union and International Communism, 1933–9. In W. Mommsen and L. Kettenacker, eds., *The Fascist Challenge and the Policy of Appeasement*. London: Allen and Unwin.

Nitzan, J. 1998. Differential Accumulation: A New Theory of Capital. *Review of International Political Economy* 5, no. 2: 169–217.

Nitzan, J. 2002. Regimes of Differential Accumulation: Mergers, Stagflation and the Logic of Globalization. *Review of International Political Economy* 8, no. 2: 226–74.

Nitzan, J., and S. Bichler. 2001. Going Global: Differential Accumulation and the Great U-Turn in South Africa and Israel. *Review of Radical Political Economics* 33, no. 1: 21–44.

Nolde, B. F. 1928. *Russia in the Economic War*. New Haven: Yale University Press.

North, D. C. 1981. *Structure and Change in Economic History*. New York: W. W. Norton.

North, D. C. 1990. *Institutions, Institutional Change, and Economic Performance*. Cambridge: Cambridge University Press.

North, D. C., and Paul Thomas. 1973. *The Rise of the Western World: A New Economic History*. London: Cambridge University Press.

Northedge, F. S. 1966. *The Troubled Giant: Britain among the Great Powers, 1916–1939*. New York: Praeger.

Nove, A. 1982. *An Economic History of the U.S.S.R.* Harmondsworth: Penguin.

Nowell, C. E. 1952. *A History of Portugal*. New York: Van Nostrand.

O'Ballance, E. 1966. *The Greek Civil War, 1944–1949*. New York: Praeger.

O'Brien, P. K. 1977. Agriculture and the Industrial Revolution. *Economic History Review* 30: 166–81.

O'Brien, P. K. 1982. European Economic Development: The Contribution of the Periphery. *Economic History Review* 35, no. 1: 1–18.

O'Connor, J. 1973. *The Fiscal Crisis of the State*. New York: St. Martin's Press.

Ogg, F. A. 1930. *Economic Development of Modern Europe*. New York: Macmillan.

O'Leary, C. 1962. *The Elimination of Corrupt Practices in British Elections, 1868–1911*. Oxford: Clarendon Press.

Olson, M. 1982. *The Rise and Decline of Nations*. New Haven: Yale University Press.

Oren, N. 1971. *Bulgarian Communism: The Road to Power, 1934–1944*. New York: Columbia University Press.

Organski, A. F. K. 1968. *World Politics*. New York: Alfred A. Knopf.

Osterud, O. 1978. *Agrarian Structure and Peasant Politics in Scandinavia*. Oslo: Universitetsforlaget.

Ovendale, R. 1975. *Appeasement and the English-Speaking World*. Cardiff: University of Wales Press.

Ovendale, R. 1983. Britain, the Dominions, and the Coming of the Second World War. In W. J. Mommsen and L. Kettenacker, eds., *The Fascist Challenge and the Appeasement Policy*. London: Allen & Unwin.

Packenham, R. A. 1992. *The Dependency Movement: Scholarship and Politics in Development Studies*. Cambridge, Mass.: Harvard University Press.

Paget, J. 1969. *Last Post: Aden*. London: Faber.

Pakenham, T. 1969. *The Year of Liberty: The Story of the Great Irish Rebellion of 1798*. London: Hodder and Stoughton.

Pallis, A. A. 1925a. Racial Migrations in the Balkans during the Years 1912–1924. *Geographical Journal* 66: 315–31.

Pallis, A. A. 1925b. *Statistical Study of the Racial Migrations of Macedonia and Thrace, 1912–24*. Athens.

Palmer, A. 1964. *The Penguin Dictionary of Modern History, 1789–1945*, 2nd ed. Harmondsworth: Penguin.

Palmer, A. 1983. *The Penguin Dictionary of Twentieth-Century History, 1900–1982*, 2nd ed. London: Penguin.

Palmer, R. R. 1944. The National Idea in France before the Revolution. *Journal of the History of Ideas* 1: 95–111.

Panitch, L. 1996. Rethinking the Role of the State. In J. H. Mittelman, ed., *Globalization: Critical Reflections*. Boulder: Lynne Rienner.

Papacosma, V. S. 1979. *The Military in Greek Politics: The 1909 Coup d'Etat*. Kent, Ohio: Kent State University.

Papadopoulos, G. 1969. *England and the Near East, 1896–1898*. Thessaloniki: Institute for Balkan Studies.

Pareto, V. 1917–19. *Traitè de sociologie gènèrale*. Paris: Payot.

Pareto, V. 1935. *The Mind and Society [Trattato di sociologia]*, trans. A. Bongiorno and A. Livingstone. New York: Harcourt, Brace.

Pareto, V. 1966 [1899]. *La Marèe socialiste*. In Pareto, *Mythes et idéologies*, ed. Giovanni Busino. Geneva: Droz.

Pareto, V. 1968. *The Circulation of the Elites: An Application of Theoretical Sociology*. Totowa, N.J.: Bedminster Press [1901].

Parker, G. 1988. *The Military Revolution: Military Innovation and the Rise of the West, 1500–1800*. Cambridge: Cambridge University Press.

Parker, R. A. C. 1969. *Europe 1919–1945*. London: Weidenfeld and Nicolson.

Parker, R. A. C. 1975. Economics, Rearmament, and Foreign Policy: The United Kingdom before 1939 – a Preliminary Study. *Journal of Contemporary History* 10: 637–47.

Parker, R. A. C. 1981. British Rearmament, 1936–9: Treasury, Trade Unions and Skilled Labour. *English Historical Review* 96: 306–43.

Parker, R. A. C. 1993. *Chamberlain and Appeasement*. London: Cambridge University Press.

Parkin, F. 1969. Class Stratification in Socialist Societies. *British Journal of Sociology* 20: 355–74.

Parkin, F. 1971. Yugoslavia. In M. Scotford Archer and S. Giner, eds., *Contemporary Europe: Class, Status, Power*. London: Weidenfeld and Nicolson.

Parmalee, M. 1924. *Blockade and Sea Power: The Blockade, 1914–1919, and Its Significance for a World State*. London: Hutchinson.

Parsons, T. 1951. The Processes of Change in Social Systems. In T. Parsons, ed., *The Social System*. New York: Free Press.

Parsons, T. 1966. *Societies: Evolutionary and Comparative Perspectives*. Englewood Cliffs, N.J.: Prentice-Hall.

Passelecq, F. 1928. *Déportation et travail forcè des ouvrierd et la population civile de la Belgique occupée*. Paris: Presses Universitaires de France.

Paton, H. J. 1924–27. *Papers Relating to the Foreign Relations of the United States: The Paris Peace Conference, 1919*, vol. 4. Washington: U.S. Department of State.

Paukert, F. 1973. Income Distribution at Different Levels of Development: A Survey of Evidence. *International Labour Review* 108: 97–125.

Pawelcznska, A. 1966. *The Dynamics of Religious Changes in the Country*. Warsaw: P.W.N.

Paxton, R. O. 1972. *Vichy France: Old Guard and New Order, 1940–1944*. New York: Alfred A. Knopf.

Payne, S. 1967. *Politics and the Military in Modern Spain.* Stanford, Calif.: Stanford University Press.

Payne, S. G. 1961. *Falange: A History of Spanish Fascism.* Stanford, Calif.: Stanford University Press.

Payne, S. G. 1975. *Basque Nationalism.* Reno: University of Nevada Press.

Peacock, A. J. 1965. *Bread or Blood: A Study of the Agrarian Riots in East Anglia in 1816.* London: Victor Gollancz.

Pearson, R. 1983. *National Minorities in Eastern Europe, 1848–1945.* London: Macmillan.

Pech, S. Z. 1969. *The Czech Revolution of 1848.* Chapel Hill: University of North Carolina Press.

Peden, G. C. 1979. *British Rearmament and the Treasury, 1932–39.* Edinburgh: Scottish Academic Association.

Peden, G. C. 1983. Keynes, the Economics of Rearmament and Appeasement. In W. J. Mommsen and L. Kettenacker, eds., *The Fascist Challenge and the Policy of Appeasement.* London: Allen and Unwin.

Peiter, Henry. 1976. Institutions and Attitudes: The Consolidation of the Business Community in Bourgeois France, 1880–1914. *Journal of Social History* 9, no. 4: 510–25.

Pelling, H. 1963. *A History of British Trade Unionism.* London: Pelican.

Pelling, H. 1968. *Popular Politics and Society in Late Victorian Britain.* New York: Macmillan.

Pempel, T. J. 1998. *Regime Shift: Comparative Dynamics of the Japanese Political Economy.* New York: Cornell University Press.

Perkin, H. 1969. *The Origins of Modern English Society, 1780–1889.* London: Routledge & Kegan Paul.

Perlmutter, A. 1970. The Myth of the Myth of the New Middle Class. *Comparative Studies in Society and History* 12: 14–30.

Perrot, Michelle. 1986. On the Formation of the French Working Class. In Ira Katznelson and Aristide R. Zolberg, eds., *Working-Class Formation: Nineteenth-Century Patterns in Western Europe and the United States.* Pp. 71–110. Princeton, N.J.: Princeton University Press.

Perroy, E. 1970. At the Origin of a Contracted Economy: The Crises of the 14th Century. In Rondo Cameron, ed., *Essays in French Economic History.* Homewood, Ill.: R. D. Irwin.

Perthes, J. 1903. *Central Europe.* New York: Heineman.

Petit-Dutaillis, C. 1947. *Les Communes francaises, caractéres et Revolution des origines aux xviiie siècle.* Paris: A. Michel.

Petrie, C. 1944. *Diplomatic History.* London: Hollis and Carten.

Petrovich, M. B. 1976. *A History of Modern Serbia, 1804–1918,* vol. 1. New York: Harcourt, Brace, Jovanovich.

Philips, D. 1975. Riots in the Black Country, 1835–1869. In R. Quinault and J. Stevenson, eds., *Popular Protest and Public Order.* London: St. Martin's Press.

Phyllis, D., and W. A. Cole. 1967. *British Economic Growth, 1688–1959: Trends and Structure,* 2nd ed. Cambridge: Cambridge University Press.

Pinkney, D. H. 1964. The Crowd in the French Revolution of 1830. *American Historical Review* 70: 1–17.

Piotrowski, R. 1933. *Cartels and Trusts*. London: Allen and Unwin.

Pirenne, H. 1900–1926. *Histoire de Belgique*, vol. 4. Brussels: Lamartin.

Pirenne, H. 1958. *A History of Europe*. Garden City, N.Y.: Doubleday.

Pirenne, H. 1969. *Economic and Social History of Medieval Europe*. New York: Harcourt, Brace.

Plumb, J. H. 1967. *The Growth of Political Stability in England, 1675–1725*. Harmondsworth: Penguin.

Poggi, G. 1978. *The Development of the Modern State: A Sociological Introduction*. Stanford, Calif.: Stanford University Press.

Polanyi, K. 1944. *The Great Transformation: The Political and Economic Origins of Our Time*. New York: Farrar and Rinehart.

Polanyi, K. 1945. Universal Capitalism or Regional Planning? *London Quarterly of World Affairs* 10: 86–91.

Polanyi, K. 1947. Our Obsolete Market Mentality. *Commentary* 3: 109–17.

Polanyi, K. 1971. *Primitive, Archaic, and Modern Economies: Essays of Karl Polanyi*, ed. G. Dalton. Boston: Beacon.

Pollard, S. 1968. *The Genesis of Modern Management: A Study of the Industrial Revolution in Great Britain*. Harmondsworth: Penguin.

Ponting, C. 1989. *1940: Myth and Reality*. London: Hamish Hamilton.

Portes, A. 1985. Latin American Class Structures: Their Composition and Change during the Last Decades. *Latin American Research Review* 20, no. 3: 7–40.

Postan, M. M. 1967. *An Economic History of Western Europe*. London: Methuen.

Potter, G. 1870. Strikes and Lockouts from the Workman's Point of View. *Contemporary Review* 15: 525–39.

Poulantzas, N. 1974. *Classes in Contemporary Capitalism*. London: New Left Books.

Poulantzas, N., and Ralph Miliband. 1973. The Problem of the Capitalist State. In Robin Blackburn, ed., *Ideology in Social Science*. Pp. 238–62. New York: Vintage.

Pounds, J. G. 1959. Economic Growth in Germany. In H. Aitken ed., *The State and Economic Growth*. New York: Social Science Research Council.

Powell, R. 1994. Anarchy in International Relations Theory: The Neorealist-Neoliberal Debate. *International Organization* 48, no. 2 (Spring): 313–44.

Poznanski, K. 1995. Institutional Perspectives on Post Communist Recession in Eastern Europe. In K. Poznanski, ed., *The Evolutionary Transition to Capitalism*. Boulder, Colo.: Westview.

Prazàk, A. 1928. The Slovak Sources of Kollár's Pan-Slavism. *Slavonic Review* 6: 579–92.

Prescott, J. R. V. 1965. *The Geography of Frontiers and Boundaries*. London: Hutchinson.

Pribicevic, B. 1959. *The Shop Stewards' Movement and Workers' Control 1910–1922*. Oxford: Blackwell.

Pribram, A. F. 1967. *The Secret Treaties of Austria-Hungary, 1879–1914*. New York: H. Fertig.

Price, R. 1972. *An Imperial War and the British Working Class*. London: Routledge and Kegan Paul.

Price, R. 1981. *An Economic History of Modern France, 1730–1914*. London: Macmillan.

Prothero, I. 1974. William Benbow and the "General Strike." *Past and Present* 63: 132–71.

Przeworski, A. 1979. The Material Bases of Consent. *Political Power and Social Theory.* 1: 21–63.

Puchala, D. J., and R. F. Hopkins. 1983. International Regimes: Lessons from Inductive Research. In S. Krasner, ed., *International Regimes.* Ithaca, N.Y.: Cornell University Press.

Pullan, B. 1968. Wage Earners and the Venetian Economy, 1550–1630. In B. Pullan, ed., *Crisis and Change in the Venetian Economy.* London: Methuen.

Rabb, T. 1975. *The Struggle for Stability in Early Modern Europe.* New York: Oxford University Press.

Randall, A., and A. Charlesworth. 1996. Industrial Protest, 1750–1850. In A. Charlesworth, D. Gilbert, A. Randall, H. Southall, and C. Wrigley, eds., *Atlas of Industrial Protest in Britain, 1750–1990.* London: Macmillan.

Reddaway, W. F., ed. 1950. *The Cambridge History of Poland,* vol. 2. Cambridge: Cambridge University Press.

Reddy, W. M. 1987. *Money and Liberty in Modern Europe: A Critique of Historical Understanding.* Cambridge: Cambridge University Press.

Reichert, R. W. 1969. *Crippled from Birth: German Social Democracy, 1844–1870.* Ames: Iowa State University Press.

Reid, A. J. 1992. *Social Classes and Social Relations in Britain, 1850–1914.* London: Macmillan.

Remak, J. 1967. *The Origins of World War One, 1871–1914.* New York: Holt, Rinehart and Winston.

Renner, K. 1902. *Der Kampf der Österreichischen Nationen um den Staat.* Leipzig and Vienna: Franz Deutike.

Retallack, J. 1988. *Notables of the Right: The Conservative Party and Political Mobilization in Germany 1876–1918.* Boston: Unwin-Hyman.

Riasanowsky, N. V. 1959. *Nicholas I and Official Nationality in Russia.* Berkeley and Los Angeles: University of California Press.

Ricardo, David. 1887. *Letters of David Ricardo to Thomas Robert Malthus.* Ed. James Bonaro. Oxford.

Rice, E. F. 1970. *The Foundations of Early Modern Europe 1460–1559.* New York: W. W. Norton.

Richards, A., and J. Waterbury. 1990. *The Political Economy of the Middle East: State, Class, and Economic Development.* Boulder, Colo.: Westview Press.

Richardson, C. O. 1973. French Plans for Allied Attacks on the Caucasus Oil Fields January–April, 1940. *French Historical Studies* 8: 130–56.

Richardson, J. L. 1988. New Perspectives on Appeasement: Some Implications for International Relations. *World Politics* 40: 289–316.

Richardson, L. F. 1960. *Statistics of Deadly Quarrels.* Pittsburgh, Pa.: Boxwood Press.

Richter, F. 1938. *Preussische Wirtschaftspolitik in den Ostprovinzen.* Königsberg.

Ricossa, S. 1973. Italy 1920–1970. In C. M. Cipolla, ed., *The Fontana Economic History of Europe,* vol. 1: *Contemporary Economies.* Glasgow: William Collins Sons.

Ridley, F., and J. Blondel. 1969. *Public Administration in France,* 2nd ed. New York: Barnes and Noble.

Rigby, T. H. 1968. *Communist Party Membership in the USSR: 1917–1967*. Princeton, N.J.: Princeton University Press.

Riggs, F. 1964. *Administration in Developing Countries*. Boston: Houghton Mifflin.

Ringer, F. K. 1979. *Education and Society in Modern Europe*. Bloomington: Indiana University Press.

Rintala, M. 1962. *Three Generations: The Extreme Right in Finnish Politics*. Bloomington: Indiana University Press.

Robbins, L. 1939. *The Economic Basis of Class Conflict and Other Essays in Political Economy*. London: Macmillan.

Robbins, L. 1968. *The Economic Causes of War*. New York: H. Fertig.

Roberts, D. L. 1984. The Origins of War in the Periphery of the International System. Ph.D. dissertation, Cornell University.

Roberts, H. L. 1951. *Rumania: Political Problems of an Agrarian State*. New Haven: Yale University Press.

Robinson, R. 1972. Non-European Foundations of European Imperialism: Sketch for a Theory of Collaboration. In R. Owen and B. Sutcliffe, eds., *Studies in the Theory of Imperialism*. London: Longman.

Robson, P. 1987. *The Economics of International Integration*, 3rd rev. ed. London: Allen and Unwin.

Rodinson, M. 1970. Histoire économique et histoire des classes sociales dans le monde Muselman. In M. A. Cook, ed., *Studies in the Economic History of the Middle East*. London: Oxford University Press.

Röhl, John C. 1976. Higher Civil Servants in Germany, 1890–1900. In James J. Sheehan, ed., *Imperial Germany*. New York: New Viewpoints.

Rokkan, S. 1975. Dimensions of State Formation and Nation-Building: A Possible Paradigm for Research on Variations within Europe. In C. Tilly, ed., *The Formation of National States in Western Europe*. Princeton, N.J.: Princeton University Press.

Romein, J. 1978. *The Watershed of Two Eras*. Middletown, Conn.: Wesleyan University Press.

Romero-Maura, J. 1977. "Caciquismo" as a Political System. In E. Gellner and J. Waterbury, eds., *Patrons and Clients*. London: Duckworth.

Roosevelt, K. 1979. *Countercoup: The Bloody Struggle for Control of Iran*. New York: McGraw-Hill.

Rose, A. G. 1957. The Plug Riots of 1942 in Lancashire and Cheshire. In A. G. Rose, ed., *Transactions of the Lancashire and Cheshire Antiquarian Society*. Manchester: H. Rawson.

Rose, J. H. 1905. *The Development of the European Nations 1870–1921*. New York: G. P. Putnam's Sons.

Rose, M. E. 1971. *The English Poor Law, 1780–1930*. Newton Abbot: David and Charles.

Rosenau, J., ed. 1969. *Linkage Politics: Essays in the Convergence of National and International Systems*. New York: Free Press.

Rosenberg, A. 1931. *The Birth of the German Republic, 1871–1918*, trans. I. F. D. Morrow. London: Oxford Press.

Rosenberg, A. 1936. *The History of the German Republic*. London: Methuen.

Rosenberg, H. 1934. The World Economic Crisis, 1857–9. *Vierteljahrschrift für Sozial und Wirtschafts Geschichte*, suppl. no. 30.

Rosenberg, H. 1966. *Bureaucracy, Aristocracy and Autocracy: The Prussian Experience, 1660–1815.* Cambridge, Mass.: Harvard University Press.

Rosow, S. J. 1994. On the Political Theory of Political Economy: Conceptual Ambiguity and the Global Economy. *Review of Political Economy* 1: 465–88.

Rostow, W. W. 1971. *Politics and the Stages of Growth.* Cambridge: Cambridge University Press.

Roth, G. 1963. *The Social Democrats in Imperial Germany: A Study in Working-Class Isolation and Nation Integration.* Totowa, N.J.: Bedminster.

Rothstein, A. 1958. *The Munich Conspiracy.* London: Lawrence and Wishart.

Rowntree, B. S. 1901. *Poverty: A Study of Town Life.* London: Macmillan.

Rowntree, B. S. 1913. *How the Labourer Lives.* New York: Arno Press.

Rowse, A. L. 1947. *End of an Epoch: Reflection on Contemporary History.* London: Macmillan.

Rowse, A. L. 1961. *Appeasement: A Study in Political Decline, 1933–1939.* New York: Norton.

Royle, T. 1999. *Crimea: The Great Crimean War, 1854–1856.* Boston: Little, Brown.

Rubinstein, W. D. 1981. *Men of Poverty: The Very Wealthy in Britain since the Industrial Revolution.* New Brunswick, N.J.: Rutgers University Press.

Rubinstein, W. D. 1983. Entrepreneurial Effort and Entrepreneurial Success: Peak Wealth-Holding in Three Societies, 1850–1930. *Business History* 25: 11–29.

Rubinstein, W. D. 1987. New Men of Wealth and the Purchase of Land in Nineteenth Century Britain. In W. D. Rubinstein, ed., *Elites and the Wealthy in Modern British History.* New York: St. Martin's Press.

Rudé, G. 1959. *The Crowd in the French Revolution.* London: Clarendon.

Rudé, G. 1967. English Rural and Urban Disturbances on the Eve of the First Reform Bill, 1830–1831. *Past and Present* 37: 87–102.

Rudin, H. R. 1944. *Armistice, 1918.* New Haven: Yale University Press.

Rueschemeyer, D., et al. 1992. *Capitalist Development and Democracy.* Chicago: University of Chicago Press.

Ruggie, J. 1982. International Regimes, Transactions, and Change: Embedded Liberalism in the Postwar Economic Order. *International Organization*, 36, no. 2.

Ruigrok, W., and R. Van Tulder. 1995. *The Logic of International Restructuring.* London: Routledge.

Rummel, R. 1963a. Dimensions of Conflict Behavior within and between Nations. *General System Yearbook* 8: 1–50.

Rummel, R. 1963b. Testing Some Possible Predictors of Conflict Behavior within and between Nations. *Peace Research Society (International) Papers* 1: 79–111.

Rummel, R. 1968. The Relationship between National Attributes and Foreign Conflict Behavior. In D. J. Singer, ed., *Quantitative International Politics.* New York: Free Press.

Rummel, R. 1969. Dimensions of Foreign and Domestic Conflict Behavior: A Review of Empirical Findings. In D. G. Pruitt and R. C. Snyder, eds., *Theory and Research on the Causes of War.* Englewood Cliffs, N.J.: Prentice-Hall.

Rummel, R. 1983. Libertarianism and International Violence. *Journal of Conflict Resolution* 27: 27–71.

Rupert, M. 1995. *Producing Hegemony: The Politics of Mass Production and American Global Power.* Cambridge: Cambridge University Press.

Russell, F. S. 1877. *Russian Wars with Turkey.* London: Henry S. King.

Russet, B. 1993. *Grasping the Democratic Peace: Principles for a Post–Cold War World.* Princeton, N.J.: Princeton University Press.

Russet, B. M., 1964. Inequality and Instability: The Relation of Land Tenure to Politics. *World Politics* 16: 442–54.

Russet, B. M., et al. 1964. *World Handbook of Political and Social Indicators.* New Haven: Yale University Press.

Ryder, A. J. 1963. The German Revolution, 1918–19. In W. N. Medlicott, ed., *From Metternich to Hitler: Aspects of British and Foreign History.* New York: Barnes and Noble.

Saint-Jours, Y. 1982. France. In P. A. Kohler and H. F. Zacher, eds., *The Evolution of Social Insurance, 1881–1981: Studies of Germany, France, Great Britain, Austria and Switzerland.* New York: St. Martin's Press.

Ste. Croix, G. E. M. de 1981. *The Class Struggle in the Ancient Greek World.* Ithaca, N.Y.: Cornell University Press.

Saladino, S. 1966. Italy. In H. Rogger and E. Weber, eds., *The European Right.* Berkeley: University of California Press.

Sally, R. 1994. Multinational Enterprises, Political Economy and Institutional Theory: Domestic Embeddedness in the Context of Internationalization. *Review of Political Economy* 1: 161–92.

Salter, J. A. 1921. *Allied Shipping Control: An Experiment in International Administration.* Oxford: Clarendon Press.

Samuelsson, K. 1968. *From Great Power to Welfare State.* London: Allen and Unwin.

Sayer, A. 1992. *Methods in Social Science: A Realist Approach*, 2nd ed. London: Routledge.

Schachtman, M. 1962. *The Bureaucratic Revolution: The Rise of the Stalinist State.* New York: Donald Press.

Schapiro, L. 1960. *The Communist Party of the Soviet Union.* London: Constable.

Schatz, S. P. 1956. A Dual Economy Model of an Underdeveloped Country. *Social Research* 4: 419–32.

Schechtman, J. P. 1946. *European Population Transfers 1939–1945.* New York: Oxford University Press.

Schmidt, G. 1986. *The Politics and Economics of Appeasement: British Foreign Policy in the 1930s.* London: Berg.

Schneer, J. 1982. The War, the State and the Workplace: British Dockers during 1914–1918. In J. E. Cronin and J. Schneer, eds., *Social Conflict and the Political Order in Modern Britain.* New Brunswick, N.J.: Rutgers University Press.

Schneider, J., and P. Schneider. 1976. *Culture and Political Economy in Western Sicily.* New York: Academic Press.

Schonfield, A. 1965. *Modern Capitalism: The Changing Balance of Public and Private Power.* London: Oxford University Press.

Schorske, C. E. 1955. *German Social Democracy 1905–1917: The Development of the Great Schism.* Cambridge, Mass.: Harvard University Press.

Schuman, F. 1937. *Germany since 1918.* New York: H. Holt.

Schuman, F. 1942. *Europe on the Eve: The Crises of Diplomacy, 1933–1939.* New York: Alfred A. Knopf.

Schumpeter, J. A. 1955. *Imperialism and Social Classes: Two Essays.* New York: Meridian Books.

Schumpeter, J. A. 1976 [1950]. *Capitalism, Socialism and Democracy*. London: Routledge.

Schwartz, H. 1994. *States versus Markets: History, Geography, and the Development of the International Political Economy*. New York: St. Martin's Press.

Schwartz, H. 2002–3. Hobson's Voice: American Internationalism, Asian Development, and Global Macro-economic Imbalances. *Journal of Post-Keynesian Economics*, 25, no. 2 (Winter): 321–51.

Scott, W. R. 1924. *The Industries of the Clyde Valley during the War*. Oxford: Clarendon Press.

Sée, H. 1942. *Histoire économique de la France*, vol. 2: *Les Temps modernes, 1789–1914*. Paris: Colin.

Seers, D. 1949. *Changes in the Cost-of-Living and the Distribution of Income since 1938*. Oxford: Blackwell.

Sefer, B. 1968. Income Distribution in Yugoslavia. *International Labour Review* 97: 371–89.

Sen, A. 1960. *Choice of Techniques: An Aspect of the Theory of Planned Economic Development*. Oxford: Basil Blackwell.

Sereni, E. 1968. *Il Capitalismo Nelle Campagne (1860–1900)*. Turin: Einaudi.

Serge, V. 1972. *Year One of the Russian Revolution*, trans. P. Sedgwick. Chicago: Holt, Rinehart and Winston.

Seton-Watson, C. 1967. *Italy from Liberalism to Fascism, 1870–1925*. London: Methuen.

Seton-Watson, H. 1945. *Eastern Europe between the Wars, 1918–1941*. Hamden: Archon Books.

Seton-Watson, H. 1951. *The East European Revolution*. New York: Praeger.

Seton-Watson, H. 1977. *Nations and States: An Inquiry into the Origins of Nations and the Politics of Nationalism*. London: Methuen.

Seton-Watson, R. W. 1911. *Corruption and Reform in Hungary: A Study of Electoral Practice*. London: Constable.

Seton-Watson, R. W. 1934. *A History of the Roumanians*. London: Cambridge University Press.

Seton-Watson, R. W. 1938. *Britain in Europe, 1789–1914*. Cambridge: Cambridge University Press.

Sewell, W. 1980. *Work and Revolution in France: The Language of Labour from the Old Regime to 1848*. Cambridge: Cambridge University Press.

Seymour, C. 1926–28. *The Intimate Papers of Colonel House*, 4 vols. Boston: Houghton Mifflin.

Shachtman, T. 1982. *The Phony War, 1939–1940*. New York: Harper and Row.

Shapiro, David, ed. 1962. *The Right in France 1890–1891*. Carbondale: Southern Illinois University Press.

Shaw, S. J., and E. K. Shaw. 1977. *History of the Ottoman Empire and Modern Turkey*, vol. 2. Cambridge: Cambridge University Press.

Sheehan, James J. 1976. Conflict and Cohesion among German Elites in the 19th Century. In James J. Sheehan, ed., *Imperial Germany*. New York: New Viewpoints.

Shils, E. 1960. Political Development in the New States. *Comparative Studies in Society and History* 2: 265–92.

Shimko, K. L. 1992. Realism, Neorealism and American Liberalism. *Review of Politics* 54 (Spring): 281–301.

Shorter, E., and C. Tilly. 1974. *Strikes in France, 1830–1974*. London: Cambridge University Press.

Shotwell, J. T. 1924. *Economic and Social History of the World War: Outline of Plan, European Series*. Washington: Carnegie Endowment for Peace.

Shuglett, P. 1970. *Britain in Iraq, 1914–1932*. London: Oxford University Press.

Sigelman, L., and M. Simpson. 1977. A Cross-National Test of the Linkage between Economic Inequality and Political Violence. *Journal of Conflict Resolution* 21: 105–28.

Silver, B. J. 1995. Labor Unrest and World Systems Analysis. *Review* 18: 7–24.

Silver, B. J., and E. Slater. 1999. The Social Origins of World Hegemonies. In G. Arrighi and B. J. Silver, eds., *Chaos and Governance in the Modern World System*. Minneapolis: University of Minnesota Press.

Simon, M. 1968. The Pattern of New British Portfolio Investment, 1865–1914. In A. R. Hall, ed., *The Export of Capital from Britain 1870–1914*. London: Methuen.

Simpson, C. 1994. *The Science of Coercion: Communication Research and Psychological Warfare 1945–1960*. New York: Oxford University Press.

Simpson, C. 1999. *Universities and Empire: Money and Politics in the Social Sciences during the Cold War*. New York: New Press.

Singer, D. J., and M. Small. 1972. *The Wages of War, 1816–1965: A Statistical Handbook*. New York: Wiley.

SIPRI. 1969. *SIPRI Annual Yearbook 1969*. Oslo: Stockholm International Peace Research Institute.

Skendi, S. 1953. Beginnings of Albanian Nationalist and Autonomous Trends: The Albanian League, 1878–1881. *American Slavic and East European Review* 12: 219–32.

Skidelsky, R. 1981. Keynes and the Treasury View: The Case for and against an Active Unemployment Policy in Britain 1920–1939. In W. J. Mommsen, ed., *The Emergence of the Welfare State in Britain and Germany*. London: CroomHelm.

Skilling, H. G. 1971. Groups in Soviet Politics: Some Hypotheses. In H. G. Skilling, and F. Griffiths, eds., *Interest Groups in Soviet Politics*. Princeton, N.J.: Princeton University Press.

Skocpol, T. 1979. *States and Social Revolutions: A Comparative Analysis of France, Russia, and China*. Cambridge: Cambridge University Press.

Slack, P. 1988. *Poverty and Policy in Tudor and Stuart England*. London: Longmans.

Slack, P. 1990. *The English Poor Law, 1531–1782*. London: Macmillan.

Small, M., and J. David Singer. 1982. *Resort to Arms: International and Civil Wars, 1816–1980*. Beverly Hills: Sage.

Smelser, N. J. 1963. *Theory of Collective Behavior*. New York: Free Press.

Smith, A. 1976a. The Formation of Nationalist Movements. In A. D. Smith, ed., *Nationalist Movements*. London: Macmillan.

Smith, A. 1976b. *Wealth of Nations*, ed. E. Cannon. Chicago: University of Chicago Press.

Smith, A. 1987. State-Making and Nation-Building. In J. A. Hall, ed., *States in History*. London: Basil Blackwell.

Smith, A. 1991. *National Identity*. Reno: University of Nevada Press.

Smith, A. D. 1993. The Ethnic Sources of Nationalism. In M. Brown, ed., *Ethnic Conflict and International Security*. Princeton, N.J.: Princeton University Press.

Smith, D. M. 1959. *Italy: A Modern History*. Ann Arbor: University of Michigan Press.

Smith, D. M. 1971. *Victor Emmanuel, Cavour, and the Risorgimento*. London: Oxford University Press.

Smith, P. H. 1978. The Breakdown of Democracy in Argentina, 1916–1930. In J. Linz and A. Stepan, eds., *Breakdown of Democratic Regimes: Latin America*. Baltimore: Johns Hopkins University Press.

Snell, K. D. M. 1985. *Annals of the Labouring Poor: Social Change and Agrarian England, 1660–1900*. London: Cambridge University Press.

Snell, K. D. M., and J. Millar. 1987. Lone-Parent Families and the Welfare State: Past and Present. *Continuity & Change* 2: 387–422.

Snyder, G. H., and P. Diesing. 1977. *Conflict among Nations*. Princeton, N.J.: Princeton University Press.

Snyder, L. 1964. *The Dynamics of Nationalism*. Princeton, N.J.: D. Van Nostrand.

Snyder, L. 1982. *Global Mini-Nationalisms: Autonomy or Independence*. Westport: Greenwood Press.

So, A. Y. 1990. *Social Change and Development: Modernization, Dependency, and World-System Theories*. Newbury Park, Calif.: Sage.

Soboul, A. 1958. *Les Sans-Culottes*. Paris: Clavreuil.

Sohn-Rethel, A. 1978a. *Economy and Class Structure of German Fascism*. London: CSE Books.

Sohn-Rethel, A. 1978b. *Intellectual and Manual Labour: A Critique of Bourgeois Epistemology*. London: Macmillan.

Sontag, R. J. 1971. *A Broken World, 1919–1939*. New York: Harper and Row.

Sorokin, P. 1927. *Social Mobility*. London: Harper.

Sorokin, P. 1928. *Contemporary Sociological Theories*. New York: Harper and Row.

Sorokin, P. 1969. *Society, Culture, and Personality: Their Structure and Dynamics*. New York: Cooper Square.

Soucy, R. 1972. *Fascism in France: The Case of Maurice Barrès*. Berkeley and Los Angeles: University of California Press.

Spencer, H. 1898. *Principles of Sociology*, vol. 3. New York: D. Appleton.

Spencer, H. 1902. *Facts and Comments*. London: Williams and Norgate.

Spencer, H. 1981 [1884]. The Man versus the State. In *The Man versus the State, with Six Essays on Government, Society and Freedom*, ed. Eric Mack. Indianapolis: Liberty Classics.

Spring, D., ed. 1977. *European Landed Elites in the Nineteenth Century*. Baltimore: Johns Hopkins University Press.

Spruyt, H. 1996. *The Sovereign Territorial State and Its Competitors*. Princeton, N.J.: Princeton University Press.

Standing, G. 1997. Globalization, Labour Flexibility and Insecurity: The Era of Market Regulation. *European Journal of Industrial Relations* 3, no. 1.

Stavrianos, L. 1958. *The Balkans since 1453*. New York: Rinehart and Winston.

Steefel, L. C. 1932. *The Schleswig-Holstein Question*. Cambridge, Mass.: Harvard University Press.

Steiner, Z. S. 1969. *The Foreign Office and Foreign Policy, 1898–1914*. London: Cambridge University Press.

Stern, F. 1977. Prussia. In D. Spring, ed., *European Landed Elites in the Nineteenth Century*. Baltimore: Johns Hopkins University Press.

Stevenson, J. 1975. Food Riots in England, 1792–1818. In R. Quinault and J. Stevenson, eds., *Popular Protest and Public Order*. London: St. Martin's Press.

Stewart, P. 1950. Soviet Interest Groups and the Policy Process. *World Politics* (October).

Stillman, W. J. 1966. *Articles and Dispatches from Crete*, ed. G. G. Arnakis. Austin: Center for Neo-Hellenic Studies.

Stojanovic, M. D. 1939. *The Great Powers and the Balkans*. New York: Cambridge University Press.

Stone, J. 1932. *International Guarantees of Minority Rights*. London: Oxford University Press.

Stone, K. 1974. The Origins of Job Structures in the Steel Industry. *Review of Radical Political Economics* 6: 61–97.

Stone, L. 1965. *The Crisis of the Aristocracy, 1558–1641*. Oxford: Oxford University Press.

Stone, L. 1972. *The Causes of the English Revolution, 1529–1642*. London: Routledge and Kegan Paul.

Stone, L. 1981. The Results of the English Revolutions of the Seventeenth Century. In J. G. A. Pocock, ed., *Three British Revolutions: 1641, 1688, 1776*. Princeton, N.J.: Princeton University Press.

Stone, N. 1983. *Europe Transformed, 1878–1919*. London: Allen and Unwin.

Stover, C. C. 1970. Tropical Exports. In W. Arthur Lewis, ed., *Tropical Development, 1880–1913*. Pp. 46–63. Evanston, Ill.: Northwestern University Press.

Strachey, J. 1959. *The End of Empire*. New York: Praeger.

Strayer, J. R. 1970. *On the Medieval Origins of the Modern State*. Princeton, N.J.: Princeton University Press.

Strikwerda, K. 1993. The Troubled Origins of European Economic Integration: International Iron and Steel Migration in the Era of World War I. *American Historical Review* 98 (October): 1106–29.

Struve, W. 1973. *Elites against Democracy: Leadership Ideals in Bourgeois Political Thought in Germany, 1890–1933*. Princeton, N. J.: Princeton University Press.

Stubbs, W. 1967. *Seventeen Lectures on the Study of Medieval and Modern History and Kindred Subjects*. New York: Fertig.

Sugar, P. F. 1971. *Native Fascism in the Successor States, 1918–1945*. Santa Barbara: ABC-Clio.

Suleiman, M. 1967. *Political Parties in Lebanon*. New York: Cornell University Press.

Sunkel, Osvaldo. 1973. Transnational Capitalism and National Disintegration in Latin America. *Social and Economic Studies* 22: 132–76.

Sunkel, Osvaldo. 1993. From Inward-Looking Development to Development from Within. In Osvaldo Sunkel, ed., *Development From Within: Toward a Neostructuralist Approach for Latin America*. Boulder, Colo.: Lynne Rienner.

Supple, B. 1973. The State and the Industrial Revolution: 1700–1914. In C. M. Cipolla, ed., *The Fontana Economic History of Europe*. Harmondsworth: Penguin.

Sutton, M. 1982. *Nationalism, Positivism and Catholicism*. Cambridge: Cambridge University Press.

Swann, W., and M. Lissowska. 1996. Capabilities, Routines, and East European Economic Reform. *Journal of Economic Issues* 30: 1031–57.

Sweezy, P. 1976. A Critique. In P. Sweezy et al., eds., *The Transition from Feudalism to Capitalism*. London: Verso.

Sweezy, P. et al., eds. 1976. *The Transition from Feudalism to Capitalism*. London: Verso.

Swire, J. 1929. *Albania: The Rise of a Kingdom*. London: Williams and Ungate.

Sykes, C. 1953. *Two Studies in Virtue*. London: Collins.

Taborsky, E. 1961. *Communism in Czechoslovakia, 1948–1960*. Princeton, N.J.: Princeton University Press.

Taine, H. A. 1962 [1872]. *The Ancient Règime*, trans. J. Durand. Gloucester, Mass.: Peter Smith.

Taithe, B. 2001. *Citizenship and Wars: France in Turmoil, 1870–1871*. London: Routledge.

Tamke, J. 1981. Bismarck's Social Legislation: A Genuine Breakthrough? In W. J. Mommsen, ed., *The Emergence of the Welfare State in Britain and Germany*. London: CroomHelm.

Tannenbaum, E. R. 1977. *1900: The Generation before the Great War*. Garden City, N.Y.: Anchor.

Tanter, R. 1966. Dimensions of Conflict Behavior within and between Nations, 1958–1960. *Journal of Conflict Resolution* 10: 41–64.

Tarlé, E. V. 1910. *L'Industrie dans le campagnes en Franceà la fin de l'ancien régime*. Paris: F. Alcar.

Tarrow, S. 1989. *Democracy and Disorder: Protest and Politics in Italy, 1965–1975*. London: Oxford University Press.

Tasca, A. 1966. *The Rise of Italian Fascism, 1918–1922*. New York: H. Fertig.

Tawney, R. H. 1952 [1931]. *Inequality*, rev. ed. London: Allen and Unwin.

Taylor, A. J. P. 1957. *The Trouble Makers: Dissent over Foreign Policy, 1792–1932*. London: Hamish Hamilton.

Taylor, A. J. P. 1961. *Origins of the Second World War*. New York: Fawcett.

Taylor, G. V. 1967. Noncapitalist Wealth and the Origins of the French Revolution. *American Historical Review* 72: 469–96.

Teeple, G. 1995. *Globalization and the Decline of Social Reform*. Atlantic Highlands, N.J.: Humanities Press.

Teichova, A. 1974. *An Economic Background to Munich: International Business and Czechoslovakia 1918–1938*. London: Cambridge University Press.

Temperley, H. W. V., ed. 1920–24. *A History of the Peace Conference of Paris*, 6 vols. London: Henry Frowde, Hoddard Stoughton.

Temperley, H. W. V. 1925. *The Foreign Policy of Canning, 1822–1827: England, the Neo-Holy Alliance and the New World*. London: G. Bell and Sons.

Thane, P. 1990. Government and Society in England and Wales, 1750–1914. In *The Cambridge Social History of Britain, 1750–1950*, vol. 3: *Social Agencies and Institutions*. Cambridge: Cambridge University Press.

Thane, P. 1998. Histories of the Welfare State. In W. Lamont, ed., *Historical Controversies and Historians*. London: UCL Press.

Thirsk, J. 1978. *Economic Policy and Projects: The Development of a Consumer Society in Early Modern England*. Oxford: Clarendon Press.

Thomas, J. A. 1939. *The House of Commons: 1832–1901: A Study of Its Economic and Functional Character*. Cardiff: University of Wales Press.

Thomas, R. P., and D. N. McCloskey. 1981. Overseas Trade and Empire, 1700–1860. In R. C. Floud and D. N. McCloskey, eds., *The Economic History of Britain since 1700*, vol. 1. Cambridge: Cambridge University Press.

Thompson, E. P. 1965. *The Making of the English Working Class*. London: Victor Gollancz.

Thompson, E. P. 1975. Standards and Experiences. In A. J. Taylor, *The Standard of Living in Britain in the Industrial Revolution*. London: Methuen & Co.

Thompson, E. P. 1993. The Moral Economy of the English Crowd in the Eighteenth Century. Reprinted in *Customs in Common*. Pp. 185–258. New York: New Press.

Thompson, F. M. L. 1963. *English Landed Society in the Nineteenth Century*. London: Routledge.

Thompson, F. M. L. 1977. Britain. In D. Spring, ed., *European Landed Elites in the Nineteenth Century*. Baltimore: Johns Hopkins University Press.

Thompson, J. E. 1990. State Practice, International Norms, and the Decline of Mercenarism. *International Studies Quarterly* 34: 23–47.

Thompson, J. M. 1966. *Russia, Bolshevism, and the Versailles Treaty*. Princeton, N.J.: Princeton University Press.

Thompson, K. 1974. Church of England Bishops as an Elite. In P. Stanworld and A. Giddens, eds., *Elites and Power in British Society*. London: Cambridge University Press.

Thompson, N. 1971. *The Anti-Appeasers: Conservative Opposition to Appeasement in the 1930s*. London: Oxford University Press.

Thomson, D. 1984. The Decline of Social Welfare: Falling State Support for the Elderly since Early Victorian Times. *Ageing and Society* 44: 451–82.

Tihany, L. C. 1976. *A History of Middle Europe*. New Brunswick, N.J.: Rutgers University Press.

Tilly, C. 1964. *The Vendée*. Cambridge, Mass.: Harvard University Press.

Tilly, C. 1973. Does Modernization Breed Revolution? *Comparative Politics* 5: 427–47.

Tilly, C. 1975a. Reflection on the History of European State-Making. In C. Tilly, ed., *The Formation of National States in Western Europe*. Princeton, N.J.: Princeton University Press.

Tilly, C. 1975b. Revolutions and Collective Violence. In F. I. Greenstein and N. W. Polsby, eds., *Handbook of Political Science*, vol. 3. Reading, Mass.: Addison-Wesley.

Tilly, C. 1984. *Big Structures, Large Processes, Huge Comparisons*. New York: Russell Sage Foundation.

Tilly, C. 1989. Theories and Realities. In L. Haimson and C. Tilly, eds., *Strikes, Wars, and Revolution in an International Perspective: Strike Waves in the Late Nineteenth and Early Twentieth Centuries*. Cambridge: Cambridge University Press.

Tilly, C. 1990. *Coercion, Capital, and European States, AD 990–1992*. London: Blackwell.

Tilly, C. 1998. *Durable Inequality*. Berkeley and Los Angeles: University of California Press.

Tilly, C., L. Tilly, and R. Tilly. 1975. *The Rebellious Century, 1830–1930.* Cambridge, Mass.: Harvard University Press.

Tipton, F. B. 1976. *Regional Variations in the Economic Development of Germany during the Nineteenth Century.* Middletown, Conn.: Wesleyan University Press.

Tipton, F. B., and R. Aldrich. 1987a. *An Economic and Social History of Europe, 1890–1939.* Baltimore: Johns Hopkins University Press.

Tipton, F. B., and R. Aldrich. 1987b. *An Economic and Social History of Europe, from 1939 to the Present.* Baltimore: Johns Hopkins University Press.

Tismeneanu, V. 1989. Democracy, What Democracy? *East European Reporter* 4.

Titmuss, R. M. 1958. *Essays on the Welfare State.* Boston: Beacon Press.

Tocqueville, A. de 1955. *The Old Regime and the French Revolution.* Garden City, N.Y.: Doubleday Anchor Books.

Tomasevich, J. 1955. *Peasants, Politics and Economic Change in Yugoslavia.* Stanford, Calif.: Stanford University Press.

Tool, M. R. 1994. Institutional Adjustment and Instrumental Value. *Review of Political Economy* 1: 405–44.

Touraine, A. 1971. *The May Movement: Revolt and Reform.* New York: Random House.

Toynbee, A. 1890. *Lectures on the Industrial Revolution of the Eighteenth Century in England,* 3rd ed. London: Longmans, Green.

Toynbee, A. 1915. *Nationality and the War.* London and Toronto: J. M. Dent.

Trebilcock, C. 1981. *Industrialization of the Continental Powers 1780–1914.* London: Longmans.

Trevelyan, G. M. 1919. *Garibaldi and the Making of Italy.* London: Longmans, Green.

Tribe, K. 1981. *Genealogies of Capitalism.* London: Macmillan.

Trimberger, E. K. 1978. *Revolution from Above: Military Bureaucrats and Development in Japan, Turkey, and Peru.* New Brunswick, N.J.: Transaction Books.

Troeltsch, E. 1960. *The Social Teaching of the Christian Churches,* trans. O. Wyon. New York: Harper.

Trotsky, L. 1957. *The History of the Russian Revolution.* London: Victor Gollancz.

Türk, K. 1898. *Böhmen, Möhren und Schlesien.* Munich: J. F. Lehmann.

Tussman, J. 1960. *Obligation and the Body Politic.* New York: Oxford University Press.

Ulam, A. B. 1977. *In the Name of the People: Prophets and Conspirators in Revolutionary Russia.* New York: Russia.

United Nations, Department of Economic and Social Affairs. 1956. *Economic Survey of Latin America.* New York.

Urusov, S. D. 1908. *Memoirs of a Russian Governor,* trans. H. Rosenthal. London: Harper.

van der Pijl, K. 1984. *The Making of an Atlantic Ruling Class.* London: Verso.

van der Pijl, K. 1998. *Transnational Classes and International Relations.* London: Routledge.

Vandervelde, E. 1925. Ten Years of Socialism in Europe. *Foreign Affairs* 3: 556–66.

Vansittart, P. 1984. *Voices, 1870–1914.* London: Jonathan Cape.

Vaughan, M. 1971. Poland. In Margaret Scotford Archer and Salvador Giner, eds., *Contemporary Europe: Class, Status, Power.* London: Weidenfeld and Nicolson.

Veblen, T. 1904. *The Theory of Business Enterprise.* Clifton, N.J.: Augustus M. Kelley.

Veblen, T. 1915. *Imperial Germany and the Industrial Revolution.* London: Macmillan.

Veblen, T. 1923. *Absentee Ownership and Business Enterprise in Recent Times: The Case of America*. Boston: Beacon Press.

Veblen, T. 1959. An Inquiry into the Nature of Peace and the Terms of Its Perpetuation. In M. Lerner, ed., *The Portable Veblen*. New York: Viking Press.

Verney, D. V. 1957. *Parliamentary Reform in Sweden 1866–1921*. Oxford: Clarendon Press.

Vicinich, W. S. 1967. The Serbs in Austria-Hungary. *Austrian Yearbook* 3: 3–47.

Vigness, M. 1913. Le Bassin de Briey et la politique de ses enterprises sidérurgiques ou minières. *Revue d'économie politique* 27.

Vincent, J. 1969. *Costume and Conduct in the Laws of Basel, Bern, and Zurich, 1370–1800*. New York: Greenwood.

Volgyes, I. 1980. Economic Aspects of Rural Transformation in Eastern Europe. In I. Volgyes, R. E. Lonsdale, and W. P. Avery, eds., *The Process of Rural Transformation: Eastern Europe, Latin America and Australia*. New York: Pergamon Press.

Voltaire. 1935. *The Age of Louis XIV*. London: Everyman's Library.

Von Bismarck, O. 1924–32. *Die Gesammelten Werke*, 15 vols. Berlin: Stollberg.

Von Lazar, J. 1966. Class Struggle and Socialist Construction: The Hungarian Paradox. *Slavic Review* 25.

Waites, B. 1987. *A Class Society at War: England 1914–1918*. Leamington Spa: Berg.

Walaszek, Z. 1986. An Open Issue of Legitimacy: The State and the Church in Poland. *Annals of the American Academy of Political and Social Science* 483: 118–34.

Wallerstein, E. 1996 [1983]. *Historical Capitalism*, 2nd ed. W. W. Norton.

Wallerstein, I. 1974. *The Modern World System I: Capitalist Agriculture and the Origins of the European World Economy in the 16th Century*. New York: Academic Press.

Wallerstein, I. 1980. *The Modern World System II: Mercantilism and the Consolidation of the European World Economy, 1600–1750*. New York: Academic Press.

Wallerstein, I. 1997. The Unintended Consequences of Cold War Area Studies. In N. Chomsky, et al., *The Cold War and the University: Toward an Intellectual History of the Postwar Years*. Pp. 195–231. New York: New Press.

Walsh, D. 1996. The Disturbances of 1826 in the Manufacturing Districts of the North of England. In A. Charlesworth, D. Gilbert, A. Randall, H. Southall, and C. Wrigley, eds., *An Atlas of Industrial Protest in Britain, 1750–1990*. London: Macmillan.

Walters, P. 1986. The Russian Orthodox Church and the Orthodox State. *Annals of the American Academy of Political and Social Science* 483: 135–44.

Waltz, K. 1970. The Myth of National Interdependence. In C. P. Kindleberger, ed., *The International Corporation*. Cambridge, Mass.: MIT Press.

Waltz, K. 1979. *Theory of International Politics*. Reading, Mass.: Addison-Wesley.

Waltz, K. 1990. Realist Thought and Neorealist Theory. *Journal of International Affairs* 44: 21–37.

Warriner, D. 1950. *Revolution in Eastern Europe*. London: Turnstile Press.

Warwick, P. 1985. Did Britain Change? An Inquiry into the Causes of National Decline. *Journal of Contemporary History* 20: 99–133.

Watkins, K. W. 1963. *Britain Divided: The Effect of the Spanish Civil War on British Public Opinion*. London: Thomas Nelson and Sons.

Watt, D. C. 1975. *Too Serious a Business*. Berkeley: University of California Press.

Webb, S., and B. Webb. 1920. *The History of Trade Unionism* Rev. Ed. London: Chiswick.

Weber, E. 1959. *The National Revival in France, 1905–1914.* Berkeley: University of California Press.

Weber, E. 1962. *Action Francaise.* Stanford, Calif.: Stanford University Press.

Weber, E. 1964. *Varieties of Fascism.* Princeton: Princeton University Press.

Weber, E. 1965a. France. In H. Rogger and E. Weber, eds., *The European Right: A Historical Profile.* Berkeley: University of California Press.

Weber, E. 1965b. Romania. In H. Rogger and E. Weber, eds., *The European Right: A Historical Profile.* Berkeley: University of California Press.

Weber, E. 1976. *Peasants into Frenchmen: The Modernization of Rural France, 1870–1914.* Stanford, Calif.: Stanford University Press.

Weber, E. 1994. *The Hollow Years: France in the 1930s.* New York: Norton.

Weber, M. 1921. On the Conditions of Bourgeois Democracy in Russia. In *Gesammelte Politische Schriften.* Munich: Drei Masken Verlag.

Weber, M. 1924. Die Sozialen Gründe des Untergangs der Antiken Welt. In *Gesammelte Aufsätze Zur Sozial- Und Wirtschaftsgeschichte.* Tübingen: J. C. B. Mohr.

Weber, M. 1978. *Economy and Society*, vol. 2, ed. G. Roth and C. Wittich. Berkeley: University of California Press.

Webster, S. C. K. 1925. *The Foreign Policy of Castlereagh, 1815–1822: Britain and the European Alliance.* London: G. Bell and Sons.

Weede, E. 1984. Democracy and War Involvement. *Journal of Conflict Resolution* 28: 649–64.

Wehler, H.-U. 1969. *Bismarck und der Imperialismus.* Cologne: Kiepenheuer.

Wehler, H.-U. 1985. *The German Empire, 1871–1918.* Leamington Spa, Warwickshire: Berg.

Weiner, M. J. 1981. *English Culture and the Decline of the Industrial Spirit, 1850–1980.* Cambridge: Cambridge University Press.

Weiss, J. 1977. *Conservatism in Europe 1770–1945: Traditionalism, Reaction, and Counter-Revolution.* New York: Harcourt Brace Jovanovich.

Wells, H. G. 1934. *Experiment in Autobiography: Discoveries and Conclusions of a Very Ordinary Brain.* New York: Macmillan.

Wells, R. 1990. The Development of the English Rural Proletariat and Social Protest, 1700–1850. In M. Reed and R. Wells, eds., *Class, Conflict and Protest in the English Countryside, 1700–1880.* London: Frank Cass.

Wendt, B. J. 1983. Economic Appeasement: A Crisis "Strategy." In W. J. Mommsen and L. Kettenecker, eds., *The Fascist Challenge and the Policy of Appeasement.* London: Allen and Unwin.

Werth, A. 1968. *France in Ferment.* New York: Harper and Brothers.

Wertheimer, M. S. 1924. *The Pan-German League, 1890–1914.* New York: Columbia University Press.

Wesolowski, W. 1969. The Notions of Strata and Class in Socialist Society. In A. Béteille, ed., *Social Inequality.* Harmondsworth: Penguin.

Wesseling, H. L. 1997. *Imperialism and Colonialism: Essays on the History of European Expansion.* Westport: Greenwood Press.

Wesson, R. G. 1978. *State Systems: International Pluralism, Politics and Culture.* New York: Free Press.

Westergaard, J., and H. Resler. 1975. *Class in a Capitalist Society: A Study of Contemporary Britain*. London: Heinemann.

Westergaard, J. H. 1972. Sociology: The Myth of Classlessness. In R. Blackburn, ed., *Ideology in Social Science: Readings in Critical Social Theory*. New York: Random House.

Wexler, A. 1989. *Emma Goldman in Exile: From the Russian Revolution to the Spanish Civil War*. Boston: Beacon Press.

Wheatcroft, A. 1983. *Atlas of World Revolutions*. New York: Simon and Schuster.

White, G. F. 1909. *A Century of Spain and Portugal*. London: Methuen.

Whiteside, A. G. 1965. Austria. In H. Rogger and E. Weber, eds., *The European Right: A Historical Profile*. Berkeley: University of California Press.

Wight, M. 1977. *Systems of States*, ed. H. Bull. Leicester: Leicester University Press.

Wight, M. 1979. *Power Politics*, ed. H. Bull and C. Holbraad. London: Penguin Books.

Wilensky, H. 1975. *The Welfare State and Equality*. Berkeley: University of California Press.

Williams, A. 1911. *Life in a Railway Factory*, 2nd ed. London.

Williams, D. 1955. *The Rebecca Riots: A Study in Agrarian Dissent*. Cardiff: University of Wales Press.

Williams, K., J. Williams, and C. Haslam. 1989. Do Labour Costs Really Matter? *Work, Employment, and Society* 3: 281–305.

Williamson, J. G. 1965. Regional Inequality and the Process of National Development: A Description of the Patterns. *Economic and Cultural Change* 13: 3–44.

Williamson, S., Jr. 1979. Theories of Organizational Process and Foreign Policy Outcomes. In P. G. Lauren, ed., *Diplomacy*. New York: Free Press.

Wilson, C. H. 1941. *Anglo-Dutch Commerce and Finance in the Eighteenth Century*. Cambridge: Cambridge University Press.

Winch, D. 1969. *Economics and Policy*. London: Hodder and Stoughton.

Wiskemann, E. 1956. *Germany's Eastern Neighbors: Problems Relating to the Oder-Neisse Line and the Czech Frontier Regions*. London: Oxford University Press.

Wolf, E. R. 1982. *Europe and the People without History*. Berkeley: University of California Press.

Wolff, R. L. 1974. *The Balkans in Our Time*. Cambridge, Mass.: Harvard University Press.

Wood, E. M. 1995. *Democracy against Capitalism: Renewing Historical Materialism*. Cambridge: Cambridge University Press.

Wood, E. M. 1998a. Labor, Class, and State in Global Capitalism. In E. M. Wood, P. Meiksins, and M. Yates, eds., *Rising from the Ashes? Labor in the Age of "Global Capitalism."* New York: Monthly Review Press.

Wood, E. M. 1998b. *The Retreat from Class: A New "True" Socialism*, rev. ed. London: Verso.

Woodhouse, C. M. 1952. *The Greek War of Independence: Its Historical Setting*. London: Russell.

Woodhouse, C. M. 1968. *Modern Greece: A Short History*. London: Faber and Faber.

Wrench, S. E. 1955. *Geoffrey Dawson and Our Times*. London: Hutchinson.

Wright, E. 2000. Workers' Power, Capitalist Interest and Class Compromise. *American Journal of Sociology* 105, no. 4: 957–1002.

Wright, E. O. 1999. Working Class Power, Capitalist Class Interests, and Class Compromise. Unpublished paper, Department of Sociology, University of Wisconsin.

Wright, G. 1964. *Rural Revolution in France: The Peasantry in the Twentieth Century.* Stanford, Calif.: Stanford University Press.

Wright, Q. 1965 [1942]. *A Study of War*, vol. 1. Rev. ed. Chicago: University of Chicago Press.

Wrigley, C. 1990. *Lloyd George and the Challenge of Labour.* London: Harvester Wheatsheaf.

Youngson, A. J. 1973. Introduction. In A. J. Youngson, ed., *Economic Development in the Long Run.* New York: St. Martin's Press.

Youngson, A. J. 1976. Britain 1920–1970. In C. C. Cipolla, ed., *The Fontana Economic History of Europe*, vol. 1: *Contemporary Economies.* Glasgow: William Collins Sons.

Zauberman, A. 1976. Russia and Eastern Europe 1920–1970. In C. M. Cipolla, ed., *The Fontana Economic History of Europe*, vol. 2: *Contemporary Economies.* Glasgow: William Collins Sons.

Zavalani, T. 1969. Albanian Nationalism. In P. F. Sugar and I. J. Lederer, eds., *Nationalism in East Europe.* Seattle: University of Washington Press.

Zeitlin, M. 1984. *The Civil Wars in Chile (or the Bourgeois Revolutions That Never Were).* Princeton, N.J.: Princeton University Press.

Zeldin, T. 1977. France. In D. Spring, ed., *European Landed Elites in the Nineteenth Century.* Baltimore: Johns Hopkins University Press.

Zeldin, T. 1979. *France, 1848–1945: Politics and Anger.* London: Oxford University Press.

Zèllner, D. 1982. Germany. In P. A. Kohler and H. F. Zacher, eds., *The Evolution of Social Insurance, 1881–1981: Studies of Germany, France, Great Britain, Austria and Switzerland.* New York: St. Martin's Press.

Zernatto, G. 1944. Nation: The History of a Word. *Review of Politics* 6: 351–66.

Zilliacus, K. 1946. *Mirror of the Past: A History of Secret Diplomacy.* New York: A. A. Wyn.

Zimmerman, L. J. 1962. The Distribution of World Income. In E. De Vries, ed., *Essays on Unbalanced Growth.* The Hague: Mouton.

Zimmermann, E. 1983. *Politics, Violence, Crises and Revolutions: Theories and Research.* Cambridge, Mass.: Schenkman.

Zimmermann, E., and T. Saalfield. 1988. Economic and Political Reactions to the World Economic Crisis of the 1930s in Six European Countries. *International Studies Quarterly* 32: 305–34.

Zolberg, A. R. 1986. How Many Exceptionalisms? In I. Katznelson and A. R. Zolberg, eds., *Working-Class Formation: Nineteenth-Century Patterns in Western Europe and the United States.* Princeton, N.J.: Princeton University Press.

Index

Abrams, Philip, 146, 156, 157, 158, 247
Abramsky, C., 293
absolutism: absolutist state, emergence of, 51–55; and capitalist development, 28–29
Abyssinia, and imperialist conflict, 136–143
Adelman, M. A., 241
Aden, and decolonization, 266–267
Afghanistan, and imperialist conflict, 136–143
Aglietta, M., 282
Alapuro, R., 259
Albania, and imperialist conflict, 136–143
Albo, Greg, 289
Albrecht-Carrié, R., 212, 216
Aldcroft, D. H., 237, 238, 240, 252, 253, 255
Aldrich, Robert, 183, 192, 193, 216, 225, 238, 253, 255, 256, 291
Algeria: and decolonization, 266–267; and imperialist conflict, 136–143
Alsace-Lorraine: and circuit of capital, 108–109; and imperialism, 40–42; imperialist rivalry over, 147–148
Anderson, Perry, 29, 52
Angola, and decolonization, 266–267
Annual Register, 133
Anti-Comintern Pact, 210, 211, 213, 220

appeasement, 200–231
Archer, J. E., 127
Argentina, 242; and imperialist conflict, 136–143
aristocracy: and class change, 176; decline of, 150–153; decline of wealth of, 153; and land redistribution, 152–153; and land transfers, 151–152
Arnold, Matthew, 175
Aron, R., 251
ASEAN, 239
Ashton, T. S., 85
Assam, and imperialist conflict, 136–143
Augé-Laribé, H., 100
Australia: and circuit of capital, 111; post–WWII change in balance of class forces in, 244–245
Austria, 6, 46; annexation of, 170; and concert of Europe, 297; and custom wars, 149–150; and democracy, 159; enfranchisement conflict in, 131–134; ethnic conflict in, 134–136; European wars involving, 119–125; peasant protest in, 189–190; post–WWII economic planning in, 255–262; post–WWII peace and prosperity in, 236–251; and Quadruple Alliance, 1; repression of left in, 193–194; socialist parties in, 181; Three Emperors League, 148

Austro-Hungarian Empire, 39; Archduke Franz Ferdinand, 136; ethnic conflict in, 134–136; and German nationalism, 56; and imperialism, 45; and imperialist rivalry, 146–147

Bade, K., 240
Badie, B., 55, 259
Bairoch, Paul, 103–104, 239, 242, 251, 252
Baker, Ray Stannard, 204, 205
Baldwin, F. E., 105
Baldy, E., 100
Balkans: Balkan Wars, 142, 264; and custom wars, 149–150; imperialist rivalry over, 146–147, 149–150; unskilled workers and labor movement in, 188–189
Banks, A., 242
Barnett, C., 223
Barraclough, G., 45, 141, 180, 241
Barratt Brown, M., 109, 112, 115
Becker, G., 92
Belgium, 39; enfranchisement in, 131–132, 263–264; ethnic conflict in, 134–136; and imperialism, 45, 136–143; nationalism in, 57; post–WWII peace and prosperity in, 236–251; post–WWII welfare system in, 261; socialist parties in, 180; strikes in, 128–131
Benns, L., 207–208, 209
Benson, L. 94, 97–98, 155
Betts, R. R., 235, 254
Beveridge, Sir William, 250
Bialer, U., 223
Bigo, R., 100
Block, F., 282
Boer War, 114, 155
Bolshevism: British foreign policy and, 228, 202–231; Nazi Germany as bulwark against, 221–222
Bond, B., 223
Bonnell, A. T., 201, 220, 221
Bonnet, Georges, 212, 216
Bosnia-Herzegovina, 148; enfranchisement conflict in, 131–134

Bouvier, J., 100
Boyce, R., 248
Brazil, 242, 243
Brecher, J., 291
Brest Litovsk, 186
Brewer, J., 85
Briggs, Asa, 245, 249
Britain, 6, 21, 39, 64; agrarian reform, 87–88; Anglo-Soviet trade agreement, 207; appeasement policies of, 201–202, 228–231; British Employers Defence Union, 182–183; capital investment in, 99–104; changes in labor movement of, 181–182; Charles II, 55; Chartism, 133, 178; class divisions in, 181; class interests and appeasement by, 217–221; and Concert of Europe, 297; and decolonization, 266–267; early welfare measures in, 65–66; enfranchisement in, 131–132; enfranchisement conflict in, 131–134; ethnic conflict in, 134–136; European wars involving, 119–125; foreign policy of, 200–231; and hegemony, 18; Home Office "Survey of Revolutionary and Class Interests," 10–11; and imperialism, 45; and imperialist conflict, 136–143; industrial development in, 82–108; industrial organization in, 88; Industrial Revolution in, 27; intraclass conflict in, 25; Labour Party, 181, 208, 209; market privileges in, 53; parliamentary reform movement in, 21; and "Phony War," 213–214; post–WWII changes in social structure in, 251–255; post–WWII demand management in, 240–241; post–WWII economic planning in, 246–251, 255–262; post–WWII peace and prosperity in, 236–251; post–WWII welfare system in, 249–250, 261; production for export in, 85–86; and Quadruple Alliance, 297; repression of left in, 193–194; and Russian civil war, 124; and Russo-Finnish War, 214–215;

socialist parties in, 181; and Spanish civil war, 194, 211; strikes in, 128–131, 177, 186, 190–191; structure of landholding in, 87–88; "Swing movement" in, 128; trade policies of, 10; Zinoviev letter, 208

Brown, P., 96–97

Buci-Glucksman, C., 293

Bulgaria: and autonomy, 149; class conflict in, 194–199; and imperialism, 45, 136–143; nationalism in, 57–58, 61–64; peasant protest in, 189–190; and postwar migration, 264–265; repression of left in, 193–194; strikes in, 291

Burma, and decolonization, 266–267

Burnbaum, B., 55, 259

Butler, Rab, 214

Byzantine Empire, 64

Cadogan, Alexander, 228

Cain, P. J., 113

Callwell, C. E., 205

Cambodia, and decolonization, 266–267

Campbell, P., 177, 178

Canada: and circuit of capital, 111; post–WWII change in balance of class forces in, 244–245

Cannadine, D., 87, 118, 179, 251

capital, circuit of, 108

Cardoso, F. N., 80, 243

Carlsbad Decrees, 177

Carr, E. H., 205, 246

Carstairs, A. M., 134, 159

Carsten, F. L., 185, 186

cartelism, 144; origins of, 89; prevention of, 260–262

Castlereagh, V. R. S., 8

Castles, S., 290

Catherine the Great, 54

Ceylon, and decolonization, 266–267

Chamberlain, Neville, 214, 227; and responsibility for appeasement policies, 229

Chandler, A. D., 282

Chernow, R., 203, 218

Chile, 242

China: and imperialist conflict, 136–143; and spread of communism, xii

Chirot, D., 81

Christensen, T. J., 222

Churchill, Winston, 210, 212, 213, 223, 225, 226

citizen armies, 46; in France, 46, 72–73

City of London, 88

class: antagonism between classes, 75; and appeasement, 217, 200–221, 231; class agency, 33–38; class-based analysis, xiv–xv, xx–xxi, 19–21; class structure, 21–33, 176–178; and imperialism, 42–44; intraclass conflict, 25, 148–149; and nation, 20–21; post–WWII change in balance of class forces, 244–245; and social change, 18, 15–18, 38; and state, 37–38; transnational structure of, 29–33

Claude, I., 136, 165, 266

Clegg, H., 182

Clemenceau, 205

Clough, S. B., 116

Coates, David, 26

Colbertism, *see* mercantilism

Cole, A., 177, 178

Cole, G. D. H., 85, 142, 237

Cole, W. A., 85

Cole, W. H., 82–85

Collas, H., 100

Collins, H., 293

Colombia, 242

commodification, 3

communism, spread of, xii

Concert of Europe, 78, 123, 177, 297; and international markets, 5–9

conflict: enfranchisement, 131–134, 263–264; ethnic, 134–136, 163–164, 264–266; imperialist, 136–143, 266–267; labor, 125–131

Congo, and imperialist conflict, 136–143

Corn Bill, 127

Corn Laws, 22, 27

Corporatism, 12, 257; and labor
   movements, 123
Cox, R., 283
Crete, and imperialist conflict, 140
Crimean War, 119, 140
Croatia, nationalism in, 58, 61–64
Crotty, J., 283
Crowe, Sir Eyre, 200
Cuba, 242, 243; and imperialist conflict,
   136–143
Curtis, M., 261
Curzon, Lord, 191–192, 206, 208
Czechoslovakia: annexation of
   Sudetenland, 212; creation of, 163;
   peasant protest in, 189–190;
   post–WWII changes in social
   structure in, 251–255; post–WWII
   land reforms in, 253–255; and
   postwar migration, 264–265; and
   Russian civil war, 124; social unrest
   in, 289; strikes in, 291; unskilled
   workers and labor movement in,
   188–189; "velvet revolution," 263

Daladier, Édouard, 196
Dallas, G., 154
Daphnas, G., 64
Darwin, J., 206
Davin, L. E., 259
Davis, Lance, 102
De Gaulle, Charles, 203
De Vries, J., 256, 259
Deane, P., 85, 106
Dedijer, V. I., 189
democracy: and class, 179; definition of,
   159; during interwar years, 158–162
Denison, Edward, 239
Denmark, 6; enfranchisement in,
   131–132; enfranchisement conflict in,
   131–134; European wars involving,
   119–125; political structure of, 31;
   socialist parties in, 180; strikes in,
   191–192
dependency theory, 279–281
Deutsch, J., 159
Djordjevic, D., 189, 196
Dobb, M., 68
Dockrill, M.L., 204, 206

Dorwart, R., 105
Droz, J., 177, 178
Dunbabin, J. A. D., 224

Ecuador, 242
Eden, Sir Anthony, 201, 218, 226, 227
Egypt, and imperialist conflict, 136–143
Einzig, P., 201, 216, 218, 219, 220
Eisner, Kurt, 187
enclosures, 67
Engels, Friedrich, 88–89, 134
Engerman, S., 82–85
enlistment: and labor, 154–155; and
   poverty, 155
Epstein, G., 283
Erickson, J., 225, 226
Estonia, peasant protest in, 189–190
Europe: "American model," 25;
   aristocratic decline in, 150–153;
   definition of, 297–298; and
   democracy, 159; ethnic conflict in,
   163–164; industrial capitalist
   development in, 8, 14–15, 24;
   Keynesianism in, 282–283; and
   Marshall Plan, 237–238; and
   minorities, 162–165; polarization of,
   175–199; postwar migration in,
   264–265; post–WWII change in
   balance of class forces in, 244–245,
   280; post–WWII changes in social
   structure in, 251–255; post–WWII
   economic planning in, 246–251,
   255–262; post–WWII land reforms
   in, 253–255; post–WWII peace and
   prosperity in, 236–251; rise of left in,
   187–192; rise of right in, 192–194;
   and social legislation, 156–157, 261;
   social theory of, xi–xii; socialist
   parties in, 180–181; transnational
   elites in, 29–33
European Coal and Steel Community,
   238, 260–261
European Economic Community, 239
European Free Trade Area, 239

Falletto, E., 80, 243
Feiling, K., 229
Ferris, J. R., 224

feudalism, 26; crisis of, 51–55
Finland: class conflict in, 194–199; and imperialist conflict, 136–143; nationalism in, 61–64; peasant protest in, 189–190; and Russo-Finnish War, 214–215
First International, 123, 180
"first transformation," xix, 276
Fischer-Galati, S., 189, 196
Floud, R., 116
Fohlen, C., 255
Fordism, 282–283
Foster, J., 75, 94
Four Power Pact, 210, 212
France, 6, 64; administrative apparatus in, 28; bureaucracy in, 11; capital investment in, 99–104; class conflict in, 182–183, 194–199; and class interests, 10–11; "continental system" of, 110; and decolonization, 266–267; early welfare measures in, 65–66; enfranchisement conflict in, 131–134, 263–264; ethnic conflict in, 134–136; European wars involving, 119–125; fall of, 215–216; foreign policy of, 209–210; Fourth Republic, 11; Franco-Soviet Pact, 204; and imperialism, 44–45, 136–143; and imperialist rivalry, 147–148; and interwar democracy, 160–161; labor conflict in, 125–131; market privileges in, 53; Monnet Plan, 255; nationalism in, 55, 61–64; Paris Commune, 46; peasant protest in, 189–190; and "Phony War," 213–214; post-WWII changes in social structure in, 251–255; post-WWII demand management, 240–241; post-WWII economic planning in, 246–251, 255–262; post-WWII peace and prosperity in, 236–251; post-WWII welfare system in, 261; reforms of Louis XV, 55; repression of left in, 193–194; and Russian civil war, 124; and Russo-Finnish War, 214–215; Second Republic, 178; social unrest in, 71–72, 289; socialist parties in, 180; and Spanish civil war, 194, 211;

strikes in, 128–131, 186, 191–192; unskilled workers and labor movement in, 188–189; "White terror" in, 176
Franco-Prussian War, 147
French Revolution, xxi, 22, 55, 72–73, 176; European reaction to, 176–177; *sans-culottes'* role in, 72–73
Friedberg, A. L., 224
Fromkin, D., 206
Fukuyama, Francis, 271
Furtado, C., 242

Gallacher, W., 184
Galtung, Johan, on imperialism, 114
Gay, P., 193
Geary, D., 127, 188
General Agreement on Tariffs and Trade, 239
George, H., 215, 217, 218, 222
Germany, 6, 39, 40; *Anschluss*, 170, 220; appeasement of, 200–231; and Bolshevism, 210, 221–222; bureaucracy in, 11; class conflict in, 183, 194–199; and class interests, 10–11; and democracy, 159, 161; enfranchisement in, 131–132; enfranchisement conflict in, 131–134; ethnic conflict in, 134–136, 164–165; European wars involving, 119–125; German-Soviet Pact, 204; German-Soviet trade agreement, 204; and imperialism, 45, 136–143; and imperialist rivalry, 147–148; intraclass conflict in, 148–149; and invasion of Europe, 170; Junkers in, 148, 222; King Frederick William IV, 134, 178; labor conflict in, 125–131; *Lebensraum*, 115; market privileges in, 53; nationalism in, 61–64; Nazi-Soviet Pact, 212–213; Pan-German League, 112; peasant protest in, 189–190; and "Phony War," 213–214; and postwar migration, 264–265; post-WWII changes in social structure in, 251–255; post-WWII demand

Germany (*cont.*)
management in, 240–241;
post–WWII economic planning in,
255–262; repression of left in,
193–194; revolution in, 186–187;
and Russian civil war, 124; social
consequences of WWI in, 185; social
unrest in, 289; socialist parties, 180;
and Spanish Civil War, 124, 194, 211;
strikes in, 128–131, 186, 191–192;
Three Emperors League, 148;
unskilled workers and labor
movement in, 188–189; Weimar
Republic, 208
Gerschenkron, A., 241
Gilbert, M., 200, 201, 225, 228
Gill, D., 154
Gillis, J., 69, 188
Gilpin, Robert, 16; "uneven
development," 17; *War and Change in
World Politics*, 17
globalization, xv, xvii, xxvi, 270–271,
281, 287–291, 294
Glyn, A., 291
gold standard, 4, 6, 25, 78, 235
Goldsmith, R. W., 225
Goldstone, J. A., 126
Goold, J. D., 204, 206
Gott, R., 201, 225, 228
Gramsci, Antonio, 33, 175
Gravier, J.-F., 259
Great Depression, 126, 141, 145, 189,
192, 244, 282
Great War, *see* World War I
Greece, 6; class conflict in, 194–199;
European wars involving, 119–125;
and imperialism, 45, 136–143;
nationalism in, 57; post–WWII
changes in social structure in,
251–255
Greenfeld, Liah, 34

Halifax, Lord, 214
Halperin, S., 242
Hamilton, Ian, 155
Hammond, T., 253
Hapsburg Empire: cultural diversity in,
61; enfranchisement conflict in,
131–134; and market privileges, 53;
monarchy, 54; reforms of Joseph II,
55
Hardach, G., 166, 167, 183, 185, 186,
256
Haslam, C., 285
haute finance: and "Hundred Years'
Peace," 5, 6, 7; and war, 8
Haxey, S., 217, 222
Hecksher, E. F., 138
hegemonic transition, theories of,
208
Henderson, W. O., 241
Herbert, U., 240
Herndon, James 225, 226
Hobsbawm, E., 8, 58, 94, 95, 98, 181,
182, 183, 211, 213, 237
Hobson, John, 8, 286, 287, 288; on
capital investment, 100–103
Hoffman, S., 182, 246, 250, 252
Hopkins, A. G., 113
Howard, M., 223, 224
Huguenots, 54
"Hundred Years' Peace," 4, 119, 278;
and markets, 5–9
Hungary: class conflict in, 194–199;
enfranchisement conflict in,
131–134, 263–264; Magyar
nationalism, 55, 57, 134–136;
"March Laws," 178; nationalism in,
61–64; peasant protest in, 189–190;
post–WWII changes in social
structure in, 251–255; post–WWII
land reforms in, 253–255; unskilled
workers and labor movement in,
188–189
Hunt, A., 105
Huttenback, Robert, 102
Hyde, H. M., 223

imperialism, 114; and absolute
surplus value, 40–42; and class,
42–44; imperialist conflicts,
136–143; imperialist rivalry, 146;
interwar years, 165–170; "New
Imperialism," 171; and production,
112; structural basis of, 113–115; and
war, 44–47

India, 224; and decolonization, 266–267; and imperialist conflict, 136–143
Indonesia, and decolonization, 266–267
Industrial Revolution, 27; and enclosures, 67; and industrial capitalist development, xxi, 24–25; and mechanization, 93–95; and productivity, 95–98; social unrest resulting from, 69–72
International Labour Office, 155
International Working Men's Association, 180, 293
Ireland: enfranchisement conflict in, 131–134; surplus value extraction in, 91; "Tithe War" in, 128
Italy, 6, 39; class conflict in, 183; and democracy, 159; enfranchisement conflict in, 131–134, 263–264; ethnic conflict in, 134–136; European wars involving, 119–125; Francesco Crispi, 136; and imperialism, 45; and Imperialist conflict, 136–143; labor conflict in, 125–131; nationalism in, 59, 61–64; and postwar migration, 264–265; post–WWII demand management in, 240–241; post–WWII economic planning in, 255–262; repression of left in, 193–194; social unrest in, 289; socialist parties in, 181; and Spanish Civil War, 124, 194, 211; strikes in, 128–131, 186, 191–192; unskilled workers and labor movement in, 188–189

Jackson, R. H., 253, 256
Japan: and Chinese Bolshevism, 221; post–WWII change in balance of class forces in, 244–245; and Russian civil war, 124
Jarman, L., 193
Jaurès, Jean, 153
Johnson, A. A., 237
Jörberg, L., 241

Kalecki, Michael, 245

Kautsky, Karl, 37
Keeble, S. C., 203, 205, 207, 208, 211, 213, 216
Keegan, J., 216
Kehr, Eckart, 148
Kennan, G., 206, 207, 208, 212, 213
Kennedy, Paul, 102, 168, 170, 184, 208, 212, 221, 223, 224, 225
Keynesianism, 282–283
Kindleberger, Charles, 99–100, 239
Korea, and imperialist conflict, 136–143
Kulischer, E. M., 264
Kundera, Milan, *The Unbearable Lightness of Being*, 269
Kurth, J. R., 25, 117
Kuznets, Simon, 240, 242, 275

labor, 42, 153–158; and consumption, 98–99; and enlistment, 154–155; and globalization, 291; labor conflict, 125–131; mobility of, 9–10; parties in Europe, 160; strikes, 128–131; unskilled workers and labor movement, 188–189; and violence, 153–154; and the war effort, 154–155
Ladas, S. P., 264
Lampe, J. R., 253, 256
land redistribution, 152–153
Landes, David, 89, 147, 171, 190, 240, 290
Landy, P., 290
Langer, W. L., 112–113, 141, 146
Laos, and decolonization, 266–267
Laquer, W., 253
Latvia: minorities in, 163; peasant protest in, 189–190
Laval, Pierre, 216
League of Nations, 156, 209–211, 220
Lefebvre, C., 55, 56
Lenin, V. I., 8, 26–27; on capital investment, 100–103; on commodities, 98; on imperialism, 43, 114
Lentin, A., 228
Lewis, Arthur, 101–102, 237, 242, 243
liberalism, 178–179

Libya: and decolonization, 266–267; and imperialist conflict, 136–143

Lipietz, A., 275, 282, 291

Lipski, J. J., 291

Lis, C., 94

Lithuania: and imperialist conflict, 136–143; minorities in, 163; peasant protest in, 189–190

Lloyd George, David, 169, 227; and agrarian reform, 87–88, 118; anti-Bolshevist policies of, 204, 205, 222; resignation of, 207

Louis XIV, 54

Luck, J. M., 196

Ludendorff, General, 169

Luxemburg, Rosa, 27–28

Macartney, C. A., 163–165

MacDonald, C. A., 201

MacDonald, M., 159

MacIver, R. M., 131

Macmillan, Harold, 247

Macshane, D., 282

Madagascar, and imperialist conflict, 136–143

Maddison, A., 236, 242

Magyar, *see* Hungary

Maier, C., 153, 160, 190

Malaysia, and decolonization, 266–267

Marglin, S. A., 258, 276

market, home, industrial development and, 82–85

market privileges, 53

Marsh, D. C., 237

Marshall Plan, 237–238, 244

Marwick, A., 185–186, 247, 248, 249

Marx, K., 23, 24, 134; and mass production, 106–107; productivity and wages, 98; surplus value extraction in Britain, 93

Marxism: and class analysis, xiv; and state theories, 37–38; surplus value, xvii

mass mobilization, 145–146, 151

Masterman, C. F. G., 118

Mathias, P., 95, 241

Mayer, Arno, 40, 188

Mazour, A., 112

McClellan, W. D., 189

McClosky, D. N., 109

McHenry, D. E., 160, 208, 209

McKendrick, N. J., *et al.*, 85

McKeown, T. J., 224, 225

McLean, I., 184

McNeill, William, 89

Meacham, S., 181, 182

Medlicott, W. H., 201, 225

Menderhausen, H., 158

mercantilism, 54, 88, 105–106

Mexico, 242

Meyer, H. C., 112, 142, 167, 169

Meyers, R., 224

Milward, A. S., 236, 252, 258, 261

Minorities, 162–165, 169–170; and imperial expansion, 163–165

Mokyr, J., 259

Monnet, Jean, 261

Montagu, L., 151, 179

Montenegro, and sovereignty, 149

Moore, Barrington, 29, 81, 280

Morgan, K. O., 206, 224

Morocco: and decolonization, 266–267; and imperialist conflict, 136–143

Morris, Cynthia, 21, 95, 241

Mowat, R. B., 167, 209

Mozambique, and decolonization, 266–267

multinational corporations, 32

Munger, F., 127

Murray, W., 223

Muskett, P., 128

Mussolini, 193, 212

Napoleon, Louis, 178

Napoleonic Wars, 8, 22, 31, 43, 44, 46, 47, 286; "citizen armies," 46; Continental System, 138; and "Hundred Years' Peace," 119–120; as imperialist conflict, 136–143

National Transport Workers Federation, 184

nationalism: and the bourgeoisie, 58–59; and class antagonism, 75–76; and imperialism, 61–64; origins of (Europe), 55

Naumann, Friedrich, 168

Netherlands, the: class conflict in, 194–199; enfranchisement in, 131–132; and imperialism, 45; and imperialist conflict, 136–143; political structure of, 31; post–WWII economic planning in, 255–262; post–WWII peace and prosperity in, 236–251; post–WWII welfare system in, 261; social unrest in, 71–72, 191–192; socialist parties in, 180

New Zealand, post–WWII change in balance of class forces in, 244–245

Nicholson, Sir Harold, 200, 211

Nietzsche, Friedrich: *The Eternal Recurrence*, 269

Nitzan, J., 285, 286

Northern Ireland, ethnic conflict in, 264–266

Norway: enfranchisement in, 131–132; nationalism in, 58; post–WWII economic planning in, 255–262; repression of left in, 193–194; and Russo-Finnish War, 214–215; socialist parties in, 181; strikes in, 191–192

O'Brien, P. K., 103

Ogg, F. A., 157, 180, 181

O'Leary, C., 159

Organisation for European Economic Cooperation, 239

Osterud, O., 259

Ottoman Empire: and Balkan nationalism, 56, 59, 61–64; and circuit of capital, 110; cultural diversity in, 60–61; effects of collapse of, 169–170; ethnic conflict in, 134–136; European status of, 1–2; and imperialist conflict, 138, 136–139, 143; and imperialist rivalry, 146–147

Owen, Robert, 123

Pallis, A. A., 264

Palmer, A., 180, 201

Pareto, Vilfredo, 11, 229

Parker, R. A. C., 192, 224, 227, 228

Parkin, F., 290

parliamentary reform movement, 21

Parsons, Talcott, 37

Paukert, F., 237

Peacock, A. J., 128

Peden, G. C., 224

Pelling, Henry, 114

Persia, and imperialist conflict, 136–143

Peru, 242

"Phony War," 213–214

Plumb, J. H., 85

Poland: class conflict in, 194–199; ethnic conflict in, 134–136; and imperialism, 45, 136–143; invasion of Soviet Union by, 205–206; market privileges in, 53; nationalism in, 61–64; peasant protest in, 189–190; political structure of, 31; and postwar migration, 264–265; post–WWII changes in social structure in, 251–255; and Russian civil war, 124; strikes in, 291; unskilled workers and labor movement in, 188–189

Polanyi, Karl: class analysis, xvi–xvii; and democracy, 179; embedded and disembedded markets, 270–271; *The Great Transformation*, xv–xxiv, 269, 276–279, 296; World War I, 235

Ponting, C., 214, 216

Poor Law, 71

Portugal, 39; civil war in, 177; and decolonization, 266–267; enfranchisement conflict in, 131–134; and imperialism, 45, 136–143; "Miguelite Wars," 133; Queen Maria II, 133

Postgate, R., 85, 142

Pounds, J. C., 241

Pribicevic, B., 184

Price, R., 114, 241, 259

proletarianization, 23, 122

protectionism, 13–14

Prussia: and Concert of Europe, 1; early welfare measures in, 65–66; enfranchisement conflict in, 131–134; ethnic conflict in, 134–136; European wars involving, 119–125; and imperialist conflict, 136–143; and Quadruple Alliance, 1;

Prussia (*cont.*)
  reforms of Frederick II, 54; reforms
  of Frederick William I, 54
Przeworski, A., 282
Puchala, D., 113

Reddy, W. M., 117–118
Resher, H., 237
Richardson, C. O., 203, 215
Ricossa, S., 237, 260
Riggs, F., 259
Romania, 252; and expansionism,
  168–169; and imperialism, 45,
  136–143; and postwar migration,
  264–265; and sovereignty, 149; class
  conflict in, 194–199;
  enfranchisement conflict in, 131–134;
  loss of Bessarabia, 149; nationalism
  in, 57, 61–64; peasant protest in,
  189–190; post–WWII changes in
  social structure in, 251–255;
  post–WWII land reforms in, 253–255;
  strikes in, 291
Rowse, A. L., 223, 227, 228, 231
Rueschemeyer, D., xx, 280
Ruggie, J., 270
Rupert, M., 283
Russia, 6, 39; Alexander II, 46; and
  "Army of Europe," 297; Bolshevik
  revolution, 192; bureaucracy in, 12;
  and circuit of capital, 111; class
  conflict in, 194–199; and class
  interests, 10–11; and Concert of
  Europe, 297; ethnic conflict in,
  134–136; European status of, 1–2;
  European wars involving, 119–125;
  and imperialism, 45; and imperialist
  rivalry, 146–147; nationalism in,
  61–64; Nicholas I, 132; pan-Slav
  movement, 137, 146; post–WWII
  demand management in, 240–241;
  and Quadruple Alliance, 297; social
  consequences of WWI in, 185; strikes
  in, 128–131, 291; Three Emperors
  League, 148; trade union movement
  in, 183; *see also* Soviet Union
Russian Revolution, 185–186; solidarity
  with, 154

Russo-Finnish War, 214–215
Russo-Turkish War, 148, 149
Ryder, A. J., 186

Saladino, S., 193
Salter, J. A., 167
Sayles, J., 85
Schachtman, M., 215
Schechtman, J. P., 162, 163
Schmidt, G., 201, 218, 224
Schonfield, A., 237, 263, 283
Schor, J. B., 258, 276
Schuman, F., 193, 196, 201, 202, 222,
  227
Schumpeter, Joseph, 113, 245, 246
Schwartz, H., 285, 287, 288
Scott, W. R., 184
Second Internationale, 293
Seers, S., 237
self-regulating market, 3; and class
  antagonism, 75; and Concert of
  Europe, 5–9; dismantling of, 75; ideal
  of, 9; and protectionism, 4
Senegal, and imperialist conflict,
  136–143
Serbia, 6; European wars involving,
  119–125; and imperialism, 45,
  136–143; and sovereignty, 149
Serge, V., 194
Seton-Watson, C., 135
Seton-Watson, H., 56, 189, 254, 256
Seven Years' War, 54
Seymour, C., 205
Sierra Leone, and imperialist conflict,
  136–143
Silver, B., 122
Skocpol, Theda, 16; *States and Social
  Revolutions*, 16–17
slave trade, 110
Snyder, J., 222
social change, relationship between
  domestic and international in study
  of, 4
social order, social theory and the
  maintenance of, xi–xii
social structure, 175–176; and decline
  in wealth, 153
social theory, in Europe, xi–xii

socialism: electoral success of left, 188; and enlistment, 154–155; and labor, 153–158; and labor violence, 153–154

Sohn-Rethel, A., 25, 295

Soly, H., 94

Sontag, R. J., 212, 213

South Africa, and imperialist conflict, 136–143

Soviet Union: Anglo-Soviet trade agreement, 207; and British foreign policy, 201–202, 221–222; change in balance of class forces in, 244–245; Franco-Soviet Pact, 204; German-Soviet Pact, 204; German-Soviet trade agreement, 204; New Economic Policy, 241; Polish invasion of, 205–206; post–WWII demand management in, 240–241; and Spanish civil war, 211; *see also* Russia

Spain, 6, 39, 263–264; Carlists, 134; civil war in, 194, 211; enfranchisement conflict in, 131–134; ethnic conflict in, 134–136, 264–266; European wars involving, 119–125, 251–255, in, 193–194; and imperialism, 45; and imperialist conflict, 136–143; King Alphonso XII, 134; King Amadeo, 134; King Ferdinand, 132; political structure of, 31; post–WWII changes in social structure repression of left in, 193–194

Spencer, Herbert, 11

Ste. Croix, G. E. M. de, 15, 19

Standing, G., 293

state: autonomy of, 16–17, 37–38; and class interests xiv–xv, xviii

Stevenson, J., 127, 128

Strachey, J., 101

Strikwerda, K., 240

Sudan, and imperialist conflict, 136–143

suffrage, changes in, 177–178

Sunkel, O., 80, 279

Supple, B., 241

surplus value: and imperialist expansion, 40–42; production of absolute, 91–93; production of relative, 91–93

Sweden: bureaucracy in, 11; and class interests, 10–11; enfranchisement in, 131–132; and imperialism, 45; and imperialist conflict, 136–143 King Charles XIV, 138; repression of left in, 193–194; and Russo-Finnish War, 214–215; socialist parties in, 181; strikes in, 191–192

Switzerland: enfranchisement in, 131–132; ethnic conflict in, 134–136; post–WWII peace and prosperity in, 236–251; repression of left in, 193–194; socialist parties in, 180; strikes in, 128–131, 191–192

Taborsky, E., 291

Tasmania, and imperialist conflict, 136–143

Teeple, G., 293

Temperley, H. W. V., 155; *The Unbearable Lightness of Being*, xx

Third International, 187; and CPGB, 208–209

Thomas, J. A., 109

Thompson, E. P., 20–21

Thompson, F. M. L., 181

Thompson, J. M., 204

Thompson, N., 222

Tilly, C., 186, 191, 194, 196

Tipton, F. B., 183, 192, 193, 216, 225, 238, 253, 255, 256, 291

Tismeneanu, V., 291

Titmuss, R. M., 249

Tocqueville, Alexis de, 29, 176

trade, and European imperialism, 166–169

Trebilcock, C., 101–102

Triple Alliance, 149

Triple Entente, 149

Tunisia: and decolonization, 266–267; and imperialist conflict, 136–143

Turkey: enfranchisement conflict in, 131–134; and imperialist conflict, 136–143

Uganda, and imperialist conflict, 136–143
unionism, 181
United States: American civil war, 32, 141; and circuit of capital, 111; and class analysis, xiv; "development project" of, xii–xii; Fordism in, 282–283; and hegemony, 18; immigration into, 190; Marshall Plan, 237–238; and Russian civil war, 124; and self-regulating market, 4–5; social theory of, xi–xii
Uruguay, 242
Urusov, S. D., 135

van der Pijl, Kees, 24, 25, 247; transnational class, 32–33
Vaughan, M., 254
Venezuela, 242
Vietnam: and decolonization, 266–267; war in and U.S. economy, 283, 295
Vignes, M., 240
Vincent, J., 105
Von Bismarck, Otto, 148, 149
von Lazar, J., 291

Wallerstein, Immanuel: and underdevelopment, 243; world systems theory and colonial trade, 103
Waltz, Kenneth, 222
Warriner, D., 254
Warwick, P., 117, 250
Watkins, K. W., 194, 211
Watt, D. C., 223
Weber, Max, 88; and class interests, 11
Wehler, H.-U., 116
Weiner, M. J., 107
Weiss, J., 192, 221

welfare systems, 28; early welfare measures, 65–66; eighteenth-century dismantling of, xvi, xviii–xix, 261; post–WWII expansion of, 245–246, 249–250; revisionist history of, xiii–xiv
Wells, R., 127
Wells, H. G., 41
Wendt, B. J., 224
Wertheimer, M. S., 112
Wesseling, H. L., 114, 116
Westergaard, J., 237
Williams, A., 285
Williams, D., 128
Williamson, J. G., 259
Williamson, S., Jr., 136
Wilson, Sir Henry, 205
Winch, D., 282
Wiskemann, E., 265
world systems theory, 103, 243, 279–281
World War I, 35–36, 40, 44–45, 179; and the aristocracy, 150–153; and class conflict, 183–187; and labor, 153–158
World War II, 38
Wrench, S. E., 213, 215
Wright, E., 21, 291, 293
Wright, G., 189
Wright, Quincey, 119

Youngson, A. J., 255
Yugoslavia: and imperialist conflict, 136–143; peasant protest in, 189–190; and postwar migration, 264–265; post–WWII land reforms in, 253–255; repression of left in, 193–194; strikes in, 291

Zeitlin, M., 243